MAR 2 4 2005

Donated by the Friends
of the
Olathe Public Library

OLATHE PUBLIC LIBRARY
201 EAST PARK
OLATHE, KANSAS 66061

Descendants of
John Messer Lowell

Revolutionary Soldier
Who Changed His Name to

John Reed

by

Laurel K. Chapman

North Syracuse, New York
1992

Copyright © 1992
Laurel K. Chapman

For additional information about this publication
contact the author at
115 Castle Road
North Syracuse, New York 13212

Library of Congress Catalgoue Card Number 92–74059
ISBN: 1–55787–087–X

Quality book production by
Heart of the Lakes Publishing
Interlaken, New York 14847

Contents

Dedication		5
Introduction		7
Chapter 1	The Ancestry of John Messer Lowell	9
Chapter 2	John Lowell Reed	5
Chapter 3	Children of John Lowell Reed	25
Chapter 4	The Third Generation	33
Chapter 5	The Fourth Generation	95
Chapter 6	The Fifth Generation	135
Chapter 7	The Sixth Generation	199
Chapter 8	The Seventh Generation	309
Chapter 9	The Eighth Generation	419
Appendix	The First Family of Joshua Wadley	435
	The Family of Lyman Austin	441
Addendum		445
Index		447

Illustrations

Photographs of third and fourth generation family members will be found following page 94.

Dedication

To my husband
Glenn M. Chapman
for his constant support
and encouragement.

Introduction

This genealogy of the descendants of John Messer Lowell, better known to us as John Reed, has been a labor of love, over a period of more than fifteen years. While my husband Glenn was living we spent our vacations and later our leisure time traveling around the country to the states and localities where early Reeds lived and where many descendants are now living. We spent many hours in court houses, cemeteries and local libraries searching for local records of the early generations. At the same time we were meeting many descendants in person in many localities around the country. Each of them welcomed us as relatives and gladly shared records, pictures, memories and stories, giving us a better understanding of what they were like, how they lived, what their hardships were, and how they lived out their lives. I am sharing with you whatever I can to make them come alive as much as possible. Beside these personal visits, I have spent countless hours sending out questionaires and writing for records around the country.

Since the death of my husband in 1985, I have felt a great compulsion to complete the book and make available to all who have shown an interest. I have since written the eighth and concluding chapter. Although it is far from complete, I felt I wanted to share with you what I do have, with the thought that building upon this information you can complete the information on your own families.

I am bringing down three lines of Reeds, the three children of John Lowell (Reed) who grew up and had families; Ella Fear Cheeseman's, Pauline Austin's family, and son John Reed's family and descendants.

I am much indebted to my grandmother, Ida Reed Canfield, for saving the precious letters sent to her by her brothers Cyrus and Morris Reed and others. I owe much to my mother, Alta Canfield Kennedy, for passing on to me the knowledge of where the Reed boys moved when they left Mexico, New York and moved west; also that Pearl Wadley went to Portland, Oregon, etc. My grandfather visited them in his travels. Also my mother and father took a trip to Seymour, Wisconsin and the other localities where Bert Reed and family lived in 1938. It all came together when Ruth Mentz talked about the professor from back east who came to visit her family and, impressed with her, said she should go to college . . .

that was my father in 1938, at her home at Lake Tomahawk, Wisconsin.

I am indebted to the two sisters, Cheeseman descendants, we visited in Conneaut, Ohio, Ellen and Ruth Johnson, who shared their records of early Cheesemans.

I owe *much* to Patricia Pryor, whom we visited in Kansasville, Wisconsin. She is a descendant of Morris Reed and has lovingly preserved the scrap book which contains letters he wrote to the newspaper, and others of his writings such as the fascinating accounts of the early trip of the young Reed family in wagon train to Wisconsin to possibly start a new life after Sarah died, and the return by schooner to Mexico. Also Morris accounts of his early life and Civil War experiences. It would appear that perhaps he had thoughts of writing his biography.

Many thanks go to Euloda Fetcha, Historian, Town of Mexico, NY and to John Castle of Mexico who loves history and gleaned many important facts from early issues of *The Mexico Independent*. Also to Page Thorpe, who is compiling Wadley materials and Vera Runyan, who shared her Austin family history. I cannot forget the Onondaga County Public Library in Syracuse, where I spent many, many hours in the Local History and Genealogy Department; their outstanding collection enabled me to resolve the connection beteween the early Lowells and John Reed.

I am most appreciative to the many in the present generation who have replied to my queries with a wealth of information, to make this genealogy possible. I hope they will feel rewarded as they have a chance to see the results.

Thank you also to Walt Steesy, my publisher, and his able assistant, Laura Argus for editing and pulling it all together into proper genealogical format.

Sincerely,
Laurel (Kennedy) Chapman

Chapter 1

The Ancestry of John Messer Lowell

The Lowell family has been traced back to eleventh century England, when in 1066 a member of the family fought on the side of William the Conqueror during the Norman Invasion of England. One-hundred fifty years later they were found in 1220 in the person of William Lowle of Yardley in Worcestershire. From then on the line was continuous to Percival, the son of Richard[c] Lowle.

Percival[b] Lowell, born in 1571, was brought up in North Somerset County at Kingston-Seymour on the shore of the Severn Sea. He had a thorough classical education. He married well and was appointed, at age 26, to the office of Assessor of Lands, a position previously held by his father. Upon his father's death he received a sizable inheritance.

Percival, his wife and children moved to the busy seaport of Bristol where he became a very successful wholesale trader in exports and imports. Percival's sons, John and Richard, as well as a family friend, William Gerrish, joined the firm: Percival Lowle and Company.

Beginning in 1630 the British government began imposing stiff taxes and tight controls over the economic life of the country, which hurt the shipping trade. Large numbers of people began to emigrate to the new world.

Percival Lowell was 68 years old on April 12, 1639 when he and his party set sail for America. There were his wife Rebecca, his sons John and Richard, with their wives and four children, his daughter Joan and her husband John Oliver, as well as his partner William Gerrish, a total of sixteen in the party. They landed at Newbury, Massachusetts, north east of Boston, where Percival bought 100 acres of land in a choice section, purchasing more land later. His wife Rebecca died soon after their arrival, and in 1649 he relocated two miles north of Newbury at Newburyport, where he lived to the age of 93, dying in 1664. He was buried in a small graveyard at Newbury not far from the town green.

Percival's son John,[a] born 1595 in England, had eight children: John "The Elder" (b. 1629 in England), who married Hannah Proctor; Mary (b. 1633 in England); Peter (b. 1635 in England); James (b. 1637 in England); Joseph (b. 1639 in Newbury, MA); who married Abigail Proctor, sister of John's wife; **Benjamin**[1] (b. 1642 in Newbury); Thomas (b. 1644 in Newbury); and Elizabeth (b. 1646 in Newbury).

Sons John "The Elder" and Joseph moved to Boston, Massachusetts and started a cooper business, making crates and barrels, and later adding a shoemaking business. This lucrative establishment in turn was passed to John "The Elder's" son, Ebenezer. Ebenezer's son, the future Rev. John Lowell (b. 1704), was the first of the Lowell family to afford a college education, entering Harvard University at Cambridge Massachusetts in 1717, at age 13. Rev. John Lowell was a distinguished scholar and became minister of First Congregational Church of Newburyport.

Rev. John Lowell's son, Judge John Lowell (1743–1802), was a member of the Massachusetts Constitutional Convention in 1780 to draft a constitution for Massachusetts. He introduced into the Bill of Rights a phrase from the Virginia Bill of Rights "All men are created free and equal," thus freeing all the slaves of Massachusetts. After the new nation was founded, Judge John Lowell was appointed the first judge of the district court.

Judge John Lowell married three times and from each marriage there emerged a son who was destined to start an illustrious line of Lowell's. By Sarah Higginson he had two daughters and a son John, "The Rebel." Down the line from this son was the well known and eccentric poetess Amy Lowell (1814–1925), who was portly due to a glandular imbalance, and who smoked long black cigars in public. She introduced imagism to American poetry and won posthumously the Pulitzer Prize for a collection of her poems entitled "What's O'Clock," published in 1925. One of her brothers, Abbott Lawrence Lowell was president of Harvard University and another, Percival Lowell, an astronomer.

Judge John Lowell's second wife, Susanna Cabot, a descendant of the famous Massachusetts Cabots, gave him two children, including Francis Cabot Lowell, the pioneer of cotton manufacturing in this country, America's first factory town, Lowell, Massachusetts, was named for him.

Judge John Lowell's third wife, Mrs. Rebecca Tyng, bore him three daughters and a son Charles who was Rev. Charles Lowell, pastor of West Church (Unitarian), Boston, more than forty years. He had six children, the youngest of whom was Honorable James Russell Lowell (1819–1891), the poet. In his day he was the most highly regarded man of letters. From James Russell Lowell's brother, Rev. Robert Traill Spence Lowell descended the eminent poet, Robert Traill Spence Lowell IV (1917–1977), who won the Pulitzer prize for his second book entitled "Lord Weary's Castle," published in 1946.

These branches of the Lowell family were and are wealthy, having made wise investments, but being accustomed to this security through the generations, have been more interested in contributing good works to their community. They have founded and/or contributed to many outstanding Massachusetts institutions, such as Harvard University, with which they have close ties, Boston Museum of Fine Arts, Massachusetts Institute of Technology, Boston Symphony Orchestra, Massachusetts General Hospital, Perkins Institute for the Blind, The Lowell Institute and many others. The Lowell Observatory was founded by Amy Lowell's brother, Percival, in Flagstaff, Arizona.

To find *our* line of descent, we must go back to the first American generation John "The Elder" and his brother Joseph, the Boston coopers. Their younger brother, Benjamin[1] Lowell, born 12 September 1642 in Newbury, Massachusetts was our direct ancestor, with his descendants coming down parallel to the illustrious Lowells, and being cousins to them. Benjamin declared his marriage intentions with Ruth Woodman, daughter of Edward and Joanna Woodman, 17 October 1666. Ruth's father was a wealthy and prominent man. Benjamin was listed as a "blacksmith."

Benjamin[1] and Ruth Lowell had nine children, the youngest being John[2] Lowell, born in Newbury, 22 February 1682. This John Lowell married about 1707 Mary Davis, daughter of John and Sarah (Carter) Davis. John was listed as being a blacksmith, like his father.

John[2] and Mary (Davis) Lowell had nine children, the youngest of whom was Stephen[3] Lowell, born 10 February 1729, recorded in Haverhill, MA. Stephen married Lydia Messer 10 January 1755 (church records of First Church of Christ in Nottingham West, NH, 1921). Lydia probably was the Lydia Messer born to John and Sarah (Barker) Messer in Methuen, Essex Co., MA, the second of four children. She was baptized 6 August 1732. Methuen is just across the border from Nottingham West,

N.H. (Genealogy of the Messer Family and Descendants of Richard Mercer.) Stephen and Lydia (Messer) Lowell had eight children, all born in Nottingham West (now Hudson), NH. Stephen, b 28 February 1756: Ruth b 1758; Mollie, b 1760, these recorded in Christ Church records; the fourth was *John Messer Lowell*, b 6 August 1762; the fifth child Susan, b 5 September 1767; the sixth Hannah, b 23 October 1768 and married to William Cofern; the seventh Asa Lowell, b 1769, who for several years was a prosperous farmer in Canada, forfeiting all his property during the War of 1812, to settle in Oriskany Falls, Oneida Co., NY; the eighth child was Lydia, b 27 December 1783. She died 8 December 1867 at Concord, NH, having never married.

The fourth child of Stephen and Lydia Lowell, **John Messer Lowell**, was our direct ancestor. He was fourteen years old when he enlisted for the Revolutionary War 1 May 1777 at Cambridge, MA for three year service. He was a private in a company commanded by Captain Lemuel Trescott in Colonel Henry Jackson's Regiment in the Massachusetts line of the Continental Army. In trying to ascertain why he enlisted at Cambridge instead of Nottingham West, where his father and brother enlisted, it was thought he might have been enrolled at Harvard University as a student; his cousins routinely enrolled there. However, a check with Harvard University Archives, which does have records as far back as early 1770s, dashed that hope. The reason is still a mystery, unless this was the closest station at the time he was ready.

The following is the description of John Messer Lowell's military service, taken from his Revolutionary War Pension File:

Colonel Jackson some time in October marched his regiment to a place called White Marsh in Pennsylvania and here found Washington's Main Army and from thence marched to Lancaster, in the same state.

There we quartered during the winter of 1777 and 1778 until April of the last year and from thence in the spring of 1778 we marched to Gulph Mills (Gulf Mills), 13 miles from Philadelphia. We then stayed until June of the same year, until the British left there. We then followed them to Monmouth in the state of New Jersey and [June 28, 1778] gave the British battle. From thence we marched to White Plains in the state of New York and stayed about two weeks, and from there we marched to Rhode Island. Sometime in August [August 29, 1778], near Newport, Rhode Island the British attacked our Regiment, and that was called the "Rhode Island Battle." Our Regiment, Gen'l Glover's Brigade and Gen'l. Barnum's Brigade, was in the engagement, and one independent Company from

Boston. They were all under the command of General Sullivan and General LaFayette, who were present during the engagement. The winter of 1778 and 1779 we quartered at Pawtuxet, five miles from Providence in Rhode Island. In the summer (July) of 1779 there was an expedition fitted out and commanded by Commodore Hopkins to go to Penobscot River to dislodge the British from Bagaduce and our Regiment was ordered to march there to his assistance and we marched to Portland in the now state of Maine. We then heard of Commodore Hopkins' defeat, his fleet taken and all destroyed. We then marched back to Boston and from thence back to Morristown in the state of New Jersey and thence we continued until May 1, 1780, when I was discharged.

    The reader is encouraged to study the charts located on the end sheets to clarify the relationships within the family.

Chapter 2

John Lowell Reed

After, or during, the Revolutionary War, John Messer Lowell changed his name to John Reed, for what reason we have not been able to determine.

Among the papers of John's great-granddaughter, Eva Belle Reed Plasteur of Long Beach, California, was found a copy of a letter sent from the Bureau of Pensions in Washington, DC to Morris Reed, Eva's uncle. It listed facts in regard to John Lowell's military career, with the simple statement, "After the war he assumed the name of John Reed." At the bottom of the document is an additional paragraph entitled,

Remarks:

It is a matter of record, at Washington, DC that while in the service of his country John Lowell was captured by the British and held prisoner in the Indies. After seven years he escaped and for REASONS GOOD AND SUFFICIENT WAS GIVEN THE NAME OF JOHN REED.

John's pension file gives no indication of this or any other explanation.

I met another descendant of Percival Lowell, not of our line, while researching at Newbery, Mass. and he indicated that the Lowell family was loyal to England during the Revolution, and were very unfriendly to any members who became rebels; this could have possibly have been a factor in the case.

Under the name of *John Reed*, then a resident of Stockbridge, Massachusetts, he married *Elizabeth Crocker* of Lee, MA, on 24 August 1794 in Lee. This fact appears in his Revolutionary War Pension file and is confirmed in the vital records of Lee.

The following children were born to John and Elizabeth Reed, as listed in his pension file.

"Manda" Read	Born May 21, 1795
Fear Read	Born May 26, 1796
Anne Read	Born December 24, 1797
Pauline Read	Born June 28, 1799
Ruth Read	Born April 26, 1802

John Read　　　　　　　Born April 14, 1804

Recorded in the Vital Records of Lee, Amanda, Fear, Anne and Pauline were born there. The 1800 Federal Census for New York State we find the family living in Chenango County. In 1806 Madison Co. was taken off Chenango Co., so when we find the family living in the Town of Eaton, Madison Co. in the 1810 Census, it could be in the same location. Children Ruth and John were born in Madison Co. according to later censuses.

In the 1820 Census John (Lowell) Reed and his family are listed in Oswego Co., Town of Mexico, NY. This is where his wife and family continued to live. John (Lowell) Reed did not appear in a census again with his family. He could not be found in any New York Census in 1830 and 1840, he probably was moving around a great deal in his chosen trade as a peddler. He applied for a Revolutionary War pension on 4 October 1831, while living in Frankfort, Herkimer Co., NY. The pension was allowed 6 March 1832. His nephew Asa Lowell and family were living in that area. He died in Frankfort 10 May 1840 and is buried in Oak View Cemetery, Frankfort, under the name John Lowell. Buried with him is his nephew, Rev. Asa Lowell (1804–22 Sep 1866), Asa's wife, Aurillo Cross Lowell (1800–6 June 1883) and Asa's son, Reuben Lowell (1832–1855), all the names on the same large monument.

When applying for his Revolutionary War Pension, John (Lowell) Reed stated "I have no wife to support. I have no children able to support me. I have no real estate. I have a Sunday suit and an every day suit of clothing."

John's widow, Elizabeth (Crocker) Reed, applied for a widow's pension March 24, 1849, living in Mexico, Oswego Co., NY. She was referred to as "Elizabeth Reed, alias Lowell" in documents in John's pension file. There were letters in the file from their son John and daughter Ruth, establishing her identity as wife of John Lowell. In his letter son John described his father thus: "was only occasionally at home, that the said John Lowell, alias Reed, was a sort of a peddler, a roving sort of a man and was from home much of the time and made very little provision for his wife or family and that he might with propriety have stated in his affidavit in 1831 "that he had no wife to support." Ruth, their daughter wrote in her letter that her "said father went by the name of John Reed, though his real name was John Lowell," that he had informed her when a child of his real name.

John's brother Asa Lowell, also sent an affidavit, acknowledging his brother as the claimant.

We can find no record of Elizabeth's parents or of her death or of her burial. A letter from her grandson, Morris Reed, of Seymour, WI to Pearl Wadley of Portland, OR, Morris' nephew, dated 10 October 1905, says: "Here is a partial history. This John Lowell is my father's father and Elizabeth was Grandma Reed who died at Stone Quarry or Arthur in 1853." Arthur, originally Stone Quarry, is a settlement in the Town of Mexico. Elizabeth may be buried in the Arthur Cemetery or in the Mexico Village Cemetery in an unmarked grave. The only other record of Elizabeth was her son John's petition to be administrator of his mother's estate on 28 March 1855, she having died without a will. John named Fear, wife of Duran Cheeseman of Springfield, Erie Co., PA, Ruth Reed, of Mexico and himself, of Mexico as the only surviving family members.

Children, surname LOWELL:

2. i. Amanda,^{2} b May 21, 1795, Lee, Berkshire Co., MA. She was with her family in Madison Co., NY. in the 1800 Census. The only other record of Amanda is possibly in an 1850 Census for Oswego Co., Town of Mexico, NY; this Amanda was living with Peter Schermerhorn and family as: Amanda Reed, aged 52 years and "insane." She must have died between 1850 and 1855, when her brother John applied for administration of their mother's estate.

+ 3. ii. Ella Fear, b May 26, 1796, at Lee.

+ 4. iii. Anne Reed, born December 24, 1797, at Lee, MA. She is not in census with her family after 1800, Town of Eaton, Madison Co., NY. She would have been 3 years old.

+ 5. iv. Pauline Reed, b June 28, 1799, at Lee.

6. v. Ruth Reed, b April 26, 1802 in Madison Co., NY. She lived at home with her mother in Mexico through the 1850 Census, she 48 and her mother 87. The 1855 State Census shows her, age 52 living there yet; her nephew Morris Reed (#28), age 8, was with her. In the 1860 Census she is listed living in Mexico with Benjamin Davis and his family, she 54, evidently working for her keep. She lived alone from then on. She bought property in the Village of Colosse, Town of Mexico on 18 July 1862, a town lot. She sold the same property 1 April 1875. According to records of the Oswego County Poor House, she entered the home 16 October 1884, and died there 10 August 1889 of paralysis; she is buried, according to the same records, in the Mexico Village

Cemetery, but there is no stone. She never married.

+   7. vi. John Reed, born April 14, 1804, Town of Eaton, Madison Co., NY.

—COPY—

O.W.& N. Div. 3-525
A.E.P. Dept. of the Interior
Wid. file, 2166 Bureau of Pensions
Washington, D.C. Sept. 26, 1905
M. Reed—Seymour, Wis.

Sir:

In reply to your request for a statement of the Military History of John Lowell, a soldier of the Revolutionary War: You will find below the desired information as contained in his widow's application, for pension on file in this bureau.

Date of enlistment, May 1st., 1777. Term of service 3 years

Officers under whom he served:
Captains: Trescott, North and Fox
Colonels: David Henlrey and Henry Jackson State Continental.

Battles engaged in: Monmouth, N.J. & Rhode Island
Date of application for pension: Oct. 4th, 1831
Residence at date of application: Herkimer Co., N.Y.
Age at date of application: 70 years

Remarks: His claim was allowed

After the war he assumed the name of John Reed. He died May 10th., 1840 at Frankfort, Herkimer County, N.Y.

He married Elizabeth— Aug. 24th., 1794 in Lee, Berkshire Co., Mass.— She applied for pension Mar. 26th, 1849 at which time she lived in Oswego Co., N.Y., aged 80 years. Her claim was allowed.

V. Warner
Commissioner
Morris Reed [Bro. of Cyrus]
R.F.D. 35 Seymour, Wis.

REMARKS

It is a matter of record, at Washington, D.C. that:

While in the service of his country John Lowell was captured by the British, and held prisoner in the Indies. After seven years he escaped and FOR REASONS

John Lowell Reed 19

GOOD AND SUFFICIENT was GIVEN the name of John REED.

It is further recorded that: "His wife, Elizabeth, FOUGHT with and BESTED a British Officer, at the Boston Tea Party."

Cyrus Reed was the son of John Reed. He served his country in the Indian wars. He did scout duty under William "Buffalo Bill" Cody. He moved about from Wyoming to Colo. to Calif. to N. Dak, (where he exercised his Homestead right) to Washington State. Between moves from Colo. to Calif. he owned a general merchandise store in Milford, [MO] and farmed, extensively in Columbus Co., Kansas.

Eva B. Plasteur was the daughter of Cyrus Reed.

Oswego Surrogate Court

In the matter of the administration
of Elizabeth Reed alias
Elizabeth Lowell

To the Surrogate of Oswego County

The petition of John Reed of the Town of Mexico, Oswego County, NY respectfully shows that he is the son of Elizabeth Reed alias Elizabeth Lowell late of the said town of Mexico deceased, that the said Elizabeth dies intestate as your petitioner believes, That your petitioner has to the best of his ability estimated and ascertained the value of the personal property of the said deceased and that the sum does not exceed the value of $20 in value. That the sum intestate left Kindred entitled to her estate whose names and places of residence are as follows: Fear, wife of Duran Cheeseman of Springfield, Erie Co. and state of Pennsylvania. Ruth Reed of Mexico aforesaid, your petitioner the said John Reed, being all the children of the said deceased and of full age, that the said deceased left no husband her surviving.

Your petitioner further shows that the said deceased at the time of her death was a resident of Oswego County, that your petitioner is of full age and he prays that letter of administration be granted to him pursuant to the statement and your petition will ever . . .

Dated March 28, 1855

John Read

Know all men by these present, that we, John Reed, Starr Clarke and Silas Clarke are held and firmly bound, unto the people of the State of New York, in the sum of fifty dollars. lawful money of the United States of America, to be paid to the said people. To which payment well and truly to be made, we bind ourselves, our and each of our heirs, executors and administrators, jointly and severally, firmly by these present. Sealed with our seals.

Dated the 28th day of March in the year of our Lord one thousand eight hundred and fifty five.

The condition of the above obligation is such, that if the above bounden

John Reed

administrator of all and singular the goods, chattels and credits of Elizabeth Reed alias Elizabeth Lowell deceased, shall faithfully execute the trust reposed in him as such administrator and also shall obey all orders that may from time to time be made by the surrogate of the County of Oswego, touching the administration of the estate of the said Elizabeth, deceased, committed to him. Then this obligation to be void, otherwise to remain in full force and virtue.

John Reed
Starr Clark
Silas Clark

State of New York
Oswego County

Ruth Reed, whom I certify is a respectable person and says that John Reed late a pensioner of the United States was her father and that the present applicant for a pension Elizabeth Reed is this deponent's mother, that her said father went by the name of John Reed, though his real name was John Lowell. That this deponent had when a child been informed that her father's name was John Lowell and that so he often told her, but he assumed the name of John Reed and lived and died under that name, that he was pensioned under the name of Lowell, that her said father John Reed or John Lowell died in Frankfort, Herkimer Co., N.Y. on the 10th day of May 1840, leaving his widow the sworn and subscribed before me this 26th day of March, 1849

Signed Ruth Reed

State of New York
Oswego County

John Reed or John Lowell, aged forty-five years (whom I certify is a respectable person) after being duly sworn, deposed and says that he is the son of the late John Lowell alias Reed, who went by the name of John Reed, who was a Revolutionary pensioner under the name of John Lowell, and who died at Frankfort, Herkimer Co., New York May 10, 1840, and that Elizabeth Reed, alias Lowell, the present applicant for a pension as the widow of said John Lowell alias Reed, the said pensioner is the deponent's mother. That she is now a widow and the widow of said John Lowell, alias Reed, the said pensioner, that the said Elizabeth Reed, alias Lowell, who is the deponents's mother and was the wife of said John Lowell, alias Reed, lived in the town of Mexico, in the county of Oswego

John Lowell Reed 21

in the year 1831, that this deponent lived with his mother, the said Elizabeth Reed, alias Lowell at that time and mainly supported her the said Elizabeth Reed alias Lowell and that the said John Lowell the said pensioner, this deponent's father, was only occasionally at home, that the said John Lowell alias Reed, was a sort of a peddler, a roving sort of a man and was from home much of his time and made very little or no provision for his wife or family and that he might with propriety have stated in his affidavit in 1831 "that he had no wife to support," that the said Elizabeth Reed alias Lowell, this proponent's mother and the present applicant for a pension from said County of Oswego, NY was his then wife and whom this proponent knew lived together as man and wife and said John Lowell alias Reed was recognized as the husband of said Elizabeth Reed alias Lowell by all the neighbors and never disputed and the said Elizabeth Reed alias Lowell was always recognized by said John Lowell and the neighbors as his lawful wife and that he never was divorced from her and that she remained his wife till his death. He left her as his widow and sent her his pension certificate. What money he had (about one hundred and fifty dollars) to her and his daughter and this deponent says that she is the identical person who had recently applied for a pension from Oswego County, under the name of Elizabeth Reed alias Lowell, as the widow of the said John Lowell alias Reed, the said pensioner and that she is still his widow.

15th day of May 1849

John Reed
(signature)

Microfilm Record of John Lowell's pension record

Declaration

In order to obtain the benefit of the act of Congress passed on the 29th of July 1848, State of New York and County Oswego.

On the 24th day of March 1849 personally appeared before the subscriber the county Judge of said county Elizabeth Reed of said County, aged eighty __ years, who being first duly sworn according to law doth on her oath make the following declaration, in order to obtain the benefit of the provision made by the act of Congress, passed July 29, 1848.

That she is the widow of John Lowell who was a pensioner of the United States and who went under the assumed name of John Reed, that her said husband served in the war of the Revolution under his then name of John Lowell, the name that his father, brothers and sisters bore at that time, but that owing to circumstances, he changed his name and assumed the name John Reed, and that this deponent was married to him under the name of John Reed in Lee, Berkshire County, Massachusetts by Rev. Alvin Hyde, that for some twenty years she supposed his real name to be John Reed. When she was informed that his real name was John Lowell, that her children bear the name of Reed, that her said husband, the late pensioner John Reed or John Lowell, died at Frankfort, Herkimer Co., N.Y. May 10, 1840. That she was married to him August 24, 1794. Subscribed and sworn before me the 26th day March 1849.

Signed Elizabeth Reed

[July 23, 1849 received $80 per year]
[April 16, 1850 increased to $96 per year]

M. REED
Pension Claim Agent
Seymour, Wis.
Oct. 10, 1905

Say Pete, are you yet alive?

Well old Boy where are you? Can't see a thing of U in 4 dogs ages. Hope you are well, and hope you will be so much interested in the contents of the other side this sheet, you will write a fellow. And just how much this thing means to all of us of Mohawk Blood—can't say yet. Here is a partial history. This John Lowell is my father's father and Elizabeth was grandma Reed who died at Stone Quarry or Arthur in 1853. I was living with Aunt Ruth when she died there. I had heard her tell when I was about 6 or 7 years old that our name was once Lowell. The change I was told grew out of the Rev. War on our side. Well, when I was in Wash. Cyrus told me that when I was in the army, 2 ladies & a man came to the Potash to see Father, and called him Uncle John. They were finely dressed and seemed wealthy. They said "Uncle John, this place and business is not for you; come with us and you shall have your proper place & fare." They came twice and urged him hard but he refused and Cy said he asked Father about them & what they wanted. Father would say but little, only that they was rich & he poor, and he wanted to be his own boss.

When I came here from work, I was introduced to a man in Seymour by a merchant here, and when he heard my name, he said, Reed, Reed. Why I have a brother-in-law in Chicago by that name, and he has been some years looking up his Ancestry—and there is some missing links. I will give him you ad. and you may hear from him and I did. He gave me some of his family history and said his people was from Herkimer Co., NY and that a John Reed once lived in Mexico, Oswego Co., NY. And wanted to know my Grandfather & Mother Reed's names. I did not know at the time, so wrote Cousin Jack Austin at Sparta, Wis. He's very old. He said Grandma's name was Elizabeth and he thought Grand Pa's was John, not certain. So I wrote the Dept. and asked for the military history of the Husband of Elizabeth Reed as I knew she drew a Pension from Rev. War as late as 1852 or 3. The Dept. letter gives the answer.

I Spect to find, perhaps, that we are related to the Hon. James Russell Lowell and Thomas B. Reed, Speaker of House.

R.S.P. & B.M. Heap Punkins. I have for many years had something in my head (if it did crawl) and may work it out. I have written my Chicago man & sent him a duplicate of Dept. letter. He wrote me awhile ago that he was then on his way to Herkimer Co., N.Y. & Mexico, to see what he could find. So I have not yet heard from him. Now, can you throw any light on any of this? Did you ever hear your mother mention it? But I don't know as she ever heard of it.

Well, a word of us—I Bought the 40 acres East of Berts. Am fixing it up to sell the whole place, Berts and this too. We was in hopes to sell and get out of this before Winter. I have never seen such a year as the one now passed. The hardest and longest Winter last Winter I ever saw, and this summer—Rain 2/3 of time til last 3 weeks. We have Hay & that's about all. Very little Potatoes in the state. Grain badly spoiled by excessive rain. But had near 3 acres of cabbage he depended on to pay his debt on his house. He got nearly 35 dollars out of it, and not even potatoes to feed the many mouths. One man has 20 acres cabbage here, all rotted. We must get out of here. Marinda is willing now to go West. I have sunk money coming back, but had to on her account. Where is Mildred? and how are you making it & what doing. Tell me all about it. Write soon, what you think of Dept. letter.

M. Reed.

Chapter 3

The Children of John Reed

3. ELLA[2] FEAR REED (d/o John[1] Lowell), born 26 May 1796 at Lee, Berkshire Co., MA. She was with her family in Madison Co., NY until her marriage to **Duran Cheeseman**, 28 Jan 1818, at Eaton, Madison Co. Duran was the son of Benjamin Cheeseman, who was born in Braintree, MA, 20 September 1756, a Revolutionary War soldier. Duran's mother was Sarah Howe; His great grandparents, George and Jane (Duran) Cheeseman are documented in Church's *History Town of Middlefield, Massachuetts*. Duran was born 1 June 1797 in Middlefield, Hampshire Co., MA and died 10 September 1859 in Springfield, PA age 62 years, about 7 years after his father's death, 29 March 1852.

Benjamin bought 40 acres of land in the Town of Nelson, Madison Co., 3 September 1807 and sold it 12 November 1824, at the time he moved to Erie Co., Pennsylvania with his son and daughter-in-law.

Ella Fear died 1 February 1865, age 68 years, and is buried in the Springfield Cemetery at East Springfield, PA with her husband and father-in-law. They were the parents of eight children:

Children, surname CHEESEMAN:

+ 8. i. William[3] B., b. October 11, 1819 .
+ 9. ii. John Smith, b. February 3, 1821 .
   10. iii. Isaac Dwight, b. 6 November 1822, Nelson. He died there 6 October 1824.
+ 11. iv. Willis Hiram, b. 23 January 1824.
   12. v. Mary Etta, b. 6 August 1827, Springfield, Erie Co, PA; m 8 August 1864 **Ira Simpson**, b June 1825 in New York State. According to 1900 Census for Ashtabula Co., Town of Conneaut, OH, Mary E. Simpson, then 70 years, which would have them married 1849. They had no children. There is a record of a Mary A. Simpson buried in Amboy Cemetery, west of Conneaut, OH, who died 30 July 1902, aged 73 years. This is Mary Etta Cheeseman, according to Cheeseman records held by Ellen and

Louise Johnson of Conneaut.
- 13. vi. Sarah Ann, b. 28 October 1829, Springfield. In her brother William's obituary there was mention of a sister surviving him listed as Mrs. Snow of Girard, Erie Co., PA. Sarah seems the most likely to be that sister; no further records are available.
- 14. vii. Calvin Allen, b. 18 March 1832; d. 10 August 1832, Springfield.
- + 15. viii. Lucien Duran, b. 18 November 1833.

5. PAULINE[2] REED (d/o John[1] Lowell) b. Lee, Berkshire Co., Mass. 28 June 1799: last appeared with family in 1810 Census in Eaton, Madison Co., NY, m. **Lyman L. Austin** (s/o Elihu and Abigail Austin) b. 1799 in Conn. They appear in the Town of Mexico, Oswego Co., NY. in 1820 and 1830 Census. Lyman bought land 25 November 1828 in Town of Parish, sold 11 February 1829; sold more 7 March 1836. [Parish was formed from Mexico 20 March 1828.] In 1840 Census were listed in the Town of Springfield, Erie Co., Pa., as were Pauline's sister and brother in law, Duran and Ella Fear Cheeseman. Lyman bought land 30 January 1838 from Orrin Lyman, 12 acres, 8 October 1843. They moved to Mackford, Green Lake Co., WI, in 1844. (Heiple, Robert. *A Heritage History of Beautiful Green Lake, Wisconsin* (1976); "an area of rolling land and rich soil." "The first religious service was held at the home of Lyman Austin in 1846, with Dr. Randall, a methodist, officiating.") On 24 September 1845 Lyman and Pauline sold 12 acres in Springfield. He bought several acres of land in Town of Mackford, Green Lake Co., WI not far from Lake Maria, one of 40 acres and one of 140 acres in 1848. Pauline died in Town of Mackford September 8, 1854 at age 55. She is buried in Lake Maria Cemetery, Town of Mackford.

Lyman L. Austin married second in Town of Harden, Green Lake Co., **Cornelia (Cooper) Smith**, 31 March 1855. He had two sons by her: Emmett Austin, born 3 June 1855, at Mackford, and Nelson C. Austin, born 1860. He divorced her and married third **Eliza Austin**, d/o Ebenezer and Mary (Bickford) Austin January 8, 1866. He divorced her and married fourth February 18, 1869, **Lucinda (Hooper) Peterson**, d/o David and Nancy Hooper, born Livingston Co., NY; he later divorced her. Lyman L. Austin died October 28, 1871 in Town of Mackford, Green Lake Co., WI and is buried with Pauline in Lake Maria Cemetery. The later marriage of Lyman and his other descendants are more fully covered in the appendix.

Children, surname AUSTIN:

Children of John Reed

+ 16. i. Angeline,[3] b 14 July 1820.
+ 17. ii. Lyman, b 26 October 1821.
+ 18. iii. Amanda Melissa, b 29 September 1823.
+ 19. iv. Minerva, b 4 October 1825.
+ 20. v. Theron S., b March 14, 1828.
+ 21. vi. Andrew Jackson, b 28 February 1830.
   22. vii. Melinda, b 1832, New York State; m Benjamin F. Baker, b 10 July 1826 at New Hudson, Allegany Co., NY. He enlisted in the Civil War at Winona, Minnesota on 1 April 1865 as Corporal in Co. H, 1st Regiment of Minnesota Volunteer Infantry, age 39. He was discharged at Jeffersonville, IN 14 July 1865. Benjamin appeared in the First Ward of the City of Winona, MN in the 1870 and 1880 U.S. Census with Melinda. He was a builder and developer in Winona. Baker and North Baker Streets were named for him. He bought, moved, remodeled, and sold old houses in the west end of the city. He also platted the Baker and Balcom additions to the city. Melinda died 26 July 1896, "age 67, at her home near Lackey Coleman's, west of the city. She was an invalid for many years. The funeral took place from the Olive Branch M. E. Church." Benjamin married second Rachel Minerva Dougherty at the Olive Branch M. E. Church, Winona on 10 December 1896, according to his Civil War file. Benjamin was admitted to National Home for Disabled Volunteer Soldiers at Wood, Wisconsin, near Milwaukee 10 March 1908, age 82, and he died there 27 May 1909. Both Melinda and Benjamin are buried at Woodlawn Cemetery, Winona. No records of any children found. She took Nelson Austin into her home after he [Lyman L.] died in 1871.
+ 23. viii. Elizabeth, born circa 7 May 1836.
+ 24. ix. Matilda, b 1838.
+ 25. x. William Harrison, b 1840.

7. JOHN[2] REED (John[1] Lowell), born 14 April 1804 at Town of Eaton, Madison County, NY. He came to Mexico, Oswego Co., NY. with his parents and sister Ruth about 1820. John was a potash boiler according to the 1855 Census, working in an ashery, where wood ashes from trees burned in clearing the land were processed into lye for making soap and glass. These products were shipped out in oak barrels, a good cash crop of the time. Some farmers nearly paid for their land by the sale of ashes to the asheries. The 1855 Census says John and children lived in a house of logs. We only have a record of a short time when John owned land. On

20 November 1862 he bought 13–39/100 acres, part of Lot 103 on Stone Road, three miles south of Mexico village, for $401.70, borrowed from Joshua Wadley, his future son-in-law, with a mortgage of $93.94 due that date. Less than four years later he sold this land to his son Michael, for $400, on 11 April 1866, carrying a mortgage in his son Morris' name for $130, bearing the date 10 April 1864. As an interesting sidelight, we came across a bit of information on a money order that was sent from New Lancer, PA by the Eastern Adams Express Company from Morris Reed, dated 3 April 1865 to his father for $200. This may have been to pay off the mortgage. Morris was serving in the army in the Civil War at the time. Where exactly the family lived in the Town of Mexico, for all the years, is unknown.

John was living with his mother and sister Ruth at the time of the 1840 Census, age 36. It must have been fairly soon after this that he married **Sarah Ann Hotchkiss**, d/o Stephen and Tryphena (Daniels) Hotchkiss. Sarah was born in 11 Feb 1824 in Mexico and lived not far from the Reed family, according to the census. By the 1850 Census all their children had been born, except Ida. Sarah Ann died 3 May 1853, probably of Tuberculosis and is buried in Mexico Village Cemetery as "Sarah Ann, wife of John Read, Died May 3, 1853, age 28 years." At the bottom of the monument which has a large carved weeping willow tree and urn at the top, is the following verse:

> Death thou has conquered,
> But Christ has conquered thee
> And I will rise again.

After Sarah's death the family was partially broken up, with Morris, age six, going to live with his Aunt Ruth Reed at Colosse, a few miles from Mexico. Ida, the youngest child, nineteen months old, was taken into the home of friends of the family, Asa and Mary Westcott, who brought her up as their own child; she went by the name of Westcott.

According to an 1898 account written by John's son Morris, in about 1854 or 55, with hope of starting a new life in Wisconsin, John and four of his children left Mexico.

Alta Kennedy, daughter of Ida Reed Canfield, visited Morris' son Bert and his wife at Seymour, WI in 1938. While there she was told about this first journey made by John and his children. It seems that they walked the whole distance from the family home in New York to Wisconsin. John was 51, Michael 13, Martha 11, Morris 9, Mary 7, and Cyrus 6.

We know from Morris' account, given to me from a descendant in Wisconsin, that Mackford, in Green Lake County, in the central part of the state, was their first destination. Recent research reveals that John's sister Pauline and her husband, Lyman L. Austin, also lived there. Morris went on to say:

My father's nephew [probably Lyman and Pauline's son, Jack, in Sparta, from Morris' letter to Pearl Wadley dated 10 October 1905] had preempted some land for him away up in the wilds of Chippewa and the next year finds my father and myself and youngest brother in company with two other emigrant families on the way to see our possessions along the bluffs of Chippewa.

Our train was composed of five large covered wagons drawn by oxen, and one covered light wagon drawn by horses for the ladies' use. We had also some stock to drive at which I assisted my father what I was able. We cooked at the open campfire and some of us slept under the wagons upon the ground. Game was plenty—such as deer, some elk and wolves beside smaller game.

We often saw wild Indians with their blankets around them and armed with bow and arrow. They were all friendly and we had no fear of them.

In due time we reached our destination and camped away up on a bluff near the road that wound around the bluff in the coulie or valley making a sharp bend at the place called the Devil's Elbow. This is where some of those we were with owned land, while Father's was some miles further on.

Father at once pitched our camp which consisted of two crotched sticks drove into the ground and a ridge pole across, and over this a couple of blankets with the corners fastened to the ground with stakes. My brother and I kept house and father went to see his new farm. On his return he said "We will have to get out of this—that land is one half sand and rock bluff and the balance clear sand where a gopher could not live."

We remained there a few days and provisions began to get scarce all around. And my father decided to leave us boys there and foot it back to Sparta, a distance I believe of about 100 miles. He had a relative there and wanted to get his team to move us out. He returned without the team, having made about 50 miles a day on foot. But before he started on his journey, our provisions had given out and he had taken some seed corn from his trunk and boiled it and that lasted us til nearly the time of his return. The other families had not enough for their own use and could not help us.

Once in a long time an old stage coach or ark as it was called, made a trip through that country and in it we managed to reach civilization again after a time. Father then determined to return to our old home on Salmon River in York State [Mexico] as soon as possible. And the next year found us aboard boat making the run of the chain of Big Lakes—homeward bound, or to what we called Home.

On our way we stopped at Erie, PA and visited some relatives for a week or two [John's sister, Fear Cheeseman], then boarded a schooner and made sail for Oswego, NY. A big storm and then a big calm made our passage slow but at last we landed in the desired haven and was glad.

Father resumed his old occupation in the ashery, and all but my youngest brother and oldest sister went to work for farmers as we could find places.

While Morris Reed was away fighting in the Civil War, according to a letter he wrote 10 October 1905 to Pearl Wadley, his cousin, The Lowell family tried to entice John to go live with them. Cyrus, Morris' younger brother told him "That when I was in the army, two ladies and a man came to the Potash to see Father, and called him Uncle John. They were finely dressed, and seemed wealthy. They said, "Uncle John, this place and business is not for you; come with us and you shall have your proper place and faire." They came twice and urged him hard but he refused and Cy said he asked Father about them and what they wanted. Father would say but little, only that they were rich and he poor, and he wanted to be his own boss.

Of this incident, there was another account written by Cyrus' son, Floyd Reed in which he says,

My Father was just about 4-1/2 years old, but remembers quite a little of the incident that I am going to describe. The father of the two boys, Cyrus and Morris, your great grandfather, was a Potash maker, He made it out of wood ashes that he had teams gathering up around the country. One day a splashing sorrel team drove up hitched to an underslung buggy, with both coachman and driver in stove pipe hats. With them was some delightfully dressed ladies (for that day) and a distinguished looking gentleman. One of the ladies alighted from the carriage and called, or addressed Uncle Morris, my father's father, as Uncle. He turned on her and told her that he had told them before that he never wanted to see John Russell again as long as he lived. He absolutely refused to have anything to do with them. Now I do not understand this myself. The gentleman that refused to see the party in the carriage, was my grandfather and it was his father that changed his name to Reed.

In reality, Cyrus must have been at least 12 years old if his brother Morris was in the army. The callers without much doubt must have been some of the Lowell family living in Herkimer Co., NY., namely John (Lowell) Reed's brother Asa Lowell's family. Asa Lowell, Jr. and his wife Aurilla and one of their daughters probably, who were living in Frankfort, Herkimer Co., NY then, and with whom John (Lowell) Reed was buried as John Lowell. Through the years the family became obsessed by the idea that they were related to James Russell Lowell, the poet. This relationship has been touched on in the preceding chapter.

John Reed's youngest daughter, Ida, was only nineteen months old. when her mother died. Friends of the family, Asa and Mary Westcott, then living in Mexico, NY took her into their home when she was a baby and raised her as their own child. Asa was a soldier in the Civil War and died 25 July 1863 in the south. Ida's daughter, Alta Canfield Kennedy, said that after Mary Westcott became a widow, John Reed approached her with a proposal of marriage, he having been a widower since 1853. However, she did not care to marry again, but said he was always welcome to come and visit Ida. He did visit from time to time, sometimes for a week or more at a time, helping with the farm work, as Mary and Ida were still living on the farm.

John was still living in Mexico at the time of the 1865 Census; John was 55, Michael was 22 and Morris, 20. Cyrus was away working at a flax factory at the time and enlisted in the army in 1866 and left with the army for Wyoming.

In 1868 Morris and his young family left for Seymour, WI by wagon. Michael left sometime later, about 1869, for Wisconsin. John was left alone. His granddaughter Eva Belle Plasteur applied for membership in the D.A.R. years later, on the basis of John Lowell's Revolutionary War record. She stated that grandfather John Reed died in 1880.

Until recently we had no knowledge of what happened to John. His son Morris, living in Seymour, Wisconsin, tried hard to find out about his father as evidenced in a letter to his sister, Ida, dated December 17, 1885. "I have written to Syracuse again to see if I can find father." He and Ida believed he worked in the salt industry in Syracuse. Also while again going through Grandmother Ida Canfield's papers I happened on a note written by her on the back of a bill for blacksmith supplies the following:

> John Reed, the Father of
> Mrs. Ida Canfield
> Father went to Syracuse
> July 5, 1878
> Died December 10, 1880
> H. R. Knapp, Keeper—
> State Asylum,
> Syracuse, NY.

A check of the Proceedings of the Board of Supervisors of Onondaga County for 1881, page 205, has the following report on the Poor.

The following named inmates of the Poor House died during the year:
John Reed, December 10, 1880.

John must have entered the home shortly after he left Mexico in 1878; he was listed as being there all through 1879. The Poor House was located at Onondaga Hill, Syracuse. It is uncertain where the inmates, at that time, were buried; there is a graveyard behind the Poor House, but there is no record showing John was buried there. As a ward of the state and because he was from out of county; no Onondaga County village was responsible for his support.

Children, surname REED, all born at Mexico, NY:

+ 26. i. Michael,[3] b 4 March 1842.
+ 27. ii. Martha, b about 1844.
+ 28. iii. Morris, b 13 July 1846.
+ 29. iv. Mary Marie, b about 1848.
+ 30. v. Cyrus, b 6 September 6, 1849.
+ 31. vi. Ida Adella, b 17 August 1851.

Chapter 4

The Third Generation

8. WILLIAM[3] B. CHEESEMAN (s/o Ella[2] Fear (Reed) Cheeseman, #3), b 11 October 1819 at Town of Eaton, Madison Co., NY. Lenna Johnson's records indicate William married Emy D. Ricky, 22 April 1845; no record of this marriage was found. The only marriage verified is to **Lorina Emeline Jackson**, probably d/o Royal G. and Sophie Jackson, b 5 August 1826; d 12 March 1901, age 75 years, at Milesgrove [Lake City], Town of Girard, Erie Co., PA. In the 1850 and 1860 Census the family was located in Town of Conneaut, Erie Co., PA with William listed as a farmer. They appear in the 1870 Census living in Town of Albion, Erie Co., PA., William listed as Justice of Peace and Lorina as a Milliner. In 1880 Census, still in Town of Albion, William was listed with the occupation of "wooden handle factory." On 14 November 1888 they sold Lots 4–10 in Block 17 in Town of Albion, containing 2 acres, formerly owned by Royal Jackson, while living in the village of Milesgrove. William died in 1889, age about 70 years, and he and Lorina are buried in the Girard Cemetery.

Children, surname CHEESEMAN:

    32. i. Pauline[4] L., b about 1846 at Milesgrove. According to an obituary in *Erie* [PA] *Observer* of May 7, 1869, she died in Albion, 17 April 1869, age 23 years.

+   31. ii. Royal D., b about January 1848.

    32. iii. Elda E., b about 1850. Married and lived in Sedalia, MO.

    34. iv. Eva M., b about 1852. Married and lived in Sedalia. I visited there and found no records of either Elda or Eva.

    36. v. Mary Adella, b about 1854; d 17 January 1882 at Albion, about 28 years of age.

+   37. vi. Jennie C., b about 1859.

+   38. vii. Carrie I., b about 1866.

9. JOHN[3] SMITH CHEESEMAN (s/o Ella[2] Fear (Reed) Cheeseman, #3) b 3 February 1821 in Town of Nelson, Madison Co., NY. He was in Springfield, Erie Co., PA by 1830 with his family. In 1850 U.S. Census, Town of Girard, Erie Co., he was a clerk, age 29, working for John

Guilford, a merchant. John m 18 April 1855 **Elizabeth** "Betsy or Bess" **E. Sherman**, d/o John Sackett and Polly (DeWolf) Sherman, b 31 July 1831. John died 1 July 1893 at Conneaut, Ashtabula Co., OH, age 72 years and 5 months. Ellen and Louise Johnson say he was a "loan shark." Elizabeth d about 4 February 1916, according to her will, registered in Ashtabula Co. Court House, Jefferson, OH. John and Elizabeth are both buried at Conneaut City Cemetery.

Child, surname CHEESEMAN:

    39. i. Nellie Louise, b November 1862 at Conneaut. She did not marry and lived at home. She d 2 February 1902 of Typhoid Fever, age 40 and is buried at Conneaut City Cemetery.

10. WILLIS[3] HIRAM CHEESEMAN (s/o Ella[2] Fear (Reed) Cheeseman, #3) b 23 January 1824 at Nelson, Madison Co., NY.; m 28 September 1862 **Valnette Miriam Durkee**, d/o James H. and Huldah (Carpenter) Durkee, b 15 March 1836 in PA. They sold 41 acres of land in Springfield Township, Erie Co., PA in 1866. They were located in the Town of Conneaut, Erie Co. according to the 1870 U.S. Census, where Willis listed as a merchant. Willis died in Monroe, Ashtabula, OH, now known as Kelloggsville, on 20 March 1903, age 79 years. Grandson Homer Marble believes he is buried in Conneaut; no record found. Valnette d 27 August 1894, age 58, at Monroe, OH of Typhoid Fever and is buried in Conneaut City Cemetery on the Durkee lot.

Children, surname CHEESEMAN:

    40. i. James[4] D., b 18 November 1863; he died the same day.
    41. ii. Alburtus "Bertie," b 8 April 1866: d 14 November 1872.
+   42. iii. Alice Juliet, b 4 October 1868.

15. LUCIEN[3] DURAN CHEESEMAN (s/o Ella[2] Fear (Reed) Cheeseman, #3) b 18 November 1833 at Springfield, Erie Co., PA: m **Deborah Elizabeth Sherman**, d/o John S. and Polly (DeWolf) Sherman, b 8 February 1840 at East Springfield, Erie Co. The 1895–96 *Conneaut City Directory* show Lucien and Deborah Cheeseman living at 247 Buffalo St., Conneaut, listed as a furniture dealer. The building which housed the furniture business is still in possession of the family. Lucien died 31 July 1907; Deborah died 17 November 1909 in Conneaut. They both are buried in Conneaut City Cemetery.

Children, surname CHEESEMAN:

    43. i. Lizzie,[4] b 1873: d 1882, age 9 years.

+   44.   ii.   Lenna Sherman, b 16 January 1886.

16. ANGELINE[3] **AUSTIN** (d/o Pauline[2] (Reed) Austin, #5), b 14 July 1820 in New York State, probably at Mexico, Oswego Co.; m 17 February 1849, probably at Green Lake Co., WI, **Henry Crouch**, b in England 24 February 1818. They were together in Green Lake Co., Town of Middleton [later part of Green Lake Township] in the 1850 Census, he 33 and she 30. Their first child was born later that year. The 1860 Census lists them in Town of Sparta, Monroe Co., WI and were still there at the time of the 1870 Census. Angeline's brother, Andrew Jackson Austin lived in Sparta, as well as her sister Matilda. They were at Wasioja, Dodge Co., MN at the time of the 1880 U.S. Census. Angeline died of "paralysis" 25 February 1898, age 77 years and is buried in Wildwood Cemetery, Wasioja, as is Henry, who died 1 November 1895, age 77 years, 8 mo, 7 days. According to Angeline's obituary they were parents of 7 children.

Children, surname CROUCH:

+   45.   i.   George[4] Henry, b 3 June 1850.
+   46.   ii.   Nelson Reasoner, b 7 December 1851.
+   47.   iii. Emma A., b 12 August 1854.
     48.   iv.   Charles Wesley, b 10 August 1856 at Sparta, WI; d 14 February 1893, age 36 years, 6 mo., 4 days: buried at Wildwood Cemetery.
     49.   v.   John Wesley, b 10 August 1856 (twin); d 15 September 1856; buried on Crouch lot at Big Creek Cemetery, near Sparta.
     50.   vi.   James Harrison, b 2 August 1862 at Sparta; d 30 August 1862, 29 days old; buried on Crouch Lot in Big Creek Cemetery, near Sparta.
     51.   vii. Walter Irvin, b 25 July 1865; d 9 September 1865.

17. LYMAN[3] **AUSTIN** (s/o Pauline[2] (Reed) Austin, #5) b 26 October 1821 at Mexico, Oswego Co., NY.; m 18 September 1845 at Albion, Erie Co., PA, **Lou Emma Church**, d/o Joshua and Sophronia (Shurtleff) Church, b about 1824 at Springfield, PA. His land possessions at one time aggregated more than 1200 acres, situated in Eau Claire, Buffalo and Green Lake counties, WI and a 165 acre tract in Faribault Co., MN. The 1850, 1860, 1870, 1880, and 1890 U.S. Census show them living in Town of Mackford, Green Lake Co., WI. The 1900 Census does not reveal where they were then or thereafter. They had one adopted daughter, according to the 1880 U.S. Census.

Child, surname AUSTIN:

+ 52. i. Emma, born about 1856.

18. AMANDA[3] MELISSA AUSTIN (d/o Pauline[2] (Reed) Austin, #5) b 29 September 1823 in Mexico, Oswego Co., NY; m 25 December 1845 in Dodge Co., WI, **Lansing Martin**, b about 23 November 1817 in western New York. He came to Wisconsin about 1843. He lived in Troy, Kingston, Manchester and Lake Maria, before moving to Ripon, Fond du Lac Co., about 1871. He died 10 August 1891, age 72 years, 8 mo., 17 days, at Ripon and is buried at Lake Maria Cemetery, Town of Mackford, Green Lake Co., WI. Amanda died 24 September 1904, age 81, at Town of Trenton, Dodge Co., WI at the home of Howard Quick, a grandson. She is also buried at Lake Maria Cemetery. According to her obituary she had eight children, seven of whom can be accounted for. One was born before her marriage, and may have been from an earlier marriage; Amanda was called his second wife in his obituary.

Children, surname MARTIN:
  53. i. Marriett,[4] b about 1842 according to the 1850 U.S. Census.
  54. ii. Worthy or Wesley, b about 1847 as listed in the 1850 and 1860 U.S. Census.
  55. iii. Esther M., b about 1850; died 14 June 1862, age 11 years, buried Lake Maria Cemetery.
+ 56. iv. Ellen M., b 19 August 1851.
  57. v. Loren, b about 28 October 1854; d 10 November 1854, age 14 days; buried Lake Maria Cemetery
+ 58. vi. Amanda Elizabeth, b 29 June 1858.
  59. vii. Adelbert, b about June 1859; d 4 October 1859, 4 month 18 days. Buried Lake Maria Cemetery.

19. MINERVA[3] AUSTIN (d/o Pauline[2] (Reed) Austin, #5) b 4 October 1825 at Mexico, Oswego Co., NY. She moved with her family to Green Lake Co., WI about 1845.; m 19 April 1846 at Marcellon, Columbia Co., WI, **Peleg Lawton Peckham**, b 24 May 1819 in Madison Co., NY. He was probably s/o Stephen and Ruth (Lawton) Peckham. He was a lifelong farmer in Town of Marcellon, since 1846 when he arrived from New York State. Minerva d 22 November 1894, age 69 years. Peleg d 26 November 1886, age 67 years. Both are buried in Marcellon Cemetery, Columbia Co., WI. One child who died in infancy, is not listed.

Children, surname PECKHAM:
+ 60. i. John[4] Eber, b 22 July 1850.

The Third Generation

+   61.   ii.   Lucretia M., b 18 March 1854.
+   62.   iii.   Elizabeth, b 21 November 1858.
+   63.   iv.   Charles Wesley, b 20 November 1861.
+   64.   vi.   William Harrison, b 13 November 1864.

20. THERON[3] S. AUSTIN (s/o Pauline[2] (Reed) Austin, #5) b. 14 March 1828 at Mexico, Oswego Co., NY; m/1 **Lorilla Mershom** 8 May 1850 at Springfield, Erie Co., PA, b about 21 December 1829: d 25 February 1854, age 24 years, 2 mo., 4 days, probably as a result of the birth of her second child, and is buried at Lake Maria Cemetery Green Lake Co., WI. Theron m/2 **Frances Jane Leach** 10 December 1856 at Springfield, Erie Co., PA. Theron enlisted in Co. I, 14th Penn. Cavalry 28 October 1862 and was killed 14 Aug 1863, age 35y, 5m, near Petersburg, VA while on picket duty. Affidavit of son Myron Austin states death was on 15 August. Theron and Lorilla are buried in Lake Maria Cemetery, Town of Mackford, Green Lake Co., WI. Frances Leach received a pension until March 1871, living in Springfield, PA.

    Children, surname AUSTIN:

    65.   i.   Myron,[4] b 31 December 1851/2, probably in Springfield, He was very young when his mother died in 1854 and not quite 12 years when his father was killed in the Civil War. An affadavit in Theron's Civil War Pension file, written by Sarah Hyatt and dated 30 April 1898, a resident of Lodi, Madison Co., OH, says she, sister of Lorilla (Theron's wife), raised him from the age of four years until he was 21 years old. She also says "I obtained the date of his birth from a letter written me by my mother. Said letter is now lost but I can remember distinctly that the date was 31 December 1852 . . ."

    On 2 March 1896 Myron married Mrs. Kate Kepley in Delaware County, Indiana. The WPA Index to Supplemental Record Marriage Transcript, Delaware Co. 1882–1911 lists Myron Austin, 47, son of Theron and Clarissa Mershon.

    In Emerson's *Muncie Directory for 1897–98* Myron Austin and wife Kate appeared, with notation that he worked for Whiteley Malleable Castings Co., home NW corner Madison and 8th. The 1899–1900 Directory showed just Mrs. Kate Austin living there.

    A check of deaths, probates, land and Cemetery records in the Muncie (Delaware Co.) IN Court House gave no answers as to his fate.

66. ii. Melvin M., b 17 February 1854; d 29 August 1854.

21. ANDREW[3] JACKSON AUSTIN (s/o Pauline[2] (Reed) Austin, #5) b 28 February 1830 in Town of Parish, Oswego Co., NY. He m 17 November 1858 at Sparta, Monroe Co., WI, **Edna Brown**; probably d/o Lucian and Ann (Whitcomb) Brown, b 10 March 1836 in Vermont; d 5 March 1898. Andrew farmed for many years at Big Creek, Monroe Co., WI. and lived the last years in Sparta, WI. He died 6 February 1911 in Sparta, both are buried there in Mount Hope Cemetery.

Children, surname AUSTIN:

+ 67. i. Ann Janette, better known as Nettie, b 18 September 1859 at Big Creek, Monroe Co., WI. near Sparta.

68. ii. Edson L., b 27 January 1860 at Big Creek; he lived and worked in Minneapolis, where he died 3 March 1932, age 72 years, 1 mo., 16 days. He is buried in Mount Hope Cemetery in an unmarked grave; The only record was at cemetery office. No record was ever found of marriage or children.

69. iii. Alice Melinda, b 10 May 1868, Big Creek, Monroe Co., WI. The city Directory of LaCrosse, Wisc. lists Alice as a teacher of drawing from 1888 to 1891 in the city schools. She married 24 October 1906 Charles Frank Hutson, s/o John and Mary Hutson, at Sparta, Wisc., her age listed as 38 years. Charles was b about 1864 at Jamestown, NY. Both were active members of the Methodist Church, teaching in the Sunday School, and he acted as Financial Secretary on the Official Board of the church for twenty years. Alice d 24 March 1941 at Sparta, Wisc., not quite 73 years old, and Charles d 29 March 1942, also at Sparta. Both are buried in Big Creek Cemetery, near Sparta. They had no children.

+ 70. iv. Allen M., born 10 May 1868 a twin to Alice. From a descendant of Allen came the information that Allen during part of his life was a Forest Ranger based in the Jackson Hole, WY area. The only information available on Allen is from a letter written by Mrs. Esther B. Allan, wife of the Ranger, about 1940, obtained from Cheyenne, Wyoming archives. There are errors in regard to his family, so all may not be entirely accurate. The following are excerpts from the letter:

"The Austin family lived close to a tribe of Blackfoot Indians and Lizzie Monroe, a half breed, took Al to take care of because his mother couldn't feed and care for the two babies and her two other small children.

"His father was a carpenter who went up and down the river to different posts on a raft first and later in a boat or canoe, doing jobs wherever he was needed.

"Al was raised as an Indian boy and many of his beliefs and habits were formed at this period and which influenced his entire life. He learned to hunt, live and think as an Indian. He believed, for one thing, he had developed an ability to photograph animals like the Indians hunted with bow and arrow and the results of his method make this easy to believe. He also thought he had developed a sixth sense from close association with animals and this enabled him to get pictures up closer and in more unusual poses as he instinctively seemed to know, in many cases, just when there would be an animal around the next bend of the trail and he would have his light reading and camera all set for the picture.

"1885. Al was helping the Blackfoot Indians near Mt. McCloud in the Louis Riel Rebellion and was wounded in the neck.

"1888–1889. Al worked in the Ferris Haggerty Mine in southern Wyoming, then in Bob Tail Mine at Ouray, Col. He went into Jackson Hole Country for the first time and worked there a few years.

"1894–1897. He was in Alaska, but he never revealed what he did there. He had a hard time and nearly starved. He said that if he ever wanted to die, that after the first few days of hunger, it isn't an unpleasant sensation, to die of starvation.

"1899–1900. He was in Butte, Montana working as a mechanic in a mine. Here he met his wife and met the great tragedy of his life, when she died a year later in Prescott , Arizona. For several years after that he wandered from place to place on horseback, working when it became necessary. He ended up in Jackson Hole as he had liked it so much on his first visit. In the early 1900s acted as guide for different well known men on different expeditions but mostly to search for pictures and facts on animal life. Eastman was one of these. He took him out on several trips and Eastman became Al Austin's lifelong friend, and gave him many gifts of cameras and equipment. It was one of these, a telephoto lens , that enabled Al to get some tooth hunters convicted that had long been killing many elk both in this country and in Yellowstone Park.

"1914. He was building a road over Teton Pass when the war started.

"1914, 1915, 1916. He worked summers on the Teton Pass Road and in winters did things he enjoyed such as photography and studying wildlife. He worked with leather and made himself and his friends many fine leather articles."

Sometime between 1900 and 1920 he guided W.T. Horneday on a trip to study and photograph wildlife. Horneday was head of the New York Zoo, and wrote a book on natural history.

"1917. Al Austin ran a garage in Jackson. He was a first class mechanic and did a great deal of work on cars and machinery when he needed a grub stake.

"1918–1920. He was a mechanic for Skinner & Eddy (the big ship building men) at the Hatchet Ranch, which he built up the Buffalo River some 15 miles above Moran, Wyo. It is still known by that name.

"1920–1922. After the war, he was an instructor mechanic at the Russell Air Fields. A pilot friend of his, Pilot Leese, taught him to fly. Then he and another man started a flying company, the LeGrande Air School at LeGrande, Oregon, but it failed.

"1922. He returned to Jackson Hole and worked on road construction. He helped build the road from Moose to Moran until the year 1925. From 1922 on, Al was a mechanic here and there in Jackson Hole; did Road work and other jobs; was one of the early Forest Rangers; and acted as photographer and guide. He was the first mechanic in Teton Park and he also took pictures for them and gave talks at their campfire programs for the tourists and showed his animal movies. He took wildlife pictures for the Forest Service, also. He made some excellent movies of wildlife at this period and later.

"Al was a friend of all wild life and was well known for his unusual pictures of animals both in stills and motion picture. He spent weeks living with them and studying and had a wealth of material concerning them and their habits. He hated hunters and liked people who felt the same way.

"His early experiences in Jackson Hole; his first-hand knowledge of animals and picture experience; his personal information on mysteries of the country and his fund of history, made him an interesting companion. He didn't like many people but those he did, were his life long friends and he was completely loyal.

"LAST YEARS. The past few years of his life he acted as mechanic for Teton Park until about 1939 and also as caretaker for the Woodburys in the winter. The last two summers he lived in the Arizona Guard Station on the Jackson Lake Ranger District about ten miles above Moran towards Yellowstone Park. This was his favorite spot in Jackson Hole and he had spent many days in the area behind the cabin looking for animals to visit with and take pictures of. My husband, who is ranger of this district gave him permission to use the cabin there and he spent his last summers either in the cabin or when the weather was good, in his tent-camp a couple of miles back of it. He spent the last years doing the thing he loved most, camping out and near his best friends, the wild creatures, and communing with nature. He took a few of us out on his beloved cook-outs and would serve us Dutch oven lunches in some of his favorite spots and tells us tales of his life or recite some of his own poetry.

"He had long expressed his desire to die when his time came like an old bull elk away from the herd and in his favorite spot. He had long been sick and believed he had cancer. He had planned to die and had picked his spot. He didn't want to be a nuisance to his friends. He sorted out all his possessions and gave them to each of his friends over the last two years of his life. On the twentieth of October (1940), a year ago, Al came down and spent the entire day with us and it seemed very special, but I didn't know why at the time. Now I know it was his way of telling us goodbye. He returned on the 28th of October to bring us some of his things to keep for him, he said, as he was going to Montana for the winter in a day or so. That was the last time anyone saw him so we know he just went back up to the Arizona and drove his car back a half mile into the timber and hid it. He then walked back over to the camp he had been preparing for months. He didn't want any of us to start worrying about him and searching. If we had seen his car, we would have thought that is what he had done, so he hid it well, took off the tail-light reflector and all things that might attract attention, and partially covered it with pine-boughs.

"None of us thought anything about his not having gone to Montana, as he had said, until the next spring. When his mail kept coming back to Jackson Hole, undelivered, and the snow had long been gone and still he didn't show up, two or three who knew him well began to wonder if he had ever gone outside. My husband, Sunny Allan, was sure that he was back of the Arizona Station in his last camp. So he asked two of his fire-guards who were then working trails in that area to spend some time extra and keep a look-out for Al's camp just in case he might be there. They looked for days before they found him. On June 11th, 1941, the two boys came in to report that they found Al's body. In his camp was plenty of wood and tea but only two unopened cans of meat—no other cans or signs of food. He hadn't eaten or taken any food with him but the meat which was untouched. This brings to mind the experience he had in Alaska when he nearly starved and thought it an easy death. He was in great pain with his sickness and perhaps chose that way out. His diary had only one page in it and on this he had enumerated the dates it snowed but that is all. The last entry was the second week in November. Note: The local sheriff's office in Jackson, Wyoming, has this diary and complete information on it."

23. ELIZABETH[3] **AUSTIN** (d/o Pauline[2] (Reed) Austin, #5) b about 7 May 1836, probably at Springfield, Erie Co., PA. Her parents sold land in Town of Parish, Oswego Co., NY 7 March 1836, and moved to Springfield. She married 26 November 1856 at Kingston, Marquette Co., WI, **Edward Ames**, s/o Phineas and Hannah (Leonard) Ames, at the home of the minister, Rev. William Sturges. Edward was born 11 November 1832 at Haverill, NH. As a child he moved to the Province of Ontario, Canada, then with parents to Wisconsin, where they settled in Mackford, Green Lake Co. in 1850. He spent the last year of his life with his daughter, Mrs. Crane, in Oshkosh, WI, where he died 11 Oct 1919, age 86 years; he was reported to be buried at Markesan, Green Lake Co., WI but no such record has been found. Elizabeth preceded her husband in death, 9 October 1889, in Dodge Co., WI, age 53 years, 5 Mo. and 2 days, and she is buried at Lake Maria Cemetery, Green Lake Co. Very little information on this family was available.

Children, surname AMES:
- 71. i. Rhoda,[4] b about 1858 at Green Lake Co. According to her father's obituary she was Mrs. Butler of Minnesota.
- + 72. ii. Mary Ann, b July, 1863.
- 73. iii. Amy Elizabeth, b about 1869 at Green Lake Co. Her father's obituary lists her as Mrs. Freeman of Oshkosh.
- 74. iv. Edward M., b about 1872 at Green Lake Co. He was not living when his father died in 1919.

24. MATILDA[3] **AUSTIN** (d/o Pauline[2] Reed Austin, #5) b about 1 July 1838 at Springfield, Erie Co., PA where the family were living at the time; m 3 November 1858 in Monroe Co., WI (probably Sparta), **Thomas Boston Phillips**, b 21 April 1832 near Pittsburgh, PA. In the 1870 Census there was a Jonathan Phillips, age 68, living with Thomas, perhaps his father. Thomas came to Sparta as a young man in 1856; on account of poor health the doctor ordered him to Missouri in 1870. He returned to Wisconsin in 1874 and four years later they moved to Wasioja, Dodge Co., MN. Matilda's brother, Andrew J. Austin and her sister Angeline (Austin) Crouch lived at Sparta, too; Angeline also moved to Wasioja. Matilda d 20 March 1882, age 43 years, and Thomas d 12 April 1899, age 67 years, both at Wasioja where they are buried in Wildwood Cemetery, next to Angeline and Henry Crouch. A record of the Phillips children was found in possession of Mrs. Clara Hanson, West Concord, MN; who had copied the data from the Phillips family bible.

Children, surname PHILLIPS:

    75. i. Lyman[4] Addison, b 22 August 1859 at Sparta; d 5 February 1932, age 72 years, 5 Mo., 14 days. At the age of 19 he went with his parents to Wasioja; five years later he went to Mellette SD, where he made his home until c. 1920 when he made his home with his sister, Mrs. James Abel of Claremont, MN. He had no wife or children.

    76. ii. Lorena Delina, b 6 September 1861 at Sparta; d. 1863 and is probably buried at Big Creek Cemetery, near Sparta according to records of the cemetery in local history room at the Monroe Co. Library.

+   77. iii. Malinda Alvaretta, b 7 April 1863.

+   78. iv. Lorilla Ann, b 12 July 1865.

    79. v. Estrina Louesta, b 16 December 1867 at Sparta; d 6 January 1871, age 4 years

    80. vi. Martha Emma, b 19 March 1873 at Sparta; d 13 July 1873, and is probably buried with Lorena.

+   81. vii. Nelson Ray, b 25 October 1875.

25. WILLIAM[3] HARRISON AUSTIN (s/o Pauline[2] Reed Austin, #5) b 25 August 1840 at Springfield, Erie Co., PA. He moved to Green Lake Co. WI about 1845 with the family; at age 21 he enlisted on 2 August 1861 at Fox Lake, WI in the Union Army in Co. D, 8th Regiment of Wisconsin Infantry and was promoted to Corporal in August of 1864, shortly before he mustered out 16 September 1864 at Memphis, TN; he fought in many battles, including Fredericktown, MO, Corinth, MS, Siege of Vicksburg, MS, Mechanicsburg, MS, Reed River Expedition and Abbyville, MS.

William m 9 November 1864 at Mackford, Green Lake Co., WI. **Hannah Marie Currie**, born 7 August 1846 in Columbus, Ontario, Canada, d/o Robert and Hannah (Ames) Currie. Her grandfather, John Currie, was born at Yetholm, Roxboroughshire, Scotland and her grandmother, Hannah (Lockey) Currie, was born in Ilderton, Northumberland, England. Robert, her father, was also born in Scotland; her mother, Hannah, was born in Columbus, Canada, according to his death certificate. Robert and Hannah came to the U.S. in 1849 and settled near Lake Maria, WI. In 1876 they moved to Solomon City, KS.

At one time William went to Coronado, CA and purchased property in the tent city; however, he didn't like it there, so he sold it and returned to the midwest. He was a builder by trade and they moved frequently because of his work. According to land records in Texas Co. Court House, Houston, MO, William and Hannah bought 120 acres of land in Texas Co. as early as 4 October 1888 (Deed Book 8, p.247) for $300: on 30 April 1895 they sold this land for $1200 (Book 36, p. 178); 26 June 1895 they bought Lot 25 in Block A, Town of Cabool, Texas Co., MO for $500. William died 17 April 1897, age 56, at Cabool, and is buried there.; on 5 January 1903 Hannah sold property at Cabool for $3500 (Book 54, p.124) and 17 November 1906 she sold Lot 25 in Cabool for $650 (Book 69,p.90.) Perhaps this is when she moved to Torrington, WY; her son Willie was working near Chugwater, WY. Hannah died at the home of her daughter, Gertrude McDaniel, in Torrington, on 8 March 1928, age 81, and she is buried at Valley View Cemetery, Torrington.

Children, surname AUSTIN:

+ 82. i. Llewelyn[4] Edward, b 4 July 1868.
+ 83. ii. Gertrude P., b 19 January 1873.
   84. iii. Mabel D., b 9 November 1876 at Holland. She spent her childhood in Cabool. She was bitten by a snake when she was about five years old and had to have her leg amputated. She suffered from this experience, then was further weakened by the flu, all of which affected her mind. She finally was so confused that her brother Willis had her committed to a sanitarium in Denver, CO, where she lived only a few days, dying 10 October 1926 and is buried in Valley View Cemetery, Torrington.
   85. iv. Minnie, b 9 November 1876, a twin to Mabel; she died in infancy.
   86. v. Willis Wilbur, b 23 August 1880.

26. MICHAEL[3] REED (s/o John[2] Reed, #7) b 4 March 1842 at Mexico,

Oswego Co., NY; d 30 January 1898, just short of 56 years, while logging with his son DeWitt at Town of Spruce, Oconto Co., WI. Michael was ten years old in 1853 when his mother died. (See account of early trip to Wisconsin included with his father biography.) Upon his return, according to descendants, much of his life was spent working for local farmers and his education was very limited. Michael enlisted as Private in Company E, 110th Regiment, 11 August 1862, later being transferred to Company C, 3rd Regiment. The following is an account of his military career, from his Civil War Pension File:

While a member of the organization in the line of duty at Carlton, near New Orleans, Louisiana in 1863 he was attacked with measles and in 1864 while on a transport (under Gen. Banks) at Galveston, Texas, he was attacked with chills and fever. Said diseases have caused malarial poisoning and general debility for which he claims pension. Was treated in Marine Hospital at New Orleans some three or four months, then transferred to Veterans Reserve Corp. in consequence of disability 9 February 1864.

He was discharged from the service 10 July 1865 at Burlington, Vermont. Michael married at Mexico, in October or November 1865 **Martha J. Morton**, probably d/o Gad W. and Betsy Morton. According to his Civil War Pension Record, he only lived with her about 3 months and there were no children; divorced 15 May 1869. Martha buried in Mexico Village Cemetery with her parents under the name Martha J. Morton; she d 14 December 1872, age 23 years, 3 months. On the same day as the divorce Michael sold the 13–39/100 acres he bought, near Mexico, from his father on 11 April 1866.

According to Morris Reed's affidavit, in his Civil War Pension File, Michael

lived in the same house with him after his separation from Martha. In May 1868 we, [Morris, wife and son] came to Wisconsin and early in the spring of 1869 he [Michael] came to this place and settled one half mile from us and lived there until some time in 1871 when he returned to the State of New York near where we came from and married the Claimant, Marietta F. Reed and at once returned to this place.

Michael m/2 **Marietta Smith** 11 April 1871 at the Town of Albion, Oswego Co., NY, the ceremony conducted by Elder Johnson. Marietta was living in Sand Banks, later Altmar, NY., with her brother, Samuel Smith, 27, and his wife Juliana, 20, Marietta, 19 years, Emma, 3 years, and Arthur, 1 year. Samuel was her brother, listed in Census as a lumberman; since this was also Michael's occupation, probably it was through Samuel that Marietta met Michael. Marietta Smith b 13 August 1851 in Peekskill, Westchester Co., NY., d/o Isaac and Annise (Frost) Smith, both parents born in England. A record of Marietta's early marriage to a Donilay or Donnelly hasn't been found. This name shows up in her daughter Emma's marriage record in Aspen, CO as her maiden name. The 1880 U.S. Census for Seymour, Outagamie Co., WI. lists Emma and Arthur as Michael's step-children. They were brought up with the subsequent children as one big family.

Michael bought 40 acres of land 5 June 1883 at Seymour, WI. for $950; his sons Fred and Arthur assumed payment on it 13 March 1895, then sold it 4 October 1898.

Michael's obituary in a newspaper clipping states, "Michael Reed, of Cicero, was almost instantly killed Monday by a tree falling on him which he had cut down; the tree lodged in another one, and while Mr. Reed was working it loose it fell on him and broke his back." Fourteen year old DeWitt drove the sleigh carrying his father to town for medical aid. Another obituary states, "Michael Read, killed January 30, was buried February 3. The funeral took place from the Christian Church. Mr. and Mrs. Reed came from New York to Seymour, where they have lived twenty-five years, and removed to Hickory about one year ago."

After Michael's untimely death on 5 October 1899, Marietta m George Henry Trecartin, s/o John and Mary (Lord) Trecartin, a farmer of Maple Valley, WI, b February 1828 at Deer Isle, New Brunswick, Canada. Marietta d 26 March 1915 at Appleton, WI, while living with her daughter, Julia Verwey, and is buried at Hickory Corners Cemetery, Hickory, WI as is Michael.

Children, surname REED:
+ 87. i. Emma Augusta Donnelly, b February 1868.
+ 88. ii. Arthur James Reed, b 11 March 1870.
+ 89. iii. Jennie Adell, b 27 February 1872.
+ 90. iv. Fred, b 4 January 1875.
+ 91. v. Julia Agnes, b 11 November 1877.
+ 92. vi. Ida May, b March 1880.
+ 93. vii. Dewitt Cornelius, b 27 January 1883.
+ 94. viii. Roy Albert, b 17 February 1887.
+ 95. ix. Effie Maud, b 7 February 1890.

27. MARTHA[4] REED (d/o John[3] Reed, #7), born about 1846 at Mexico, Oswego Co., NY.; m about 1864 **Joshua Wadley** (s/o Moses and Beda (Glass) Wadley), b April 1816 at Watertown, Jefferson Co., NY. Joshua had been married previously to Elizabeth — , by whom he had a son, Joshua L. Wadley, Jr.; for information on his first marriage and descendants, see the appendix. In several census Joshua is listed as a lawyer. Mr. John Castle of Mexico, NY found in some old town records that on 3 May 1858 and again on 3 May 1859 Joshua was appointed Pound Master. A definition of the term Pound in the Oxford English Dictionary states "In the early days the lock-up of criminals and debtors was called a Pound." Thus, he was Master of the Pound. Also an examination of the land records in Oswego County Court House reveals that Joshua was something of a land speculator, buying and selling several pieces of land in the Mexico area. There was a mention in one land deal of the "Wadley Sawmill." Mr. Castle found that in 1883 several men in Mexico submitted bids for the job of lighting the village lamps; Joshua Wadley's bid of $60 won; he was appointed 29 June 1881. Joshua was received into full membership the Mexico Methodist Church 3 October 1880; his wife Martha was received April 1880 and daughter Jennie 18 April 1883.

Martha died 12 January 1881, age 35 years, probably of tuberculosis Joshua died, also of TB according to his death certificate, on 10 October 1900 at Mexico; both are buried in Mexico Village Cemetery, with Joshua's first wife Elizabeth and daughter "Lizzie."

In the lot next to Joshua is buried Lera Wadley (d 23 Mar. 1885, ae 63 years) and his wife Rebecca (d 30 Oct 1869, ae 51 years). He might be Joshua's brother—no records have been found—Joshua's son Pearl's middle name is Lera and Pearl named a daughter Lera; additionally, Joshua's son Joshua has the middle initial "L."

Children, surname WADLEY:
+   96.   i.   Pearl[4] Lera, b 25 June 1865.
+   97.   ii.   Jennie L., b about 1868.
       98.   iii.   William "Willie," b November 1870 at Mexico, NY. He was with the family in the 1875 census, age 7 and 1880 Census, age 10. Mr. Castle of Mexico recently, while researching the early issues of the *Mexico Independent*, found an obituary for "Willie." He died at Seymour, WI 16 August 1891 and he is buried in his Uncle Bert Reed's cemetery Lot, about three months short of 21 years. He probably died of tuberculosis, as did his father, mother

and two sisters.
99. iv. Elizabeth "Lizzie" May, b November 1879 at Mexico. She would have been about two years old, when her mother died, living at home with her father and the two Hollister sisters, Frances and Lydia, who kept house for them. They probably were the people, who, feeling compassion for her, very ill, cut some grass from the lawn and strewed it around her bedroom floor, so she could walk on the grass, which she was unable to do outdoors. She died 10 July 1906 at Mexico at age 26 years, 7 months, of Pulmonary Tuberculosis. She is buried in the Mexico Village Cemetery.

28. MORRIS³ REED (s/o John² Reed, #7) b 13 July 1846 at Mexico, Oswego Co., NY. Morris enlisted 26 August 1861 in Company A.U.W, 14th Infantry, at Oswego, for three years and was made Corporal in September 1862. He was promoted to Sergeant after the battle of Chancellorsville for bravery in action; he received final discharge 23 June 1865 at Fort Trumbull, New London, CT. The list of battles he was engaged in include: Siege of Yorktown, Gaines Mills, Malvern Hill, second Bull Run, Antietam, Leetown, and Gettysburg.

Morris m 24 August 1866 at the residence of George W. Putnam, Mexico, **Marinda Wingate,** d/o John and Rebecca (Conklin) Wingate, born 16 May 1850, Onondaga Co., NY. In 1868, when their son Adelbert was about a year old, Morris and Marinda set out in a wagon train for Wisconsin. Until recently, Norman Reed's family had the old sewing rocker Marinda sat in on the trip to the midwest, so she could rock her baby. For six months they tried growing hops at Kilbourn City, WI. They then moved permanently to Seymour, Outagami Co., WI, a rough logging commuity, with but two log cabins as recorded in Gordon Bubolz's *The Land of the Fox* in 1949. Morris engaged in farming in a limited way, as a war wound in his abdomen left him partially incapacitated, with frequent illnesses when he engaged in heavy lifting. He became a Seventh Day Adventist preacher, with quite a following. He also acted as Pension Agent, assisting veterans and widows in acquiring pensions as Civil War claimants. Morris died 11 November 1913, age 67, at Seymour; Marinda died 18 July 1928, at Seymour, age 79; both are buried at Seymour City Cemetery.

In his own words we hear of his early life:

Another boy, said my parents, and we will call his name Morris. That was 52 years ago, and I am yet alive and move among the people of the earth. My life

The Third Generation

has not been altogether an uneventful one, and for this reason I write. As I sit in my western home today and look from my window into the snow of another Wisconsin winter, my mind wanders to my old home on the bank of Little Salmon River in Oswego County, NY. How well I know even at this late date all the rapids—crooks and bends of the river from the place of my birth to where it empties into Lake Ontario 5 miles below; every eddy and deep pool where I have so many times caught the lazing fish, are as well known to memory as when I was a boy and rather fish than work. At the age of 4 years I used to stand upon the bank below the old mill dam near the end of the Tannery and with a willow wand for a fish pole and twine and a bended pin for tackle, I used to catch little shiners of a finger's length; that was very large business for me then. Two years later I stood at Mother's death bed and wondered, What is Death? A large family and poor circumstances made it necessary for some of the children to separate and I went to live with a maiden aunt." Two years later I find myself with my father and four of the children in Mackford, WI. My father's nephew had preempted some land for him away up in the wilds of Chippewa and the next year finds my father and myself and youngest brother in company with two other emigrant families on the way to see our possessions among the bluffs of Chippewa. [See John Reed #5 for rest of description of trip to Wisconsin].

After the return home to Mexico, Morris goes on to say:

Father resumed his old occupation in the ashery, and all but my youngest brother and oldest sister went to work for farmers as we could find places. And that was hard for me to do—that is to find a staying place. I was very ambitious about anything but work. I was not born under that planet. I shifted about continually and sometimes remained only 3/4 of a day in a place.

When about thirteen years old I went to live with Sol Peck. Mr. Peck was an old soldier of 1812 War. He was considered a very hard man for boys to get along with. But there was some attraction there that I could not resist. And I have since been told that he also took quite a fancy to me for I had many traits of character that was so much like Sol's when he was a boy that he perhaps treated me better on that account. He was very decrepit and used to go around with a crutch and a cane. He had been wounded in some British and Indian shooting match while a soldier and was a pensioner. He had a sword which it was claimed he took from a Redcoat and then run him through the body with it. And that act was a very large testimony in his favor for me in those days. Now I used to handle that sword when no one was around and many an imaginary Redcoat and Indian I slew. And then old Sol used to sit in front of the large kitchen fireplace evenings, twirl his crutch on his knees and spin yarns to me of many kinds. It was said by old residents there that he was a very ugly customer to run afoul of in times gone by—I know he was a man of violent temper even then, also of terrible strength. One day the man he had hired to build a stone wall for a driveway upon the barn floor had drawn some large stones up with old Rah—for that was the name of the old horse that Uncle Sol drove nearly everyday to town—and one was so large and heavy that the combined efforts of the man and myself could not get the stone up. Old Sol stood and watched us and gave orders for a time. Then his temper flew and the crutch and the cane too! Down on his knees he went, onto the stoneboat and picked the stone up bodily and placed it on the wall. Whew, but that made a big man of Sol in a moment in my eyes! I was equally careful to keep out of reach of the old cane when even inclined to be a little independent and run business to suit myself, because there was one thing Uncle Sol could not do and that was to run and I could. One day in rummaging around in the woodshed I found an old salmon spear that had once been used by Sol in spearing the fine salmon that before the days of mill dams and civilization, used to run up the river from which the river took its name. I got a stick for a handle and away to the river I ran without permission. I ran out on the boom that crossed the river near the back end of Sol's land. The river was quite rapid there and a lot of foam had gathered on the upper side of the timber. As I stood there I heard a queer sucking noise in the foam and in looking sharp could see it rise in a place where the noise came from. I made a terrible lunge with the blunt rusty spear and fetched out a large sucker. And then I felt I was almost as large a man as old Sol and no time was lost in getting where I could let old Sol see my catch. He was proud of me at once and could see a great future for a boy that could spear a fish he could not see. Among the stories he used to tell was one about the buck deer which ran about as follows:

"Well," said he, "When I first came here it was a wild country. I tell you. I had got a little clearing and had sown some wheat and when it came time to harvest that wheat I had to cut it all with a sickle. There was no cradle in them days and an acre was a good days work to cut and tie up. One day as I was reaping away at the wheat, I heard a noise in the grain and looked up and there went a fine buck deer on the jump through the grain. I grabbed up my sickle and ran after him. He jumped over the fence and landed on a large snowdrift and before he could get out I ran up and cut his throat with the sickle." Well, of course, if anyone else in the world had told that I would have doubted it. But Sol was a different man to me then than anyone else. He said he used to be a great hand to swallow things but the hardest thing he ever swallowed was a lantern. I have sometimes thought I might have learned some of my "orations" of those times and also some years later of Sol. But almost all things come to an end and so did my stay with Uncle Sol. One day late in the fall after a year's sojourn there, I was trying to drive his sheep home from a neighbors. They did not care to leave the lot where they were and several times ran by me as I tried to head them off. And, Oh, how I did run, and oh, how Sol would yell "Run, you _ _ _!" Well, I can't just spell it all out but after awhile I got tired of it—Ol Sol, sheep and all and I started out for town a mile away. No roaring could stay my feet. I was nearly fourteen years old and, as I thought, old enough and big enough to up and run away if I wanted to and I did want to then. I soon went to work for Mr. B[iddlecome], Sol's nearest neighbor and there I had a good home which I am sorry to say I did not appreciate as I should and have often wondered how they kept me on the place as I often practiced Uncle Sol's kind of teaching practice, but not in lantern swallowing, however.

During the campaign of Lincoln and Douglas in the fall of 1860, I belonged to a company of young fellows called Republican Cadets and as I paraded the streets evenings to the sound of a fife and drum, I felt I was a very large factor in the coming presidential election even if I wasn't a voter. In 1861, when the Ball opened at Fort Sumter, I was full of patriotism if not years, and as later in the season some of the Mexico boys began to enlist, I was terrible uneasy and wanted to be older. In August '61 I could stand it no longer and went on French leave to Oswego City 15 miles away. I found some of the boys who were already soldiers and got posted by them—what to say to the recruiting officer, how old I must be and all about it. At that time I was fifteen years and six weeks old. When an hour later I went to the Recruiting office I was a full 18, the youngest anyone could be taken into the army. When I entered the office, I found 8 or 10 who had already enlisted to put down the rebellion but the officer was absent. In a short time he entered and then everyone jumped to their feet and saluted as he marched toward his office at the far end of the room. I gazed at him in amazement for he was the first military officer I had ever seen. But there he was in all his military glory of blue uniform, and sash, and clanking sword. Oh, my! that took me by storm and I hastened after him. As he reached the stopping place, I said, "Captain, I want to enlist." He was a large fine looking man and as he looked me over, I could see a big smile as he said, "You want to enlist, do you?" "Yes, Sir," said I. "Well, hardly, I guess. How old are you?" Of course, I did not have time to think of the hatchet and cherry tree just then and said, "Eighteen, Sir." "Oh, no, not yet," said he. "Yes, Sir, and just a little over." "Well, step under this standard here." I knew I had to be 5 feet, 4–1/2 inches to pass and I made all the stretch in my anatomy as well as conscience came out and could just feel the hair touch the standard on top, and was jubilant. Then after a long talk, he said, "You are too young and small for a soldier but I guess you will grow to it." "Oh, yes, Sir, I am growing fast, Sir," said I. "You will do for an orderly for me for awhile then you will be all right." "Oh, yes, Sir, I am good at that," I replied, not having the least idea in the world what "Orderly" was. He sat down, wrote on a paper a moment and handed it to me and said, "You go to this address and hand it to Dr. So-and-so." I found the doctor and he took me into an upper room and told me to pull off all my clothes. I did so and he gave me a thorough examination, tried all my joints, and made me jump around to see if I was sound, tested teeth, eyesight and finally said, "That will do. Put on your clothes and come on." As we entered the office, the Captain said, "How is he, Doctor?" "Sound as a brick but rather slim and small," he replied. Then the Captain wrote for sometime and handed me a large envelope and some papers and said, "You say you have a father.

Well, you must get him to sign those papers or I cannot take you. And now you will have to take the stage at the Munger House at 4 P.M., go to Mexico fifteen miles away and get them signed and be back here tomorrow for we leave for Fort Trumbull, Conn. tomorrow evening." Oh, how the chills did run up and down my back, for I well knew my father would not willingly sign those papers. But no use; I must act. And soon I was rumbling out in the old stage for home. When I reached the forks in the road a mile short of Mexico, I got out and made my way to Mr. B's where I was set to work the last they saw of me. It was beginning to be dark and as I entered the house, Mrs. B. said, "Why, Morris, where in the world have you been?" The two girls came up—Annie and Mary—and said, "What did you go off and not tell us for?" Mr. B. (probably H. [Harvey, 1860 U.S.Census] Biddlecome) came in and said, "Well, you got back." "Well, hurry up and get my duds packed up," said I. "I must be going now. I have little time to spare." "Why, what's the matter, Morris? Don't we use you well? You going to leave us? You better go to work again." "Work," said I, contemptuously, "Oh, I've got beyond that now—I'm a soldier!" and pulled the big envelope out with a flourish and said, "Look there." "Oh, you foolish boy!" said the girls, "you are not large enough or old enough to enlist and you must not go!" "Oh, I can't get out of it now," said I, but did not tell them that my prospects of soldiering rested on Father's signature. Well, the few belongings I had was made up and some presents from the family and girls and a hurried goodbye and I was off to see how I was to come out with the signing business. Father had not yet retired when I reached home. I dared not broach the matter that evening but as the stage left for Oswego at 7 A.M., I was very anxious and at the first peep of day was up and got my sister up to get breakfast. Oh, how I did watch the hands fly around the dial on the old clock! It seemed as though time never moved as fast before. At last the meal was over and Father was moving back from the table when I made a desperate effort and threw the big envelope on the table in front of him. He picked it up, glanced at the papers and sprang to his feet and roared out, "You rascal, you! What have you been doing, sir? You go back to your place and go to work and no more of this, sir!" And off he went into the ashery nearby. I picked up the papers and followed and said, "Now, Father, you must sign these papers at once as I have to take the seven o'clock stage for Oswego: we leave for the field this evening." "I will not sign them, sir! Go back to your work, I tell you! You are a pretty fellow to be a soldier, ain't you, a little boy like you. Clear out to your work, I tell you!" I did not move but said, "Father, I have worked out all my life and now you can lick me or tie me up or do what you want to me, but I am going to be a soldier when I get loose." Father knew that I would keep my word and that threatening would do no good and so he began to reason the matter and told me what a soldier would have to meet—hardships, hunger and bullets if it was actually war. I told him I thought that all over and was going. He finally said, "Well, I will have to sign them," and did and he handed them to me and he said, "There, I feel as though I had signed your death warrant."

"I was just in time to catch the stage and away we whirled to Oswego—which was reached in due time and I with the others was sent to a hotel to dinner. Oh, wasn't that fine—a fine hotel dinner and Uncle Sam to pay the bill. Supper came the same and I was happy. I was no longer a boy working a farm—not by any means—I was a man. And more than a man, a soldier in the Regular Army, 14th U.S. Infantry, and was soon going to have a gun all my own and a suit of blue. That evening we boarded a train and started for New York, ran up to Albany and took a steamer, the *Daniel Drew*, to the city, landed at Governor's Island, and there I saw huge piles of cannon balls, piled up in long heaps; each heap topped out with a single ball or row of balls. Then they took us up into a very large upper room inside the big round fort or tower and left us all to ourselves. In a short time an old Regular Sergeant came up and told us to make ourselves comfortable. They looked around the large bare room, not a thing in it, only a few chairs. Then the sergeant happened to see where one of the boys had spit on the floor and sang out—"Who did that?" No one did, of course, and that old fellow got a broom, handed it to one of the boys and said, "You sweep this whole room now and don't you dare spit again." we thought he was putting on a good many frills but did not dare to tell him so. He seemed so savage and besides, he was an old soldier and we didn't know but he had seen shooting sometime in his life. It was afternoon and by and by we was all marched downstairs and into a long room with a table made of boards and benches for chairs and was told to eat our supper. We looked at each other and then at our fare which consisted of a tin plate, knife and fork. On the plate was a large slice of fat boiled pork and a hunk of bread. Beside our plate stood a pint tin cup of awful black coffee. I did not care for much of that kind of grub and thought I would wait 'til something else was brought on before eating. But as I saw some who had evidently been there for sometime get up and leave after disposing of their rations, I concluded it was not hotel fare we was to get and ate a little government fare for the first time and got up and left.

The end.

The preceding account written by Morris Reed, dated 1912; in possession of Patricia Reed Pryor, Kansasville, WI., a great-granddaughter.

Invalid Pension Claim No. 366903
Seymour, Outagamie Co., Wis.
March 12, 1883
Mr. Dudley, Commissioner of Pensions:

Dear Sir:

I got a letter from the Dept. today requiring me to make a statement under oath of my case, which I have done I think once or twice before and sent them to my atty. and supposed you had them long ago. With the exception of the two years before I joined the army in 1861. But I will now try and give as true and accurate a statement of events and dates as I can.

I was born and lived in Mexico, Oswego Co., NY. til 26 of Aug. 1861 when I enlisted, and had lived for about two years before that with a Farmer named Harvey N. Biddlecom, P.O. address Mexico, Oswego Co., NY and worked on a farm. I was unusually healthy as I never had a Dr. or any sickness but measles and whooping cough in my life til in army, and never have had a run of fever or any disease in my whole life up to present. And never was in Hospital in army till 1864 and never on sick report but very little before that. And was in every battle and skirmish the Reg't. was up to move for the wilderness in 1864. Some months before the Battle of Chancelorsville, VA, May 1, 1863 I was detailed from my Co. A. and put on the color guard as Corpl. of the guard in the center of the regt. and served there in the front of the fight where I received a contused wound in my right side by the explosion of a shell in our midst—which killed and wounded 9 I think, a piece striking me on the side of the Bowells near the hip. It must have been a glancing blow or would have went into me. The skin was not broken but I was hurt inside and doubled up like a jack knife. The Regt. then marched by the left flank and brought my Co. past me and when Lt. James Henton of my Co. gave me orders to go to the rear if I could get there in about 2 hours after the Regt. marched. Back near where I was at an old log house being used as field Hospt. and he saw me & talked with me again so did the Co. boys and told me to get out of that if I could as the Rebs might be in there at any time. I followed after as best I could. After the Battle the Regt. went back to our old Camp near Falmouth, VA where I joined them and went to the large Hospt. tent before Dr. Starrow, I think his name was, am not sure. Nothing was done for me but leave me off duty. I expected then to be all right in a few days again. I done no duty for several days and often after that had to leave ranks for my tent on inspection or Drill. I never got over it, but done duty most of time til Jan. 1864 when got wet on duty and took cold which settled in that side and was compelled to go on sick rept. about the middle of Jan. and came near dying. I was in terrible pain in right side and right leg was drawn up. Seemed like tearing side open to try to straighten it. I was so bad they could not move me to the Hospt. about 20 rods. I was attended by Dr. Coles of our Regt. This was at Camp John F. Reynolds, VA about the 14th of the next month, Feb. The Regt. moved up to Camp near Cattlett Station, VA about 3 miles. Here I was still on sick rept. off duty under Dr. Coles care all the time til about April 30th 1864. When the Regt. started on the Wilderness Campaign and I was sent off with others to Carver Hospt., Washington, D.C. There I saw no Dr. nor had any treatment—for about two weeks, when I was sent off to McClellan Hospt. near Philadelphia, PA. Got there about May 15, '64. Was put in ward 14 under Dr. Cleeman most of time, sometimes other physicians attended the Ward—don't know their names. There I took medicine and suppose it was for trouble in side as there was never anything else the matter with me. Was sent from there to Fort Trumbull, New London, CT., our Regimental head quarters. Some time in Aug. or Sept.—have forgotten. I was Sergt. of the Guard once or twice, was then set to drilling Recruits, then sent off to Detroit, Michigan after a Deserter and got him, then was sent with Prisoners from the Ft. to the Regt. several times. Then was put in charge of a Co. of Recruits in the Ft. I did not carry a musket but a non-commissioned officer's sword. In May or June there came an order from Genl. Dix then Commdg. the eastern Dept. to discharge all soldiers not fit for field service. And I was discharged June 23rd, 1865, my discharge reading: Discharged in Consequence of Surgeons Certificate of Disability on account of wounds received in action.

I then returned to Mexico, NY and the next month in July hired out in haying. I worked two days and a half, I think it was and could not stand the work. Pain in side. I got $1.50 per day I believe and the others $1.75 at same work. I then done no work of any consequence that summer or fall. Some of the time I lived with a brother about 3 miles out of Mexico. I had no home anywhere as Mother was dead. In the fall I bought 20 acres of Swamp Land 3 miles from Mexico and lived in a shantie on it that winter. Was intending to set out wood and cedar posts but done but very little and sold it again. Then I was *all* over. Sometimes to my Brothers a few days, then in Mexico or different places around it. At one time I hired out on a Brick Yard; worked about 3/4 of a day and quit. I was there nearly or quite 3 years. Got married in meantime and in 1868 moved to Wisconsin and went to near Kilbourne City, WI. Did not like it there and came to Seymour, WS and settled down and here I have been since 1868 and am well known by everyone here. First work here was chopping fallow. It was all woods here then. And if you have got all the proof of my condition that I have sent in since 1878 while here you have plenty of it. And here I will state that about two months ago I sent in to my atty. at Chicago a statement of my condition from the Town Board of Officers of this town that have known me and lived near me for past 14 years and over. Also the P.M. [Postmaster] and City Clk & Notary of Seymour City & both physicians here and suppose he sent them to you with the affadavit of Genl. or Capt. Vernon. My work while here has been chopping—logging, of this I could do but little as lifting hurts my side and laid me up from two days to two weeks. It would be impossible for me to tell you every time I was laid up by that side, but will state it was as often as once in every six weeks or about that. Some dates I can remember well, In about June 1870 I was chopping on a job my brother had taken and strained my side in felling a large oak. So I had to leave the work and Mr. Holcomb whose affadavit you have, took my place. I done no more at it, was laid up about 6 weeks that time. And I don't know how to state it any different shape but will say that is just the way hard lifting or straining work has always served me since I got the injury in army. And often after lifting at logging or hard work at pitching hay or such work fresh blood would fill my bowels. I have not ben treated by Drs. for til in past two years or more since I got so bad and in so much pain I was obliged to have help. But have often talked with Dr. B. T. Strong years ago about. He has been here about 8 years or more I think. Dr. Strong and Kerwin whose statement & affadavit you have are the only physicians that have ever treated me since I left army. About 4 or 5 years ago Dr. Strong gave me medicine for Dyspepsia and catarrah symptoms, that is all. I know I am making this statement very long but I want to write just as I would talk it if I was there and tell it as near as my memory will let me as I have nothing else to go by. I started this yesterday but have to stop and lay down every little while. Until in the last few years this injury has been confined to a spot in my right side less than the size of your hand. Since it has gone all through my right hip and down into right thigh and up under ribs that side. Two years ago last Jan. I had to give up work; have done but little since and since last fall have been confined to the house so that I do nothing at all and seldom walk to the nearest house 40 rods away. For the last two months the pain from side has gone up into my chest and troubles me _____. The only relief I get is to put cloths rung out of hot water on my chest, then the pain goes back into my side worse again. The Drs. can't help me here. I have got so bad that a few weeks ago I wrote to the medical and surgical Sanitarium at Battle Creek, Michigan, telling all about my injury in 1863 and present trouble in chest and asked them if they thought they could help one if I could come there and I will send their reply to you enclosed in this letter. I thought if I got my pension of going there and be treated. It must come down if it helps me. Life is as dear to me as anyone. I have no means to go of my own. I have a just claim from the nature of the injury being all inside. I have had but little treatment as while in army I did not have to go to Dr. to get off duty as my Co. officers knew how I was and how I got it and favoured one I fully expected until late years to outgrow it but here I am. And now can you help me, Col. D. I know you have to be careful. Can my discharges do you any good by sending them to you. I don't know of any more I can do. I can talk but I can't write. If you can help me Please do at once. We need it for proper food & clothing as well as medical help.

Morris Reed

Sworn to and subscribed before me, this 13th day of March, A.D. 1883

Seymour, Wisconsin
Wm. Michelstetter,
Notary Public, WI.

Send the check this time without further delay.

   (Pension appears to have been increased from $4 to $6 per month after this letter)

A PREMONITION
By M. Reed of Seymour, Wisconsin.

To the Editor, *Green Bay Review*.

A premonition or warning of impending danger or evil is believed in by few and discredited by the many, and yet it can not be doubted that coming events do sometimes cast their shadows before.

In this life there are many things we cannot account for, and yet they really exist. The Great Apostle Paul in 1st Cor. 13:12, tells us that in this life we see thorugh a glass, darkly; but in the future we will see face to face and know even as we are known.

I acknowledge that I was very skeptical regarding such warnings before I was a personal witness, and in one sense an actor in the event which I wish to relate.

History has told all the world of the great foot-race of the Union and Confederate Armies from the seat of the war along the Rappahanock River in Virigina to Gettysburg, PA, in 1863, and of the terrible fighting and slaughter on that hard contested field, where 54,000 men were put out of action.

When the battle opened, our corps, the 5th army corps, had not yet arrived, but was rushed forward by long forced marches almost day and night, and when within sound of the firing, we were halted beside the road to find where we were most needed in the contest. We were lying on the ground in all positions, some munching a hardtack, some with the deck of cards out, playing poker or old sledge, and others hunting a chew of tobacco, for it had been impossible for the boys to secure a supply on our rapid march from Virginia and nearly all were out, and all users of the weed known that a soldier will even trade his scant supply of hardtack for a chew. The sound of the cannon and musketry was a couple miles away, and we knew that soon we would be taking a hand.

In my company, Co. A, 14th U.S. Infantry was a man of about 30 years of age, called Nathaniel Copp. Nat, we always called him. It was known that he had some tobacco, and one of the boys came to him and said, Nat, can you let me have a chew. Nat handed him a long plug of Navy, he took a liberal chew and handed the plug back to Nat. No, said he, you can keep it. I have no more use for it. This was noted by many, and it was also noted that Nat was looking rather melancholy and sad, and took no part in any thing that was said or done. Some of the boys chaffed him, and said, why, Nat, you are not getting scared yet, are you? We haven't got where the Minnies are flying yet. You may laught all you want to, boys, said he, but I have taken my last chew of tobacco in this world. At that moment the officers sang out, fall in fall in lively here, and away we went at at double quick for the front. Cannon was booming, musketry was crashing, and above all we could hear the rebel yell.

Something was doing out there right smart, and all the dogs of war seemed let loose and there was need of being in a hurry. General G. K. Warren, had discovered that little Round Top, was the key to the battle, and must be held at all hazards. The Rebel General Longstreet had made the same discovery, and wanted it bad. As we neared Little Round Top, we left the road, filed to the left and formed line of battle in a cleared field, the order was, forward, guide center, and we advanced to near the base of Round Top and just as we reached a rail fence that ran parallel with our line, and every man had sent the rails over the ground with a push of his feet, the order came, Halt, we were standing among the rails waiting for futher orders.

And now comes the most singular part of it all. Dan Cole, was in the rear rank, directly behind Nat. Dan said I wish I was in the front rank. I would rather be in front than the rear, and as strange as it may seem, there seemed to more danger in rear, than the front rank. Nat said, Dan, I will change with you. I had rather be in the rear rank. My position as second Sergt. of the company was two paces in rear of the line to see that every man kept his place and did his duty, And I sanctioned the change and Dan stepped to the front and Nat, into Dan's place in the rear rank. The moment he stepped into Dan's place a bullet from off to the left, from most likely a rebel sharp shooter in the Devil's Den, hit him in the neck, and he fell a corpse among the rails. At the moment the Command rang out, forward, guide center, and over Little Round Top, down the other side and across Plum Run to the edge of the timber where we met Longstreet's Division face to face. They never got any nearer Round Top but in less than the time it takes to tell it, Nat had lots of company from both sides. We were greatly outnumbered and the line pressed back on our right and left for a moment we were alone. Major Gittings was in command of our regiment there and seeing we all would be killed or taken prisoners, he ordered us to fall back to the foot of Round Top, about 12 rods in our rear, where we could screen ourselves among the great boulders which lay scattered over the ground from the Round Top. We fell back, firing as we went. The Pennsylvania bucktails were our supporting line and lay looking over the crest of the top. They rose up and gave three cheers. You done well, boys, said they and we will fix them. They came in a charge over us and lit into them Johnnys as tho they were used to such things. There is nothing on earth that can stand Northern still and all was soon quite in our front in short order. Such are the strange facts in regard to Nat's premonition. Thirteen years ago, Dan Cole came from his home in Iowa and made me a week's visit. One night Dan and I were sitting by the stone, near midnight, building our campfire of long ago. When I said to him, Dan, whatever became of Nat Copp. Dan turned and looked at me a minute and said, Reed, why do you ask that question? You know as well as I do all about that, and we went to bed.

FIGHTING THEM OVER
December 9, 1897

What Our Veterans Have To Say
About Their Campaigns

A TIMELY SPRINT
How Two Yankees' Legs Carried Their
Owners to a Safe Place

Editor *National Tribune*: In your issue of Nov. 20 I saw an article from Comrade Thomas P. Allen on Gaines's Mill. He was formerly a member of Co. D. 14th U.S. Well, When I saw one of the old 14th had written on that subject I could feel my memory jog 14 cogs a second.

Our regiment, not a large one, as only our 1st battalion was then in existence, lost heavily—about 248—on that 27th day of June, 1862, between 9 A.M. and dark. Early that morning we were ordered to fall in, and be expeditious about it. We were at Camp Lovel about nine miles from Richmond.

We all soon mounted, and moved out toward Gaines's Mill, some two or three miles distant. We were none too soon for the Johnnies were not far behind.

We passed through a neck of low, swampy land near Gaines's Mill, and forced line in a rise of ground in a cleared, sandy field.

The swamp and timber land below us, where we had just come through, was in a semi-circular form, and came up well to our right and farther away to our left.

The old 5th N.Y. Zouaves were formed on our left. They were good ones, too. At this time there were no troops on our right in touch with us.

We had just formed line and been ordered to lie down, when we could see through the road we had passed the swamp on, a battery of rebs coming on a keen run to a rise of ground on the other side of the swamp.

In a moment they had unlimbered, a shot came over our heads, and the battle of Gaines's Mill had opened. Their range was too high, and about the second shot found a log cabin about 15 rods in our rear, where a lot of darkies and others had congregated to be out of the way of the shooting. Well, I have to laugh yet, at the way those fellows tumbled over themselves in trying to get out and away to a more congenial clime.

About this time "Old Paddy"—Col. J. D. O'Connell—called us to attention, and said he wanted two men to volunteer for a scout into the swamp in our front, and find out the enemy's position, and where first to expect an attack.

Serg't Patrick Kerens, Co. A., at once stepped to the front. It was a dangerous piece of business, and all knew it; no one else made a move.

In a moment Pat looked over his shoulder and called out: "Come out here, Morris! Ye'r a good shot. Come out here!"

Of Course, when called out before the whole regiment I was as brave as a lion all at once, and took my place at Pat's side. We then got our instructions, and took the timber on our right and worked our way down to the front and came out near the swamp.

We saw a large oak out in the clearing, about 12 rods from the timber, and on a little higher ground than we were. We made our way to the tree, and could see the rebel skirmish-line just coming out of the woods on the left and in front of the 5th N.Y.

One fellow had on a large white hat. Pat at once drew his gun out to fire then took it down and said: "Morris, you try him; you are a better shot than I." "All right, Pat; I'll get him," I said, and, resting my left hand against a tree, sighted for the hat. Just as I was going to pull the trigger, ping! came something into the tree near me. I did not yet know the kind of music the minie made. I sighted again. Just then I saw Pat jump and yell like a bog-trotter: "Run for your life, Morris! Run!"

I took one look and yelled, "Got it, Pat; I'm after you!" The swamp near us was full of Johnnies, who didn't intend I should impair the usefulness of that old white hat, and sent in a lively remonstrance. Pat and I ran for the timber we had come out of about 12 rods away.

I never saw a man run so well as Pat did. He was the finest built soldier I think I ever saw, and had served in the English army before he came our way. As he ran his body was as straight as if on parade.

The ground around us seemed alive with lead. As we neared the timber we saw a log-and-pole fence. Pat yelled to me: "Don't stop to climb, Morris, or ye'r' a dead man."

We got over the fence, but I certainly never had any idea how. We did not go under it and we did not climb it.

Just then Co. A came up to us on the skirmish line. We told them not to step into that clearing, or they wouldn't live a minute. Two men stepped out, and in a moment went down. But as I can almost hear the Editor grit his teeth at the length of this article, and know that a long manuscript and the wastebasket are apt to be near of kin, I fear I shall have to choke off till another time. But, land sakes alive! I had only just got started, and would like to go on indefinitely.

I think all the old 14th will remember me, as I was, I think, the youngest and smallest Sergeant in the regiment from '61–'65, and was 15 years and six weeks old in August, 1861, when I enlisted at Oswego City, N.Y.

M. Reed, Sergeant, Co. A, 1st battalion, 14th U.S.
Seymour, Wis.
Washington D.C.
December 20, 1900

FIGHTING THEM OVER
Still Aanother Regular

A 14th U.S. Man Sends a Breezy Story About Second Bull Run
Editor, *National Tribune*: :

In your issue of Oct. 18 I saw another regular had written. I refer to the article of E. J. Kilmer, of Corpus Christie, TX and when I saw he once belonged to the bully old 14th U.S., I was all attention at once, I can assure you. For be it known that same old command had the honor to include the writer in its ranks from August 1861 to near the same time in 1865.

First of all I will say to Comrade K., "Let s shake, old boy; glad to meet you again, if only on paper."

I have found that when a comrade writes up his recollections of "de wah" some other lad will "jump" him and give a different version of the affair. Now, we must all remember it has been many long years since we stood in the ranks in Dixie, shoulder to shoulder, in support of the old flag, and memory fails even the best of us sometimes. I am willing to let charity cover all the mistakes I may make in writing this article.

Comrade Kilmer wrote of his recollection of "Second Bull Run." There are some statements I can hardly understand. Comrade Kilmer says he belonged to Capt. Locke's Company, G, of the 2nd Battalion, 14th U.S. and was in that company at Bull Run fight, and saw Capt. Coppinger wounded. Now, here is my trouble, to understand how that can be, but explain it in this wise: Comrade Kilmer must have mistaken the 1st Battalion for the 2nd Battalion, unless the 2nd was formed on the left of our 1st at that battle, which I fail to remember.

Now, I will give my recollection of that Gentleman-Cow Run affair as I saw it from the standpoint of our 1st Battalion.

Not later than 8 o'clock A.M. on the morning of August 30, 1862, we filed to the left from the road on which we had reached the historic field, formed line of battle in a large field, advanced about 60 rods, and halted on the edge of a large corn field, near two or three large apple trees. We at once commenced to break our fast on the ears of green corn. There was some scattering musketry and a few heavier shots in our front, which gave us to understand that Johnny Reb was on hand as usual.

We lay there awaiting orders perhaps 20 minutes, and lost our first man, from Co. E, I think it was, by a cannon shot from the front.

Capt. John D. O'Connell ("Old Paddy") was in command of us at the time, and no better officer ever wore a sword in action than he. He had a voice you could hear above the roar of the artillery, and for fear, I do not think he knew what it was; he led us on many fields, and I never saw him exhibit the least sign of it.

Soon the commands, "Attention-Battalion," "Forward, guide center," were given, and away we went through the corn, then advanced through a strip of timber, across a road into a large field and halted our line and what a sight met our gaze: about 50 rods in our front on a rise was a rebel battery, and at the foot of the knoll on the slope lay a line of red breeches. We thought at first sight they were there to gobble that battery, but soon found they were dead soldiers of a Brooklyn Regiment, we were told.

The rebel battery turned its attention to our line, and we fell back to the road about four rods in the rear and lay down, our right resting near a log cabin. Then there was music in the air. Shells burst all around, and on the sandy land in our front it looked like taking a handful of gravel and small stones and throwing them onto the surface of a mill-pond. I suspect it was grape and canister they were feeding us there.

I witnessed one of the coolest things I ever saw during the war. "Old Paddy" rode his old stocking-leg horse about five rods to the front of our line, wheeled and said,

"Oh, Adj't Lucifee, come out here."

Our Adjutant rushed out to the old Captain's side, expecting some order, when "Old Paddy" drew his sword, pointed to the rebel battery, and said, "Adjutant, just see those rebellious people up there." Well, it was worth a haversack of monkeys to see that Adjutant. He turned, and with a look of the most intense disgust I ever saw made a dash to the rear of the line again.

Now occurred another little event to keep our spirits up. Many of us had our blankets rolled, one end tied, and over one shoulder and under the arm on the other side, which made a roll as large as your leg. On my right lay a tall New Englander. A missile struck that roll over his right shoulder a smart slap. All heard it and looked to see the damage it might have done. The New Englander shut his eyes, straightened out his arms and legs, just as a frog will when hit with a club, and yelled:

"Oh, I'm dead."

We could see that it was the blanket and not John it had hit, and set up a yell. I have no doubt most of us would have done as he did, but it was fun for us. John still lives in New Hampshire.

I never knew why we were not ordered to go for that battery, but soon it was evident the rebs were coming in on our left and rear, and we were ordered back to meet this new condition. We about-faced and fell back to the strip of timber, halted, about-faced, and lay down again. The Johnnies kept up their practice on us all the time. A shell burst over and in front of my company. A piece as large as my hand came tumbling along and stopped a little before it reached my head. Another solid shot cut a tree nearly through near the right of the company. I had much rather go fishing than be where it was so unhealthy. In about two minutes we were called to "Attention," and back we went again.

There was with our company a young man named Kendall. He had his hand crushed in a bump on our march here, and had turned in his gun, as he carried his arm in a sling. He had followed us into the fight, but was not required to be there at all. When we now fell back through this strip of timber he was in our rear. When we had nearly reached the other side of the wood we heard Kendall yell, and looking back saw him standing bent over and a stream of blood running from above the belt. A reb stood with a smoking gun in his hand a little distance from him; he had just shot poor Kendall. A yell went up from the whole regiment to shoot him. The rebel turned to run, then held up his hands and cried: "Don't shoot; I'll surrender." But poor Kendall was mustered out.

We fell back about 80 rods, went in on the left flank and we struck a yellow jacket nest for sure.

Old Paddy saw there was to be some heavy work here, and seeming to have more fear for his old horse than himself he dismounted, turned the animal around and said:

"Go to the rear; you will get hurt here."

As he turned to lead us on the old horse would follow him up with his head over his shoulder. Rebel lead was coming then like a hail storm. Again the Captain turned, stopped the horse and said: "Go to the rear, you old fool; you will get shot here."

The old horse would not leave him, and soon got it in the head and keeled over. Even a large Newfoundland dog that followed us was killed there.

We halted and worked those old Springfields for all they were worth. The old Captain kept in front of the line till he got so full of lead he could do nothing more, and then called out:

"Capt. Brown, you will have to take charge of my little battalion. I can't do any more." I remember his exact words. He clambered onto the rear step of an ambulance in rear of our line and rode from the field, and Capt. Brown took command.

About this time I looked down the line of our regiment—I was in Co. A the head of the regiment—and about three or four companies to my left I saw Capt.—now Gen. Coppinger—his neck and shoulders covered with blood. I did not notice him as he left the field, as I was too busy, and I am certain that Coppinger and Locke belonged to my 1st Battalion at the time.

I was acting file closer at this time, and my place was two paces in rear of the company, to see that every man kept his position and did his duty. We had recently had a batch of recruits to make up the losses on our Chickahominy campaign a few months before and I saw one of them step from the ranks and squat down in rear of the company. I stepped up to him and saw he was not shot, and said:

"Get up and attend to your business."

He said: "I can t."

"Get up or I will put a head off you with the butt of my musket."

He held up the gun and said: "See there." A ball had struck his gun near the muzzle and jammed it in so it could not be used. I saw he was all right and good stuff, too, so I said:

"Well, drop it. There are lots more all over the ground that the owners will never call for."

He picked up one and was all right again.

The rebel fire slackened in our front, we advanced and they fell back. Soon we halted and lay on our arms. In a short time McDowell and some of his staff came near our company, advanced about 6 rods, and took observations. I well remember the hat he wore—a large white thing, that looked like an inverted turtle shell. There was no firing at the time on our part of the line. In a few moments he rode away.

Capt. Brown, now in command, was sitting on his large gray horse a few feet in rear of my company. A solid 12-pound shot came over, struck the sand about three rods in front of us, rose, and we watched its flight over our heads as it made straight for Brown. It did not seem to go very fast, but the old Captain did not get out of its range, nor did the horse. It struck the old gray just in front of the Captain s left leg and stood the horse on his head as neatly as you ever saw plantation darky dance the "Juba." The Captain managed to clear himself, and rolled to one side as the old horse fell over. The horse jumped to his feet, whirled around two or three times as a dog does after its tail, and then bolted for the rear like a Kansas cyclone. The Captain jumped up too, drew his blade and shouted:

"Catch him! Shoot him! Any way to get him. There are two bottles of whiskey in the saddle-bags."

About three days after the fight one of our drum corps fetched the horse into camp, but not the whiskey, and the last time I saw the old horse there was a welt where the cannon ball cut, just in front of the collar bone, full as large, or larger, than the ball was. I was told, but will not vouch for it, that they could never get the old beast into a fight after that, and I don't blame him.

We stayed there about an hour or so, and then, as most of the troops and trains were out of the way, fell back to Centerville that night, and from there to near Chain Bridge, and skedaddle No. 2 was over.

I never have believed there was the least use in the world for our being "whipped" out at that time. I saw at least a whole division of our troops to our rear, massed in a large field, half or three-fourths of a mile in rear of us, that I did not see called into action at all. As we left the field that afternoon there were some signs of a rout along our way—some smashed-up baggage-trains, a dismounted cannon, etc. but we were not pressed at all, and did not hurry much either; neither were we driven a rod at any time, but drive the Johnnies back as I have mentioned. I speak only of our regiment or battalion.

Nine months later we followed the rebs over the same ground and camped near where we fought the Summer before for a single night, and as it was not dark yet three other boys of my company and I went over the field. First we went to the two old apple trees where we had first formed our line and lost our first man. There I picked up a skull. The teeth were loose, and I pulled one out with my fingers and said: "Boys, I am going to keep this tooth to remember the fight," and each one of us took a tooth; I have mine now. Then we visited the strip of timber where Kendall was killed, and along the line of a rail fence near where the right of our regiment had been was a thicket of saplings, and in this was nearly a wagon-load of bones—whole skeletons. Then went up to the railroad cut a short distance from the right of our regiment where we lay in front of the rebel battery. There also were plenty of signs of war. I found the thigh bone of a man—rebel, we supposed—who must have been very tall, for when we compared it with others it was about a third longer.

We had camped for the night near where our greatest loss was sustained, and all over the ground were small mounds where the soldiers were quietly sleeping the sleep that can only be awakened by the last bugle-call. Let us hope we may all meet there, where war and strife are no more.

I shall be glad to hear from any of the old boys who may see this article. Let me assure them I have a soft place in my heart and memory yet.

M. Reed, Sergeant Co. A., 1st Battalion, 14th U.S. Brigade, Second Division, Fifth Corps, Seymour, Wis.

FIGHTING THEM OVER
What the Veterans Have to Say About Their Campaigns
TOO BUSY TO RUN
Comrade Reed say's the 14th U.S. Stood Their Ground at Gains Mill

Editor, *National Tribune*:

Although a reader for several years, I never realized how far it could reach until I wrote an article on "Second Bull Run" in your issue of Dec. 20 last. Sometimes something has to open our eyes to the magnitude of things, or we never would comprehend them. I have lived about 200 miles from the city of Chicago for the last 82 years, but it did not seem so big a town, after all, until I was on my return trip from the National Encampment held at Buffalo, NY three years ago.

Well, since that article on Bull Run came out I have been made to see that the old *National Tribune* has a "right smart" list of readers, as I have been opening, reading and answering letters since, from New Jersey to Minnesota, and all good ones, and I expect more to follow.

But, Mr. Editor, what a grand mistake I made in not finding out if any of the good old 16th N.Y. yet existed before I ventured to write on a war subject. I am reminded of what the good book tells us in Proverbs 18:17. "He that is first in his own cause seemeth just; but his neighbor cometh and searchest him." And one Friday, as I came from the post office, I stood my old bike on the front porch, kicked off my shoes, hung up my coat and tumbled into the old arm chair to see how Si and Shorty were making it, and the Spy of the Rebellion, and the comrades of the Fighting Them Over column, when, Way down in the northeast corner, I saw Jim Allen, of the 16th N.Y. Jim had his fists all doubled up and blood in his eye. Jim is my neighbor, you see—just look on the map and you will find it so—and here in the West, the man who tells the first story in a lumber camp don't stand a ghost of a show. I don't know just how big Jim is. So I will go slow. For we might meet at some encampment, you know, and I might be as scared as I was at Gaines's Mill on June 27, 1862; and I can assure Jim I am a man of peace, every time. This would not have been written if Jim hadn't told of the old 14th running at Gaines's Mill.

But as Jim has jumped on with both feet I will wiggle out if I can and run again.

Jim begins by saying he noticed a letter from one of the 14th Regulars In *The National Tribune*, and then, just as polite, as can be, he says: "I would like to ask him, what his regiment did on June 27, 1862, at Gaines's Mill."

Now Jim, you know some people don't like to answer all the questions that are asked on some subjects, but I will do the best I can to comply with your demand. You must promise me you will not ask any more such questions. If you have a file, just turn to the issue of Dec. 9, 1897, and you will find what two of the 14th did, at least.

To answer your question, I will go back to our first line of battle, formed about 8 or 9 o'clock [the 14th] on a sandy piece of ground which descended to a low, swampy piece of timber in our front. This timber was in rectangular form, and came up near our right and farther on our left where the splendid old N.Y. Zouaves were lined up.

Straight in our front was a road through this piece of swamp, and we could see the higher land beyond. In a moment a rebel battery came in view, on the run, and opened up on the 14th. Well, we didn't run then, did we, Comrade Jim? The Johnnies had too high a range, and about the second shot stirred up a nest of darkies who had made headquarters in an old log building a little in our rear and there were many rounds of juba danced to get over each other and away.

To get out of this running scrape individually I will have to say that I was in the regiment but little that day until sundown. After I refer to my article on Gaines's Mill of Dec. 9, 1897, which fully explains all that, and that Was written before I ever knew the 14th had run at that battle. Serg't Kerns and I had volunteered as scouts at the call of our old commander (Old Paddy), took to the timber on our right, and worked our way to the front, feeling out the advance of the enemy.

Near night I was advanced far toward the rebel line. I saw what I took to be graycoats coming in on our right, and at that time the 14th was the right of the line, as no other troops were in touch with us on the right. I ran back and gave the alarm of our right being turned, and I am sure I was the first one to serve that notice. A fine new regiment was rushed in and formed on our right. This was at dark. It was a large regiment, and each man wore a white straw hat. I had now fallen back into my company, and was doing some tall shooting at a large column of men in gray on our front. The Johnnies opened upon the white hats from the timber, only a few rods in their front. They stood like men, or rather fell, for that line of white hats was a splendid mark for shooting in the dark, and I remember I yelled:

"Throw those hats away!" We were told at the time that the straw hats were worn by the 16th N.Y. I know they did not run at that time, and I know the 14th did not. I know the 14th was on the same ground near dark where Kerns and I left them in the forenoon, when we took to scouting.

Now I know of my own personal knowledge that some little time before dark I was in line for a short time, and while there the rebels made three or four advances on our line and came out of the swamp in our front, it seemed to me six deep, and advanced part way to the battery we were supporting. The big guns did not seem to stop them, and each time the 14th advanced through the guns, which ceased firing, and put Johnny back where he belonged. Then as they came out again we fell back behind the guns and let them pound.

I will not deny that the 14th may have been forced back, as other troops were that day, but I do deny they ever broke like a flock of sheep, as Comrade Jim says. I have never heard it from any source before, and had it been so it seems as though I certainly should know it. Somehow we held our line all day, and were there at night, and lay on the field until late in the night, when we fell back over the Chickahominy, and marched and fought a week, back to Harrison's Landing. At Malvern Hill, near the close of the seven days' fight, we did good shooting. Comrade Jim tells his regiment lost about 300 at Gaines's Mill. I think the 16th N.Y. was nearly twice as large as the 14th, and the loss of the 14th was 248, on that day, when Jim says we ran. The above figures I took from *The National Tribune* a few years ago, when the Fifth and some other corps were written up by the Editor.

I filed the papers away, but fail to find them at this writing, or could give the loss of the 16th as well. I have never forgotten the old 16th coming to our aid; at Gaines's Mill and believe they did their duty there.

About five years ago I was in the bank in this place and a man came in who had on part of a Grand Army suit. I noted him at once as an old soldier, and saw he had lost the left eye.

I always made it a point to greet every old soldier, whether I know him or not, so I stepped up and held out my hand and said, "How are you, Comrade?" Then I said, "What was your command?" "16th N.Y.," said he. Well, I felt he was a comrade, indeed, and said, "Where did you lose your eye?" "Gaines's Mill," said he. "Say," said I, "I never saw you or heard of you before, but I will tell you all about it, and what time of day it was you lost it. Your regiment came into line on the right of the 14th regulars just at dusk on June 27, 1862. Every man wore a white straw hat and made a fine mark for the Johnnies, and they dropped a lot of you in a hurry."

"Gospel," said he. "Where or how on earth do you know all that?"

"Well, I was in Co. A., the right flank company of the 14th, and saw the whole shooting-match." And we shook hands again.

"Yes," said he, "I lost that eye there, and here is where the lead came out." He showed me a large scar on his throat. And I was shot in both legs at the same time, and remained on the field all night."

His name is Perry. I do not remember his first name, or what company he belonged to, but he lived about 20 miles north of Seymour, the last I knew of him.

I inferred from what he told me that evening was the first time the 16th was under fire. If so, when did the 14th break? Not then, certainly, as I was in ranks then and know they did not even waver. I know we all did our duty, and the Fifth Corps and about one division of another Corps, fought the rebel army all day and held our own against big odds.

Now, Comrade Jim, there is enough honor (if we can call war honor) to go all around, and don't let a volunteer jump a Regular because he was in the Regular Army, or a Regular put on frills over a Volunteer, because he sometimes wore white gloves when not campaigning.

Let me speak of one little circumstance. On my way to the Buffalo Encampment, three years ago, I had been down in Oswego Co., NY to my old birthplace a couple of weeks before Encampment time. The first day of the Encampment I boarded a special at Syracuse loaded with old vets for Buffalo. I took my seat, and soon one crossed the aisle, and bending over the back of my seat, said, "Where are you from, Comrade?" I took that to mean what command, and touched my large badge, which read in large letters, "Syke's Brigade, Fifth Corps."

"Oh, pshaw!" said he, for the badge had given me away as a Regular. He stood there awhile talking of battles, etc. and Gettysburg was mentioned.

"Yes," said I, "I Was there." "Not much you weren't," said he; "Sykes' Regulars weren't in it." "Oh, beg your pardon, comrade, but we were. We held Little Round Top, the key of the battle."

Well, I say you weren't there."

I reached in my side pocket, brought out a long pocket-book and took out two parchment discharges, with battles, all from the records, and said: "Comrade, it may not be any of your business, but will you look them over?" He took them, read them carefully, and said: "Say, comrade, you were there; and say, you have a splendid record."

"Well," said I don't have to take a back seat for anything on this train." "And you needn't," said he. And the war was over; it was all right.

I expect to do more writing but will serve notice that it will not be in defense of myself or the 14th. It's too late, comrades, to pick up the hatchet every time someone thinks you or your command failed to do all that was done to put down the rebellion. And, say, Comrade Jim, if you ever strike Seymour, 15 miles west of Green Bay, WI, call and see me, and we will have it out at dinner-time over the johnny-cake and potatoes we may be fortunate enough to have at that time.

As some comrades have found me through my article of Dec 20, I will state that I was also a member of Co. B, 2nd Battalion, 14th U.S., a while before discharge, in 1865.

M. Reed, Sergeant, Co. A,
14th U.S. and Co.B, 14th
U.S. Seymour, Wisc.

A Letter from Washington
From M. Reed, formerly a resident in this vicinity

Editor *Times*, Black Creek, Wis.
January 1904

Dear Sirs:

I am pleased to tell you that a copy of the first issue of the Times—has made a bold dash in its Infancy; it has crossed the vast plains of the great west, skipped over the Rocky Mountains and found all us Seymourites, on the Pacific Coast where winter is not, and where the tater bug ceases from troubling the weary who want to rest. And where old Sol takes his final plunge beneath the waves of the Pacific Ocean, as he bids us good night. We left Seymour the 3rd of last Aug. on our westward journey and the last we saw of Black Creek was reached from the car and shook the hands of our Comrade Justice McKee and wife. We reached St. Paul at 5 P.M. and at once took Great Northern train for our long journey. The rest of the daylight was spent in watching from the car window the country we was passing through, then as daylight faded we called the porter who made our births in the sleeper and all retired.

About 4 o'clock the next morning we passed through a big hail storm as we neared Devils Lake, Minn. The scenery of the great wheat fields of Minn. and the eastern part of Dakota was fine. But soon the scene changed as we sped on, stations and dwellings were further between; vegetation was dried up and grain was short and more scant. We had reached a point where the Rancher considered time wasted in trying to make a home. Alkili pools were on every side as we whirled along on the old iron horse. As far as the vision could reach the great plains spread out in every direction, where once the mighty herds of Buffalo roamed, and the red man was lord of all here surveyed, but how times have changed. Prairie chickens, and ducks fly away as we invade thier lonely homes. Now and then as we get more to the west, a herder appears as he herds his band of cattle or horses. And then appears in the distance a village of Indians with their teepies, dogs, and ponies. Soon we pass the great Muddy, the old Missouri River, which is fringed as far as we can see, with cottonwood timber, and with these scenes night sends us to our births again.

The day finds me at the window in the car, as I had been told to be on the lookout at that time by the conductor. Away to the NW I saw a great bank of clouds rising, and I thought now for a big thunder shower, but as the first rays of the sun struck them a great change came over them; mighty masses of rock and earth appeared, and then above the mass of clouds that in some cases reached nearer the ground appeared the snow capped summits of the mighty old Rockies.

The Back Bone of North America, the rays of the rising sun guilding their rugged pinacles, was a grand spectacle which the beholder will never forget. It is needless to say that I had a late breakfast that morning, as I was feasting on the Beauties of Nature, one which makes man feel his own insignificence and the Mighty, Power and Wisdom of the great God who made them.

We passed villages of Flat Head and Black Feet Indians as we neared the base of the Rockies. When first we sighted them, it seemed that we were at the very base of the mountain range, but some hours elapsed before we could see that we were really on the climb to the top. When we reached a stopping placed called Summit, we were then 5,500 feet altitude. I swung from the car and picked some mountain flowers and mailed back to Seymour.

We had passed through Montana and would soon be in Idaho. When we had passed the Rocky Mountains proper and began the descent into the great valley that separates the Rocky Mountain and Cascade Range.

We were not allowed to see but little of the great Cascade Range as we were sleeping when we crossed them the next night.

The next evening at dark we struck Spokane, Washington and was in the state we had come so far to see, but the trip was not yet ended. That night we had a breakdown, and delayed us some. So we did not reach Everett, where we was to change cars for the final pull to Ferndale.

We was behind time so had the Conductor telegraph ahead and hold the train at Everett, until we could reach there which was one hour behind, and all steam had been crowded on, that the nature of the mountain road would allow.

The change of bag and baggage were made from the track, and we was whirled away on to Puget Sound, where we landed at 1:10 P.M. the 6th of August last.

My Brother Cyrus and family were at the depot to greet us and we were glad to meet, I can assure you, as we met but once before in 28 years.

Ferndale is a new place of over 500 inhabitants and is situated on the banks of the Nooksack River which empties into Puget South 6 miles to the south. It is well named Ferndale; Ferns grow to ten feet high here. The river is navagable and a line of Steamers will soon run here from the city of Whatcom, our county seat ten miles to the south. It is a city of 27,000 inhabitants, so you can see we are not clear out of civilization.

My son-in-law S. D. Rider and his parents have bought a 75 acre ranch one and one half miles from Ferndale for which they paid $5,000. Good buildings, a splendid spring of clear cold water near the house which runs to the barn lot and waters all the stock. A fine orchard of apples, pears, prunes, plums, peaches, cherries of different varieties and etc. They have a fine place.

Wife and I have rooms with them as we do not intend to buy until son Bert comes from Seymour, where he has a fine farm to sell to the first man who wants to buy.

We are not in the midst of winter as they call it here, but no such a thing has yet struck us here.

In November we had one fourth inch of snow which lasted three hours and for three days had cold, windy and rainy weather. Ice froze one half inch thick on puddles in the fields. Since that there has been no cold weather but considerable rain for the last ten days especially, but roads are not so bad as they would be in Wisconsin. My son-in-law took 1,160 lbs. of hay to Whatcom with a pair of 11 hundred lb. horses and an 18 hundred lb. wagon, 11 miles. So you see we are neither mudded or snowed in.

Lands are high here, that is, good improved lands. Timber is very large on the up lands, fir and cedar from six to nine feet in diameter.

Salmon and trout can be had in the river and lakes here, ducks are here also; I shot a fine one today in sight of the house.

But perhaps I have said enough to thaw you Wis. Badgers out of your holes so will desert for this time at least.

                I am your truly,
                M. Reed, Ferndale, Wash.
                85 yrs. a resident of Seymour, Wisc.

M. REED
Pension Claim Agent
Seymour, Wis.

Feb. 8, 1906

My dear Pearl:

Yours of Dec. 4th was duly rec'd and much pleased to hear from you. Glad to find you happy.

Please convey our kind regards to Mrs. W. I am a long time in making reply I admit. Cause—Since the 9th of Nov. last I have been in very poor health, I do not think I mentioned it to you—But have been to City—Seymour only 3 times since Nov. 9. And for several weeks do not leave the house. I over did the thing, in improving this place since I came here, and as you know work & I don't agree, with old War Wounds, etc. I am on the shelf. Sometimes I am unable to Write but very (few) letters for weeks at a time. We have a fine place here now and Hope to Sell—Bert & all—and go West again—The sooner the <u>Better</u>. I printed some hand bills & will enclose one—You send a man here to buy and as soon as sale is sure I mail you a check for $100—Marinda is now willing to go west. I never was so heavy in my life as when I was in Wash. And I do not see how I can stand this climate another winter. Bert says I must go west if we sell or not—But I have put nearly all in land and improvements here. I am not able to do but little at my Pension Biz now for some months.

What Photo—you spoke of—no I did not get__?__ (one?) Last winter was terrible here—not so back this—only 20 below today—some days 34 above & 14 below the next. How's that for changes—too much for me.

The Reed in Chicago, I heard from him recently. His Brother-in-law was in Seymour. And inquired of me and told Mr. Graham our merchant that he was instructed to see me if I was in town. I was not able to be there—He told Mr. Graham that his Brother-in-law said, there was no doubt there was relationship between us and he thought Cousins. We will watch developments.

That we have rich and influential relatives, I am sure—and that we came of good stock.

Cyrus told me when in Wash. that when I was in the army, and he a small boy with Father, that a gentleman and two ladies all finely dressed came to see Father—and called him Uncle John and tried to persuade him to leave there and take his proper station for said they this is no place for you. But you know how independent he was—and would not go. Cyrus said he asked father who they were & what they wanted. Father said oh—they are some rich people & I am poor & rather stay here. Cyrus said they came there twice to see father and tried hard to have him go.

This man in Chicago and I may unravel the matter yet. Our name was formerly Lowell no doubt of that. See Dept. letter—But I see I am getting so I can not write much more & must quit. Bert's whole family are getting over whooping cough. All had scarlet fever last fall. Bert not well of it yet. Marinda's health very good for her. We hear often from Myrt, don't want to leave there—Want us to come. Send that buyer along. Love to wife and all. Write again soon.

BM Uncle & Hant M & M

(The original letter owned by Bill Wadley, Yakima, WA.)

The History of My Life

Yes, I'm getting old and rickety and weak in the knees. I was 30 years old in my present form in March 1899. I was born in the old Anderson Sawmill, in the wilderness town of Seymour, Wisconsin in the winter of 1869. I was purchased by Mr. Peter Tubbs of said town at the rate of $7.00 per 1000. But Peter being of a generous turn of mind and willing to assist a comrade who lived in a small shanty on his land at the that time, I was presented to Mr. Morris Reed, and with the aid of a plane, handsaw and hammer, and a few nails all donated by the said Peter. The finances of Mr. Reed not being equal to such an expenditure at that early date, I was speedily converted into my present shape—minus my two leaves which were added later as riches increased. I was not altogether a thing of Beauty, but was much prized by my owners who by some hook or crook obtained sufficient bluing to color my legs—and then I was a dandy, and the envy of our wilderness neighbors.

That season I was moved into a small rough board house 12x18 foot one mile north of the present city of Seymour, Wis. where I did daily duty for Johnny cake, wild gooseberries and deer meat for 18 long years. Oh, yes, I was happy in those olden times, never was overburdened and feared no rivals. But said to relate a change came in 1881. I was moved across the road in another house. Master then owned a horse and a cow and began to put on airs, and I was considered hardly up to date with my leather hinges and blue legs and a rival was purchased of Mr. P. W. Evans for a jar of butter and I was consigned to a lonely room to do duty as a Center Table.

But my disgrace was not yet complete. In a short time a little affair in paint and varnish took my place and I was relegated to the back kitchen to wash dishes on and other menial duties.

But oh, dear, will you please wipe the water from my eyes and I will tell you the rest; that is if I can. Mistress she went to the city one day with a little red-headed man and came back with a big ugly extension table, and I was put out of doors, and the red-headed man took me away, and today the 24th day of August, 1899,

I was ushered into a fine new home about 1/2 of a mile further west and I became the property of Master's daughter. They call her Myrtle and there was a nice little girl of 4 summers they called Marion and Baby Ellen and PaPa Sidney. They seemed real glad to see me and I hope to spend my days in peace at last, and I hope they won't begin putting on airs as Mistress did with her five cent calico dress and as Master did with his bicycle and 10 cent watch chain.

Well, I guess that's all, so good night and a happy future to you all.

Yours turly,
Mrs. Reed's First Table

June 19, 1909

My Adventure With Wolves
By M. Reed of Seymour, Wisc.

Editor *Green Bay Review*:

In 1868, I became one of the early pioneers in Seymour in the northern part of Outagamie County, I had been one of Uncle Sam's kids for four years from August 1861–65. Having enlisted when 15 years and six weeks old in Oswego, NY, and I felt I was capable of being a pioneer in almost any undertaking.

I had married a curly headed girl in 1866, and in 1868 we and the boy hiked out west to grow up with the country. We reached the present site of Seymour city in November 1868, all was standing timber at that time where now stands the city, no sign of a railroad. Green Bay and Appleton was our trading post then, and three days was consumed in a trip with an ox-team to replenish our store goods.

We had neither team nor cash—not even a hen or a cow to bother with, not even the filthy lucre to obtain them with, but we had ourselves and the boy—now a family of eight of his own, and a fine farm near Seymour.

My first venture was a job of cutting ten acres of this heavy timber in logging length for C. E. McIntosh at ten dollars per acre. We had writings specifying that no logs should be cut more than eighteen feet long. We moved into Mr. McIntosh's house, and he and family went to Madison, as he was elected that fall to the Legislature. Now it happened that McIntosh and his neighbor, Tom Ausbourne, did not love each other, according to the golden rule, and when McIntosh left for Madison, Tom was a frequent visitor to where I was chopping on my job. One day Tom said, what is the use of your cutting all them big red oak all up eighteen feet long; I would never do that way, I'd fall them across the brush heaps and when they burn the fellow, they will all burn off and save you a big lot of work. I knew absolutely nothing about such things at that time, and no more cutting big timber for me, I took Tom's advice.

The next spring when McIntosh came to look over the job, we first inspected my part where I had not yet made Tom's acquaintance. Well, you have done a good job, said he, but when we came to another post, he said, Say Morris, I guess there is a red oak you failed to cut, and there is another on that heap. Oh, I said, I left them on purpose. You see, I was very careful to leave them only where I could fall them on a brush heap and when you burn the fellow, the logs will all burn off. You see, I did cut them all till I learned it was no use. Tom Ausbourne was up here and told me they always done that way—Now every one who has ever cleared land among oak timber knows that a green red oak a thousand brush heaps would no more than scorch the bark on them. Well, the name of Tom Ausbourne was too much for McIntosh, he just literally exploded all over at once and I thought of Bull Run, and a whole lot of other places where I wanted to get a way from. He looked me over critically to where the joke came in, and concluded I was an innocent party to the transaction, finally cooled down enough to say Morris, if Tom ever comes on this place again, you order him out in a hurry, and go cut all them trees up as per contract.

I find I have wandered from my design to tell about my terrible experience with wolves. That awful time has made an impression on my mind that time will not suffice to erase it either from my own or my neighbor's minds. Having come from an old settled part of York state, I knew little about large game. I had often heard old settlers there tell of the awful panther, wolves and bear and had read of the great western hunters, and their narrow escapes from wolves and Indians, ect., and when I was doing that chopping I was mentally calculating that as soon as I could get some spare time I would take my rifle—about the only thing I did own and explore some of the almost unbroken forest to the North. I could see there was deer here and they came into my chopping rights and Tom had told me some tales of what was to be seen and heard in the big woods. One day in the winter, or the next spring for I remember it was caucus day at the old log school house, I shouldered my trusty rifle, a muzzle loader of about 44 calibre and struck into the tall timber in a northeast direction toward Toad Creek. It was a dark cloudy day with quite a body of snow in the wood. I had no compass, but thought if Daniel Boone could travel the woods night and day and kill varmints and Indians, I could do a little of that, too. I had not gone far when my eye caught the glimpse of a move in the brush about fifteen rods ahead, and partially behind a windfall, I stopped and soon made out a large animal looking at me over a fallen log. I was in a hard position to shout without stepping to one side a little and I did not dare stir as I saw it was a fine deer. I had never had a shot at a deer, and wanted one bad. I leaned to the left all I could to escape some brush but saw there was not much chance as all I could see was the neck of the deer who was standing facing me. I hesitated to shoot but did not dare to move and had heard that a man never gets the first deer he shoots at. At last I made a venture and cut loose at the deer and at the crack of the rifle the deer hit the snow and I was a hunter—but in a moment it jumped to its feet and started off. I commenced to reload but I did not have the ready made cartridges of army times so it was slow work and before I was loaded, my deer was gone. I went to where it had stood and found I had cut hair clear along its neck and side. I grabbed up a handful and trust it into my pocket and started on the track. I would run it down if I could not shoot it. I have since expected I had a slight touch of buck fever, but I think this was a doe. I followed it into a swampy country where I never was before and was making good time on the track when I hear a low dismal howl. I paid little attention to it at first but in a moment it sounded much nearer and louder. I stopped short, and listened, there it was again, and rapidly coming nearer, a croaking howl, it sounded bad in the lonely wood and all the tales of wolves and panthers I had heard or read, came to mind and now it had come my turn to have a hand in such things. But somehow I kept thinking of the little woman and the boy at home, what would become of them if anything happened to me. I had little time to speculate on those things for the howls was very near and I must be doing things. I now knew a pack of large timber wolves was coming, and unless I made a move toward protection or safety at once, the curly headed girl and the boy would wait and watch in vain for my homecoming. But whew, that last howl was a loud one, almost on me, the timber was thick and I could see but a short distance. I made a jump for a small white beech tree that stood near me, the limbs grew down to near the ground, I took my rifle in one hand and up I went. I located in a crotch of the tree about twelve feet from the ground and as I had quite a lot of powder and balls along, I felt quite safe and made up my mind I could kill as many of them as they could of me. I had no more than got my position in the tree than they was on me. I cocked my trusty rifle and peered down through the branches to see the advance of the pack when all at once there was a terrible howl or racket over my head and I yanked up my head to see a large flock of ravens going over me croaking for all there was out. Well, I just climbed down and went home, and later in the afternoon I went down to the old log school where the neighbors were attending caucus and told the story of my terrible narrow escape from the wolves and when I got to the ravens, there was a big old time doing, I have not heard the last of it yet.

Children, Surname REED:
+ 100. i. Adelbert Lowell, b 4 May 1867.
+ 101. ii. Myrtle Minnie, b 7 October 1870.

29. MARY[3] **MARIE REED** (d/o John[2] Reed, #7) b about 1848 at Mexico, Oswego Co., NY.; m in 1866/67 **John Wingate**, s/o John S. and Rebecca (Conklin) Wingate, b March 1839 in NY. Mary and John were together in Seymour, WI in the 1870 U.S. Census near his parents, and they had one child at the time, Charles. In the 1880 Census of Seymour, John, age 40, was living with his parents and Cyrus Wingate, age 12, was boarding with Alonzo and Harriet Stevenson. This Cyrus could be the Charles in the 1870 Census, as the age agrees. At the same time Mary Wingate, age 31, appears in Town of Richland, Oswego Co., NY living with Lewis Conant, 74, widower and his daughter Betsey Conant. With Mary is son George Wingate, age 6; Anna Wingate, age 8, born WI, is boarding with Eli and Sophina Caswell, also in Richland; this could be her daughter. The 1900 Soundex Census for Wisconsin revealed the presence of a John Wingate, age 61, born NY, living in Shawano Co., Town of Lessor, living alone. Also living in the same town was Cyrus Wingate, spelled Syrus in Census, age 31, b NY, boarding with John S. Courtice. There was a record of the death of this John Wingate on 7 May 1909 in Shawano, Town of Lessor, WI with burial in Rose Lawn Cemetery, in an unmarked grave. A visit to Rose Lawn Cemetery in 1980 was somewhat fruitful, in that Mrs. Eugene Goerl, keeper of Cemetery records, revealed that he was indeed buried there, and Cyrus Wingate was the purchaser of the lot. She consulted her aged mother, who remembered John Wingate living alone in a log cabin on Country Trunk W on corner of Silver Lane. There was no record of the burial of Cyrus there. This is purely circumstantial evidence, but I feel reasonably sure this is our John Wingate.

Mary apparently was divorced from John Wingate, because on 30 December 1887 Mary Marie Reed m **Lorenzo Cook**, s/o George W. and Eunice (Dayton) Cook, b 28 December 1858 at Volney, Oswego Co., NY. The first marriage to John Wingate was indicated.

Mary died 4 September 1894 at Mexico, NY, age 45, and is buried in Mexico Village Cemetery as "Mary Wingate." Lorenzo died 12 February 1900 at Volney, NY and is buried in Volney Center Cemetery. As far as is known, Mary and John Wingate appear to have had three children.

Children, surname WINGATE:
  102. i. Cyrus[4] Charles (or Charles Cyrus), b April 1869 in New York, probably Mexico.
  103. ii. Anna, b about 1872 in Wisconsin, probably Seymour.
  104. iii. George, b about 1874 in Wisconsin, probably Seymour.

30. CYRUS[3] REED (s/o John[2] Reed, #7) b 6 September 1849 at Mexico, Oswego Co., NY. He was a little under four years old when his mother died, and for a couple of years he lived with his Aunt Ruth. About 1855 the whole family journeyed to visit relatives of his father's in Wisconsin. A full account of the trip is found in his father's entry.

As a result of the Civil War there was a shortage of cotton. According to the *Mexico Independent* newspaper of 16 April 1863 a company was formed at Oswego to "cottonize and manufacture" flax. Seed would be furnished to farmers at cost and a good price paid them for their crops, to replace the cotton formerly raised in the south. Mexico farmers did begin the cultivation and conditioning of flax; a flax mill was opened in 1865 near the Harlow Ames place on the Colosse Road just south of the village. The women spun and wove the linen, some of it surviving the wear and tear of time to this day as sheets, towels, and tablecloths. Cyrus was living with his Aunt Ruth at Colosse at the time. When he enlisted in the Indian Wars 28 May 1866 as Private, Co. E., 4th U.S. Infantry at Oswego, age 17 years, his enlistment paper listed his occupation as "Flax Dresser." In his Army Pension file are letters about his duties protecting army wagon trains carrying supplies between Fort Fetterman and Fort Laramie, WY and protecting the workers building the Union Pacific Railroad, against attacks by Sioux Indians. He evidently had some close calls, only suffering one wound by an Indian arrow through his left wrist, leaving a scar which his grandchildren remembered seeing. He claimed injuries to his knees, as well, from donkey kicks. There are many accounts of his army experiences, making it difficult to sort out fact from fiction. Several will be included here. He was discharged 26 May 1869 at Fort Fetterman, returned to Seymour, WI to spend time with his brothers, Michael and Morris.

Cyrus m 4 July 1870 **Louise Harris**, probably in Seymour, WI; she b 8 March 1846 at Monith City, Monmouthshire, England. According to his Pension file they moved quite a bit; in 1875 they moved to Winona City, MN; located in 1877 at Deadwood, SD; and then in 1880 located at Aspen, CO. In this same document there is the information that Louise died at Belle Fourche, SD May 1881. One of her granddaughters gave me an account of her supposed death thus: "She was at home on their ranch, perhaps in Colorado: a heavy rain caused high water in the local streams, cutting off their herd of horses. When Louise ordered the ranch hands to ride across the swollen stream to drive the horses back across, they refused. She, calling them 'Lily-livered,' attempted to rescue the horses riding her horse across the water and was swept away in the swift current, her body never recovered." According to the pension file she had divorced him before her death. No records of her death place have been found.

Cyrus Reed m/2 **Susan Belle Hardwick**, d/o John Milton and Sarah Higgins (Chandler) Hardwick, at Aspen, CO, 3 October 1883. The following is the announcement of their marriage in *The Aspen Times* of 6 October 1883: "On the evening of 1 October at the residence of H.P. Noble, Esq. in Aspen, Mr. Cyrus Reed, of Middle Roaring Fork Valley, Pitkin Co., Col. to Miss Susan Belle Hardwick, of Four Mile, Garfield Co." Four Mile is near Glenwood Springs. Susan (or Susie), better known as Belle, was born 13 January 1861 at Kansas City, Mo. the 8th child of 13 children. According to the grandchildren interviewed, this marriage was a stormy one, Susie Belle occasionally asserting her independence, far ahead of her time. According to Cyrus' Indian Wars Pension file Susie was involved with Charles Barton, previous to her marriage to Cyrus. This evidently was a bogus marriage, and resulted in the birth of a daughter, Pearl; Cyrus accepted her as his own daughter.

The war records go on to say Cyrus was located at Milford, MO in 1888. Records at LaMar, Barton Co., MO indicate he did own property there a few years. A tintype of his store there was sent me by Leota Nickle of Long Beach, CA, a granddaughter. The sign on top said:

<blockquote>
C. REED
Dealer In
Dry Goods, Groceries,
Hats, caps, boots, Shoes,
Clothing, Hardware, et.
</blockquote>

Cyrus and Susie bought first on 20 September 1888 land in Township 33 and sold it 7 October 1889. At that time he bought Lots 8, 9, 10 in Town of Milford, where he had the store. On 5 December 1892 they sold these lots, having moved to Weir City, KS. Their next stop was Long Beach, CA; then came Portal, ND in 1894; 1900 U.S. Census for ND found them living next to their daughter Maud and family. They finally located at Ferndale, WA at first on a farm and later moved into the village. Here they remained until 1923 when on 22 October they applied for admission to the Retsil Soldier's Home in Retsil, WA. There Cyrus, aged 87, died 5 February 1937 and Susie died 16 April 1939; both buried in military cemetery there. Cyrus was remembered by relatives who met him as a flamboyant man, usually dressed in buckskins, with long, flowing white hair, reminding them of Buffalo Bill Cody, with interesting stories of his experiences. His young grandchildren remembered a jolly man in baggy trousers who liked to take them on his lap and always had lemon drops in his pocket for them. Below are a number of newspaper accounts, Pension letters and personal letters written by him.

                              Emma P.O.
                              Pitkin Co.
                              Colorado

Dear Brother Morris:

    At last I have got around to answer your kind and welcome letter. Morris, I am almost ashamed to write after putting it off so long. I have been drove all the fall with work it is true, but nevertheless I could have wrote if I had tryed very hard when I first got your letter but on the second day of this month I started acrost the mountains to buy cattle. I crossed the grate continental divide that divides the eastern and western slopes. I stood 12,000 feet above the level of the sea where I could see the waters flow one way to the mighty Pacific and on the other hand on its way to the Atlantic. It makes ones' lungs ache to travel on a slow walk there for a few miles the altitude is so high. Then went down Lake Crick. Struck twin lakes, then from there on the old Arkansaw River, and there, Morris, for the first time in four years I saw the cars go apuffing up along the Arkansaw Valley. Sat on my horse and swang my hat till I guess the passengers thought I was crazy. I forded the Arkansaw and made for the western pass, It snowed while crossing the pass. I reached South Park on the West Platte River all right. There I bought 21 head of cattle, 17 lambs and 4 calves. I crossed the western pass again, encountered some snow, reached the old Arkansaw again, turned up the Arkansaw, traveled to the head of it, crossed Tennesse Park. Then went over Tenessee Pass, altitude about 10,000 ft. Struck the head of Eagle River, trailed down it through Malta to Red Cliff then over Battle Mountains. Encountered hard snow storms as I ever saw. Feed poor for the cattle one month. Slept in the snow. Struck the Eagle again at foot of Battle Mountain, down Eagle then down to Bellyache Mountain. There encountered heavy snow again and Man and Beast Suffered some. Struck Eagle again, down till I come to Gifesunse Creek. Thare turned in direction of home acrost Cottonwood Pass. Thare cattle found some grass, Man found Snow for drink a small portion, a cracker. On top of Cottonwood Pass I knocked my forefinger on my right hand out of joint at the knuckle joint and broke some of the bones in the back of my hand. Then came the pass; had to put the bride reins over my neck and use the corn whip in the left hand, but thank God I reached home the next day with all of my stock and my hand in a bad shape. I had a man with me that has been to work for me all summer by the name of Nelson Ectes. He sends his best respects to you. I don't know as this will interest you but I know it did me and so I thought it would you. I have got now 31 head of cattle altogether.

    Belle sends her love to you all and wants you to write soon. I shall write as soon as I hear from you again. I will write to Bertie in a few days. Morris, give this to Mike's folks after you read it. I will write them soon. I want them here as soon thay can get here. Help them, Morris, to sell their place if possible.

Write soon. From your brother,
Cyrus Reed.

dated Nov. 26, 1885.

On upper edge of Cyrus' letter is written,

Please send me your picture in your next letter. Don't forget, send one of your pictures if you can. I must have your this time.

Morris I forgot to date this letter but it is the 26th day of Nov. hand pains me so I guess I must quit.

Whoop it up Liza Jane.

In envelope with Morris' letter, envelope dated Dec. 18, 1885 and addressed to Mrs. Ida Canfield, Kasoag, NY. Letter dated Nov. 26, 1885.

DEPOSITION
a case of
Cyrus Reed
No. 662644

On this 29 day of May, 1895 at Pentwater, County of Oceana, State of Michigan, before me, G. T. Fitzsimons, a Special Examiner of the Pension Office, personally appeared Augustus Jacobs, who, being by me first duly sworn to answer truly all interrogatories propounded to him during this Special Examination of aforesaid pension claim, deposes and says:

I am 50 years old, formerly a shoemaker, am not able to work now. P.O. address & residence Pentwater, Oceana Co., Mich. I have lived in Pentwater about 22 years. I enlisted in Co. E, 4th U.S. Inf. Jany. 17, 1866, and was discharged from that service Jany. 17, 1869. I was a Corporal. I never served after that. Prior to that service I had served in Cos. H & E, 151st. NY. Infantry. The first time I recollect Cyrus Reed, the soldier, was sometime after my enlistment in Co. E, 4th Inf. He was a member of my company. To the best of my knowledge when I first knew him in the service he was a healthy man. I bunked with him some and when we would be guarding the mails & supply train from one fort to another, I would be with him two or three weeks at a time. While we were on our way between Fort McPherson and Fort Laramie in the spring of 1867, he was attacked with the measles and was left at Fort McPherson. I knew that he had the measles because that is what the doctor & everybody else said was the matter with him; there were several others who had the measles about the same time. I was not bunking with him at that time, but saw him while he had the measles there in the camp. After he was taken out of the camp I did not see him again until he came back to duty. When he came back to duty, he seemed to be alright, but some little time after that he was bothered with the rheumatism. I knew he had the rheumatism because he complained of it and I bunked with him some while he was suffering from it, and saw his feet & legs swelled up and he was excused from duty a good deal on account of the rheumatism. I don't know how he contracted the rheumatism unless it came on from the measles. No, I can't say that I ever heard him say how he contracted the rheumatism. I remember in the fall of 1868 at Fort Fetterman I was detailed for duty under the Q.M. Dept. and had entire charge of the corrals. Reed was one of the men under me, and he was driving team, hauling logs, and he got one of his hands hurt in handling logs, I don't remember which hand it was. I was right there when the accident occurred. He was unloading logs & got his hand caught in some way. I cannot recollect the exact details. I remember right the bones in the palm of his hand were broken. I know that it left his hand in a crippled shape. He was excused from duty on account of this injury for a month or six weeks or something like that, but I don't remember whether he went to the hospital. He returned to duty but his hand was crippled & in bad shape. Also, while at Fort Fetterman. I can't say whether it was after or before the accident to his hand, but it was in the same year, a mule or a horse kicked him in the knee, I don't know which knee. It bruised his knee badly and it swelled up. I saw the kick and also his bad knee after the kick was received. He was breaking some unruly horses or mules. I cannot say whether he was riding or driving at the time or exactly how he came to get kicked.

He was laid off duty for some time on account of this injury but I don't think he went to the hospital, but I know he was limping around a considerable time afterwards but he seemed to have gotten over it alright when he returned to duty. In the Summer of 1867 towards the Fall he got hurt in a fight with the Indians. That was between Fort Laramie & Fort Fetterman. An arrow struck him on the front of the wrist & cut some of the arteries, I think. We were on detail guarding the mail or supply train between the said forts when the Indians made a sudden swoop down on us & let some arrows fly & then rode off. One of the arrows struck him as I have told you. He was the only man hurt that I remember. I don't remember who was in charge of the detail. I cannot recall the names of any of the other men who were on the detail. The wound was bound up the best way possible until we got to Fort Fetterman, where he went into the hospital & had it attended to by the doctor. I do not remember who the doctor was. After he got hurt he rode in the wagon most of the time. I saw him after he was in the hospital. He was there quite awhile, I could not say how long. I cannot remember his ever suffering from any other disability in the service. It seems to me that I met him once since my discharge, but I cannot be positive.

QUESTION: Cyrus Reed states that when he received the wound by the arrow, the detail was out Scouting for Indians. You have stated that you were on the march guarding the mail or supply wagon. Who is right?

ANSWER: I think that he is mistaken. I don't remember being out scouting for Indians. Our duty was almost entirely guarding the mail & supply trains. The Cavy. did most of the scouting.

QUESTION: He says that the Indians charged right through the detail killing two or three men of his regiment. You have told me that he was the only man who was hurt. Which one of you is correct?

ANSWER: He has got things all mixed up.

QUESTION, Do you remember when Sgt. Ray of Co. A. was killed?

ANSWER: Yes, but that was a different time. There were one or two others killed on that occasion but I was not with that detail. I don't recollect our doing any scouting duty about that time or any other time.

QUESTION: The hospital record shows that Reed was in the hospital at Ft. Laramie on account of wound of left wrist caused by glass bottle accident. Have you any recollection of this?

ANSWER: No. The only thing I ever heard of any men being hurt by a glass [the next page was not sent to me] (Deponent's statement continued) He was disabled on account of the injury to his wrist after he got back to duty.

I recognize my signature to the affidavit which you have shown me. [b.j.] when I stated in that affidavit that he contracted rheumatism by getting wet while crossing the Platte R. I mean that is what I heard at that time in the Camp. I was not with him then & had no personal knowledge of the matter.

I received a letter from him about the time he made application for pension and he asked me if I recollected about his disabilities and I wrote to him telling him what I could remember. I am not related to the claimant and I have no interest in the prosecution of his claim. I cannot find the letter he wrote me. I have heard the foregoing read and I am correctly recorded.

Augustus Jacobs. Deponent.

Sworn to and subscribed before me this 29 day of May, 1895 and I certify that the contents were fully made known to deponent before signing.

G. F. Fitzsimons,
Special Examiner.

Orig. Inv'd. 662644

The Third Generation

Cyrus Reed, Co. E., 4
Regt. U.S. Inf. Weir,
Cherokee Co., Kansas

Notice waived
Grand Rapids, Mich.

May 31, 1895

Hon. Wm. Lochnew,
Commissioner of Pensions
Washington, D. C.

Sir:

I have the honor to return the papers in the claim above indicated and to submit my report.

The claim was referred to T.E.W. to determine incurrence of alleged injury to right hand and left wrist. It came to me on further examination for the testimony of Augustus Jacobs. Witness bears a good reputation for veracity but I believe is willing to strain a point to assist a comrade. After he had made the preliminary statements in his deposition, he excused himself and went out of the room for a few minutes. His action gave ground for the belief that he did this in order to refresh his memory by some memorandum of his affidavit. I wanted him to let me see the letter which he said claimant wrote him. I think that he was probably coached in that letter. He made a show of looking for it and then said that he could not find it. Though the claimant has in a letter, Apr. 23, 1895 (see loose papers) corrected his statement made to Special Examiner Burger that the wound by arrow was incurred in fight with Indians when Sgt. Ray was killed. I thought it best in cross examining Jacobs to call attention to the discrepancy. As it appeared under oath, this being the most satisfactory manner of bringing out the facts. Jacob's testimony seems to sustain claimant's corrected statement except that he was positive that he never engaged in scouting for Indians. He corroborates claimant's statement as to the time of the only glass bottle incident mentioned by these two men is connected with the injury to left wrist. It will have to be shown, either that they are mistaken as to the time of the incident, or else that the injury affected claimant's wrist in such a way that it had to receive hospital treatment some months afterwards.

The claim at present seems to be of doubtful merit. I recommend further examination as follows:

Origin
James Nolen [b.j. II] Hanover, Washington County, Kans.
Sam'l Lampson, Lampson's Depot, NY.

Martin Hogen, Oswego City, Oswego Co. NY.
Sam'l O'Neil, Tully, Onondaga Co., NY.
Harvey Stowel, Fullerton, Dickey Co., N. Dakota.
and others on list if necessary.

> Very respectfully
>
> G. T. Fitzsimons,
> Special examiner.

CLAIM OF SOLDIER FOR SERVICE PENSION INDIAN WARS

State of Washington

County of Whatcom

On this 28th day of March, A.D. 1917, personally appeared before me, a Notary Public within and for the county and State aforesaid, Cyrus Reed, aged 67 years, a resident of Ferndale, County of Whatcom, State of Washington, who, being duly sworn according to law, makes the following declaration for the purpose of obtaining pension under the act of Congress granting pensions for service in various Indian Wars of the United States from 1817 to 1891.

That he served under the name of Cyrus Reed, as a Private in Captain Henry H. Patterson's company, Bvt. Colonel Wm. McE. Dye, regiment of Fourth U.S. Infantry Volunteers; that he entered said organization at Fort Ontario, Oswego, NY, on or about the 28th day of May, 1866 and was honorably discharged at Fort Fetterman, Wyoming on or about the 28th day of May 1869, having served thirty days or more in the war or disturbance with the Sioux Indians in the State or Territory of Wyoming.

That his personal description at date of first enlistment was as follows' age, 21; height 5 ft. 5-1/4 in.; complexion, Dark; color of eyes, grey; color of hair, brown; that his occupation was flax dresser; that he was born Sept. 6th, 1849 at Mexico, Oswego Co., NY.

That his several places of residence since leaving the service have been as follows: Mexico, New York, from 1869 for about a month; and then to Seymour, Wisconsin, leaving Wisconsin 1875 for Winona City, Minn.; located then in Deadwood, S.D. in 1877; located in Aspen, Colorado in 1880; located in Milford, Missouri 1888; located Weir City, Kansas 1892; located in Long Beach, Cal. 1892; located in Portal, N.D. 1894; located Ferndale, Washington 1901, and has resided at Ferndale, Washington since that time.

That he is a married man; that the maiden name of his wife, to whom he was married in Aspen, Colorado, on the 2nd day of October, 1883, was Susie Belle

Hardwick, that she is living; that he was previously married to Louisa L. Harris, who died at Belle Fouche, S.D. on the_____day of May, 1881.

That he is not a pensioner of the United States; that he has heretofore applied for pension; that he has not applied for bounty, land, etc.

That he is an actual and bona fide resident of the U.S.; that his post-office address is Ferndale, County of Whatcom, State of Washington.

Cyrus Reed
Claimant's signature

Also personally appeared H. E. Campbell, residing at Ferndale, Wash. personally certified to be respectable and entitled to credit, and who, being by me duly sworn, say that they were present and saw Cyrus Reed, the claimant, sign his name to the foregoing declaration, etc.

CYRUS LETTER

Long Beach, Cal.
April 10, 1898

My dear Sister Ida & Family:

Your good and welcome letter of February 18 reached me all right and to tell you the truth I was as tickled as a spotted pup to hear from you. Many times, Ida, for the last 28 years I have often thought of writing to you and thus I would get careless or lazy and put it off and so on until the next time. But as you say I have often heard of and from you through Morris' letters. But you must excuse me for this time and hereafter will try and do better. My life has been one roaring life you know on a small scale. I have been in nearly all of the large cities of the United States, have lived in a few of the states and traveled through many more and traveled many more, for inst. New York, Ohio, Penn., Mich., WI., Indiana, Ill., Minn., Wyoming, Montana, Nebraska, Mo., Kansas, the Indian Nation, through different tribes in the nation; also Dakota, Colorado, Utah, Nevada, and California, and Iowa, perhaps more if I could think of them. I have went by rail, by steam boat and sailing vessel, have traveled by team, mules, horses and oxen. Have traveled a foot and horseback, have traveled hungry & dry, have traveled well fed and wet. Have been rich and poor 3 or 4 times. Have been married twice. Two girls from my first wife; 2 boys and 2 girls from my last wife. I made my first wife a big present one day. I gave her one half of the world. I took the other half. I have a good wife to share it with me. We feed out of the same manger and sleep under the same sidewalk. Her name is Belle, she weighs 165 lbs., is 5 ft. 6 tall and is 37 years old, and can whip her weight in wild cats. As for the country, Ida, this is the finest climate that I was ever in. The thermometer stood all winter about 45 above zero, flowers in bloom all winter, ripe oranges, green oranges, oranges in bloom, all at the same time and on the same tree, lemons the same. They raise here grapes, figs, apricots, olives, apples, pears, plums, cherries, berries and many kinds of nuts and all kinds of vegetables, barley, corn, oats, wheat without end, alfalfa, hay and other things. But the country has one drawback—that is the drought. They are not sure of a crop here every year, unless in some places where they can irrigate and this is one of their dry seasons. The crops in many parts is already gone. It is the driest year for 10 or 12 years, so they tell me. It is healthy here, we get the sea breeze and we are about 300 yds. from the clean beach. We can walk on the beach and pick many funny shells, see many funny things and hear the sea lion roar and see him swim and dive. As for the blacksmith trade here, it is about the same everywhere, like everything else, but I suppose pays as well as anything else, in these present Hard Times. Now, Ida, it would not do for me to advise you, and Scott. What is best in regard to coming here nor going anywhere, for I would not wish to be instrumental in your making a move and your getting dissatisfied and homesick. You have been in old Oswego County all your life and if you should leave there & moved I bet a four year old new moon that you would cuss the best country in the world for a year or two until you got over being sea sick or sick of you would know what. This ole gal is a big world, a wide world, a good world, and a hard world and very few get through it alive, you know. So be careful before you jump. Of course, Ida, I would like to see you and your family more than you will ever know but send Scott to look before you sell what you have got there. As for me and what I know of New York, I would not live in the state if I was to be made a present of the whole state. But do not let that have any influence on you because as you know I am part Mohawk Indian, and the world is my home. In fact, I am at home wherever I take off my hat. Now, if I was a blacksmith and could beat some one out of the lumber & would put me into a shop right here in this end of town, as there is none here. Will explain further in next letter. Say, Ida, has Scott a brother by the name of L. H. Canfield? He was in the army with me. He said he knew you. If so, where is he now? Give our love to your children and keep some for yourself. Member your old Indian brother and tell me to behave myself, and do better. Write soon.

Cyrus Reed

P.S. Have Scott and the boys write. Where is Al Westcott and everyone else that I wish to know.

Cy, Belle, Pearl, Eva, Clyde & Floyd

SEYMOUR PIONEER RECALLS DAYS OF INDIAN WARFARE

About 1931

Capt. Cyrus Reed, 82 years old, Seymour pioneer, recalls the days of Indian warfare on the western frontier, the laying of the great Union Pacific Railroad and remembers Jim Bridger and Buffalo Bill as his contemporaries. Capt. Reed, who is spending his annual vacation with his nephew, B. L. Reed of Seymour, came from the Veteran's home at Retsil, Wash. where he has been for the past eight years.

Capt. Reed enlisted in the army when he was 17 years old and fought Indians on the western frontiers. When he was guarding the men laying the rails for the western railroad, he was shot through the wrist with an Indian arrow. Another time he was nearly captured by Indians. His capture was averted by the friendship of Chief White Eagle, who assisted him to escape and return to safety on his own pony.

The pioneer was born in New York in 1849 and settled in Seymour after his army enlistment expired. He lived with his two brothers Michael and Morris until he married and settled on the present Hugo Baehler farm. He went west in 1875 and has spent the last 30 years in the state of Washington.

Among his contemporaries Capt. Reed has kept the friendship of the Indian Pawnee Bill with whom he corresponds.

The Reed family held a reunion at Kelly Lake last Sunday, which was attended by nieces and nephews of the first, second and third generations.

(The clipping below is from Bill Wadley, Yakima, WA, 8-79)

Indian Fighter of 1867 Recalls Thrill Atop Pole

Captain Reed, now past 80, once afforded Redskins good target but escaped with only 17 holes in clothing.

Bang! Bang! Bang! Whizzzzz! But no Redskin hit the dust. Not that time. Instead a young American soldier, without gun or sword, scuttled down a telegraph pole and struck out for the protecting hills near Fort Fetterman, WY.

The young soldier was Cyrus Reed, then a private in the United States Army, and the incident described above occurred in 1867, at which time the army was actively engaged in quelling the warring tribes of the Sioux, Cheyenne, and Arapaho Indians.

Reed, now Captain Reed of the Soldier's Home at Retsil, Wash. related the experience yesterday on his arrival here from Los Angeles, Cal. where he attended the annual gathering of the United Indian War Veterans.

"Yes, Sir," the veteran said laughingly, "That was some time, believe me. A telegraph wire had broken down out of Fort Fetterman and I volunteered to fix it. I was sent out with a number of other soldiers and on arriving at the place discarded my gun and cartridge belt in order to make the climb easier.

"Well, sir, I just reached the top when—wham! An arrow shot by my head and I heard a series of blook-curdling yells. Looking down, I saw a band of Sioux race out from a deep ravine, all shooting arrows in my direction. I don't know how I ever got down alive, but somehow my feet touched gorund and then I ran. Reaching the fort, I found no less than 17 holes in my trousers and coat but didn't have a scratch. No, I didn't go back for my gun or belt."

That was just one of the many experiences told by Captain Reed. Though more than 80 years old, he is in perfect health and when interviewed proudly admitted that he still can dance the steps so popular in his youth.

Captain Reed enlisted at Fort Ontario, near Oswego City, NY in 1866 and for three years was in the heart of the many Indian battles. His first taste of redskin warfare was at North Platte, Nebraska, where Reed and his company were stationed while the Union Pacific was laying railroad tracks westward.

"I was asleep," he said, "when another of those whoops split the air. We didn't have to wait for the bugle. We knew what was happening. After a vicious three-hour battle the Indians retreated, suffering a heavy loss of men. We had some casualties, too."

From then, until 1869, when he was mustered out of the service, Captain Reed was in almost every major conflict. At Plattsville, he suffered his first and only wound. A speeding arrow struck his left wrist, severing the main cords and causing a serious loss of blood. He recovered, however, and soon rejoined his regiment.

While at Los Angeles, Captain Reed was presented with a medal of honor by the leader of the veterans, and yesterday also displayed a badge, identifying him as commander of the General George A. Custer Camp, No. 9. On his arrival here, he visited with his nephew, P. L. Wadley, 229 East Thirty-sixth Street.

VETERANS ADMINISTRATION

Date: December 4, 1937
MBAB-1
MEMORANDUM

From: Chief, Adjudicating Division

To: Mr. Phillips, Legal Consultant

Subject: REED, Cyrus c15-620
XC-2,581,721

QUESTION

May Susan Belle Reed be accepted as the legal widow the veteran?

FACTS

The veteran enlisted May 28, 1866, and was honorably discharged May 26, 1869, a Private, Company E, 4th U.S. Infantry. He died February 5, 1937, at Retsil, Washington.

The veteran stated on pension questionnaire received July 16, 1917, that he married Louisa Harris July 4, 1870, that she died at Bellfouche, South Dakota, that he married Susan Belle Hardwick October 2, 1883, at Aspen, Colorado. On questionnaire received from the veteran February 20, 1892, he gave the name of his first wife as Louisa O. Harris and stated she was divorced from him, the exact date being unknown. In letter received from the veteran February 20, 1892, he stated his first wife obtained a divorce from him but that he did not know the date of said divorce. The veteran married Susan Belle Hardwick at Aspen, Colorado, October 2, 1883, and a record of the marriage is on file.

The widow stated on her claim for pension that the veteran's first wife died in 1880. Proof of death of Louise Harris or of her divorce from the veteran has not been furnished. The widow stated in affidavit received November 4, 1937, that she has searched diligently for proof of death of the veteran's first wife, Louise Harris, in the states in which she has knowledge of his residence, but has not been able to obtain any evidence of proof of her death; that she died many years ago, and before the claimant's marriage to the veteran.

R. J. HINTON

Children: Surname REED

105.   i. Zoe Olive, b 25 May 1871 in Minnesota according to the obituary; about 10 years old when her mother died. She married first Jesse Thomas Zane, s/o Thomas W. and Virginia (Cummings) Zane on 17 January 1897 at Sundance, WY. She must have been living with sister Maude then. Jesse b 11 October 1868 at Schoolcraft, MI. Zoe and Jesse had a cattle ranch at Sundance. Jesse died 2 October 1915 at Sundance, at age 46. She evidently moved to Washington State to be near her family after her husband's death.

Zoe m/2 3 July 1917 at Bellingham, WA, Andrew Weston, the husband of her deceased sister, Maud; Andrew was b 31 May 1880 at Sherwood, Oregon. They lived about 20 years in an apartment house in Nampa, Idaho. Zoe d 16 April 1946, just short of 75 years of age at Nampa, Idaho and is buried in Cloverdale Memorial Park, Boise, Idaho. Andrew d 16 October 1960 at Portland, Oregon. He had spent a number of years in his hometown, Sherwood, Oregon. Zoe had no children by either marriage.

+ 106. ii. Maud Edna, b 20 November 1876.
107. iii. Pearl, b 23 April 1883 (her death certificate says 1893) at Colorado Springs, CO. According to one of Cyrus' grandsons, Susie Belle was going with a young man from an influential family who did not approve of the match and it was broken off, but she was pregnant for Pearl. Pearl was born previous to Susie Belle's marriage to Cyrus, so she must have been born in 1883; the death certificate says 1893. Pearl herself tried to find a record of Susie Belle's earlier marriage but was unsuccessful. Cyrus' Indian Wars Record says Susan Josephine Hardwick's spouse or whatever's name was Charles Barton.

The author has a copy of a picture of Pearl in a school picture at Dominquez School, Long Beach, California, dated 1899, Pearl at the far left, certainly a teen age girl, disputing the date on the death certificate. The following are remarks made by a niece of Pearl's:

"Pearl married, first, Al Roseall in Ferndale and they went to Alaska. She returned to Ferndale alone; no one knew what happened. Then she married Al Hilty and went back to Alaska, during the gold rush days before 1910. It was a bad marriage. In Alaska she fell in love with a fellow named Tony. She had made quite a bit of money in Alaska and she planned on going to South America with Tony. She trusted him with her savings—he went to South America and she never heard from him again. It nearly killed her. She went about 1914 to Sacramento to go to Business School. There she met Frank E. Fletcher, head of Pioneer Fruit Company, whose offices were located there. They married and moved to San Francisco. She never had any children. I, Leota, lived with them 3 years in San Francisco, during my last 3 years of High School (1930–1933)."

Pearl was accepted by Cyrus as one of his children, and she appears in several pictures of family gatherings at the farm at Ferndale, Washington.

According to her death certificate Pearl died 19 May 1941 at San Francisco, California and her ashes were buried in Olivet Memorial Park. She died of pulmonary tuberculosis. Her age was listed as 48 years; probably closer to 58. Her husband's age was listed as 72 years old. They had no children.
+ 108. iv. Eva Belle, b 4 April 1887.
+ 109. v. Clyde Laverne, b 4 December 1888.
110. vi. Alfred Floyd, b 6 August 1890 at Milford, Barton Co., MO. His

father was proprietor of a general store there, at that time. During his younger days Floyd worked as a brakeman on the Canadian Pacific Railroad. He m in 1932 at Moose Jaw, Saskachewan, Canada Beatrice M. Dawkins, d/o Edward and Alice Dawkins, she b 20 July 1904 in England. Floyd trained as a chiropractor and had a practice in Auburn, Washington. Like his brother Clyde he was very musical and played several instruments. When his cousin Olive visited him in 1974 when he was 84 years old, he played the accordian and sang songs to her. Beatrice d 6 June 1972 at Auburn and Floyd d 19 January 1976, also at Auburn, Washington. Both are buried in Mountain View Cemetery, in Auburn. They did not have any children.

111. vii. Gordon F., b August 1893 in Mo. The only evidence of his existence is found in the 1900 U.S. Census for Ward Co., ND with his parents.

31. IDA³ ADELLA REED (d/o John² Reed, #7) b 17 August 1851 at Mexico, Oswego Co., NY. After her mother's death in 1853, Ida was taken into the home of friends of the family, Asa and Mary Westcott when she was about five months old. Asa Westcott was b 12 October 1807 at Williamstown, NY and m Mary Wing 28 July 1829, at Mexico, NY; she b 17 December 1809. They had one son of their own, Allen, b 25 October 1832. Asa enlisted at age 54 as private, Co. F, 147th Regiment NY Volunteers, 2 September 1862; he d 25 July 1863, age 55 years, of Chronic Diarrhea in the military hospital at Portsmouth Grove, RI and was buried in the hospital graveyard. After Asa's death Mary and Ida Westcott, for Ida adopted the name although not legally adopted, moved to a small farm of about 13 acres in the Town of Albion, Oswego Co., NY. Mary Westcott died 12 December 1893 and was buried in the Baptist Church graveyard near her home.

Ida sang in the Baptist Church choir, where she met her future husband, **Scott Canfield**, s/o William and Mary Ann (House) Canfield, whom she married 27 June 1875 at Williamstown, NY; Scott born 4 November 1851 at Brighton Corners, Otsego Co., NY., Just west of Richfield Springs, NY. We have the original deed of property bought by Scott in Kasoag, NY. 10 May 1875, where they lived a number of years, where he had his own blacksmith shop, a trade he learned from his father. There were documents among Scott's effects indicating he was probably town clerk and postmaster in Kasoag, a thriving lumber town, with a big lumber mill. Thirty or forty teams of horses hauling logs all winter provided Scott with lots of business repairing wagons and shoeing horses. When Kasoag ran out as a lumbering town in the early 1900s, Scott built a new stone blacksmith shop at Altmar, Oswego Co., NY where he continued to work and live until he left Altmar.

Scott loved to travel and by way of the railroad visited many of his and Ida's relatives in Portland, OR, Bellingham, WA, Seymour, WI, and others; Ida did not care to travel. In fact, she hardly ever went so far as the stores in downtown Altmar, preferring to send Scott or the children to do her shopping. She did visit her daughter Alta near Syracuse, NY, as evidenced by letters sent her there; and her son Lucius at Verona, NY. She appeared to be in poor health through the years, with frequent sick spells. She was a very private person and at least in late years had a joyless outlook on life. As will be seen in letters written by her brother Cyrus, she at one time considered moving to Long Beach, CA which he did not encourage.

About 1932 Scott and Ida Canfield lost their home and shop in Altmar and, being in ill health, they moved to their daughter Alta Kennedy's home in Warners, near Syracuse. For several years Scott raised a big garden to help feed the family in Warners. Ida died 10 August 1937, a week short of her 86th birthday, in Warners. Scott died 27 May 1938, age 86. They both are buried at Williamstown, Oswego Co., NY.

Children, surname CANFIELD:

      112. i. Arthur[4] W., b 17 March 1878 at Williamstown; d 6 February 1881, just short of three years and is buried at Williamstown.

+   113. ii. Willis Burton, b 28 May 1879.

      114. iii. Clinton Arthur, b 2 July 1882 at Williamstown; d 24 May 1901 at 18 years, of cancer which developed from a leg injury when he jumped off a train and struck his left shin bone. He is buried at Williamstown.

+   115. iv. Lucius Leroy, b 5 November 1884.

+   116. v. Floyd Beecher, b 18 July 1886.

+   117. vi. Alta May, b 22 March 1889.

The Third Generation

William Harrison Austin
(#25) at age 20 in 1860.

Hannah Currie Austin
Taken in Torrington, WY
shortly before her death

Michael Reed (#26)
From portrait owned by
Wallace Reed's son, Philip.

Descendents of John Messer Lowell

Martha Reed Wadley (#27)

Joshua Wadley

Pearl Lera Wadley (# 96)
son of Joshua and Martha.

The Third Generation

Morris Reed (#28) and his wife,
Marinda Wingate Reed

Descendents of John Messer Lowell

Susie Belle Reed,
Cyrus' second wife

Cyrus Reed (#30)

Cyrus Reed at Retsil, WA

The Third Generation

Ida Reed Canfield (# 31)

Grandma Ida Canfield
Alta Canfield Kennedy
Grampa Scott Canfield

Chapter 5

The Fourth Generation

33. ROYAL[4] **DURAN CHEESEMAN** (s/o William[3] Cheeseman #8), b about January 1848 at Milesgrove (now Lake City), Erie Co., PA. On 21 February 1867 he married **Adelaide Marion Sargent,** d/o Alfred and Maria (Phelps) Sargent, b at Spring Trip, Crawford Co., PA. 20 November 1846. They resided at Albion, PA until the spring of 1875 when they moved to North Girard, PA for his employment with American Fork and Hoe Co., then known as Otsego Fork Mills, operated by Alfred Denio. Royal and Adelaide spent the balance of their lives in North Girard, where he was foreman of the Otsego Fork Mills for fifty years. Both were active in church work, being members of the Presbyterian Church, he being an elder in the church for 36 years and superintendent of the Sabbath School for more than 20 years. Adelaide was an active member of Bay View Club. Royal d 16 December 1920 at North Girard, PA; Adelaide died 23 November 1924 at Pittsburgh, PA while visiting their son William.

Children, surname CHEESEMAN:
+   118. i. William[5] Alfred, b 23 November 1870.
+   119. ii. Ina E., b May 1876.

37. JENNIE[4] **CHEESEMAN** (d/o William Cheeseman #8), b about 1859. She married **— TOWNER** and lived in Toledo, Ohio. She died in 1885, age 26, the same year her son was born, and is buried in Conneaut [OH] City Cemetery. Her gravestone, next to her son's grave, was hard to find under a bush. I found no records of her in Toledo.

Children, surname TOWNER:
  120. i. Jay[5] W., born in 1885, probably in Toledo, OH. He was killed when an automobile hit him near his home in Toledo, April 4, 1934.

38. CARRIE[4] **CHEESEMAN** (d/o William Cheeseman #8) b about 1866. She m **William Meyers** and lived in Toledo, Ohio, according to family records. Her father, who died in 1889, was lauded in a newspaper obituary, and it states that "he is survived by a daughter, Mrs. Will Meyers of Sterrettania, PA." There was an obituary for Jay Towner in Toledo in

1934, saying he is survived by an aunt, Mrs. William Meyers of Toledo. A trip to Toledo did not resolve the mystery of what happened to Carrie. In a letter from Hubert Cheeseman, East Haven, CT dated March 28, 1985, he states that Carrie married William Meyers, who worked at the Skinner Organ Co. in Toledo. He further stated that she had two daughters who died very young.

Children, surname MEYERS:
    121   i. Daughter^5, died young.
    122 ii. Daughter, died young.

42. ALICE^4 JULIET CHEESEMAN (d/o Willis^3 Cheeseman #11) b 4 October 1868, Plymouth Township, OH; m 21 December 1898 at Town of Monroe, Ashtabula Co., **Warren W. Marble**. He was born 2 July 1859 at Edinboro, Erie Co., PA, s/o Chauncey and Olive Marble. Chauncey was born in Onondaga Co., NY and when a young man moved with his parents, Paul and Clara (Cobb) Marble to Erie Co., PA where he engaged in farming and stock raising. He was the owner of 300 acres of land. In 1893 Warren moved to Conneaut, OH and after his marriage in early 1900s bought City View Farm, at the crest of Farnham Hill with 80 acres, overlooking the City of Conneaut, one of the largest dairy farms in Ashtabula Co. They were both active members of South Ridge Baptist Church, of which he was a deacon; he was also a member Lone Star Grange, Farm Bureau and Conneaut Chamber of Commerce. Warren died 2 November 1938 in Conneaut; Alice died 1 August 1946 and both are buried in East Conneaut Cemetery.

Children, surname MARBLE:
    123.   i. Homer^5 Wilder, b 26 August 1900 at Conneaut. He grew up on his father's farm; graduated from Ohio State University 1923. He worked three years in Canton, OH in a dairy plant making ice cream. He then worked thirteen years in Pittsburgh, PA at the North Pole Ice Cream Co. After his father's death he came home to run the family farm. He m 31 March 1956 at Troy, OH, Marguerite Hotchkiss, d/o Benjamin Vaughn and Alta (Rhodes) Hotchkiss. She was an elementary school teacher for 36 years, retiring in 1971.

              General Electric drilled three wells on their farm property to help supply gas for the local GE factory which makes bases for electric light bulbs. In payment they get free gas for heating their home. Homer and Marguerite have no children.

The Fourth Generation

124. ii. Junior[5], born and died 10 May 1902 at Conneaut.

44. LENNA[4] SHERMAN CHEESEMAN (d/o Lucien[3] Cheeseman #15) b 16 January 1886 Conneaut, Ashtabula Co, OH. She m **Floyd Perry Johnson** 20 September 1909 at Conneaut, OH. Floyd b 10 September 1887 at Vermillion, OH, s/o Frank M. and DeEtta (Hewitt) Johnson. Floyd was an electrician; Lenna was a 1908 graduate of Oberlin College and a member of Phi Beta Kappa fraternity. For a number of years she operated Johnson China Shop on Main Street, Conneaut. Floyd graduated from Ohio State University at Columbus. They lived in Columbus until 1923, when they returned to Conneaut. Lenna was born and died in the same house, 247 Buffalo St., Conneaut, once owned by her father. Lenna died 19 November 1959, age 73, and is buried in Conneaut City Cemetery.

Children, surname JOHNSON:

125. i. Ellen[5] Louise, b 29 December 1912 at Defiance, OH. Louise was a teller in a Conneaut bank, for 30 years, retiring in 1978. She and her sister, Ruth, lived when last known, with their father in the old family home at 247 Buffalo St., Conneaut. She did not marry.

126. ii. Ruth Elizabeth, b 16 August 1914 at Columbus, OH. She was a medical secretary for a doctor in Conneaut for over 30 years, retiring in 1975. She did not marry.

+ 127. ii. Louis Frank, b 5 March 1921 at Warren, Ohio.

45. GEORGE[4] HENRY CROUCH (s/o Angeline[3] Austin Crouch #16) born June 3, 1850 in Green Lake Co., WI. Together with his parents and the entire family, he moved to Minnesota in 1874, and located on the farm, where he continued to reside until his death. He m/1 **Emma Burch** in 1876; she was b about 1852. She was working as a servant for his father's family in the 1870 Monroe Co., Wisconsin Census, Town of Sparta, age 18. They had two children before she died in 1880.

George Crouch m/2 **Eliza Jane Castle** on 16 November 1882, she b 6 December 1864 at Beaver Dam, Wisconsin, d/o Sydney and Sarah (Shoemaker) Castle, and d 30 April 1954, age 89 years. George was a semi-invalid for the last years of his life. A tree fell across his chest while he was cutting winter wood, leaving him incapacitated. He d 22 October 1913 at his farm home five miles north of Dodge Center, MN. He and both wives are buried in Wildwood Cemetery, Wasioja, MN. However, we were unable to find their gravestones.

Children, surname CROUCH:
+ 128. i. Mertie[5] Ann, b 19 August 1877.
+ 129. ii. Irvin H., b 12 November 1878.
+ 130. iii. Grace May, b 31 August 1883.
+ 131. iv. Lettie Adell, b 10 March 1886.
+ 132. v. Harrison Morton, b 8 October 1888.
+ 133. vi. Vernon George, b 7 June 1891.
+ 134. vii. Lila Belle, b 30 August 1895.
+ 135. viii. Floyd Allen, b 25 July 1898.
    136. ix. Bertie Lorn, b 16 August 1901 at Wasioja. He died 9 August 1911, age 10, and buried at Wasioja.
+ 137. x. Charles Henry, b 11 December 1903.

46. NELSON[4] REASONER CROUCH (s/o Angeline[3] Austin Crouch #16) b 7 December 1851 at Big Creek, Wisconsin. He m 29 April 1885 **Hattie M. Leach**, b 5 Jan. 1864. Hattie, and her infant son, died in childbirth 21 March 1886. He m/2 **Agnes Abbie Briggs** June 1888. Agnes was b 11 February 1861, d/o John G. and Abby E. (Cook) Briggs. She d 29 November 1902, age 41 years. They had three children. Nelson m/3 Mrs. **Janet Carlaw Abernathy** on 3 Sept. 1904, b 17 April 1851. They moved to Northfield, MN about 1918, having many years in Dodge Center and Tracy, Dodge Co., MN. Nelson d 7 April 1934 at Northfield, was a member of the First Congregational Church of Northfield and active in Prohibition work. He is buried in Wildwood Cemetery, Wasioja, Dodge Co., MN and his nephew Rev. Charles Crouch of Saint Paul, MN conducted the interment ceremony.

Children, surname CROUCH, by Agnes Briggs:
+ 138. i. Mildred[5] Abby, b 9 March 1894.
+ 139. ii. John Wilbur, b 29 October 1895.
    140. iii. Frank Nelson, b 20 May 1900 in Wasioja. He graduated from high school, when his father was farming near there, at Tracy, Minn. Later lived at Northfield, MN with family. He was a banker at San Diego, CA for a number of years. He m Cecilia Cassutt at Rochester, MN. They did not have any children. Cecilia had a daughter Geraldine by a former marriage. Frank for a number of years suffered from arthritis which resulted from a football injury in high school, which became progressively crippling. Frank d 11 December 1971 at Rochester, MN and Cecilia d about 1981 or 1982.

47. EMMA[4] A. CROUCH (d/o Angeline[3] Austin Crouch #16), b 12 August 1854, in Wisconsin. She m in 1888, **William Edgar Osborn**, s/o Abraham and — (Caukins) Osborn, he b in Marengo, Morrow Co., OH 9 Dec. 1854. In 1879 he came to Wasioja, MN to attend the Wesleyan Methodist Seminary. He worked at the stonemason's trade the greater part of his life. was an active member of the Baptist Church in Wasioja. Emma d 27 March 1896, age 41, at Wasioja of Tuberculosis; William d 29 May 1929, age 74, at Wasioja. Both are buried at Wildwood Cemetery, Wasioja.

Children, surname OSBORN:
+ 141. i. Willie[5] L., b 12 December 1889.
+ 142. ii. Emma Angeline, b 24 May 1890.
+ 143. iii. Lida Elizabeth, b 22 July 1891.
+ 144. iv. Bida Bell, b 27 July 1892.
    145. v. Henry A., b about 1895, d March 1896, and is buried at Wildwood Cemetery.

52. EMMA[4] AUSTIN (d/o Lyman[3] Austin #16), b about 1856; no detailed information on her husband has been found, other than the report of the children.

Children, surname unknown:
    146. i. Edna.[5]
    147. ii. Myrtle.
    148. iii. Ernest.

56. ELLEN[4] M. MARTIN (d/o Amanda[3] Austin Martin #18), b 9 August 1851 at Town of Buffalo, Fond du Lac Co., WI; m 17 September 1872 in the Methodist Church in Ripon, Fond du Lac Co., **James R. Quick** s/o Jacob and Hannah (Crawford) Quick, he b 4 March 1846 at Scranton, PA. Ellen d 4 August 1918, age 66 years, 11 months at Mackford, Green Lake Co., WI and is buried at Lake Maria Cemetery, Mackford. Ellen and James evidently were divorced; James was m 17 November 1903 in Ripon to Ida B. Fobes Lange, d/o Charles and Elmira M. (Canfield) Fobes. The 1905 Town of Mackford Census shows James with three younger children only. James d 11 November 1922 in Arcadia, FL according to an unidentified obituary and is also buried at Lake Maria Cemetery. The 1900 Census for Town of Mackford, Green Lake Co., indicates Ellen had had six children, five then living, the sixth not known.

Children, surname QUICK:
+ 149. i. George[5] Martin, b 8 May 1874.
    150. ii. Howard, b 12 September 1877. He was a farmer and never married. He d 31 March 1958, age 80, at Black River Falls, Johnson Co., Wisc. He is buried at Riverside Cemetery, Black River Falls.
    151. iii. Esther, b 6 March 1881; she d 25 April 1922, age 41 years, Town of Brooklyn, Green Lake Co. in a fire and is buried at Lake Maria Cemetery.
+ 152. iv. Jesse James, b 2 January 1884.
+ 153. v. Eugene, b 25 May 1889.

58. AMANDA[4] ELIZABETH MARTIN (d/o Amanda[3] Austin Martin #18), b 29 June 1858 at Green Lake Co., WI. She m 2 April 1882 in Green Lake Co., **George William Clark**, s/o Steven and Susan (Popal) Clark. b 23 November 1850 at Brookfield, Madison Co., NY. He died 12 January 1929 in Town of Brooklyn, Green Lake Co. Amanda died 3 June 1913 at Brooklyn. Both are buried at Woodlawn Cemetery, Ripon, Fond du Lac Co, WI

Children, surname CLARK:
+ 154. i. Amanda[5] Maude, b 19 January 1883.
    155. ii. George Jay, b 2 February 1892. He m/1 8 July 1917 at Ripon, WI, Alice Patchett, d/o John and Julia (Sear) Patchett, b 7 April 1898 at Mackford, Green Lake Co., WI; d 21 February 1932. They adopted George Leroy Patchett, s/o his sister Amanda and her husband Clarence Maude Patchett. George m/2 **Leona Ziellow** on 14 October 1934. George d 8 April 1967/68.
+ 156. iii. Ruth May, b 8 April 1898.

60. JOHN[4] EBER PECKHAM (s/o Minerva[3] Austin Peckham #19), b 22 July 1850 at Marcellon, Columbia Co., WI. He m 25 September 1870 at Manchester, Green Lake Co., WI, **Almira Bray Staves**, d/o John and — (Bray) Staves, b 29 January 1853 at Kingston, WI and died 28 February 1933 at Alexandria, Hanson Co., SD, age 81.

    County Auditor J. E. Peckham died at his home in this city at 10:30 o'clock Wednesday morning, February 26, 1913 after a painful illness.... The deceased was an early settler of the county, coming here with his family from the state of Minnesota in 1879, settling upon a homestead a few miles east of Alexandria. About twenty five years ago he disposed of the farm and removed to Alexandria, engaging in the hardware business as successor to the firm of A. & J. McQuarters and having been engaged in different lines of business here continually since that time with the exception of a period of a few years during which he was engaged in the hardware business at Charles City, IA.

Both Bert and Sibil Peckham told me the story of the first Peckham who came to Hanson County, SD from Wisconsin. It seems that he drove a covered wagon and one horse that was not "bridle broke" so he could not "gee" or "haw" with reins, so had to lead the horse some 600 miles by the bridle bit and wore out several pair of shoes with finally bare feet on the bare ground.

Among his experiences in pioneer life was the carrying of a sack of flour on his back from Marion Junction to his home, a distance of over thirty miles, to save his family from starvation. At another time, during one of the most severe winters known in the Dakotas he assisted in shoveling a way through the drifts on the Chicago, Milwaukee & Saint Paul RR as far as Sanborn, IA with Nick Mueller, now a resident of Springlake township, this county, walked back to Alexandria, a distance of 115 miles.

He lived in Hanson County from the time he filed on his homestead, thirty-four years ago. His health was always good, and he never required the services of a physician until four years ago, while serving as postmaster of the Senate at Pierre. At that time his health gave way and he was taken to the sanatorium at Chamberlain for treatment. He soon recovered sufficiently to be able to accept the position of Deputy State Oil Inspector, which position he held until March 1, 1911, when he began serving as auditor of Hanson County, to which position he had been elected at the preceding election. Both are buried at Green Hill Cemetery, Alexandria, SD.

Children, surname PECKHAM:

    157. i. William^5 Eugene, b 5 September 1871 at Marcellon, Columbia Co., WI. He died 20 March 1873.

+   158. ii. John Wallace, b 10 March 1873.

+   159. iii. Charles Herbert, b 15 February 1875.

+   160. iv. Frank Duward, b 20 March 1877.

+   161. v. Edith May, b 16 April 1879.

    162. vi. Ida Maude, b 17 December 1883 at Emery, Hanson Co., SD. She m 8 November 1905, Rev. A. Franklin Ainsworth at Charles City, IA. When her father died in 1913, she lived at Woodbine, IA. She was not mentioned as attending her mother's funeral in 1933, but was listed as living in Fairmont, IN. In 1939 when her brother John died her location was listed as in Texas. In 1943 when her brother Frank died her location was Corpus Christi,

TX. Again in 1945 when her sister Edith died she was still in Corpus Christi. She would have been 62 years old then. No more is known about her.

163. i. Myrtle Ann, b 28 October 1887 at Emery. She m 19 August 1908 At Alexandria, SD, Fred A. Bond, b 14 February 1879 at Columbus, WI. He moved to Alexandria with his parents in 1883. His father was a pioneer lumber dealer in Alexandria. Fred was employed in a bank for some time, later engaging in the contracting business and followed the trade of carpentry, before he went into the lumber business and operated his own yard.

    In 1941 Fred and Myrtle moved to Seattle, Washington, where Fred died 9 January 1949. Myrtle died 30 August 1960 at Seattle. Both are buried in Green Hill Cemetery, Alexandria, SD. They did not have any children.

164. i. Walter Eugene, b 18 July 1891 at Alexandria. He died of Scarlet Fever on 23 February 1901, at 10 years of age.

61. LUCRETIA[4] M. PECKHAM (d/o Minerva[3] Austin Peckham #19) b 18 March 1854 at Marcellon, Columbia Co., Wisc. She m 9 November 1870, **Thomas Vining**, b November 1849, s/o Edward and Katherine (Haynes) Vining. They lived for awhile in Faribault Co., MN, then moved on to Chetek, Barron Co., WI. Lucretia d 4 March 1910 at Chetek, not quite 56 years of age; Thomas d 24 March 1927 at Chetek, aged 77 years. Both are buried in Lake View Cemetery, Chetek.

Children, surname VINING:

165. i. Charles[5], b 22 March 1873 and d 12 October 1883 at Chetek and is buried with his parents in Lake View Cemetery.

+ 166. ii. Laura May, b 26 January 1875.

+ 167. iii. Jesse L., b 28 October 1881.

+ 168. iv. Thomas Ray, b 26 October 1887.

169. v. Lester Eugene, b 6 August 1890, probably at Chetak; d 12 September 1917 at Chetek, age 27, of pulmonary tuberculosis. He was a carpenter and never married.

+ 170. vi. Harry Edward, b 27 April 1893.

171. vii. Benjamin W., b 14 March 1898, probably in Chetak. He worked the Vining family farm near Chetek after his father's death and the rest of the family left home until he moved to the Knapp Haven Nursing Home in Chetek many years later. He d 22 October 1980, at 82 years of age; he never married.

62. ELIZABETH[4] ANN PECKHAM (d/o Minerva[3] Austin Peckham #19), b 21 November 1858 at Marcellon, Columbia Co., WI. She m 11 April 1883 at Portage, Columbia Co., WI, **William Henry McElroy**, s/o William and Ann Eliza (Fuller) McElroy, he b 18 October 1860 at Buffalo, Marquette Co., WI. When he was 9 years old his parents acquired a farm in the Town of Marcellon and there he grew up. He and Elizabeth made their home on a farm adjoining his father's. In 1924 William, his wife and daughter, Joyce, chose the village of Pardeeville as their residence. Elizabeth d 15 February 1931 at Pardeeville and William d 3 May 1936. Both are buried in Marcellon Cemetery.

Children, surname McELROY:

- 172. i. Daughter[5], b and d in infancy 29 January 1884.
- + 173. ii. Alice Grace, b 4 June 1885.
- + 174. iii. Lucy May, b 13 September 1887.
- 175. iv. Myrtle Elizabeth, b 27 July 1891; she d 11 March 1924 and is buried at Marcellon Cemetery, age 32. She did not marry.
- + 176. v. William Boyd, b 27 January 1894.
- + 177. vi. Winnie Blanche, b 27 January 1894, twin to William.
- 178. vii. Edna Joyce, b 1 December 1897 at Marcellon. She did not marry, but lived at home with her parents. From about 1914 she gave piano lessons to children in the area; in the early days she hitched up her horse and buggy and drove to the homes of her pupils. Later she drove her Model A Ford car. She loved cooking, baking and canning and raised a large garden of vegetables. Her niece remembers her old fashioned house with wood stove and pantry, where she always had a cookie jar filled with her good cookies. She willed that her house be sold, with proceeds going to her church, where she played the piano, and was active in other church activities. Joyce d 30 June 1982 and is buried with her parents in Marcellon Cemetery.
- + 179. viii. Ralph Fay, b 8 January 1900.
- 180. ix. Daughter, b 14 July 1903 and died the same day.

63. CHARLES[4] WESLEY PECKHAM (s/o Minerva[3] Austin Peckham #19), b 20 November 1861 at Marcellon, Columbia Co., WI; m 7 March 1883 at Marcellon Free Will Baptist Church, **Elizabeth Jane Smith**, b Oct 1863, Portage, WI, d/o Thomas and Rhoda (Reeves) Smith. They later moved to the West, settling in Potter Co., SD. where they lived a number of years, coming to Day Co., SD. about 1890. They knew all the hardships of pioneer life. Elizabeth d 30 May 1913, age 50 years, at Bristol, SD. Charles Wesley d 3 June 1926 at Webster, Day Co, SD, nearly 65 years old. Both are buried in Webster. Cemetery.

Children, surname PECKHAM:

+ 181. i. Edna[5] Pearl, b 5 March 1885.
+ 182. ii. Maude Susan, b 2 February 1887.
+ 183. iii. Thomas Ralph, b 7 November 1891.
+ 184. iv. Raymond Charles, b 4 March 1894.
+ 185. v. Harold S., b 8 April 1895.
+ 186. vi. Gertrude Primrose, b 2 September 1898.
+ 187. vii. Floy Valanda, b 19 October 1900.
+ 188. viii. Orville Kenneth, b 19 July 1907.

64. WILLIAM[4] HARRISON PECKHAM (s/o Minerva[3] Austin Peckham #19), b 13 November 1864 at Wyocena Township, Columbia Co., WI; m 17 October 1883 at Portage, Columbia Co., WI, **Abigail Waite**, d/o Andrew and Mary Jane (Smith) Waite. William farmed his father's farm until 1920 when they moved to Portage where he was grounds keeper for Dr. Meacher. Abbie d 22 October 1926, age 62, at Portage, and William d 21 March 1940, age 77 at the same place. Both are buried in Marcellon Cemetery. Their first three children died of scarlet fever in a period of 16 days.

Children, surname PECKHAM:

189. i. Mary[5] Ina, b 15 February 1884; d 3 January 1895, age 11 years.
190. ii. Jesse Lawton, b 12 April 1886; d 7 January 1895, age 9 years.
191. iii. Vieva May, b 22 July 1892: d 19 January 1895, age 3 years.
+ 192. iv. Lela Eldora, b 28 March 1896.
+ 193. v. William Emery, b 20 March 1898.
194. vi. Orrie, b 16 December 1899: d 12 November 1922, not quite 23 years, the victim of an accidental drowning.

67. ANN[4] JANETTE AUSTIN (d/o Andrew[3] J. Austin #21), known as "Nettie" b 18 September 1859 in WI, probably in Big Creek, Monroe Co. She appeared with her family in 1860 and 1870 Monroe Co. census, Town of Sparta as Anna J. In the 1910 Census for Barron Co., WI, she appeared as Ann Janette. She m **Thomas James Powell**, s/o William and Margaret (Jones) Powell on 25 June 1889 at Sparta, at her father's home. Her residence is listed as LaCrosse, WI. Thomas was b 6 September 1860 at

Bangor, LaCrosse Co. The 1910 Census for Barron Co., City of Barron, showed Ann Janette as being a city librarian. A letter dated 6 July 1984 from Barron Public Library confirmed that she was librarian there from April 1909 to May 1913.

Thomas d in Barron 28 March 1917 and is buried in Fairview Cemetery, Bangor with his parents. Nettie d 5 January 1953, age 93 at Santa Monica, CA and is buried in Forest Lawn Cemetery, Glendale, CA. She may have been living with her grandson William at the time.

Children, surname POWELL:
+ 195. i. Edna[5] Margaret, b 4 May 1890.
    196. ii. Gladys Leona, b 1 August 1896, Bangor, LaCrosse Co. In her father's obituary in 1917 she was listed as single and a graduate nurse of Minneapolis, MN. When her mother died in Santa Monica, CA in 1953 Gladys was listed as a survivor and wife of Thorton Onley Hack, s/o Glenmore W. and Mary E. (Onley) Hack, both parents born in Maryland. Thornton b 31 January 1895 at Los Angeles, CA. He was office manager for Douglas Aircraft; he d 2 May 1952, age 57, at Santa Monica, CA. According to a grandson and granddaughter of her sister Edna, Philip and Pamela Spratt (Lee), she was a patient in a nursing home in Altoona WI, where she d 9 January 1985, age 88: she and her husband are buried at Forest Hill Cemetery, Eau, Claire, WI. She was married briefly to Jack Riley at Portland, Oregon; marriage annulled, but she kept the Riley name.

72. MARY[4] ANN AMES (d/o Elizabeth[3] Austin Ames #23), b July 1863 in Green Lake Co.; m 24 December 1884, **Charles James Crane**, s/o John and Amy (Pike) Crane at Town of Mackford, Green Lake Co., he b 17 June 1858 in Green Lake Co. The 1900 Census Soundex for Wisconsin shows them living in Town of Rushford, Winnebago Co. He d 13 March 1914 in Oshkosh, WI., age 56, his occupation listed as laborer at Crane Lumber Co. Mary d in 1939, age about 76. Both are buried at Waukau Cemetery in Winnebago Co.

Children, surname CRANE:
    197. i. Stella, b April 1886, probably in Oshkosh, WI. According to her father's obituary she was married to — Shove and lived in Duluth, MN. Her name was not in the Duluth City Directory.
    198. ii. Percy, b July 1898, probably in Oshkosh, WI. According to his father's obituary he lived in Oshkosh, but his name not in the

Oshkosh City Directory.

77. MALINDA[4] ALVARETTA PHILLIPS (d/o Matilda[3] Austin Phillips #24), b 7 April 1863 at Sparta, Monroe Co., WI. At the age of 15 years she moved with her parents to Wasioja, Dodge Co., MN. She m **James Andrew Abel** on 3 July 1884, he b 24 August 1858 in Lafayette Co., WI, s/o Morgan and Mary (Eastman) Abel. He moved with his parents to Wasioja. in 1876. In 1904, Malinda and James moved to Webster, Burnett Co., WI, by covered wagon according to a descendant. Here they were instrumental in starting the Bluff Lake Evangelical Church. They made their home here for 19 years. In 1923 they moved back to Dodge Co., where they lived the rest of their lives. James d 4 February 1934, age 75 years. Malinda d 25 October 1938 at Rochester, MN, age 75 years. James and Malinda were both buried in Wildwood Cemetery, Wasioja.

Children, surname ABEL:
- 199. i. Andrew[5] Luverne, b 1 May 1885, Wasioja. He m late in life Ethel — who reportedly forced him to sell his farm and took the proceeds before leaving him; they had no children. He moved in with his brother Lester. He was a carpenter until he retired. After that he made his home with his cousin, Mrs. Ann White, in Dodge Center, Dodge Co. He d 22 November 1960 at Owatonna, MN.
- \+ 200. ii. Delia Ann, b 30 July 1887.
- \+ 201. iii. Estina May, b 4 March 1890.
- \+ 202. iv. Thomas Morgan, b 29 May 1892.
- \+ 203. v. Lester Ross, b 3 December 1894.
- \+ 204. vi. Etta Matilda, b 16 December 1898.
- \+ 205. vii. Ethel Lorilla, b 25 November 1901.

78. LORILLA[4] ANN PHILLIPS (d/o Matilda[3] Austin Phillips #24), b 12 July 1865 at Sparta, Monroe Co., WI. She m 10 November 1900 **George Bond**. Lorilla d 19 May 1907, not quite 42 years old, at Bluff Lake, WI and is buried on the shores there. George abandoned the children after Lorilla died, and the children were brought up by James and Malinda Abel.

Children, surname BOND:
- \+ 206. i. Alice[5] May, b 21 May 1901.
- \+ 207. ii. Anna Laura, b 26 May 1903.

81. NELSON[4] RAY PHILLIPS (s/o Matilda[3] Austin Phillips #24), b 25

October 1875 at Sparta, Monroe Co., WI.; m 15 November 1905 at Saint Paul, MN, **Mabel B. Elliott** of Wasioja, MN. Nelson was raised by his sister "Retta" (Malinda Alvaretta Abel); his mother died when he was only 6-1/2 years old. He was a railway mail clerk on the run from Saint Paul to Duluth, MN. for 7-1/2 years. He moved to Anaheim, California about 1911, where he became one of the first mail carriers, which job he held 25 years until his retirement about 1935. He was a member of the White Temple Methodist Church, Anaheim, and was a member of the choir. Nelson died in 1939, age about 64, at Orange, CA. Mabel died a year later and both are buried at Orange.

Children, surname PHILLIPS
+ 208. i. Ethel^5 Edna, b 25 June 1910.

82. LLEWELYN^4 EDWARD AUSTIN (s/o William^3 H. Austin #25), b 4 July 1868 at Mackford, Green Lake Co., WI. His early years were spent on a farm near Cabool, Texas Co., MO. In 1897 the family moved to Goshen Co., WY, where he spent the remainder of his life. He m 23 February 1893, probably at Cabool, **Florence Anne "Annie" Robinson**, d/o Phillip and Annie Robinson, she b 22 November 1874. Later Annie left Llewelyn and took Grace and Irvin with her, not allowing them to see the family for many years.

Llewelyn, more familiarly known as "Lew," m/2 Mrs. **Alta (Bright) Gardner** 6 January 1917 at Torrington, WY, a widow with three daughters; it has been said that he courted her on a Harley-Davidson motorcycle and side car. Alta was Aunt of Maud Bright who married Harry Austin McDaniel. For three years Lew filled the position of chief engineer for the Torrington Electric-Light Plant. Pernicious anemia developed, eventually causing his death, 3 May 1920 at Torrington. He is buried at Valley View Cemetery, Torrington, Wyoming. Alta d 15 January 1969 at Maywood, California.

Children, surname AUSTIN:
+ 209. i. Grace^5, b 3 January 1894, probably at Licking, MO.
   210. ii. Irvin Hugh, b 21 October 1896, probably at Cabool. He moved with his family to Wyoming in 1897. Irvin m 17 July 1932 at Wheatland, WY, Laura Gertrude Mason, d/o Charles R. and Lillie (Brouillette) Mason, b 17 September 1903 at Wheatland. Irvin ran a retail hardware store. They lived 10 years in Casper, WY. Irvin d 25 June 1971 at Casper and is buried in Highland

Cemetery. When last known Gertrude still lived in Casper. Grace and Irvin did not have any children.
- 211. iii. Alfred, b 10 December 1900 at Wheatland. He died 28 December 1901.

83. GERTRUDE[4] PAULINE AUSTIN (d/o William[3] H. Austin #25), b 19 January 1873 at Holland, Dickinson Co., Kansas. She spent her childhood in Cabool, Texas Co., MO. She m at Licking, Texas Co, 9 November 1893, **William Edwin McDaniel** b 2 May 1873, at Licking, s/o William Franklin and Margaret Amanda (Barnes) McDaniel. His mother died and his father was m/2 to Mattie Enochs Rawles, by whom he had three children: Harry Lee, Frank, and Essie May.

Gertrude's brother Willis was working for the Swan Land and Cattle Co., near Chugwater, WY at this time. He urged William to come there to find work as none was available in Missouri. Gertrude was pregnant with Harry, so she could not make the long trip. William got as far as Denver and stayed there awhile working on the truck farms near Brighton. As a second job he worked as an extra in a theater walking planks in the back of the stage, sounding like soldiers marching, for which he got $5 per day. The planks were elevated above the floor and one day he fell off and broke his shoulder.

With the assistance of Willis he finally accumulated enough money to go on to Chugwater, where, he too, worked for the Swan Co. on the Whitcomb Ranch 5 miles west of town. Early in 1900, he was able to send for Gertrude and little Harry to join him.

Cattle rustling was quite wide-spread in those times and the ranchers were forced to start fencing their land to protect their cattle and horses. The saddle horses were wild stock and it was nothing for Gertrude to watch the men breaking horses from her kitchen window. She never enjoyed rodeos later on because she had seen so much of it on the Whitcomb. The horses were so wild that, even though they were broken to ride, they would still buck every time they were mounted. One day a cowboy mounted a horse that bucked its way into one end of a large machine shed about 75 feet long. As they all excitedly watched, it came bucking out of the far end of the building.

From the Whitcomb they moved into the town of Wheatland where William worked in the Wheatland Flour Mill for awhile. Next they moved to the Hat Ranch, about 18 miles northwest of Wheatland where their post office was Uva. One day when Gertrude was going for the mail she had her little five month old daughter Gertrude in the buggy with her. Something frightened the horse and it ran away fatally injuring the little baby who died shortly afterward.

Gertrude's brother Lew had gone to work for the Rock Ranch at Torrington, WY and liked the area so much that he persuaded William to come there too. He purchased the Dray Line from G. W. Thomas and preparations were made for the move. William had about thirty dray horses working about half of them at one time to haul freight from the depot to the various business places, coal and groceries to Yoder and Hawk Springs and tank wagons delivering fuel to Lingle and the various ditch camps along a canal that was being built at this time. Willis had interest in an oil well out south of town and they would haul pipe and other supplies out there. At first, all the hauling was done by team and wagon but about 1917 they acquired trucks to haul the gasoline from their bulk station for the Continental Oil Co. to the draglines working on the southside ditch. They usually had three men steady plus extra help for unloading carloads of lumber, coal, and other commodities. Their first trucks were Ford and Republic.

William and his family attended the Methodist Church when they first came to Torrington. However, William was serving on the City Council at the time they were putting the trees around in the city park and he wanted to put up a band stand there. Quite a controversy developed with some of the other Methodists who didn't want a band stand across from their church. William proceeded to build the band stand and charged his membership to the United Presbyterian Church.

One day in 1917, William was riding on the dray wagon with his legs hanging over the side. A wheel broke causing the wagon to turn over on him, smashing his body flat from the waist down. Emil Daniel had been driving the team and somehow, he managed to get William out and carry him to the house. It was months before he would let anyone handle him except Emil. He suffered so much in the two years before his death, using crutches and canes to aid him in getting around. Gertrude took him to Excelsior Springs and to Mayo Clinic but couldn't find anyone who could help him. William died 21 May, 1919 at Torrington, WY and was buried in the Valley View Cemetery on the hill north of Torrington.

Gertrude remodeled the house and added on a little bedroom, then took in boarders and roomers. Although she had running water and electricity, she did not have an electric washing machine. This meant doing wash for all these people with a hand-turned washer wringer. She sold her home about ten years later and went to work at Sherwood Hall in Laramie as a cook. She and son Don bought a Model A, which was the third one sold in Wyoming, at a cost of $777. After this she spent a summer at Devil's Gate Camp, a school for rich boys from the east which was located on the Old Roper Ranch in Devil's Gulch. In 1934 and 1935 she was in Denver working for the Harry Graham's keeping house and baby sitting. Later she worked for the Marshalls in Denver doing the same kind of work. Gertrude later lived for several years in Brush, CO to be near her daughter Mabel Robertson. When Mabel's husband Duke was transferred to Longmont, CO she moved and took an apartment there. She was unable to care for herself after she broke her hip and she spent her last years in a nursing home in Longmont, CO. She died there 11 November 1966, at the age of 93, and is buried in Valley View Cemetery at Torrington.

Children, surname McDANIEL:

+ 212. i. Harry[5] Austin, b 5 March 1898.
+ 213. ii. Mabel Margaret, b 3 September 1902.
   214. iii. Gertrude, b 12 April 1907 at Chugwater. She died 3 Sep 1907 as a result of injuries in a buggy accident.
   215. iv Donald Robert, b 11 June 1912 at Torrington, Goshen Co., Wyoming. He grew up and graduated from Torrington High School, after which he lived in CO and Arizona. He m 2 December 1935 at Loveland, CO, Leah Powell. Don enlisted in the Navy 10 June 1942 after working for Bethlehem Steel in San Francisco where Leah worked in a hospital. Don had boot camp and Quartermaster School in San Diego after which he was assigned to the U.S.S. *Fox*, a destroyer out of Seattle. He was dreadfully seasick, and later assigned to a Mine Sweeper. His illness led to transfer to shore duty. He later spent some time in a hospital in Norfolk for his eyes; he had nine ulcers of the cornea of the left eye and three on the right eye. He was given a discharge with partial disability in 1946. He lived in San Diego after the war, where he worked for Convair Aircraft Company, until his retirement. Leah died in 1970. Donald died in San Diego, 11 April 1975. He was buried in Valley View Cemetery, Torrington, WY. He and Leah did not have any children.

86. WILLIS[4] WILBUR AUSTIN (s/o William[3] H. Austin #25), b 23 August 1880 at Axtel, Marshall Co., KS. He spent his childhood on his family's farm at Cabool, Texas Co., MO. He left home in 1898, moved to WY and worked for Swan Land and Cattle Co., near Chugwater, WY. He m 5 May 1906 **Sarah Petty**, d/o John and Adeline (Woody) Petty, at the McDaniel home, probably at Wheatland, WY. Sarah was b 1 August 1883 at Skeimah, Georgia.

In 1909 Willis left the Swan Land and Cattle Co. and purchased a blacksmith shop from Charlie Ackerblade in Torrington, WY. He ran the shop for two or three years, then sold it. He and C. A. (Charlie) Elquest built a garage and they had the first Ford Automobile Agency in what was then Laramie Co. It was in this building that Willis and Charlie Elquest installed a big one-cylinder engine and generator to furnish electricity for Torrington's first picture show.

Charlie Elquest taught Willis the undertaking business and they worked together in Elquest Hardware Company and exchanged coroner jobs at County Elections. About 1916 Henry Ford shipped them a car load or two of Ford cars that they had not ordered. They had a hard time selling them so they gave up the Ford Agency. They sold Studebakers, Oaklands, and Oldsmobiles after that.

In the summer of 1918 Willis, Charlie Elquest and Harvey Slack built a hardware, furniture and undertaking business in Manville, WY. It was called Austin, Elquest, Slack Hardware Co. Willis sold his home in Torrirgton. In the fall of 1919 Willis and Charlie Elquest built the Austin Elquest Hardware Co. in Lusk, WY and closed out the store in Manville. In the spring of 1921, Willis and Charlie sold the store and he purchased the farm near Yoder, WY. It was awfully hard to make a living on a farm as it was raw land, there were no buildings, fences, no machinery. The irrigation ditches were not finished, the irrigation district was not formed or organized. It was a fight from the start for the farmers for water. The Hawk Springs Reservoir was finished, but it was a struggle to fill it with water in the winter time as other water users had prior water rights and some years the farmers were short of water. It was always a challenge to make enough money to live on, pay taxes, and water taxes, build up houses, buildings, buy machinery, and build up capital to expand on. During this time Willis served on the Horse Creek Conservation District Board to finish the irrigation ditches and make and maintain the irrigation

District. He served on the School Board for the School District, County Commissioner for Goshen County which ran and maintained the County for about eight years. In 1928 he was elected for a term of four years to the State Senate, serving 1929 and 1931, as the legislature met every other year. They were still living on the farm.

In 1939 Willis was appointed Liquor Commissioner for WY and the family moved from the farm at Yoder to Cheyenne. He was reappointed in 1943 and served until his retirement at age 65 in 1945.

Willis' hobby was fishing, and he and his wife spent many winters at Fort Isabel, Texas, fishing in the Gulf of Mexico.

Willis d 17 April 1968 at Cheyenne, WY; Sarah d 18 January 1974 at Fort Collins, CO; both are buried in Beth El Cemetery, Cheyenne.

Children, surname AUSTIN:
+ 216. i. Harry^5 Ames, b 16 February 1907.
+ 217. ii. Marjorie Ruth, b 15 June 1923.

87. EMMA^4 AUGUSTA DONNELLY (d/o Michael^3 Reed #26), b 2 February 1868 in New York State. She and her brother and mother were living with her Uncle Samuel Smith, his wife, Juliana, and Samuel's brothers, Lyman and Elias, at Sand Banks [Altmar], Oswego Co., NY in the 1870 U.S. Census. After her mother Marietta married Michael Reed in 1871, they moved to Seymour, WI.

Sometime in the late 1880s she went to Aspen, CO, with her step-father to visit Michael's brother Cyrus Reed. While there she met her future husband, **Nelson Cates**. The *Aspen Times* of November 21, 1888 stated thus: "Marriages: on Tuesday evening, November 20, 1888 at the residence of Mr. A. Goodrich, Corner of 6th St. and Hopkins Ave. by Judge Thos. A. Rucker, Mr. Nelson Cates and Miss Emma Augusta Donelly."

Nelson was born 20 April 1858, s/o William H. Cates, in Indiana. His father was born in Tennessee. While Nelson and his family were homesteading in Kansas, his parents were killed by jayhawkers. Some local Indians took Nelson and his sister to raise. The tribe traveled between Kansas and Colorado, most of the time in the latter state. When Nelson and his sister returned to the white man's world, after the Battle of Little Big Horn, they were dressed in Indian buckskins. These clothes are still

The Fourth Generation

in possession of a member of the family, a prized part of their heritage. According to Neva Brown, Nelson had a brother, Ethan, who was a wheat farmer in Nebraska.

Nelson was a teamster, driving mule teams carrying ore in and out of mines. Sometime after their marriage he was injured in a mining accident. A dynamite charge in the Leadville, CO mine did not go off on schedule. Nelson drove his wagon over the charge, exploding it, and his hand and part of his arm were blown off. Henceforth he continued to work as a teamster, with a hook in place of a hand.

Emma Cates d 6 November 1900 in Aspen, CO, of Brights Disease, and is buried in Red Butte Cemetery there. She was 32 years and 9 months old. There is a simple wooden marker on her grave, weatherbeaten and with several knot holes. If there had not been a record of her death in the court house, it would have been impossible to know the full dates.

Della Martin, of Quitman, Georgia, a Reed descendant, tells that Nelson sent Emma's fir coat to her sister, Julia Verwey, in Wisconsin after Emma's death. Julia cut up the fir and made hats and muffs for Verna Verwey and Della. She sewed the coat buttons on top of the tams for decoration.

On 16 August 1901 Nelson sold his two city blocks in Aspen. He and the children set out for Nevada, much of the time living in a covered wagon. They lived at various construction sites where Nelson was working, but the children spent the school years living with a family in a town so they could go to school. Nelson d 5 February 1917 while driving a mule team out of the Comstock Lode at Virginia City, NV, and he is buried at Luning, NV.

Children, surname CATES:
+   218.   i.   Julia[5] Mae, b 7 September 1888.
+   219.   ii.   William Henry, b 18 September 1895.
+   220.   iii.   Jessie Anna, b 3 June 1897.
+   221.   iv.   Ina Belle, b 25 September 1898.

88. ARTHUR[4] JAMES REED (s/o Michael[3] Reed #26), b 11 March 1870 at Utica, Oneida Co., NY. He was living with his mother and sister at Altmar, Oswego Co., NY in 1870 at his Uncle Samuel's home. After his mother married Michael Reed in 1871, he went with the family to Seymour, WI to live. He was brought up with Michael and Marietta's children as part of the family. Arthur m November 1896, **Elsbeth Dorothy Klein** at Menominee, Michigan. She was b 8 April 1877 in Berlin, Germany daughter of Herman and Louise (Bahn) Klein. When six years old she came with her parents to the U.S. and settled in Menominee, MI. In 1900 Arthur and Elsie moved onto a farm in the Town of Maple Valley, Oconto Co., WI. Elsie d 29 December 1964 at Oconto Falls, WI. Arthur d 28 October 1943 and both are buried at Wanderer's Rest Cemetery, Gillett, WI.

Child, surname REED:

+ 222. i. Harold[5] Arthur, b 10 July 1897.

89. JENNIE[4] ADELL REED (d/o Michael[3] Reed #26), b 27 February 1872 at Seymour, WI. She m about 1890, **Clark Wright**, s/o George McGill and Euretta (Ray or Wray) Wright. He was b 1 February 1855 at Shirley, Canada. Jennie and Clark had a big farm at Seymour. Clark deserted the family when the children were small.

Clark was at Snohomish, WA in 1910 when his daughter Gertrude went to live with him. He was on the west coast, probably in Oregon in 1915 when his son George came to visit him. In January 1920 George went to Roberts, FL, near Pensacola, where his father had already "planted watermelons on five acres of land, with a big white house he bought." Clark d 24 October 1922 at Gonzales, FL of Malaria Fever and is buried in an unmarked grave in Jeradin Cemetery, Roberts, next to his daughter Irene.

Jennie later m **Herman Schroeder** and lived on a farm near Suring, WI for 40 years. After Herman died, about 1942, she went to Oregon to keep house for her unmarried son, George. She died at Oregon City, OR, 6 May 1958 and her body was brought to Hickory Corners, Oconto County, WI for burial in the Hickory Cemetery.

Children, surname WRIGHT:

+ 223. i. Gertrude[5] Mary Etta, b 15 October 1891.
   224. ii. George, b 22 February 1894 at Seymour, Outagamie Co., WI. When asked what work he had done during his life, he wrote "Railroads, logging camps, iron ore mines, gold mines, shipyards, sawmills, farming on my own farm, worked in a factory, worked building all kinds of roads, and was in the Army in World War I. He went out to the west in 1915 and lived in Portland since 1944 but never married. George died February 1991, at age 97.

The Fourth Generation

+ 225. iii. Nellie Beatrice, b 29 February 1896.
+ 226. iv. Irene Orpha, b 5 June 1898.
+ 227. v. Thomas Martin, b 17 November 1901.

90. FRED[4] REED (s/o Michael[3] Reed #26), b 4 January 1875 at Seymour, WI. He m 27 December 1896 at Appleton, WI, **Mary Louise Marsh**, d/o John H. and Hattie (Dillon) Marsh, she b 26 March 1877 at Rose Lawn, Shawano Co., WI.

Fred was a lumberman and logger all his life. He and Mary Louise lived all their married life in the Town of Maple Valley, Oconto Co., WI. Mary Louise, better known as May, d 19 January 1924. Fred made his home with his daughter at Suring, WI, where he d 16 December 1958, rather than in the hospital at Oconto Falls, WI. Both were buried at Hickory Cemetery at Hickory Corners, WI.

Child, surname REED:
    228. i. Angeline[5] Irene, b 28 December 1895.

91. JULIA[5] REED (d/o Michael[3] Reed #26), b 11 November 1877 at Seymour, Outagamie Co., WI. "Jewell," as she was more commonly known as a young woman, went to Appleton, WI to find a job and there she met her husband, **Richard Verwey**. They were married March 28, 1896 in Appleton at the First Congregational Church. Richard was born May 17, 1872 at Appleton, son of George and Wilhelmina (Van Ooyan) Verwey, natives of Holland. George's grandfather, Peter Verwey, came to the U.S. about 1825 alone to work and save money to bring the rest of the family here. By the time he could bring them over, his wife had died, and he had to bring up his children alone. A family folk story tells that when the Verwey family got to Niagara Falls, NY they ran out of money, so they lived and worked a year on Grand Island in order to earn enough money to go on to Wisconsin. While watering the oxen attached to a wagon above the falls, the current swept the wagon and oxen away from the shore and over the falls. There were two children in the wagon—one jumped off and made it to shore and the other stayed with the wagon and was lost.

Richard was a teamster in his youth. For 17 years before his retirement in 1941 he was foreman of the cutter room at the Fox River Paper Company. Richard died December 8, 1958 in Green Bay, WI, where he had lived the last ten years of his life. Julia d December 11, 1976, age 99 years, at the Gillett Nursing Home, Gillett, Oconto Co., WI, where she had been a patient several years; she had fractured her hip at age 94. Both are buried in Riverside Cemetery, Appleton.

Children, surname VERWEY:

 229. i. George[5] Leroy, b 8 September 1897 at Appleton. He m 4 February 1921 at Waukegan, IL, Ida Maack, d/o Henry and Hedwig (Sievert) Maack; she b 24 July 1899 at Appleton. They lived in Green Bay. George was yard clerk for Milwaukee Road Railroad, 1914–1964. He received a Purple Heart medal for meritorious service overseas during World War I. George d 15 February 1971 at Green Bay and Ida d 11 October 1979 at Milwaukee. Both are buried at Riverside Cemetery, Appleton. They had no children.

+ 230. ii. Victor Richard, b 2 April 1900.
+ 231. iii. Verna, b 16 April 1903.
 232. iv. Dudley Gilbert, b 8 March 1905 at Appleton. He m 15 October 1930 at Zion Lutheran Church, Highland Park, IL. Emma Florence Benson, d/o John and Jenny (Johnson) Benson, b 4 September 1906 at Helmstad, Sweden. Dudley graduated from business college in Appleton, and was traffic manager at Kimberly Clark Company until his retirement 30 August 1968, with a total of 40 years with the company. Emma graduated from Ravenswood School of Nursing at Chicago, IL. Dud and Emma met at Jamestown, NY, where she was a nurse and he visited the Bullocks there. They lived many years at their summer home at Big Lake, Gresham, WI, until about 1988 when they moved to Shawano, WI. They have no children.

92. IDA[4] MAY REED (d/o Michael[3] Reed #26), b March 1880 at Seymour, WI. She married **David Carrie**, a livestock dealer, born about 1859 in Canada. He d in 1924; Ida d 26 March 1919, age 40, at the County Asylum at Fond du Lac, WI. Both are buried at Hickory Cemetery, Hickory Corners, WI.

Children, surname CARRIE:

 233. i. Orpha[5], b 22 May 1900 at Town of Maple Valley, Oconto Co., WI. She m 25 Aug 1924, Carl Holger Hansen, b 30 May 1901; he d 24 April 1977 and is buried in the Hickory Cemetery, Hickory Corners, WI. In 1990, Orpha was still living; they had no children.
 234. ii. Alvin E., b 1902 at Town of Maple Valley. He lived a tragic life after his father's death. He contracted TB and d in 1930 and was

The Fourth Generation 117

buried in Hickory Cemetery.
235. iii. Oliver, b about 1907 in Maple Valley. He died of a gun shot wound while hunting.
236. iv. Elmer H., b in 1911: d in 1932. He went to the doctor with a bad cold and died over night. Buried at Hickory Cemetery.

93. DEWITT[4] CORNELIUS REED (s/o Michael[3] Reed #26), b 27 January 1883 at Seymour, WI: on 16 October 1907 at the home of his sister Julia Verwey in Appleton, WI, he m/1 **Helga Lydia Heyerdahl**, b 26 February 1885 in Maple Valley, WI, d/o Clemet and Annie (Gilberson) Heyerdahl, both parents born in Norway. He was a prosperous farmer in Town of Spruce, Oconto Co., owning two farms, until 1933 when the depression hit very hard and he lost the farms. Along with farming he was also a logger. He then was located in the Town of Underhill until illness required his removal to the Gillett Nursing Home. Helga d 5 October 1943 at Gillett, at her son Alfred's home.

DeWitt was a great story-teller and kept the other patients in the nursing home cheered up, even though he had both legs amputated due to diabetes and had bad eyesight. He died at the nursing home 18 January 1977, age almost 94.

Alfred remembers stories his father DeWitt told of his childhood. He was raised mainly on corn meal mush and corn bread, with a pig butchered now and then for meat. Later a cow or two made it possible to make butter, which could be bartered for other staples. Also one Christmas, DeWitt's mother, Marietta, wanting to surprise him with a new pair of pants, cut up old mackinaws of Mikes and the older boys, and secretly sewed a new pair for him at night when he was in bed. What she didn't know was that DeWitt, in his bedroom overhead, peeked down by the stove pipe and watched his mother sewing them.

DeWitt m/2 **Myrna (Blair) Schlais** on 16 October 1951, d/o Joseph and Josephine (Burley) Blair, born 21 February 1908 at Chase, Lake County, MI.

Children, surname REED:
+ 237. i. Emerald[5] DeWitt, b 18 April 1909.
+ 238. ii. Alfred Michael, b 10 March 1911.
+ 239. iii. Wallace Clemet, b 14 May 1913.
+ 240. iv. Raymond Edgar, b 13 December 1914.

+ 241. v. June Anna Marietta, b 1 July 1918.
+ 242. vi. Norma Mae, b 7 May 1921.
+ 243. vii. Ilene Ruth, b 22 April 1925.
+ 244. viii. Arnold James, b 28 April 1927.

94. ROY[4] ALBERT REED (s/o Michael[3] Reed #26), b 17 February 1887 at Town of Cicero, Outagamie Co., WI. He married 20 October 1907 at Appleton, WI, **Florence M. Mills**, adopted d/o R. Frank and Harriet (Helson) Mills. Her real parents were Frank Raeber and Minnie Busch. She was b 29 July 1886 at Pleasant Prairie, Kanosha Co., WI, and d 9 September 1914, age 28 years, when her children were very young. Russell, about 6 years old, went to live with his Uncle Arthur Reed; Ruby, nearly 5 years old, went to live with her Aunt Julia Verwey: and Mildred, a little over two years old, went to live with her Uncle Fred Reed.

Roy may have married a second time; a record in Oconto Co. Court House shows the death of Mrs. Roy (Juanita) Reed, 11 December 1954 at little River, Oconto Co., WI; b 24 June 1918, d/o Frank Zimmerman.

Roy d 20 November 1966, age 79, at Oconto, WI. His occupation was listed as "Sailing on Great Lakes" and business listed as "shipping," on his death certificate. The present descendants do not recognize this information. They knew him only as a farmer. He is buried in Hickory Cemetery, Town of Maple Valley, Oconto Co., as is his wife Florence.

Children, surname REED:
+ 245. i. Russell[5] Sadell, b 31 May 1908.
+ 246. ii. Ruby Blanche, b 29 August 1909.
+ 247. iii. Mildred Agnes, b 26 January 1911.

95. EFFIE[4] MAUD REED (d/o Michael[3] Reed #26), b 7 February 1890 at Seymour WI. She married when only 15 years old on 5 October 1905 at Hickory, Oconto Co., WI, **Eldred Jacob Bullock**, s/o Elmer Oscar and Carrie F. (Cottrell) Bullock, b 14 March 1883 at Waushara Co. The following is an account of his early life, by Eldred Bullock:

"The Homestead"
by Eldred Bullock

My father took a homestead in the year 1881 in Shawano Co., WI. That was two years before I was born. The land, which consisted of only 40 acres was all timbered; part high-land, with hemlock, maple, and basswood trees, and part swamp with yellow cedar. This land was at that time [1881] 20 miles from the

The Fourth Generation 119

Chicago and Northwestern Railroad.

My father and his cousin Mark Cottrell walked 20 miles on a trail through the woods to the nearest town [Marion, WI] and bought 50 pounds of flour and divided it so they each had 25 pounds to carry and returned to the homestead the same day, or well into the night. A forty-nine mile trip in one day. Can you visualize two men, one with a lantern and each with 25 lbs. of flour on a woods trail after dark, footsore and weary, in a wilderness full of wild beasts, panther, bear, wild cats, lynx, and deer?

My father also walked from my Grandfather's to the homestead, 72 miles in two days. The original log house on the homestead had but one room. Chinkings were cut out with an axe and driven between the logs and then plastered with mud.

One night my mother and father found themselves sitting up in bed, wondering why? Then the Panther screamed again, a blood curdling scream. There was a window open. They sat there in bed in terror. Then they heard the panther sniffing around the house hunting for the puppy which was under the house. They were frightened but not molested.

We had a spring which my father had dug out, then sunk in a hollow basswood log, from which we dipped our water. My mother went to the spring one night and an animal behind her; she was scared but got her bucket of water and returned to the house.

When I was about 7 years old the railroad had been extended to Whitcomb or beyond and we were about 1–1/4 miles from Whitcomb. The cedar timber was valuable for telegraph poles and fence posts. My father hired men to cut the timber, which was skidded and hauled by oxen. My first sleigh ride was behind an ox team.

Effie and Eldred were in Lynchberg, VA from 1907 to 1912, then in Appleton, WI, where they stayed about two years. Then to Erma, WI, as homesteaders, where Chester was born in a log cabin. From 1919 to about 1923 they lived in Jamestown, NY; in 1925 they started their life in Florida.

Eldred Bullock left WI in 1925, driving a Model T Ford toward Sarasota, FL and the building boom. Immediately he put his house painting skills to work, and within 3 months was able to send for his family. Their new home was a 15' by 15' tent surrounded by a 6 foot high wooden wall perched high on an Indian mound overlooking the bay near Whittaker Bayou. It was their home for the next year. They lived off the land and sea. Bananas, guavas, oranges, dates, and cactus fruit were there for the picking. Oysters waited just 100 feet from their door. Often Eldred would take his stool and salt and pepper shakers, and sit on the oyster bed to enjoy a dozen or so raw. The children learned to swim, climb trees and swing on the vines. They were unaccustomed to hurricanes and were unprepared when one struck. As the water rose, they huddled on the table and bunks and the tent blew away. After the hurricane they moved back from the beach and Eldred built a wooden house, where they lived for seven years, until a deputy sheriff said the family had to move because the property owners objected. Immediately, a friend offered the family, which had now grown to seven, a house on Whittaker Bayou.

Later their daughter, Marietta, married a building contractor. They built a house for Eldred and Effie, one that was theirs for as long as they lived.

Effie died 7 May 1953 at Sarasota, FL and Eldred died on the 13th of June 1963. Both are buried at Sarasota Memorial Cemetery.

Children, surname BULLOCK:
+ 248. i. Verna[5], b 27 June 1907.
+ 249. ii. Della Elsie, b 7 September 1909.
+ 250. iii. Elmer Oscar, b 13 May 1912.
+ 251. iv. Marietta Eleanore, b 2 September 1915.
+ 252. v. Chester Jesse, b 18 September 1919.

96. PEARL[4] LERA WADLEY (s/o Martha[3] Reed Wadley #27), b 25 June 1865 in Mexico, Oswego Co., NY. He m/1 28 June 1892 in Woodland, MI, **Blanche Pearl Dillenbeck**, d/o Joshua and Jennie Dillenbeck. She was b 9 January 1873 in Michigan. Pearl was a resident of Chicago, IL at the time and his occupation was listed as bookkeeper; they had one child. Blanche was listed as "Pearly Wadley in her death certificate. She d 11 August 1896 in Woodland Township, age 23 years, 7 months, 2 days of "consumption."

Pearl's son Paul believes his father was working for the Railway Express in Chicago, later working in Minneapolis, MN. A family bible in possession of William Wadley is dated 9 January 1896, in Minneapolis, presented by Blanche to Pearl a few months before she died. He later was transferred to Portland, OR.

Pearl m/2 **Ruby Grace Farnsworth** on 4 October 1905 in Portland, d/o Nathan and Amanda (Newman) Farnsworth, b 19 September 1878. Ruby was in Portland visiting her parents from her teaching position in the Dakotas, when she met Pearl. Her parents were originally from that area. Pearl later worked for the Ladd and Tilton Bank several years, retiring at age 55. Later he worked for the U.S. Customs Service as a guard, and helped capture a rum runner on the river. Ruby d 30 May 1962 at Portland, OR and Pearl d 4 November 1945 at Portland. Both were cremated and their ashes are interred at Portland Memorial Cemetery.

Children, surname WADLEY:

+ 253. i. Mildred[5] DeSilva, b 14 February 1894.
+ 254. ii. Lera[5] Edwina, b 13 February 1907.
+ 255. iii. Edythe Martha, b 12 October 1908.
+ 256. iv. William Irwin, b 7 June 1910.
+ 257. v. Pauline Lois, b 26 June 1913.
    258. vi. Paul Lowell, b 26 June 1913 at Portland, a twin to Pauline. He m 2 November 1940 at Portland, Methodist Church Mabel Rose Halverson, d/o Charles and Christina (Swensen) Halverson, b 28 April 1913 at Woodburn, OR. Mabel's father, Charles Halverson, came with his parents from Norway, settling first in Nebraska. Charles homesteaded just outside of Spokane, WA, where he met Christina Swensen, who was born in Zumbrota, MN and came west to work. After their marriage they moved to Woodburn, where their children were born.

        Paul was a radio operator in the 110th Signal Corps during World War II. He trained two years at Leadville, CO with the ski troops, expecting to be involved in an invasion of Norway. They finally were in the forces that invaded Italy, landing at Naples and working their way up to northern Italy. After the war Paul was a teamster for Meier and Frank Department Store in Portland, for 44 years, until retirement in June 1975. They have no children.

97. JENNIE[4] L. WADLEY (d/o Martha[3] Reed Wadley #27), b about 1868 at Mexico, Oswego Co., NY. She was about 12 years old when her mother died. She m/1 25 October 1885 at Mexico, NY, **Joseph Surback**. The minister was Rev. J. Austin and witnesses were Jacob Surback and Dora Dawley. No other records on this marriage were found.

Jennie m/2 **Charles Henry Davis** 25 August 1896 at Summerland, Santa Barbara Co., CA. The marriage record indicates one of the parties was married, but the husband dead. The marriage was witnessed by Mrs. Lulu Lyon and Mrs. Maggie Calkins and performed by Rev. M. E. Taylor. In Santa Barbara County Court House was a record of the birth of a girl baby, unnamed, to Charles and Jennie Davis on 1 January 1898. No further record on the child; it may have died at birth. Jennie d 22 May 1900, age 32 of TB at Mexico; her death certificate indicated she was a dressmaker. In the 1900 Census, Charles was lodging with Charles J. Johnson, a saloon keeper, and Bertha Johnson, his wife, lodging house keeper, Charles listed as bartender, and b on September 1866 in Massachusetts. He d 29 April 1907 at Santa Barbara, and is buried in Santa Barbara Cemetery.

The author, while visiting Summerland, CA in 1979, found local historian, Mrs. Opal Lambert, who claimed her father built the ten-room hotel in Summerland in 1898, where Charles Davis was bartender; she believed Maggie Calkins, one of the witnesses to the marriage of Charles and Jennie, was a relative of Charles.

The first residents of Summerland in the late 1880s were interested in making the place a spiritualist colony and the name Summerland was taken from a spiritualist book of that title. Early houses at Summerland were built in curious ways, with false doors, blind windows, and stairs that went nowhere, in accord with its tenets; a seance room, snowy white and always full of exquisite flowers was maintained by the colony. The inhabitants numbered about 500 and the community became a mecca of all kinds of mediums. Also numerous oil wells were put down and by 1898 a new boom was in progress as oil superseded Spiritualism. If either of these interests brought Jennie and Charles to Summerland is not known.

Child, surname DAVIS:
    259   i. Daughter.[5]

100. ADELBERT[4] LOWELL REED (s/o Morris[3] Reed #28), b 4 May 1867 at Mexico, Oswego Co., NY. "Bert" traveled at about the age of two years with his parents when they moved from Oswego Co., by covered wagon in 1868, and settled at Seymour, Outagamie Co., WI. Marinda, his mother, managed to take along her sewing rocker in the wagon, in which she sat frequently rocking her little son. This chair was preserved for many years as a prized heirloom by Bert's wife and was handed down to the younger generation.

Bert m 10 March 1889, **Maydora Cecilia Robinson** at Seymour. "May" was born 7 October 1867 at Plainfield, Waushara Co., WI, d/o Francis Morris and Luana Cecilia America (Kelley) Robinson. May taught school five years previous to her marriage. They lived most of their married life in the Seymour area as farmers and Bert also did carpentry work. Where their farm was located is now a golf course; their spring is still intact, and people in the area prize its pure water. They later moved to Edmore, MI to be near their daughter. There Bert built a barn by himself when over 80 years old. Bert d 7 February 1955 and May d 7 June 1956, both at Edmore, MI and both are buried in Vinewood Cemetery, Edmore.

Children, surname REED:
+   260.   i.   Pearl[5] Eunice, b 19 June 1890.
+   261.   ii.   Roland Morris, b 6 December 1891.
    262.   iii.   Herald Lincoln, b 21 November 1893; he died 15 October 1909 of polio and is buried at Seymour City Cemetery.
+   263.   iv.   Clifford Lowell, b 8 October 1897.
    264.   v.   Geneva, b 27 January 1900, d 27 September 1917, age 17 and is buried at Seymour City Cemetery.
+   265.   vi.   Norman Wilder, b 6 February 1902.
+   266.   vii.   Olive Marinda, b 9 November 1904.
+   267.   viii.   Vivian Medora, b 25 April 1907.
+   268.   ix.   Donald Adelbert, b 10 December 1909.

101. MYRTLE[4] MINNIE REED (d/o Morris[3] Reed #28), b 7 October 1870 at Seymour, WI. She married 17 November 1894, **Sidney David Ryder**, s/o David and Amanda (Haver) Ryder. Sidney was born 28 January 1858 in Canada. Most of their married life was spent in Edmore, Montcalm Co., on their farm. Myrtle d 1 August 1954 at Cedar Lake and Sidney on 10 July 1944 at Town of Ferris, Montcalm Co. Both are buried at Richland Township Cemetery at Vestaburg.

Children, surname RYDER:
+   269.   i.   Marion[5] Jessie, b 27 June 1895.
+   270.   ii.   Ellen Marinda, b 16 February 1899.

106. MAUD[4] EDNA REED (d/o Cyrus[3] Reed #30), b 20 November 1876 at Utica, MN. She was about 5 years old when her mother died and two years later her father married Susan Belle Hardwick in Aspen, CO. She was about 15 years old when she m **William Nathan Beavert**, about 1891, who was b August 1865 in OR. Their first five children were born in Sundance, WY. In 1900 they were in Portal, ND, where they had a large cattle and horse ranch. William left her for unexplained reasons about 1902 or 1903 and was never heard from again. In January 1905 the family moved to Ferndale, WA, where Maud's parents were living.

Maud m/2 **Andrew Medford Weston**, s/o William J. and Sarah (Beavert) Weston on 6 October 1906 at Bellingham, WA, b 31 May 1880 at Sherwood, OR. Sarah Beavert Weston was sister of Will Beavert, Andrew was nephew of Will. Andrew Weston had a cream route in Laurel, WA and collected cream from farms with a wagon and team. It was brought into town to be made into butter. At one time he and a partner ran a car repair business called "Highway Garage," and had the agency for Willis Knight cars in Ferndale, WA.

Maud d as a result of complications following the birth of her last child, on 1 June 1912 at Laurel, WA. Andrew d 15 October 1960 at Portland, OR. Both are buried in Lynden, WA, Cemetery.

Children, surname BEAVERT:
+   271.   i.   Ethel[5], b 29 September 1892.
         272.   ii.   Worth Laverne, b 26 February 1894 at Sundance, WY. He helped run a restaurant in Fernwood, WA with his sisters May and Ethel, but never married. He d 1 January 1921, age 27. He is buried in Lyndon [WA] Cemetery.
+   273.   iii.   May, b 24 May 1895.
         274.   iv.   Edna Belle, b January 1897. She died young and is probably buried at Sundance.
+   275.   v.   Bertha Beatrice, b 24 July 1898.
+   276.   vi.   Warren William, b 13 November 1900.
         277.   vii.   Cyrus John, b 23 July 1902 at Portal. According to Lois Tate, Cyrus got involved with the Wobbly Movement, men who organized for union activities. He was arrested and put in solitary confinement in the latter 1910s and this seemed to be too much stress for him. He was in mental hospitals several years and died in 1942 in California and is buried at Lynden, WA.
+   278.   viii.   Frank, b 14 November 1904 at Portal.

Children, surname WESTON:
+   279.   ix.   Marvin[5] Laverne, b 2 September 1908.
+   280.   x.   Merle Vincent, b 11 May 1912.

108. EVA[4] BELLE REED (d/o Cyrus Reed #30), b 4 April 1887 at Pitkin Co., CO, probably at Glenwood Springs. When just 17 years old she married **Lee Eck**, on 29 June 1904, at Bellingham, WA. Lee was b about 1883 at Fernwood, WA, son of William N. and Mary A. (Clark) Eck.

Her parents, Cyrus and Susie Belle Reed, were witnesses to the wedding and H. B. Williams, Justice of the Peace, officiated. They lived in Ferndale during their marriage, which lasted seven years, ending in divorce about 1911; they had two children.

Eva and her son probably lived with her parents at Ferndale until she married m/2 **Rudolph Culmore Plasteur** at Bellingham, WA, December 16, 1911. Witnesses were Clyde and Neva Reed and John A. Kellogg, Judge of Superior Court, officiated. Rudolph was born about June 1889, son of John H. and Lucy Plaster. Eva added the "u" to the name because is sounded "more French."

Lucy's family tells the story of a number of Indian tribes that held a Pow-Wow in South-Western Canada, like an Indian Olympics, where tribes competed in athletic events, with 7 days of feasting. There would be several hundred people involved. Gradually the best ones would win out over the rest. On this particular occasion the contest was narrowed down to two Indians, of different tribes, and after 10 days neither one could best the other. One of these was Lucy's ancestor, a Lummi Indian. Finally his tribe got together and decided to murder the other champion, to settle this contest. They did so, and they thought the other Indians would pay obiescence and follow, but they turned on them and Lucy's ancestors had to flee. They paddled canoes down the coast and ended up in the Ferndale, WA area.

The Plasters came from France and settled in New Orleans. There were three boys and a girl, Mary. All three boys were in the legal field. John Plaster became a circuit Judge (originally called "wandering judges") in WA State. John had two wives already, but he took a third wife, Lucy, the beautiful indian maiden. When a law was passed that a man could have only one wife, he chose Lucy. After John died, Lucy married George ("Drinkwater George"), an Indian, and she had children Mary, May and Frank by him. Rudoloph Culmore Thomas Peter Plasteur, was Lucy's and John Plaster's son.

Eva Belle went to live on Rudy Plasteur's place on 14 acres in the Ferndale area. About 1918 they moved into the village of Ferndale. They then leased 160 acres of land on a corner of the Lummie Indian Reservation near Ferndale, where they stayed about three years. They separated due to Rudy's alcohol problem, and were divorced.

Eva and her son went to Yakima, WA to pick apples, then on to Seattle. During 1926–1928 Eva Belle went to the University of Oregon at Portland to get her degree. At the same time she worked for Traveler' Aide and then Boys' and Girls' Aid Society, traveling to check on living conditions of the children. In the 1930s she and her son moved in together in Los Angeles. She bought quite a bit of property, fixed it up, and sold it. She became quite a business woman.

In 1957 her daughter Leota bought her daughter her first horse, and the whole family, including Eva Belle and Casper, became very much involved with horses and horse shows. About 1968 Eva Belle bought a little horse ranch near Long Beach. Later, when they grew tired of the smog, they moved north and bought a house in Santa Ynez, CA. There Eva Belle became interested in a little library, the oldest one in CA. The building was rickety and there was talk of tearing it down. Eva Belle, then 83, went out door-to-door and collected enough money to refurbish and save the old library building.

Eva Belle was very proud of her Lowell heritage and on May 19, 1971, aged 84, wrote a letter to Robert Lowell, prominent poet, and a distant cousin, introduced herself as his cousin and enclosed the document about John Lowell from the Pension Dept. in WA. She was hoping to establish her kinship for the sake of her granddaughter.

Lakewood, CA.
May 26, 1967
Dept. of the Interior
Bureau of Pensions
Washington, D.C.

Dear Sirs:

I believe the enclosed material to be self-explanatory. On it I base my request for additional information.

I am a great granddaughter of the John Reed here-in mentioned and a niece of the Morris Reed who made application for the information.

Besides Morris Reed there were two brothers: Mike (or Michael) and Cyrus Reed. Cyrus Reed was my father.

I first learned of the details (which I am hoping to again receive) when Morris Reed, who was at that time Pension's claim agent, applied for my Father's pension.

During a time when I lived in Seattle, WA I had a trunk stolen which contained practically ALL of my important papers including the original of the copy enclosed and considerable others, on the same subject.

One of the papers contained this statement: "That John Lowell was captured and held prisoner, in the West Indies. Later, upon returning to his own country HE WAS GIVEN, for REASONS (or Cause) GOOD AND SUFFICIENT, the name of John Reed."

Another statement relating to his wife: That "she FOUGHT with and BESTED an English officer at the Boston Tea Party."

These statements may not be wholly verbatim but the gist of it is the same. I am attempting, a chronicle of our ancestry for my GRAND DAUGHTER (the only one I'll ever have) and it certainly could never be complete without the details I am humbly requesting.

I had hoped to find some horse-thieves way back there but it seems they, the Lowells were positively lily-white. All except the darling old grandmother who FIT the English officer. Of course she was NOT a member of the "CLAN."

Thanking and thanking you in advance for this favor and without apologies for facetiousness I am,

> Yours Gratefully,
> Eva B. Plasteur
> 11707 E 216
> Lakewood, Calif. 90713

No answering letter was found among her things. This love of her heritage perhaps inspired her to write poetry herself. While at the Los Alamitos Mobile Home Estates where she went to live in the 1970s, she contributed to the *Sombrero News*.

Here is one of her poems: "A Slender Blade of Grass"

> I stood before thee humbly,
> and marveled at Thy power
> To inspire, with in me
> Dreams of joy and bliss,
> As glittering with dew-drops,
> Emblazoned by the Sun
> You gaily waved your greeting
> To the Universe.
> I stooped and plucked Thee
> From the breast of Mother Earth.
> Mighty Thou art, yet fragile
> As a vase of dainty glass

> Within my trembling palm
> You lie inert—
> God's beauteous, benevolent gift.
> A slender blade of grass.

Here she lived until about 1977 when she was moved to a nursing home. She d 27 January 1978, age 90 years, at Los Alamitos, Orange Co., CA. Her ashes are buried in Memory Garden Memorial Park, Brea, CA. Rudolph later Joined the Salvation Army and became a christian. He d about 1974 at Seattle, WA.

Children, surname ECK:

281. i. Casper[5] Leroy, born December 12, 1906 at Ferndale, Whatcom Co., WA. We met Casper "Red" at the United Campground at Ferndale in 1979, which was an accomplishment, as he for a number of years had lived in his trailer and pickup truck the year round and moved around frequently. He did many interesting things in his travels such as: he worked one summer at Yellowstone National Park; for 1–1/2 years in Pascagoula, MS; picked apples at Yakima, WA, and was then planning on working as a ranch hand at a Dude Ranch in Arizona. He worked wherever he went and enjoyed meeting local people. He had many stories about the Reed family which were interesting to hear. He enlisted in the Marine Corps in 1924 and served on the Battleship *New Mexico* three years. He more recently bought a house in Fairhope, AL; he rented out the house and lived in his trailer. In the 1960s he became interested in horses and horseshows. He owned Chief Tabu, California State champion quarter horses and won the figure 8 barrel races for three years in the Santa Ynez Valley horse show. The horse died in 1970 and the Santa Ynez Valley Riders, sponsors of the annual horseshow set up the Chief Tabu Memorial Championship barrel race in his honor. He d 11 December 1990 in the Veterans Administration Hospital at Biloxi, MS. He never married.

282. ii. Claire Evan, born about 1908. He died at two years and is buried at Bellingham, WA.

Children, surname PLASTEUR:

283. iii. Cleo[5] Patra Eloise, b 16 October 1913 at Ferndale, Whatcom Co., WA. She was a fashion designer, very intelligent and Bohemian, in short, a sort of "hippy." She married four or five, times, according to her sister Leota. She traveled and for several years had a shop in New Orleans. At the last part of her life she was in San Francisco where she had a shop, and designed show costumes

The Fourth Generation 129

and night club costumes. A glamorous girl, her sister Leota thought. Leota remembers only slightly the names of her husbands: (1) Herbert Palmer; (2) Herbert (or George) Turner; (3) Arthur Thelan, and the 4th she believes was David —, who was in the Merchant Marines and brought her daughter a pearl from the orient. Cleo told Leota she was married a fifth time, but it only lasted a short time. She died in San Francisco 11 August 1963. She had no children.

+   284. iv. Leota Lorraine, b 25 May 1915.

109. CLYDE[4] LAVERNE REED (s/o Cyrus[3] Reed #30), b 4 December 1888 at Milford, Barton Co., MO where his father was running a general store.

He graduated from Bellingham Normal School and then from the University of Washington at Seattle. He taught school in Roslyn and Yakima, WA and at Santa Ynez, CA. He was attending Loma Linda School, a Seventh Day Adventist School of Medicine, when his eyesight failed just short of his finishing the course. He was very musical and played several instruments. He had a music store in Los Angeles and taught music when his eyesight failed. He m/1 **Neva Sisson**, d/o Henry Charles and Lilly (Keighly) Sisson, she b 24 April 1892. Neva was not allowed to keep her daughter; her grandparents did not consider her a fit mother. Neva and Clyde were divorced when their daughter was about one year old. Clyde enlisted in the Army 7 Oct 1918 and discharged 2 Jan 1919. Neva married 4 or 5 times. The last husband being — Rehbein. Neva d 9 June 1967 at San Mateo, CA and was buried at Skylawn Memorial Park at Half Moon Bay, CA.

Clyde Reed m/2 **Ragna Antine Anderson** of Creston, WA on 28 December 1925 at Immanuel Lutheran Church, Seattle. She was a teacher too and they met at Roslyn, WA where both were teaching. It is not known when Ragna died but she is buried at Pacific Lutheran Cemetery in Seattle. Clyde d 7 November 1964, age 85, at Seattle and he is buried with Ragna. They had no children.

Children, surname REED:
    285. i. Lorena[5], b 5 December 1913, at Ferndale, Whatcom Co., WA. She was one year old when her parents separated. She was brought up pretty much by her grandparents, Cyrus and Susie Belle Reed. Cyrus took her on his lap, gave her peppermint or lemon candy he always carried in his pocket, and told her stories of his

experiences with the Indians in WY. He showed her the scar on his wrist where an Indian arrow pierced his arm. Her grandparents were very strict with her and did not approve of her mother, Neva, and Lorena seldom saw her. She longed to be with her mother, who had carroty red hair and blue eyes. But when Lorena once visited her, Neva introduced her to her friends as a "friend." She didn't want anyone to know her age as she was married to a younger man but Lorena looked enough like her mother, so they could guess the relationship. Lorena was twelve years old when her father married Ragna. Lorena didn't get along with her step-mother, so she left home when she was sixteen years old.

During the depression Lorena rode the freight trains and worked at odd jobs, such as picking pears one time. She cooked for a logging camp at Fort Seward, CA about 1950, and also cooked for the Canadian Steamship Lines in Seattle. An old sea captain used to hold her hand and sing "Lorena" to her. She worked in the harbor, not on the ships. When Lorena applied for a job in the California shipyards during World War II, she needed a birth certificate. She had a hard time getting the certificate, and for a time thought her birth had not been recorded. She finally found out her father had registered her name as "Aurora Borealis," because the northern lights were so bright the night she was born. She legally changed her name to Lorena, which is what her mother wished her to be named. For 22 years she was an electrical installer in airplanes at Santa Monica. She worked on DC3, DC6, DC7, DC8, and DC9 planes, also on the Thor Missile, NIKI-Zeus, NIKI-Hercules missiles. The Douglas Aircraft plant closed in 1974.

Lorena was married five times, twice to the same man. Her first husband was Oa Dilts, whom she married in 1930. Her second husband was Charles Manwarren, whom she married in 1937. Her third husband was Charles Tucker, born 3 April, 1925 at Watsonville, CA, whom she married in 1947. In 1957 she married Manual Salazar, and later divorced him in 1975. She remarried Charles Tucker on 20 September, 1977. When she first met Charles in 1945 they were both driving truck for Railway Express in Los Angeles. When she married him in 1947 he had his own trucking business and they traveled together all over the country, taking turns driving. In 1980 in a letter she said

Charles talked me into buying a truck. We have been in business for three months now and are still in the red but at least we have been able to make the payments on the truck and on the insurance. Everything is much higher than when we went into the business in 1945. I find it a lot harder to drive these big diesels than the gas trucks I used to drive. He have a 1972 White Freight Liner cab over. Charles thinks he might sell it though as he got an offer for $16,500 and we only paid $10,500. Then he might get a Kenworth.

In 1981 Charles had three cancer operations and she had two operations for the same thing. On 30 July, 1982 Charles died at Livermore, CA and his ashes were scattered over Cherokee Memorial Park. Lorena died 29 September 1982 at Stockton, CA where she lived in a mobile home. Her ashes were scattered over El Dorado National Forest. She never had any children.

113. WILLIS[4] BURTON CANFIELD (s/o Ida[3] Reed Canfield #31), b 28 May 1879 at Kasoag, Oswego Co., NY. The family moved to Altmar, Oswego Co., NY in the early 1900s. In early manhood he worked for several years for Page-Fairchild, a lumber company at the Town of Montague, Lewis Co., NY where he was cutting logs, stacking lumber, and booming logs on the pond.

On 10 Oct 1905, Willis m **Gertrude Estelle Crump**, who lived at Barber's Corners, near Altmar. They went to Watertown, Jefferson Co., NY where Willis learned the mattress making trade. They moved to Syracuse, NY in 1908, where they continued to live. He worked for several companies including Penfield Manufacturing Co., Onondaga Bed Manufacturing Co., Silverstone Upholsterers, and at Onondaga Hotel, Syracuse. After his health became poor he worked as night watchman and time keeper at the hotel until August 1941. He d 15 August 1946 in Syracuse. Gertrude d there 28 May 1954. Both are buried at Pineville Cemetery in Oswego Co.

Children, surname CANFIELD:
+   286. i. Doreatha[5] Ruth, b 5 January 1908.
+   287. ii. Elton Fay, b 27 December 1909.
     288. iii. Joyce Marilyn, b 23 July 1926 at Pineville; d April 1929 in Syracuse.

114. LUCIUS[4] LEROY CANFIELD (s/o Ida[3] Reed Canfield #31), b 5 November 1884 at Kasoag, Oswego Co., NY. He learned telegraphy and started working as a telegraph operator at age 17 at nearby Altmar, at the New York Central Railroad station. He continued in this work until his death. On 10 October 1906 he m **Grace Naomi Rowell**, d/o Herbert and

Anna Augusta (Morehouse) Rowell; she b 2 March 1887 and d 25 March 1947 at Verona, Oneida Co., where they lived many years. Lucius was a trustee of the Methodist Church in Verona, as well as a member of the Board of Education. Lucius d 3 February 1920 of influenza and pneumonia. Both are buried at Verona.

Children, surname CANFIEID:
+ 289. i. Thelma[5] Ann, b 2 October 1911.
+ 290. ii. Herbert Clinton, b 13 December 1915.

116. FLOYD[4] BEECHER CANFIELD (s/o Ida[3] Reed Canfield #31), b 18 July 1886, at Kasoag, Oswego Co., NY. He m 11 March 1908 at Williamstown, Oswego Co., **Hulda Oella March**, d/o James Hiram and Ellen Oella (Murphy) March, b 10 August 1891 at Altmar, NY and d 8 November 1966 at Fulton, Oswego Co., NY.

During World War I Floyd worked for Remington Arms at Ilion, NY. Along in the 1930s he was making wooden crates in the saw mill in the rear of his father's blacksmith Shop in Altmar; he hauled logs, cut them into boards and the strips for the crates. He worked for the Nestle Chocolate Co. in Fulton as a millright from 1940 until he retired in 1958. Floyd d in Fulton 24 November 1962 and both are buried in Mount Adnah Cemetery, Fulton.

Children, surname CANFIELD:
+ 291. i. Fenton[5] Emil, b 6 June 1912.
+ 292. ii. Harold Milburn, b 18 July 1915.
+ 293. iii. Oscar Willard, b 29 July 1924.
+ 294. iv. Douglas Liston, b 30 March 1926.

117. ALTA[4] MAY CANFIELD (d/o Ida[3] Reed Canfield #31), b 22 March 1889 at Kasoag, Oswego Co., NY. She moved with her family in early 1900s to Altmar, Oswego Co. and grew up in this village. Her father was the town blacksmith. She m 10 October 1910 the minister of her church, Altmar Methodist Church, **Sherman Lloyd Kennedy**, s/o Michael and Clara (Sherman) Kennedy, at the home of a college friend, Rev. Perry Wilcox, pastor of the Fernwood Methodist Church. Sherman was b 2 November 1882 at Moravia, Cayuga Co., NY, where he grew up on a farm, graduated from the local high school in 1901, and served as the preacher at both Freetown and East Homer Methodist Churches from 1902 until the fall of 1905. He was a student at Syracuse University, working

The Fourth Generation 133

his way through college preaching weekends at East Homer, Lock Berlin, and Altmar. He majored in Philosophy and pursued an active life on campus, excelled in debating, and graduated *Cum Laude* the permanent secretary of the Syracuse Class of 1910. Because Alta's father so strenuously objected to her marrying that "Red-Faced Irishman" and expected her to stay home and take care of her ailing mother, they were married in nearby Fernwood, at the home of a college friend, Rev. Perry Wilcox.

Sherman continued at Syracuse with the appointment as assistant for a course in Public Speaking and as coach of the Debate Team, a position he held for the next fifteen years. In 1913 he was appointed instructor at the University and also admitted to full conference membership in the Methodist Church. In 1915 he was appointed to a full Professorship of Public Speaking, a position he held until his death 23 years later, on 4 December 1938. He was chairman of the School of Speech and Dramatic Art from 1931 to 1938.

Their first home was in McConnellsville, Oneida Co. where Sherman was pastor until 1913 when they purchased their home in Warners, Onondaga Co. to be nearer to the University. Alta continued living in the big family home in Warners until her death 28 March 1980. She lived a very active life and kept in touch with friends and family to the last, dying at 91 years. They are both buried in Memorial Park Cemetery, Warners.

Children, surname KENNEDY:
+ 295. i. Sherman[5] Wilbur, b 11 July 1911.
    296. ii. Amoret Ida, b 4 September 1913 at Warners. She contracted Scarlet Fever at six years and d 2 February 1920 at Warners. Buried at Memorial Park Cemetery, Warners.
+ 297. iii. Neil Dow, b 19 November 1914.
    298. iv. Laurel Nadeen, b 17 May 1919, Syracuse, NY. She graduated from Syracuse University, College of Liberal Arts, School of Speech and Dramatic Arts in 1941. She taught High School English and ran the school library at Minetto, Oswego Co., NY for 1–1/2 years. She returned to Syracuse University for a graduate degree in Library Science, which took two years, working part time at SU library, and taking courses part time, receiving her degree in library science in 1945. She was children's Librarian in Onondaga County Public Library, Syracuse, NY, 34 years, retiring September 1981.

        Laurel m 1 January 1954 at Warners Methodist Church,

Glenn Maurice Chapman, s/o Glenn Maurice and Frances Mabel (Bates) Chapman, b 21 September 1916 in Syracuse. He graduated from Central High School, Syracuse, in 1935 and attended Syracuse Collegiate Center two years. He entered service in the Army Signal Corps August 1943, as Radio and Transmitter repairman. He served in New Guinea, the Philippine Islands, and Japan, being discharged February 1946. He was employed by General Electric Co., Syracuse, first in TV Repair, then several years in Heavy Military Department, writing manuals for government equipment built by General Electric, specifically radar and sonar equipment. He retired March 1977 at first repairing TV sets, learning to use Heath Kit computer, which he built, and doing research on his Chapman and Bates genealogies.

Glenn and Laurel traveled widely around the country, first by automobile, then with their trailer, lastly with their Shasta Motor Home, researching their family genealogy in court houses, cemeteries, and libraries around the country, as well as meeting and interviewing many descendants, who gave much information and many stories and pictures to add to the interest in their genealogies. Glenn d 30 June 1985, of a heart attack, at their home in North Syracuse. He is buried in Memorial Park Cemetery, Warners. They did not have any children.

Laurel continues to live in their home in North Syracuse and has become active in community and church activities. She traveled to Israel in January 1989, and in 1990 attended the Oberommergau Passion Play in Germany with extended travel to Switzerland; in 1991 she visited Scandinavia and Leningrad. In 1991, Laurel finished this genealogy and is assisting the publisher proofreading and approval of final editing.

+ 299. v. Roger Belden, b 28 April 1923.
+ 300. vi. Martha Louise, b 4 May 1929.
+ 301. vii. Hugh Irving, b 26 February 1934.

Chapter 6

The Fifth Generation

118. WILLIAM[5] ALFRED CHEESEMAN (s/o Royal[4] Cheeseman #33), b 23 November 1870 at North Girard, Erie Co., PA; m/1 1 July 1891 at North Girard, PA, **Carrie M. Webster**, d/o Daniel and Marinda Webster, b 4 March 1871 at Albion, MI. William was a piano tuner and gave music lessons. In addition, he traveled with evangelists, leading the singing and furnishing the music for their services. Carrie didn't like William's involvement in this kind of work; this may have contributed to the breakup of the marriage in 1914. She d November 1958 at Branford, CT and is buried in Girard, PA cemetery. In 1918 he m/2 **Genevieve Stephans**, d/o Joshua Stephans, born at Findley Lake, NY, d in 1938 at Pittsburgh, PA. William d 29 June 1956 at Pittsburgh and is buried in Mount Royal Cemetery, Glenshaw, Allegheny Co., PA.

Children, surname CHEESEMAN:
+ 302. i. Roland[6] George, b 13 June 1895.
+ 303. ii. Hubert Edmond, b 21 October 1900.

119. INA[5] E. CHEESEMAN (d/o Royal[4] Cheeseman #33), b May 1876 at Milesgrove [now Lake City], Erie Co., PA; m 27 September 1899 **David Garloch**, s/o John and Catherine (Hassler) Garloch, b 19 September 1871 at East Springfield, Erie Co., PA. David was manager of a canning factory. Ina d 4 September 1937 and David d in 1946; both are buried in North Girard, Erie Co.

Children, surname GARLOCH:
    304. i. Lorena[6] A., b 28 September 1908 at North Girard, m 7 August 1936 at Waynesburg, PA, Paul Byers, s/o John and Jean Byers. He was manager of real estate for the Mellon Bank in Pittsburgh, PA. He d in 1980 in Pittsburgh. Lorena has had a long and distinguished career in the fields of Education and Library. She was a cataloger at Oberlin College (1928–29); order librarian, American Library, Paris, France (1929–31); was with University of Pittsburgh, first as reference librarian, then director of Public Services; Acting Librarian and Lecturer (1931–54); Librarian and Lecturer Library Science 1954 until her retirement. Has since

added a doctorate in Foundation of Education to a Bachelor's and two Master's Degrees. She also taught Library Science at Rutgers University, helped organize a new School of Library Science at the State University of New York. She lives in Pittsburgh, PA and had no children.

127. LOUIS[5] FRANK JOHNSON (s/o Lenna[4] Cheeseman Johnson #44), b 5 March 1921 at Warren, OH. He m 19 October 1947, **Ruth Elizabeth Stewart**, b 9 October 1918. Louis worked at Reliance Electric Co. until his retirement.

Children, surname JOHNSON:
+   305.   i.   David[6] S., b 22 May 1952.
      306.   ii.   Louis F., b 22 May 1952, twin of David; died the same day.
      307.   iii.   Cynthia S., b 24 November 1956; d 1 October 1960.

128. MERTIE[5] ANN CROUCH (d/o George[4] H. Crouch #45), b 19 August 1877 at Wasioja, Dodge Co., MN; m 6 December 1897, **Norman C. Stevens**, s/o Frank and Louisa (Sanford) Stevens. Norman d 19 October 1954 in Minneapolis, MN and Mertie d 20 February 1957. Both are buried in Hillside Cemetery, Minneapolis.

Children, surname CROUCH:
+   308.   i.   Grace[6] Mae, b 7 September 1901.
+   309.   ii.   Norman Carroll, b 18 June 1905.
+   310.   iii.   Thelma, b 14 July 1908.

129. IRVIN[5] H. CROUCH (s/o George[4] H. Crouch #45), b 12 November 1878 at Wasioja, Dodge Co., MN. He m 12 September 1900 at Wasioja, MN, **Jennie Adell Garrison**, d/o Edmond E. and Lucinda (Taft) Garrison, b 5 November 1879. Irvin d 13 January 1949 at Saint Paul, MN in a train-automobile accident, with his brother Harrison Crouch. Jennie d 6 October 1974 at Dallas, OR and is buried at Portland, OR, as is Irvin.

Children, surname CROUCH:
+   311.   i.   Clarence[6], b 27 July 1901.
+   312.   ii.   Mildred, b 30 April 1904.
+   313.   iii.   Evelyn, b 27 June 1914.
+   314.   iv.   Vernon, b 27 August 1918.

130. GRACE[5] MAY CROUCH (d/o George[4] H. Crouch #45), b 31 August 1883 at Wasioja, Dodge Co., MN.; m 24 June 1903 at Wasioja,

MN, **George Edmund Garrison**, s/o Frederick L. and Mary G. (Yearly) Garrison, b 26 September 1873 at Dodge Co., MN. George was a farmer in Brookings Co., SD from 1893 to 1924. He moved to California in 1926. He had brothers and a sister living there and wanted to live in a warmer climate. He had various jobs in California including a sugar factory, glass factory, and Douglas Aircraft. He d 16 December 1948 at Long Beach, CA and Grace d there 2 April 1978, age 94, and both are buried at Sunnyside Cemetery, Long Beach, CA.

Children, surname GARRISON:

    315. i. Anona^6 Bell, b 6 March 1905 on a farm in Brookings Co., SD; m 11 October 1946 at Reno, NV, Paul Bernie Lethco and lives in Long Beach. No children.

+ 316. ii. Lloyd Henry, b 2 February 1907.

    317. iii. Wayne, b 1 May 1909 at Bushnell, Brookings Co. He moved to California with his family in 1926. From 1941 to 1974 he worked mechanical repair and rebuilding of numerical control metal working machine tools with Northrop Aircraft in Hawthorne, Los Angeles Co., CA. He m 3 July 1950 Lois Newcomb, a widow with two children, Betty Jo and Dolores, both born in Los Angeles Co. Lois b 18 July 1910 in Los Angeles Co. Her mother, Jenny Spencer, Grandmother and great-grandmother were born in Los Angeles Co. Lois' father b in Mississippi and came to Los Angeles Co. in 1870 at age 71. Wayne and Lois live at Thousand Oaks, CA. They do not have any children.

+ 318. i. Myrtle Adell, b 10 July 1911.
+ 319. ii. Vernon, b 2 July 1916.

    320. iii. Clare Faye, b 4 March 1919 at Brookings Co, SD. He moved with his family to California in 1926. He m 12 August 1940 at Los Angeles, CA; Lillian M. Stovee, d/o Nordahl and Ella (Hauge) Stovee, she b at Howard, SD. Clare is Transportation Supervisor for Certified Grocers of California. Clare and Lillian live in Long Beach, CA. They do not have any children.

+ 321. iv. Donald, b 5 September 1921.

131. LETTIE^5 ADELL CROUCH (d/o George^4 H. Crouch #45), b 10 March 1886 at Wasioja, MN.; m 8 June 1904, **Bert Jacob Daniels**, s/o Stephen and Adele (Wyman) Daniels, b 9 August 1880 at West Concord, MN. Bert was a farmer and cattleman. He died 26 April 1952 at Long Beach, CA; Lettie d there 9 September 1956. Both are buried at Westminster Memorial Park, Westminster, CA.

Children, surname DANIELS:
+ 322. i. Juanita[6] Mae, b 10 December 1904.
+ 323. ii. Wynot Berdell, b 6 October 1912.
+ 324. iii. Bethel June, b 19 June 1919.

132. HARRISON[5] MORTON CROUCH (s/o George[4] H. Crouch #45), b 8 October 1888 at Wasioja, Dodge Co., MN; m/1 23 November 1911, **Elsie Belle Cartwright**, d/o Arron and Rosilian (Kramer) Cartwright, b 25 December 1888. She died 10 January 1931. He m/2 Mrs. **Hazel Nordstrom** on 1 December 1931. Harrison was a cattle buyer and died in a train-automobile accident 13 January 1949 at Saint Paul, MN, with his brother, Irvin. He is buried in Riverside Cemetery, Dodge Center, Dodge Co., MN.

Children, surname CROUCH:
325. i. Harvey[6], b in 1913. He died at 13 or 14 years of age.
+ 326. ii. Harlie Laverne, b 30 November 1914.
+ 327. iii. Leora Belle, b 21 November 1916.
328. iv. Anola, died before 1931 in California.

133. VERNON[5] GEORGE CROUCH (s/o George[4] H. Crouch #45), b 7 June 1891 at Wasioja, Dodge Co., MN; m 6 August 1928, **Genevieve Irwin**, d/o William H. and Mary (Porter) Irwin, b 4 June 1895, at Salem, SD. They lived in Dodge Center, MN. Vernon was self employed in real estate and insurance. He d 14 June 1959 at Dodge Center, MN. When last known she was in a nursing home.

Children, surname CROUCH:
+ 329. i. Quentin[6], b 18 July 1929.
+ 330. ii. Kermit, b 16 September 1934.

134. LILA[5] BELLE CROUCH (d/o George[4] H. Crouch #45), b 30 August 1895 at Wasioja, Dodge Co., MN.; m 20 October 1915 at her parents home in Dodge Co., MN, **Hila Vanderhyde**, s/o Frank S. and Emily (Harkum) Vanderhyde, b 18 October 1894 in Dodge Co., MN. Hila d 6 July 1957 and Lila Belle d 25 July 1977 at Excelsior, MN. Both are buried in Lakewood Cemetery, Minneapolis, MN.

Children, surname VANDERHYDE:
331. i. Melva[6], b 22 October 1916 at Wasioja, MN. She was a secretary, account clerk and shareholder receptionist at Northern States

The Fifth Generation

Power & Executive Secretary of Church Women United. She lives at Excelsior and never married.
332. ii. James L. Egan, foster son they raised.

135. FLOYD[5] ALLEN CROUCH (s/o George[4] H. Crouch #45), b 25 July 1898 at Wasioja, MN; m 24 April 1918, **Mildred Moreland**, d/o John William and Caroline Almira (Gilbert) Moreland, b 2 September 1899. Floyd farmed in Dodge Co., MN. Previous to retirement he worked eight years at Methodist Hospital as a painter. Floyd d 13 February 1983 at West Concord, Dodge Co. and is buried in Concord Cemetery. Mildred was in a nursing home in 1984.

Children, surname CROUCH:
+ 333. i. Allen[6] George, b 26 March 1919.
+ 334. ii. Ruth Mildred, b 14 November 1920.
+ 335. iii. Marie Lois, b 22 November 1922.
   336. iv. Mary Louise, b 15 December 1927; d 26 June 1931 and buried in Concord Cemetery.
+ 337. v. Elna Nadine, b 3 December 1932.
   338. vi. Donald William, b 28 May 1936 at Wasioja, Dodge Co.; m 24 February 1961 at Cloquet, MN, Elaine Marlys Peterson, d/o Albert and Frances (Lindhart) Peterson, b 20 July 1942 at Cloquet. Donald teaches in a junior high school in Kenosha, WI and Elaine works in a closing office in an abstract company. They have no children.

137. CHARLES[5] HENRY CROUCH (s/o George[4] H. Crouch #45), b 11 December 1903 at Wasioja, MN; m 12 June 1928 at Mankato, MN, **Beulah Hollingsworth**, d/o Marvin David and Myrtle Dell (Johnson) Hollingsworth. Charles served as minister in seven Methodist Churches in Minnesota from 1928–1950. They moved to Arizona in 1950 for Beulah's health, locating in Tempe in 1951; served seven years as Executive Secretary of Arizona Council of Churches and 15 years as Coordinator of Religious Affairs at Arizona State University in Tempe. Beulah was on the faculty at the same institution for 23 years. Both are retired. Charles wrote a history of his home town, Wasioja, entitled *Wasioja, Rooted Yet Growing* as well as *Let This Mind Be In You* and *Seeds of Thought*.

Children, surname CROUCH:
+ 339. i. Cheryl[6] Mavis, b 6 May 1941.

138. MILDRED[5] ABBY CROUCH (d/o Nelson[4] R. Crouch #46), b 9 March 1894 at Wasioja, MN. She was a missionary to the Hopi Indians at Second Mesa, AZ in the early 20s. While on leave she met her future husband, a school teacher, and m 31 December 1928 at Ashford, AZ, **Joseph Walker Raymond**, b 19 September 1898 at Deer Creek, OK, s/o Wilbur Hamilton and Jettie Susan Raymond. Joseph continued school teaching until 1948 when he went to the Hopi Indians as a Baptist Missionary; resumed teaching in 1952 or 1953 and they retired in 1965 to Fort Smith, AR. Mildred was a "people" person, liking people and was musically inclined. Joseph was talented in art, music, and writing. Mildred d 10 August 1966 at Fort Smith. Joseph m Ina Lee Utley at Fort Smith, 3 November 1967. He d 9 September 1982 at Fort Smith and both are buried there.

Children, surname RAYMOND:
+   340.   i. John[6] Walker, b 6 December 1929.
+   341.   ii. Thomas Hamilton, b 15 April 1931.

139. JOHN[5] WILBUR CROUCH (s/o Nelson[4] R. Crouch #46), b 29 October 1895 at Wasioja, MN; m/1 28 July 1918 **Wilberda** (or Alberda) **Lazetta Keune**, d 19 March 1920 at Albert Lea, MN. They were living on a farm on Claremont Street, a country road near Wasioja. No children.

Wilbur m/2 on 31 May 1923 at Valley City, ND, **Mildred Mary McGoon**, b 23 December 1896 at Waukon, IA, d/o John and Iola (Thibode) McGoon. They lived on his father's farm near Northfield, MN until they retired. They lived in Alpine, CA, near San Diego, then moved to Truth or Consequences, NM, where they lived until Wilbur d 25 September 1981. Mildred lives in an apartment near her daughter in Chaska, MN.

Children, surname CROUCH:
+   342.   i. Betty[6] Jane, b 12 January 1927.

141. WILLIAM[5] L. "WILLIE" OSBORN (s/o Emma[4] Crouch Osborn #47), b 12 December 1889 at Wasioja, MN. In 1920 he m **Daisie Prall**, d/o Clinton and Mary Prall, b 5 December 1896, d 15 January 1927 at age 30, in Minneapolis, MN of complications resulting from her pregnancy. Willie d 26 July 1954 at his farm at Wasioja, MN. He was a veteran of World War I and had been under treatment at the veterans hospital in Minneapolis, MN. Both were buried in Wildwood Cemetery, Wasioja,

The Fifth Generation

MN.

Children, surname OSBORN:

 343. i. Earl[6], probably born about January 1927. He was reportedly an epileptic. At the time of his father's death was living in Cambridge, MN.

142. EMMA[5] ANGELINE OSBORN (d/o Emma[4] Crouch Osborn #47), b 24 May 1890 in Dodge Co., MN., probably Wasioja; m 17 July 1915 in South Dakota, **Owen Leon Palmer**, s/o Eva Reed from Tennessee. His father died when Owen was little and the family doesn't know his name; he was b 3 June 1890 at Hillsdale, MI. Owen and Emma moved from Perkins, SD in October 1929 to take over William Osborn's farm at Wasioja, MN. Owen d 8 March 1970 at Hayfield, MN; Emma d 31 July 1971, age 81 years, at Rochester, MN. Both are buried in Wildwood Cemetery, Wasioja, MN.

Children, surname PALMER:

+ 344. i. Eva[6] Reed, b 28 November 1918.
+ 345. ii. Marian Nadean, b 8 August 1922.
+ 346. iii. Clinton (Red) Orwin, b 18 October 1927.

143. LIDA[5] ELIZABETH OSBORN (d/o Emma[4] Crouch Osborn #47), b 22 July 1891 at Wasioja, Dodge Co., MN. She m 1910, **Berkley Alvin Mason**, s/o John and Myrtle (Foote) Mason at Dodge Co., MN, b 18 September 1892. He was a carpenter and contractor. Lida d 28 November 1964 at Indio, CA; Berkley d 11 November 1977 at Chula Vista, CA; both are buried in Coachella Valley Cemetery, Riverside, CA.

Children, surname MASON:

+ 347. i. Lois[6], b 8 May 1915 in Dodge Co., MN.
 348. ii. Merle, b and died shortly after Lois
+ 349. iii. Myron, b 10 September 1917 at Perkins Co., SD.

144. BIDA[5] BELL OSBORN (d/o Emma[4] Crouch Osborn #47), b 27 July 1892 at Wasioja, Dodge Co., MN. She was not yet 4 years old when her mother died and she was raised by next door neighbors, the Masons. She m 26 May 1920 at Dodge Co., MN, **Horace Franklin**, s/o William and Sarah (Schramm) Franklin, b 17 April 1890 at Sterling Center, MN. Horace taught school for awhile, then farmed. He lived at Good Thunder, Vernon Center, and Northome, MN. Horace d 14 April 1965 and Bida d 6 October 1968 at Northome.

Children, surname FRANKLIN:
- \+ 350. i. Gordon[6] W., b 11 July 1921.
- \+ 351. ii. Donald Lincoln, b 12 February 1924.
- 352. iii. Clark Mason, b 16 December 1925 at Vernon Center. He is a ranch hand and is unmarried. His last know address was Nashua, MT.
- 353. iv. Marjorie May, b 17 April 1930 at Vernon Center; she d May 1930.
- \+ 354. v. Norman Dale, b 26 June 1932.
- \+ 355. vi. Rilla Bell, b 9 January 1933.

149. GEORGE[5] MARTIN QUICK (s/o Ellen[4] Martin Quick #56), b 8 May 1874 at Markesan or Mackford, WI; m 2 April 1899 at Blooming Rose, MO, **Mary Ethel Denison**, d/o James and America Elizabeth (Haggard) Denison, she b 2 June 1878 at Licking, MO. George was a farmer, first at Licking, later at several places in California; he d 18 March 1941 at Modesto, CA; Mary died 7 August 1970 at Modesto; both buried at Odd Fellows Cemetery, Modesto.

Children, surname QUICK:
- \+ 356. i. Eugene[6] James, b 15 January 1900.
- 357. ii. Mary Moletna, b 17 June 1901, Licking; d 4 August 1901.
- \+ 358. iii. Georgia Mae, b 9 October 1902.
- 359. iv. Harry Denison, b 17 November 1904; d 4 February 1920.
- \+ 360. v. Ellen Elizabeth, b 7 October 1906.
- \+ 361. vi. Vera Evelyn, b 20 November 1908.
- \+ 362. vii. Doris Iva, b 22 July 1914.

152. JESSE[5] JAMES QUICK (s/o Ellen[4] Martin Quick #56), b 2 January 1884 at Markesan, Green Lake Co., WI. His parents lived in Town of Mackford in 1880 and 1900 U.S. Census. In the 1905 Census he was still living with his family, a farmer, age 21. He resided in Mosinee, Marathon Co., WI. when he m 23 November 1909, **Gladys Vivian Bush**, d/o Robert Bush, b 20 April 1892 at Mineral Point, WI. He was a farmer, retiring in 1941. Gladys d 13 November 1959 at Madison, Dane Co., WI. Jesse d 11 November 1956, Green Lake, WI. Both are buried at Lake Maria Cemetery, Town of Mackford, Green Lake Co., WI.

Children, surname QUICK:
- \+ 363. i. Calvin[6], b 14 October 1912.

The Fifth Generation 143

+ 364. ii. Elmer, b 11 February 1914.
+ 365. iii. Russell, b 9 March 1916.
+ 366. iv. Leland, b 13 February 1918.
+ 367. v. Irene, b 4 July 1922.

153. EUGENE[5] QUICK (s/o Ellen[4] Martin Quick #56), b 25 May 1889 at Markesan, WI; m 14 June 1911, **Inez Johnson,** b 18 October 1890 at Waushara Co., WI, d/o Lars and Mary (Sorenson) Johnson.; d 9 February 1970, age 79, at Ripon, Fond du Lac, WI and is buried in Loper Cemetery, Ripon. They lived in Florida for 12 years before moving to Ripon. According to his obituary, he died 22 August 1980 at Ripon and is buried in the Loper Cemetery.

Children, surname QUICK:
+ 368. i. Evelyn, b 5 September 1913.
+ 369. ii. Lyle James, b 10 February 1914.
+ 370. iii. Naomi, b 9 April 1915.
+ 371. iv. Dorothy, b 24 November 1919.
   372. v. Irma L., b 28 March 1920 at Ripon; m 10 June 1944 at Oshkosh, WI, Austin Grout; they had no children. She d October 1977 and is buried at Liberty Prairie Cemetery in Pickett.

154. AMANDA[5] MAUDE CLARK (d/o Amanda[4] Martin Clark #58), b 19 January 1883; m 12 November 1916 at Ripon, WI, **Clarence H. Patchett,** s/o John and Julia (Sear) Patchett. Clarence d 12 January 1929 at Brooklyn, Green Lake Co., WI, where Amanda d 19 January 1920.

Children, surname PATCHETT:
   373. i. George[6] Leroy, b circa 1917/18, d 7 March 19—, at Chippewa, WI. He was adopted by his uncle George Jay Clark (#155).
   374. ii. Earl, died 12 June 1933.

156. RUTH[5] MAE CLARK (d/o Amanda[4] Martin Clark #58), b 8 April 1898. She m 15 January 1932, **Frank Patchett,** of Ripon, Fond du Lac Co., WI. Frank was b in 1881 and d 13 January 1966 and Ruth d 17 December 1982 and both are buried at Mackford Cemetery, Green Lake Co., WI.

Children, surname PATCHETT:
   375. i. Eleanor, b 27 December 1932; m 23 October 1965, Robert Simmons, b 6 March 1928. Eleanor reportedly lives at Oshkosh.
   376. ii. Donald, b 13 May 1935, d 14 December 1955 and is buried in

Mackford.

158. JOHN[5] WALLACE PECKHAM (s/o John[4] Eber Peckham #60), b 10 March 1873 at Portage, Columbia Co., WI. He moved to South Dakota with his parents in 1879, when he was six years old. As a young man he studied at Yankton [SD] College and later took on the editorship of the *Alexandria* [SD] *Journal* from 1893–1902. In 1904 he took over the *Parkston* [SD] *Advance* newspaper and continued as its publisher until his death.

John m/1 **Sarah Jeanette Dobson** 21 August 1895 at Alexandria, SD, b about 12 January 1877. After young Flora Miller came to work for him, they were separated and divorced. He m/2 **Flora Bell Miller** on 20 September 1902. John served as state oil inspector from 1909 to 1913; he served two terms in the State Senate, 1915 and 1917. John d 20 April 1939, age 66, at Rochester, MN and is buried in Sioux Falls, SD.

Sarah later m — Shreve and had one child by him; James Bird Shreve, b 7 August 1907 at Alexandria, SD and she raised the three children together. She d October 1968 in Sioux Falls, SD.

Children, surname PECKHAM:
- 377. i. Leith[6] James, b June 1896 at Alexandria; m Harriet Rednik from Chicago. He was an auditor. Harriet d in 1957 and Leith d in 1955 in Chicago, IL. There were no children.
- + 378. ii. Beatrice Margurite, b 31 March 1899.

159. CHARLES[5] HERBERT PECKHAM (s/o John[4] Eber Peckham #60), b 15 February 1875 at Eugene, OR. At the age of four years he moved with his family from Minnesota to a homestead farm a few miles east of Alexandria in 1879. For fourteen years he lived on the farm, moving then to the village of Alexandria, SD where he graduated from high school. Subsequently he was apprenticed to the plumbing and tinning trades. He later owned a half interest in the hardware store of Peckham & Jones and was owner of the city gas plant. Married 7 July 1897 **Sybil Vickers**, d/o John and Harriet (Dale) Vickers, b 20 August 1878 in SD. On 17 May 1914 Bert was appointed postmaster of Alexandria. Later Bert and Sybil owned and operated a grocery and meat market in Des Moines, IA. They remained there several years, until Bert suffered a stroke, when they moved to Louisville, Kentucky to be near their daughter.

Charles Herbert "Bert" d 10 February 1960 at Louisville, KY just 5

The Fifth Generation 145

days short of 85 years. Sybil d 17 July 1968 at Louisville, 89 years old. Both are buried in Resthaven Cemetery, Louisville.

Children, surname PECKHAM:

+ 379. i. Harriet[6], b 24 June 1898.

160. FRANK[5] DURWARD PECKHAM (s/o John[4] Eber Peckham #60), b 20 March 1877 at Portage, Columbia Co., WI. At the age of two years he moved with his parents to South Dakota and lived on the family homestead near Emery; he was about 11 years old when the family moved to Alexandria, SD. Here he graduated from high school; at the age of 21 he became a bookkeeper in the First National Bank of Alexandria and fifteen years later was made president of that institution and of the Emery State Bank.

On 11 May 1898 he m **Florence W. Durkee**, d/o Franklin E. and Mary (Wakeman) Durkee, she b 10 April 1879 at Clinton, Rock Co., WI. In 1907 Frank left the bank and went into an abstract office with Fred Thiel and George Ryburn, but in 1909, when a vacancy was caused by the death of Will Ryburn, he returned to the banking business.

Frank was interested in good livestock and was a breeder of shorthorn cattle and Duroc Jersey hogs. He had large herds of fine animals on his farm two miles west of Alexandria. He took an active part in the community and state, according to his obituary. He served one term in the South Dakota Senate, beginning in 1917. He gave freely of his musical talents, singing in the Methodist Church Choir and playing in the local band.

On 26 December 1933 he suffered a stroke, and for the last eight years was an invalid. Frank d 8 January 1943, age 65, in Sioux Falls, SD. Florence d 21 August 1957 at Sioux Falls, age 78 years. Both are buried in Greenhill Cemetery, Alexandria.

Children, surname PECKHAM

+ 380. i. Ellsworth[6] L., b 18 August 1899.
+ 381. ii. Donald Seth, b 7 November 1903.
+ 382. iii. Howard John, b 17 August 1905.
+ 383. iv. Norma Florence, b 27 June 1907.
+ 384. v. Francis Herbert, b 15 February 1914.

161. EDITH[5] MAY PECKHAM (d/o John[4] Eber Peckham #60), b 16

April 1879 at Owatonna, MN. She was 3 months old when her parents moved to South Dakota and located on a farm near Alexandria, Hanson Co., SD where she grew up and received her education. She m 27 April 1897 **William Legge Ryburn**, b 10 May 1872 at Rockford, Winnebago Co., IL., s/o William and Mary Mundy (Legge) Ryburn. Edith was past Matron of Eastern Star and was organist and Sunday School Teacher in Presbyterian Church of Alexandria.

William was cashier at First National Bank of Alexandria until his death 13 July 1909, 37 years, at Mitchell, SD of complications following an appendectomy eighteen months earlier. After twelve years of marriage, Edith was left a widow with three daughters to care for. Edith d 29 October 1945 at Minneapolis, MN, age 66. Both are buried in Green Hill Cemetery, Alexandria, SD.

Children, surname RYBURN:
+ 385. i. Leota[6] Vernette, b 16 February 1899.
    386. ii. Neva, b 6 April 1900: d 5 September 1900 at Alexandria.
    387. iii. Helen, b 8 June 1902 at Alexandria; m 6 December 1935 at Omaha, NE, Claude Orr. Helen d 27 February 1944 at Omaha and is buried in Green Hill Cemetery, Alexandria. No known children.
    388. iv. William, died as an infant 15 October 1904, at Alexandria.
+ 389. v. Dorothy Jeanette, b 12 February 1906.

166. LAURA[5] MAY VINING (d/o Lucretia[4] Peckham Vining #61), b 26 January 1875 near Rio, Columbia Co., WI; m 19 September 1894 at Pardeeville, Columbia Co., WI, **Benjamin Wade Palmer**, b 15 Mar 1865, s/o William and Eliza Jane (Cowley) Palmer. Ben was a resident of Flensburg, now Hillside, Douglas Co., SD at the time of his marriage, and they returned there immediately after the marriage. They farmed for several years, then moved to Mitchell, SD in 1903, where Ben had purchased a grain and coal business. In 1920 they moved to a farm 17 miles south of Miller, Hand Co., SD, where they farmed for two years, then moved to Miller to make their home.

Benjamin d 20 September 1940 at Miller and Laura d 1 January 1942 at the home of her daughter, in Huron, Beadle Co., SD. Both are buried in Graceland Cemetery, Mitchell, Davison Co., SD.

Children, surname PALMER:
+ 390. i. Nettie[6] May, b 18 July 1895.

+   391.   ii.   Chester, b 1 or 4 August 1900.

167. JESSE[5] **L. VINING** (s/o Lucretia[4] Peckham Vining #61), b 28 October 1881 at Elmore, Faribault Co., MN. He m/1, 24 November 1904, Thanksgiving Day, **Lulu Hewitt**, at his father's house in Chetek, Barron Co., WI. Lulu b 5 January 1887, d/o Elbert and Eva (Lane) Hewitt. Jesse and Lulu were divorced about 1908 at Chetek. "Late one dark night Jesse went with horse and buggy to where his former wife lived and stole his daughter, Laura May, and brought her to his sister, Laura May Palmer to live." Lulu later m 21 October 1911, Henry Forbes. Lulu d 9 April 1969, age 82, at Nekoosa, Wood Co., WI and is buried in Greenwood Cemetery, Town of Armenia, Juneau Co., WI.

Jesse m/2, **Regina Thill** in Minneapolis, MN about 1945 or 1946. They had no children. Jesse d 17 June 1950, age 68, at Mitchell, SD and is buried in Ethan Methodist Cemetery, Ethan, SD.

Children, surname VINING:
+   392.   i.   Laura[6] May, b 30 September 1905.
+   393.   ii. Ralph Jesse, b 6 October 1907.

168. THOMAS[5] **RAY VINING** (s/o Lucretia[4] Peckham Vining #61), b 26 October 1887 in Wisconsin. He m 4 September 1910 **Gertrude Michaelsen** of Parkston, Hutchinson Co., SD, b 20 April 1892, d/o Hans J. and Caroline (Nielsen) Michaelsen. They farmed in the Ethan, Hanson Co., SD. area from about 1913. Thomas d 10 January 1952, age 64, at Mitchell, Davison Co., SD. In 1984 Gertrude was still living, with son Raymond at Ethan, SD.

Children, surname VINING:
+   394.   i.   Mabel[6] Caroline, b 26 September 1911.
+   395.   ii.   Raymond Hans, b 27 November 1912.
+   396.   iii. Edward Harrison, b 3 December 1913.
+   397.   iv.   Charles Lester, b 1 February 1919.

170. HARRY[5] **EDWARD VINING** (s/o Lucretia[4] Peckham Vining #61), b 27 April 1893 at Rio, Columbia Co., WI. He was a school teacher in Wisconsin, moved to Minneapolis in 1917; was in WW I. He m/1 September 1917, at Gethsemane Lutheran Church parsonage, Minneapolis, MN, **Selma Christine Peterson**, b 8 August 1894 at Hennepin Co., MN, d/o Paul and Maren Oline (Anderson) Peterson. Harry was a bookkeeper, traveling auditor, policeman, and postal clerk. He d 28 May 1972 at Edina, Hennepin Co., MN.

Children, surname VINING:
+   398.   i.   Joyce^6 Marvel, b 8 February 1920.
+   399.   ii.   Lilas Jane, b 8 February 1922.
+   400.   iii.   Curtis Harry, b 9 January 1924.

173. ALICE^5 GRACE McELROY (d/o Elizabeth^4 Peckham McElroy #62), b 4 June 1885 at Marcellon, Columbia Co., WI. She m 6 March 1907, **Asa Christopher Roberts**, s/o Markus and Jeanette (Langdon) Roberts, he b 13 May 1883 in Town of Scott, Columbia Co., WI. They started their married life on his father's farm, later living near Pardeeville, Columbia Co., WI. Asa d 4 March 1958 and Alice d 18 July 1974, aged 89 years. They are both buried in Marcellon Cemetery.

Children, surname ROBERTS:
+   401.   i.   Beulah^6 Elizabeth, b 21 April 1908.
+   402.   ii.   Roger Wayman, b 14 August 1909.
+   403.   iii.   Ruth Janette, b 20 July 1912.
+   404.   iv.   Amber Irene, b 19 April 1917.
    405.   v.   Bernice Vernetta, b 1 July 1919, Town of Scott, Columbia Co, WI; m/1 Jaxon Miles, who d 28 February 1966; m/2 Gerry Stephson in 1970. Lives in San Francisco, CA and works for Standard Oil of California. No known children.

174. LUCY^5 MAY McELROY (d/o Elizabeth^4 Peckham McElroy #62), b 13 September 1887 at Marcellon, Columbia Co., WI; she m 30 March 1910, **Donald Jenkins** at Town of Marcellon, Columbia Co., WI, he b 16 September 1885, s/o Edward David and Sarah Elizabeth (Reynolds) Jenkins. Donald d May 1936 in Town of Scott, Columbia Co., WI and is buried in Greenwood Cemetery, Dalton, WI. He was a farmer by trade. In June 1984 Lucy was living in the Columbia Co. Home for the Aged at Wyocena, WI, aged 96.

Children, surname JENKINS:
+   406.   i.   Ronald^6 Ralph, b 27 December 1910.
+   407.   ii.   Orris Durwood, b 8 December 1915.
+   408.   iii.   Lucille Elizabeth, b 27 September 1918.
+   409.   iv.   Stanley William, b 15 February 1922.
+   410.   v.   Donald Earl, b 24 February 1925.

+ 411. vi. Vernon Jess, b 13 June 1929.
 412. vii. Gladys Fern, b 26 November 1931 at Dalton, Green Lake Co, WI. She never married. Gladys has been a public school teacher since 1953, teaching grades one and two at Fort Winnebago School, in the Portage [WI] school district. She supplied all the facts on her brothers and sisters and their families.

176. WILLIAM[5] BOYD McELROY (s/o Elizabeth[4] Peckham McElroy #62), b 27 January 1894 at Marcellon, Columbia Co., WI. He m 29 December 1915 in the village of Pardeeville, WI, **Edna Fenske**, d/o William and Lillie (Winne) Fenske, b 15 March 1897 in Town of Manchester. William was a farmer and bred purebred Duroc hogs. He was past president of the Town of Marcellon School Board, a town board member and founder of the Columbia County Swine Breeders. In 1960 he was honored by the Wisconsin Livestock Assn. William d 3 November 1978, age 82, in Portage, Columbia Co. Edna d 25 December 1978, age 79, at Portage, WI. Both are buried in Marcellon Cemetery.

Children, surname McELROY:
+ 413. i. Boyd[6] Wayne, b 16 November 1916.
 414. ii. William Gerald, b 24 October 1920 at Town of Marcellon, Columbia Co. He is a farmer, raising registered Duroc hogs and a small herd of dairy cows. He was not married, when last known.
+ 415. iii. Maxine Elizabeth, b 22 April 1925.

177. WINNIE[5] BLANCHE McELROY (d/o Elizabeth[4] Peckham McElroy #62), b 27 January 1894 at Pardeeville, Town of Marcellon, Columbia Co., WI. She m 1 August 1917, at Green Lake Co., WI, **Freeman "Freme" Wesley Gorsuch**, s/o John Wesley and Eunice (Ross) Gorsuch, b 6 May 1873 in Town of Scott, Columbia Co., WI. He was previously m to Mina Ann Fuller. Freeman and Mina moved to Chetek in 1901; after 8 years they returned to Columbia Co., where Mina d 20 September 1914. They had three children: Stuart, Wilfred and Harold.

Freeman d 14 March 1939 at Pardeeville, Columbia Co., WI. Winnie Blanche d 3 January 1972 at Wyocena, Columbia Co., where she had lived since 1967. Freeman and Blanche are buried in Comstock Cemetery, Pardeeville.

Children, surname GORSUCH:
+ 416. i. Floy[6] Beatrice, b 26 May 1918.
+ 417. ii. Maysel Elizabeth, b 29 October 1922.

179. RALPH[5] FAY McELROY (s/o Elizabeth[4] Peckham McElroy #62), b 8 January 1900 at Marcellon, Columbia Co., WI. He lived all his life on the family farm. He m 15 December 1922 at Pardeeville, WI, **Georgetta Kiefer**, d/o George and Nellie (Merrill) Kiefer, b 2 September 1904 at Pardeeville, WI. Ralph Fay d 17 October 1939 and is buried in Marcellon Cemetery. As of 1984 Georgetta was still living in Pardeeville, WI.

Children, surname McELROY:
+   418.   i.   Evalyn[6] Elizabeth, b 8 November 1923.
+   419.   ii.   Wanda Elaine, b 24 October 1925.
       420.   iii.   William George, b 2 July 1929, at Portage, WI.
+   421.   iv.   Berwin Ralph, b 22 October 1930.
+   422.   v.   Carol Ann, b 19 July 1936.

181. EDNA[5] PEARL PECKHAM (d/o Charles[4] W. Peckham #63), b 5 March 1885 at Alexandria, Hanson Co., SD. She taught school south of Webster. She m 19 October 1904, **James Arthur Chowen** at Waubay, Day Co., SD., he b 12 July 1886 at Strand, Day Co, SD, s/o William and Annie (Long) Chowen. In 1914 they homesteaded on the Peace River country of Alberta, Canada on 160 acres of farmland which could be owned by anyone willing to expend the effort to move there and clear the land, living on it for three years, when it would be their property. The Chowen homestead and the first school were at "Blue-sky," Alberta. Arthur Chowen and a neighbor, Mr. Huninston organized and built the first school in the district, a one room log structure attended by eight children. Although Pearl was a qualified teacher, she did not hold certification for Alberta. Two of the children in this school were Art and Pearl's.

Arthur d 4 December 1966 at Edmonton, Alberts, Canada, and is buried in Beacmont Cemetery, Edmonton. Pearl d 29 September 1968 at Fairview, Alberta, Canada and is buried in Waterhole Cemetery, three miles west of Fairview, Alberta.

Children, surname CHOWEN:
+   423.   i.   Luvia[6] Imogene, b 7 August 1905.
       424.   ii.   William Wesley, b 25 January 1907 at Strand, SD; m during the service in World War II. When he left the army they moved to Quesnel, BC, Canada. After his death in June 1956 at Quesnel, his wife, Mickey, remarried and the family has completely lost

The Fifth Generation 151

touch. Wesley spent most of his working years in the forest industry in British Columbia and northern Alberta. He did not have any children.

182. MAUDE[5] SUSAN PECKHAM (d/o Charles[4] W. Peckham #63), b 2 February 1887 in Potter Co., SD. She m 26 August 1906 at Webster, Day Co., SD, **Scott Merrell Bates**, s/o Edward H. and Nancy Ann (Hull) Bates, b 21 October 1883 at Paynesville, MN. Scott was a farmer for his whole life in Webster. Maude d 12 May 1963 at Webster and Scott d 20 April 1967 at Webster; both are buried in the Webster Cemetery.

Children, surname BATES
- 425. i. Darville[6] Delos, b 3 December 1907 at Webster. He did not marry but farmed with his father. He d 29 June 1952 at Webster.
- 426. ii. Goldie, b in 1911/12 at Webster; she changed her name to Greta. She m Bill Munson and has an adopted boy, Justin Scott. She lives in Fresno, CA.
+ 427. iii. Arlo Wayne, b 2 October 1917.

183. THOMAS[5] RALPH PECKHAM (s/o Charles[4] W. Peckham #63), b 7 November 1891 at Webster, Day Co., SD. He m 11 January 1913 at Bristol, SD at the bride's home, **Marie Caroline Bakken**, d/o Ole and Ann (Ellinson) Bakken. Ole came from Norway and homesteaded in Bristol. Marie was b 13 May 1889 in Lynn Township, Day Co., SD. Thomas farmed in the Bristol area and operated a well drilling business. It was while drilling a well at Ole Bakken's farm, north of Bristol, that he met Marie. He loved the out-of-doors and knew the bird songs and tracks of the animals, and loved to hunt. He was a dreamer and philosopher. Tom d 22 May 1979, 87 years; Marie d 18 September 1983, age 94 years, at the Holmes Lake Manor nursing home in Lincoln, Nebraska. Both are buried at Bristol, Day Co., SD.

Children, surname PECKHAM:
+ 428. i. Orville[6] Charles, b 6 August 1913.
+ 429. ii. Grace Elizabeth, b 8 September 1914.
+ 430. iii. Kenneth Nathan, b 18 December 1915.
+ 431. iv. Anne Rosella, b 9 July 1918.
+ 432. v. Hazel Viola, b 27 October 1919.
+ 433. vi. Gene Ralph, b 14 March 1921.
+ 434. v. Percy Donald, b 16 January 1925.
+ 435. vi. Ruth Marie, b 30 June 1927.

184. RAYMOND[5] CHARLES PECKHAM (s/o Charles[4] W. Peckham #63), b 4 March 1894 at Webster, Day Co., SD. He m 6 May 1916, **Emma Pernilla Olsen**, d/o Peter and Kjersti Olsen, b 2 August 1897 at Lily, SD. Raymond farmed near Bristol, Day Co., SD. Ray d 22 November 1988 at Webster, SD. Emma d 1 October 1979, about 82 years at Bristol and is buried in Bristol Cemetery.

Children, surname PECKHAM:
- \+ 436. i. Clayton[6] Maurice, b 28 November 1916.
- \+ 437. ii. Fern Isabell, b 22 November 1917.
-     438. iii. Marjorie May, b 25 May 1921 at Lily. She started out as a school teacher in rural South Dakota villages, graduated to Junior High School in Watertown, SD and Chico, CA. Later initiated the first guidance program at Watertown Schools and was secondary school counselor at Saint Louis Park, MN for 24 years before retiring in June 1983. She completed her career with a Masters Degree plus 65 credits in Counseling and Guidance. She never married. She provided material on the rest of her family.
- \+ 439. iv. Jesse Vernon, b 17 January 1925.
- \+ 440. v. Virginia Cleone, b 6 October 1931.

185. HAROLD[5] PECKHAM (s/o Charles[4] W. Peckham #63), b 8 April 1895 in Day Co., SD.; m 1 July 1926, **Gladys Watson**, d/o George and Tilla (Ward) Watson, she b 24 April 1901 at Craig, NB. Her father was a mail carrier in Nebraska and lived in a sod house, which he built. Harold was a well-driller; Gladys taught the lower grades in various schools for many years. They lived in Clark, Clark Co., SD, where Gladys still resided as of 1984. Harold d 24 September 1983 at Watertown, SD; he is buried at Rose Hill Cemetery at Clark, SD.

Children, surname PECKHAM:
- \+ 441. i. James, b 1 July 1937.
- \+ 442. ii. Robert, b 18 October 1938.

186. GERTRUDE[5] PRIMROSE PECKHAM (d/o Charles[4] W. Peckham #63), b 2 September 1898 at Egeland Township, Day Co., SD; m 15 November 1915 at Webster, Day Co., SD, **William A. Roseth**, he b 2 April 1887 at Lowry, SD., s/o Andrew and Anne (Karlstad) Roseth. The family moved to California in 1935 during the depression and drought, when they heard things were opening up there. William was a barber. He d 12 July 1959 at Bell Gardens, Los Angeles Co., CA; Gertrude d 26 July

The Fifth Generation 153

1963 at Bell Gardens and both are buried there.

Children, surname ROSETH
+   443. iii. Orel[6] Luvia, b 27 April 1916.
     444. iv. Billie Gae, b 4 April 1918; she d 9 June 1929, age 11 years and is buried in the Webster [SD] Cemetery.
     445. v. Minard Wesley, b 7 January 1920; he d 4 January 1942, age 20 years, in California and is buried in Forest Lawn Cemetery, Los Angeles, CA.
+   446. vi. Beryl Smith, b 15 November 1921.
+   447. vii. Beverly Peckham, b 2 August 1923.
     448. viii. Wilda Floy, b 24 September 1925 at Lily; m 3 August 1967 at Las Vegas, NV, Carl Julian, s/o Victor and Louise (Dentino) Guiliano, he b 15 August 1929. Carl is a self-employed financial & tax consultant; Wilda an office manager; they live in Brea, CA.
+   449. ix. Harold Merwyn, b 24 March 1927.
     450. x. Ronald Darwyn, b 14 June 1929, at Lily, SD; he has epilepsy and lives in a nursing home at Bell Garden, California.
+   451. xi. Jon Henry, b 30 March 1931.
+   452. xii. Elizabeth Jane, b 18 July 1933.
+   453. xiii. Nancy Dawn, b 25 March 1939.

187. FLOY[5] VALANDA PECKHAM (d/o Charles W. Peckham #63), b 19 October 1900 at Webster, Day Co., SD. She m 4 November 1916 at Lily, SD, **Hugh Linley Robertson**, better known as "Smoke," b 30 November 1888 at Newton, IA, s/o Thomas and Mary (Whitney) Robertson. He signed his name Hughston on the marriage record. Smoke was a machinist and welder. He d 9 July 1968 at Citrus Heights, CA and is buried in Sylvan Cemetery at Citrus Heights. She lives next door to her daughter.

Children, surname ROBERTSON:
+   454. i. Maxine, b 22 February 1918.

188. ORVILLE[5] KENNETH PECKHAM (s/o Charles[4] W. Peckham #63), b 19 July 1907 at Webster, Day Co., SD. He says he is usually called O. K. Peckham. He m 1 June 1929 at Brookings, SD, **Evelyn Lenoi Olson**, d/o Ole and Eva (Ash) Olson, she b 17 February 1907 at Lily, Day Co., SD. They endured grasshoppers, then dust storms in SD so they moved to California on September 1933 in a broken down Hupmobile, taking 14 days. They only had 80¢ left when they arrived in Sacramento, CA. They went into a pawn shop and asked the owner if she wanted a typewriter, guitar, or banjo and she wanted the typewriter. She emptied her purse and gave them $7.60, as her money for the day was in the safe. They had left most of their money in a South Dakota bank. "O. K." bought a 5¢ bar of soap to clean up with and they had money for gas and all fresh fruit so the kids could eat. They stayed first with an aunt in Modesto. They moved to Sonora, CA in 1938, where Kenneth started the *Sonora Daily*. He sold the newspaper in 1958. Kenneth and Evelyn were divorced 4 May 1956 and she m Charles Wesley Daniel in Carson City 17 July 1965. She divorced him 25 May 1973 and when last known they both lived at Sonora.

Children, surname PECKHAM:
+ 455. i. Elwyn^6 Kay, b 5 December 1929.
+ 456. ii. Donna Jean, b 8 June 1931.
+ 457. iii. Elizabeth Jane, b 6 November 1932.
+ 458. iv. Charles Wesley, b 4 April 1935.

192. LELA^5 ELDORA PECKHAM (d/o William^4 H. Peckham #64), b 28 March 1896 at Marcellon Township, Columbia Co., WI; m 23 June 1915, in her father's home at Marcellon, **Harold Roberts Clark**; he b 9 August 1892 at Fort Winnebago Township, Columbia Co., WI, s/o Charles and Agnes (Rodger) Clark, Lela and Harold farmed his father's farm until they moved to Pardeeville, WI in 1947. He worked for the Columbia Co. Highway Department until he suffered a heart attack and died 16 May 1961. Lela d 31 January 1965. Both are buried at Moundville Cemetery Marquette Co., WI.

Children, surname PECKHAM:
+ 459. i. Carol^6 M., b 20 May 1917.
+ 460. ii. Norma Elaine, b 24 April 1921.
+ 461. iii. Beverly May, b 11 May 1929.

193. WILLIAM^5 EMERY PECKHAM (s/o William H. Peckham #64), b 20 March 1898 at Marcellon, Columbia Co., WI; m 8 March 1920, **Nettie Hanslin**, b about 1901, and still living at Waupun, WI when last known. William d 15 July 1944, age 46 years.

Children, surname PECKHAM
+ 462. i. Merlyn^6 Emery, b about 1922.
  463. ii. Morris William, b 26 March 1930 at Portage, WI.

195. EDNA^5 MARGARET POWELL (d/o Ann^4 Janette Powell #67), b 4 May 1890 at Bangor, LaCrosse Co., WI; m 1911, **George Walter Spratt** in Minneapolis, MN, he b 16 January 1891 at Mornoville, IL, s/o Oscar and Laura (Clowen) Spratt. He was sales manager for a rubber company in Eau Claire, WI; d 18 March 1939 at Eau Claire, 48 years old. Edna graduated from Lawrence University at Appleton, WI. The 1910 Census for Barron Co., WI, Town of Barron lists Edna with her family, age 19 and a teacher in a country school. She may have continued her teaching career in Minneapolis, since this was where she was married. Edna d 2 September 1978 at Eau Claire. She and Walter are buried in Forest Hill Cemetery, Eau Claire.

Children, surname SPRATT:
+   464. i. Mary^6 Ann, b 25 September 1915.
+   465. ii. William, b 6 September 1917.

200. DELIA^5 ANN ABEL (d/o Malinda^4 Phillips Abel #77), b 30 July 1887, probably at Wasioja, Dodge Co., MN. When she was about 17 years old her family moved to Webster, Burnett Co., WI where she m 7 October 1913, **Henry Kroeplin**, a farmer, b 10 June 1873, s/o John Louis and Sophia (Hindenburg) Kroeplin. Delia d 16 July 1939 in Burnett Co. and Henry d 17 September 1957 at Stanley, WI. Both buried at Oakland Cemetery, Stanley.

Children, surname KROEPLIN:
+   466. i. Edna^6 Sophie Ann, b 16 May 1914.
+   467. ii. Elmer Thomas John, b 24 October 1915.
+   468. iii. William Henry Frederick, b 23 June 1917.
+   469. iv. Henry Albert Neil, b 17 March 1921.
+   470. v. Emma Mary Annie, b 27 March 1923 at Danbury, WI; m 28 May 1977 at Stanley, WI, Harry Frederick Klein, s/o Henry and Margrite (Junk) Klein; b 1 September 1917 at Bellevue, IA; d 12 June 1987; Harry worked for John Deere in Dubuque, IA for 29 years retiring in 1976. He has four children by a former marriage.
+   471. vi. Palmer James Louis, b 5 April 1925.
    472. vii. Cora Malinda Matilda, b 16 December 1927 at Burnett Co.; m/1 Leon John Zasyezurynski; m/2 Ferris Shaffer; m/3 Chester Strack. In 1985 living in Chicago, IL, but has not answer my letters.

201. ESTINA^5 MAY ABEL (d/o Malinda^4 Phillips Abel #77), b 4 March 1890 at Wasioja, Dodge Co., MN, m 25 November 1909 in WI, **Charles**

Robie French, he b 21 October 1882 at Cameron, Steuben Co., NY, s/o John Flavel and Anna (Roff) French. They farmed in Wisconsin until 1924, when they moved to Dodge Center, Dodge Co. They farmed in rural West Concord for many years.

Charles d 19 February 1964 at West Concord, Dodge Co. Estina d 22 July 1983 at Dodge Center; both are buried at Wildwood Cemetery, Wasioja, Dodge Co.

Children, surname FRENCH;
+ 473. i. Bessie[6] Anna, b 15 December 1910.
+ 474. ii. Allen Flavel, b 19 August 1912.
+ 475. iii. Clara Alverette, b 25 October 1914.
+ 476. iv. Dorothy Belle, b 22 August 1917.
+ 477. v. Richard Andrew, b 1 August 1922.
+ 478. vi. Evelyn Mae, b 9 July 1927.
+ 479. vii. June Carol, b 14 June 1933.

202. THOMAS[5] MORGAN ABEL (s/o Malinda Phillips Abel #77), b 29 May 1892 at Wasioja, Dodge Co., MN; m/1 21 January 1915 at West Concord, MN, **Mabel Cartwright**, she b 10 March 1886 at Owatonna, MN, d/o Aaron and Rosabell (Kramer) Cartwright.

Thomas injured his knee in 1934 and was unable to farm after that. Then he worked at setting up (putting together) farm machinery, until he moved to California in 1943. Then he worked in a sawmill until he retired. Evidently Thomas and Mabel were divorced because he m a second time and Mabel didn't die until 12 April 1974, at Newberg, OR, probably at her son's home, and she is buried in Evergreen Memorial Park, McMinnville, OR.

Thomas m/2 Katherine Olena (Hayes) Culbert on 3 November 1923 at Chinook, MT, she b 28 February 1892, d/o Henry and Alice Caroline Hayes. Thomas d 27 June 1979 at Fortuna, Hombolt Co., CA. Katherine d 21 May 1982, and both are buried in Sunrise Cemetery, Fortuna.

Children, surname ABEL:
+ 480. i. Forrest[6] Edward, b 15 May 1916.
+ 481. ii. Helen May, b 18 November 1924.
+ 482. iii. Alice, b 10 May 1934.

203. LESTER[5] ROSS ABEL (s/o Malinda Phillips Abel #77), b 3

The Fifth Generation 157

December 1894 at Wasioja, Dodge Co., MN; m/1 10 August 1927 at Dodge Center, MN, **Bertha Irene Bennett**, b 14 April 1900 in Dodge Co., MN., d/o Daniel and Lottie Irene (Dudley) Bennett. He owned and operated a garbage business in Rochester, MN for many years before moving to Missouri. Bertha d 28 March 1949 at Owatonna, MN and is buried in Wildwood Cemetery, Wasioja, Dodge Co., MN. Bertha had one child before her marriage to Lester.

Lester Abel m/2 3 October 1949 at Stewartville, MN, **Dulsie Mae (House) Taylor**, she b 13 April 1899, d/o Lysander George and Pearl Eliza (Rhodes) House. She had previously been married to Fred Taylor and had four children: Nadine, Herbert, Floyd and John. Lester and Dulsie had no children. Lester d 21 February 1976 at Buffalo, Dallas Co., MO and is buried in Lindley Cemetery, Buffalo. Dulsie d 9 May 1983 in Dodge Center, MN and was cremated. Her daughter is keeping the ashes.

Children, surname ABEL:
- 483. i. Beth^6, b 8 March 19—, adopted by Lester; m Robert Nelson and had 12 Children; reportedly divorced and living in Rochester, MN.
- + 484. ii. James Daniel, b 3 September 1928.
- + 485. iii. Leonard Orlow, b 12 May 1931.

204. ETTA^5 MATILDA ABEL (d/o Malinda^4 Phillips Abel #77), b 16 December 1898 at Wasioja, Dodge Co., MN. The family moved to Danbury, Burnett Co., WI in 1906. She m 23 December 1916, **Lamont Adelbert Baker**, s/o Adelbert and Emma (Gay) Baker, he b about 1897. They made their home at Webster, Burnett Co. until Lamont's death in June 1924 at about 27 years of age, of a burst appendix. He is buried in Webster. The youngest child was about 9 months old, and Matilda went to live with her parents at Claremont, Dodge Co., MN.

Matilda d 4 February 1963 at Owatonna, Steele Co., MN at the home of her daughter-in-law, Esther Baker. She is buried at Wildwood Cemetery, Wasioja, Dodge Co.

Children, surname BAKER:
- + 486. i. Chester^6 L., b 16 December 1917.
- + 487. ii. Beatrice I., b 6 May 1919.
- + 488. iii. Lorraine A., b 11 September 1921.
- + 489. iv. Claudia L., b 1 September 1923.

205. ETHEL[5] LORILLA ABEL (d/o Malinda[4] Phillips Abel #77), b 25 November 1900 at Wasioja, Dodge Co., MN. She moved with her family to Danbury, Burnett Co., WI in 1906; m 15 January 1933, **Ingvard Wester**, s/o Jensen Christian and Kirsten (Nielsen) Wester, at Bennett, Douglas Co., WI; he b 14 December 1889 at Alsted Maro, Denmark. Ingvard worked for Great Northern Railroad. He d 17 December 1974 and is buried in Bennett Cemetery. When last known Ethel was still living at Bennett.

Children, surname WESTER:
+ 490. i. Donald[6], b 17 January 1934.
+ 491. ii. Phillip, b 19 March 1935.
+ 492. iii. Harry, b 7 March 1936.
+ 493. iv. Linda, b 8 September 1938.
+ 494. v. Victor, b 19 May 1941.
+ 495. vi. Leota, b 2 October 1942.

206 ALICE[5] MAY BOND (d/o Lorilla[4] Phillips Bond #78), b 21 May 1901 at Wasioja, MN; m July 1932 at Lake Nebagamon, WI, **Iver Otto Johnson**, b 21 February 1889 at Hawthorne, WI; he d 15 February 1979 at Superior, WI. Alice d 12 March 1983 at the same place. Iver was a farmer, carpenter, shoemaker and musician.

Children, surname JOHNSON:
+ 496. i. Ruth[6] Ann, b 19 May 1933.

207. ANNA[5] LAURA BOND (d/o Lorilla[4] Phillips Bond #78), b 26 May 1903 at Wasioja, MN; m 10 November 1928, **Richard White**, b 24 February 1905. Before their child was born, Richard left her. She worked for a number of years at Collins Produce in Dodge Center, MN. Later Richard returned, with a new family and under the name of Wesley Conant. He worked at the Mayo Clinic at Rochester, MN. He d April 1970 at Rochester; Anna d 5 August 1977 and is buried in Wildwood Cemetery, Wasioja.

Children, surname WHITE:
+ 497. i. Alice[6] Ivena, b 15 August 1929.

208. ETHEL[5] EDNA PHILLIPS (d/o Nelson[4] Ray Phillips #81), b 25 June 1910 at Garden Grove, CA; m 14 August 1930 at Riverside, CA, **Donald Eisenhauer**, he b 14 April 1909 at Los Angeles, CA, s/o Frank and Bessie (Curtiss) Eisenhauer. Donald was a pharmacist. He d 10 December 1974 at Los Angeles and is buried in Forest Lawn Memorial Park, Glendale, CA. Ethel was still living in Los Angeles when last known.

Children, surname EISENHAUER:
+   498.   i. Donald[6] Leslie, b 9 January 1933.
+   499.   ii. Patricia Jean, b 22 October 1935.

207. GRACE[5] AUSTIN (d/o Llewelyn[4] Austin #82), b 3 January 1894 at Licking, Texas Co., MO. In 1897 the family moved to Goshen Co., WY. She m 31 July 1913 at Wheatland, WY, **Leon Goodrich**. He was an architect. He d 17 December 1968 at Casper, WY. Grace d 30 August 1982 at Casper and both are buried in Highland Cemetery, Casper.

Children, surname GOODRICH:
+   500.   i. Anne[6], b 25 December 1929.
+   501.   ii. Jane, b 10 April 1934.

212. HARRY[5] AUSTIN McDANIEL (s/o Gertrude[4] Austin McDaniel #83), b 5 March 1898 at Naylor, Ripley Co., MO, in his grandmother Austin's home. Early in 1900 he moved with his mother to Chugwater, WY in Platte County, to join his father, who was working on the Whitcomb Ranch for the Swan Company.

Harry recalls the early morning spring roundups when the Swan Company crews of 100 to 120 men would ride as far north as Douglas and as far south as Colorado, rounding up the horses. There would always be a few orphaned colts in the herd that the children were allowed to bottle feed until they were old enough to run with the herd. When the four or five hundred head of horses were rounded up, each rancher would cut out those bearing his brand; the Whitcomb brand was the Two Bar (=).

One day his folks gave Harry a new pony and he was so elated over it that he rode out where the men were working to show it off. All the cowboys called his Dad "Mac," so he thought he would try to too. He called out, "Hi, Mac," which didn't set too well with his father at all, even resulting in a spanking.

In order to enjoy any fellowship or companionship, they had to travel many slow, bumpy miles. Harry recalls their loading everyone into the wagon for the long ride to a neighboring ranch for a night of dancing, visiting and eating. The children were bedded down while the grown-ups enjoyed the festivities until breakfast time when all enjoyed a hearty breakfast before climbing into the wagons for the long return home.

Harry and his sister Mabel attended poorly disciplined schools with sometimes three different teachers in one year. Harry recalls that he rode behind his teacher's saddle for the three and one half miles to school during one term.

When World War I started, Harry felt badly that all his friends were going to war and he couldn't because of his father's illness and death. He ran the Dray [Torrington, WY] and kept the Continental Bulk station for about a year. The Company would measure the tanks in Casper when they were hot and as they cooled enroute they would lose volume and the company would bill him on the Casper measurement. Harry finally grew weary of hassling with them over it and gave up the station.

Harry and Maud Avery Bright were married 22 December, 1920 at her parents home on London Flats. Maud was born 22 October 1894 near Fort Laramie, Goshen Co., Wyoming, daughter of Emery Ulysses and Vena (Kuhnast) Bright. Harry, with his mother and Don, was driving up from Torrington along the road that followed the ditch bank. They became firmly stuck in a snow bank and had to call for help. We had asked Rev. Mehaffey to marry us and he was at the farm when they called, so he went to their assistance. Finally, everyone was gathered for our dinner followed by the ceremony. For the occasion, Harry wore a blue serge suit and I was attired in a brown suit with two-toned brown high buttoned shoes.

Harry had a robe made of Rattler's hide [Rattler had been a favorite horse] in the car to keep us warm on our drive to Lingle to board the train for Denver. However, the weather was so bad that we stayed in Cheyenne a couple of days instead before returning to Mother McDaniel's. We had the east room upstairs and ate with her, paying rent and for half of the groceries. I continued teaching until the end of the term.

In the summer of 1923, Harry decided to go to Casper and find work in the booming oil industry. He went ahead and I remained in Torrington to sell the Dray Line before Roberta and I joined him. He worked at the Standard Oil Refinery pulling wax molds and later for the railroad round house as a mechanic. While he was working for the railroad a railroad car ran over his foot requiring surgery to repair the damage.

In March of that year I returned to Torrington, where our second daughter was born at Mother McDaniel's. In the spring of 1925 Harry decided to try farming so we returned to Torrington and moved our things to the Pruitt farm near Yoder. In the spring of 1926 Mr. Pruitt died and we were told that the place was up for sale, so Harry bought a relinquishment on a homestead nearby and we moved over there.

Harry rode the ditch and farmed with Uncle Billy and in the fall of 1926, he worked as tare man and I weighed beets at the dump on the Union Pacific Railroad.

This was the first year that the factory was open in Torrington and Tom Bracken was the field man for the Holly Sugar Company. I had to leave the children with a sitter.

I became critically ill after the birth of our daughter with childbirth fever; the doctor carried the fever from one new mother to another.

We moved into Grandma Austin's little house and Harry would go to work at the sugar factory. He worked for two years steady, then for 11 campaigns after that.

The struggles and depravity of the depression were compounded by the drought that hit us in '33. The winds would blow the dirt from the plowed field west of our house until the drifts would completely cover the yard fence. Although we stuffed old rags around the windows and hung wet sheets over them, we would still have drifts of sand sifted into the house. We would actually have to use a scoop shovel to pick up the sand and put it in buckets to carry out. On the bad days, the sun would be like a red ball through the black sky.

The drought killed most of the timber below the ditch and along the river banks and most of the trees around the house died out for lack of water. We did plant more in the yard and formed a bucket brigade to carry water from the well below the ditch when the yard pump was broken.

Harry farmed our place alone in the spring of 1934 and 1935 continuing to work at the factory during campaigns. Times were so bad during these dark days that it was all we could do to keep clothes on our backs. If it hadn't been for our chickens and garden we would have starved. It was a family joke that we had "eggs and potatoes" for one meal and "potatoes and eggs" for the next.

By the spring of 1936, Harry decided to give up the struggle to keep the farm since we were so heavily in debt. We let it go back to the loan company and, together with many others in our situation, lost everything we had. We moved to a rented house in Torrington and Harry did odd jobs, then for awhile took over custodial work at the United Presbyterian church.

Harry went out to Ogden, Utah to work at the Navy Supply Depot as a guard from March until December 1943. He then worked for the city of Torrington for six months. In 1944 he took the job of driving truck for Safeway Stores, which he continued until his retirement in 1963.

Harry d 29 June 1991 of Parkinson's Disease. Maud Bright McDaniel, who wrote the family account, died 22 June, 1984 in Torrington, WY. She is buried in Valley View Cemetery, Torrington, as is Harry.

Children, surname McDANIEL:
+ 502. i. Frances[6] Roberta, b 22 January 1922.

>   503. ii. Vena Margaret, b 22 March, 1924 at Torrington; m 24 December 1946 at Torrington, Thomas Wayne Runyan, s/o Thomas and Margie Obedience (Scott) Runyan, b 20 June 1927 at Texhoma, OK. Thomas Wayne is an electronic engineer and they lived at Spring Valley, CA until moving to Loveland, CO. They have no children. Vena is the author of *And Now the Golden Years*, an account of early Austins, cited extensively above. See Addenda.
> + 504. iii. Ward Emery, b 23 September 1925.
> + 505. iv. Betty Jo, b 25 January 1928.
>   506. v. Robert Austin, b 11 August 1929 at Scottsbluff, NE. He is a retired Professor from Michigan University at Lansing now living in Boulder, CO.

213. MABEL[5] MARGARET McDANIEL (d/o Gertrude[4] Austin McDaniel #83), b 3 September 1902 at Chugwater, Platte Co., WY; m 5 March 1924, **Thomas Earl "Duke" Robertson** at Carter Lake, IA, he b 6 July 1901 at Gering, NB, s/o Asahal (Ace) B. and Mary (Sandercook) Robertson. Their old minister friend, Rev. Mehaffey, was living in Omaha at the time and they wanted him to marry them. When they arrived, they found that some legal technicality kept them from being married in Nebraska, so they went across the line to Mr. Mehaffey's brother's home for the ceremony. Duke was working at the Penny Store in Independence, KS at this time so they went there to make their home. Later they lived in Windsor, Brush, Longmont and Denver, CO. "Duke" d 13 May 1988; Mabel d in Aurora, CO 14 February 1991. She is buried at Littleton, CO.

Children, surname ROBERTSON:
> + 507. i. Thomas[6] Earl, b 7 March 1925.
> + 508. ii. Mary Gertrude, b 11 September 1928.

216. HARRY[5] AMES AUSTIN (s/o Willis[4] Austin #86), b 16 February 1907 at Wheatland, Platte Co., WY. He moved with his family from Chugwater, WY to Torrington, WY in 1909. He went to the University of Wyoming at Laramie, WY two years, fall of 1927 to spring of 1929, when he had to quit to earn a living. He became a field man for Holly Sugar Company, in the spring of 1934 at Hawk Springs. Just before that on 26 February 1934 he m Alice Guthrie at Scottsbluff, NE, b 7 October 1907 at Platteville, CO, d/o James B. and Edith Harriet (Smith) Guthrie. After being laid off from the Sugar Company, in the fall of 1939 he tried farming and real estate, but didn't like either. Then they moved to Cheyenne, WY where he worked briefly for the Union Pacific Railroad, installing boilers on locomotives. During the war he went to San Diego, CA and got a tacking job in Solar Aircraft. He learned welding in high school and did gas and atomic-hydrogen welding on stainless steel until July 1945, when it became necessary to join a union; he went back to Cheyenne, where he worked for Wyoming Highway Patrol, setting and administering driver's license act. Later he was Chief Clerk, Fiscal Agent, Chief of Radio Communications, was Governor Milward L. Simpson's chauffeur for two years, and set up budgets to run the Patrol. When the Highway Department obtained a computer, he learned to be a programmer, and wrote programs for the Patrol. He retired from the Patrol 2 March 1972 and purchased a travel trailer and he and Alice lived in Arizona in the winter and Cheyenne in the summer from then until her death 11 June 1980 in Cheyenne. She is buried in Riverside Cemetery, Denver, CO, in her Grandfather Smith's lot. Harry is still living in Cheyenne.

Children, surname AUSTIN:
+ 509. i. Joyce[6], b 20 February 1937.
+ 510. ii. Robert Ames, b 26 September 1944.

217. MARJORIE[5] RUTH AUSTIN (d/o Willis[4] Austin #86), b 15 June 1923 at Yoder, Goshen Co., WY. She lived with her family on the farm at Yoder until she was about sixteen, in 1939, when they moved to Cheyenne. She m 7 February 1948 at Kimball, NE, **James Bertil Olson**, s/o Verner and Ada (Norling) Olson, he b 14 April 1922 at Lindsborg, KS. They lived in Texas from 1958 to 1964, moved to Colorado in 1964, then returned to Texas in 1977, where they now live in Harlingen. In 1983 James retired after working in the construction industry for 42 years. Marjorie was employed as secretary for 7 years while living in Fort Collins, CO and ever since 1981 in Texas.

Children, surname OLSON:
- 511. i. John[6] B., b 18 July 1953 at Cheyenne, WY; m 19 December 1982 at Austin, TX. Dianne Rathgeber, d/o Edward Richard and Esther L. (Kiesschnick) Rathgeber, b 9 April 1953 at Vernon, TX. John is a construction sheet metal worker; Dianne is a Real Estate Secretary; living in Port Isabel, TX. They have no known children.
- 512. ii. Marcelle R., b 10 January 1956 at Cheyenne, WY; m 31 March 1974 at Greeley, CO. Ronnie Lee Garison, s/o Gerald Kenneth and Wilma Jean (Hart) Garison, b 21 March 1948 at Lakeport,

CA; Ron is a carpet layer; they live in Green River, WY; no known children.

218. JULIA[5] MAE CATES (d/o Emma[4] Donnelly Cates #87) b 7 September 1888 at Aspen, CO; m 28 September 1907 in Grand Junction, **Thomas Jefferson Rogers**, (s/o Robert Bruce and Elizabeth (Mathis) Rogers) b 18 March 1872 at Waynesville, NC; d 5 June 1957 at his cabin in Jack's Canyon, Unaweep, Mesa Co., CO according to his death certificate, of self-inflicted gunshot wound through the chest. He was listed as a farmer. Julia, more commonly known as "May," d 13 May 1962 at Teller Arms Nursing Home; both are buried at Orchard Mesa Cemetery, Grand Junction, CO.

Children, surname ROGERS:

+ 513. i. Gladys[6], b 20 May 1911.
+ 514. ii. Elsie, b about 1919.
    515. iii. George, b about 1922 at Grand Junction; m 20 June 1940 Julia Hooker. Hale Tognoni says he, George, came to Eureka, Nevada, where the Tognoni's lived, and worked as a highway maintenance man just before WW II; he was drafted, went to the Philippine Islands, was killed in action 22 May 1944. There were no children.
+ 516. iv. Elizabeth Jane, b about 1929.
+ 517. v. Margery W., b 29 April 1931.
    518. vi. Helen, b in Grand Junction; m a Pierson. She may live in Las Vegas, FL; the family has lost touch with her.

219. WILLIAM[5] HENRY CATES (s/o Emma Donnelly Cates #87), born 18 September 1895 at Aspen, CO. He m 16 June 1916 at Ely, NV **Lydia Bruno**, d/o Anthony and Lucy Martha (Bradley) Bruno. According to Neva Brown, William Cates became a Bishop in the Mormon Church. Lydia b 15 February 1897 at Nephi, Juab Co., Utah. He farmed in Preston, Nevada and hauled freight to Ruth and Ely before 1930. About 1930–35 he worked on U.S. Highway 6; during 1941–49 at the Kennecott Copper Mines, Kimberly, NV; during 1950–59 at Kennecott Copper Mines, McGill, NV. William d 4 February 1966 at Ely, NV and Lydia d 16 February 1966 at Las Vegas, NV; both are buried at Ely.

Children, surname CATES:

+ 519. i. Lucy[6] Margaret, b 26 March 1917.
+ 520. ii. Emma Esther, b 31 March 1919.

+   521. iii. Arlina (Aroline) Bell, b 23 November 1920.
+   522. iv. Willetta, b 6 June 1922.
+   523. v.   Deloris Jane, b 6 February 1924.
+   524. vi. Sylvia Joy, b 25 February 1926.
+   525. vii. June, b 17 June 1928.
+   526. viii. Gordon Bruno, b 30 March 1930.
+   527. ix. Geneil, b 24 July 1933.

220. JESSIE[5] ANNA CATES (d/o Emma[4] Donnelly Cates #87), b 3 June 1897 at Aspen, CO; m **Gerald Crawford**. They lived in Bishop, Inyo Co., CA, where Gerard ran a trucking company. There are no additional record of him. Jessie d 22 June 1952, age 55, at Bishop, CA and is buried in Bishop Pioneer Cemetery.

Children, surname CRAWFORD:
   528. i. Jessie[6]. She married an — Ernst; her last known address was Venice, CA.
   529. ii. Gerard N., b 2 June 1925; d 13 September 1971.

221. INA[5] BELLE CATES (d/o Emma[4] Donnelly Cates #87), b 25 September 1898 at Aspen, CO; m 26 February 1916, **Joseph Russell Tognoni** at Goldfield, Esmeralda Co., NV, b 23 February 1889 at Duckwater, NV, s/o Joseph Christopher and Jesse Myrtle (Jacques) Tognoni. Joseph's father was born in Naples, Italy and migrated to Nevada in 1880, taking the surname Tognoni from the name of his mountain village in Italy.

He started the Monte Carlo Stock Farm in Duckwater Valley and struggled many years to gain water rights in this arid region. Joseph Christopher, as did other ranchers, moonlighted in the mountains as prospector. His first claim was in 1903 at the Goldfield District near Tonopah. A protracted illness in Tonopah caused him to lose his claim through lack of assessment work. The ranch was heavily mortgaged to buy prospecting and mining equipment and was foreclosed in 1921. During this time he developed a silver mine at Silverton.

Joseph Russell Tognoni was not a strong man, and died 27 February 1934, age 45, at Eureka, NV and buried at Silverton. After Joseph Christopher's death in the 1930s, Ina's mother-in-law Myrtle took possession of the mine in Silverton. She planted her rocking chair on the front porch of their house, built on black lava, looking out onto broad, white salt flats of Railroad Valley and the blue granite mountain range rising steeply out of the sage brush. Here she guarded the claim for her children and grandchildren for the next six years. She buried her husband, Joseph Christopher and son, Joseph Russell there.

The Togroni family still owns the claim to the Silverton Mine, for sentimental reasons, and hoping the value of silver may increase someday. Her grandson, Hale Tognoni, in early years spent time there working on the claim, to retain the family rights. Hale says now the claim is leased to Inspiration Gold Co.; they are drilling for silver and gold.

Ina Tognoni served as postmaster in Gold Hill during World War II and delivered mail on contract to mountain ranches around Eureka. She married again in 1945, to **Leslie R. Conway**. Ina d 30 August 1959 at Phoenix, Arizona and she, too, is buried in the graveyard at the Silverton Mine between Ely and Tonapah, NV.

Children, surname TOGNONI:
+   530.   i.   Nye[6] Woodrow, b 28 November 1917.
+   531.   ii.   Neva June, b 23 October 1919.
+   532.   iii.   Hale Christopher, b 16 April 1921.
+   533.   iv.   Robert Louis, b 19 March 1925.

222. HAROLD[5] ARTHUR REED (s/o Arthur[4] J. Reed #88), b 10 July 1897 at Menominee, MI; m/1 24 July 1918, **Pearl Young**, d/o Graham and Augusta (Procknow) Young, b 13 March 1892 at Gillett, Oconto Co., WI. Harold was a farmer for 28 years before moving into Gillett. He was elected Sheriff of Oconto Co., WI in 1954, after several years as Undersheriff, and served two terms, or four years, in that capacity. Pearl d just after he was elected Sheriff, on 31 October 1954, in Gillett. She is buried in Wanderer's Rest Cemetery, Gillett, WI.

On 29 December 1956 Harold m/2 **Florence S. Dunton**, d/o Cornelius and Mary Ann (Allcox) Serier, she b 28 February 1902 at Suring, WI. Florence was Oconto County Register of Deeds. Harold d 30 May 1972 at Gillett and is also buried in Wanderer's Rest Cemetery.

Children, surname REED:
    534.   i.   Glynn[6], b 4 November 1919, d in 1948.
+   535.   ii.   Gertrude E., b 11 October 1920.
+   536.   iii.   Gordon Elmer, b 11 October 1920.

223. GERTRUDE[5] MARY ETTA WRIGHT (d/o Jennie[4] Reed Wright

#89), b 15 October 1891 at Seymour, Owtagamie Co., WI. She was named for her grandmother Marietta Reed. She moved out to Snohomish, WA in 1910 to live with her father, Clark Wright, who had left the family when she was young. Her boyfriend, **Henry Beekman**, followed her to Washington and they were married at Snoqualmie Falls, WA, 25 January 1910. Henry was b 24 January 1887 at Oconto, WI, s/o Jacob and Elizabeth (DeLowe) Beekman. Henry was engaged in logging and blacksmithing. He d 31 May 1956, age 69, at Anaconda, MT where they lived many years, and is buried in Sunset Memorial Park, Anaconda, MT. Gertrude died at age 99 on 6 May 1991.

Children, surname BEEKMAN:

537. i. Beatrice[5] May, b 10 May 1910 at Snohomish, m 21 December 1932, Frank Fessler, s/o Wilbur Nicholas and Flora Etta Fessler, b 13 Aug 1892, Iowa. They had no children. He owned his own trucking business and hauled ore for the Trout Gold Mines at Phillipsburg, MT. He died 12 Feb 1967 at Hamilton, MT; Beatrice d 4 May 1967 at Anaconda; both are buried at Phillipsburg.

538. ii. Royal Buhel, b 9 June 1912 at Everett, WA; he d 28 September 1914.

539. iii. Elmer Dewey, b 16 August 1913 at Nelson Gulch, Deer Lodge Co., MT. He worked at Anaconda Copper Mines and later worked a ranch. He lives at Philipsburg and is unmarried.

+ 540. iv. Geneva Viola, b 31 December 1916, d 24 Jan 1988.

225. NELLIE[5] BEATRICE WRIGHT (d/o Jennie[4] Reed Wright #89), b 29 February 1896 at Seymour, Outagamie Co., WI. When a young woman she left Seymour for Illinois to do housework for wealthy families. Here she met her husband, **Oscar Wennell**, s/o Peter and Caroline Wennell, and they were married 4 March 1916. Oscar was b 30 January 1888 at Regno, Sweden. They lived in Evanston, IL, where Oscar was a machinist, working for Clayton Mark Steel Company. Nellie d 4 December 1958 at Evanston and Oscar d 27 September 1967 in Portland, OR, while living with George Wright; they are buried in Memorial Park Cemetery, Evanston.

Children, surname WENNELL:

+ 541. i. Mary Caroline, b 14 May 1919.
+ 542. ii. Hazel Jennie, b 3 April 1921.

226. IRENE[5] **ORPHA WRIGHT** (d/o Jennie[4] Reed Wright #89), b 5 June 1898 at Seymour, Outagamie Co., WI. She m/1 **James Carey**. Later divorced him. She m/2 about 1925 **John Norman Thompson**, s/o John and Eliza (Johnson) Thompson, he b 27 September 1890 and d 15 July 1970. He is buried in Jeradin Cemetery, Gonzales, FL. Irene d May 1960 at Mena, AR and is buried in the Jeradin Cemetery. Irene m/3 **Elston Thompson**, brother of John, in 1954 at Colorado Springs, CO.

Children, surname CAREY:
+   543. i. Tony[6] James, b 28 July 1921.
+   544. ii. June Adeline, b 29 October 1925.

Children, surname THOMPSON:
+   545. iii. John[6] Norman, b 4 February 1927.
    546. iv. Marion Robert, b 23 December 1937, Roberts, FL
    547. v. Mary Louise, b 24 December 1937, Roberts.

227. THOMAS[5] **MARTIN WRIGHT** (s/o Jennie[4] Reed Wright #89), b 17 November 1901 at Seymour, Outagamie Co., WI. He m 27 January 1926 at Saint Mary's Catholic Church, Iron Mountain, MI, **Margaret Eva Lake**, d/o John and Theresa (Reidenger) Lake. They farmed all their life at Suring, WI. Tom died November 1990.

Children, surname WRIGHT:
+   548. i. Clarice[6] Eva, b 17 June 1926.
+   549. ii. Lylis Margaret, b 20 December 1928.
+   550. iii. Dalores Dorothy, b 9 April 1929.
+   551. iv. Eugene Thomas, b 14 October 1930.
    552. v. Janet, b 20 March 1933. She was b with bronchial pneumonia and died a week later.
    553. vi. Alice, b 6 November 1936; died 27 February 1937.
    554. vii. Robert Herman, b 13 March 1939 at Suring, WI; m 24 June 1978 at Saint Michael's Catholic Church, Suring, WI, Judith Ann Carroll, d/o George Francis and Lillian May (Handlin) Carroll, b 16 December 1943 at Uniontown, PA. He ia a construction worker and when last known had no children.
+   555. viii. Thomas Martin, b 9 July 1941.
+   556. ix. Patricia Ann, b 30 December 1947.

228. ANGELINE[5] **IRENE REED** (d/o Fred Reed #90), b 28 December 1895 at Town of Maple Valley, Oconto Co., WI; m 28 May 1913, **Lars**

The Fifth Generation

Christian Johnson, s/o Lars Christian Phillipson and wife Karen (Peterson) Phillipson. Lars' father was swept overboard from the ship he was working on in the North Sea. Karen brought her son Lars to America and kept house for her brother, Rasmus Peterson, in Town of Spruce and Kelly Brook. She later married John C. Johnson, who adopted Lars and gave him his surname. Lars was a life-long farmer. Lars was b 25 January 1891 in Copenhagen, Denmark. He d 14 December 1976 at Bismark, ND, while visiting his daughter Laurel Herick. While raising a large family, Angeline was active in their church, Our Redeemer Lutheran Church in Maple Valley and taught a Sunday School class for 35 years. She d 13 April 1972 at Green Bay, WI; both are buried at Hickory Cemetery, Hickory Corners, WI.

Children, surname JOHNSON:
+ 557. i. Wilma^6 Fern, b 3 October 1914.
+ 558. ii. Lars Christian, b 31 January 1916.
+ 559. iii. Ronald Eugene, b 9 May 1918.
+ 560. iv. Kenneth Leroy, b 12 February 1920.
+ 561. v. Clyde Lyle, b 2 January 1922.
+ 562. vi. Neva Angeline, b 28 October 1923.
+ 563. vii. Mae Carolyn, b 16 November 1924.
+ 564. viii. Dora Jeanette, b 23 December 1925.
+ 565. ix. Audrey Dorothea, b 28 July 1928.
+ 566. x. Virgil Arling, b 9 March 1930.
+ 567. xi. Beverly June, b 8 September 1932.
+ 568. xii. Laurel Gay, b 29 July 1934.
+ 569. xiii. Dale Raymond, b 21 January 1938.

230. VICTOR^5 RICHARD VERWEY (s/o Julia^4 Reed Verwey #91), b 2 April 1900 at Appleton, WI. He m 15 October 1925 at Zion Lutheran Church, Appleton, **Laura C. Rohde**, d/o Paul and Anna (Post) Rohde, she b 8 April 1900 at Appleton. Laura d 25 April 1956 at Appleton, and is buried at Highland Memorial Park Cemetery, Appleton. Victor was a wire anealer at Appleton Wire Works. As of 1983 he was confined at a nursing home in Little Chute, WI as the result of a stroke.

Children, surname VERWEY:
+ 570. i. Gloria^6 Ann, b 2 January 1928.

231. VERNA^5 VERWEY (d/o Julia^4 Reed Verwey #91), b 16 April 1903 at Appleton, WI. She married about 1924 at Gillett, WI, **Roy Paulsen**, s/o Christopher and Lena (Christiansen) Paulsen, both parents born in Copenhagen, Denmark. He was b 22 September 1896 at Denmark, Wisconsin. Roy and Verna were divorced about 1955 and Verna lives in Green Bay, WI. Roy d 4 August 1967 at Green Bay and is buried in Highland Memorial Cemetery, Appleton, WI. Roy was a railroad employee, as building and bridge foreman.

Children, surname PAULSEN:
+ 571. i. Harold^6 R., b 25 January 1925.
+ 572. ii. June Ione, b 7 May 1926.
+ 573. iii. Lois Elaine, b 3 July 1927.

237. EMERALD^5 DeWITT REED (s/o DeWitt^4 Reed #93), b 18 April 1909 at Hickory, WI. He m 29 September 1934 at Waukegan, IL, **Leona Bashina**, d/o Frank And Bertha (Schiding) Bashina, b 12 February 1914 at Timber lake, SD. They lived a number of years in Rogers, AR, where they were in the Real Estate business. They are retired now and live on a farm at Breed, WI in the Gillett area.

Children, surname REED:
+ 574. i. Vincent^6, b 7 July 1935.
   575. ii. Sidney, b 24 November 1936 at Brookfield, WI. He is not married.
+ 576. iii. Rosalie, b 5 December 1937.

238. ALFRED^5 MICHAEL REED (s/o DeWitt^4 Reed #93), b 10 March 1911 in Town of Spruce, Oconto Co., WI. He m 30 May 1939 at Suring, WI, **Emily Hulda Shuettpelz**, d/o Carl and Matilda (Nitzband) Shuettpelz, b 5 April 1919 in Town of How, Oconto Co., WI. Alfred had 97 holstein milk cows on a 360 acre farm with 65 additional acres rented. The barn burned August 1981, and a new barn was built with "free stall and parlor." Alfred and Emily now live in a different house away from the farm, at Hintze, and the sons, Wayne and David work the farm.

Children, surname REED:
+ 577. i. Marvin^6 Lee, b 18 June 1939.
+ 578. ii. Warren James, b 7 December 1940.
+ 579. iii. Marcella Mae, b 22 October 1942.
+ 580. iv. Norma Jean, b 9 July 1945.
+ 581. v. Alfred Allen, b 12 July 1946.

The Fifth Generation 171

+ 582. vi. Wayne Carl, b 3 October 1947.
   583. vii. David Dewitt, b 2 May 1951 at Oconto Falls; m 28 September 1974 at Saint James Lutheran Church, Shawano, WI. Judy Flaig, d/o Edward H. and Deloris L. (Utke) Flaig, b 15 March 1951 at Shawano; they live near Alfred.
+ 584. viii. Beverly Ann, b 3 November 1956.
+ 585. ix. Barbara Sue, b 10 January 1957.
+ 586. x. Lorna Joy, b 17 February 1960.

239. WALLACE[5] CLEMET REED (s/o Dewitt[4] Reed #93), b 14 May 1913 at Town of Spruce, Oconto Co., WI. He m 30 October 1937 at Christian Church, Hickory, WI, **Freda Rose Vorpahl**, d/o Edmund John and Elizabeth (Grams) Vorpahl, b 16 October 1918 in Town of Underhill, Oconto Co., WI. Wallace was a farmer and logger until his retirement.

Children, surname REED:
+ 587. i. Vivian[6] Ann, b 6 June 1938.
+ 588. ii. Wallace James, b 22 February 1940.
+ 589. iii. Philip Edmund, b 1 April 1942.
+ 590. iv. Stanley Dewitt, b 15 February 1943.
+ 591. v. Valerie Joyce, b 30 March 1945.
+ 592. vi. Maureen Martha, b 2 March 1947.
+ 593. vii. Dwight Dale, b 27 August 1951.
+ 594. viii. Colleen Kay, b 5 January 1956.

240. RAYMOND[5] EDGAR REED (s/o DeWitt[4] Reed #93), b 13 December 1914 at Town of Spruce, Oconto Co., WI. He m/1 **Eva Hetts**, who divorced him during World War II. He m/2 **Irma Jean Burdeau**, 20 July 1946 in Milwaukee, WI. Ray had his own cement construction company in Milwaukee. Later he bought and sold lots at Lakewood, Oconto Co., WI. He moved to Rogers, AR and bought a boat dock, which he later sold after two years. They still live in Arkansas, are retired, when last known. Ray and Irma had one child of their own and three adopted children.

Children, surname REED:
+ 595. i. Sylvan[6], b 5 February 1951.
   596. ii. Virginia, adopted daughter. In 1968 she married Paul Orlando.
   597. iii. Tom, adopted son.
   598. iv. Lynelle, adopted daughter who married on 29 May 1982 Richard

A. Sandon.

241. JUNE[5] ANNA MARIETTA REED (d/o DeWitt[4] Reed #93) b 1 July 1918 at Town of Spruce, Oconto Co., WI. She m 23 September 1935 in Shawano, WI, **Clyde Gust Schroeder**, s/o Gust and Bessie (Wilson) Schroeder, b 27 August 1911 in Town of Underhill, Oconto Co., WI. Clyde had a farm of 360 acres, some in swamp and good stands of hardwood. He retired and rented out his land. He would upon occasion render a concert of old time tunes on his mouth organ. Clyde died suddenly 30 May 1983 at his home at Gillett, WI. June remembers when she was a child her mother took the backs out of two of her father's black and white checked shirts and made her an underskirt which she wore all winter. June lives in Shawano, WI now.

Children, surname SCHROEDER:
+ 599. i. Donna[6] Rae, b 2 April 1937.
+ 600. ii. Vernon Clyde, b 16 April 1940.

242. NORMA[5] MAE REED (d/o DeWitt[4] Reed #93), b 7 May 1921 at Town of Spruce, Oconto Co., WI. She m/1 at Milwaukee, WI, 9 March 1937, **Cecil Siegel**, b about 1911, s/o John and Ella Siegel; Norma divorced Cecil and m/2 **Aldo Kuhn** 8 December 1962 at Wautoma, WI. Norma and Aldo live at Wautoma, WI.

Children, surname SIEGEL:
+ 601. i. Raymond[6] Cecil, b 21 February 1938.
+ 602. ii. Jordan Lee, b 21 August 1939.
+ 603. iii. Sandra Jane, b 25 October 1944.

243. ILENE[5] RUTH REED (d/o DeWitt[4] Reed #93), b 22 April 1925 at Town of Spruce, Oconto Co., WI. She m 28 June 1943, **Ralph Clayton Hawkins**, s/o George and Artie (Name) Hawkins, he b 12 July 1921 at Warsaw, IN. Ralph d 10 May 1971. Ilene m/2 — Fazenden. She died 2 October 1990 and is buried in Hickory Cemetery.

Children, surname HAWKINS:
+ 604. i. Ralph[6] George, b 5 March 1945.
+ 605. ii. Gale Michael, b 13 August 1946.
+ 606. iii. Linda June, b 6 January 1948.
+ 607. iv. Robert Carl, b 26 May 1949.

244. ARNOLD[5] JAMES REED, known as "Whitey" (s/o DeWitt[4] Reed

#93) b 28 April 1927, at Gillett, WI. He m 2 July 1949 in Milwaukee, WI, **Audrey Ethel Becker**, d/o Alfred Fredric John and Margaret Emma (Keipper) Becker, b 29 November 1926 at Milwaukee. Arnold was employed in construction 32 years in Milwaukee, where they lived until 1979 when they returned to the Gillett area and built a home. The house burned February 1980 and they rebuilt it. Arnold was working in logging for Vernon Schroeder until he became ill with cancer; after a long fight he d 4 July 1986.

Children, surname REED:
- 608. i. Janice[6] Margaret, b 22 January 1950 at Milwaukee; she is an elementary school teacher in Milwaukee and a reading specialist. She is not married.
- + 609. ii. Ronald James, b 9 December 1950.
- + 610. iii. Joyce Lynn, b 1 January 1953.
- + 611. iv. Jayne Marie, b 2 April 1955.
- 612. v. Janine Ann, b 24 August 1962, at Milwaukee; m 21 May 1983 Todd Johnson, b August 1951; secretary at the *Milwaukee Journal*.
- 613. vi. Joanne May, b 18 November 1963, at Milwaukee.
- 614. v. Roger Allan, b 19 April 1967 at Milwaukee.

245. RUSSELL[5] SADELL REED (s/o Roy[4] Reed #94), b 31 May 1908 at Hickory Corners, Oconto Co., WI. He m 14 June 1930 at Racine, WI, **Ruby Blanche Coryell**, d/o Charles and Martha Jane (Ingle) Coryell, b 6 December 1911 at Caldwell, KS. Russell was a farmer. Ruby d 4 June 1977. Since then Russell lives in Racine, spending his summers at his camp at Anderson Lake at Mountain, WI.

Children Surname REED:
- + 615. i. Ruth[6], b 29 April 1931.
- + 616. ii. Russell, 3 October 1933.
- 617. iii. Charles, b 20 November 1935; he d 4 September 1959, in an automobile accident and was never married.
- + 618. iv. Jaqueline Jane, b 5 November 1937.
- + 619. v. Darla, b 10 February 1940.
- + 620. vi. Judith, b 15 May 1949.

246. RUBY[5] BLANCHE REED (d/o Roy[4] Reed #94), b 29 August 1909 at Appleton, WI. She m 18 June 1929 in Ilinois, **Wayne John Nygard**, adopted son of Victor Nygard, Wayne's original surname being Erickson.

Wayne worked for Banta Publishing Company for 34 years. They lived in Menasha, WI. Ruby d 24 August 1966 at Menasha and Wayne d 19 July 1966 at Neenah, WI.

Children, surname NYGARD:

+ 621. i. Delores, b 5 February 1930.

247. MILDRED[5] AGNES REED (d/o Roy[4] Reed #94), b 26 January 1911 at Maple Valley, Oconto Co., WI. She m 19 April 1930 at Chicago, IL, at the office of Church of Epiphany (Episcopal) **Raymond Charles Erickson**, s/o Charles A. and Hilma (Anderson) Erickson, b 4 June 1907 at Chicago, IL. His father was born in Dalsland, Sweden. Raymond was blind a number of years before his death 29 January 1981 at Wausau, WI, where Mildred still lives, when last known.

Children, surname ERICKSON:

+ 622. i. Jean[6] Mildred, b 18 January 1931.
+ 623. ii. William Charles, b 13 June 1932.
+ 624. iii. Janet Marie, b 27 November 1943.

248. VERNA[5] BULLOCK (d/o Effie[4] Reed Bullock #95), b 27 June 1970, Foss, Wisconsin. She m/1 — **Adel**; m/2 1924 **Joe Snyder**; m/3 **Charles LeBaron** 2 August 1933, he b 23 October 1898. She was married to him about 25 years; he dropped dead. She m/4 **Ace Carl Brooks**, b 9 October 1911. He d 26 February 1976 and is buried in Sarasota Memorial Park. Verna was already married to Joe Snyder, when the family left Wisconsin for Florida, so she didn't go with them then. She later joined the family in Sarasota, FL when she was married to Charles LeBaron. She now lives in Sarasota, but does not see the family.

Children, surname SNYDER:

625. i. John[6] A., b 23 July 1925 at Jamestown, NY. Marietta Springman says John was inspector for Marlin Rockwell Corp. more than 26 years. Reportedly married late in life to a woman who had children. He d 9 December 1975 at Jamestown, and is buried in Lakeview Cemetery, Jamestown.

249. DELLA[5] ELSIE BERDINE BULLOCK (d/o Effie[4] Reed Bullock #95), b 7 September 1909 at Lynchburg, VA. She m 27 June 1935 at Bradenton, FL, **Carroll Lee Martin**, s/o William E. and Phoebe (Fiveash) Martin, b 17 February 1905 at Hahira, Lownes Co., GA. Della and Carroll farmed between Adel and Nashville, GA, where both children were born.

Carroll worked as a painter in shipyards at Panama City, FL during World War II, and later the same work at North Madison, OH. Later they ran a chicken farm near Quitman, GA, from 1948–1965, and maintained a large delivery route for eggs. Then together they ran in turn two different 7–11 stores in Valdosta, GA, then two motels in the same area. They lived in Quitman, GA from about 1972 until 1983 when Carroll wanted to travel more after they sold their home.

Children, surname MARTIN
+   626.   i.   Louise^6, b 2 April 1939.
+   627.   ii.   Forrest Lee, b 7 September 1940.

250. ELMER^5 OSCAR BULLOCK (s/o Effie^4 Reed Bullock #95), b 13 May 1912 at Lynchburg, VA. He m 15 June 1943 at Madison, OH, **Mae Martin**, d/o Bert and Mary (McDermott) Martin, b 26 January 1921 at Barton, FL. Elmer was a house painter. He d 12 December 1971. When last known Mae was still living Sarasota, FL.

Children, surname BULLOCK:
+   628.   i.   Peggy^6, b 19 January 1945.
     629.   ii.   Richard, b 19 January 1947, Sarasota. He is a paraplegic and never married.
+   630.   iii.   Bonnie, b 29 May 1948.

251. MARIETTA^5 ELEANORE BULLOCK (d/o Effie^4 Reed Bullock #95), b 2 September 1915 at Appleton, WI. Marietta was 10 years old when the family moved to Florida. She m 16 May 1936 at Sarasota, FL, **Otto Springman**, s/o Johann Georg and Friederike (Keck) Springman, he born 22 November 1906 at Lossburg, Germany. He was a successful building contractor, first at Bradenton for 14 years, then in the Sarasota area, where he built many houses. He d 7 January 1977 at Sarasota and is buried in Palm Memorial Cemetery, Fruitville, FL. Marietta lives a very active life in Sarasota.

Children, surname SPRINGMAN:
+   631.   i.   Sandra^6 Lorraine, b 4 October 1941.
     632.   ii.   Paul, b 19 January 1945 at Sarasota; m/1 Martha —; she left him before their first anniversary to take care of her sick mother and never returned; m/2 24 November 1976 Carolee Christian, d/o Robert and Barbara Christian, b 20 September 1954; they are divorced and no children. When last known Paul was working for Florida Power and Light Co., as lineman.

252. CHESTER[5] **JESSE BULLOCK** (s/o Effie[4] Reed Bullock #95), b 18 September 1919 at Irma, Lincoln Co., WI, in a log cabin; his parents were homesteading there then. He m 18 June 1942 **Betty Carpenter**, d/o Paul and Virgie (Robinson) Carpenter, b 19 September 1924 at Anastin, AL. Chester is a painting contractor in the Sarasota, FL area.

Children, surname BULLOCK:
+   633.   i.   Ronald[6], b 25 August 1945.
+   634.   ii.   Gary, b 4 February 1949.
       635.   iii.   Gail, b 22 April 1953 at Sarasota; m Dale Reichard, b 10 May 1955. Divorced.
       636.   iv.   Steven, b 9 March 1959. He is not married.

253. MILDRED[5] **DESILVA WADLEY** (d/o Pearl[4] Wadley #96), b 14 February 1894 at Chicago, IL. She m **Ford Everitt**, s/o Malanthken and Ida (Corbett) Everitt, b 7 March 1890 at Payne, OH. Mildred was killed in an automobile accident 28 May 1975 and she is buried at Clear Lake, CA. Ford d 10 March 1945 at San Francisco, CA and his ashes were scattered outside the Golden Gate.

Children, surname EVERITT:
       637.   i.   Lee[6], b 6 August 1912: m 16 April 1955, Martha Pauline Rieumes, b Reimes, France, 19 April 1927; Lee a retired as skipper of an Army Corps of Engineers dredge ship, d 1990.
       638.   ii.   Irma Jean, b 23 December 1913; m 1/Lyman Johnson; m/2 Hank —; m/3 Paul Florey.
       639.   iii.   Floyd, b 16 December 1923 at Oakland, CA; m/1 Ida Landis; m/2 Olley —; d; m/3 Betty Jo —.
+   640.   iv.   Audrey, b 23 April 1925.

254. LERA[5] **EDWINA WADLEY** (d/o Pearl[4] Wadley #96), b 13 February 1907 at Portland, OR; m 17 August 1927 at Portland, **Paul Hilbert Foster**, s/o Hilbert Joyce and Marie (Thomson) Foster, b 29 November 1904 at Portland, OR. Paul was office manager for Baxter Fir Treating Co., first in San Francisco, then in San Mateo, CA, before his retirement. Lera as a young girl played the cello and piano well and when a teenager toured on the Pantages Circuit with an orchestra, from Portland to Los Angeles. She later was a stenographer at the court house in Portland, OR. Lera d 24 July 1984, after three years in a nursing home, a victim of Alzheimer's Disease.

Children, surname FOSTER:

The Fifth Generation 177

+ 641. i. Lera[6] Jean, b 16 February 1930.
+ 642. ii. Robert Paul, b 16 October 1934.

255. EDYTHE[5] MARTHA WADLEY (d/o Pearl[4] Wadley #96), b 12 October 1908 at Portland, OR; m 31 December 1932 at Portland, OR, Episcopal Church, **Harold Weyburn Ticknor**, s/o Harry W. and Blanche (Mentch) Ticknor, b 20 July 1908 at Portland, OR. He owned and ran a printing business in Woodburn, OR, until his death 28 February 1979 at Woodburn. He is buried at Belli Passe, Woodburn. Edith still lived in Woodburn when last known.

Children, surname TICKNOR:
+ 643. i. John[6] Weyburn, b 16 April 1934.
+ 644. ii. William Alan, b 4 June 1939.
+ 645. iii. Nancy Ann, b 12 October 1942.

256. WILLIAM[5] IRWIN WADLEY (s/o Pearl[4] Wadley #96), b 7 June 1910 at Portland, OR; m 20 September 1933 at Portland, OR, **Virgie Norine Wolfe**, d/o Maxwell Leo and Ida Edna (Modrell) Wolfe, b 13 October 1911 at McCook, Red Willow Co., NB. Bill was a cook in the U.S. Navy, stationed all through World War II at Farragut, ID. He retired from his auto supply business at Yakima, WA, in 1978 to Portland. Vergie d 9 March 1989 and William d 24 March 1992.

Children Surname WADLEY:
+ 646. i. Richard[6] Norlin, b 13 April 1943.
+ 647. ii. Douglass Lee, b 2 January 1947.

257. PAULINE[5] LOIS WADLEY (d/o Pearl[4] Wadley #96), b 26 June 1913 at Portland, OR, a twin to her brother Paul; she m 29 August 1936 at Portland, **Roland Grassens**, s/o Joseph John and Johanna Amelia (Engelmann) Grassens, b 8 August 1909 at Grants Pass, OR. His father was born at Gemert, Holland and his mother at Teneswar, Austria. Roland was a structural steel worker and steel estimator in buildings.

Child, surname GRASSENS:
+ 648. i. Marlene[6] Ellen, b 9 July 1938.

260. PEARL[5] EUNICE REED (d/o Adelbert Reed #100), b 19 June 1890 at Seymour, Outagamie Co., WI. She trained as a registered nurse at Saint Vincent's Hospital, Green Bay, WI. While working as a nurse in Green Bay she met her first husband, **John Christopherson**, s/o Nels and

Johanna (Jensen) Christopherson, b about 1880. They were m 1 June 1911 and they lived in Green Bay. Both of his parents were born in Denmark. John was listed as a brakeman. This marriage ended in divorce. Pearl was a private duty nurse in Milwaukee, WI, and one of the wealthy families brought Pearl with them to Florida. Her second husband, **Peter Sones** was in the service at the time and later joined her in Florida, where they were married. They lived not far from Haines City, FL. He bought property in Haines City and went into the garage and machine shop business and had the Nash Agency. Pearl divorced Pete about 1924. Later she m/3 **Thomas Pack**. Tom was a plumbing contractor and got big contracts with builders such as the Paul Smith Construction Company. They adopted one son. This marriage ended in divorce, too. She moved to Gainesville, FL about 1934. Pearl was a great collector of family information and memorablia, which filled her home in Gainesville. While she was away on a visit to her adopted son at Haines City, the house burned down, destroying all the precious family mementos. She regretted especially losing a hand carved wooden doll with jointed arms and legs which had a wig made from her grandmother Marinda Reed's hair. About 1944 she moved to Tampa, FL, where she owned a very successful and exclusive nursing home. Pearl d 3 July 1958 of Leukemia at age 68 years, at Tampa. She is buried in Forest Hill Cemetery, Haines City. She did not have any children of her own, but adopted one child. Her obituary stated "Survivors include two sons: Harold L. Pack of Flint, MI, and Col. Charles M. Pack of Baltimore, MD; a daughter Mary Lou Swindle of Palatka; . . . and 6 grandchildren. I assume that Charles and and Mary Lou are children of her husband by a previous marriage.

Child, surname PACK:

+ 649. i. Harold[6] Lloyd, b 12 December 1927.

261. ROLAND[5] MORRIS REED (s/o Adelbert[4] Reed #100), b 6 December 1892, Seymour, Outagamie Co., WI. He was rebellious as a boy and left home at an early age. He had many exciting experiences riding the rails around the country. He was out west working on the railroad when a stranger approached him and told him his brother was ill back home and needed him. After he recovered from his surprise at this news, he asked others in the crew if they had seen the stranger, and no one had seen any strangers. He had a strong feeling that he should go home and did so. He was grieved to find out that his brother Herald had died of polio.

Roland m 7 December 1916 at the Methodist Church in Rhinelander, WI, **Eva Lonea Lyannas**, d/o George and Mary (Gustag) Lyannas. she b 22 February 1898 at Wisconsin Rapids, WI. She was half Indian; her parents came from Canada. Roland and Eva moved early to a wild part of the state, to Lake Tomahawk, Oneida Co., WI. They lived a primitive existence in a tent until Roland could build them a house, and developed farm land. Because of their isolation from other families the children grew up knowing all about the forests and its animals.

Eva d 21 July 1975 and Roland d 21 November 1976 at Lake Tomahawk. Roland and Eva are buried in Wilderness Rest Cemetery at Lake Tomahawk.

Children, surname REED:
+ 650. i. Ruth[6] Elizabeth, b 18 February 1918.
    651. ii. Robert Adelbert, b 17 August 1920; he was stillborn and is buried on the farm at Lake Tomahawk.
+ 652. iii. Richard Morris, b 27 July 1921 at Lake Tomahawk.
    653. iv. Isabelle Jane, b 22 July 1924 at Lake Tomahawk; m 26 November 1949 at Dubuque, IA Frederick Dies, s/o Charles and Anna (Mertens) Dies, b 28 February 1909 at Milwaukee Co., WI; Frederick d 5 February 1977; when last known Isabelle lived at Oconomowoc, WI. They had no children.
+ 654. v. Roland Lowell, b 27 May 1932.

263. CLIFFORD[5] LOWELL REED (s/o Adelbert[4] Reed #100), b 8 October 1898 at Seymour, Outagamie Co., WI; m 1 January 1921 at Seymour, WI, **Dora Marie LaMarche**, d/o Delore and Pauline LaMarche, b 10 April 1903 at Nedeau, MI. Since Dora was a Roman Catholic and Clifford a Seventh Day Adventist, they were married by a Justice of the Peace. From the time he was 17 years old Clifford did logging at Long Lake in northern Wisconsin. Clifford and Dora moved to Florida in 1922. They had a hard time during the depression years; he had a truck and he collected old auto batteries and radiators and rebuilt them and resold them to make a little money. He bought quite a bit of land at auctions, from people who defaulted on their payments. He later bought heavy equipment and worked preparing the land for ranchers who were developing citrus groves and grazing land. He was very resourceful and built in his own machine shop special equipment for special needs in this development period, such as 18-foot wide disks and equipment for squeezing and sectioning grapefruit. He became very successful, and built his present home near Haines City in 1957.

Children, surname REED:
- 655. i. Delbert[6] Lowell, b 24 September 1922 at Seymour, WI; he d 27 September 1922.
- + 656. ii. Joyce Ann, b 15 January 1925.

265. NORMAN[5] WILDER REED (s/o Adelbert[4] Reed #100), b 6 February 1902 at Seymour, WI; m 27 August 1925 at Menominee, MI, **Amy Rosina Andrus**, d/o Herbert Mortimer and Mary Jane (Maier) Andrus, she b 16 April 1908 at Chippewa County, WI. Amy and Norman lived a few years in Seymour, then worked a farm at Shiocton, Outagamie Co., WI for ten years. Then they moved to Rochester, WI in 1942 while Norman was working in a war industry in Milwaukee, WI. After the children were grown up, Norman and Amy moved to Edmore, MI and bought a stone house. There Amy divorced Norman and moved to California to visit her daughter Janet and stayed there almost 17 years. She kept house for a wealthy family at Westwood, a suburb of Los Angeles from 1958 to 1964. She lived in a senior citizen's housing in Union Grove, WI, until her death 4 April 1984. Norman was in a nursing home near Edmore five years before his death on 12 March 1967, at Edmore. Both are buried at Union Grove Cemetery.

Children, surname REED:
- + 657. i. Virginia Charlotte, b 1 April 1927.
- + 658. ii. Morris Herbert, b 31 October 1929.
- + 659. iii. Patricia Jean, b 27 November 1930.
- + 660. iv. June Rose, b 31 May 1932.
- + 661. v. Janet Loraine, b 4 August 1933.
- + 662. vi. Marilyn Carol, b 26 April 1935.
- + 663. vii. Arlene May, b 2 January 1939.
- + 664. viii. Sue Bernadine, b 21 August 1940.

266. OLIVE[5] MARINDA REED (d/o Adelbert[4] Reed #100), b 9 November 1904 at Seymour, Outagamie Co., WI.; m/1 9 April 1925 at Seymour, WI, **Sanford Staeben Simmons**, s/o William Alfred and Emma Rose (Staeben) Simmons, he b 3 November 1904 at Chicago, IL. They moved to Gainesville, FL in March 1941, bringing the cattle and machinery from their farm in Illinois. When the pasteurization of milk became a law in about 1943, they sold them off. Sanford d 26 July 1951 in New

The Fifth Generation

York City and is buried at Evergreen Cemetery, Gainesville. Olive m/2 at Gainesville, 27 September 1957 **Edwin Hearn**, s/o Edwin Boderstein (who was adopted by Daniel Hearn) and Louise (Van Keuren) Hearn. Olive and Edwin lived in New Jersey until 1971. He worked for Wagner Electric on power tubes (Gov't. contracts—Dew Line), etc. In 1971 Ed retired and they moved to Deerfield Beach, FL, where they owned a duplex and lived in one of the units. About 1983 Olive and Ed built a home on part of the land owned by her son Sanford and given to her (5–1/2 acres of choice wooded land) by Sandy, her son, near Micanopy, Alachua Co., FL. Ed d 18 June 1988, and Olive still lives there.

Children, surname SIMMONS:

    665. i. Jacqueline[6] Mae, b 9 August 1927 at Chicago, IL; m/1 Ralph Reinhart at Tampa, FL when she was 18, in 1945; they lived at McDill Field, Tampa, an army base; she divorced him and resumed the name Simmons; m/2 15 June 1956 at New Orleans, LA, Warren Greene; b NY City in early 1920s; d 21 June 1973 at West Palm Beach, FL. Warren managed a furniture store and she had a nursery in West Palm Beach. She had no children. When last known she was living at Pompano Beach, FL.

+ 666. ii. Beverly Jean, b 20 December 1928.
+ 667. iii. Shirley Gay, b 12 November 1933.
   668. iv. Sanford, b 22 October 1938 at LeMont, IL; m for about 8 years to Guytha H—, who had previously been married to a Fielding and two others. No children. He is in Real Estate. He brought up Guytha's children. He bought the 400 acres in 1962 at Micanopy, FL near Gainesville, originally bought by Olive and Sanford in 1941.
   669. i. Judith Lee, b 3 August 1943 at Gainesville, Florida.

267. VIVIAN[5] MEDORA REED (d/o Adelbert[4] Reed #100), b 25 April 1907 at Seymour, WI; m 10 November 1938 at Tampa, FL **Bruce Bennington Morehead**, s/o Charles Francis and Alene Eleanor (Taylor) Morehead, b 2 April 1913 at DeKalb, IL. Vivian taught school in Wisconsin several years; came to Florida because sister Pearl and brother Clifford were there. Bruce's last job before retirement about 1977 was as Branch Manager of Florida Equipment Co., at Tampa. For years they had raised orchids as a hobby at Tampa. After retirement they moved to the mobile home they had at their orange grove at Brandon on Route 60 in Florida; in addition to orchids they grew three kinds of grapes, with automatic watering and fertilizing system for both. Bruce was an American

Orchid Society judge. Bruce d 18 December 1982 at Lake City, FL. According to her son, in 1988, she is living at Dover, FL and is active in the Tampa Orchid Club.

Children, surname MOREHEAD:

    670.   i. Bruce[6] Reed, b 6 August 1940 at Winter Haven, FL. He received an Associate Degree from Saint Petersburg Junior College in 1961; joined the Air Force 1963 as personnel specialist; stationed at Royal Air Force Station, Wethersfield, England until 1967; received B.A. Degree from University of South Florida in Business Administration, with specialty in personnel management; hired by Hillsborough Co. Aviation Authority as Personnel Specialist in 1971 to Staff Tampa International Airport, which opened in 1971. He is now Management Services Coordinator and in charge of their microcomputers, computer training and video production. He has been active in sports car racing for 27 years and is active in local sports car clubs. Also active in Explorer Scouts for 17 years and an advisor to the post sponsored by Aviation Authority; received the Silver Beaver Award from Boy Scout Council. Has been active in other community activities as well. He never married. He lives at Tampa, FL.

+   671. ii. Ernest Lee, b 6 January 1944.

268. DONALD[5] ADLEBERT REED (s/o Adelbert[4] Reed #100), b 10 December 1909 at Seymour, WI; m 1 April 1933 at Bartow, FL, Gladys Lastrella Allman, d/o George and Annette (Johns) Allman, she b 6 April 1917 at Kissimee, FL; she d 1 June 1955 at Orlando, FL and is buried at Forest Lawn Cemetery, Orlando. Here is Donald's account of his life:

    When I was 7 I drove the wagon to deliver my father's milk to the cheese factory in Seymour, WI. When I was 9 I started smoking. I stole eggs from the nests and sold them to get tobacco. My father couldn't understand why the hens weren't laying more eggs. I was the youngest child in my family and I was supposed to stay nights with my Grandmother Marinda Reed, a widow. When I got older I wanted to go out nights, so after Grandmother had gone to sleep I would sneak out through the woodbox. The woodbox was built into the side of the house, and had lids on the inside and outside the house. After being out late I was upset when Grandmother pounded on the stove pipe at 4:00 in the morning to wake me up to do the chores. After I finished High School I bought a four cylinder Buick for $25, which I had saved up from working in a canning factory, and started out for Florida to live with my brother Cliff. I had car trouble and stopped in Milwaukee. The man asked me where I was going, and he told me I'd never make it. I crossed the Ohio River and slept all night in the car. The car kept smoking all day and I had no brakes when I reached High Springs, Florida. I parked the car and went to a dance. The next morning I set out for Haines City. I stopped and had the gas tank filled and gave the station attendant a $5 bill. The man had a jar of money which he got out to give me my change—a regular Florida Cracker—when I got away I counted the change and found I had over $10. Smoke was rolling out of the car when I reached Cliff's and Cliff said, "Don't stop." and I ran it out into the woods. Part of the time after that I went home during summers. From the time I was 21 to 23 I drifted all over the country, in my Pontiac roadster, even into Mexico. I lived on vegetables and slept in the car. I worked in the vegetable fields in California and Mexico. I finally started hauling vegetables from 1931–32. I worked my way up to Oregon and Washington and over into Montana and on home.

I met my first wife at a gas station when I stopped for gas. I had taken fruit to Jacksonville and I was on my way back to Winter Haven. I got a date with her, and a friend dared me to marry her. We woke up a judge and got married. I stole roses from the Judge's garden for her wedding bouquet. I found out afterward she wasn't quite 16 years old. We lived together 22 years until her death, 1 June 1955 at Orlando, Florida. She had a brain tumor and was sick 8 or 9 years. I was hauling heavy equipment then and was away a lot.

For awhile he returned to Wisconsin and stayed 12 years. He bought a farm and had 55 head of cattle. During the war he worked building submarines in a shipyard in Green Bay, WI. He tried to join the army the day after Pearl Harbor, but he had the farm and worked at the shipyards so they wouldn't take him. He left the farm in 1945. He bought diesels for rebuilding and worked for Allis Chalmers for 17 years, demonstrating their equipment. In 1971 he retired from Construction Equipment Company in Orlando where he had lived 32 years.

Donald m/2 16 December 1958 at Orlando, **Irene Hanak Genesy**, b 27 August 1914 at Cleveland, Ohio, d/o John and Elizabeth (Bahari) Genesy. For a number of years Donald and Irene lived in a mobile home at Franklin, Macon Co., NC, a beautiful spot in the Smokey Mountains. Donald d 29 October 1986.

Children, surname REED:
+   672.   i.   Adelbert[6] George Lowell, b 31 July 1934.

269. MARION[5] JESSIE RIDER (d/o Myrtle[4] Reed Rider #101), b 27 June 1895 at Seymour, WI; m May 1917 at Cedar Lake, MI in the Seventh Day Adventist Church, **Karl Stanley Hall**, s/o Charles S. and Cynthia (Rowland) Hall. Karl and Marion had a farm at Elm Hall, Gratiot Co.,

MI, 15 miles from Edmore. Marion d 23 June 1974 at Alma, MI and is buried in Richland Township Cemetery, Vestaburg, MI. Karl is still living as of 1983 on his farm. Marion and Karl had four stillborn babies.

Children, surname HALL:
- 673. i. Wayne[6] C., b 12 June 1918; m Beatrice Rose; reportedly had 4 children.
- 674. ii. E. Leona, b 18 March 1921. Was a teacher at Kent State University in Ohio; retired 1978 to Lewiston, Michigan; d 26 Feb 1987.

270. ELLEN[5] MARINDA RIDER (d/o Myrtle[4] Reed Rider #101), b 16 February 1899 at Seymour, WI; m 17 June 1916 at Stanton, MI, **William Bryan Jorgensen**, s/o Chris Jorgensen, by a Justice of the Peace, b 28 October 1896 at Sidney, MI. They farmed a number of years at Cedar Lake, MI. During the 1920s and 1930s Bryan was employed by Pere Marquette Railway Bridge and Building Co. at Edmore, MI. Ellen d April 1973 and is buried at Richland Township Cemetery at Vestaburg, MI. Bryan has lived in Edmore for many years and his daughter Irene makes her home with him. During the winter months he is with his daughter Irene and her husband in their large motor home, parked on a lot next to Clifford Reed's home near Haines City, FL.

Children, surname JORGENSEN
- \+ 675. i. Pearl[6] Irene, b 15 February 1917.
- \+ 676. ii. Robert Stanley, b 26 February 1920.
- \+ 677. iii. Reed Carlyle, b 9 March 1922.
- \+ 678. iv. Betty Rae, b 26 February 1925.

271. ETHEL[5] BEAVERT (d/o Maud[4] Reed Beavert #106), b 29 September 1892 at Sundance, WY. She was 20 years old when her mother died, and the oldest of eight children. She mothered her three youngest brothers, Warren, Cyrus and Frank. As a young woman Ethel and her sister Bertha worked as waitresses in the logging camp of McCoy Logie Timber Co., 20 or 30 miles east of Bellingham, WA. At one time Ethel, with May and Worth Beavert, ran a restaurant in Ferndale, WA. Cyrus Reed, their grandfather, liked to come to their restaurant especially for their calf brains.

Ethel m/1 **Ray Colby**; m/2 **Henry Carl Beyers**, s/o Henry and Pauline Beyers, in 1918, b 26 October 1889 at Seattle, WA. Henry was on the police force in Seattle. Later Ethel boarded college boys in Bellingham, WA, where there was a teacher's college. Ethel loved children and she would buy yards of material before Christmas and work long hours sewing stockings and all the children around Ferndale would receive filled stockings from her. She did not have any children of her own. Ethel d in 1955 in Bellingham. Henry was married briefly after Ethel's death. He d 29 June 1975. Both are buried at Woodlawn Cemetery, Ferndale. Ethel and Henry adopted a little girl in 1932:

Children, surname BEYERS:

    679. i. Patsy^6; m Morris Johnson.

273. MAY^5 BEAVERT (d/o Maud^4 Reed Beavert #106), b 24 May 1895 at Sundance, WY; m in 1915 **James A. McCormick**, s/o William and Elizabeth McCormick, he b 12 June 1887 at Arkansas City, KS. May ran a restaurant in Ferndale, WA with sister, Ethel, and brother, Worth, in the early days. May and James worked for the Carnation Company in California for a time. James d in 1955 at Seattle, WA. May d 19 April 1973 at Bremerton, WA. Both are buried in Woodlawn Cemetery, Ferndale.

Children, surname McCORMICK:

    680. i. Laura^6 May, b 2 November 1916 at Ferndale; m 25 November 1950, William Henry McMullen, s/o William Henry & Gertrude (McNeely) McMullen, b 16 August 1920. William is a truck driver and they have no children.

+   681. ii. Donald Albert, b 8 May 1922.

275. BERTHA^5 BEATRICE BEAVERT (d/o Maud^4 Reed Beavert #106), b 24 July 1898 at Sundance, WY. She was 6 years old when her father, William Beavert, disappeared and 14 when her mother died. As a young girl Bertha was a waitress at McCoy Logie Timber Company, 20 or 30 miles east of Bellingham, WA. Waitresses were called "flunkies" in logging camps. She met her husband, **Orin Louis Archibald**, and married him there. Orrin was b 26 March 1896 at Matapedia, New Brunswick, Canada, s/o William and Elizabeth (Ryan) Archibald. Bertha and Orin's first home at the logging camp was a tent fitted over a wooden floor with wooden sides. Orin worked in the timber industry nearly all his life, starting at age 9, when he fed horses used in logging. He worked for Bloedel, Donovan and Crescent Logging Company on the Olympic Peninsula, Washington for many years. In 1940 they moved to Skyhomish to manage Bloedel' logging operations there. From 1950 until he retired in 1965 he was West Coast Manager for Empire Millwork Corp., a New York lumber Company. Bertha d 23 June 1964 at Everett, WA. Orin m/2 22 May 1967 at Everett, Elizabeth (Winklesky) Titus, d/o Paul and Irene (Peacha) Winklesky, b 22 November 1907 at Bemidji, MN. She was previously married to Arthur Titus, by whom she had three children: Dianne Short, Nancy Schoner and David Titus; David drowned in a sailboat accident 15 November 1981. Orin d 29 April 1979 at Everett and is buried in Cypress Lawn Memorial Park, Everett.

Children, surname ARCHIBALD:
+   682. i. Lois[6], b 10 June 1921.
+   683. ii. Donna Jean, b 30 November 1923.

276. WARREN[5] WILLIAM BEAVERT (s/o Maud[4] Reed Beavert #106), b 13 November 1900 at Portal, ND. He was about 12 years old when his mother died and he went to live with his sister Ethel. He m August 1925 **Ruby Clark**, d/o Theodore and Anna Marie (Knapp) Clark, b 24 November 1906 at Wolfpoint, MT. Warren and his sister Bertha were playing in ashes dumped from the wood stove when quite young, putting ashes in a bottle with a spoon. Warren's dress caught fire and he was badly burned. Later Warren and his wife and two children were living in Thermopolis, WY. Warren's wife was crippled and walked with a limp. It was very cold and she put Beverly near the wood cook stove to keep her warm. She left the room and Beverly fell on the stove and cooked one side of her face. Being crippled her mother couldn't get to her quickly. It left a very bad scar. She has had plastic surgery and looks okay now.

Warren was a longshoreman, working on the Seattle docks; he loved fishing, especially at the mouth of the Columbia River. When he d 7 April 1977 at Long Beach, CA, his body was cremated and his ashes were scattered at the mouth of the river he loved. Ruby d 19 April 1974 at Redmond, WA. Her body was donated to the University of Washington at Seattle for research.

Children, surname BEAVERT:
+   684. i. Beverly[6] Anne, b 3 March 1928.
+   685. ii. Warren William, b 4 March 1930.

278. FRANK[5] BEAVERT (s/o Maud[4] Reed Beavert #106), b 14 November 1904 at Portal, ND; m 3 April 1926 at Everett, WA, **Elizabeth**

The Fifth Generation

McDonald, d/o Angus M. and Emily (Yecny) McDonald, b 11 January 1904 at Clearlake, WA. Frank's father was really Andrew Weston, Will Beavert's nephew who was working on the ranch. Will had left the family and Maud had to wait seven years to declare him legally dead so she could marry Andrew Weston. Frank was 7 years old when his mother died. The family stayed together a couple of years, then split up. Frank did hard farm work for an old couple in Laurel, WA until he was 14 years old. Then worked for another couple by the name of Wynn for his board. Frank moved to Monroe and worked for the Carnation Company in Monroe, WA and his father, Andrew Weston, was chief engineer. He worked first in the factory, then as assistant engineer. He transferred with the company to Gustine, CA. He became affiliated with Mobil Oil in 1935, retiring in 1966. Elizabeth d 19 December 1974 and is buried in Washington Memorial Cemetery, Seattle, WA. Frank had triple bypass surgery in 1984; he d 25 May 1992 at Seattle and is buried with his wife.

Children, surname BEAVERT:
+   686.   i.   Frank[6], b 24 January 1927.
+   687.   ii. Betty May, b 9 September 1933.

279. MARVIN[5] L. WESTON (s/o Maude[4] Reed Beavert Weston #106), b 2 September 1908 at Laurel, Klickitat Co., WA; m 6 August 1937 at Davenport, Lincoln Co., WA, **Gladys Pauline Baurer**, d/o Fred George and Martha Josephine (Dick) Baurer, b 27 March 1914 at Sherwood, Washington Co., OR. After his mother died, when he was 3–1/2 years old, Marvin was raised by his Aunt Cecil Weston at Sherwood. Marvin d 10 January 1969 at Portland, OR and is buried in Crescent Grove Cemetery, Tigard, OR. Gladys m/2 19 December 1979 to a Nicholson and lives in Clovis, CA.

Children, surname WESTON:
+   688.   i.   Marvys[6] Jane, b 20 October 1939.
+   689.   ii. Sharon Lee, b 21 June 1942.
+   690. iii. Steven Craig, b 26 September 1950.

280. MERLE[5] VINCENT WESTON (d/o Maude[4] Reed Beavert Weston #106), b 11 May 1912 at Laurel, Klickitat Co., WA. He was just a tiny baby when his mother died and he was raised by his father's maiden sister, aunt Cecil Weston, at Sherwood, OR. Merle was a farmer and livestock dealer. He bought beef on the hoof for several meat companies and also bought young cattle in the spring and fattened them up for market in the fall at Portland. Merle m 9 October 1936 at Vancouver, WA, **Esther Marie Walls**, d/o James H. and Mable Marie (Replogle) Walls, she b 30 May 1916 in Hollidaysburg, Blair Co., PA. She had just recently come out to Portland to live with her mother, who had left her husband in Pennsylvania when Esther was 12-1/2 years old. She met Merle at a New Year's celebration in Portland, 1 January 1936. Merle died 23 February 1972 at Estacada, OR, and is buried there. Esther is living in Estacada, OR.

Children, surname WESTON:

+ 691. i. James[6] Merle, born 3 February, 1938.

284. LEOTA[5] LORRAINE PLASTEUR (d/o Eva[4] Belle Reed Eck Plasteur #108), b 25 May 1915 at Ferndale, WA. She married 25 July, 1934 at Los Angeles, CA, **Stanton Harrison Nickle**, son of Stanton Alexander and Nellie Sarmia (Harrison) Nickle. Stanton was born 20 June, 1910 at Winnipeg, Canada. Leota met Stanton at Long Beach, CA while visiting her mother and sister there for the summer. She went to Miss Miller's Business College for a year in San Francisco and married Stanton right after she finished. Leota claims Stanton was a descendant of Edward M. Stanton, Secretary of War for President Lincoln. His Grandmother, Martha Jane Stanton, married George Nickle in Detroit; he was a close friend of Henry Ford, and Leota claims they used to tinker together before the Model T Ford was invented. Stanton Nickle owned and operated his own pharmacy in Long Beach a number of years. Stanton died 18 January, 1975 and is buried at Westminster, CA. Leota m/2 on 27 April, 1984 at Santa Barbara, CA, **Richard D. Tead**, a Pharmacist and friend of her husband's. They live in Long Beach; Leota and Stanton were parents of one child.

Child, surname Nickle

692. i. Penelope[6] Lee, b 2 July, 1947 at Long Beach, CA.

286. DOREATHA[5] RUTH CANFIELD (d/o Willis[4] Canfield #113), b 5 January 1908 at Watertown, Jefferson Co., NY; m 29 July 1926 in North Syracuse, NY, **Leonard Robert Clarke**, s/o Leonard Robert and Louise (Taft) Clarke, b 1907 at Johnson City, NY. Except for a few years after 1940 when they lived in Sidney, Delaware Co., NY, they lived in Syracuse, where Robert was an automobile salesman. Doreatha d 18 August 1978 in Syracuse and Robert d 21 May 1983 at Van Duyn Home, Syracuse.

Children, surname CLARKE:
- 693. i. Richard[6] Winston, b 4 September 1927, Syracuse. He d 18 July 1943 from accidental electrocution and is buried in Morningside Cemetery, Syracuse.
- + 694. ii. Leonard Robert III, b 18 September 1929.
- + 695. iii. Diane Elyse, b 21 December 1930.
- + 696. iv. Bruce Bailey, b 21 June 1935.
- + 697. v. Prudence Penelope, b 4 December 1936.
- + 698. vi. Roger Walter, b 14 February 1938.
- 699. vii. Wendy Lou, b 28 July 1941 at Oeonta, Otsego Co., NY.; d 10 December 1967. She m Sherrill Weeks about 1960/61. Lived in Seneca Falls, NY, but had no children.
- + 700. viii. Gary Scott, b 26 November 1942.

287. ELTON[5] FAY CANFIELD (s/o Willis[4] Canfield #113), b 27 December 1909 at Watertown, Jefferson Co., NY; m 27 August 1931 at East Syracuse, NY, **Loretta Marie Wynn**, d/o Hiram and Pearl Amelia (Piper) Wynn, b 4 March 1915 at Kirkville, Onondaga Co., NY. Elton worked for many years for the American Stores Company, d 23 December 1958 in Syracuse, NY, and is buried in Woodlawn Cemetery, Syracuse. Loretta was still living in East Syracuse, when last known.

Children, surname CANFIELD:
- + 701. i. Robert[6] Gene, b 12 January 1932.

289. THELMA[5] ANN CANFIELD (d/o Lucius[4] Canfield #115), b 2 October 1911 at Verona, Oneida Co., NY; m 28 July 1928 at Oneida, Madison Co., NY, **Kenneth Newell Oatman**, s/o Newell and Mabel Oatman, b 19 February 1909 at Oneida. This marriage ended in divorce. Kenneth d in 1963 at Oneida.

Thelma m/2 April 1946 at Melrose, PA, **Eugene Dills Lane**, s/o Clarence and Hazel (Collins) Lane, b 8 April 1909 at Syracuse, NY. Eugene worked as an assembler at Oneida Limited, a silver manufacturer. He d 11 August 1968 at Syracuse. Thelma has for many years run her own beauty parlor business from her home in Oneida.

Children, surname OATMAN:
- + 702. i. Roger[6] Newell, b 3 July 1933.

Children, surname LANE:
- + 703. ii. Marcia Jean, b 11 March 1947.

+ 704. iii. Joyce Marie, b 6 August 1948.
705. iv. Janice Lynn, b 17 May 1952 at Oneida. She d 22 November 1956 at Syracuse and is buried at Valley View Cemetery, Sherrill, NY.

290. HERBERT[5] CLINTON CANFIELD (s/o Lucius[4] Canfield #115), b 13 December 1915 at Verona, Oneida Co., NY.; m 15 August 1934 at Constantia, Oswego Co., NY, **Gladys Kent**, d/o Edward and Tiny (Wood) Kent, b 23 April 1917 at Vienna, NY. This marriage ended in divorce in 1950 in Mexico, NY; she d 21 September 1987. He m/2 in 1950 at Las Vegas, NV, **Ruth Portner**, b in 1910 at Rome, NY. They moved to California in 1952 and live in Westlake Village.

Children, surname CANFIELD:
+ 706. i. Herbert Edward, b 26 February 1936.
+ 707. ii. Thelma Grace, b 2 January 1940.
708. iii. Richard Lucius, b 30 May 1942 at Oneida, NY; m/1 in Rome, NY on 23 May 1964, Anna Marie Salvaggio, d/o Frank and Angeline Salvaggio, b 15 August 1944 at Rome, NY; marriage annulled 1 December 1964 at Rome; m/2 3 August 1968 at Marcy, NY, Lynette Joan Mathers, d/o William and Doris (Johnson) Mathers, b 15 December 1940 at Utica, NY. Lynette had two sons by former husband Kenneth Youngs: Bruce Brian, b December 1961 at Utica and Jeffery Scott, b 8 December 1963 at Utica. This marriage ended in divorce 2 October 1979 at Rome. Richard is an occupational therapist at Marcy State Hospital, Marcy, NY; he lives in Rome and has no children.

291. FENTON[5] EMIL CANFIELD (s/o Floyd[4] Beecher Canfield #116), b 6 June 1912, Adams, Oswego Co, NY; m 31 September 1933, Adams, **Margaret Isabell Schubert**, d/o Paul F. and Agnes Newell (Leitch) Schubert, b 31 August 1913, d 30 March 1957. He m/2 at Catholic Church in Fulton, Oswego Co., 11 April 1964, **Esther Turchiarulo**, d/o Lawrence and Lucretia (D'Amico) Turchiarulo, b 5 April 1920, Fulton.

Fenton worked for the Hunter Arms Co., in Fulton, and learned the gunsmith trade and later worked several years at the Ithaca Gun Co. While there he took several courses at Cornell University. After his second marriage he moved to Pittsford, Monroe Co, NY, where he worked for General Motors until his retirement in 1974. While at GM he also attended Rochester Institute of Technology. Fenton and his wife live in Pittsford, NY.

The Fifth Generation

Children, surname CANFIELD:
- 709. i. Jean[6] Martha, b 14 October 1940 at Ithaca, Tompkins Co., NY; was involved in an early unfortunate marriage which ended in divorce. She m/2 4 June 1966 at the home of his sister in Trumansburg, NY, George Taylor Denison, s/o E. Glenn and Grace (Taylor) Denison, b 24 September 1931 at Brocton, NY. George retired due to ill health and died 20 February 1990. Jean is employed by the Xerox Corporation in Rochester and resides in Ontario, Wayne Co., NY. She is very active in genealogical research, especially of the Canfield family. They had no children.
- + 710. ii. Donald Fenton, b 29 May 1945.

292. HAROLD[5] MILBURN CANFIELD (s/o Floyd[4] Canfield #116), b 18 July 1915 at Altmar, Oswego Co., NY.; m (1) 6 July 1937 at Pulaski, Oswego Co., NY, **Agnes Martha Hurlbut**, d/o John Clinton and Mildred Marie (Rice) Hurlbut, b 21 February 1919 at Lewisburg, NY. Harold was Furnace Maintenance Foreman at Revere Copper and Brass Co., Rome, NY. The company also sent him to install new furnaces in California and Alabama. Additionally, he ran his own used car business. Harold and Agnes were divorced and Agnes d at Tulsa, OK on August 1980.

Harold m/2 14 September 1956 in California, **Mabel Sarah Light**, d/o Clifford and Mabel Alberta (O'Dell) Light, b 22 January 1927 at Rome, NY. Harold and Mabel have one daughter and now live in Orlando, FL.

Children, surname CANFIELD:
- + 711. i. Carol[6] Ann, b 3 June 1938.
- + 712. ii. Jean Kitty, b 30 December 1940.
- + 713. iii. John Harold, b 13 March 1946.
- + 714. iv. Bette Eileen, b 7 January 1948.
- + 715. v. Jim Scott, b 14 August 1950.
- 716. vi. Caren Alice, b 5 January 1952, Rome.
- 717. vii. Carrie[6] Light, b 27 April 1964 at Oneida, NY. She graduated from college in 1988 and has a public relations business.

293. OSCAR[5] WILLARD CANFIELD (s/o Floyd Canfield #116), b 29 July 1924 at Altmar, Oswego Co., NY; m 9 June 1951 at Wellsville, Allegany Co., NY, **Dorothy Ellen Mead**, d/o Lloyd James and Esther Clara (Northrup) Mead, b 12 April 1929 at Wellsville. Oscar has worked for many years at the Nestle Company, now in Quality Control, in Fulton,

Oswego Co., where they live. Dorothy runs the "Gospel Book Center," a bookstore in their home.

Children, surname CANFIELD:
- 718. i. William[6] James, b 26 November 1953 at Fulton.
- + 719. ii. Linda Jane, b 21 August 1955.
- 720. iii. Sandra Joyce, b 6 July 1959 at Fulton; m 6 July 1984 at Fulton, Ralph Jammen, s/o Eddie and Sadie Jammen, b 27 May 1959.

294. DOUGLAS[5] LISTON CANFIELD (s/o Floyd[4] Canfield #110), b 30 March 1926 at Altmar, Oswego Co., NY., m 12 November 1950 at Fulton Methodist Church, **Helen H. Babikian**, d/o Haig M. and Nevart (Shahinian) Babikian, b 25 December 1928 at Fulton, NY. Douglas is in business for himself and has a machine shop in Fulton.

Children, surname CANFIELD:
- + 721. i. Douglas[6] Jonathan, b 5 November 1952 in Fulton, NY. He buys antiques in New York State in the summer and takes them to Florida to sell. He teaches 7th grade at Hobe Sound [FL] Bible College. See Addenda.
- 722. ii. Christopher Dwight, b 14 October 1955 at Fulton; m 20 August 1977 at Lakewood Chapel, Mays Landing, NJ, Debra Beth McKay, d/o Stanley A. and Ruth L. (Clemenson) McKay, b 22 March 1955 at Philadelphia, PA. They live between Fulton and Oswego; Christopher is supervisor of his father's machine and tool company in Fulton. They have no children.
- 723. iii. David Liston, b 15 March 1962 at Fulton. Is a fireman in Fulton and never married. On 16 June 1992 he rescued a woman from her car which plunged into the Oswego Canal in Fulton.
- 724. iv. John Paul, b 26 December 1968 at Oswego. Works in a machine and tool Co., for his father; not married.

295. SHERMAN[5] WILBUR KENNEDY (s/o Alta[4] Canfield Kennedy #117), b 11 July 1911 at McConnellsville, Oswego Co., NY. He graduated from Syracuse University, College of Business Administration, majoring in Economics, in 1934. He earned his Masters Degree in Education in 1938. He m 25 June 1936 at Newfield, Tompkins Co., NY, **Florence Elizabeth Minnie Baker**, d/o Rev. Walter and Jennie (McBain) Baker, b 23 November 1910 at the Lutheran Parsonage of Chatham, Columbia Co., NY. She graduated from Russell Sage College in Troy, NY and was teaching foreign languages at Newfield, where Sherman was teaching commercial subjects. They went on to Mexico, Oswego Co., NY where

Sherman taught commercial subjects four years (1938–1946). He was instructor in accounting at Syracuse University for three years, when he left to go into the business world. He was business manager at "Grandma's" Browns Beans in Mexico for three years, then at Sealright Corporation, Fulton, NY, later being transferred to Phillips Petroleum Company at Kansas City, MO after the two companies merged. His last employment was as business manager at a private school, The Barstow School, Kansas City from which he retired in 1978. He now works during income tax time for an accounting firm in Kansas City, preparing income tax returns for their clients. After raising her family, Florence returned to work as a School Librarian at Fulton and continued in this capacity when they moved to Kansas City, and retired in 1978. She is now actively pursuing a new career in art. They live in Leawood, KS, a suburb of Kansas City.

Children, surname KENNEDY:

725. i. Sherman[6] Walter, b 10 October 1937 at Ithaca, Tompkins Co., NY. He is employed at University of Kansas, College of Health Science and Hospital, as medical technologist.
+ 726. ii. Brant Dow, b 26 April 1939.
727. iii. Mark William, b 16 November 1943 at Oswego. When last know was employed in the computer field in Baltimore, Maryland.
728. iv. Bonnie Jane, b 31 August 1947 at Syracuse; m 19 March 1988 at John Street Methodist Church, New York City, Paul Edward Cox, s/o Paul Edward and Dorothy Elizabeth (Morris) Cox, b 15 December 1943 at Glen Cove, NY; Paul previously m 31 July 1965 at Glen Cove, Eileen Rooney, by whom he had two children: Sheila Marie Cox, b 22 September 1967 and Paul Edward Cox Jr., b 17 May 1971; Paul and Eileen were divorced 31 May 1980 in New Jersey.

Bonnie is a 1969 graduate of Russell Sage College, Troy, NY; she has been employed in New York since 1974, first at Shaw-Walker Furniture and later at by Ashland Desk Company as a office decoration and furnishings planner; she is now employed by Prudential Bache; Paul works for Chase Manhattan Bank. They live in Brooklyn and have no children.
729. v. Eric Paul, b 21 October 1948 at Syracuse, Onondaga Co., NY. Eric lived on and helped operate a horse breeding farm and has worked as a welder near Ottawa, KS; he is currently employed in the Kansas City area and lives in the Leewood suburb.

297. NEIL[5] DOW KENNEDY (s/o Alta[4] Canfield Kennedy #117), b 19 November 1914 at Warners, Onondaga Co., NY. He graduated from Syracuse University, College of Engineering, with an Electrical Engineering degree in 1937 and worked for Westinghouse Electric Company at Long Island City and Albany, NY., Saginaw, MI, and Baltimore, MD. He enlisted in the U.S. Army Signal Corps September 1942 as Second Lieutenant in the Aircraft Warning Battalion. He spent three months at Harvard University and three months at MIT before being sent overseas to the China-India-Burma theater of War. He was in India about three months and then in Chengtu, China about 1–1/2 years, where he set up a peripheral radar station which monitored U.S. cargo and military planes, as well as Japanese planes. He was discharged from the service in 1946. Neil m 9 February 1946 at Memphis, NY, in the Baptist Church, **Helen Sarah Peterson**, d/o Charles and Hazel (Jacobson) Peterson, b 18 September 1919 at her parents home, "Twin Brook Farm," on Bennetts Corners Road, Camillus, NY. She graduated from Syracuse University, College of Business Administration, in 1945. The last few years she has been Library Aide at Jordan-Elbridge Central School, Jordan, NY. She has been very active in her church at Memphis as teacher, choir member, etc.

Neil and Helen lived at Baltimore, Maryland when first married, then from December 1953 to January 1955 at Churchville, Monroe Co., NY., still with Westinghouse. He later joined the General Electric Co. in Syracuse, NY. spending the last few years of his employment at Schenectady, NY. He retired in 1976, and they live in the Peterson homestead, "Twin Brooks Farm" Camillus, NY.

Children, surname KENNEDY:
+   730.   i.   Neil[6] Craig, b 30 January 1948.
+   731.   ii.   Karen Jean, b 13 September 1952.

299. ROGER[5] BELDEN KENNEDY (s/o Alta[4] Canfield Kennedy #117), b 28 April 1923 in Syracuse, Onondaga Co., NY. He entered Syracuse University in the fall of 1941 and his education was interrupted by his service experiences. He served in the Second Armored Division in Germany where he worked in the division Post Office in Occupied Germany. He was privileged to attend Cambridge University in England for one Semester. He was discharged 1 February 1946. He returned to Syracuse University, graduating in 1951. He then went to Southern

Methodist University, Perkins School of Theology in Dallas, Texas 1951–1954. His first ministerial appointment was a Varna and Forest Home churches in 1954. He was ordained Elder and received into full membership in Central New York Methodist Church 27 May 1956 at Oneida, NY. He served at Euclid and Morgan (1957), and McGraw and East Freetown (1959), in New York State. His father, Sherman L. Kennedy, had many years before served at the East Freetown charge and had received as a gift from the congregation a chair. Roger had this chair in his parsonage, and older members of the church remembered Sherman Kennedy, and the chair. In 1964 Roger transferred to the Northeast Ohio Methodist Conference where he served first at Green Springs and Pleasant Ridge, followed by Brilliant and Ruth Run, Ohio (1969); Nova, Ohio (1976); and took a sabbatical leave July 1974–July 1976; Pavonia, Ohio (1976). He served at Melmore, Ohio, Methodist Church from 1980 to 1984. He retired from the church in Jewett, Ohio.

Roger m 5 June 1955 at Marcellus Methodist Church, **Gloria Carolyn Schanzle**, d/o Arthur and Hazel (Lucas) Schanzle, she b 2 September 1932 at Syracuse, Onondaga Co., NY. She graduated from the National College of Christian Workers at Kansas City, MO in 1954. She was religious Education Director at Elmira, NY, Methodist Church until her marriage. She continued to be active in each church they served and in her present church at Jewett, where they live.

Children, surname KENNEDY:
+ 732. i. Roger^6 Bruce, b 19 May 1956.
+ 733. ii. Gloria Dawn, b 14 April 1957.
+ 734. iii. Sharon Joy, b 20 March 1959.
+ 735. iv. Stephen Scott, b 17 May 1960.
+ 736. v. David Martin, b 15 October 1961.

300. MARTHA^5 LOUISE KENNEDY (d/o Alta^4 Canfield Kennedy #117), b 4 May 1929 at Warners, Onondaga Co., NY. She graduated from Syracuse University, College of Home Economics in 1952. She taught Home Economics at Palmyra, NY for three years, later at Greece, NY. Left teaching and worked at Sibleys, Singer Co., and Edwards Dept. Store in Rochester, NY. She m **Leroy Jerome DeSeyn**, s/o Jacob and Lillian (Beach) DeSeyn, he b 5 July 1929 in Palmyra, NY, where he attended Palmyra High School. He enlisted in the Army in 1952, receiving additional training in Japan, before being sent to Korea, fought in the Battle for Pork Chop Hill, where he received two wounds, for which he received the Purple Heart. For several years he was Scoutmaster of Troop 113 at Bridgeport, NY. Later he ran his own welding business from their home in Warners, NY, which formerly was the Kennedy family home, which they bought in 1980. Roy built a smaller log cabin type house on the same land in 1989. Roy d in the hospital in Syracuse of heart failure 28 November 1990. Martha continues to live in the smaller house, amid evergreen trees.

Children, surname DeSEYN:
+ 737. i. Marla^6 Ann, b 20 August 1963.
    738. ii. Roy Jerome, b 13 December 1964 in Syracuse.
    739. iii. Sharon Leigh, b 22 February 1966, Syracuse. She graduated from West Genesee High School in 1984 and became a Home Aide. She m 30 June 1990 at Casowasco, Moravia, NY, Robert Preske, s/o Raymond and Mary Lou (Slack) Preske, b 6 September 1953 in Syracuse. They reside at Warners, in the Kennedy family homestead; both work for Crystal Photo.
    740. iv. Melanie Mae, b 19 June 1969.
    741. v. Scott William, b 12 February 1971, Syracuse, NY.

301. HUGH^5 IRVING KENNEDY (s/o Alta^4 Canfield Kennedy #117), b 26 February 1934 at Warners, Onondaga Co., NY. He graduated from High School in Warners in 1952 and had about two years of college at Syracuse University when he enlisted in the U.S. Air Force and was stationed at Lowry Air Force Base at Denver, Colorado, being discharged 4 October 1960. He m 7 September 1957 at Walden, CO on her father's sheep ranch, in an outdoor ceremony **Effie Lou Wade**, d/o Robert and Grace (Metcalf) Wade, she b 26 July 1936 at Laramie, WY. After discharge from the army Hugh and family moved back to Onondaga Co., NY and returned to Syracuse University in 1962. He finally completed his degree requirements at Greeley, CO in 1963. Hugh taught High School Social Studies at Worland, WY from 1964 to 1972, returning to Lou's father's ranch at Walden, CO, bought a lot from her father and built a log cabin, making a living for awhile selling stakes from fallen trees and guiding hunting parties. He then worked for the U.S. Geological Survey in Cheyenne, WY and traveled around Wyoming, inspecting the quality and condition of the water supply in rivers and streams. Hugh and Lou were divorced 26 February 1979.

Hugh m/2 29 September 1979 in the Lutheran Church in Cheyenne,

WY, Florence Theresa Moen, d/o Olaf and Borghild Nicholina (Nelson) Moen, b 18 December 1935 at Ward Co., ND. "Florey" was previously married to Dwayne Brown and has three children from this marriage: Steven Dwayne Brown, b 12 November 1955; Wanda Faith (Brown) Richardson, b 4 April 1957; David Gary Brown, b 7 April 1958; she was divorced. Until recently she was employed at a local department store. They own 30 acres of land in suburban Cheyenne where they have built a log cabin and several shelters for the calves, milking cows, pigs and chickens they raise. They have several beef cows in their herd and every year buy several nursing calves which they fatten for market. They also grow a large garden, from which they freeze and can on a large scale for the winter months. Hugh is still working for the U.S. Geological Survey at their Cheyenne headquarters. They have no children.

Children, surname KENNEDY:
+ 742. i. Cynthia Kay, b 19 April 1958
+ 743. ii. Gwen Ann, b 20 June 1959.
+ 744. iii. Tami Louise, b 21 December 1960.
+ 745. iv. Julie Lynn, b 7 February 1963.
    746. v. Hugh Scott, b 23 October 1967 at Worland, WY. He graduated high school in 1986; enlisted in service 1989; and was on active duty in Germany in 1990.

Ina Cates Tognoni (#221) and
Joseph Russell Tognoni

Chapter 7

The Sixth Generation

302. ROLAND[6] **GEORGE CHEESEMAN** (s/o William[5] Alfred Cheeseman #118), b 13 June 1895 at North Girard, Erie Co., PA; m in 1919 at Pittsburg, PA, **Eleanor Merle Hamilton**. Roland d April 1948 in Birmingham, AL, and his ashes are buried in Hollywood Memorial Park, Union, NJ. Merle d in NJ in 1958 and is buried with her husband.

Child, surname CHEESEMAN:
+   747.   i.   Dorothy[7], b 5 October 1920.

303. HUBERT[6] **EDMOND CHEESEMAN** (s/o William[5] Alfred Cheeseman #118), b 21 October 1900 at North Girard, PA; m 27 October 1924, **Marion Edna Reynolds**, d/o John Francis and Hannah (Warner) Reynolds, b 15 October 1898 at New Haven, CT. Hubert was a realtor, licensed in the City of New York and Nassau Co., NY. Hubert is retired and living in East Haven, CT.

Children, surname CHEESEMAN:
+   748.   i.   John[7] Royal, b 13 August 1927.
+   749.   ii.   Carol Edna, b 17 November 1933.

305. DAVID[6] **S. JOHNSON** (s/o Louis[5] Johnson #127), b 22 May 1952; m 5 April 1975 at Amboy United Methodist Church, Conneaut, Ashtabula Co., OH, **Carol Ann Micelli**. David has a burglar alarm company, "John-Tronics Security Co." in Ashtabula. They live in Geneva, OH.

Child, surname JOHNSON:
    750.   i.   Crystal[7] Ann, b 19 August 1981 at Ashtabula.

308. GRACE[6] **MAE STEVENS** (d/o Mertie[5] Crouch Stevens #128), b 7 September 1901 in Dodge Co., MN; m 14 April 1920, **Earl Wiedendorf**, s/o Andrew and Julia Wiedendorf, b 23 March 1900 in Dodge Co., MN. For many years Earl was a farmer, then had his own cattle hauling truck; he trucked cattle to Saint. Paul stockyards. Grace d 7 October 1952 at Kasson, Dodge Co., MN. Earl d 19 July 1959 at West Concord, Dodge Co.

Children, surname WIEDENDORF:
- 751. i. David[7], died young.
- + 752. ii. Norma Ruth, b 5 October 1922.
- + 753. iii. Geryl Earl, b 2 November 1924.
- + 754. iv. Wayne Andrew, b 15 September 1939.

309. NORMAN[6] CARROLL STEVENS (s/o Mertie[5] Crouch Stevens #128), b 18 June 1905 at Dodge Co., MN; m **Myrtle Kleven**, d/o Matthew and Anna Kleven, she b 5 April 1904. Norman d March 1973 at Minneapolis, MN. Myrtle lives in Minneapolis, MN. She refused to give us any information on her family.

Child, surname STEVENS:
- + 755. i. Lea[7] Etta.

310. THELMA[6] BELLE STEVENS (d/o Mertie[5] Crouch Stevens #128), b 14 July, 1908 in Dodge Co., MN; m 20 May 1930 in Minneapolis, MN, **William Paul Schuffenhauer**, s/o Otto and Louise (Stopp) Schuffenhauer, b 2 August 1900 in Germany. He was a truck driver. William d 18 November 1952 and is buried in Hillside Cemetery, Minneapolis. Thelma lived in Minneapolis, when last known.

Children, surname SCHUFFENHAUER:
- 756. i. William[7] Paul, b 24 April 1931. He m at Aberdeen, MD, 8 May 1952, Charlotte Lauren DeMars, b 11 May 1920 at Columbia Heights, MN, d/o Mitchell and Anita DeMars. William works for Ed Phillips & Son Distillery.
- + 757. ii. Kenneth Roy, b 20 August 1933.
- + 758. iii. Jo Ann, b 9 June 1934.
- 759. iv. Gayle James, b 10 July 1936 at Minneapolis; m 28 November 1975 Carole Ann Frank at Northfield, MN. He works for Board of Education.
- 760. v. Norman Charles, b 4 August 1938. He works at the Minneapolis Post Office. He is not married.
- + 761. vi. Betty Jane, b 8 July 1940.
- + 762. vii. Robert Donald, b 19 September 1941.
- + 763. viii. Ronald Dean, b 19 September 1941.

311. CLARENCE[6] CROUCH (s/o Irvin[5] Crouch #129), b 27 July 1901 at Mantorville, Dodge Co., MN; m 27 June 1923 at Miltonvale, KS, **Maud Pearl Griffin**, d/o John and Catherine Griffin, b 26 September 1901 at

Hollis, KS. Clarence was a machinist. He d 6 January 1976 at Vancouver, WA.

Children, surname CROUCH:
+   764.   i.   Clarene[7] Elmina, b 23 June 1926.
+   765.   ii.   Lavon Elaine, b 8 August 1931.

312. MILDRED[6] ADELL CROUCH (d/o Irvin Crouch #129), b 30 April 1904 at Mantorville, Dodge Co, MN; m 19 August 1925 at Topeka, KS, **Howard Monroe Lee**, s/o W. F. and Rosa Bell (Turley) Lee, b 27 November 1903 at Bison, OK. He was an accountant with Oklahoma Gas and Electric Co., then an electrician at the shipyards in Portland, OR during World War II, then retired as a carpenter and builder. He had open heart surgery with four by-passes 12 May 1983. Mildred and Howard are living in Corvallis, OR.

Children, surname LEE:
+   766.   i.   Lynn[7] Monroe, b 20 January 1936.
+   767.   ii.   Beverly Ann, b 12 May 1941.

313. EVELYN[6] CROUCH (d/o Irvin[5] Crouch #129), b 27 June 1914 at Miltonvale, Cloud Co., KS; m **Clayton Brammer**, s/o Robert and Bessie (Jones) Brammer, b 26 November 1911 at Muses Mills, Fleming Co., KY. Evelyn and Clayton live at Leesburg, FL where he is a carpenter.

Children, surname BRAMMER:
+   768.   i.   Robert[7], b 9 August 1936.
+   769.   ii.   Janice Adell, b 6 December 1939.
+   770.   iii.   Ronald Allen, b 29 November 1947.

314. VERNON[6] CROUCH (s/o Irvin[5] Crouch #129), b 27 August 1918 at Ames, KS; m 24 November 1940 at Wichita, KS, **Evelyn Faith Garlow** d/o Joshua Franklin and Ruby Minnie (Cyr) Garlow, b 27 March 1922 at Ames. Vernon is a retired music teacher, vocal and band. They live at Leesburg, FL.

Children, surname CROUCH:
+   771.   i.   Sharon[7] Lu, b 30 October 1942.
+   772.   ii.   Linda Kay, b 28 March 1947.
      773.   iii.   Richard Jay, b 1 September 1954 at Marion, IN. He was killed in a plane crash 20 April 1974 at Herrington, KS.

316. LLOYD[6] HENRY GARRISON (s/o Grace[5] Crouch Garrison #130), b 2 February 1907 at Brookings Co., SD; m 12 April 1929 at Santa Ana, CA, **Dora Hodge**, d/o Fred and Millie (Allen) Hodge. Lloyd was an automobile painter; they live at Rialto, CA.

Children, surname GARRISON:
+   774.   i.   Donald[7] Lloyd, b 19 September 1929.
+   775.   ii.   Nona Lou, b 6 July 1935.

318. MYRTLE[6] ADELL GARRISON (d/o Grace[5] Crouch Garrison #130), b 10 July 1911 at Brookings Co., SD. She moved to California with her family in 1926; m 3 December 1928 at Santa Ana, CA; **Chester Kenneth Meeker**, s/o Charles and Dora (Pearson) Meeker, he b 29 July 1908 at Wapello Co., IA. Chester Kenneth was a mechanic and aircraft worker, now deceased. Myrtle lives at Long Beach, CA.

Child, surname MEEKER:
+   776.   i.   Betty[7] June, b 5 July 1929.

319. VERNON[6] GARRISON (s/o Grace[5] Crouch Garrison #130), b 2 July 1916 in Brookings Co., SD. He moved to California with his family in 1926. He m **Lillian Leseuer**(?) They live at Long Beach, CA.

Children, surname GARRISON:
  777.   i.   Barbara[7].
  778.   ii.   Judy.
  779.   iii.   Vicky.

321. DONALD[6] GARRISON (s/o Grace[5] Crouch Garrison #130) b 5 September 1921 at Brookings Co., SD. He moved to California with his family in 1926. Married 12 April 1942 at Salome, AZ, **Dorothy Carol Smith**, father not known by Donald, but mother's name Hazel Delight Newcomb. Dorothy born 22 December 1924. Donald and Dorothy divorced in 1947, Long Beach, CA.

Donald m/2 24 September 1955 at Glendale, CA, **Patricia Ann Petrick**, d/o John Frank and Ida Florence (Woodworth) Petrick, born 23 September 1932 at Los Angeles, CA. Donald and Patricia live at Lakeport, CA.

Children, surname GARRISON:
+   780.   i.   Donald[7], b 26 July 1944.
+   781.   ii.   David, born 4 November 1946.

The Sixth Generation

+ 782. iii. Kathy La Vonne, b 22 June 1956.
 783. iv. John Michael, b 16 November 1959, at Lake Port, CA; he graduated 1984 from Chico State College with a degree in Communication; he lives in Chico.

322. JUANITA[6] MAE DANIELS (d/o Lettie[5] Crouch Daniels #131), b 10 December 1904 at Wasioja, Dodge Co., MN; m August 1932 in IA, **Glenn William Evans**, s/o Ira and Sarah (Paul) Evans, b 9 March 1910 at Shelby, IA. Glenn came to Wasioja to attend college and become a teacher; instead got married. Juanita was hospitalized 8 years in mental hospitals for a nervous breakdown six months after the birth of her fifth child; while in hospital a sixth unnamed female child was born and died young. Juanita's mother took her from the hospital to Long Beach, CA where she lived 29 years. Glenn divorced Juanita after 7 years, about 1949 and m/2 Fern Carlson, who died two or three years later, in 1953, of cancer. He was employed at Tassee Bakery. On 18 June 1966 he m/3 Joyce Duran. They live at Bloomington, MN. Juanita moved from Long Beach, CA to Oseo, MN in 1980 to be near her children. When last known she lived in a Residential Home called Berkshire.

Children, surname EVANS:
+ 784. i. Richard[7] Allen, b 21 January 1933.
+ 785. ii. David Wayne, b 11 February 1935.
+ 786. iii. Thomas Glenn, b 5 December 1938.
+ 787. iv. Sarah Adell, b 7 March 1940.
+ 788. v. Sharon Elizabeth, b 5 October 1943.

323. WYNOT[6] BERDELL DANIELS (s/o Lettie[5] Crouch Daniels #131) b 6 October 1912 at Cannon Falls, Goodhue Co., MN; m 19 October 1933 at Minneapolis, MN, **Edna Anita Gunnufson**, d/o Edward Andrew and Aletta Sophia (Anderson) Gunnufson, b 10 July 1916; Wynot died 5 June 1947 at Lancaster, CA; is buried at Westminster, CA, Memorial Park; Edna lives at LaMesa, CA.

Children, surname DANIELS:
+ 789. i. David[7] Wynot b 13 June 1935.
+ 790. ii. Constance Diane, b 18 December 1938.
+ 791. iii. Robert Blake, b 11 September 1943.

324. BETHEL[6] JUNE DANIELS (d/o Lettie[5] Crouch Daniels #131), b 19 June 1919 at Red Wing, Goodhue Co., MN; m 12 February 1939 at

Long Beach, CA, **Jack Reed Hunt**, s/o Smith and Blanche (Seefelt) Hunt, b 17 May 1918 in Iowa. They were divorced December 1955 in Florida. Jack died 7 January 1984 at Daytona Beach, FL.

Bethel m/2 15 April 1963 at Las Vegas, NV, **Henry Louis Valette**, s/o Henry Clement and Viola Marie (Miller) Valette, he b 9 February 1916. Henry had a Furniture Manufacturing Company which he sold and retired in 1973. He is now semi-retired as a consultant. They have a home near Wickenburg, AZ, where they may move permanently. Presently they live at Rolling Hills Estates, CA. They have no children.

Children, surname HUNT:
+ 792. i. Ricky[7] Reed, b 2 September 1944.
+ 793. ii. Gary Dean, b 23 March 1946.

326. HARLIE[6] LAVERNE CROUCH (s/o Harrison[5] M. Crouch #132), b 30 November 1914 at Wasioja, Dodge Co., MN; m 18 February 1951 at the Lutheran Church at Rock Dell, MN, **Bernice Holtan**, d/o Alfred and Minnie Holtan, of Kasson, MN, b 23 July 1927 at Wasioja, Minn. Harlie is a retired farmer who bought and sold livestock. Harlie and Bernice live at West Concord, MN.

Children, surname CROUCH:
+ 794. i. Garth[7], b 13 March 1952.
+ 795. ii. Elizabeth, b 10 September 1953.
+ 796. iii. Kathryn, b 5 March 1956.

327. LEORA[6] BELLE CROUCH (d/o Harrison[5] M. Crouch #132), b 21 November 1916 at Wasioja, Dodge Co., MN; m 21 July 1938 at Blooming Grove MN, **Burdette Hart**, s/o Grover Franklin and Johanna Magdalena (Pfeiffer) Hart, he b 30 April 1917 at Davis, ND. Burdette worked at a lumber yard at Pine Island, MN. Leora d 28 August 1981 at Mesa, AZ. Burdette still lives at Mesa.

Children, surname HART:
+ 797. i. David[7] Burdette, b 28 May 1939.
+ 798. ii. Larry Duane, b 22 July 1941.
+ 799. iii. Cherelyn Lea, b 31 December 1943.
+ 800. iv. Nancy Kay, b 11 February 1948.
+ 801. v. Sue Ranal, b 18 January 1953.

329. QUENTIN[6] CROUCH (s/o Vernon[5] Crouch #133), b 18 July 1929 at Rochester, MN; m 21 August 1953 at Rochester, MN, **Lois Marie Peterson**, d/o Clarence D. and Eunice M. (Humrickhouse) Peterson, she b 21 January 1932 at Minneapolis, MN. Quentin graduated Hamline University, Saint Paul, MN. He is Public Relations Coordinator for the Minnesota Dept. of Transportation. He and Lois live in Rochester, MN.

Children, surname CROUCH:
- 802. i. Steven[7] Douglas, b 24 October 1954 at Minneapolis, MN. He is unmarried and works for Boeing Aircraft as an Aerospace Engineer.
- \+ 803. ii. Marcia Jean, b 16 April 1957.
- \+ 804. iii. Brenda Eileen, b 20 January 1959.

330. KERMIT[6] CROUCH (s/o Vernon[5] Crouch #133), b 16 September 1934 at Rochester MN; m 6 April 1957 at Minneapolis, MN, **Elizabeth Louise Ross**, d/o Donald Alexander and Mary Alice (Day) Ross, b 29 May 1933 at Minneapolis. Quentin graduated from University of Minnesota. "I am an Urban planner. I consult on an advisory basis to out state and suburban communities which do not have full time staff planners. I founded my own firm, Crouch Consultants, in April 1982." Elizabeth was previously married: the first two children were hers by that marriage, and adopted by Kermit. Together they had the last three children.

Children, surname CROUCH:
- \+ 805. i. Virginia[7] Lee, b 7 May 1954.
- \+ 806. ii. Byron Ross, b 27 July 1955.
- \+ 807. iii. Vincent Kevin, b 13 October 1957.
- \+ 808. iv. Kurt Jeffrey, b 19 November 1958.
- 809. v. Todd Gregory, b 23 May 1961. When last known was a student in college at Mankato, MN.

333. ALLEN[6] GEORGE CROUCH (s/o Floyd[5] Crouch #135), b 26 March 1919 at Wasioja, Dodge Co., MN; m 19 March 1942 at Las Vegas, NV, **Bette Germaine Draper**, she b 1921. In 1984 were living in Fontana, CA.

Children, surname CROUCH;
- 810. i. Jerald[7] Allen, b in 1943; m Connie Van Der Borgh.
- 811. ii. Carol Diane, b in 1945; m Robert Kenneth Padgett, b 1945.
- 812. iii. Debra Sue, b in 1955; m Gary Fisher.

334. RUTH[6] MILDRED CROUCH (d/o Floyd[5] Crouch #135), b 14

November 1920 near Mantorville, Dodge Co., MN; m 15 May 1941 at Dodge Center, **Gordon Ralph Miller**, s/o Ralph Vernon and Nellie Elizabeth (Proper) Miller, b 3 June 1914 at Milton Township, Dodge Co. Ruth and Gordon live in Dodge Center.

Children, surname MILLER:
- 813. i. Unnamed female child, born dead November 1946, Owatonna, MN.
- 814. ii. Kenneth[7] Gordon, b 26 June 1948, Owatonna. He lives in Denver, CO, and is Supervisor of Laboratory Technicians in a hospital. He is not married.
- + 815. iii. Pamela Ruth, b 3 April 1950.
- + 816. iv. Steven Douglas, b 20 November 1953.

335. MARIE[6] LOIS CROUCH (d/o Floyd[5] Crouch #135), b 22 November 1922 at Wasioja, MN; m/1 at Claremont, MN, 31 December 1941, **Edwin Marquette**. They were divorced 13 April 1952 at Burbank, CA. She m/2 **Eugene William Dubois**, 24 January 1955 at Las Vegas, NV, b 5 November 1914 at Rumford, Maine, s/o Frederick and Philomine (Desroches) Dubois. He was manager and cook at his V.F.W. Eugene d 20 August 1977 at Sun Valley, CA. Marie is a waitress, and lives at Sun Valley.

Child, surname DUBOIS:
- 817. i. David[7] Arthur, b 2 August 1955 at Burbank. He is a punch press operator and musician.

337. ELNA[6] NADENE CROUCH (d/o Floyd[5] Crouch #135), b 3 December 1932 at Dodge Co., MN; m/1 **Charles Geise** at Red Bank, NJ in 1950. They were divorced in Dodge Co. in 1958, and there were no children. She m/2 at Denver, CO, 30 November 1959, **Neil Vincent Romano**, b 29 November 1929 at New York, NY; s/o John and Carmella (Madonna) Romano. Neil and Elna own and run an Italian restaurant, Elna being the bookkeeper.

Children, surname ROMANO:
- 818. i. Susan[7] Carmella, b 18 June 1960; m Edward Bartlett at Littleton, CO, 2 June 1984. They live at Lakewood, CO. Susan is employed in the promotion department of the local NBC TV station; Ed is a CPA and is employeed in a construction company.
- 819. ii. John Anthony, b 3 July 1962; he was to marry Rachelle Schwalm, 28 September 1985. He works at the restaurant.

820. iii. Nicholas Allen, b 10 November 1965.

339. CHERYL[6] MAVIS CROUCH (d/o Charles[5] H. Crouch #137), b 6 May 1941 at Waseca, Waseca Co., MN. She moved with her family to Arizona in 1950 where she m 27 December 1957 at Tempe, **Wayne Gay**, s/o Wilton Kenneth and Mary (Coker) Gay, b 17 August 1938 at Corsicana, TX. Wayne and Cheryl run their own plumbing firm, Gay Plumbing, in Payson, AZ, where they live.

Children, surname GAY, all born at Tempe:
+ 821. i. William[7] Kenneth, b 10 July 1958.
+ 822. ii. Carolyn Elaine, b 3 July 1959.
   823. iii. Thomas Charles, b 18 July 1960.
   824. iv. Kevin Wyatt, b 10 November 1967.

340. JOHN[6] WALKER RAYMOND (s/o Mildred[5] Crouch Raymond #138), b 6 December 1929 at Long Beach, CA; m 16 October 1976 at West Point, NY, **Rolande Marie Elie**, d/o Edmond Joseph and Aldea Marie (Dore) Elie, she b 1 January 1950 at Biddeford, ME. John was a Medical Specialist in the U.S. Army until he retired 31 December 1975. He now is messenger at the Portsmouth Naval Shipyard. They live at Biddeford, ME.

Children, surname RAYMOND:
   825. i. Jonathan[7] Moses, b 8 August 1979.

341. THOMAS[6] HAMILTON RAYMOND (s/o Mildred[5] Crouch Raymond #138), b 15 April 1931 at Kingman, AZ; m 11 August 1952 at Wichita, KS, **Anna Ruth Loewen**, b 31 January 1934 at Buhler, Kansas. Tom graduated from Wichita University in 1955 and Kansas University School of Medicine in 1958. He is a specialist in ear, nose and throat medicine at Fort Smith, AR.

Children, surname RAYMOND;
   826. i. Linda[7] Gail, b 8 January 1954 at Wichita, KS. She taught school for 4 years. Went to University of Arkansas Medical School.
   827. ii. Laura Abby, b 17 March 1961 at Kansas City, KS; m 31 December 1983 at Fort Smith, Keith Allen Rayl. She is a graduate of Baylor University, Waco, TX in business and psychology. Keith has a masters degree in Gerontology.
   828. iii. Peter Thomas, b 11 September 1963 at Fort Sill, Lawton, OK. Currently attending (1985) the Journalism School at University

of Missouri; wants to be a photo-Journalist.

342. BETTY[6] JANE CROUCH (d/o John[5] W. Crouch #139), b 12 January 1927 at Northfield, Rice Co., MN; m 7 April 1947 at University of Minnesota Chapel, Minneapolis, MN, **Gerald Phillip Schoenfelder**, s/o William Alfred and Mary Ann (Fogarty) Schoenfelder, b 20 March 1926, on a farm outside of Rochester, MN; they were divorced April 1972.

Betty Jane m/2 **Cleon "Bud" W. Main**, s/o William A. and Maybelle Gertrude (Gilmer) Main on 5 July 1975 at Jonathan, MN, near Chaska, b 26 October 1925 at Delano, MN. There have no children.

Children, surname SCHOENFELDER:
+ 829.   i. Patrick[7] Gerald, b 22 November 1947.
+ 830. ii. Daniel John, b 7 June 1949.
+ 831. iii. Timothy William, b 9 July 1950.
+ 832. iv. Kevin Peter, b 28 February 1952.
+ 833.   v. Bridget Mary, b 3 September 1953.
  834. vi. Mary Elizabeth, b 28 September 1956 at Davenport, IA.
  835. vii. Nora Anne, b 26 August 1958 at Shakopee, MN. She graduated from Antioch College and was going to medical school at University of Minnesota in the fall of 1984.
  836. viii. Sheila Marie, b 15 August 1961 at Shakopee. She graduated from MacAllister College and is in the Peace Corps in Dominican Republic until December 1985.
  837. ix. Kathleen Carmel, b 7 February 1963 at Shakopee. June 1985 graduates from Dartmouth College, Hanover, NH as a Math major.

344. EVA[6] REED PALMER (d/o Emma[5] Osborn Palmer #142), b 21 November 1918 at Strool, SD; m 17 November 1937 at Kasson, MN, **Reuben Phelps**, s/o Guy and Hattie A. (Burk) Phelps, b 2 December 1904 at Dodge Co., MN and was a farmer. Eva d 13 July 1981 at Red Wing, MN. and is buried in Wildwood Cemetery, Wasioja, MN. When last known Reuben was still living at Bay City, WI.

Children, surname PHELPS:
+ 838.   i. Lawrence[7], b 10 December 1938.
+ 839. ii. Shirley, b 11 August 1941.

345. MARIAN[6] NADEAN PALMER (d/o Emma[5] Osborn Palmer #142), b 8 August 1922 at Wasioja, Dodge Co., MN; m 24 December

The Sixth Generation 209

1940 at Northwood, IA, **Kyle Markie Stafford**, s/o Markie and Isabelle (Bartholomew) Stafford, b 21 September 1920 in Olmstead Co., MN. Kyle has a large farm of 160 acres and rents about 140 acres more. From 1950 to 1967 he sawed lumber, in addition to farming. He raises oats, soy beans and corn primarily.

Children, surname STAFFORD:
+ 840. i. Maxine[7] Paula, b 23 October 1941.
+ 841. ii. Bonita Jean, b 1 March 1945.
+ 842. iii. Betty Kay, b 21 July 1947.
    843. iv. Mark Owen, b 3 September 1951 at Dodge Center; m 30 June 1979, Nancy Ellen Quast, b 27 January 1953. They graduated from Saint Cloud University; she teachers 10th grade history and he is a supervisor for inventory control for Grace, Inc.
+ 844. v. Marvin Kyle, b 11 November 1953.

346. CLINTON[6] "Red" OWEN PALMER (s/o Emma[5] Osborn Palmer #142), b 18 October 1927 at Perkins Co., SD; m 13 April 1957 at Mason City, IA, **Allie Rieken**, d/o Michael and Kate Rieken, b 15 March 1935 at Renova, Mower Co., MN. Clinton works at the Saint Paul Union Stockyards; Allie works for Foto Mark Anodizing Plant.

Children, surname PALMER:
+ 845. i. Dale[7], b 17 January 1958.
+ 846. ii. Nancy, b 10 August 1959.

347. LOIS[6] MASON (d/o Lida[5] Osborn Mason #143), b 8 May 1915, Dodge Co, MN; m 4 July 1936, **Harley Lewis**, s/o William James and Mary (Barthelow) Lewis, he b 17 December 1907. Harley had a barber shop at Dodge Center, MN. He d 23 September 1950 and is buried in Wasioja, MN. Lois was Special Education teacher in Indio, CA until her retirement in 1982. She lives in Indio, CA when last known.

Child, surname LEWIS:
+ 847. i. Rowena[7] Harlene, b 12 April 1940.

349. MYRON[6] MASON (s/o Lida[5] Osborn Mason #143), b 10 September 1917 at Perkins Co., SD; m 20 August 1938, **Florence Hazel Lee** at Cresco IA, b 7 April 1917 at Dodge Co., MN. Myron owns two businesses: Mason's Auto Clinic and Mason's Precision Wheel and Brake Service at Imperial Beach, CA. Myron and Florence live in Joshua Tree, CA, when last known.

Children, surname MASON:
+ 848. i. Darlene[7] Faye, b 4 July 1939.
+ 849. ii. Robert Myron, b 9 April 1943.
+ 850. iii. John Gerald, b 13 March 1947.

350. GORDON[6] WILLIAM FRANKLIN (s/o #139 Bida[5] Osborn Franklin #144), b 11 July 1921 at Mankato, MN. He graduated from Union College at Lincoln, NE; went through Army Special Training in Morgantown, WV. He received his medical degree at Loma Linda University, Loma Linda, CA. He is a general practitioner in Northome, MN. Gordon m 14 October 1948, Chapel of the Roses, at Pasadena, CA, **Marjorie Helen Kaldahl**, d/o Clarence and Jesse (Forney) Kaldahl, b 14 February 1925 at Rolling Forks, MN.

Children, surname FRANKLIN:
851. i. Marcia[7] Jane, b 10 March 1950, Saint Paul, MN. She graduated from Loma Linda University Medical School, Loma Linda and is in family practice at Karlstad, MN. She is not married.
852. ii. Paul Dwight, b 12 January 1951 at Little Fork, MN. He works in building construction in Alaska in the summer and in winter, logs at Mispah, MN. Unmarried.
853. iii. Kent Gordon, b 18 December 1952 at Bemidji, Minn. He lives at Mizpah, MN. Summers he does carpentry work and farming. In the winter he logs with brother Paul. He is not married.

351. DONALD[6] LINCOLN FRANKLIN (s/o Bida[5] Osborn Franklin #144), b 12 February 1924 at Good Thunder, MN; m 12 August 1959 at Delta, CO, **Esther Lois Curtis**, d/o Lyman and Lois Iciphene (Puleston) Curtis, b 3 February 1929 at Cedar Edge, CO. Donald is a custodian and part time farmer and lives at Northome, MN.

Children, surname FRANKLIN:
854. i. Roberta[7] Lois, b 11 December 1960 at Farmington, NM; m 12 August 1984 at Benidji, MN, Eugene Roger Clausen. She has a batchelors degree in education and works in the Union College Library. Eugene teaches math at the University of Nebraska and is taking additional course work. They live in Lincoln and have no children.
855. ii. Albert Lloyd, b 22 October 1962 at Farmington, NM. He works for College View Printers in Lincoln, NE, operating a folding, addressing machine. He went to college part time when last know about him.

354. NORMAN[6] DALE FRANKLIN (s/o Bida[5] Osborn Franklin #144), b 26 June 1931/32 at Vernon Center, MN; m **Alice Sylvia Miller**, d/o John Edward and Lillian Maria (Watson) Miller, she b 9 April 19— at Fairton, NJ. Norman was a Laboratory Technician at Walter Reed Hospital, Washington, DC. He d 1 March 1976 at Silver Springs, WV and is buried at Millville, NJ. Alice is living in Bridgeton, NJ.

Child, surname FRANKLIN:
- 856. i. Rie[7], b 17 July 1966 at Frederick, MD. Was a senior student at Highland View Academy, Hagerstown, MD in 1985.

355. RILLA[6] BELL FRANKLIN (d/o Bida[5] Osborn Franklin #144), b 9 January 1933 at Vernon Center, MN; m 28 November 1959 at Sacred Heart Church, Melrose Park, IL, **John Walenga**, b 11 December 1933 at Harvey, IL, s/o Edward Leo and Minnie Mary (Albert) Walenga. John is computer systems analyst at Dept. of Mental Health for State of Illinois. They live in Springfield, IL.

Children, surname WALENGA:
- 857. i. Mark[7] Gregory, b 5 November 1955 at Portland, OR. He graduated from college in 1985 with a degree in Russian.
- 858. ii. Jaqueline Kay, b 1 May 1960 at Chicago, IL. She has a degree in Social Sciences.
- + 859. iii. Elizabeth Jo, b 17 July 1961.
- + 860. iv. Lora Marie, b 6 August 1962.
- 861. v. Yvonne Carol, b 2 July 1964 at Chicago.

356. EUGENE[6] JAMES QUICK (s/o George[5] Martin Quick #149), b 15 January 1900 at Licking, MO; m/1, 25 May 1928, **Zula Cope** in Nevada. He was a farmer. Eugene m/2 **Mabel Dow** in the 1940s and they live at Waterford, CA.

Child, surname QUICK:
- + 862. i. Virginia[7] Jean, b in the 1930s.

363. GEORGIA[6] MAE QUICK (d/o George[5] Martin Quick #149), b 9 October 1902 at Licking, MO; m 1 May 1925 at Colorado Springs, CO, **James Wood McCloskey**, he b 8 May 1900 at Lawrence, KS, s/o William Herbert and Minnie (Sanderson) McCloskey. He worked for Borden's Creamer at Modesto, CA until his death in 1964. Mae lives at Modesto.

Child, surname QUICK:

+ 863. i. Betty[7] Mae, b 28 October 1926.

360. ELLEN[6] ELIZABETH QUICK (d/o George[5] Martin Quick #149), b 7 October 1906 at Texas Co., MO; m 24 August 1928, **Paul Brown** in California; he is deceased. Ellen m/2 **Jack Whitlock** and m/3 **Herman Niebaum**. They lives at Turlock, CA.

Child, surname BROWN

864. i. Paul[7] Shryer, b 1 July 1933 at Modesto, CA. See Addenda.

361. VERA[6] EVELYN QUICK (d/o George[5] Martin Quick #149), b 20 November 1908; m in California, 20 July 1927, **Kenneth Perry**, b August 1906.

Child, surname PERRY:

865. ii. Ronnie, adopted in 1945/46; d about 1961 at age 16.

362. DORIS[6] IVA QUICK (d/o George[5] Martin Quick #149), b 22 July 1914 in Calhan, CO; m 24 December 1935 at Hilmar, CA, **James Vernon Houghton**, b 11 March 1912 at Hollister, CA, s/o James V. and Jessie Fremont (Sharp) Houghton. Doris and James live at Santa Maria, CA.

Children, surname HOUGHTON:

866. i. Marian[7] Delores, b March 1939; d April 1939.
+ 867. ii. Lois Jean, b 30 June 1940.
+ 868. iii. Ann Louise, b 8 October 1943.

363. CALVIN[6] QUICK (s/o Jesse[5] James Quick #152), b 14 October 1912 at Markesan, WI; m 26 April 1936, **Margaret Mary Jodarski**, d/o Martin and Martha (Tramph) Jodarski, b 22 August 1914 at Berlin, WI. Calvin worked for L.P. Gas Co. before his retirement. He d 14 March 1987.

Child, surname QUICK;
+ 869. i. Dennis[7] Lee, b 25 February 1939.

364. ELMER[6] QUICK (s/o Jesse[5] James Quick #152), b 11 February 1914 at Markesan, WI; m 31 August 1940 at Waupun, WI, **Bernice Trowbridge**, d/o Frank and Agatha (Klugen) Trowbridge, b 7 July 1917 at Waupun, Wisconsin. Elmer was an engineer for 45 years with John Deere Co., at Horicon works. He is now a consultant for them in Florida.

Children, surname QUICK:

870. i. Patricia[7] Louise, b 23 April 1942, Horicon, WI; m Wallace

The Sixth Generation 213

                Koehler at Milwaukee, WI. He works for a cheese manufacturer in Wacipaca, WI.

+   871.   ii. Jeanne Ann, b 17 May 1945.

365. RUSSELL[6] E. QUICK (s/o Jesse[5] James Quick #152), b 7 March 1915 at Markesan, WI; m 6 April 1941, **Dorothy Margaret Dalke**, d/o Andrew and Magdalene (Sina) Dalke, b 17 April 1917 at Princeton, WI. Until his retirement Russell was lineman for Wisconsin Power and Light Co. They are retired and live in Florida in the winter and Green Lake, WI in the summer.

Children, surname QUICK:
+   872.   i. James[7] Russell, b 20 October 1946.
+   873.   ii. Robert Alan, b 1 October 1948.

366. LELAND[6] QUICK (s/o Jesse[5] James Quick #152), b 13 February 1918 at Markesan, WI; m at Green Lake, WI, 29 July 1944, **Mary Maldari**, b 21 June 1918 at Red Granite, WI, d/o Philip and Pasqualina (D'Agostino) Maldari. Leland was a plumber and pipe fitter; they live at Hughson, CA.

Children, surname QUICK:
+   874.   i. Mary[7] L., b 23 August 1946.
+   875.   ii. David, b 1 May 1948.
+   876.   iii. Bruce, b 24 July 1951.

367. IRENE[6] QUICK (d/o Jesse[5] James Quick #152), b 4 July 1922 at Markesan, WI; m 5 February 1944, **Joe S. Ilgen**, s/o James and Carrie (Snook) Ilgen. he b 6 November 1919 at Cedarville, IL. Irene was a biology teacher before her marriage; she worked as an academic support specialist in the Zoology Department, University of Wisconsin from 1962 until she retired in 1985. Joe worked as remote control specialist for Wisconsin Power and Light. He d 12 June 1975 while in Greece visiting one of many foreign students who made their home with the Ilgens while in the U.S. Irene still lives at Madison, WI.

Children, surname ILGEN:
+   877.   i. Thomas[7] Lee, b 13 February 1946.
+   878.   ii. Jane Ellen, b 22 July 1948.

368. EVELYN[6] QUICK (d/o Eugene[5] Quick #153), b 5 September 1913 at Markesan, WI; m 21 December 1934, **Ervin Grahn**, s/o Henry and

Emma (Sanders) Grahn, he b 1 May 1912 at Ripon, WI.

Child, surname GRAHN:

+ 879. i. Gary[7], b 7 February 1942.

369. LYLE[6] JAMES QUICK (s/o Eugene[5] Quick #153), b 10 February 1914 at Markesan, WI; m 27 February 1943, **Lois Lorraine Kimble**, d/o Merwin and Josephine (Lichtenberg) Kimble; she b 24 November 1924 on a farm near Markesan. Lyle was a farmer. His residence at the time of his marriage was Town of Nepeuskun, Winnebago, WI. Lyle died in Fulton, MO, 18 March 1974 and is buried in Liberty Prairie Cemetery, Picket, WI. On his death certificate he was listed as night watchman at Fulton State Hospital.

Children, surname QUICK:

    880. i. Darlene[7] Lois, b 21 July 1944; d 3 September 1964.

+ 881. ii. Phyllis, b 8 November 1945.

370. NAOMI[6] MARY QUICK (d/o Eugene[5] Quick #153), b 9 April 1915 at Markesan, WI; m 22 September 1936, at Picket, WI, **Gordon Heckes**, s/o Fred and Ida (Splitgerber) Heckes, b 29 July 1910 in Town of Rosendale. He was a farmer.

Children, surname HECKES:

+ 882. i. Sharon[7] Mae, b 19 March 1938.
+ 883. ii. Ronald Gordon, b 26 November 1941.

371. DOROTHY[6] MARY ELLEN QUICK (d/o Eugene[5] Quick #153), b 24 November 1919 at Ripon WI; m 4 December 1937, Ripon, **Arnold Garhard Valentine Badtke**, s/o Albert and Marie (Bolter) Badtke, b 29 March 1914 at Ripon. He is a farmer.

Children, surname BADTKE:

+ 884. i. Caroline[7] Dorothy, b 6 August 1938.
+ 885. ii. James Arnold Albert, b 12 June 1940.
+ 886. iii. Tom Norbert, b 20 February 1945.
+ 887. iv. Jon Dennis, b 16 April 1946.

378. BEATRICE[6] MARGUERITE PECKHAM (d/o John[5] W. Peckham #158), b 31 March 1899 at Alexandria, SD; m 14 July 1917 at Belvedere, IL, **Arthur Randolph Shipton**, s/o George and Edith Shipton, he b 19 December 1893 at Mitchell, SD, Arthur was President of Midwest

The Sixth Generation

Oil Co., Sioux Falls, SD. He d 7 April 1958 at Sioux Falls. Beatrice still living at Sioux Falls when last known.

Children, surname SHIPTON:
- \+ 888. i. Beverly[7] Jeanette, b 8 October 1919.
- \+ 889. ii. Virginia Lola, b 25 September 1922.
- \+ 890. iii. Artha Jane, b 16 February 1932.

379. HARRIET[6] PECKHAM (d/o Charles[5] H. Peckham #159), b 24 June 1898 at Alexandria, Hanson Co., SD. She moved to Des Moines, IA with her parents in 1919; m 10 August 1920 at Boone, IA, **Clarence Millard Hathorn**, s/o Frank E. and Lida (Smith) Hathorn, b 13 February 1899 at Cedar Rapids, IA. Clarence worked for Glens Falls Insurance Company in Des Moines, IA and Louisville, KY from 1927 to 1963, when he retired. Harriet was an accomplished pianist, having studied piano at Northwestern University at Evanston, IL. Harriet d 15 September 1978 at Louisville and is buried at Resthaven Memorial Park there. Clarence remarried, in 1979, Anita Richardson and in 1984 they were living in Louisville. Clarence claims descent from the famous author Nathaniel Hawthorn.

Children, surname HATHORN:
- \+ 891. i. Betty[7] Jean , b 15 April 1921.
- 892. ii. John Clarence, b 4 February 1927, Des Moines, IA; m 1945, at New Albany, IN, Betty Hock, d/o Paul & Margaret Hock.

380. ELLSWORTH[6] L. PECKHAM (s/o Frank[5] D. Peckham #160), b 18 August 1899 at Alexandria, Hanson Co., SD; m 15 August 1925, **Thelma Maytum**, d/o Dr. Wellington James and Lillian Mae (Syferd) Maytum, b 25 August 1900 at Alexandria, SD. Ellsworth was Clearance Officer for Wisconsin State Employment Service, at Madison. Ellsworth d 28 July 1983 at Madison and is buried in Sunset Memorial Cemetery at Madison. Thelma was still living in 1984.

Children, surname PECKHAM:
- \+ 893. i. Phillip[7] Durward, b 6 March 1927.
- \+ 894. ii. John Richard, b 14 April 1930.

381. DONALD[6] SETH PECKHAM (s/o Frank[5] D. Peckham #160), b 7 November 1903 at Alexandria, SD; m **Crystal Maytum**, sister of Thelma who m his brother Ellsworth, b 16 June 1903 at Alexandria, SD.

She was a science teacher, then Superintendent of Schools in several school systems. Donald d October 1973 at Oceanside, CA. Crystal was living in 1984 in Oceanside.

Children, surname PECKHAM:
+   895. i. Donald[7] Dean, b 8 February 1932.
+   896. ii. Janet May, b 30 July 1934.
    897. iii. Nancy Ann, b 30 September 1937.
+   898. iv. James Maytum, b 13 December 1938.

382. HOWARD[6] JOHN PECKHAM (s/o Frank[5]D. Peckham #160), b 17 August 1905 at Alexandria, SD; m 11 October 1930 at University Baptist Church at Minneapolis, MN, **Mary Kathryn Price**, d/o Dr. Walthal Wooldridge and Elia Leigh (Newsome) Price, b 12 October 1910 at Centerville, Turner Co., SD. Howard was employed by Midwest Oil Company, 40 years first as office manager and secretary, the last twenty years as President of the company (1927–1967). Howard d 1 November 1980 at Sioux Falls, SD and is buried in Hills of Rest Cemetery, Sioux Falls. Kathryn still living as of 1984.

Children, surname PECKHAM:
+   899. i. Howard[7] John, b 25 March 1934.
+   900. ii. Mary Elia, b 16 March 1938.
    901. iii. Kathryn Leigh, b 15 December 1950 at Sioux Falls; m 29 May 1972, Marc Steven Aune; divorced in 1981. m/2 at Captiva Island near Fort Myers, FL, on 3 July 1982, Kenneth John Gooderham, s/o William and Janet Gooderham. Kenneth is in the advertising business at Fort Myers and Kathryn is secretary of the Captiva Erosion District Engineering Co. in Fort Myers, where they live.

383. NORMA[6] FLORENCE PECKHAM (d/o Frank[5] D. Peckham #160), b 27 June 1907 at Alexandria, Hanson Co., MN; m 8 August 1928, **Francis R. Olsen**, s/o Chris and Serena (Nasby) Olsen, b 15 November 1900 near Dell Rapids, SD. Francis was coach and athletic director for twelve years, then in management at John Morell Co., in Sioux Falls, SD, until his retirement in 1965. In 1970 they moved to California, where Norma d 20 January 1980 at Calimesa. Her ashes are interred in Francis' family cemetery at Dell Rapids, SD. When last known Francis still living at Calimesa; he has Parkinson's Disease.

Children, surname OLSEN:
+   902. i. Dean[7] Stanton, b 22 April 1935.

+ 903. ii. David Peckham, b 27 May 1939.
+ 904. iii. Barbara Joanne, b 21 August 1940.

384. FRANCIS[6] HERBERT PECKHAM (s/o Frank[5] D. Peckham #160), b 15 February 1914 at Alexandria, Hanson Co., SD; m 26 August 1939 at Luverne, MN, **Beulah M. Arneson**, d/o Albert O. and Berthanna (Gudahl) Arneson, b 22 September 1916 at Howard, SD. Francis was local manager of livestock Transit Dept. at Sioux Falls Livestock Exchange and almost 42 years with Hartford Fire Insurance Co. Beulah d 23 September 1983 at Sioux Falls, SD and is buried at Hills of Rest Cemetery, Sioux Falls. As of 1984 Francis was still living at Sioux Falls.

Children, surname PECKHAM:
    905. i. Robert[7] Frank, b in 1940; died in infancy.
    906. ii. Joan Elaine, b 1941; died in infancy.
+ 907. iii. Carole Jane, b 6 February 1943.
    908. iv. Barbara Lee, b 14 January 1944; m Bart Friedhoff whom she divorced shortly before her death 9 April 1974, while waiting for a heart transplant.

385. LEOTA[6] VERNETTE RYBURN (d/o Edith[5] Peckham Ryburn #161), b 16 February 1899 at Alexandria, Hanson Co., SD; m 3 February 1921 at Alexandria, **Omar Hilligoss**. Omar was a Chevrolet dealer. Leota d and is buried in Lakewood Mausoleum, Minneapolis, MN. Omar still living in 1984.

Children, surname HILLIGOSS:
    909. i. Billy[7].
    910. ii. Donny.
    911. iii. Jerry.

389. DOROTHY[6] JEANETTE RYBURN (d/o Edith[5] Peckham Ryburn #161), b 12 February 1906 at Alexandria, SD; m **Arthur Fox**. Last known address was Great Falls, MT.

Child, surname FOX:
    912. i. John[7] Richard, b 27 June 1930 at Mitchell, SD.

390. NETTIE[6] MAY PALMER (d/o Laura[5] Vining Palmer #166), b 18 July 1895 near Hillside, SD; m 19 April 1919 at Mitchell, SD, **Berger Sjursen Jelmeland**, s/o Sjur Knutsen and Britha (Instefjord) Jelmeland; b 17 July 1883 near Bergen, Norway. Berger was a tailor, a trade he learned in his native land and had been plying since 1900. He even continued the trade in the nursing home, Violet Tschetter Memorial Home. His hobby was gardening. He d 5 February 1980 at Huron, SD. Nettie d 6 July 1955 at Huron, SD. Both are buried at Graceland Cemetery, Mitchell.

Children, surname JELMELAND:
- 913. i. Bernetta[7] May, b 29 May 1920; d 16 February 1924.
- + 914. ii. Wilma Maxine, b 2 November 1921.
- + 915. iii. Donald Kenneth, b 12 January 1924.
- + 916. iv. Harvey Vincent, b 9 November 1925 at Miller, SD; m 31 January 1956 at Colorado Springs, CO, Ethel Jennings, d/o William and Marie (Hardin) Jennings; they are divorced and had no children. He retired from Denver Post.

391. CHESTER[6] PALMER (s/o Laura[5] Vining Palmer #166), b 1 or 4 August 1900; m about 1922 at Mitchell, SD, **Ethel Miller**. The last his sister heard from him he was in Anamosa, IA, where he ran a feed store. He had no children, but he and his wife adopted a little girl, probably in the late 1920s.

Child, surname PALMER:
- 917. i. Marilyn[7], m —, who farms in Iowa.

392. LAURA[6] MAY VINING (d/o Jesse[5] L. Vining #167), b 30 September 1905 at Chetek, Barron Co., WI; m/1 at Minneapolis, MN, 3 October 1923, **George Alfred Peterson**, b 10 August 1897 at Bayfield, WI, d September 1949. Laura m/2 at Minneapolis, 6 October 1951, **Melvin John Swanson**, who d August 1968.

Children, surname PETERSON:
- + 918. i. Donald[7] Gordon, b 11 June 1924.
- + 919. ii. Dona Jane, b 15 December 1925.
- + 920. iii. Beverly Ann, b 17 January 1932.

393. RALPH[6] JESS FORBES (s/o Jesse[5] L. Vining #167), b 6 October 1907 at Rusk Co., WI; m/1 at Minneapolis, MN, 15 October 1932, **Vivian Beck**; divorced 22 December 1933 in Wisconsin Rapids, WI. Ralph m/2 31 July 1939 **Elenor Mattner** at Des Moines, IA. Ralph was a barber. He d 23 April 1981 at Wisconsin Rapids, and is buried in Greenwood Cemetery, Town of Armenia, Juneau Co., WI.

The Sixth Generation

Children, surname FORBES, both born at Wisconsin Rapids:
+ 921. i. Wayne[7] b 16 January 1933.
+ 922. ii. Danny, b 9 October 1946.

394. MABEL[6] CAROLINE VINING (d/o Thomas Ray Vining #168), b 26 September 1911 at Chetek, WI; m 10 February 1932 at Mitchell, SD, **William Adams**, b 17 June 1910 at Modesto, CA s/o Edward and Jennie (Brink) Adams. They live at Parkston, SD.

Children, surname ADAMS:
+ 923. i. David[7], b 28 February 1934.
+ 924. ii. Alvin, b 17 October 1936.
+ 925. iii. Larry, b 22 December 1947.

395. RAYMOND[6] HANS VINING (s/o Thomas[5] Ray Vining #168), b 27 November 1912 at Chetek, Barron Co., WI; m 31 March 1935, **Velma Ruth Ashley**, d/o Arthur (born Buffalo, NY) and Emma (Oatman) Ashley, b 20 October 1918 at Plankinton, SD. Raymond was a farmer and in building construction; later street and water commissioner at Marshall. After a heart attack, he took a correspondence course in TV repair.

Children Surname: VINING:
+ 926. i. Shirley[7] Ann, b 2 June 1936.
+ 927. ii. Carolyn Rae, b 23 March 1939.

396. EDWARD[6] HARRISON VINING (s/o Thomas[5] Rae Vining #168), b 3 December 1913 at Alexandria, Hanson Co., SD; m 1 September 1939 at Lake Andes, Charles Mix Co., SD, **Martha M. Wudel**, d/o Nathaniel and Dora Thea (Harnish) Wudel, b 30 November 1919 at Parkston, SD. They live in Alexandria SD.

Children, surname VINING:
+ 928. i. Helen[7] Marie, b 26 April 1940.
+ 929. ii. Thomas William, b 25 January 1943.
+ 930. iii. Edward Warren, b 21 April 1944.
+ 931. iv. Mary Margaret, b 21 May 1947.

397. CHARLES[6] LESTER VINING (s/o Thomas[5] Ray Vining #168), b 1 February 1919 at Isanti, MN; m 25 October 1939, **Lenora Elder** in IA, she from Grandy, MN.

Children, surname VINING:

+ 932. i. Judy[7], b 31 July 1941
+ 933. ii. Joanne.
+ 934. iii. Linda.
    935. iv. Laurie, b 2 February 1960; m 1981, Dennis Norburg.

398. JOYCE[6] MARVEL VINING (d/o Harry[5] Edward Vining #170), b 8 February 1920 at Minneapolis, MN; m 20 March 1942 at Bethany Lutheran Church, Minneapolis, **John Glenn Wilson**, b 1 March 1919 at Saint Charles, Kane Co., IL, s/o John Walter and Matel Erma (Glenn) Wilson. John was a mechanical engineer for Control Data Corporation before his retirement.

Children, surname WILSON:
+ 936. i. Barbara[7] Joyce, b 26 January 1944.
+ 937. ii. John David, b 4 December 1946.
+ 938. iii. James Richard, b 12 March 1948.

399. LILAS[6] JANE VINING (d/o Harry[5] Edward Vining #170), b 8 February 1922 at Minneapolis, MN; m 7 September 1946 at Minneapolis, **Raymond Joseph Koch**, s/o Joseph August and Margaret Ann (Schuth) Koch, b 2 June 1917 at Wabash, MN. Lilas was employed as receptionist at various hospitals and doctors' offices; Raymond retired in 1982 as a social worker.

Children, surname KOCH:
+ 939. i. Sheryl[7] Ann, b 15 January 1949.
+ 940. ii. Joyce Carol, b 20 April 1952.
    941. iii. Jody Lynn, b 20 February 1957; d 7 September 1978 at Rochester, MN, during lung surgery.

400. CURTIS[6] HARRY VINING (s/o Harry[5] Edward Vining #170), b 9 January 1924 at Minneapolis, MN; m 13 August 1948 at Minneapolis, **Virginia Sutherland**, d/o David and Ruth Elizabeth (Erickson) Sutherland, b 23 October 1925; Curtis d 11 October 1990 and is buried at Hillside Cemetery.

Children, surname VINING, all born at Minneapolis:
+ 942. i. Mary[7] Curtis, b 24 April 1955.
+ 943. ii. Nancy Dale, b 18 June 1957.
    944. iii. Anne Elizabeth, b 1 May 1961; m 31 August 1985 Nathaniel Pedersen.

The Sixth Generation

401. BEULAH[6] **ELIZABETH ROBERTS** (d/o Alice[5] McElroy Roberts #173), b 21 April 1908 in Town of Scott, Columbia Co., WI; m 11 September 1929, **Everett J. Pogue**, s/o John and Pearl (Stocks) Pogue, b 31 January 1901; d 17 November 1961.

Children, surname POGUE:
- \+ 945. i. Vernon[7] Everett, b 22 October 1931.
- \+ 946. ii. Roy Roger, b 21 May 1933.
-    947. iii. Arlene, b 1936; d in 1937.
- \+ 948. iv. Ione Pearl, b 23 October 1938.
- \+ 949. v. Irene C., b 23 October 1938.

402. ROGER[6] **WAYMAN ROBERTS** (s/o Alice[5] McElroy Roberts #173), b 14 August 1909 in Town of Scott, Columbia Co., WI; m 7 June 1940, **Verna Noble**, d/o Carlton and Bess (Jenkins) Noble, b 8 October 1911. Roger retired from the refrigeration business and Verna from N.B.C. They live in Milwaukee, WI.

Children, surname ROBERTS:
- \+ 950. i. Janice[7], b 7 September 1940.
- \+ 951. ii. Roger William, b 11 January 1943.

403. RUTH[6] **JANETTE ROBERTS** (d/o Alice[5] McElroy Roberts #173), b 20 July 1912 at Town of Scott, Columbia Co., WI; m 6 May 1933 at Waukegan, IL, **Orin D. Dalton**, s/o Mark and Etta (Smith) Dalton, b 14 September 1908. He was a painter and operated a permit drug store and is now retired. They live at Dalton, WI.

Children, surname DALTON:
- \+ 952. i. Dolores[7] Janette, b 23 December 1933.
- \+ 953. ii. Monna Elaine, b 4 October 1937.
- \+ 954. iii. Richard Orin, 15 March 1940.
- \+ 955. iv. Russell Charles, b 5 February 1946.

404. AMBER[6] **IRENE ROBERTS** (d/o Alice[5] McElroy Roberts #173), b 9 April 1917 at Town of Scott, Columbia Co., WI; m 8 February 1936, **George Stollfus**, s/o Fred and Bertha (Nehring) Stollfus, b 19 May 1909 in Columbia Co.,WI. George was a farmer.

Children, surname STOLLFUS:
- \+ 956. i. Marilyn[7], b 22 October 1937.
- \+ 957. ii. Wayne George, b 15 May 1944.

406. RONALD[6] RALPH JENKINS (s/o Lucy[5] McElroy Jenkins #174), b 27 December 1910 at Dalton, Green Lake Co, WI; m 1 December 1937, **Mary Lois Cuff**, d/o Lester and Clara (Day) Cuff, in the Baptist parsonage at Pardeeville, WI. Ronald ran the home farm at Dalton for many years. He d 9 June 1984.

Children, surname JENKINS:
    958. i. Elaine[7] Mary, b 24 January 1939; not married.
    959. ii. Harold Kenneth, b 29 August 1940; not married.
    960. iii. George Ronald, b 12 April 1944; not married.
+   961. iv. Gordon Lyle, b 6 September 1945.
    962. v. Howard.
+   963. vi. Neal Edward.

407. ORRIS[6] DURWOOD JENKINS (s/o Lucy[5] McElroy Jenkins #174), b 8 December 1915, Dalton, Green Lake Co., WI; m 26 October 1940 at the Baptist parsonage, North Scott, Town of Pardeeville, WI, **Natalie Ruth Wagner**, d/o Edwin and Clara (Have) Wagner. Orris farmed at Markesan, WI; he d 10 September 1973.

Children, surname JENKINS:
+   964. i. James[7] Orris, b 10 January 1942.
+   965. ii. Stephen Roy, b 15 April 1948.
+   966. iii. Linda Rae, b 18 August 1949.
+   967. iv. Douglas Lee, b 5 June 1952.
+   968. v. Vivian Carol, b 11 April 1954.
    969. vi. Cynthia Sue, b 31 October 1958, Waupun, WI.
    970. vii. William Donald, b 13 June 1960, Waupun.

408. LUCILLE[6] ELIZABETH JENKINS (d/o Lucy[5] McElroy Jenkins #174), b 27 September 1918, Dalton, Green Lake Co., WI; m 2 February 1946 at Pardeeville, WI, **Stanley Haynes**, s/o Howard and Emma (Hughes) Haynes. Stanley retired as a farmer and school janitor.

Children, surname HAYNES:
+   971. i. Caroline[7] May, b 23 March 1948.
+   972. ii. Colleen Joyce, b 26 July 1952.
    973. iii. Debra Lucille, b 24 December 1958.

409. STANLEY[6] WILLIAM JENKINS (s/o Lucy[5] McElroy Jenkins #174), b 15 February 1922, Dalton, Green Lake Co., WI; m 9 June 1945

Winifred Holden at Sheboygan Falls WI; d/o Clarence and Eunice (Ramaker) Holden, b 17 December 1920 at Sheboygan Falls. Stanley was a truck driver and worked at a lumberyard; he d December 1990.

Children, surname JENKINS:
+ 974. i. Kenneth[7] Duane, b 1 April 1946.
+ 975. ii. Beverly Jean, b 27 August 1948.
+ 976. iii. Alan Ray, b 30 April 1951.
+ 977. iv. Dennis Lee, b 26 March 1954.
    978. v. Michael Wayne, b 7 January 1959; m 12 May 1984 Debra Kaas.
    979. vi. Kathryn Ann, b 24 January 1962, Sheboygan Falls.

410. DONALD[6] EARL JENKINS (s/o Lucy[5] McElroy Jenkins #174), b 24 February 1925, Dalton, Green Lake Co, WI; m 25 October 1952 at Endeavor, WI, **Mary McTier**, b 6 December 1933 at Endeavor, WI.; Mary d 25 December 1989 in a car accident; Donald was a carpenter and roofer before his retirement; he d 26 December 1989.

Children, surname JENKINS:
    980. i. Sharon[7] Louise, b 25 May 1955, Madison, WI.
+ 981. ii. Russell Earl, b 11 December 1956.
    982. iii. Donalee Ann, b 25 February 1960, Madison.
    983. iv. Lucy Jean, b 10 July 1962, Madison.

411. VERNON[6] JESS JENKINS (s/o Lucy[5] McElroy Jenkins, #174), b 13 June 1929 at Dalton, Green Lake Co., WI; m 7 May 1956 at Adams, WI, **Noreen Sweet**, my informant only knowing her mother's maiden name, Mary Baumgartner. Vernon is a builder.

Children, surname JENKINS:
+ 984. i. Gary Lee, b 6 August 1956.
+ 985. ii. Larry Lynn, b 7 August 1958.
    986. iii. Cheri Ann, b 14 June 1968, Waupun, WI.
    987. iv. Jerry Vern, b 7 April 1970, Waupun.

413. BOYD[6] WAYNE McELROY (s/o William[5] B. McElroy #176), b 16 November 1916 at Town of Marcellon, Columbia Co., WI; m 1957 **Edith Rye** at Rock Prairie Presbyterian Church, Johnstown, WI; d/o Ralph and Clara (Duess) Rye, b 23 October 1931 at Avalon, WI. Boyd d 6 October 1969 on his farm and is buried in Marcellon Cemetery.

Children, surname McELROY:

988. i. Lois[7] Ann, b in Portage, WI; m 8 May 1980, Terence Lindell in Lincoln, Nebraska.
989. ii. Donna Kay.

415. MAXINE[6] ELIZABETH McELROY (d/o William[5] B. McElroy #176), b 22 April 1925, Town of Marcellon, Columbia Co., WI; m **Lloyd J. Hoppe**, b 23 January 1908 at Tarpon Springs, FL. He delivered a Saint Petersburg, FL newspaper and lived at Palm Harbor. He d 9 April 1984 at Tarpon Springs, FL and is buried there.

Child, surname HOPPE:
990. i. Boyd[7] Mark, b 6 November 19—.

416. FLOY[6] BEATRICE GORSUCH (d/o Winnie[5] McElroy Gorsuch #177), b 26 May 1918 at Pardeeville, WI; m 20 May 1939 at Pardeeville, **Roy Breneman**, s/o Henry and Amelia (Hackbarth) Boelk, but at age 5 he was adopted by Walter and Mary Jane (Whirry) Breneman. Floy and Roy bought her parents' farm at RR 1, Pardeeville, WI and raised corn, hay, grain, beef cattle and hogs.

Children, surname BRENEMAN, all were born in Portage, WI:
991. i. Sharon[7], b 17 May 1940. She teaches special education at Allen School at Hutchinson, Kansas.
+ 992. ii. Douglas, b 7 October 1942.
+ 993. iii. Richard, b 9 February 1950.
+ 994. iv. Beth, b 22 July 1955.

417. MAYSEL[6] ELIZABETH GORSUCH (d/o Winnie[5] McElroy Gorsuch #177), b 29 October 1922 at Pardeeville, WI; m 7 April 1956 at Madison, **Howard Berendsen**, s/o Mr. and Mrs. Jerome Berendsen, b 18 August 1931 at Neenah, WI. Maysel and Howard manage a Howard Johnson motel at Indianapolis, IN.

Children Surname BERENDSEN
995. i. Robin[7] Maysel, b 26 November 1957, Neenah, WI.
996. ii. Vicki Lou, b 31 July 1960 at Neenah.

418. EVALYN[6] ELIZABETH McELROY (d/o Ralph[5] Fay McElroy #179), b 8 November 1923 at Pardeeville, WI; m 11 September 1948, **Lloyd Miller**, s/o Bernard Miller.

Children, surname MILLER:
997. i. Gary[7] Ralph, b 26 August 1949, Portage, WI.

998. ii. Kathleen Evalyn, b 14 December 1950 at Portage.
999. iii. Nina Sue, b 16 November 1956 at Portage.

419. WANDA[6] ELAINE McELROY (d/o Ralph[5] Fay McElroy #179), b 24 October 1925 at Pardeeville, WI; m 23 March 1946, **Ronald Barden**, s/o Reginald Barden.

Children, surname BARDEN:
- 1000. i. Sandra[7] Lee, b 25 August 1946 at Milwaukee, WI.
- 1001. ii. Judith Ann, b 2 April 1948 at Millwaukee.
- 1002. iii. Joan Marie, b 11 July 1949 at Pardeeville.
- 1003. iv. Richard Ralph, b 8 December 1953 at Portage, WI.
- 1004. v. David William, b 30 November 1962 at Ripon, WI.

421. BERWIN[6] RALPH McELROY (s/o Ralph[5] Fay McElroy #179), b 22 October 1930 at Portage, WI; m 20 September 1950, **Muriel Comstock**, d/o Donald Comstock. They live at Portage, WI.

Children, surname McELROY:
- 1005. i. Susan[7] Marie, b 7 September 1951.
- 1006. ii. Ralph Donald, b 30 October 1954.
- 1007. iii. Steven Edward, b 10 August 1961.

422. CAROL[6] ANN McELROY (d/o Ralph[5] F. McElroy #179) b 19 July 1936 at Portage, WI; m 23 February 1957, **James Thompson**, s/o Vail Thompson.

Children, surname THOMPSON, all born at Madison, WI:
- 1008. iv. Jane[7] Ellen, b 2 July 1958.
- 1009. v. Mark Vail, b 24 November 1960.
- 1010. vi. Timothy James, b 5 November 1962.
- 1011. vii. Julie Ann, b 19 June 1964.

423. LUVIA[6] IMOGENE CHOWEN (d/o Edna[5] Peckham Chowen #181), b 7 August 1905 at Strand, SD., near Lilly. She was 7 years old when she and her parents moved to Canada; m/1 at Edmonton, Alberta, Canada, 16 December 1927, **Clifford Carlyle Williamson**, s/o Edward Thomas and Lizzie (Buchanan) Williamson, b 28 October 1896 at Smith Falls, Ontario, Canada. Clifford farmed during the early years of marriage and during World War II became a heavy equipment operator. He followed this line of work until his death 22 January 1960 at Berwyn, Alberta, Canada; he is buried at Berwin Municipal Cemetery. She m/2 at the United

Methodist Church at Fairview, 11 November 1964, **John Henry Nichols**, s/o Charles Oscar and Sara (McTavish) Nichols, b 3 November 1904 at Detroit, MI, and d 29 June 1974 at Edmonton, Alberta, Canada. Luvia d 22 August 1991 at Stony Plain, Alberta, Canada; her cremated remains are buried at Edmonton, Alberta.

Children, surname WILLIAMSON:
+ 1012. i. Clifford^7 Carlyle, b 10 June 1930.
+ 1013. ii. Carole Mavis, b 9 December 1939.

427. ARLO^6 WAYNE BATES (s/o Maude^5 Peckham Bates #182), b 2 October 1917 at Webster, SD; m **Anna S. Grinley**, d/o Ben and Audrene (Skarperrid) Grinley, b 13 December 1917 at Portland, ND. He was a farmer in South Dakota; during the war worked in a defense plant in California, after he sold Studebakers, etc. Arlo d 3 February 1970 at Waubay, SD where his widow still lives.

Children, surname BATES:
+ 1014. i. Nancy^7, b 23 December 1945.
+ 1015. ii. Judy, b 10 May 1947.
+ 1016. iii. Susan, b 19 March 1949.
+ 1017. iv. Sonja, b 24 August 1953.
+ 1018. v. Kathy, b 16 December 1955.
    1019. vi. Scott, b 7 August 1965 at Watertown, SD. My last knowledge of him was when he was attending Northern State Teachers College at Aberdeen.

428. ORVILLE^6 CHARLES PECKHAM (s/o Thomas^5 R. Peckham #183), b 6 August 1913 at Bristol, SD; m 5 July 1932 at Sisseton, SD, **Irwina Wahl**, d/o Edwin and Florence (Johnson) Wahl, b 8 November 1914, at Roslyn, SD. Orville d 5 March 1982 at Bristol, SD and is buried in Bristol Cemetery. In 1984 Irwina was living in Saint Paul, MN.

Children, surname PECKHAM:
+ 1020. i. Delores^7 Helen, b 16 February, 1933.
+ 1021. ii. Jean Carolyn, b 25 March 1934.
+ 1022. iii. Donald Orville, b 5 September 1936.
+ 1023. iv. Rex Maynard, b 22 October 1939.
+ 1024. v. Wayne Russell, b 9 November 1943.

429. GRACE^6 ELIZABETH PECKHAM (d/o Thomas^5 R. Peckham

#183), b 8 September 1914 at Bristol, SD; m 23 March 1933 in SD, **Joseph L. Sparrow**, s/o William Walter and Ella (Hendron) Sparrow, b 13 November 1903 at Louisville, Kentucky. Joseph was a baker and Grace was a teacher. As of 1984 they were still living at Spearfish, SD.

Child, surname SPARROW:
+ 1025. i. William[7] Donald, b 24 February 1934.

430. KENNETH[6] NATHAN PECKHAM (s/o Thomas[5] R. Peckham #183), b 18 December 1915 at Bristol, SD; m 4 July 1938 at Ipswich, SD, **Geraldine Sanders**, d/o Michael G. (born Russia) and Hattie (Rapp) Sanders, b 12 April 1919 at Aberdeen, SD. Kenneth d 1 December 1989 at Spearfish.

Children, surname PECKHAM, all born at Aberdeen:
 1026. i. Kenneth[7], b 28 March 1942.
 1027. ii. Keith, b 28 March 1942 (twin).
 1028. iii. Patty, b 11 August 1944; d May 1951 at Denver, CO.
 1029. iv. Kay Lynn, b —, d —.

431. ANNE[6] ROSELLA PECKHAM (d/o Thomas[5] R. Peckham #183), b 9 July 1918, Bristol, SD; m about September 1937, **Lynn Shelp**, s/o George and Florence Shelp, b 6 December 1915 at Brookings, SD. Anne d 29 January 1974 at Spearfish, SD and is buried in the Bristol, SD cemetery. In 1984 Lynn was wintering at Brownsville, TX and summering at Thermopolis, WY.

Children, surname SHELP:
 1030. i. Richard[7], b 30 March 1938; died in infancy.
+ 1031. ii. Ralph, b 30 September 1939.
+ 1032. iii. John, b 25 June 1942.
 1033. iv. Glenn, b 1 July 1945. He was a pianist and taught Band at Wall, then Menno, SD. Died of a brain hemorrhage at Rochester, MN on 26 November 1971.
+ 1034. v. David Scott, b 12 March 1948.
+ 1035. vi. Jean, b 10 November 1951.

432. HAZEL[6] VIOLA PECKHAM (d/o Thomas[5] R. Peckham #183), b 27 October 1919 at Lynn Township, north of Bristol, SD; m 24 June 1945, **Ellis Milton Day** at the Bethesda Lutheran Church in Bristol, s/o Charles Herbert and Sylvia B. (Fogelberg) Day, b 5 August 1916 at

Belleville, KS. Hazel and Ellis ran a Coast-to-Coast franchise in Belle Fourche, SD until their retirement in 1984. They now spend winters at Sun City, AZ and summer months at Lead, SD.

Children, surname DAY:
+ 1036. i. Mary[7] Sue, b 28 August 1948.
+ 1037. ii. Barbara June, b 24 May 1951.
+ 1038. iii. Martha Joan, b 19 August 1954.

433. GENE[6] RALPH PECKHAM (s/o Thomas[5] R. Peckham #183), b 14 March 1921 at Bristol, SD; m/1 **Rilla Margaret Hanson**; they had four children. M/2 **Areta Virginia Caldwell**; they have one daugter. He lives Provo, UT.

Children, surname PECKHAM:
    1039. i. Mary[7] Margaret, b 14 November 1946 at Duluth, MN.
    1040. ii. Thomas Arthur, b 22 December 1947 at Rapid City, SD.
    1041. iii. Audrey Susan, b 18 July 1950 at Leadville Co., SD.
    1042. iv. Ronnie Kirk, b 24 November 1951 at Leadville Co.
    1043. v. Margaret.

434. PERCY[6] DONALD PECKHAM (s/o Thomas[5] R. Peckham #183), b 16 January 1925 at Bristol, SD; m 16 September 1945 at Bristol, **Bette Olsen**, d/o Otto Gottlieb and Rika Sophia (Tvite or Twite) Olsen, b 16 October 1924 at Frederick, SD. Percy is Professor of Educational Psychology in College of Education at University of Washington, his specialty is Statistics and Research Methods. They live at Seattle, WA.

Children, surname PECKHAM:
+ 1044. i. Matthew[7], b 28 July 1955.
    1045. ii. Sara, b 10 July 1957 at Denver; not married; is a layout artist in a print shop. She lives in Costa Mesa, CA.
    1046. ii. Sally Ann, b 10 July 1957 (twin).
    1047. iv Thomas, b 28 July 1958 at Denver.

435. RUTH[6] MARIE PECKHAM (d/o Thomas[5] R. Peckham #183), b 30 June 1927 at Bristol, SD; m **Royce Russell Ronning**, b 19 April 1927 at Westport, SD, s/o Oscar and Amy (Bazeley) Ronning. Royce is Professor of Educational Psychology at the University of Nebraska. He received his Ph.D. degree from Ohio State University. He taught previously at Miami [OH] University, University of California at Berkley and

SUNY at Buffalo, NY. Ruth is an elementary school librarian in Lincoln, NE where they live.

Children, surname RONNING:
+ 1048. i. Kristin[7] Amy, b 6 May 1949.
+ 1049. ii. Kari Ann, b 6 May 1949 (twin).
+ 1050. iii. Richard Royce, b 19 December 1950.

436. CLAYTON[6] MAURICE PECKHAM (s/o Raymond[5] C. Peckham #184), b 28 November 1916 at Lily, SD; m 14 February 1942 at Portland, OR, **Vera Etta Roth**, d/o George and Helena (Marx) Roth, b 4 March 1918 at Bristol, SD. Clayton was a farmer until his death 28 July 1966 at Aberdeen, SD. Vera d 15 December 1982 at Aberdeen and both are buried at Bristol Cemetery.

Children, surname PECKHAM:
+ 1051. i. Darwin[7] Dennis, b 20 September 1947.
   1052. ii. Daryl Dean, b 10 August 1957 at Aberdeen, SD. As of 1984 he was unmarried and working as a cabinet maker in Webster, SD.

437. FERN[6] ISABELLE PECKHAM (d/o Raymond[5] C. Peckham #184), b 22 November 1917 at Lily, SD; m/1 **Robert Acker** on 12 January 1937. She m/2 **William Antognini**, 11 September 1955. Fern lived as of 1984 at Rochester, MN, a widow for 2nd time.

Children, surname ACKER, both born at Patterson, CA:
   1053. i. Robert[7] Charles, b 24 March 1939; he married Pansy —.
   1054. ii. Carole Jane, b 2 January 1942; she m Joaquin Azevedo.

Children, surname ANTOGNINI:
   1055. iii. Cindy, b 29 May 1958 at Patterson; she m Terry Kohn.
   1056. iv. Kent, b 14 October 1961 at Patterson; m Kim —.
   1057. v. Keith, b 14 October 1961 (twin) at Patterson.

439. JESSE[6] VERNON PECKHAM (s/o Raymond[5] C. Peckham #184), b 17 January 1925 at Lily, SD; m 14 October 1950 at Bergen Lutheran Church, Pierpont, SD, **Donna M. McKittrick**, d/o Glen and Mildred McKittrick, b 10 March 1930. Jesse was last known to be farming near Bristol, SD.

Children, surname PECKHAM:
+ 1058. i. Vicki[7] Renee, b 2 March 1952.
+ 1059. ii. Rebecca Lynn, b 2 April 1956.

1060. iii. Douglas Jesse, b 23 February 1962. He is single and works in a bank in Missoula, MT.

440. VIRGINIA[6] CLEONE PECKHAM (d/o Raymond[5] C. Peckham #184), b 6 October 1931 at Crocker, Clark Co., SD; m 10 August 1953 at Aberdeen, SD, **Leo Arntz**, s/o James F. and Olga Gamena (Lee) Arntz, b 10 May 1925 at Aberdeen. Leo teaches business courses at Fresno, CA.

Children, surname ARNTZ:
+ 1061. i. Karen[7] Joy, b 13 May 1954.
   1062. ii. Susan J. b 14 December 1956, at Fresno, CA.
   1063. iii. Charles Ray, b 28 January 1958 at Fresno.

441. JAMES[6] PECKHAM (s/o Harold[5] Peckham #185), b 1 July 1937 at Clark, SD; m 16 October 1958 at Clark, **Jacqueline Urdahl**, d/o Oscar and Myrtle Urdahl, b 3 July 1940 at Bradley, SD. James originally did well drilling with brother Robert; when work became scarce in that field, he became janitor at a local school. They live at Clark, SD.

Children, surname PECKHAM:
+ 1064. i. Diana[7], b 23 January 1961.
   1065. ii. James, b 31 March 1962, Oakes, ND
   1066. iii. Richard, b 16 January 1967, Oakes.

442. ROBERT[6] PECKHAM (s/o Harold[5] Peckham #185), b 18 October 1938 at Clark, SD; m 16 July 1952 at Louisville, KY, **Marcella Hess**, d/o Nick and Delina Hess, b 6 July 1933 at Clark. Robert is a well driller and lives at Clark.

Children, surname PECKHAM:
+ 1067. i. Marie[7], b 15 June 1953.
+ 1068. ii. Cindy, b 8 November 1955.
+ 1069. iii. Linda, b 3 May 1962.
   1070. iv. Dale, b 30 September 1963, Watertown, SD.
   1071. v. Douglas, b 20 August 1967, Watertown.
   1072. vi. David, b 20 August 1967, (twin) at Watertown.

443. OREL[6] LUVIA ROSETH (d/o Gertrude[5] Peckham Roseth #186), b 27 April 1916 at Lily, Day Co., SD; m 3 October 1936 at Huntington Park, CA, **Marvel Gustav Kruse**, s/o Henry Herman and Amanda Christine (Meyer) Kruse, b 15 July 1914 at Lily and d 19 July 1966 at Lily, buried Lily Cemetery. For 30 years they ran a farm at York

Township, Day Co. She and 3 children moved to Denver, CO after Marvel's death; for 15 years worked in the cafeteria at Swedish Hospital at Englewood, CO.

Children, surname KRUSE:
- + 1073. i. Marvel[7] Keith, b 10 August 1938.
- + 1074. ii. James Wesley, b 13 April 1942.
- 1075. iii. Nancy Orel, b 16 May 1946 at Webster, SD; m 2 January 1971 at Denver, CO, Robert Porter, Jr., s/o Robert Porter, b 11 February 1942. Bob and Nancy live in East Bernard, TX; Bob is a grocery store manager.
- + 1076. iv. Leslie William, b 17 January 1952.
- 1077. v. David Alan, b 15 February 1957 at Webster, SD; m 16 December 1978, Cathy Elizabeth Comer at Reno, NV, b 27 December 1959. They live in Littleton, CO.

446. BERYL[6] SMITH ROSETH (d/o Gertrude[5] Peckham Roseth #186), b 15 November 1921 at Lily, Day Co., SD; m 4 March 1938 at Santa Barbara, CA, **Walter Theodore Sigmont**, s/o Walter and Bertha (Stemelski) Sigmont, b 17 February 1919 at Riverside, NJ. He was a foundry Superintendent before retirement. They live at Littleton, CO. In 1969 Beryl developed Rheumatoid Arthritis, severly limiting her activity.

Children, surname SIGMONT:
- + 1078. i. Walter[7] Theodore, b 9 January 1939.
- + 1079. ii. William Charles, b 23 June 1940.
- + 1080. iii. Jo Ann, b 21 December 1942.
- + 1081. iv. Beryl Jo, b 25 March 1949.

447. BEVERLY[6] PECKHAM ROSETH (d/o Gertrude[5] Peckham Roseth #186), b 2 August 1923 at Lily, Day Co, SD; m/1 26 June 1948 at Huntington Park, CA, **Lorin Waite**; divorced 1975; m/2 **Edwin J. Filek**, May 1976 at Virginia City, CA; divorced 1980. Beverly worked 19 years for the State of California, 16 years with the Dept. of Housing Finance Agency in Culver City, CA. She lives at Los Angeles, CA.

Children, surname Waite, both born a Huntington Park, CA:
- 1082. i. Randy[7], b 27 December 1949; is unmarried and lives in Malibu, CA so as to be near the ocean to sail his boat. He is active in Renaissance Faire, is a would-be artist, but more practically in construction/remodeling business.
- + 1083. ii. Laurie, b 18 January 1952. She trains and shows horses and

Labrador and terrier dogs.

499. HAROLD[6] MERWYN ROSETH (s/o Gertrude[5] Peckham Roseth #186), b 24 March 1927 at Lily, Day Co, SD; m 31 March 1948 at Las Vegas, NV, **Doris Virginia Mortensen**, d/o Jack and Muriel (Noonan) Mortensen, b 3 December 1929 at Los Angeles, CA. Harold is a building contractor. They live at Hesperia, CA.

Children, surname ROSETH:
+ 1084.   i.   James[7] Harold, b 18 January 1949.
+ 1085. ii.   Kathleen Dawn, b 19 February 1952.
+ 1086. iii.   Debra Lynn, b 5 January 1954.
+ 1087. iv.   Thomas William, b 12 September 1956.

451. JON[6] HENRY ROSETH (s/o Gertrude[5] Peckham Roseth #186), b 30 March 1931 at Lily; d 22 February 1963 at Seattle, WA and buried at Renton, King Co., WA; m 17 December 1954 at San Luis Obispo, CA, **Dolores Anna Bellenbaum**, d/o William Frederick and Elizabeth Mary (Pilon) Bellenbaum; b 22 January 1930 at Langian, Saskatchewan, Canada. Jon was a carpenter.

Children, surname ROSETH:
+ 1088.   i.   Inez[7], b 1 June 1957.
+ 1089. ii.   Annette, b 11 September 1959.

452. ELIZABETH[6] JANE ROSETH (d/o Gertrude[5] Peckham Roseth #186), b 18 July 1933 at Lily, Day Co, SD; m/1 26 September 1952 at Las Vegas, NV, **Charles A. Casey**, s/o Charles Allen and Alice (Whiteside) Casey, b 17 August 1933 at Memphis, TN; divorced December 1963.

Elizabeth Jane m/2 12 May 1968, **John Engelman**, s/o Morton Valentine and Gladys Otha (Holt) Engelman; b 18 December 1923 at Detroit, MI. John is owner of National Processing Equipment Co., manufactures of bulk storage tanks in Chino, CA. Elizabeth keeps the books for the company and makes out the payroll. They don't have any children.

Children, surname CASEY:
+ 1090.   i.   Gregory[7] Lynn, b 18 November 1956.
+ 1091. ii.   Caren Elizabeth, b, 28 May 1959.

453. NANCY[6] DAWN ROSETH (d/o Gertrude[5] Peckham Roseth #186), b 25 March 1939 at Bell, CA; m 10 June 1961 at Las Vegas, NV, **Albert George Strachan III**, s/o Albert George II and Rena Annette (Farrara) Strachan, b 22 March 1929 at Everett, MA. He is Aerospace engineer and marketing consultant; divorced 1 July 1984. Nancy is a secretary; lives at Manhattan Beach, CA.

Children, surname STRACHAN:
- 1092. i. Dawn[7] Alison, b 6 October 1963 at Redondo Beach, CA. In 1985 was attending college in MA.
- 1093. ii. Adam Winston, b 3 January 1966 at Mountain View, CA. In 1985 he was a cadet at the U.S. Air Force Academy.
- 1094. iii. Drew Marshall, b 9 June 1968 at Redondo Beach. In 1985 was a sophomore at Mira Costa High School at Manhattan Beach.

454. MAXINE[6] ROBERTSON (d/o Floy[5] Peckham Robertson #187), b 22 February 1918 at Lily, Day Co, SD; m 29 July 1938, **Earl Horace Bell**, s/o John Wesley and Jane (Burkett) Bell, b 13 November 1910. Earl d 9 July 1968 at Citrus Heights and is buried there in the Sylvan Cemetery. Maxine lives at Citrus Heights, CA.

Children, surname BELL:
- 1095. i. Cynthia[7] Diane, b 2 April 1943 at Huntington Park, CA. She m — Short, but now divorced with no children.
- 1096. ii. Robert Earl, b 14 November 1953 at Citrus Heights, CA. He is a computer processor. He m 17 February 1990, Wynnie Sirage.

455. ELWYN[6] KAY PECKHAM (s/o Orville[5] K. Peckham #188), b 5 December 1929 at Watertown, SD; m 29 March 1953 at Salt Lake City, UT, **Dianne O'Donnell**. Elwyn bought into a Taxi business and he drives taxi in San Francisco, CA.

Children, surname PECKHAM:
- \+ 1097. i. Anthony[7] James, b 1 February 1950.
- \+ 1098. ii. Samuel Charles, b 6 October 1953.
- 1099. iii. David Elwyn, b 4 November 1954 at Oakland.
- 1100. iv. Benjamin James, b 5 March 1956 at Walnut Creek, CA.
- 1101. v. Daniel Jonathan, b 7 June 1957 at Martinez, CA.
- 1102. vi. Aaron Kenneth, b 5 April 1960 at Martinez. He only lived 50 hours.

456. DONNA[6] JEAN PECKHAM (d/o Orville[5] Kenneth Peckham

#188), b 8 June 1931 at Aberdeen, SD; m 27 August 1949 at Methodist Church at Sonora, CA, **Wayne Paul Dawson**, b 26 July 1930 at Pacific Grove, CA. Wayne teaches at the state college in Chico, CA; Donna teaches in Paradise, CA.

Children, surname DAWSON:
- 1103. i. Brooke[7] Allyn, b 3 January 1954 at King City, CA; an officer in the Navy.
- 1104. ii. Blake Alyn, b 22 May 1955 at King City; a model in Southern California.
- 1105. iii. Dawn Paige, b 10 November 1956 at Paradise.
- + 1106. iv. Kimberly Layne, b 23 January 1958 at San Francisco, CA.

457. ELIZABETH[6] JANE PECKHAM (d/o Orville[5] Kenneth Peckham #188), b 6 November 1932 at Redfield, SD; m **Robert Laverne Mitchell**, 1 June 1952 at Methodist Church, Sonora, CA, b 12 December 1932. Robert retired at age 55 from a Gas and Oil Distributor from Redwood City, to San Francisco, CA; also owns a service station and repair business.

Children, surname MITCHELL:
- + 1107. i. Pamela[7] Ann, b 7 May 1953.
- + 1108. ii. Mark Steven, b 5 June 1954.
- 1109. iii. Matthew Brant, b 16 March 1957, Berkeley, CA.
- 1110. iv. Tamara Allyson, b 10 June 1958, Berkeley.

458. CHARLES[6] WESLEY PECKHAM (s/o Orville[5] K. Peckham #188), b 4 April 1935 at San Francisco, CA; m **Yvonne Speer** 13 December 1955 at Episcopal Church, Sonora, CA, b 11 November 1934 at Garden City, KS. Charles is Director of Printing Dept. at Corvallis State College, OR. They adopted three children.

Children, surname PECKHAM:
- + 1111. i. Peri[7] Anne, b 16 January 1960.
- 1112. ii. Kirk Andrew, b 28 February 1962, Berkeley, CA; he is a car salesman in Modesto, CA.
- 1113. iii. Kenneth Eric, b 28 February 1962, twin; is in business with his brother.

459. CAROL[6] ANN CLARK (d/o Lela[5] Peckham Clark #192), b 20 May 1917 at Fort Winnebago Township, Columbia Co., WI; m 8 April 1939, Fort Winnebago Township, **Sheldon Dewsnap** b 31 October 1914

The Sixth Generation

at Town of Moundsville, Endeavor, WI, s/o Freeman and Carolyn Henrietta Elizabeth (Eager) Dewsnap. As of 1985 Sheldon had been retired 15 years from Madison Newspapers as District Supervisor, and still has dealership for the newspapers. They live in Endeavor, WI.

Children, surname DEWSNAP:
+ 1114.   i.   Calvin[7] Roger, b 31 January 1940.
+ 1115.   ii. Douglas Wayne, b 20 August 1941.
  1116.   iii. David Charles, b 31 October 1943, Portage, WI. Not married as of 1985; lived at New Bedford, MA. Received degree in Floriculture from University of Wisconsin and employed at Olsen's Greenhouses, Raynham, MA.
+ 1117.   iv. Dennis Dean, b 7 April 1947.
  1118.   v.   Linda Diane, b 1 June 1953; m 29 December 1973, Larry Krueger, b 25 November 1953, s/o Marvin and Florence Krueger. Larry is a maintenance person with the Portage School system; they live at Endeaver.
+ 1119.   vi. Stewart Harold, b 15 December 1958.

460. NORMA[6] ELAINE CLARK (d/o Lela[5] Peckham Clark #192), b 24 April 1921 Fort Winnebago, Columbia Co., WI; m **Eldon Audiss**, s/o William and Anna (Hanson) Audiss, 1 January 1943; Eldon b 23 October 1919 Town of Moundville, Marquette Co., WI.

Children, surname AUDISS:
+ 1120.   i.   Nancy[7] Marie, b 4 November 1944.
+ 1121.   ii. Jeffrey Clark, b 6 December 1949.
+ 1122.   iii. Sally Jane, b 27 July 1956.

461. BEVERLY[6] MAY CLARK (d/o Lela[5] Peckham Clark #192), b 11 May 1929 at Portage, WI; m 21 October 1950, **Orville Karow**, s/o Walter and Myrtle Karow.

Children, surname KAROW:
+ 1123.   i.   Lorence[7] Orville, b 17 June 1952.
  1124.   ii. Richard Clark, b 10 June 1956.
  1125.   iii. Gregory Lee, b 4 April 1958.

462. MERLYN[6] EMERY PECKHAM (s/o William[5] E. Peckham #193), b about 1922 at Beaver Dam, Dodge Co., WI; m **June Barbara Henry**, b Grant Co., WI; c. 1926. Merlyn a private in the army when son was born.

Child, surname PECKHAM:

1126.   i.   Merlyn[7] Clyde, b 1 August 1945 at Endeavor, WI.

464. MARY[6] **ANN SPRATT** (d/o Edna[5] M. Spratt #195), b 25 September 1915 at Sioux Falls, SD; m **Eugene Joseph Hartwell**, s/o Eugene Joseph and Alice Edna (Preston) Hartwell, 18 November 1939 at Waukon, IA. Eugene b 24 December 1908 Marshfield, WI; d 18 December 1949 at Eau Claire, WI; Mary Ann d 1 January 1964 and buried Forest Hill Cemetery, Eau Claire.

Children, surname HARTWELL:

+ 1127.   i.   Betty[7] Jean, b 18 August 1940.
    1128.   ii.   Stephen Walter, b 20 May 1943 at Eau Claire. In 1985 was unmarried, working as sales associate at Frederick-Nelson Co. in Seattle, WA; a department store.

465. WILLIAM[6] **SPRATT** (s/o Edna[5] M. Spratt #195), b 6 September 1917 at Sioux City, IA; m 3 February 1946 at Witchita, KS, **Edith Marie Reece**, b 7 December 1926 at Chanute, KS, d/o Homer Adam and Edith Marie (Largent) Reece. William, a mechanical design engineer, d 20 October 1971 at Eau Claire, WI and is buried in Forest Hill Cemetery, Eau Claire, WI. On 9 March 1974, Edith m Alfred Willard Johnson at Eau Claire.

Children, surname SPRATT:

+ 1129.   i.   Pamela[7] Louise, b 21 March 1948.
+ 1130.   ii.   Phillip Reece, b 18 January 1954.

466. EDNA[6] **SOPHIE ANN KROEPLIN** (d/o Delia[5] Abel Kroeplin #200), b 16 May 1914 Town of Union, Burnett Co., WI; m/1, in Town of Taft, Taylor Co., WI on 17 January 1931, **Cecil Emmett Meeker** s/o George Anthony and Elsie May (Parker) Meeker; b 3 June 1910 at Wapelo Co., IA; d 31 May 1979 at Stanley, WI. Edna m/2 at Stanley, 2 September 1982, **Clarence Samplawski**, s/o Edward and Hazel (Hatfield) Samplawski; b 12 June 1915 at Stanley.

Children, surname MEEKER:

+ 1131.   i.   Waneta[7] Beth, b 14 March 1932.
+ 1132.   ii.   Rose Blanche, b 15 December 1933.
+ 1133.   iii.   Marvin Cecil, b 18 October 1935.
+ 1134.   iv.   George Henry, b 2 December 1937.

The Sixth Generation 237

+ 1135. v. Chester Eugene, b 7 February 1940.
+ 1136. vi. Lester David, b 9 January 1942.
+ 1137. vii. Judith Ann, b 14 January 1944.
+ 1138. viii. Sharon Alice, b 22 April 1951.

467. ELMER[6] THOMAS JOHN KROEPLIN (s/o Delia[5] Abel Kroeplin #200), b 24 October 1915 at Burnett Co., WI; m 18 June 1949 at Stanley, WI, **Esther May Warner** d/o Claude and Bessie (Smith) Warner b 18 October 1913 at Stanley. Elmer was a truck driver and worked for a bag company about 15 years; worked at a grain elevator for over 12 years.

Children, surname KROEPLIN:
+ 1139. i. Bessie[7] May, b 26 December 1952.
    1140. ii. Kevin Elmer, b 26 December 1952, Minneapolis, MN (twin). Not married in 1984; lives in Richfield and works for the state.

468. WILLIAM[6] HENRY FREDERICK KROEPLIN (s/o Delia[5] Abel Kroeplin #200), b 23 June 1917 at Burnett Co., WI; m 15 August 1941 at Dodge Center, MN, **Lorraine Baker** d/o Lamont Adelbert and Etta Matilda (Abel) Baker b 11 September 1921 at Webster, Burnett Co.

Children, surname KROEPLIN, all born at Stanley, WI, with the exception of Luvern Adelbert:
    1141. i. Luvern[7] Adelbert, b 3 October 1941 at Dodge Co., MN; m Betty —.
    1142. ii. Delano James, b 27 April 1943.
    1143. iii. Leona Marie, b 4 June 1945; m Gerald Turner.
    1144. iv. Robert Neil, b 3 December 1946.
    1145. v. Violet Louise, b 11 July 1950.
    1146. vi. Mark William, b 13 June 1953.
    1147. vii. Martin Louis, b 12 December 1954.
    1148. viii. Jason Ernest, b 4 August 1956.
    1149. ix. Randy Edward, b 13 January 1963.

469. HENRY[6] ALBERT NEIL KROEPLIN (s/o Delia[5] Abel Kroeplin #200), b 17 March 1921 at Burnett Co., WI; m 17 January 1946 at Cleveland, OH, **Dorothy Elizabeth Hadala**, d/o Jacob and Mary (Telatko) Hadala; b at Cleveland, OH. He is a retired farmer; in 1985 Dorothy was an institutional aide at Northern Center for Developmentally Disabled at Chippewa Falls, WI.

Children, surname KROEPLIN:
+ 1150. i   Mary[7] Elizabeth, b 8 March 1947.
+ 1151. ii. Thomas William, 20 December 1949.
+ 1152. iii. Timothy Warren, b 20 November 1952.
+ 1153. iv. Margaret Elaine, b 1 February 1953.

471. PALMER[6] JAMES LOUIS KROEPLIN (s/o Delia[5] Abel Kroeplin #200),b 5 April 1925 at Burnett Co., WI; m 7 December 1957 at Stanley, WI, **Ilene Joyce Richardson**, d/o Isaac Bruck and Blanche (Brown) Richardson, b 30 January 1929 at Stanley, WI. Palmer works at Cardinal Corp. making chairs and tables. Palmer does not have children, only a step daughter.

Child, surname RICHARDSON:
+ 1154. i.   Karen[7] Joyce, b 6 June 1950.

473. BESSIE[6] ANN FRENCH (d/o Estina[5] Abel French #201), b 15 December 1910 at Danbury, WI; d 25 January 1979 at Kalispell, MT; m **Francis Lee Culbert**, s/o Charles Edward and Katherine (Hayes) Culbert, b 9 June 1910 at LeRoy, KS, d 6 February 1976 at Kalispell, MT; both are buried in Lone Pine Cemetery, Big Fork, MT.

Children, surname CULBERT:
+ 1155. i.   Charles[7] Lee, b 12 October 1931.
+ 1156. ii. Jerald Lance, b 4 August 1933.
+ 1157. iii. Mary Layne, b 27 July 1940.

474. ALLEN[6] FLAVEL FRENCH (s/o Estina[5] Abel French #201), b 19 August 1912 at Danbury, Burnett Co., WI; m 19 May 19— in West Concord, MN area, **Nyla June Martin**, d/o Edward Martin, b 18 June 1911; Allen d 6 December 1970 at West Concord and is buried in Old Concord Cemetery there; he farmed some, road construction, hauled milk, and served in WW II.

Children, surname FRENCH:
    1158. i.   LeRoy[7] Edward, b 4 December 1934 at West Concord; m Helene —. They live in San Francisco; he works in planning for State Transportation Dept; no children.
+ 1159. ii. Dennis Allen, b 13 June 1936.
+ 1160. iii. Beverly Ann, b 5 May 1938.
+ 1161. iv. Danal Charles, b 25 July 1947.

+ 1162. v. Ronald Richard, b 3 May 1950.

475. CLARA[6] ALVERETTE FRENCH (d/o Estina[5] Abel French #201), b 25 October 1914 at Danbury, Burnett Co., WI; m 19 January 1933 at Kasson, MN, **Edward Jefferson Hanson**, s/o LeRoy and Laura (Pierce) Hanson; he b 18 December 1912 at Trego, WI. They live in Concord, MN.

Children, surname HANSON:
- 1163. i. Rodney[7] E., b 1933, Owatonna, MN; d 1937. He had polio.
+ 1164. ii. Larry Kay, b 15 October 1935.
+ 1165. iii. Glenn Eldon, b 18 December 1938.
+ 1166. iv. Loren Richard, b 26 March 1942.
+ 1167. v. Roger Arlen, b 5 March 1944.
+ 1168. vi. Phillip, b 25 July 1945.
+ 1169. vii. Anna Louise, b 2 November 1946.
+ 1170. viii. Anola Gayle, b 11 September 1949.
+ 1171. ix. David Bruce, b 11 April 1951.
- 1172. x. Steven Joel, b 13 April 1953, Owatonna, MN; d 14 August 1974 in a traffic accident at Lucas, IA. He graduated from Moody Bible Institute in Chicago and had worked for the Arkansas Highway Dept.
- 1173. xi. James Mark, b 26 July 1957, Owatonna, MN; in 1984 was living at home and attending Northwestern College in Roseville, MN.
+ 1174. xii. Timothy Clayton, b 14 October 1959.

476. DOROTHY[6] BELLE FRENCH (d/o Estina[5] Abel French #201), b 22 August 1917 at Danbury, Burnett Co., WI; m 25 March 1936 at Dodge Center, MN, **Frederick Phelps**, s/o William Henry and Katherine Elizabeth (Thomas) Phelps, b 22 March 1917 at Claremont Township, Dodge Co., MN; in 1984 they were living at West Concord, MN.

Children, surname, PHELPS:
+ 1175. i. Darrel[7] Frederick, b 7 February 1937.
+ 1176. ii. Dale Loren, b 27 July 1938.
+ 1177. iii. Constance Faye, b 12 November 1943.

477. RICHARD[6] ANDREW FRENCH (s/o Estina[5] Abel French #201), b 1 August 1922, Danbury, Burnett Co, WI; m/1 **Emma Viola Lampland**, d/o Henry and Emma Lampland.

Richard m/2 La Verna (Tienter) Westphal, d/o Ben and Gertrude (Urieze) Tienter who had two children by her former husband, Walter Westphal: Phyllis, b 13 August 1949, and Darrell, b July 1952 and d October 1970.

Richard drove a semi-truck and was killed in a truck accident at Weldon, NC, 14 December 1967 and is buried in Grand View Memorial Cemetery, Rochester, MN. In 1984 Emma was living at Hayfield, MN.

Children, surname FRENCH:

+ 1178. i. Ruth[7] Lilyan, b 15 March 1945.
   1179. ii. Sharyn Lynn, b 28 September 1954. Lives in CO; was married, but divorced and took back maiden name; no children.
+ 1180. iii. Evon Lynette, b 12 October 1956.
+ 1181. iv. Dawn Renee, b 21 January 1958.
   1182. v. Craig Charles, b 6 September 1959 at Owatonna, MN; m May 1981 at Bartow, FL, Toni Grant Wilkinson; are separated and no children. He served in the US Air Force for 4 years as a Staff Sergent and in 1984 worked as electronic Technician at Crenlo at Rochester, MN; they build cabs for tractors.
+ 1183. vi. Scott Benjamin, b 14 February 1961.
   1184. vii. Rodney Lee, b 4 November 1962 at Owatonna. In 1984 not married; worked at M.T.M., Dodge Center; lived at Wasioja, MN.

478. EVELYN[6] MAE FRENCH (d/o Estina[5] Abel French #201), b 9 July 1927, Dodge Center, WI; m 1 August 1944 at West Concord, MN, **Harvey Urch**, s/o Fred G. and Mattie (Griffin) Urch; b 9 August 1929. In 1984 was in research and development at Wengers, a firm that produces equipment for musicals, dramatics, and automatic risers; lived in West Concord, MN.

Children, surname URCH:

+ 1185. i. Carol[7] Ann, b 25 January 1946.
+ 1186. ii. Lowell Earl, b 28 April 1947.
+ 1187. iii. Vicki Lea, b 9 October 1953.
   1188. iv. Barbara Jean, b 16 February 1957, Owatonna, MN. In 1984 was single and living in Rochester, MN in school for Dental Assistant.
   1189. v. Rebecca Marie, b 15 September 1958, Owatonna; m 16 June 1979 Loren Montague at West Concord, MN; she is an insurance agent; he works for 3-M; live in Pine City, MN (1984); no children.

The Sixth Generation 241

    1190. vi. Frederick Charles, b 6 June 1964, Owatonna. In 1984 single, living at home; worked at Wengers.

479. JUNE[6] **CAROL FRENCH** (d/o Estina[5] Abel French #201), b 14 June 1933 at Dodge Center, MN; m 7 December 1957, at West Concord, **Harold Troff**, s/o Hemme and Frances (Alberts) Troff, b 13 July 1928. He works at IBM in Rochester, MN on assembly (Inf. from Mrs. Troff).
Children, surname TROFF:
    1191. i. Wayne[7] Harold, b 22 April 1960 at Owatonna, MN. In 1984 single; living at home; works in retailing.
    1192. ii. Bryan Jeffery, b 12 July 1962 at Owatonna; in 1984 was in Northwestern Bible College, Roseville, MN.
    1193. iii. Gary Allen, b 31 December 1963; in school in 1984.

480. FORREST[6] **EDWARD ABEL** (s/o Thomas[5] M. Abel #202), b 15 May 1916 at West Concord, Dodge Co, WI; m 23 September 1945 at Newberg, OR, **Edith Velma Trueax**, d/o Charlie Miller and Susie Lessie (Sullivan) Trueax, b 25 July 1925 at Bridgeport, OR. He is a mechanic and mill worker; they lives at Willamina, OR.
Children, surname ABEL:
+ 1194. i. Forrest[7] Edward, b 21 October 1946.
+ 1195. ii. Sharon Nadine, b 19 July 1950.

481. HELEN[6] **MAY ABEL** (d/o Thomas[5] M. Abel #202), b 18 November 1924 at Chinook, Blaine Co., MT; m 7 November 1945 at Eureka, CA, **Jerold LeRoy Goutermont**, s/o John and Nettie (Barber) Goutermont, b 22 November 1921 at Glenwood, MN. He worked in a saw mill as shipping clerk 15 years after separation from service in WW II, had a service station for 15 years until a heart attack; since has been sales person for a building supply store in Garberville, CA; where they live.
Children, surname GOUTERMONT:
+ 1196. i. Loretta[7] Alice, b 22 July 1948.
+ 1197. ii. Roy Luverne, b 17 January 1951.

482. ALICE[6] **ABEL** (d/o Thomas[5] M. Abel #202), b 10 May 1934, Wasioja, Dodge Co., MN; m 3 November 1952 at Carson City, NV, **Imo Pardini**, s/o Guisippie (Joe) and Isolina (Giannoni) Pardini, both born in Italy; Imo b 18 May 1924 at Healdsburg, CA; a retired carpenter.
Children, surname PARDINI:

+ 1198. i. Kathy[7] Lynn, b 3 December 1953.
+ 1199. ii. Keith Thomas, b 20 October 1954.
+ 1200. iii. Karen Marie, b 21 June 1958.

484. JAMES[6] DANIEL ABEL (s/o Lester[5] R. Abel #203), b 3 September 1928 at Dodge Center, Dodge Co., MN; m 18 April 1954 at Luverne, IA, **Elsie Hinz**, d/o Michael and Amanda Mathilda (Schmidt) Hinz, b 17 December 1926 at Luverne, IA.

Children, surname ABEL:
+ 1201. i. Ross[7], b 20 January 1955.
+ 1202. ii. Kim, b 13 July 1960.
    1203. iii. John, b 6 December 1963, Rochester, MN; m 10 July 1982 at Kasson, MN. Ann Boyum. No children as of 1984.
    1204. iv. Chris, b 1 October 1965, Rochester, MN; graduated H.S. 1984.

485. LEONARD[6] ORLOW ABEL (s/o Lester[5] R. Abel #203), b 12 May 1931 at Dodge Co., MN; d 13 April 1979 at Rochester, MN; m 3 June 1951 at First Methodist Church, Rochester, **Marilyn Dorothy Stucky**, d/o Donovan Daniel and Dorothy Olga (Sandberg) Stucky; b 4 October 1933 at Kasson, Dodge Co., MN. Leonard was driver-salesman for Marigold Foods; was in scouting for 19 years, first as Cubmaster then Scoutmaster; received many meritorious awards for his work in scouting and other community volunteer activities. All three of his boys are Eagle Scouts and his daughters are first class Girl Scouts.

Children, surname ABEL:
+ 1205. i. Daniel[7] James, b 14 January 1952.
+ 1206. ii. Mary Jane, b 16 April 1953.
+ 1207. iii. Melinda Jo, b 1 March 1955.
    1208. iv. Mark Leonard, b 18 November 1958, Rochester; m 18 August 1979, Sharon Amanda Briggs at Christ Methodist Church, Rochester.
    1209. v. Paul Eric, b 18 February 1963 at Rochester. Not married in 1984; driver and maintenance at Southwest Minnesota Educational Cooperative Service Unit.

486. CHESTER[6] LAMONT BAKER (s/o Etta[5] Abel Baker #204), b 16 December 1917 at Webster, Burnett, Co., WI; m/1 15 July 1942 at Salvation Army Chapel, Saint Paul, MN, **Esther Meeks** d/o Arthur and Ruth Meeks. While in the army Chester divorced Esther in 1957 and m/2

Amanda E. **Oftedall** at Yankton, SD; in 1958.

Children, surname BAKER:
- \+ 1210. i. Thomas[7] Edward, b 20 April 1942.
- \+ 1211. ii. Eugene Arthur, b 2 June 1944.
- \+ 1212. iii. Faye Etta, b 17 May 1946.
- \+ 1213. iv. Ruth Lucille, b 10 August 1947.
- 1214. v. Roger Lamont, b 5 September 1948 at Stanley, WI; m 6 September 1969, Sandra Lee Larson at Austin, MN.
- \+ 1215. vi. Gladys Irene, b 23 August 1952.
- \+ 1216. vii. Rose Alveretta, b 30 September 1953.

487. BEATRICE[6] BAKER (d/o Etta[5] Abel Baker #204), b 6 May 1919 at Webster, Burnett Co., WI; m 10 October 1936, **Ray Fate**, b 10 July 1910 at Swedesburg, MO, s/o Martin James and Mattie (Langdon) Fate. Mattie was adopted by the Shurtleffs. Beatrice had 11 children, but lost most because she has the RH blood factor. She lives in Mantorville, MN.

Children, surname FATE:
- 1217. i. Irene[7] Anne, b 2 March 1939; m Marvin Cecil Meeker (#1134).
- \+ 1218. ii. Chan, b 19 November 1940.
- 1219. iii. Starr, b 29 September 1952, Rochester, MN; m 15 September 1979, Francis Burton. Starr teaches in Assembly of God School; he is youth pastor at West Bend, WI, Assembly of God.
- \+ 1220. iv. Troy Allen, b 3 January 1962.

488. LORRAINE[6] BAKER (d/o Etta[5] Abel Baker #204), b 11 September 1921 at Webster, Burnett Co., WI; m 15 August 1941 at Dodge Center, WI, **William Kroeplin**, s/o Henry and Delia Ann (Abel) Kroeplin; he b 23 June 1917. See also page 237.

Children, surname KROEPLIN:
- 1221. i. Luvern[7] Adelbert, b 3 October 1941 at Dodge Co., MN; m Betty —.
- 1222. ii. Delano James, b 27 April 1943, Stanley, WI.
- 1223. iii. Leona Marie, b 4 June 1945, Stanley.
- 1224. iv. Robert Neil, b 3 December 1946, Stanley.
- 1225. v. Violet Louise, b 11 July 1950, Stanley.
- 1226. vi. Mark William, b 13 June 1953, Stanley.
- 1227. vii. Martin Louis, b 12 December 1954, Stanley.
- 1228. vii. Jason Ernest, b 4 August 1956, Stanley.

1229. viii. Randy Edward, b 13 January 1963, Stanley.

489. CLAUDIA[6] L. BAKER (d/o Etta[5] Abel Baker #204), b 1 September 1923, Webster, Burnett Co, WI; m **Edward Pepin** about 1943 at Dodge Center, WI; when he was in the service. They live in Milwaukee, WI.

Children, surname PEPIN:
    1230. i. Nina[7], m — Engen; lives in Minneapolis.
    1231. ii. Karen, m Donald Blaschaka; lives in Milwaukee.
    1232. iii. Aaron; lives in Milwaukee.
    1233. iv. Edward; lives in California.
    1234. v. Janice, m — Handricki; lives in Milwaukee.

490. DONALD[6] WESTER (s/o Ethel[5] Abel Wester #205), b 17 January 1934 at Bennett, Douglas Co., WI; m 8 June 1957 in TX, **Jean Marie East**. Donald was in the U.S. Air Force 20-1/2 years; in 1984 was driving a school bus and living in Durango, CO.

Children, surname WESTER:
+ 1235. i. Deborah[7] Kay, b 25 September 1958.
    1236. ii. Glen Andrew, b 15 January 1961 at Altus, OK.
    1237. iii. Keith Douglas, b 2 June 1963 at Altus.

491. PHILLIP[6] WESTER (s/o Ethel[5] Abel Wester #205), b 19 March 1935 at Bennett, WI; m 4 August 1954 at Solon Springs, WI, **Carol Susan Drake**. Phillip is in construction work; lives in Solon Springs.

Children, surname WESTER:
+ 1238. i. Mitchell[7] Allen, b 28 June 1955.
+ 1239. ii. Michael Lee, b 12 February 1957.
+ 1240. iii. Victoria Lynn, b 19 August 1958.
    1241. iv. Brian Phillip, b 25 August 1960, Superior, WI; m 11 April 1981 at Solon Springs. Tena Nelson. No children as of 1984.
    1242. v. Lee Anne, b 3 January 1966, Superior, WI.

492. HARRY[6] WESTER (s/o Ethel[5] Abel Wester #205), b 7 March 1936 at Bennett, Douglas Co., WI; m 23 September 1961 at Solon Springs, **Mary Edith Botton**. As of 1984 he did maintenance work at Solon Springs School, and lived at Bennett, WI.

Children, surname WESTER:
    1243. i. Curt[7] Allen, b 7 March 1963 at Superior, WI.

The Sixth Generation 245

    1244. ii. Ann Marie, b 29 July 1967 at Superior.

493. LINDA[6] **WESTER** (d/o Ethel[5] Abel Wester #205), b 8 September 1938 at Bennett, Douglas Co., WI; m/1 5 October 1957 at Bennett, **John Gustoff Theien**; m/2 26 June 1972 at Peoria, IL, **John Ernst**. They live in Metamora, IL; he works for Caterpillar and she is in insurance.

Children, surname THEIEN:
+ 1245. i. Gail[7] Marie, b 27 April 1958.
    1246. ii. Brenda Lee, b 5 July 1959 at Superior, WI; m 2 August 1980 Greg Brackett; now divorced.
    1247. iii. Theresa Kay, b 2 September 1961; Superior; d 1964 at Rochester, MN.
    1248. iv. John Kevin, b 10 February 1963 at Superior.

494. VICTOR[6] **WESTER** (s/o Ethel[5] Abel Wester #205), b 19 May 1941 at Bennett, WI; m 24 January 1961 at Solon Springs, **Doris Evelyn Leitha**; Victor is a road construction worker; in 1984 was laid off and is working in Wester Garage.

Children, surname WESTER:
+ 1249. i. Tammara[7] Kay, b 26 September 1962.
    1250. ii. Scott Allen, b 1 July 1964, Superior, WI.
    1251. iii. Julie Ann, b 25 November 1966, Superior.
    1252. iv. Barry Victor, b 1 March 1974, Superior.

495. LEOTA[6] **WESTER** (d/o Ethel[5] Abel Wester #205), b 2 October 1942 at Bennett, Douglas Co., WI; m/1 February 1964 at Bennett, **David Johnson**; Leota lives at Kewatin, MN.

Children, surname JOHNSON:
    1253. i. Dean[7] Patrick, b 19 May 1966, Milwaukee, WI.
    1254. ii. Lynn Renea, b 23 January 1968, Milwaukee.

496. RUTH[6] **ANN JOHNSON** (d/o Alice[5] Bond Johnson #206), b 19 May 1933 at Hawthorne, WI; m 16 June 1956 at Hawthorne, **Herbert Carl Schmidt**, s/o Carl Albert and Vivian May (Severson) Schmidt; he b 5 November 1925 at Greenwood, WI; Herbert is a car dump operator at Farmers Union Grain Terminal. Lives in Bennett, WI.

Children, surname SCHMIDT:
+ 1255. i. Dennis[7] James, b 15 July 1958.
    1256. ii. Duane Herbert, b 27 May 1961, Superior, WI; is a computer

programmer at Western National Mutual Insurance Co. at Edina, MN; lives at Richfield, MN.

497. ALICE[6] IVENA WHITE (d/o Alice[5] Bond White #207), b 15 August 1929 at Dodge Co., MN; m 21 May 1947 at Old West Concord, MN, **Marland Grover Ingersoll**, b 21 October 1924; d 26 December 1976; Alice divorced Marland, remarried him, divorced him, remarried him and divorced him again; he married Marge? Reportedly Marge shot him to death 25 December 1972. Alice lives at Dexter, MN.

Children, surname INGERSOLL:
+ 1257. i. Nancy[7] Kaye, b 31 July 1948.
+ 1258. ii. Joyce Ann, b 21 August 1951.
   1259. iii. Ilene Ruth, b 30 March 1957; d 5 June 1975 at Bartow, FL.
   1260. iv Kenneth Marland, b 12 August 1963; single in 1984.
+ 1261. v. Cindy Lou, b 22 August 1961.
   1262. vi. Steven Ray, b 31 July 1965.

498. DONALD[6] LESLIE EISENHAUER (s/o Ethel[5] Phillips Eisenhauer #208), b 9 January 1933 at Los Angeles, CA; m 12 June 1953 at Los Angeles, **Mary Sue Peckham**, d/o Ralph William and Gladys Evelyn (Randall) Peckham, b 2 March 1933 at Quinn, SD.

Children, surname EISENHAUER:
+ 1263. i. Donald[7] Keith, b 20 April 1954.
+ 1264. ii. Terri Ann, b 12 November 1957.

499. PATRICIA[6] JEAN EISENHAUER (d/o Ethel[5] Phillips Eisenhauer #208), b 22 October 1935 at Los Angeles, CA; m 6 April 1963 at Los Angeles, **Donald Christian Haugen**, s/o Oscar Christian and Margarette (Howell) Haugen, b Central Bethpage, NY.

Children, Surname HAUGEN:
+ 1265. i. Dena[7], b 1 February 1959.
   1266. ii. Danny, b 7 August 1964 at Sylmar, CA.
   1267. iii. Linda, b 17 July 1965 at Sylmar.

500. ANNE[6] GOODRICH (d/o Grace[5] Austin Goodrich #207), b 25 December 1929 at Casper, Wyoming; m 2 April 1952 at Fort Collins, CO, **Daniel Alexander McAtee**, b 29 October 1925 at Casper, WY. Dan is a heavy equipment operator; lives in Casper.

The Sixth Generation 247

Children, surname McATEE:
- 1268. i. Leon[7] Paul, b 5 December 1954; does car repair work in Casper.
- + 1269. ii. Mark Daniel, b 31 January 1957.
- 1270. iii. Margaret, b 5 June 1958.
- 1271. iv. Thomas Austin, b 21 December 1959; m 29 September 1985, Jane Petty. Thomas is a commercial diver at Houna, LA.
- 1272. v. John Christopher, b 19 November 1961; works on lawn maintenance; Casper.

501. JANE[6] GOODRICH (d/o Grace[5] Austin Goodrich #207), b 10 April 1934 at Casper, WY; m 2 April 1955 at Casper, **Thomas Powell Clemmons**. Tom is an engineer for Boeing Aircraft; lives in Bellevue, WA.

Child, surname CLEMMONS:
- 1273. i. Bradley[7], b 6 September 1955 at Denver, CO; lives at Olympia, WA; does graphic art.

502. FRANCES[6] ROBERTA McDANIEL (d/o Harry[5] Austin McDaniel #212), b 22 January 1922 at Torrington, WY; m 14 July 1946 at Torrington, **Harold Noble**. Harold a teacher and carpenter. They live at Vancouver, WA.

Children, surname NOBLE:
- + 1274. i. Lila[7] Jean, b 11 May 1947.
- 1275. ii. Russell Eugene, b 30 June 1955 at Seattle, WA; m Patricia Ann Risor 11 January 1979 at Vancouver; divorced; no children.
- + 1276. iii. Grant Lee, b 18 January 1962.
- + 1277. iv. Lora, b 19 January 1964.

504. WARD[6] EMERY McDANIEL (s/o Harry[5] Austin McDaniel #212), b 23 September 1925 at Yoder, WY; m 28 December 1950 at Torrington, WY, **Katherine Thomas**, d/o William Eugene and Marthena (Smith) Thomas. In 1984 Ward was Deferred Giving Representative for Central College, Pella, IA. Ward was previously working for Wearever in the Saint Louis area.

Children, surname McDANIEL:
- + 1278. i. Thomas[7] Lane, b 1 June 1952.
- + 1279. ii. Lucinda Jean, b 14 July 1954.
- 1280. iii. Jay Scott, b 1 August 1961 at Saint Louis, MO; m 3 September 1983, Collette Ann Graber, b 19 January 1964, Ames, IA, d/o

Leland Graber. Jay is a golf instructor and Collette is an U.S. Army interpreter.

505. BETTY[6] **JO McDANIEL** (d/o Harry[5] Austin McDaniel #212), b 25 January 1928 at Torrington, WY; m 29 June 1947 at Torrington, **Myrlan L. Hertzler**, s/o Glen Jay and Hazel (Schwab) Hertzler. Myrlan is a successful farmer at Veteran, WY; active in the Republican Party, Farm Bureau, and other organizations.

Children, surname HERTZLER:
- 1281. i. Gary[7] Lee, b 14 August 1948; m 22 August 1970, Eileen Higgins of Cheyenne, WY. Now divorced. Gary is a Pathologist at Atlanta, GA. No children.
- 1282. ii. Gregory Lloyd, b 21 November 1950 at Torrington, WY; m 15 March 1981, Diana Gail Douglas, d/o John and Alice Douglas, b 18 March 1957; Greg is Professor of Agricultural Economics, at University of Western Australia; Diana is animal nutritionist.
- + 1283. iii. Dean Brent, b 21 November 1955.

507. THOMAS[6] **EARL ROBERTSON** (s/o Mabel[5] McDaniel Robertson #213), b 7 March 1925 at Independence, KS; m 28 December 1950 at Morganfield, KY, **Lucille Norman**, b 27 June 1927, d/o Rudy Norman; she lives at Aurora, CO.

Children, surname ROBERTSON:
- + 1284. i. Cynthia[7] Lucille, b 9 July 1955.
- 1285. ii. Janice Ranee, b 30 March 1957. Trained as decorator; changes jobs frequently.

508. MARY[6] **GERTRUDE ROBERTSON** (d/o Mabel[5] McDaniel Robertson #213), b 11 September 1928 at Fort Collins, CO; m 2 July 1950 at Brush, CO, **Bob Courtney**, s/o J.W. and Cleora (McNamie) Courtney, b 7 October 1927 at Denver, CO. Bob worked for Otis Elevator Co. for 35 years; retired 1982, age 55.

Children, surname COURTNEY, all born at Denver CO:
- 1286. i. Mark[7] Alan, b 16 November 1951; not married. Lives at Idaho Springs, CO at Loveland Basin Ski area in winter. Missionary in Guatemala Summer 1988.
- 1287. ii. Sandra Lynn, b 31 August 1953; m 21 September 1974, Vernon Sanderson, s/o John and Valda Sanderson, b 27 December 1944; no children. Both employed by Honeywell in Littleton, CO, where they live.

The Sixth Generation 249

+ 1288. iii. Deborah Ann, b 9 April 1956.
    1289. iv. Pamela Sue, b 30 June 1957. An accountant for Ensign Oil and Gas Co.

509. JOYCE[6] AUSTIN (d/o Harry[5] A. Austin #216), b 20 February 1937 at Torrington, WY; m 11 May 1957 at Cheyenne, WY, **Bernard Lee Lindburg**, s/o Donald Maxwell and Mabel (Stegeman) Lindburg, b 18 March 1936 at Chappel, NE. Joyce and Bernard own their own furniture upholstery business in Cheyenne; they also have custom made drapes.

Children, surname LINDBURG:
    1290. i. Ronald[7] Lee, b 30 March 1963, Cheyenne. Graduated University of Wyoming; in 1987 working at Fort Collins, putting in runways at the airport.
+ 1291. ii. Karen Lynn, b 13 February 1966.

510. ROBERT[6] AMES AUSTIN (s/o Harry[5] A. Austin #216), b 26 September 1944 at San Diego, CA; m 7 July 1968 at Cheyenne, WY, **Ada Carol Agee**, d/o Richard Spriggs and Helen Agnes (Harper) Agee, b 15 April 1948. Robert is regional sales manager for Temtex Products, Inc; travels eastern half of U.S; graduated from University of Wyoming with Commission of 2nd Lieutenant; lives in Plano, TX northeast of Dallas.

Children, surname AUSTIN:
    1292. i. Nina[7] Noel, b 5 January 1969 at Andrews AFB, MD; engaged to marry in 1993 in Plano, TX, Casey John Lambright.
    1293. ii. Richard Ames, b 31 March 1970 at Fort Irwin, CA.
    1294. iii. Halley Agee, b 29 August 1975 at Oklahoma City, OK.
    1295. iv. Andrew Harper, b 20 October 1977 at Dallas, TX.

513. GLADYS[6] ROGERS (d/o Julia[5] Cates Rogers #218), b 20 May 1911 at Grand Junction, CO; m/1 **James Roots**; d 1936. Jim worked for a union, distributing money to unemployed, was also a boxer. According to Hale Tognoni he died in a fight in a bar. Gladys m/2 in 1956, **George Carlson** at Jackson, CA. Gladys d 31 May 1984.

Children, surname ROOTS:
+ 1296. i. Chadrick[7] Arthur, b 21 May 1932.
+ 1297. ii. Beauford Alba.
+ 1298. iii. Wilford Accord.

514. ELSIE[6] ROGERS (d/o Julia[5] Cates Rogers #218), b at Grand

Junction, CO about 1919; m 20 July 1939 at Grand Junction, **John Hooker**. He was a police officer.

Child, surname HOOKER:
- 1299. i. Robert[7] N., b —; d in the Philippine Islands in WWII. His stone is in Orchard Mesa Cemetery with grandparents Julia and Thomas Rogers. See Addenda.

516. ELIZABETH[6] JANE ROGERS (d/o Julia[5] Cates Rogers #218), b about 1929 at Grand Junction, CO; a personal visit revealed little about her; m 9 March 1945 at Grand Junction, CO, **Frank Virgil Coley**, s/o Frank and Minnie (Vaughn) Coley. Martin Mortuary gave her new name as Mrs. Glen Siminoe; I found Glen and he said the were married in 1964 and later divorced; no record of marriage or divorce found. Record in Grand Mesa Cemetery of her burial there 16 January 1973, age 44, no stone. Glen said he was b 1908 at Grand Junction, s/o Fred and Josephine (Vincent) Siminoe.

Child, surname COLEY:
- 1300 i. Robert[7], b —; Glen Siminoe and Mrs. Calvin Coley, sister-in-law of Frank, said Robert was in the army in NC; he married a woman with two children.

517. MARGERY[6] W. ROGERS (d/o Julia[5] Cates Rogers #218), b 29 April 1931 at Grand Junction, CO; m 22 May 1949 at Grand Junction, **Arthur Lee Roberts**.

Children, surname ROBERTS:
- 1301. i. Carol[7] Ann, b 10 March 1950 at Newport News, VA.
- 1302. ii. Diana Lee, b 29 July 1951 at Grand Junction, CO.
- 1303. iii. Arthur Thomas, b 15 December 1955.
- 1304. iv. Janette Danean, b 31 August 1964 at Jackson, CA.

519. LUCY[6] MARGARET CATES (d/o William[5] H. Cates #219), b 26 March 1917 at Preston, White Pine Co., NV; d 12 June 1978 at Bremerton, WA; buried Quilcene, Washington Cemetery; m **Donald A Perchetti**, s/o Joseph Anthony and Mary Louise (Boot) Perchetti, b 9 May 1909 at Lehigh, OK; Donald was a butcher, then worked in a mine, after that a carpenter. She m/2 **Pete Covert**.

Child, surname PERCHETTI:
- \+ 1305. i. Joan[7] Gayle, b 8 May 1936.

520. EMMA[6] **ESTHER CATES** (d/o William[5] H. Cates #219), b 31 March 1919 at Preston, White Pine Co., NV; m **Raleigh O'Key Coleman**, b 8 June 1900, d 2 September 1970, buried at Salt Lake City, UT. They homesteaded on a ranch in southeastern Utah. Her home is in Craig, CO.

Children, surname COLEMAN:
- 1306. i. Marcus[7] Anthony, b 8 March 1937.
- 1307. ii. John, b 15 July 1939.
- 1308. iii. Michael, b 17 April 1941.
- 1309. iv. Howard Alan, b 9 June 1943.
- 1310. v. Austin, b 7 March 1945; d 13 April 1947.
- 1311. vi. Willard Enoch, b 13 October 1946.
- 1312. vii. Miriam, b 12 August 1948; m Floyd Winnery, last known living in North Highlands, CA.
- 1313. viii. Merle, b 6 July 1950 at Monticello, UT; d 5 August 1981 in New Mexico.

521. ARLINA[6] or Aroline **BELL CATES** (d/o William[5] H. Cates #219), b 23 November 1920 at McGill, White Pine Co., NV; d 10 May 1987 at Safford, AZ; m 1 July 1939 at Lordsburg, NM, **Vernon Oliver Hart**, s/o Gustave Andrus and Emma Mary Magdaline (Weber) Hardt, b 18 October 1918 at Bisbee, AZ. Vernon divorced Aroline 7 August 1957; he d 23 January 1988 at Tucson, AZ. Aroline was House Mother at Copper Queen Hotel for 8 years; the rest of the years she worked at Copper Queen Hospital, all jobs but nursing, part time in the lab; all her family are Mormons. Both places are run by Phelps Dodge Mining Corp, Bisbee, AZ.

Children, surname HARDT:
- \+ 1314. i. David[7] Oliver, b 14 April 1940.
- \+ 1315. ii. Vernaline Marie, b 9 May 1941.
- 1316. iii. Elayne Jeanne, b 27 June 1943 at Hawthorne, NV; she is not married; has been a devoted teacher on the elementary level in California a number of years; lives in Los Angeles, CA. Does part time duty in the Navy.
- \+ 1317. iv. Ronald Michael, b 1 January 1946.
- \+ 1318. v. Linda Susan, b 2 May 1948.
- 1319. vi. Gary James, b 7 November 1949 at Bisbee, AZ; d 19 January 1955 of Hemophilia.
- \+ 1320. vii. Phillip Joel, b 3 March 1956.

522. WILLETTA[6] **CATES** (d/o William[5] H. Cates #219), b 3 June 1922 at Preston, White Pine Co., NV; d 5 January 1985; m about 1939, **Lawrence McCowen** in Iowa; was married 4 or 5 times; her last husband was **Gordon McDaniels**.

Children, surname McCOWEN, all born in IA:
    1321.   i.   Charlotte[7] Ann, b 1 July 1940.
    1322.   ii. Donna Kay.
    1323.   iii. Katherine.

523. DELORIS[6] **JANE CATES** (d/o William[5] H. Cates #219), b 6 February 1924 at Preston, Whie Pine Co., NV; d 3 September 1972 at Ely, NV; m/1 **John J. Weeteling**. Delores m/2 **Gordon B. Cue**.

Children, surname WEETELING, both born in NV:
    1324.   i.   Richard[7].
    1325.   ii. Terrance.

524. SYLVIA[6] **JOY CATES** (d/o William[5] H. Cates #219), b 25 February 1926 at Preston, White Pine Co., NV; m 20 December 1941 at Waterloo, IA, **Louie Miller**, b 16 May 1921 at Dumont, IA. Louie was a carpenter for Kennecott Copper at Ruth, NV until retirement.

Children, surname MILLER:
+   1326.   i.   Gloria[7] Jean, b 30 May 1942.
+   1327.   ii. Judy Kay, b 15 August 1944.
+   1328.   iii. Doris Geneil, b 29 June 1947.

525. JUNE[6] **CATES** (d/o William[5] H. Cates #219), b 17 June 1928 at Preston, White Pine Co., NV; m/1 **Avald Zunino** 12 March 1946; he adopted her two children after marring her. June m/2 **Walt Peterson**, m/3 **Merrill Wolford**, m/4 **James Wakeling**, and she m/5 **Herbert A. Covert**, March 1984 in Washington State.

Children, surname ZUNINO, both born at Oakland, CA:
    1329.   i.   William[7], b 9 August 1944.
    1330.   ii. Gordon, b 9 August 1944, twin.

Children, surname PETERSON:
    1331.   iii. Carol[7].
    1332.   iv. David.

Children, surname WOLFORD, born at Ely, NV:

1333. v. Keith[7].
1334. vi. Colleen.

526. GORDON[6] **BRUNO CATES** (s/o William[5] H. Cates #219), b 30 March 1930 at Preston, White Pine Co., NV; m 20 July 1952 at Eureka, NV, **Martha Jane Thrasher**, d/o Norman Glen and Edna Marie (Williams) Thrasher, b 26 November 1936 at Monte Vista, Rio Grande Co., CO. Gordon is in Ann's Nursing Home in Salt Lake City, UT.

Children, surname CATES, all born at Ely, NV:
1335. i. Gordon[7] Anthony, b 20 July 1953.
1336. ii. Donald Alan, b 4 August 1954.
1337. iii. Jerry Ray, b 20 March 1956.
1338. iv. Leslie.

527. GENEIL[6] **CATES** (d/o William[5] H. Cates #219), b 24 July 1933 at Preston, White Pine Co., NV; m/1 at Eureka, NV, 9 March 1949, **Avery Ferdnand Bass**; one child from this marriage; annulled 13 January 1950; m/2 at Ely, 14 January 1950, **Arthur William Carling**, s/o Norval and Florence Evelyn (Farnsworth) Carling, b 1 January 1924 at Ely. Arthur was mechanical supervisor, Kennecott Copper, Ruth, NV until his retirement; he had three children by a previous marriage; Arthur Eugene, b 28 January 1946; Anna Louise, b 30 November 1946; and Kathleen Jeanette, b 21 January 1948.

Child, surname BASS:
+ 1339. i. Pauline[7] Yvette, b 13 February 1950.

Children, surname CARLING:
+ 1340. ii. Barbara[7] Lydia, b 14 February 1951.
+ 1341. iii. Mary Ellen, b 18 October 1954.
+ 1342. iv. Karen Geneil, b 10 August 1956.

530. NYE[6] **WOODROW TOGNONI** (s/o Ina[5] Cates Tognoni #221), b 28 November 1917 at Preston, NV; m 25 December 1944, **Neva Faye Gergen**, d/o Bill Gergen, b 21 November 1927. Nevada State Library states that Nye was an assemblyman from Eureka County in the 1941 Legislative session, and became a State Senator during the 1943 and 1945 sessions; this while still in college. From a telephone conversation March 1983 I found that he was a mining engineer until about 1972, when he started the Tags Tri-State Tax Service with several offices, one in Grants,

NM where he lives. He divorced Neva and she is married to Sam Bida and lives in Ely, NV; m/2 **Susie Jesusito** on 7 December 1963; she died of cancer 3 December 1975; m/3 **Shirley Frazer** in 1976 and divorced her 16 January 1980.

Children, surname TOGNONI:
+ 1343. i. Louis[7] Christopher, b 16 August 1945.
   1344. ii. Nye Woodrow, b January 1946 at Eureka, NV; d 29 November 1946.
   1345. iii. Robert Joseph, b 19 December 1947 at Ely, NV.
+ 1346. iv. Patricia Linda, b 13 May 1950.
   1347. v. Michael Angelo, b 6 January 1952.

531. NEVA[6] JUNE TOGNONI (d/o Ina[5] Cates Tognoni #221), b 23 October 1919 at Preston, White Pine Co., NV; m 5 January 1938 at Salt Lake City, UT, **John George Mendez**, s/o Joseph Navarro Mendez, b 12 June 1917 at Atlantic, IA; d 24 October 1943 at Salt Lake City; m/2 4 June 1945 at Eureka, NV, by the Justice of the Peace, **Archie Pruett Richey**, s/o John Frank and Nancy (Ballinger) Richey, b 12 May 1892 at Waco, TX; d 1968; m/3 11 August 1968 at Denver, CO, **Victor Raymond Brown**, b 11 August 1917 at Herndon, KS; now divorced. Neva received her bachelor's degree in Social Sciences in California; has written fictional accounts of the lives of her grandfathers, Joseph Tognoni and Nelson Cates. A telephone call to her brother Hale Tognoni in 1988 revealed the she was working for the Peace Corps on the Island of Granada.

Children, surname MENDEZ, all born at Eureka, NV:
+ 1348. i. Joey[7] Ann, b 12 May 1939.
+ 1349. ii. Antonio Joseph, b 15 November 1940.
+ 1350. iii. John Frank, b 12 September 1942.
+ 1351. iv. Cindy Jill, b 31 March 1944.

Children, surname RICHEY:
+ 1352. v. Maureen[7] Patricia, b 7 May 1946.
+ 1353. vi. Nancy Lynn, b 14 February 1948.

532. HALE[6] CHRISTOPHER TOGNONI (s/o Ina[5] Cates Tognoni #221), b 16 April 1921 at Preston, NV; m 13 March 1947 at Reno, NV, **George-Ann Neudeck**, d/o Louis Merrill and Eva (Carey) Neudeck, she b 18 February 1920 at Fort Dodge, IA. Hale enrolled in the McKay School of Mines, University of Nevada, Reno, in 1939. In 1942 WW II brought an interruption to his education, but in 1946, after his tour of duty with the Army Corps of Engineers, he returned home to Eureka and then to Reno and then to the University. In 1947, George-Ann Neudeck came to Reno from her family's Iowa farm to marry the insistent young Lieutenant whom she had met while serving in the Red Cross in the Philippine Islands. Together they worked for the U.S. Geological Survey at Steamboat Springs, CO 1946-1948; then Anaconda Copper, Butte, Montana while Hale finished college as a Geological Engineer at the University of Nevada in 1948. He continued on in law school at the American University 1950–52, taking his bar examination in AZ. He has served in many capacities for government and service organizations as well as an expert in evaluating many mining districts for their potential production of minerals. He is a registered Arizona Professional Engineer, with proficiency in mining engineering. Also he is an attorney licensed to practice in Arizona; the Arizona, California and Colorado Federal District Courts; the 9th and 10th U.S. Circuit Courts of Appeal; and the US Supreme Court. He is in private practice in Phoenix, AZ. His wife, George-Ann is a professional sculptor, specializing in creating large bronze horses and ponies, on commission.

Children, surname TOGNONI:

+ 1354. i. Becky[7] Lou, b 3 January 1949.
+ 1355. ii. Brian Hale, b 18 November 1950.
+ 1356. iii. David Quentin, b 4 March 1952.
+ 1357. iv. Sandra Ann, b 21 July 1953.
+ 1358. v. Jeffery R., b 21 January 1957.

533. ROBERT[6] LOUIS TOGNONI (s/o Ina[5] Cates Tognoni #221), b 19 March 1924 at Eureka, Eureka Co., NV; m 16 March 1957 at Glenwood Springs, Garfield Co., CO, **Pearl Marie Porter**, d/o Joseph Aubrey and Iola Gladys (Abney) Porter; b 8 August 1929 at Arthur, NE. Robert joined his brothers Nye and Hale at University of Nevada in 1942, studying mining engineering. He joined the Army Specialized Training Program (ASTP) at Fort Benning. He was slated for officer training when the Battle of the Buldge occurred and he was sent to the Blackhawk Division (86th), with whom he served in the European and Asiatic theaters. While in the army he carried a correspondence course in law from La Salle University and had his degree by the time he left the army. Not satisfied with a correspondence school degree, he went on to Washington, DC and with the help of Senator Pat McCarran, he worked his way through law school, graduating in 1951. He moved to Littleton, CO, became a member of the Colorado Bar and made an unsuccessful bid for district judge. Thereafter he practiced law, with an office in Denver, CO. and became the champion of the poor and unfortunate. He was stricken with a fatal heart attack while on a case in the Golden District courtroom. He died 21 July 1978 at Denver.

It is interesting to note that in the same Eureka Sentinel newspaper as the above appears, there is an interesting account of how the Tognoni boys helped support the family in their own unique way, written in 1932 by Edna Beaman.

> Nobody ever thinks of a scavenger business being very interesting or exciting. But in Eureka, NV, a boy named Robert Tognoni has built up a profitable industry, which may well be considered the most unusual in Nevada. Robert or "Ty" as he is called by the rest of the fellers, makes the rounds of Eureka with a cart which is drawn by four or five dogs. He gathers up the garbage cans at all the back doors, loads them in his cart, and yells at the dogs, who move on to the next place. They know all the stops. Some times they break the monotony by giving chase to the stray cat or remonstrating with some dogs that made sneering remarks about them.
>
> Two or three carts have been broken, harnesses destroyed and garbage spilled all over Eureka's hill. Then Robert and his cousin who helps him gather up the pieces, doctor the pups and take it in good part as just one of those things.
>
> The garbage is used to feed pigs kept in a pen outside the town's limits. this has been a money-making scheme for several years, nothing big, just a nice steady income for a boy trying to help a widowed mother.
>
> The business was originally started by Nye, the oldest boy and handed down first to Hale, then to Robert in turn. Becky Boudway, Hale's daughter, says it started in 1928, when her grandfather, Joseph R. Tognoni bought two coon hounds for trapping coyotes. Coyote hide were valuable, if not for selling or personal use, then for bounty from the government trappers who were killing them to protect the local sheep and cattle. The two dogs, Kayo and

Brownie were to trap coyotes for Joseph. Brownie fell by the wayside, but Kayo was with the family for close to 20 years. One day when Joseph went out with his Model T Ford, he found two stray pigs running along the road. He gave the tiniest of the two to the kids, and the penned it up in the backyard, and to feed it they persuaded the cook at the Eureka Hotel to save his garbage, which they would pick up regularly in a couple of five gallon cans loaded on a little wagon. Kayo liked to accompany them on these trips in town, and then they fastened the wagon to his collar and he began pulling the wagon. Their father was sick and at home a lot, and he made Kayo a harness. The pig business began to grow; they got more pigs and began collecting garbage from the neighbors as well. After their father's death they expanded in a full blown business to help out the family finances, meanwhile moving the pig business outside the town limits, after neighbors complained. The whole interesting story is too long to tell here.

Children, surname TOGNONI:
+ 1359. i. Lynne[7] Marie, b 28 July 1958.
   1360. ii. Keith Irvin, b 3 November 1961 at Denver.

535. GERTRUDE[6] E. REED (d/o Harold[5] Reed #222), b 11 October 1920 at Gillette, WI; m 6 July 1946 in Gillette at the home of the bride, **Clarence Cox**, s/o Jesse and Mayme (Frank) Cox, he b 28 May 1915 at Underhill, WI; d 28 August 1985. Gertrude still lives in Gillette.

Children, surname COX:
+ 1361. i. Kenneth[7] Allen, b 19 April 1947.
+ 1362. ii. Alan Wayne, b 18 January 1949.
+ 1363. iii. Carol Jean, b 30 July 1950.
+ 1364. iv. Gloria Mae, b 31 May 1952.

536. GORDON[6] ELMER REED (s/o Harold[5] Reed #222), b 11 October 1920 at Gillette, WI; m 26 August 1956 at Webster City, IA, **Patricia Ann Riley**, d/o John Harold and Elsie (Hall) Riley. Gordon resided at Bethesda, MD while employed in the Pentagon in Washington, DC, in the State Department, now retired according to Gertrude, in 1990. Recently Gordon and Pat moved to Arizona.

Children, surname REED:
   1365. i. Maureen[7] Jo, b 21 June 1957 at Arlington, VA; she graduated

from Iowa State University; she is structural Engineer with Harris-Smariga.
+ 1366. ii. Sharon Lynn, b 25 January 1959.
    1367. iii. Mitzi Kay, b 5 May 1960 at Bethesda, MD; was with the Peace Corps in Jamica in 1988.
    1368. iv. Candace Pearl, b 23 October 1962 at Bethesda; plans on going into Teaching Administration.
    1369. v. Gordon Harold, b 22 January 1969 at Bethesda.

540. GENEVA[6] VIOLA BEEKMAN (d/o Gertrude[5] Wright Beekman #223), b 31 December 1916 at Twin Lakes Flume, Deerlodge Co., MT, west of Anaconda; m 24 July 1937 at Butte, MT, **Russell Milo Lester**, s/o Clarence and Grace (Putman) Lester, b 4 May 1910 at Reliance, SD; Russell a smelterman at Anaconda Copper Mines. Geneva d 24 Jan 1988.

Children, surname LESTER:
+ 1370. i. Loraine[7], b 9 January 1939.
+ 1371. ii. Lawrence Arthur, b 31 October 1942.

541. MARY[6] CAROLINE WENNELL (d/o Nellie[5] Wright Wennell #225), b 14 May 1919 at Evanston, IL; m 19 July 1941 at Seattle, WA, **Charles Brady Musgrave**, s/o Clarence Arthur and Versa (Barker) Musgrave, b 31 July 1915 at Oblong, IL. Charles is a 30 year veteran of the U.S. Air Force; he was a pilot during WW II and stayed in after the war with permanent rank of Master Sergeant, in the supply field. Mary is a Licensed Practical Nurse; worked at Scott AFB, IL in Pediatrics and Ob-Gyn. Also did secretarial work in several places and at retirement was working at Scott AFB.

Children, surname MUSGRAVE:
+ 1372. i. Charles[7] Anthony, b 13 April 1947.
+ 1373. ii. Diane Lee, b 1 April 1944.

542. HAZEL[6] JENNIE WENNELL (d/o Nellie[5] Wright Wennell #225), b 3 April 1921 at Suring, Oconto Co., WI; m/1 26 April 1941 at Evanston, IL, **Robert Anton Brandenhoff**, s/o Anton and Christene (Nissen) Brandenhoff, b 16 January 1919 at Duluth, MN.

Hazel Wennell m/2 8 June 1967 at Chicago, IL, **John Atlee Stearn**, adopted son of James and Lucy (Stevens) Stearn, b 19 May 1928 at Portland, OR. Hazel has worked for Illinois Bell Co. many years as a repair clerk; John works for AT&T.

The Sixth Generation

Children, surname BRANDENHOFF:
+ 1374. i. Carol[7] Lynn, b 30 June 1943.
+ 1375. ii. Donna Jean, b 23 January 1947.

543. TONY[6] JAMES CAREY (s/o Irene[5] Wright Carey #226), b 26 July 1921 at Raymond, WA; m/1 does not tell her name; m/2 14 November 1968 at Miami, FL, **Carolyn Campbell**, d/o Lee Harrison and Maxine (Collier) Campbell, b 15 April 1945 at Viper, KY.

Children, surname CAREY:
    1376. i. Bruce[7] Richard, b 31 January 1950 at Washington, DC. In 1982 not married and a writer at U.S. Department of Labor, Washington, DC.
    1377. ii. Gayle Nancy, b 18 March 1953 at Washington, DC, where she is now a secretary.
    1378. iii. Tony Steven Ray, b 29 April 1969 at Atlanta, GA.
    1379. iv. Robbin Lee James, b 29 May 1971 at Maimi, FL.

544. JUNE[6] ADELINE CAREY (d/o Irene[5] Wright Carey #226), b 29 October 1925 at Roberts, Escambia Co., FL; m/1 November 1951 at Great Falls, MT, **Jesse Lee James III**, s/o Jesse James II and Maggie ?, b 27 April 1905 in Mo. He claims to be a direct descendant of "the Jessie James," but has no proof and the James Family Museum does not acknowledge him. They were divorced in 1966.

June m/2 3 February 1967, **Bobbie Ray Donaldson**, s/o T. J. and Myrtle Adelia (Mosley) Donaldson, b 14 July 1934 at Waco, TX. Bobbie has three children from his former marriage: Susan R., Michel, and Alan; he drives truck for Central Freight Lines.

Children, surname JAMES:
+ 1380. i. Olympia[7] Laura, b 1 December 1952.
+ 1381. ii. Jesse Franklin, b 21 April 1955.
+ 1382. iii. Woodson Lee, b 29 April 1956.

545. JOHN[6] NORMAN THOMPSON (s/o Irene[5] Wright Thompson #226), b 4 February 1927 at Gonzales, FL; m 11 March 1950 at Lucedale, MS, **Frances Dolores Reese**, d/o Absalom Hobcomb and Clara Mae (Rutherford) Reese, b 12 February 1932 at Ferry Pass, FL.

Children, surname THOMPSON, all born at Pensacola, FL:
    1383. i. Donald[7] Andrew, b 17 December 1950; m 14 October 1977,

Brenda Suzanne Stone.
1384. ii. Dennis, b 29 April 1952; d 1 May 1976.
+ 1385. iii. John Calvin, b 2 September 1953.

548. CLARICE[6] EVA WRIGHT (d/o Thomas[5] Wright #227), b 17 June 1926 at Niagara, Marinette Co., WI; m 20 July 1946 at Gillett, WI, **Clifford William Missall**, s/o Otto and Alvina (Robenhorst) Missall, b 17 September 1919 at Breed, WI. Clifford has logged most of his life, except for 10 years in a factory. He had a heart attack in 1977, and has limited activity since. They live at Suring, WI.

Children, surname MISSALL:
    1386. i. Jean[7] Marie, b 8 January 1947 at Suring, WI; m 17 June 1967 Melvin Chris Quandt, s/o Chris and Ann (Ziereis) Quandt.
+ 1387. ii. Lois Ann, b 9 October 1948.
    1388. iii. Dennis John, b 19 July 1950 at Milwaukee, WI; m 23 September 1972. Peggy Jean Weber; d 6 May 1974 at Oconto, WI.

549. LYLIS[6] MARGARET WRIGHT (d/o Thomas[5] Wright #227), b 20 December 1928 at Niagara, Marinette Co., WI; m 12 September 1960 at Dubuque, IA, **James Jeffalone**, s/o Angelo and Ann Jeffalone, b 1 May 1926 at Beloit, WI. When last known were managing an apartment complex in Green Bay, WI.

Child, surname SCHOOL (by first husband Norman School):
    1380. i. Margaret[7] Ann, b 26 September 1947; she only lived a few hours after birth; her mother fell while carrying her baby and broke her back.

550. DELORES[6] DOROTHY WRIGHT (d/o Thomas[5] Wright #227), b 9 April 1929 at Niagara, Marinette Co., WI; m 14 June 1947 at Saint Michael's Church, Suring, WI, **Junior Louis Vancaster**, s/o Louis Joseph and Alice (Boehm) Vancaster, b 26 December 1926 at Green Bay, WI; he was railroad worker until he became disabled with Parkinson's Disease; they live in Denmark, WI.

Children, surname VANCASTER:
+ 1390. i. Donald[7] Raymond, b 7 August 1948.
+ 1391. ii. Ellen Marie, b 10 July 1952.
    1392. iii. Mark Andrew, b 15 January 1959 at Green Bay; m 9 May 1980 to Rebecca Saykally.
    1393. iv. Barbara Jean, b 6 August 1960 at Green Bay; m 13 June 1981 to

Robert Daus.
1394. v. Mike James, b 30 January 1965 at Green Bay.

551. EUGENE[6] THOMAS WRIGHT (s/o Thomas[5] Wright #227), b 14 October 1930 at Suring, WI; m 11 September 1954 at Saint John Lutheran Church, How, WI, **Lois Marie Jansen**, d/o Frank and Nora (Schuettpeltz) Jansen, b 28 January 1934 at Suring. Eugene is a cheese factory employee.

Children, surname WRIGHT:
1395. i. Randall[7] Eugene, b 6 January 1956 at Oconto Falls,WI; m 29 August 1981 Mary Hansen; Randall is a police officer.
1396. ii. Rhonda Jean, b 20 June 1960 at Shawano, WI.
1397. iii. Richard Frank, b 20 June 1969 at Shawano.

555. THOMAS[6] MARTIN WRIGHT (s/o Thomas[5] Wright #227), b 9 July 1941 at Suring, WI; m 16 April 1966 at Saint Agnes Church, Green Bay, WI, **Carol Bernadette Schroeder**, d/o Bernard W. and Violet (Wren) Schroeder, b 20 August 1945 at New Castle, England. Thomas a Vietnam veteran; when last known had trouble with his head from "Agent Orange." He is a Bank Manager in the computer Dept. in Green Bay, WI.

Children, surname WRIGHT, both born at Green Bay, WI.
1398. i. Ronald[7] Thomas, b 8 June 1967.
1399. ii. Kim Marie, b 27 May 1968.

556. PATRICIA[6] ANN WRIGHT (d/o Thomas[5] Wright #227), b 30 December 1947 at Suring, WI; m 1 October 1966 at Saint Michael's Catholic Church, Suring, **Wayne Lewis Stayback**, s/o Lewis and Quanita (Short) Stayback, b 28 February 1941 at LaPorte, IN; they live at Rolling Prairie, IN.

Children, surname STAYBACK, all born at LaPorte:
1400. i. Joseph[7] Wayne, b 11 September 1967.
1401. ii. Jeffery Paul, b 27 October 1970.
1402. iii. Julie Ann Margaret, b 20 April 1973.

557. WILMA[6] FERN JOHNSON (d/o Angeline[5] Reed Johnson #228), b 3 October 1914 Town of Maple Valley, Gillett, WI; m 3 September 1938 at Bethel Lutheran Church, Green Valley, WI, **Joseph Peter Valenta**, s/o John and Melvine (Brazeau) Valenta b 22 May 1915 at Town of Spruce, Gillett, WI. Wilma graduated from Wisconsin State University in 1965 and taught school 30 years, 10 of them on the Menominee Indian

Reservation. They have 80 acres of farm land and raise beef cattle on Holiday Inn Road, Suring, Joseph has a polka orchestra which performs at local functions and has a regular radio program.

Children, surname VALENTA:
+ 1403. i. Joseph[7] Clyde, b 25 November 1942 at Oconto Falls, WI.
+ 1404. ii. Laurel Fern, b 5 January 1946 at Oconto Falls.
   1405. iii. Sherry Jean, b 5 March 1955. When last in touch Sherry not married; was teaching school in Oconto Falls.

558. LARS[6] CHRISTIAN JOHNSON (s/o Angeline[5] Reed Johnson #228), b 31 January 1916 at Maple Valley, WI; d 13 December 1960 at Kelly Lake, WI; he is buried in Hickory Cemetery, Hickory, WI; m 25 June 1938 at Brookside Lutheran Church, **Verna Bartz**, d/o Henry and Carolyn (Prausa) Bartz, b 23 March 1917 at Pound, WI.

Child, surname JOHNSON:
+ 1406. i. Larry[7] Lars, b 18 July 1950.

559. RONALD[6] EUGENE JOHNSON (s/o Angeline[5] Reed Johnson #228), b 9 May 1918 at Maple Valley, WI; d 6 October 1981; m 25 September 1939 in North Dakota, **Wilhelmina Grabanski**, d/o Alexander and Albina Grabanski, b 18 December 1913 at Minto, ND; Ronald owned several cheese factories and won many prizes for the quality of his cheese both locally and nationwide; he once had an order for cheese from President Johnson.

Children, surname JOHNSON:
+ 1407. i. Marlene[7] Josephine, b 22 July 1941.
+ 1408. ii. Bonnie Louise, b 20 January 1945.
+ 1409. iii. Merlynn John, b 23 November 1949.
+ 1410. iv. Karen Kathryn, b 14 August 1953.

560. KENNETH[6] LEROY JOHNSON (s/o Angeline[5] Reed Johnson #228), b 12 February 1920 at Town of Maple Valley, WI; m 20 October 1943, **Alice Szymanski**, d/o Frank and Mary (Kozou) Szymanski, b 9 October 1925 at Stevenrose, MI; Kenneth suffers from Kidney disease and has frequently dialysis treatments. Previously he worked for 22 years with the Culvert Supply Co., in Green Bay, WI.

Children, surname JOHNSON:
+ 1411. i. Cecilia[7] Jean, b 6 March 1944.

The Sixth Generation 263

+ 1412. ii. Patricia, b 12 November 1947.
   1413. iii. Rebecca, b 22 February 1960 at Green Bay, WI.

561. CLYDE[6] **LYLE JOHNSON** (s/o Angeline[5] Reed Johnson #228), b 2 January 1922 at town of Maple Valley, WI; d 3 June 1974; buried in Hickory Cemetery, Hickory, WI; m 9 June 1943 at Oconoto, WI, **Doris Lilian Noel**, d/o Wilfred and Mae (VerBunker) Noel, b 4 November 1923 at Oconto; Clyde was in the cheese making business along with brother Ronald; and owned a number of factories himself.

Children, surname JOHNSON:
+ 1414. i. Fay[7] Ann, b 2 August 1946.
+ 1415. ii. Gary, b 9 October 1948.
+ 1416. iii. Linda, b 25 January 1949.
   1417. iv. Jeffery Allen, b 4 May 1955 at Viroqua, WI. When last known was carpenter and cheesemaker in Prairie du Chien, WI and unmarried.
   1418. v. Valerie, b 11 June 1958 at Prairie du Chien; when last known was working at the University in La Crosse, WI.

562. NEVA[6] **ANGELINE JOHNSON** (d/o Angeline[5] Reed Johnson #228), b 28 October 1923 at Town of Maple Valley, WI; m 14 September 1944 at Sheboygen, WI, **Robert Neal Hodge**, s/o John Henry and Margaret (Gahagan) Hodge, b 17 June 1921 at Plymouth, WI. Neva was principal of Elkhart Lake School near Plymouth, WI, where she lives. She received her Master's Degree in Education from University of Wisconsin in Milwaukee, WI. Robert worked for Borden Foods in the cheese industry located in Plymouth, WI; he d December 1, 1989. Neva spent much time and energy collecting all the information on her whole Johnson clan; it is much appreciated.

Child, surname HODGE:
   1419. i. Daniel[7] Robert, b 12 November 1946; d 13 November 1946.

563. MAE[6] **CAROLYN JOHNSON** (d/o Angeline[5] Reed Johnson #228), b 16 November 1924 at Suring, WI; m 5 October 1944 at Our Redeemer Lutheran Church, Suring, **Virgil Olick**, s/o Emil Olick, born Volhynia Province, Jitomir Co., in Toporischtsch, Rudnia and Martha Schwittay, b Pound, WI. Virgil b 25 May 1923 at Milwaukee, WI. They live at Saint Francis, WI.

Children, surname OLICK:

1420. i. Randall[7], b 28 September 1950 at Milwaukee, WI. Not married when last in touch; worked at A.D. Smith Co. as inspector; enjoys skiing, diving, and hunting and fishing.
+ 1421. ii. Pamela, b 17 May 1955.

564. DORA[6] **JEANETTE JOHNSON** (d/o Angeline[5] Reed Johnson #228), b 23 December 1925 Claywood, Town of Maple Valley, WI; m 12 August 1944 at Danish Luthern Church of the Redeemer, Suring, WI, **Orvil John Slang**, s/o James Oscar and Amanda Carolyn (Ericcson) Slang b 8 August 1919 at Maple Valley, WI. Dora is deeply involved in Rosemaling, a Norwegian folk art, hand painting marked by flowing, intertwining scrolls and impressionistic flowers. Her whole house is decorated with it and she teaches it to others.

Children, surname SLANG:
+ 1422. i. Jeanette[7] Carol, b 24 June 1945.
+ 1423. ii. Carol Lea, b 6 January 1948.
+ 1424. iii. Lora Jean, b 10 February 1952.

565. AUDREY[6] **DOROTHEA JOHNSON** (d/o Angeline[5] Reed Johnson #228), b 28 August 1928 at Town of Maple Valley, WI; m 27 January 1951 Reedeemer Lutheran Church, Suring, WI, **Henry Kralovetz Jr.**, s/o Henry and Lorrene (Kalloth) Kralovetz b 11 May 1931 at Pound, WI. Henry is in the cheese business; Audrey d 21 November 1989.

Child, surname KRALOVETZ:
 1425. i. Gregory[7] Virgil, b 9 February 1961 at Milwaukee, WI. He was adopted by Audrey and Henry.

566. VIRGIL[6] **ARLING JOHNSON** (s/o Angeline[5] Reed Johnson #228), b 9 March 1930, Oconto Co., WI; m 1 July 1947, **Marie (Mary) Alice Krause**, d/o Arthur Gustave and Elsa Josephine (Eggebrecht) Krause b 6 April 1930 at Gillett, WI, Township; Virgil has been self employed 31 years (1982); "Timber Lake Cheese Co. in Timber Lake, SD manufactures longhorn cheese from milk purchased from 78 farmers; sold to Alpha Beta Chain stores in Los Angeles. Selfridge Cheese Co. in Selfridge, ND manufactures cheddar cheese from milk purchased from 150 farmers. This is sold to Pauly Cheese Co. in Green Bay, WI. Cheese Hauling in Manden, ND trucks milk to Selfridge and hauls the cheese to Green Bay."

Children, surname JOHNSON:

+ 1426. i. David[7] Virgil, b 6 December 1947.
  1427. ii. Daniel Arling, b 17 December 1950 at Prairie du Chien, WI.
+ 1428. iii. Cynthia Marie, b 2 August 1955.
  1429. iv. Mark Andrew, b 16 November 1963 at Lancaster.
  1430. v. John Robert, b 10 July 1967 at Lancaster.

567. BEVERLY[6] JUNE JOHNSON (d/o Angeline[5] Reed Johnson #228), b 8 September 1932 at Town of Spruce, Oconto Co., WI; m 27 January 1951 at Our Redeemer Lutheran Church, Suring, WI, **Erling Donald Arneson**, s/o Elmer Wesley and Lenice Margaret (Torgerson) Arneson, b 13 September 1930 at Soldiers Grove, Utica Township, WI. Erline is manager of Morgan Coop Dairy of Oconto Falls; Beverly graduated from Marinette Teachers College and taught school for 5 years. After marriage Erling served 2 years 32nd Medium Tank Batallion of Fort Knox, KY and 1 year in Fulda, Germany in Co. Baker as a Corporal. He is second generation cheese maker.

Children, surname ARNESON:
+ 1431. i. Tyrone[7] Erling, b 23 May 1952.
  1432. ii. Delra Lenice, b 11 May 1955 at Green Bay, WI; m Michael James Olsen of Shawano 25 September 1976, s/o LaVerne and Elaine (Gudmondson) Olsen, b 7 January 1952. They were married at Saint Johns Lutheran Church, Morgan, Oconto Falls. Delra is 3rd generation cheese maker; 2nd in command Morgan Coop Dairy. Michael employed at Shawano Paper Mill. They live at Cecil, WI; no children.
+ 1433. iii. Keith Dale, b 21 February 1957.
+ 1434. iv. Kim Donald, b 5 September 1958.
  1435. v. Steven Neal, b 22 November 1961 at Sheboygan, WI; m Antoinette Marie Foral of Gillette, WI, 15 August 1982 at Saint Johns Lutheran Church at Morgan, Oconto Falls. She was b 11 March 1961 at Oconto Falls, d/o Harlan and Barbara (Graff) Foral. Steven is 3rd generation cheese maker; employed at Morgan Coop Dairy. No children.
  1436. vi. Darryl Ronald, b 15 August 1963 at Sheboygan, WI. Bulk truck driver for Morgan Coop Dairy. He m 20 October 1984, Kathleen Marie Hunt d/o Orvil & Winifred (Igoe) Hunt, b 19 January 1965 at Ashland, WI.
  1437. vii. Lisa Angeline, b 25 July 1965 at Oconto Falls. When last known (1983) she is High School graduate and employed part time as cheese wrapper Morgan Coop Dairy. She m 25 May 1984 at

Oconto Falls, Gregory John Onesti s/o Carl John and Florence Margaret (Kreischer) Onesti, b 21 December 1962 at Milwaukee, WI. No children.

568. LAUREL[6] GAY JOHNSON (d/o Angeline[5] Reed Johnson #228), b 29 July 1934 at Kelly Brook, WI; m 7 October 1961 at Our Redeemer Lutheran Church, at Suring, WI, **Arnold Alfred Herich**, s/o Emil Peter and Maria Vilma (Piovarchy) Herich, b 17 April 1932 at Forest Park, IL. Arnold is a Lutheran minister; they were in Rahan, ND for awhile; in 1982 were moving to Illinois, probably Waukegan.

Children, surname HERICH:
- 1438. i. Mark[7] John, b 6 September 1962 at McHenry, IL.
- 1439. ii. Christian Peter, b 3 June 1964 at McHenry.
- 1440. iii. Gay Laurel, b 11 January 1966 at McHenry.
- 1441. iv. Holly Anissa, b 9 January 1970 at Waukegan, IL.

569. DALE[6] RAYMOND JOHNSON (s/o Angeline[5] Reed Johnson #228), b 21 January 1937 at Kelly Brook, WI; m 17 June 1968 at Tulsa, OK, **Judith Lynne Huntington**, d/o Parke Frederick and Mildred (Kupke) Huntington, b 25 January 1942 at Casper, WY; in 1982 Dale was an airline pilot and Judy was working on cancer research and they lived at Ypsilanti, MI.

Children, surname JOHNSON:
- 1442. i. Heidi[7] Elizabeth, b 28 February 1972 at Ann Arbor, MI.
- 1443. ii. Karsten Dale, b 20 August 1974 at Plymouth, IN.

570. GLORIA[6] ANN VERWEY (d/o Victor[5] Verwey #230), b 2 January 1928 at Appleton, WI; m 11 April 1950 at Little Chute, WI at Saint John church parsonage, **Robert Vanden Boogart**, s/o Arnold and Margaret Vanden Boogart, b 2 August 1928 at Little Chute, Wi; when last known Robert was maintenance supervisor at Appleton Paper Co.

Children, surname VANDEN BOOGART:
- + 1444. i. Sharon[7] Lynn, b 30 October 1950.
- + 1445. ii. Rick Charles, b 15 May 1953.
- + 1446. iii. Jay Martin, b 16 May 1958.
- 1447. iv. Scott Robert, b 30 May 1959 at Appleton, WI.
- 1448. v. Todd Joseph, b 5 July 1961 at Appleton.
- 1449. vi. David John, b 3 October 1962 at Appleton.

1450. vii. Kim Marie, b 16 November 1968 at Appleton.

571. HAROLD[6] R. PAULSEN (s/o Verna[5] Verwey Paulsen #231), b 25 January 1925 at Appleton, WI; m 13 May 1950 at Trinity Lutheran Church, Green Bay, WI, **Caroline Horn**, d/o Charles L. Horn, b 12 June 1930 at Shawano, WI.

Children, surname PAULSEN:
+ 1451. i. Randall[7] Roy, b 4 April 1951.
+ 1452. ii. Scott, b 19 July 1953.
   1453. iii. Christopher Harold, b 11 July 1964 at Green Bay.

572. JUNE[6] IONE PAULSEN (d/o Verna[5] Verwey Paulsen #231), b 7 May 1926 at Appleton, WI; m 12 June 1948 at Saint Mary of the Angels Church parsonage, Green Bay, WI, **Donald John Verriden**, d/o Alvin and Albine (DeMain) Verriden, b 31 October 1926 at Green Bay, WI. June d 24 November 1987. Dan worked for 35 years for Charmin Paper Co.

Children, surname VERRIDEN:
+ 1454. i. Barbara[7] Jean, b 18 April 1949.
+ 1455. ii. Allan Roy, b 8 June 1951.
+ 1456. iii. Karen Marie, b 8 August 1952.
   1457. iv. Larry John, b 18 November 1954 at Green Bay; m 18 September 1981 at Green Bay, Karen Nuthals, d/o Bernard and Millie (Bissick) Nuthals, b April 1954 at Green Bay. No children known.
   1458. v. Lisa Ann, b 28 December 1961 at Green Bay; m 30 October 1982 at Green Bay, Kevin Paul Malnor, s/o Lawrence and Agnes Irene (Karasti) Malnor, b 20 December 1960 at Green Bay. No Known children.

573. LOIS[6] ELAINE PAULSEN (d/o Verna[5] Verwey Paulsen #231), b 3 July 1927 at Appleton, WI; m/1 on 2 December 1950 at Saint Mary of the Angels Church, Green Bay, WI, **Clifford Robert Hyska**, s/o Alphonse and Rosalie (Boulanger) Hyska b 8 January 1924 at Green Bay. When last known Clifford worked for a sporting goods store in Tucson, AZ; they were divorced. Lois m/2 **Drue Wilson** and they live in Tucson.

Children, surname HYSKA:
+ 1459. i. Diana[7] Lynn, b 4 December 1953.
   1460. ii. Maria Ann, b 11 April 1956 at Green Bay.

574. VINCENT[6] REED (s/o Emerald[5] Reed #237), b 7 July 1935 at Brookfield, WI; m 26 January 1963, **Janet Zandt**. When last known they lived at Olney, MT, where he was working in a sawmill.

Child, surname REED:
    1461. i. Bradley[7], b 10 February 1964 at Hartford, WI.

576. ROSALIE[6] REED (d/o Emerald[5] Reed #237), b 5 December 1937 at Brookfield, WI; m 11 May 1957, **Walter Babicky**.

Children, surname BABICKY:
    1462. i. Kenneth[7], b 20 November 1959.
    1463. ii. Jacqueline, b 9 January 1962; m 4 March 1978 Kevin Barnett.
    1464. ii. Deven, b 28 October 1966.

577. MARVIN[6] LEE REED (s/o Alfred[5] Reed #237), b 18 June 1939 at Town of How, Oconto Co., WI; m 23 October 1965 at Milwaukee, WI, **Susie Lusardi**, d/o Matthew and — (Scholz) Lusardi, b 19 January 1943 at Milwaukee, WI; Marvin worked at Lakeside Bridge & Steel Co., Milwaukee until retirement; they live at Collins, Manitowac Co., WI.

Children, surname REED, both born at Milwaukee, WI:
    1465. i. Lance[7], b 28 April 1973.
    1466. ii. Gregory, b 21 January 1974.

578. WARREN[6] JAMES REED (s/o Alfred[5] Reed #238), b 7 December 1940 at Town of How, Oconto Co., WI; m 28 November 1970 at the Court House at Oconto, **Bonnie Warschkow**, d/o Gordon and Elizabeth (Liswoe) Warschkow, b 7 October 1948 in Oconto Co. Warren works at North Port (Mirro Plant) at Gillett, where they make bolts; live in Suring, WI.

Children, surname REED, both born at Oconto Falls, WI:
    1467. i. Ronda[7], b 18 September 1971.
    1468. ii. Scott, b 7 August 1973.

579. MARCELLA[6] MAE REED (d/o Alfred[5] Reed #238), b 22 October 1942 at Town of How, Oconto Co., WI; m 12 June 1971 at Lena, WI, Catholic Church, **Wayne Pirlot**, s/o Edward and Evelyn (Early) Pirlot, b 13 September 1946 at town of Little River, WI. Wayne works at North Port (Mirro Plant) at Gillett, WI and live at Lena.

Children, surname PIRLOT:

The Sixth Generation

1469.   i.   Jodie[7], b 23 November 1972 at Oconto Falls, WI.
1470.   ii. Wade, b 30 April 1975 at Green Bay, WI.

580. NORMA[6] JEAN REED (d/o Alfred[5] Reed #238), b 9 July 1945 at Gillett, WI; m 1964, **Allen Miller**, s/o Walter H. and Anna (Konop) Miller, b 16 December 1943 at Oconto Falls, WI. Allen is employed in construction work and they live in Town of Underhill.

Children, surname MILLER:
+ 1471.   i.   Bruce[7] Allan, b 5 December 1964.
  1472.   ii. Lisa, b 13 August 1965 at Two Rivers, WI.

581. ALFRED[6] ALLEN REED (s/o Alfred[5] Reed #238), b 12 July 1946 at Gillett, WI; d 12 January 1983 at Milwaukee, WI; he had three kidney transplants; m 10 August 1968 at Gillett; Saint John's Lutheran Church, **Susan Gehm**, d/o Victor and Lydia (Sorenson) Gehm, b 19 August 1948 at Oconto Falls, WI; they had three children. Susan married second, Myron Hillman.

Children, surname REED, all born at Green Bay, WI:
1473.   i.   Alan[7], b 21 January 1971.
1474.   ii. Clinton, b 3 March 1973.
1475.   iii. Grant, b 1 May 1975.

582. WAYNE[6] CARL REED (s/o Alfred[5] Reed #238), b 3 October 1947 at Oconto Falls, WI; m 7 July 1969 at Milwaukee, WI, **Joan Flaig**, d/o Edward H. and Delores L. (Utke) Flaig, b 17 July 1948 at Shawano, WI. Wayne and Joan live next door to Alfred; Wayne and his brother David run Alfred's farm since his semi-retirement.

Children, surname REED:
1476.   i.   Timothy[7] Wayne, b 17 November 1969 at Shawano.
1477.   ii. Tami Jo, b 24 November 1972 at Shawano.
1478.   iii. Bradley Michael, b 12 October 1976 at Shawano.
1479.   iv. Brandon Jay, b 21 November 1985.

584. BEVERLY[6] ANN REED (d/o Alfred[5] Reed #238), b 3 November 1956 at Oconto Falls, WI; m 11 August 1972 at Saint Anthony's Catholic Church, Oconto Falls, **Kenneth Van Ark**, s/o Clarence and Margaret (Walske) Van Ark, b 10 May 1952 at Oconto Falls; Kenneth works at Pound, WI at Gretz Manufacturing Co., which makes farm machinery; they live at Oconto Falls.

Children, surname VAN ARK:
- 1480. i. Bobbie[7] Jo, b 24 June 1976 at Oconto Falls, WI.
- 1481. ii. Adam John, b 5 January 1974 at Oconto Falls.
- 1482. iii. Lee Michael, b 20 October 1980 at Oconto Falls.
- 1483. iv. Kiva Marie, b 2 July 1982 at Oconto Falls.
- 1484. v. Joseph James, b 29 September 1985.

585. BARBARA[6] SUE REED (d/o Alfred[5] Reed #238), b 10 January 1957 at Oconto Falls, WI; m 11 April 1980 at Hintz Church, Hintz, WI, Town of Underhill, **Ralph Fischer**, s/o Robert and Martha (Krueger) Fischer, b 11 April 1955 at Shawano, WI. Ralph works a large farm with his father.

Children, surname FISCHER:
- 1485. i. Chad[7] Lee, b 22 July 1980 at Oconto Falls, WI.
- 1486. ii. Katie Marie, b 27 March 1982 at Shawano.
- 1487. iii. Stephen, b 3 March 1986.
- 1488. iv. Aaron, b 22 February 1988.
- 1489. v. Heather Sue, b 16 March 1989.

586. LORNA[6] JOY REED (d/o Alfred[5] Reed #238), b 17 February 1960 at Oconto Falls, WI; m 14 April 1978 at Gillett Lutheran Church, Gillett, WI, **Russell Mueller**, s/o Walter and Doris (Buhrandt) Mueller, b 16 March 1957 at Oconto Falls. Russell works for French Debarking Co., where bark is peeled from logs; dried, then sent to a paper mill and the logs go to Proctor and Gamble. When last known Lorna worked at the Mirro plant in Gillett.

Children, surname MUELLER:
- 1490. i. Cory[7] Robert, b 15 August 1978 at Shawano, WI.
- 1491. ii. Ryan Russell, b 7 January 1981 at Shawano.
- 1492. iii. Lacey Nicole, b, 26 August 1985.

587. VIVIAN[6] ANN REED (d/o Wallace[5] Reed #239), b 6 June 1938 at Town of How, Oconto Co., WI; m 29 September 1956, **Frank Nardiello**, s/o Nicholas and Josephine (Loreno) Nardiello, b 25 August 1933 at Rockford, IL. Frank works at Chrysler Corp. at Belvidere, IL; they live at Rockford.

Children, surname NARDIELLO, all born at Rockford, IL:
- 1493. i. Frank[7] Nicholas, b 12 July 1957; m 29 April 1982 Fiona Skinner

in London, England. He worked in a clothing store in England; is good at designing and all art work; Fiona was married before and has children.
- 1494. ii. Cynthia Lee, b 9 December 1958.
- 1495. iii. Renee Jean, b 12 June 1964.

588. WALLACE[6] JAMES REED (s/o Wallace[5] Reed #239), b 22 February 1940 at Maple Valley, WI; m 25 July 1959, **Karen Marie Schultz** at Saint John Catholic Rectory, Gillett, WI; d/o Edward William and Mary Elizabeth (Bricco) Schultz, b 24 December 1941 at Gillett. Wallace works as a logger and operates his own saw mill; built a house in early 60s and sold it in 1976; built another where they live in Town of Underhill, Oconto Falls, WI.

Children, surname REED:
- + 1496. i. Kym[7] Marie, b 21 December 1959.
- 1497. ii. Treana Lea, b 18 July 1962 at Oconto Falls, WI.
- 1498. iii. Shawn James, b 14 March 1964 at Oconto Falls.
- 1499. iv. Sharlene Lyn, b 9 August 1965 at Oconto Falls.
- 1500. v. Ethan Dewitt, b 3 February 1980 at Oconto Falls.

589. PHILLIP[6] EDMUND REED (s/o Wallace[5] Reed #239), b 1 April 1942 at Town of Underhill, Oconto CO., WI; m 1 February 1964, **Janice Marie Heath**, d/o Allen and Christine (Warrington) Heath and a Native American, b 8 February 1944 at Menominee Indian Reservation, Keshena, WI. Phillip is a self employed logger, builder, carpenter, and is a guitar player; had his own band in early years; built their home at Town of How, Oconto Co.

Children, surname REED, all born at Oconto Falls, WI:
- 1501. i. Yvette[7] Marie, b 1 March 1966.
- 1502. ii. Michele Faye, b 19 September 1968.
- 1503. iii. Lowell Vaughn, b 21 March 1976.
- 1504. iv. Jolene Leigh, b 18 October 1977.
- 1505. v. Heather Lynne, b 9 March 1979.

590. STANLEY[6] DEWITT REED (s/o Wallace[5] Reed #239), b 15 February 1943 at Town of Underhill, Oconto Co., WI; m 4 June 1966 **Ruth Ann Chapin**, d/o Leo Glen and Naomi Esther (Case) Chapin, b 6 March 1949 at Oshkosh, Winnebago Co., WI. Stanley is involved in logging, pulp cutting and building houses; lives in Town of Underhill,

Oconto Co.

Children, surname REED, both born at Shawano, WI:
    1506. i. Linette[7] Fay, b 17 December 1974.
    1507. ii. Isaiah Ashlin, b 19 October 1980.

591. VALERIE[6] JOYCE REED (d/o Wallace[5] Reed #239), b 30 March 1945 at Town of Underhill, Oconto, CO., WI; m 9 November 1963, **Roger Louis Fernandez**, s/o Francis and Josephine (Corn) Fernandez, b 21 April 1940 at Menominee Indian Reservation, Keshena, WI. Roger is a self-employed logger on the Reservation, where they live. He contracts for the Menominee Tribal Enterprises. Originally he worked on the Reservation Police Force. He has his own trucking business. In early years he was a drummer in a Rock & Roll Band with two of his brothers and a drummer in a country-western band. Valerie worked 8 years as a teacher-aide at Neopit School on the Reservation.

Children, surname FERNANDEZ:
    1508. i. Wendy[7] Mae, b 5 May 1964 at Illinois Masonic Hospital, Chicago.
    1509. ii. Quintin Roger, b 17 September 1965 at Shawano, WI.
    1510. iii. Elisa Joy, b 4 July 1980 at Shawano.

592. MAUREEN[6] MARTHA REED (d/o Wallace[5] Reed #239), b 2 March 1947 at Town of Underhill, Oconto Co., WI; m 18 April 1964, **Robert Francis Fernandez**, s/o Francis and Josephine (Corn) Fernandez, b 14 June 1943 at Menominee Indian Reservation, Keshena,WI. When last known Robert worked installing pipelines for natural gas for the Michigan-Wisconsin Pipeline at Mountain Station; they live on Highway 55 on the Reservation. He likes to hunt, fish, trap, and is handy at many trades and is good at art, as are his children.

Children, surname FERNANDEZ, all born at Shawano, WI:
    1511. i. Dawn[7] April, b 29 April 1966; a guitar player.
    1512. ii. Wade Robert, b 9 November 1968; also a guitar player.
    1513. iii. Virgil Francis, b 23 August 1972; wants to be an electrical engineer.
    1514. iv. Travis Lee, b 29 October 1978.
    1515. v. Angela Rose, b 16 September 1981.

593. DWIGHT[6] DALE REED (s/o Wallace[5] Reed #239), b 27 August 1951 at Town of Underhill, WI; m 25 September 1971 **Geraldine Ann**

The Sixth Generation 273

Wesolowski, d/o Norbert and Antoniette (Kaczmarowski) Wesolowski, b 6 May 1949 at Green Bay, WI. Dwight works for Nu-Line Industries, a factory that makes baby furniture at Suring, WI. Geraldine worked for many years at Elliott Glove Factory, in Gillett, WI. Dwight's two brothers built his house at Maple Valley, Oconto Co., WI. He plays drums in a band, when last known.

Children, surname REED, all born at Shawano, WI:
    1516. i. Aaron[7] Lee, b 28 August 1972.
    1517. iii. Joel Gene, b 25 April 1977.
    1518. iv. Rachelle Lynn, b 30 November 1979.

594. COLLEEN[6] KAY REED (d/o Wallace[5] Reed #239), b 5 January 1956 at Oconto Falls, WI; m 24 May 1975, **Brian Larry Birr**, s/o Nathan and Bernice (Schliep) Birr, b 4 July 1953 at Green Bay WI. Brian works for Skelgas Co. in Shawano, driving truck as a propane gas salesman; he attended Stevens Point College at Stevens Point, WI for 2-1/2 years. Colleen's brothers Wallace Jr. and Phillip built their house.

Children, surname BIRR, all born at Shawano, WI:
    1519. i. Landon[7] Dale, b 7 June 1976.
    1520. ii. Monica Ann, b 26 September 1978.
    1521. iii. Owen Rinehart, b 22 May 1981.

595. SYLVAN[6] REED (s/o Raymond[5] E. Reed #240), b 5 February 1951 at Milwaukee, WI; m 12 June 1971, **Bonnie Starks**; they live at Kingston, WA and Sylvan is in the United States Navy, when last known.

Children, surname REED:
    1522. i. Heather[7], b 22 September 1971 at Green Bay, WI.
    1523. ii. Holly Ann, b 24 January 1974.
    1524. iii. Heath Allan, b 10 November 1976.

599. DONNA[6] RAE SCHROEDER (d/o June[5] Reed Schroeder #241), b 2 April 1937 at Town of Underhill, Oconto, Co., WI; m 5 December 1956 at Court House, Green Bay, WI, **Norman "Billy" Corn**, s/o August and Elizabeth (Bucklew) Corn, b 1 January 1933 on Menominee Indian Reservation, Keshena, WI. They were divorced in 1958.

After her divorce from Corn, Donna went to Chicago to work and left her two small children with her parents, who raised them for 10 years; Donna returned, bought a house and took her children back. Donna m/2

25 March 1961 at Chicago, IL, **Patrick Grignon**, s/o Michael and Inez (Adams) Grignon, b 17 March 1940 at Menominee Indian Reservation. Patrick's great grandmother was a white child left on the doorstep of an Oneida Indian family and raised by them. Donna divorced Patrick in 1971. Donna m/3 19 October 1990 Richard Schultz. She is director of a Day Care Center.

Children, surname CORN:
+ 1525. i. Laurie[7] June, b 7 January 1956.
+ 1526. ii. Cheryl Lynn, b 2 September 1958.

Children, surname GRIGNON:
+ 1527. iii. Selena[7], b 25 September 1961.
+ 1528. iv. Tammy, b 6 October 1963.
+ 1529. v. Darla, b 4 July 1965.
    1530. vi. Darwin, b 6 July 1966 at Chicago.

600. VERNON[6] CLYDE SCHROEDER (s/o June[5] Reed Schroeder #241), b 16 April 1940 at Town of Underhill, Oconto Co., WI; m 30 August 1958 at Gillett, WI, **Laurel Chapin**, d/o Joseph and Mary Gertrude (Jackling) Chapin, b 10 March 1939 at Oshkosh, WI; Vernon has a very successful logging and trucking business, employing a number of people.

Children, surname SCHROEDER:
+ 1531. i. Bannon[7] James, b 17 September 1958.
+ 1532. ii. Duran Vernon, b 13 January 1960.
+ 1533. iii. Shane Sheldon, b 24 June 1965.
    1534. iv. Faron Reece, b 6 August 1967 at Oconto Falls, WI.

601. RAYMOND[6] CECIL SIEGEL (s/o Norma[5] Reed Siegel #242), b 21 February 1938 at Gillett, WI; m December 1961, **Geraldine Krueger**, d/o Martin & Caroline (Vegue) Krueger. They live in Watertown, WI.

Children, surname SIEGEL:
+ 1535. i. Caroline[7], b 7 August 1962.
    1536. ii. Rhonda, b 19 September 1966; planned to marry 9 April 1988.
    1537. iii. Heidi, b 27 July 1971.

602. JORDAN[6] LEE SIEGEL (s/o Norma[5] Reed Siegel #242), b 21 August 1939 at Milwaukee, WI; m/1 12 November 1960, **Judith Ann Peterson**, d/o Mr. & Mrs. Victor Woodrow Peterson; later divorced her and m/2 **Donna** — in 1979. Jorden worked at Best Block Factory in Milwaukee. Jorden d 29 July 1988.

Children, surname SIEGEL:
- \+ 1538. i. Jeffery[7], b 15 March 1961.
- 1539. ii. James Brian, b 14 May 1962 at Milwaukee; m 12 May 1984 Sandra Jean Courchaine.
- \+ 1540. iii. Jon, b 17 December 1963.
- 1541. iv. Jolene Lee, b 6 September 1980.
- 1542. v. Donaven Louis, b 12 August 1981 at Milwaukee.

603. SANDRA[6] JANE SIEGEL (d/o Norma[5] Reed Siegel #242), b 25 October 1944 at Milwaukee, WI; m 23 November 1963 at Gillett, WI, **Bob Molgner**. He worked for the Kohler Co; they live in Sheboygan, WI.

Children, surname MOLGNER:
- 1543. i. Craig[7], b 2 September 1964 at Milwaukee; m 26 July 1986 Barbara Ann Visser, Sheboygan, WI.
- 1544. ii. Steven, b 10 July 1968 at Milwaukee.
- 1545. iii. Troy, b 24 September 1970 at Sheboygan.

604. RALPH[6] GEORGE HAWKINS (s/o Ilene[5] Reed Hawkins #243), b 5 March 1945 at Milwaukee, WI; m 28 December 1963, **Sharon Lou Brauer**, d/o Clarence E. and Leona E. (Wilke) Brauer, b 3 April 1947 at Shawano, WI. Ralph has his own electrical business and they live at Bonduel, WI.

Children, surname HAWKINS:
- 1546. i. Scott[7] Allen, b 21 August 1964 at Cherry Point, NC; m 7 may 1986 Jackie Klumb.
- 1547. ii. Rodney Ralph, b 31 July 1966; m 11 May 1987 Jackie Rodefer.
- \+ 1548. iii. Sheryl Lynn, b 18 May 1968.
- 1549. iv. Randal Clarence, b 13 March 1973 at Shawano, WI.
- 1550. v. Shawn Michael, b 16 February 1974 at Shawano.
- 1551. vi. Shannon Ralph, b 19 November 1976 at Shawano.
- 1552. vii. Rochelle Marie, b 22 July 1978 at Shawano.

605. GALE[6] MICHAEL HAWKINS (s/o Ilene[5] Reed Hawkins #243), b 13 August 1946 at San Rafael, CA; m/1 **Nancy Grant**; m/2 4 December 1976, **Nancy Engebose**, d/o Edmund Louis and Ruth Ann (LeGrave) Engebose, b 26 June 1952 at Kewaunee Co., WI; m/3 6 September 1986,

Diane Efferdahl. When last known Gale was stock clerk with Appleton, WI, School system, where he lived.

Children, surname HAWKINS, all born at Appleton, WI:
- 1553. i. William[7] Michael, b 30 June 1971.
- 1554. ii. Sara Lee, b 5 July 1978.
- 1555. iii. Ruth Ann, b 30 June 1980.

606. LINDA[6] JUNE HAWKINS (d/o Ilene[5] Reed Hawkins #243), b 6 January 1948 at San Rafael, CA; m 1 June 1968, **Randall Gordon Neuens**, s/o Peter and Maxine (Bouressa) Neuens, b 18 July 1949 at Iron Moutain.

Children, surname NEUENS, all born at Appleton, WI:
- 1556. i. Amy[7] Lynn, b 21 February 1969.
- 1557. ii. Robb Randall, b 20 January 1970.
- 1558. iii. Nicole Ruth, b 2 August 1974.

607. ROBERT[6] CARL HAWKINS (s/o Ilene[5] Reed Hawkins #243), b 26 May 1949 at South Bend, IN; m 14 December 1970, **Barbara Wright**, d/o Clarence Alfred and Irene Minnie (Calkins) Wright, b 7 March 1951 at Beaver Dam, WI; Robert is an electrician for Pierce Manufacturing Co., manufacturers of fire fighting equipment; they live at Neenah, WI.

Children, surname HAWKINS, both born at Appleton, WI:
- 1559. i. Tonya[7] Jean, b 19 September 1973.
- 1560. ii. Jennifer Irene, b 21 March 1977.

609. RONALD[6] JAMES REED (s/o Arnold[5] J. Reed #244), b 9 December 1950 at Milwaukee, WI; m 11 September 1982 at Kenner, LA, **Nelda Jean Varnell**, d/o Edward Leon and Bessie Louise (Marcy) Varnell, b 20 January 1942; Ronald works on an oil rig in the Gulf of Mexico and lives in Kenner, LA.

Child, surname REED:
- 1561. i. Melissa[7] Jean, b 13 August 1980 at Kenner.

610. JOYCE[6] LYNN REED (d/o Arnold[5] J. Reed #244), b 1 January 1953 at Milwaukee, WI; m 13 October 1974, **Nestor Ernesto Hinajosa**, s/o Nestor and Veda (Vela) Hinajosa, b 19 December 1952; Joyce graduated from Fresno State College, CA December 1982; moved to Norfolk, VA in 1983 to be stationed four years as 2nd Lieutenant in the

Air Force.

Child, surname HINAJOSA:

1562. i. Consuelo[7] Guadalupe, b 11 October 1987.

611. JAYNE[6] MARIE REED (d/o Arnold[5] J. Reed #244), b 2 April 1955 at Milwaukee, WI; m 2 April 1976, **Richard French**, b August 1951 s/o Mary French and Robert Hurdle. As of 1983 Jayne worked in Sage Nursing Home in Milwaukee and Richard worked for Marquette Electronics, Milwaukee. They live in Milwaukee.

Children, surname FRENCH, both born at Milwaukee, WI:

1563. i. Erika[7], b 9 September 1976.
1564. ii. Richard, b 24 November 1980.

615. RUTH[6] REED (d/o Russell[5] Reed #245), b 29 April 1931 at Racine, WI; m/1 19 October 1949 at Our Savior's Luthern Church, Racine, **Miles Prothero**, s/o Russell and Edna (Killips) Prothero, b 21 July 1927 at Waukesha, WI; m/2 3 June 1963 at Waukegan, IL, **Fred Neve**, b 1932 at Mason City, IA; annulled 1974; m/3 6 July 1974 at Messiah Lutheran Church, Racine, WI, **Erich Pudell**, b 12 December 1930 at Pomen, West Germany; Eric, trained in Germany as a stone cutter, now works for J. D. Case Tractor Co. as a core maker; Erich's parents are Edward and Berta (Walter) Pudell. Erich has two children by a former marriage, to Ilsa, who d 23 September 1972 of a cerebral hemorage: Barbel Ingried, b 26 June 1957 at Racine and Peter Eric, b 1 June 1960 at Racine. Barbel had a child, Daniel James, which the state took away from her. Ruth and Erich are now raising him.

Children, surname PROTHERO:

+ 1565. i. Melinda[7] Sue, b 16 April 1950, at Racine.
+ 1566. ii. Russell LeRoy Scott, b 24 February 1951, at Racine.
+ 1567. iii. Ruby Lynn, b 21 January 1954, at Racine.

616. RUSSELL[6] SADELL REED (s/o Russell[5] Reed #245), b 3 October 1933 at Racine, WI; m/1 22 January 1955 at Racine **Mary Litrenta**, b 18 April 1930 at Racine, d/o Tony and Sophie (Romano) Litrenta; divorced 12 July 1979; m/2 2 February 1980, **Joyce Larsen**, maiden name Lehman, d/o George and Margaret (Victoor) Lehman, b 5 January 1943.

Children, surname REED:

+ 1568. i. Bonnie[7] Ann, b 13 October 1956.

+ 1569. ii. Jeffrey Allen, b 1 April 1958.
+ 1570. iii. Charles Anthony, b 4 September 1961.

618. JACQUELINE[6] **JANE REED** (d/o Russell[5] Reed #245), b 5 November 1937 at Racine, WI; m 25 March 1956 at Topelo, MS by the Justice of the Peace, **Patrick Rock**, s/o Harold and Frances (Pitsch) Rock, b 11 April 1936 at Kenosha, WI. When they returned home they were married May 1955 by a priest, moved to California for a better job for Patrick as machine shop foreman. When last known Jackie was in training for nursing, and they lived at Burbank, CA. Patrick is in Money Management and Investing.

Children, surname ROCK:
+ 1571. i. Patrick[7], b 25 March 1957.
    1572. ii. Kevin, b 29 June 1958 at Kenosha, WI.
+ 1573. iii. Erin, b 10 July 1960.
    1574. iv. Colin, b 21 June 1962 at Kenosha.
    1575. v. Kathleen Mary, b 23 June 1964 at Racine.

619. DARLA[6] **REED** (d/o Russell[5] Reed #245), b 10 February 1940 at Racine, WI; m 2 November 1957 at Racine, **Edmund Beyer**, s/o Edmund and Leona (Frey) Beyer, b 10 January 1934 at Racine; Edmund is a millwright at J. I. Case Co., in Racine where they live.

Children, surname BEYER:
+ 1576. i. Sharon[7], b 21 June 1958.
    1577. ii. Pamela, b 3 February 1960 at Racine, WI; d 24 June 1960, of sudden crib death.
    1578. iii. Steven, b 25 September 1961 at Racine.
    1579. iv. John, b 25 September 1963 at Racine.

620. JUDITH[6] **REED** (d/o Russell[5] Reed #245), b 15 May 1949 at Racine, WI; m 11 August 1969 at Waukegan, IL, **John Haney**, s/o John Louis and Marjorie Janet (Woodward) Haney, b 12 February 1947 at Racine. John is an auto mechanic and owns his own garage.

Children, surname HANEY, both born at Racine, WI:
    1580. i. Alan[7], b 27 march 1970.
    1581. ii. Elizabeth, b 24 November 1978.

621. DELORES[6] **NYGARD** (d/o Ruby[5] Reed Nygard #246), b 5 February 1930 at Appleton, WI; m 16 June 1951 at Sacred Heart Church,

The Sixth Generation

Appleton, WI, **Edward Schauman**, s/o Alfred Schauman, b 25 June 1928 at Appleton. Edward owns the farm of Grandfather Roy at Suring, WI; he is a semi truck driver for Kimberly Clark at Neenah.

Children, surname SCHAUMAN:
+ 1582. i. Terry[7], b 16 October 1955.
   1583. ii. Sandra, b 12 January 1960 at Appleton.
   1584. iii. Randy, b 10 August 1961 at Appleton.
   1585. iv. Cathy, b 17 June 1966 at Appleton.

622. JEAN[6] MILDRED ERICKSON (d/o Mildred[5] Reed Erickson #247), b 18 January 1931 at Wausau, WI; m 2 June 1951 at Saint Mary's Catholic Church, Wausau, WI, **Theodore Burger**, s/o Theodore and Marie L. Burger, b 29 January 19–. Ted employed at Drott Manufacturing Co., maker of large road equipment.

Children, surname BURGER:
+ 1586. i. Theodore[7], b 7 July 1952.
   1587. ii. Barbara Ann, b 6 July 1955 at Wausau.
   1588. iii. Patrick, b 13 May 1958 at Wausau.
   1589. iv. John, b 23 May 1961 at Wausau.
   1590. v. Sandra Jean, b 15 May 1962 at Wausau.

623. WILLIAM[6] CHARLES ERICKSON (s/o Mildred[5] Reed Erickson #247), b 13 June 1932 at Wausau, WI; m 8 November 1952 at Saint Stephen's Evangelical Reformed Church, Merrill, WI, **Georgia Plautz**, d/o Rhinehard and Elisie (Shultz) Plautz, b 9 August 1934 at Wausau. William worked at American Can Co. until retirement due to blindness.

Children, surname ERICKSON:
+ 1591. i. Cynthia[7] Lee, b 22 May 1955.
   1592. ii. Gary Allen, b 2 May 1957 at Wausau; m Cheryl Wolf, 24 March 1978 in Hawaii, where he was in the Marines; no children.
   1593. iii. Michael, b 15 May 1960 at Wausau.
   1594. iv. Craig, b 9 May 1961 at Wausau.

624. JANET[6] MARIE ERICKSON (d/o Mildred[5] Reed Erickson #247), b 27 November 1943 at Wausau, WI; m 18 April 1964 at First Methodist Church, Wausau, **Dale L. Schlueter**, s/o John and June Schlueter.

Children, surname SCHLUETER:
   1595. i. Ronald[7] Todd, b 31 July 1966 at Wausau.

1596. ii. Joel R., b 19 November 1970 at Wausau.

626. LOUISE[6] MARTIN (d/o Della[5] Bullock Martin #249), b 2 April 1939 at Adel, Brooks Co., GA; m 28 December 1958 at Hickory Head Church, Quitman, GA, **Hilman Alexander Walden**, b 26 October 1939 at Thomasville, GA; Hilman a retired army man who served in Korean War; now works for Powell Feed and Seed Co. They are very active in Church of God as deacon and teacher.

Children, surname WALDEN:
1597. i. Hillman[7] Alexander III, b 26 January 1963 in Hawaii.
1598. ii. Teresa Luan, b 24 February 1966 at Fort Bragg, NC.

627. FORREST[6] LEE MARTIN (s/o Della[5] Bullock Martin #249), b 7 September 1940 at Adel, Cook Co., GA; m 12 April 1963 at Atlanta, GA, **Opaline Fendley**, b 10 November 1939. Forrest worked at United States Government Archives until he retired on disability. They live in Atlanta.

Children, surname MARTIN:
1599. i. Deborah[7] Denise, b 27 December 1964 at Atlanta.
1600. ii. Laurie Michelle, b 29 November 1971 at Atlanta.

628. PEGGY[6] BULLOCK (d/o Elmer[5] Bullock #250), b 19 January 1945 at Sarasota, FL; m/1 **William Ash**; m/2 **Steve Howser**.

Child, surname HOWSER;
1601. i. Stacey[7], b 26 June 1970 at Sarasota, FL.

630. BONNIE[6] BULLOCK (d/o Elmer[5] Bullock #250), b 29 May 1948 at Bradenton, FL; m/1 **Pete Pietsch**; m/2 **William Campbell**.

Children, surname PIETSCH:
1602. i. William[7], b 3 May 1969.
1603. ii. Robert, b 25 February 1972.

631. SANDRA[6] LORRAINE SPRINGMAN (d/o Marietta[5] Bullock Springman #251), b 4 October 1941 at Sarasota, FL; m 15 December 1962 at Christ Methodist Church, Bradenton, FL, **Lawrence M. Rhodes**, s/o George and Minnie Rhodes, b 7 August 1942 at Saint Augustine, FL. Sandra is a dental hygienist; when last known Lawrence was mosquito control Director for Manatee Co., FL.

Child, surname RHODES:
1604. i. Jennifer[7] Ellen, b 11 January 1965 at Bradenton, FL.

The Sixth Generation

633. RONALD[6] **BULLOCK** (s/o Chester[5] Bullock #252), b 25 August 1945 at Sarasota, FL; m **Jacqueline Cole**; divorced her; married again; separated last known. At that time was manager of an Exxon Station. One child by Jacqueline.

Child, surname BULLOCK:
    1605. i. Tammie[7], b 16 August 1968 at Sarasota FL. She was born with one bad kidney and the other one was damaged in an auto accident.

634. GARY[6] **BULLOCK** (s/o Chester[5] Bullock #252), b 4 February 1949 at Sarasota, FL; m **Earlyne Moore**, d/o Earl and Martha (Penley) Moore, b 19 June 1946 at Hemet, CA; he is a painting contractor and lives in Sarasota.

Children, surname BULLOCK:
    1606. i. Christopher[7] Lance, b 1 June 1975 at Sarasota.
    1607. ii. Robin Slade, b 13 December 1978 at Sarasota.

640. AUDREY[6] **EVERITT** (d/o Mildred[5] Wadley Everitt #253), b 23 April 1925 at Oakland, CA; m/1 **Ray Lord**, m/2 **Bill Simmons**.

Children, surname unknown:
    1608. i. Vanya[7].
+ 1609. ii. Linda.

641. LERA[6] **JEAN FOSTER** (d/o Lera[5] Wadley Foster #254), b 16 February 1930 at Portland, OR; m 13 August 1955, **Paul Nagel**, s/o Jacob F. and Sara W. (VanWinkle) Nagel, b 8 July 1927 at Portland.

Children, surname NAGEL, both born at Portland:
    1610. i. Steven[7], b 11 March 1957; he is an insurance photographer.
    1611. ii. Lori Jean, b 16 July 1959; works for a Camarillo, CA firm.

642. ROBERT[6] **PAUL FOSTER** (s/o Lera[5] Wadley Foster #254), b 16 October 1934 at Portland, OR; m 28 April 1956, **Lois Ann Griffeth**, d/o Jacob W. and Pearl E. (Wiggs) Griffeth, b 14 April 1936 at Portland.

Children, surname FOSTER:
    1612. i. Greg[7] Robert, b 20 January 1960 at Portland; m April 1983, Patricia Kay Hawkins, b 2 October 1961 at Madras, OR. Greg a salesman for Bekins Van Lines, when last known.
    1613. ii. Dana Kay, b 31 August 1962 at Portland.

643. JOHN[6] **WEYBURN TICKNOR** (s/o Edythe[5] Wadley Ticknor

#255), b 16 April 1934 at Portland, OR; m 30 July 1960 at Episcopal Church at Baker, OR, **Belva Maxwell**, d/o Omer and Pansy (Long) Maxwell, b 11 April 1937 at Baker. John d 25 July 1991, age 57 years.

Children, surname TICKNOR:
- 1614. i. Cynthia[7] Diane, b 24 January 1963 at Portland; Graduated University of Oregon School of architecture. Joined Broome, Oringdulph, O'Toole, Boles and Associates: architectural planning and interior design of Portland.
- 1615. ii. Christopher Weyburn, b 26 May 1966 at Portland.
- 1616. iii. Tamara Jeanne, b 5 September 1967 at Portland; m 10 August 1992 at Portland, Alec Victor Wilken.

644. WILLIAM[6] ALAN TICKNOR (s/o Edythe[5] Wadley Ticknor #255), b 4 June 1939 at Portland, OR; m 28 May 1965 at Bethel Congregational Church, Beaverton, OR, **Karon Rae Danne**, d/o Lawrence William and Nona Marion (Ruthroth) Danne, b 6 August 1940 at Sioux City, IA.

Children, surname TICKNOR, all born at Portland:
- + 1617. i. Steven[7] William, b 29 November 1962.
- 1618. ii. Scott Alan, b 7 August 1966 at Portland.
- 1619. iii. Tiffany Rae, b 8 March 1969 at Portland; m 11 April 1992 at Beaverton, Jason Spelce, b 7 June 1969, s/o Gary and Cynthia (Vance) Spelce. Jason is Sous Chef for Newport Bay Restaurant at Beaverton; Tiffany is a certified dental assistant.

645. NANCY[6] ANN TICKNOR (d/o Edythe[5] Wadley Ticknor #255), b 12 October 1942 at Salem, OR; m 29 June 1963 at Episcopal Church, Silverton, OR, **Gerald Garth Johnson**, s/o Charles Garth and Violette Marie (Brewer) Johnson, b 13 March 1937 at Portland. Gerald works for the state of Oregon Children's Services Division, Salem, OR. He received Bachelor's and Master's Degree in Education from Willamette University, Salem; Doctorate in Public Administration from California Western University, Santa Ana, CA. Nancy Ann attended Oregon State University, Corvallis, OR, in nursing; she is operations supervisor for Commercial Bank, Salem.

Children, surname JOHNSON:
- 1620. i. Le[7] Anne Michelle, b 29 July 1965 at Salem; m 23 July 1988 at Portland, OR, Michael Andrew Shaw, b 19 June 1965, s/o Herbert and Barbara Shaw. LeAnne graduated from the Univer-

sity of Oregon, June 1987 with a major in TV production. When last known she was working as a group life supervisor for the Hillcrest School of Oregon, an institution serving delinquent children. Michael graduated from University of Oregon in 1988 with a major in journalism and a minor in business administration; he is a fine pianist.

1621. ii. Lisa Marie, b 12 January 1968 at Portland; joined U.S. Navy and as of 1988 was stationed at Cecil Field, Jacksonville, FL, working as plane captain on the tarmac. She m at Gatlinburg, TN, 17 December 1989, Robert H. Ford, b 19 April 1960, s/o Robert Shields and Judy (Bond) Ford of New Jersey. Robert is an accountant and Lisa is now a nurse; they live in Indianapolis, IN.

1622. iii. Geoffrey Garth, b 30 May 1972 at Portland.

646. RICHARD[6] NORLIN WADLEY (s/o William[5] I. Wadley #256), b 13 April 1943 at Portland, OR; m 13 August 1965 at Salem, OR, **Mary Lou Diaz**, d/o Manuel Enreques and Guadalupe (Unzueta) Diaz, b 26 September 1943 in Colorado. Originally lived in Tempe, AZ, when last known lived in Thousand Oaks, CA, where he is Vice-President of State Farm Insurance Co.

Children, surname WADLEY:

1623. i. Marianne[7] Kay, b 16 May 1968 at Bloomington, IL; she graduated in 1991 from the University of Colorado at Boulder.

1624. ii. Deborah Chere, b 4 August 1970 at Bloomington; she graduated from California Poly Tech in San Luis Obispo in 1991.

647. DOUGLAS[6] LEE WADLEY (s/o William[5] I. Wadley #256), b 2 January 1947 at Portland, OR; m 6 June 1965 at Vancouver, WA, **Patricia Ann Dettling**, d/o Nick and Veronica Mary (Perrault) Dettling, b 18 December 1949 at Yakima, WA; they live at Kennewick, WA where Douglas has his own business selling business forms; Doug and Pat were divorced.

Children, surname WADLEY:

1625. i. Laurie[7] Anne, b 5 November 1971 at Lewiston, ID.

1626. ii. Brent William, b 9 October 1974 at Walla Walla, WA.

648. MARLENE[6] ELLEN GRASSENS (d/o Pauline[5] Wadley Grassens #257), b 9 July 1938 at Portland, OR; m 17 August 1963 at Portland Air Force Chapel, **William Esselstein**, s/o Walter and Jane Esselstein, b 2 November 1936; Marlene was killed in an automobile accident at Honolulu, HI, where her husband was stationed, 16 February 1965; she is buried in Williamette National Cemetery, Portland; William remarried and lived at Menlo Park, CA when last known.

Child, surname ESSELSTEIN:
- 1627. i. Lynn[7] Ellen, b 10 March 1964 at Honolulu, HI. In 1984 was a sophomore at University of California at Berkley, living with her father at Menlo Park, CA.

649. HAROLD[6] LLOYD PACK (d/o Pearl[5] Reed Pack #261), b 12 December 1927 at Jacksonville, FL; m/1 **Barbara Kathelene Sweeney**, b 1928 at Flint, MI, d/o James and Kathelene Sweeney; Barbara died 14 May 1961 at Flint; they had three children. Harold m/2 **Grace Ferrill**, b 5 March 1935, at Flint. When last known, Harold lived near Orlando, FL after his retirement from the Chevrolet plant in Flint.

Children, surname PACK:
- 1628. i. Gail[7] Ann, b 20 May 1948 at Flint; m David Lagness, b 31 March 1946.
- 1629. ii. Harold Laurence, b 29 July 1952, Flint; m Mary Alice McCellan, b 28 July 1952.
- + 1630. iii. Thomas Alexander, b 12 December 1957.
- 1631. iv. Rhonda Marie, b 10 September 1962 at Bay City, MI.
- 1632. v. Terry Lynn, b 20 June 1968 at Bay City.

650. RUTH[6] ELIZABETH REED (d/o Roland[5] M. Reed #261), b 18 February 1918 at Lake Tomahawk, WI; m 8 June 1939 at Merrill, WI, **Gilbert Michael Mentz**, s/o Michael and Matilda (Hanson) Mentz, b 11 October 1905 at Loona, WI; Gil worked for the State of Wisconsin as a Forest Ranger for 38 years, retiring in 1966. They lived across the road from Lake Tomahawk, with a secluded pond, teeming with wildlife, beside them; both love nature and wildlife. Ruth's hobbies are knitting and reading. Gil died 13 March 1991.

Child, surname MENTZ:
- + 1633. i. Mary[7], 10 March 1943.

652. RICHARD[6] MORRIS REED (s/o Roland[5] M. Reed #261), b 27 July 1921 at Lake Tomahawk, WI; m 10 July 1953 at the home of the bride's parents, at Woodruff, WI, **Nola Mae Fuller**, d/o Darwin Follett and Oreada Emgard (Peterson) Fuller, b 1 March 1927 at Lessor Town, Shawano Co., WI; Richard is an electrician and TV Technician; Nola worked for the Department of Natural Resources, Wisconsin Conservation Department before retiring in 1992.

Children, surname REED:
- \+ 1634. i. Brian[7] M., b 3 June 1954.
- 1635. ii. Janis, b 19 March 1956 at Woodruff; when last known she was legal assistant at Arnold, White, Durkee, a legal firm in Houston, TX.
- 1636. iii. Daniel, b 5 March 1962 at Woodruff, where he is now an orderly.

654. ROLAND[6] LOWELL REED (s/o Roland[5] M. Reed #261), b 27 May 1932 at Lake Tomahawk, WI; m 26 June 1952 at Waukeska, WI, **Arlene Leair**, d/o William Albert and Elsie Tunie (Visser) Leair, b 15 February 1935 at Waukesha City, WI; "Ike" is employed by Hein & Werner Corp. in personal dept.; they live in New Berlin, WI.

Children, surname REED:
- \+ 1637. i. Sherry[7] Lynn, b 1 May 1956.
- \+ 1638. ii. David Roland, b 27 May 1954.
- 1639. iii. Brenda Jean, b 19 October 1964, adopted 25 January 1978.

656. JOYCE[6] ANN REED (d/o Clifford[5] L. Reed #263), b 15 January 1925 at Haines City, FL; m/1 3 February 1943, **Linton Elkins**, s/o Oscar Asbury and Mary Louise (Crawford) Elkins, b 9 February 1921 at Fitzgerald, Georgia; Joyce divorced him in 1956; m/2 28 May 1960, **Orville Morris** Boulder, CO, s/o William Newton and Mary Evaline (Witcher) Morris, b 7 June 1912 at Pocahontas, AR; d 2 December 1980 at Haines City.

Child, surname ELKINS:
- \+ 1640. i. Jo[7] Lynn, b 18 November 1943.

Child, surname MORRIS:
- 1641. ii. William[7] Reed, b 28 November 1962 at Tampa, FL.

657. VIRGINIA[6] CHARLOTTE REED (d/o Norman[5] W. Reed #265), b 1 April 1927 at Chetek, WI; m 8 December 1944 at Fort Pierce, FL, **Thomas John Minor**, s/o Thomas Aloyisius and Margaret (Murphy) Minor, b 8 November 1926 at Jersey City, NJ; Virginia, better known as "Ginger" told a story about her experience during WW II, when her husband was a machinists mate on a tanker, which furnished fuel for U.S. ships in the Atlantic. He was in the tanker on his way home, when they discovered a German Submarine chasing them. They didn't worry too much because the high powered engines on the tanker could keep them out of range of the submarine. However, one of their engines failed, slowing them down. Tom was small and was able to get into the small compartment and repair the engines, in time to get up full speed again and pull away from the submarine. At the very time that Tom was in danger, Virginia woke up in the night feeling jittery and nervous as though something was wrong. Later she found out her experience happened at the same time as her husband's. He is retired from a career in the US Navy.

Children, surname MINOR:
+ 1642. i. Thomas[7] John, b 21 September 1945 at Jersey City.
  1643. ii. Richard Charles, b 19 June 1947 at Racine, WI; m 12 September 1970 Pamela Weber, d/o Michael and Julanne Weber of Nashville, TN; divorced and no children. When last known he was field service manager for a laser firm.
+ 1644. iii. Gerald Anthony, b 9 August 1948.
+ 1645. iv. Michael Herbert, b 8 February 1950.
+ 1646. v. Mary Ann, b 29 October 1951.
+ 1647. vi. William David, b 4 February 1953.
+ 1648. vii. Douglas Allen, b 20 August 1954.
+ 1649. viii. Dyanne Patricia, b 1 May 1956.
+ 1650. ix. Donna Marie, b 1 May 1956, (twin).
+ 1651. x. Darlene Margaret, b 26 March 1958.
+ 1652. xi. Donald Gerard, b 19 January 1960.
+ 1653. xii. John Thomas, b 11 May 1961.

658. MORRIS[6] HERBERT REED (s/o Norman[5] W. Reed #265), b 31 October 1929 at Seymour, WI; m 1 November 1958 at Irvingwood Community Presbyterian Church, Chicago, IL, **Sylvia Ironima**, d/o Nicholas and Cherubina (Fascia) Ironima, b 1 January 1933 at Chicago. In 1982 Morris was a self employed air conditioning engineer; plans and installs equipment for industries; Sylvia worked for Inez Jenkins Real Estate Co. Morris was in the Air Force in WW II, stationed in Alaska; he went to University of Wisconsin and graduated from Greer Institute in Chicago; he left home at 15; is a loner and does not communicate much with his siblings; is close to his own family. They live at Boca Raton, FL.

Children, surname REED, both born at Chicago, IL:
  1654. i. Cynthia[7] Amy, b 23 August 1959; m 16 September 1978 Timothy

Mark Tress; divorced; in 1982 she was a technical writer with IBM in Boca Raton.

1655. ii. Gerald Scott, b 20 September 1961; in 1982 was attending Florida Atlantic University, preparing for a business career.

659. PATRICIA[6] JEAN REED (d/o Norman[5] W. Reed #265), b 27 November 1930 at Seymour, WI; m 26 March 1949 at Evangelical United Brethren Church, Racine, WI, **James Robert Pryor**, s/o Virgil Robert and Bernadine (Meadows) Pryor, b 9 July 1926 at Benton, IL; d 2 September 1975 at Kansasville, WI; he is buried in Union Grove, [WI] Cemetery. Patricia works as night supervisor at Southern Wisconsin Center for Developmentally Disabled; she lives at Union Grove, WI.

Children, surname PRYOR:
+ 1656. i. Cheryl[7] Lynn, b 25 December 1950.
+ 1657. ii. James Robert, b 19 November 1951.
    1658. iii. Mary Jean, b 18 March 1957 at Racine; was told in 1983 that she went to Trinity Bible Institute, Ellendale, ND two years; then planning on entering nursing at Gateway Technical Institute in Kenosha, WI; she lived at home, and with her boyfriend, edited the church newspaper.
+ 1659. iv. Marcia Joan, b 18 March 1958.
    1660. v. Janet Louise, b 29 March 1960 at Racine. Works for Racine Journal Times; composing room.
+ 1661. vi. Judith Lorraine, b 13 September 1962.

660. JUNE[6] ROSE REED (d/o Norman[5] W. Reed #265), b 31 May 1932 at Shioctin, Outagamie, CO., WI; m/1 26 March 1949 at Racine, WI, **Paul Herman Kutzner**, s/o Adolf Anton and Hulda (Hefke) Kutzner, b 12 July 1927 in NY State. She divorced him 2 May 1966.

June Rose Reed m/2 1 June 1968 at Racine, **Burdette Gulbrand**, s/o Hans Hansen (changed his name to Gulbrand) and Emma (Benhke) Gulbrand, b 26 March 1937 at Denmark, WI. They live on a farm at Union Grove, WI. They have 10 acres and have several animals. June is quite involved as Supervisor of Hatcheries at C&D Foods nearby; Burdette was a Lieutenant in the Sheriff's Department; he d 15 July 1989 in an auto accident.

Children, surname KUTZNER:
+ 1662. i. Clifford[7] Henry, b 30 June 1948.
+ 1663. ii. Katherine Sue, b 15 October 1950.

1664. iii. Barbara Kay, b 14 October 1953 at Chicago. When last known about she was single and living in Phoenix, AZ.
+ 1665. iv. Elizabeth[7] Ann, b 30 November 1956.
1666. v. Jennifer[7] Jean, b 3 December 1961 at Racine.

Child, surname GULBRAND:
1667. vi. Sarah[7] Esther Patricia, b 23 April 1970 at Racine.

661. JANET[6] LORAINE REED (d/o Norman[5] W. Reed #265), b 4 August 1933 at Bovina Township, Shiocton, WI; m 21 March 1953 at Vallejo, CA, **Richard Dean Crouthers**, s/o William and Lula (Blake) Crouthers, b 22 September 1930 at Independence, MO. Janet does child care work and Richard is an industrial mechanic; they live, when last known, at Norwalk, CA.

Children, surname CROUTHERS, both born at Lynwood, CA:
1668. i. Karen[7], b 26 September 1955. When last known she was unmarried and a computer controller in TN.
1669. ii. Betty, b 14 September 1957. When last known she was single and a computer operator.

662. MARILYN[6] CAROL REED (d/o Norman[5] W. Reed #265), b 26 April 1935 at New London, WI; m/1 25 July 1952, **Jack Deyarmond**, s/o William Deyarmond, b 31 October 1933 at Alma, MI; they were divorced 2 May 1964 at Lansing, MI.

Marilyn m/2 at Lansing, 7 November 1964, **Clarence "Buck" Henry Roberts**, s/o Thomas Henry and Eathel Maude (Williams) Roberts, b 12 February 1916 at Negaunee, MI. Buck is retired from Motor Wheel Co. He adopted Jeffery, who took the name Roberts.

Children, surname DEYARMOND:
1670. i. Jack[7], b 22 July 1953 at Edmore, MI; he died at a young age.
1671. ii. Roger, b 29 July 1954 at Lansing.
1672. iii. Gregory, b 2 May 1957 at Lansing.
1673. iv. John William, b 28 July 1959 at Lansing; m Lynne Marie Grosshams.
1674. v. Jeffery Lee, b 24 April 1963 at Lansing.

Children, surname ROBERTS:
1675. vi. Marilyn[7] Eathel, b 28 February 1965 at Lansing.
1676. vii. John Henry, b 28 February 1965 at Lansing; d same day.
1677. vii. Mellissa "Missy" Carroll, b 4 May 1966 at Lansing.

663. ARLENE[6] MAY REED (d/o Norman[5] W. Reed #265), b 2 January 1939 at Town of Bovina, Shiocton, WI; "TRUDY" m/1 at Edmore, MI, 11 February 1956, **Richard Snively**, s/o Leo and Dorothy (Perkins) Snively, b 2 September 1936 at Mason, MI; divorced 18 November 1977; m/2 at Tullahoma, TN, 3 July 1982, **Joe Paul Hill**, s/o James Russell and Ruby Louise (Atkins) Hill, b 11 January 1937 at Bullard, Smith Co., TX; Joe is a journeyman pipe-fitter welder for Pan Am A.E.D.C., Tullahoma.

Children, surname SNIVELY:
- 1678. i. Julie[7], b 7 December 1958, Sheridan, MI; when last known she was an optician, employed by Pearl Vision Optical Co.
- 1679. ii. Richard, II, b 11 March 1960 at Sheridan; m 10 July 1983 at Tullahoma, TN, Heidi Marie Binion, b 10 July 1959 at Manchester, TN, d/o Travis and Helga Binon. Richard is in the US Navy in the submarine service, stationed in Holy Lock, Scotland; the family lives in Jewett City, CT.
- 1680. iii. Bradley Allen, b 7 October 1962 at Belding, MI; d 4 February 1966.
- 1681. iv. Dennis, b 5 February 1964 at Sheridan. In 1983 was a college student at Andrews University, Berrien Springs, MI; and a student missionary serving in Transkie, South Africa; to return to college in 1984.

664. SUE[6] BERNADINE REED (d/o Norman[5] W. Reed #265), b 21 August 1940 Town of Bovina, Shiocton, WI; m 5 September 1959 at Edmore, MI, **John "Jack" Bruce David**, s/o Jay Drexel and Irma Belle (Lowry) David, b 1 November 1932 at Edmore, MI; Jack is retired from the U.S. Coast Guard. In 1983 Sue had worked at Gibsons (Greenville Products) for 18 years as an aluminum heli-arc weld repair worker; she was also Financial Secretary at her local union.

Children, surname DAVID, both born at Milwaukee, WI:
- 1682. i. Jacklin[7] Kim, b 14 July 1960. In 1983 was 2nd year graduate student at Michigan State University.
- 1683. ii. John Bruce II, b 15 may 1962. In 1983 was working at Gibsons (Greenville Products) doing various jobs; had been there 3 years.

666. BEVERLY[6] JEAN SIMMONS (d/o Olive[5] Reed Simmons #266), b 20 December 1928 at Haines City, FL; m **Ronald Wallace Holden**, s/o Grant Holden, b 13 February 19— in IL. When last known she lived at Davenport, FL.

Children, surname HOLDEN:
- 1684. i. Ronda[7] Jean, b 15 January 1952 at Lakeland, FL; when last known was a waitress at Disney World; had an apartment in Orlando.
- 1685. ii. Mark Wallace, b 1 November 1956 at Lakeland; m Sharon —.

667. SHIRLEY[6] GAY SIMMONS (d/o Olive[5] Reed Simmons #266), b 12 November 1933 at Downers Grove, IL; m/1 **J.B. Webb**, in 1945 at Tampa, FL; m/2 18 April 1969, **William Hall**; d 21 June 1973. Last known she lived at Boynton Beach, FL; she had a company called Associated Traffic Markings, Inc.; son Michael worked for her.

Children, surname WEBB:
- + 1686. i. Michael[7] David, b 31 August 1956 at Gainesville, FL.
- 1687. ii. Steven Clark, b 10 November 1957 at Gainesville.
- 1688. iii. Daniel Scott, b 29 July 1961 at Gainesville.

669. JUDITH[6] LEE SIMMONS (d/o Olive[5] Reed Simmons #266), b 3 August 1943 at Gainesville, FL; m 30 November 1968 at Pompano Beach, FL, **Larry Eugene Clauss**, s/o Fred and Mildred (Huguelet) Clauss, he b 22 May 1939 at Dayton, OH. Larry was a Narcotics Agent until an auto accident; can't work now. They live near her mother Olive at Micanopy, FL.

Child, surname CLAUSS:
- 1689. i. Tonya[7] Michelle, b 1 May 1973 at Fort Lauderdale, FL. Has won many prizes competing in horsrback riding meets, riding western style, trained by her father.

671. ERNEST[6] LEE MOREHEAD (s/o Vivian[5] Reed Morehead #267), b 6 January 1944 at Tampa, FL; d 5 March 1977; m 8 June 1964, **Brenda Gail Grant**, d/o Francis LeBaron and Grace Katherine (Stackley) Grant. She b 5 April 1943 at Florence, Peedee Co., SC. Brenda is a teacher in the business department at the H.B. Plant High School, Tampa; Ernest also works at the school.

Children, surname MOREHEAD, both born at Tampa, FL:
- 1690. i. Wesley[7] Lebaron, b 26 February 1966; graduated from Abraham Baldwin Agricultural College, Tifton, GA with a degree in Forestry in 1988 and has a second degree from the University of Southern Florida and will be teaching in 1992 in Tampa.
- 1691. ii. Clayton Bennington, b 30 April 1971; he graduated from

Hillsborough Community College and will attend the University of Southern Florida.

672. ADELBERT[6] GEORGE LOWELL REED (s/o Donald[5] A. Reed #268), b 31 July 1934 at Green Bay, WI; m/1 in 1953 at Kissimee, FL, **Donna May Marring**; they were divorced; she married another three times after and contact has been lost. He was in submarine service while married to her and away much of the time.

Adelbert G. L. Reed m/2 11 October 1958 at Brewton, AL, **Betty Fillmore**, d/o John Allen and Liza May (Gleason) Fillmore, b 19 January 1941 at Brewton. He resigned from the Navy and worked as a civilian after that; 1962 to 1972 at Cape Canaveral, from the Mercury Space program through the Skylab Project; it was dangerous work and he got sick from handling the propellants while refueling the space craft. They wore no protective clothing, not knowing the chemicals were bad for their health. He went to China Lake in Death Valley for a year; this is a Navy Test Site for weapons, including lasers. His lungs are some what better. He is Progressman at the Pensacola Naval Base; he checks on the progress of the engineers in their various research and helps them solve their problems. Adelbert has chemicals in his bones; his condition is slowly deteriorating. At the time of our interview (1982) he was selling cars part time, building one house and remodeling the old farm house where he lived.

Children, surname REED:
- 1692. i. Dale[7] Adelbert, b 1954 at Orlando, FL. His father does not know where he is.
- 1693. ii. Kim Teresa, b 11 August 1959 at Pensacola, FL. In 1982 taught at Liberty Christian School, Pensacola. Engaged to Dennis Hoosh.
- 1694. iii. Kelly Marie, b 9 October 1960 at Key West, FL. Was going to Liberty Bible College in 1982.
- 1695. iv. Katie Lynn, b 14 April 1962 at Charleston, SC. Was going to Liberty Bible College in 1982.
- 1696. v. Donald Allen, b 10 June 1966 at Daytona Beach, FL. Was attending Liberty Christian School in 1982; gifted in speaking; wants to become a minister.

675. PEARL[6] IRENE JORGENSEN (d/o Ellen[5] Rider Jorgensen #270), b 15 February 1917 at Cedar Lake, MI; m 12 October 1946 at

Bryon, OH, **Austin Claire McMannis**, s/o Walter Edgar and Rosetta (Herrington) McMannis, b 21 February 1905 at Bellevue, MI. They lived in Battle Creek, MI until her mother got sick and she came home to take care of her in Edmore, MI. They spend their winters in Haines City, FL next to Clifford and summers in Edmore.

Child, surname McMANNIS:
+ 1697. i. Colene[7] Ann, b 8 October 1947.

676. ROBERT[6] **STANLEY JORGENSEN** (s/o Ellen[5] Rider Jorgensen #270), b 26 February 1920 at Richland, MI; m/1 at Battle Creek, MI, 11 August 1944, **Louise Arlene Rockafellow**, d/o Earl and Cora (Marcy) Rockafellow, b 1 April 1924 at Carson City, MI; lives in Edmore, MI; m/2 at Grant, MI, 21 December 1974, **Majel Gustavison**, b 15 January 1927 at Edmore. No children.

Children, surname JORGENSEN:
+ 1698. i. Bryan[7] Wayne, b 17 August 1945.
+ 1699. ii. John Reed, b 6 May 1947.
+ 1700. iii. Sherry Rae, b 25 December 1948.

677. REED[6] **CARLYLE JORGENSEN** (s/o Ellen[5] Rider Jorgensen #270), b 9 March 1922 at Edmore, MI; m 1 February 1942 at Carson City, MI, **Irene Lucille Richardson**, d/o Oscar and Eva (Jameison) Richardson, b 10 September 1924 at Boyne City, MI. Reed is a carpenter; they live in Edmore.

Children, surname JORGENSEN:
   1701. i. Christopher[7], b 10 September 1946 at Carson City; m 12 February 1977 at Loveland, CO. Donna —. No children; they live in Oregon.
+ 1702. ii. Curtis, b 12 May 1948.
+ 1703. iii. Cheryl, b 1 April 1953.

678. BETTY[6] **RAE JORGENSEN** (d/o Ellen[5] Rider Jorgensen #270), b 26 February 1925 at Vestaburg, MI; m 26 September 1942 at Bryon, OH, **Benjamin Nestle**, s/o Benjamin and Mabel (Mudge) Nestle, b 4 February 1922 at Detroit, MI. Ben retired in 1982 as a USPS mail carrier; they live at Edmore.

Children, surname NESTLE:
+ 1704. i. Constance[7] Ellen, b 2 October 1945.

+ 1705.   ii.   Carl, b 16 June 1947.

681. DONALD[6] **ALBERT McCORMICK** (s/o May[5] Beavert McCormick #273), b 8 May 1922 at Lynden, WA; m 1950, **Ina Fae Schneider**, d/o Benjamin and Gertrude Johanna (Lefferdink) Schneider, b 28 May 1926 at Holland, NE. Donald has a wrought iron business in Bremerton, WA.

Children, surname McCORMICK:
+ 1706.   i.   David[7], b 28 October 1947 at Bremerton.
  1707.   ii.   Nancy, b 3 November 1950 at Bremerton; she m 18 December 1971 James David Nave; they have no known children.

682. LOIS[6] **ARCHIBALD** (d/o Bertha[5] Beavert Archibald #275), b 10 June 1921 at Ferndale, WA; m/1 1940, **Charles Thompson** at Port Angeles, Olympic Penninsula, WA; he was a refrigeration engineer; she divorced him in 1946; Lois m/2 14 April 1947 at Mount Vernon, WA, **Hubert Adair Raleigh**, s/o James Ebert and Ava (Moore) Raleigh, b 3 March 1920; d April 1976 at Silverton, OR; she divorced him in 1965; Hubert was in the navy at Sand Point, Seattle the last 7 years and the children were born here; m/3 July 1966 at Phoenix, AZ, **Dr. Lynn Hammerstad**. He was married previously in Salem, OR; he was a flight surgeon in the navy; his specialty was ophthalmology. He and Lois were flown in by an American Indian Missionary society to a little village in Mexico where he operated on 8 elderly blind people for cataracts; she divorced him in Phoenix in 1967 and he still lives there. She m/4 11 December 1967 at Ellensburg, WA, **Robert Tate**, s/o Jesse and Delmar (Worthington) Tate, b 22 June 1916 at Mesa, WA; Bob was working in Alaska for National Park Service as a road maintenance worker at Mount McKinley; he was on his way to the airport for a trip home when he suffered a fatal heart attack in April 1976; his ashes were scattered on Mount McKinley. Lois m/5 on 5 July 1977 at Edmonds, WA, **Palmer Pearson**; divorced him in 1978; m/6 — **Marshall**, September 1987 and moved to Kelso, WA; divorced him 1988 and moved back to Everett, WA.

Children, surname RALEIGH:
  1708.   i.   Richard[7] Orin, b 7 September 1948 at Seattle, WA.
+ 1709.   ii.   Roxanne Lee, b 11 October 1951.

683. DONNA[6] **JEAN ARCHIBALD** (d/o Bertha[5] Beavert Archibald #275), b 30 November 1923 at Bellingham, WA; m 1 July 1946 at Seattle,

WA, **Earl William Gibson**, s/o Joseph Harold and Annie Gertrude (Edmonds) Gibson.

Children, surname GIBSON:
- 1710. i. Steven[7] Earl, b 17 May 1947 at Seattle, WA; m 12 July 1975 Dianne Lee Stroud, d/o Norman Frederick and Juanita May (Page) Stroud, b 21 August 1948 at Everett, WA; Steven was in 1982 self-employed in his own trucking business.
- \+ 1711. ii. Douglas Loy, b 22 September 1952.
- \+ 1712. iii. Sharilyn Autumn, b 10 October 1955.

684. BEVERLY[6] ANNE BEAVERT (d/o Warren[5] W. Beavert #276), b 3 March 1928 at Thermopolis, WY; m/1 17 February 1950, **John Vallentyne**, s/o Howard Judson and Mildred (Davenport) Vallentyne, b 22 January 1928 at Seattle, WA; they were divorced April 1973 at Vernon, WA; m/2 20 July 1974, **Ray Enselman**, s/o Joseph and Iris (Ball) Enselman, b 9 June 1917 at Arlington, WA. They live at Bellevue, WA.

Children, surname VALLENTYNE, all born at Seattle WA:
- 1713. i. Debra[7], b 25 December 1952.
- 1714. ii. Diane, b 26 August 1954.
- 1715. iii. Shannon, b 4 June 1956.

685. WARREN[6] WILLIAM BEAVERT II (s/o Warren[5] W. Beavert #276), b 4 March 1930 at Thermopolis, WY; m 8 times before 1988; had children by wife **Pearl** but no futher information on her. He was a longshoreman originally; last known location was New Zealand.

Children, surname BEAVERT, both born at Seattle WA:
- 1716. i. Warren[7] William III, b about 1957 or 58.
- 1717. ii. John, b about 1959 or 60.

686. FRANK[6] BEAVERT (s/o Frank[5] Beavert #278), b 24 January 1927 at Monroe, WA; m 30 June 1951, **Betty Jane O'Connor**, d/o Daniel K. and Margaret A. O'Connor, she b 8 February 1932 at Poplar, MT. Frank d 17 February 1962; Betty Jane then married **Ken Snyder**.

Children, surname BEAVERT:
- \+ 1718. i. Gary[7], b 19 August 1952.
- \+ 1719. ii. Gail, b 5 June 1955.

687. BETTY[6] MAY BEAVERT (d/o Frank[5] Beavert #278), b 9 September 1933 at Seattle, WA; m 28 February 1953 at Seattle, **John E.**

The Sixth Generation

Dunn, s/o John F. and Gladys Dunn, he b 14 October 1933 in ND; they live in Seattle and John works for Southgate Ford there.

Children, surname DUNN:
- 1720. i. Jeannie[7], b 15 June 1960 at Seattle; teachers in a large day care center.
- 1721. ii. John Frank, b 22 November 1962 at Seattle; teachers junior and senior high school and also coaches basketball at a nearby junior college.
- + 1722. iii. Judy, b 30 June 1965.

688. MARVYS[6] **JANE WESTON** (d/o Marvin[5] L. Weston #279), b 20 October 1939 at Portland, OR; m 8 October 1960, **Donald E. Chitwood**; they live at Coos Bay, OR; Don is a principal of a grade school.

Children, surname CHITWOOD:
- 1723. i. Lori[7] M., b 3 August 1961.
- 1724. ii. Rick E. b 23 December 1964.

689. SHARON[6] **LEE WESTON** (d/o Marvin[5] L. Weston #279), b 21 June 1942 at Portland, OR; m 15 June 1963 **Donald A. Telen**; they live at Fresno, CA.

Children, surname TELEN:
- 1725. i. Daniel[7] A., b 15 September 1968.
- 1726. ii. Erik J., b 20 November 1974.

690. STEVEN[6] **CRAIG WESTON** (s/o Marvin[5] L. Weston #279), b 26 September 1950 at Portland, OR; d 11 February 1977; m 8 October 1970, **Linda L. Hanson**. Linda has remarried since Steve's death and has her daughter with her in Beaverton, OR.

Child, surname WESTON:
- 1727. i. Mindi[7] A., b 9 June 1971.

691. JAMES[6] **MERLE WESTON** (s/o Merle[5] V. Weston #280), b 3 February 1938 at Altoona, PA; m 15 April 1955 at Estacada, OR, **Sharon Louise Hayden**, d/o Lester Raymond and Florence Helen (Montgomery) Hayden, b 21 August 1937 at Portland, OR. Jim's company is "Jim Weston's Pontiac" at Gresham, OR.

Children, surname WESTON, all born at Portland, OR:
- 1728. i. Jay[7] Bradley, b 24 June 1956; m 8 August 1981, at Gresham, OR, Patricia Lee Schmidt, d/o Robert and Lillian (Pulsinelli)

Schmidt, b in Portland. Jay works for his father at the Pontiac Co. No known children.

+ 1729. ii. Jan Michael, b 5 August 1959. See Addenda.
   1730. iii. Jeni Marie, b 13 July 1970.

692. PENELOPE[6] **LEE NICKLE** (d/o Leota[5] Plasteur Nickle #284), b 2 July 1947 at Long Beach, CA; m/1 1 October 1969 at Long Beach, CA, **Herman Norwood Philhower**, s/o Herman and Claire Philhower, b 18 October 1935 at Viro Beach, VA; she divorced him. Penelope m/2, 14 February 1977 at Las Vegas, NV, **Ronald Dispanza**, parents unknown; b November 1941. Penelope operates a home beauty parlor.

Child, surname PHILHOWER:
   1731. i. Amber[7] Lee, b 1 December 1971 at Long, Beach, CA.

Child, surname DISPANZA:
   1732. ii. Brent Stanton, b 27 September 1978 at Lakewood, CA.

694. LEONARD[6] **ROBERT CLARKE III** (s/o Doreatha[5] Canfield Clarke #286), b 18 September 1929 in Syracuse, NY; m 24 July 1954 at Saint Peter's Church, Syracuse, NY, **Natalie Squadrito**, d/o James L. and Jennie (Campolo) Squadrito, b 17 March 1934 at Syracuse, NY. Leonard is in charge of the supply department at Crouse Irving-Memorial Hospital in Syracuse. Natalie works as a teacher's aide in North Syracuse, Junior High School. They live in North Syracuse.

Children, surname CLARKE:
   1733. i. Richard[7] David, b 24 April 1955 at Syracuse; works at La Jolle, CA at a laboratory doing cancer research; m 23 April 1983 at Saint Rose Church, North Syracuse, Phyllis Kawanabe, d/o Thomas and Hisayo Kawanabe, an Japanese-American whom he met at college in Colorado.
+ 1734. ii. Patricia Ann, b 1 April 1957.
+ 1735. iii. Elizabeth Jane, b 13 October 1959.

695. DIANE[6] **ELYSE CLARKE** (d/o Doreatha[5] Canfield Clarke #286), b 21 December 1930 at Syracuse, NY; m 24 August 1951 in Liverpool, NY, **Robert W. Dausman**, s/o John Arthur and Ruth Claire (MacGowan) Dausman, b 18 February 1925 at Portsmouth, NH. Before retirement, Robert was a maintenance supervisor at Bristol Labs; Diane an antique dealer. They live at Burlington, NC.

Child, surname DAUSMAN:

The Sixth Generation 297

    1736.   i. Kirk[7] William, b 3 May 1965 at Syracuse; graduated SUNY Geneseo, NY, May 1987 with a B.A. in communications. He m July 1989, Wanda — and when last known was working for a pharmacutical company; Wanda is a special education teacher.

696. BRUCE[6] BAILEY CLARKE (s/o Doreatha[5] Canfield Clarke #286), b 21 June 1935 at Syracuse, NY; m/1 21 June 1966 at Albany, NY, **Jill Misner**, d/o Louis and Fern (Rose) Dick; Fern and Louis were divorced and she m William Misner, who adopted Jill; b 4 December 1944 at North Tonawanda, NY; divorced September 1974. Bruce graduated from State University at Albany, NY with a Bachelor of Arts in 1957. He taught High School in the Syracuse School System until he returned to Albany to complete his Master's Degree in 1962. He began teaching at Alfred University, Alfred, NY but returned to Albany as a doctoral fellow from 1964–1966; then worked for NY State Department of Education evaluating college programs until he returned to teaching at Alfred in 1968. He is a Professor in the English and Humanities Department.

After the divorce Kevin lived with his mother at Massena, NY and Christopher lived with his father. Bruce m/2 20 January 1979, **Marcia Louise Young**, d/o Michael and Evelyn (Bamberg) Young, b 4 November 1950 at Newport, RI. Her father is Medical Director for Kodak in Rochester, NY. Bruce met Marcia at Alfred University in 1975; they live at Hornell.

Children, surname CLARKE:
    1737.   i. Christopher[7] Bruce, b 6 March 1967 at Niskayuna, NY. He received his B.A. from SUNY-Binghamton and a M.F.A. in acting from the University of Missouri at Kansas City in 1992 and made his professional debut in "Merry Widow" at the Paper Mill Playhouse in New Jersey.
    1738. ii. Kevin William, b 5 September 1969 at Hornell, NY. He graduated from Geneseo State University College and is now attending the University of Buffalo working towards a masters degree.

697. PRUDENCE[6] PENELOPE CLARKE (d/o Doreatha[5] Canfield Clarke #286), b 4 December 1936 at Syracuse, NY; m 14 September 1957 at Saint Vincent DePaul Church, Syracuse, NY, **Charles Aloisius Carmody**, s/o Aloisius Carmody, Charles works for Parke-Davis Pharmaceutical Co. in the financial department; they live at Flanders, NJ. Prudence graduated from Crouse-Irving School of Nursing in Syracuse and worked as a nurse in a nursing home until she was injured in a fall.

Children, surname CARMODY:
- 1739. i. Clarke[7] Christopher, b 2 March 1960 at Big Rapids, MI; m June 1991, Jennifer —.
- 1740. ii. Drew Charles, b 18 March 1971 at Mount Clemmons, MI. He graduated from Syracuse University in 1993.

698. ROGER[6] WALTER CLARKE (s/o Doreatha[5] Canfield Clarke #286), b 14 February 1938 at Syracuse, NY; m/1 12 May 1958 at Kirkwood, NY, **Sylvia Morris** from Kirkwood. They were divorced and she took all but the oldest child with her to Storm Lake, IA. He m/2 **Ava** —. When last know he was living in El Paso, TX; he had moved west early because of his asthma.

Children, surname CLARKE:
- 1741. i. Brent[7], b 9 May 1959 at Binghamton, NY.
- 1742. ii. Leonard Robert, b 29 September 1961 at Tucson, AZ.
- 1743. iii. Keith, b 12 May 1965 at Tucson.
- 1744. iv. Stacia, b 29 September 1964 at Tucson.
- 1745. v. Kamela Kar, b 3 June 1971 at Tucson.
- 1746. vi. Jeremy, b 17 February 1973 at El Paso.
- 1747. vii. Ryan Shea, b 6 December 1974 at El Paso.

700. GARY[6] SCOTT CLARKE (s/o Doreatha[5] Canfield Clarke #286), b 26 November 1942 at Bainbridge, Chenango Co., NY; m/1 21 July 1961, **Phoebe Bailey**; divorced her and she remarried to Robert Hoskins and living in Florida. Gary m/2 at Syracuse, NY, 9 May 1986, **Louise St. Pierre**, d/o Alfred and Ruth (Gordon) St. Pierre, b 3 May 1951. Gary is quality control inspector at Nixon Gear Co. and Louise is bank teller at Chase Lincoln bank, Syracuse; they live in Solvay, NY.

Child, surname CLARKE:
- 1748. i. Mara[7] Michelle, b 1 December 1961 in Syracuse; is a bank teller in Tampa, FL and going to school at University of Southern FL, Tampa; working for Masters Degree in Human Services.

701. ROBERT[6] GENE CANFIELD (s/o Elton[5] F. Canfield #287), b 12 January 1932 in Syracuse, NY; m 29 November 1952 at Portsmouth, VA, **Anna May Schwartz**, d/o George L. and Anna May (Murphy) Schwartzotte; b 8 June 1934 at Syracuse. Robert is a salesman for Morgan Recreational Supplies of Rochester, NY; Anna works for VIP Companion

The Sixth Generation

Care, and goes into homes of retarded, handicapped and elderly people to give them services.

Children, surname CANFIELD:
- + 1749. i. Robert[7] Thomas, b 3 April 1953.
- + 1750. ii. Mark Francis, b 19 June 1956.
-   1751. iii. Scott Thomas, b 24 February 1959 at Syracuse; very musical; piano player; manages a restaurant.
- + 1752. iv. David Joseph, b 9 June 1960.
-   1753. v. Christopher Jude, b 24 December 1961; he was born dead.
-   1754. vi. Christopher Jude, b 12 August 1963 at Syracuse; interior designer; plays french horn.
-   1755. vii. Patrick Sean, b 12 August 1963 at Syracuse; in marines.
-   1756. viii. Joseph Francis, b 18 March 1966 at Syracuse.

702. ROGER[6] NEWELL OATMAN (s/o Thelma[5] Canfield Oatman #289), b 3 July 1933 at Oneida, NY; m 1962, **Shirley Eckhard**. Believed to live in Oneida area.

Child, surname OATMAN:
  1757. i. Roger[7] Kevin, b October 1963 at Oneida.

703. MARCIA[6] JEAN LANE (d/o Thelma[5] Canfield Oatman Lane #289), b 11 March 1947 at Oneida, NY; m 25 September 1965 at Saint Paul's Evangelical United Brethren Church (now United Methodist Church) at Oneida, **Joseph Leroy West**, s/o Joseph Charles and Edna Elizabeth (Congdon) West, b 24 October 1942 at Oneida. Joseph works for Oneida Limited as a machine operator; Marcia works there as a billing Clerk.

Child, surname WEST:
  1758. i. Lisa[7] Marie, b 22 November 1966 at Oneida.

704. JOYCE[6] MARIE LANE (d/o Thelma[5] Canfield Oatman Lane #289), b 6 August 1948 at Oneida, NY; m/1 at Oneida, NY, 17 April 1971, **Giacomo "Jack" DiSalvo**, s/o Frank and Rosa DiSalvo, b 12 March 1947 at Bagheria, Italy; she divorced him June 1973; m/2 18 November 1978 at Saint Paul's United Methodist Church, Oneida, **Robert C. Olmsted**, who has one child by his former marriage, s/o George LeRoy and Elsie Viola (Ingham) Olmsted, b 25 August 1938 at Chittenango, NY; Robert works for Carrier Corporation in Syracuse, NY. Joyce is a nurse and they live at Canastota, NY.

Child, surname DiSALVO:
1759. i. Janice[7] Lynn, b 16 May 1972 at Cornwall, NY.

706. HERBERT[6] EDWARD CANFIELD (s/o Herbert[5] C. Canfield #290), b 27 February 1936 at Verona, NY; m 18 December 1957 at Richfield Springs, NY, **Mary Jane Cole**, b 23 October 1935 at Cooperstown, NY; Herbert is a therapy aide at Marcy Psychiatric Hospital, Marcy, NY; they live at Blossvale, NY; they adopted two children.

Children, surname CANFIELD:
1760. i. Alan[7] Kent, b 27 January 1964.
1761. ii. Susan Alta, b 30 May 1965.

707. THELMA[6] GRACE CANFIELD (d/o Herbert[5] C. Canfield #290), b 2 January 1940 at Verona, NY; m 30 June 1956 at Camden, NY, **Richard Donald Chase**, s/o Donald Paul and Lula-Mae (Trudell) Chase, b 2 March 1936 at South Colton, NY. He is a self-employed mechanic. Thelma drives school bus for the city of Oneida; sells Real Estate; is manager of Blue River Band and is lead singer. She is raising her handicapped granddaughter Loretta Sue, Dawn's daughter. Thelma divorced Richard 18 March 1976.

Children, surname CHASE:
+ 1762. i. Leona[7] Norene, b 13 February 1957.
+ 1763. ii. Richard Donald, b 30 June 1958.
+ 1764. iii. Daniel Edward, b 20 August 1960.
+ 1765. iv. Mathew Ronald, b 23 December 1962.
   1766. v. Donald Paul, b 29 May 1964 at Rome; m 8 May 1982 Marilyn Johnson, d/o Charles and Ester Johnson. Donald is a factory worker in Gray Syracuse factory. They didn't have any children as of 1988.
+ 1767. vi. Dawn Paulette, b 29 May 1964.
   1768. vii. Elizabeth Thelma, b 15 December 1967 at Rome; she is in college and works at K-Mart in Herkimer, NY.

710. DONALD[6] FENTON CANFIELD (s/o Fenton[5] E. Canfield #291), b 29 May 1945 at Rochester, NY; m 5 August 1967 at The Lutheran Church, Pittsford, NY, **Linda Eileen Esker**, d/o Robert Raymond and Shirley Eileen (Hulbert) Esker; b 27 March 1947 at Rochester. For a number of years he ran a photography business in conjunction with computers in the Rochester area. He has just recently moved to Jackson-

The Sixth Generation 301

ville, FL where he expects to find a wider field for his specialty. He and his wife are divorced.

Child, surname CANFIELD:
   1769. i. Piper[7] Lynn, b 1 June 1972 at Rochester.

711. CAROL[6] ANN CANFIELD (d/o Harold[5] M. Canfield #292), b 3 June 1938 at Rome, NY; m 4 July 1964 at Camden, NY, **Edward Arthur Kent** at McConnellsville, NY. Edward is semi-retired, is a custodian for a school and runs a lawn mower repair business. Carol d 26 November 1991 of lung cancer.

Children, surname KENT:
+ 1770. i. Sharon[7] Beth, b 12 June 1965.
   1771. ii. Susan Maria, b 1 November 1969 at Rome; m Christopher Shawn Ellis; she is employeed at a nursing home.

712. JEAN[6] KITTY CANFIELD (d/o Harold[5] M. Canfield #292), b 30 December 1940 at Rome, NY; m 1 November 1958 at Camden, NY, **Robert Fred Marshall**, s/o Harry William and Grace Irene (Fetterely) Marshall, b 10 May 1936 at Rome. Robert works in a wire mill as a strander. They live at Cleveland, NY.

Children, surname MARSHALL:
+ 1772. i. Brenda[7] Lee, b 22 January 1960.
+ 1773. ii. Patti Sue, b 1 September 1964.
+ 1774. iii. Robert Fred, b 1 August 1970 at Oneida, NY.

713. JOHN[6] HAROLD CANFIELD (s/o Harold[5] M. Canfield #292), b 13 March 1946 at Rome, NY; m/1 29 July 1968 at Camden, NY, **Linda Jean Collins**, d/o Walter and Mildred Lorraine (Hillman) Collins, b 26 May 1949 at Oneida, NY; Linda and John divorced May 1975 at Tulsa, OK; m/2 21 May 1977, **Toni Lynn Wathen**, d/o C. Wathen; m/3 6 July 1987, **Syotha Jean Driggs**, d/o Bob la Dian Driggs. John lives at Coveta, OK and he works at the Tulsa Police Dept., has about 20 years and plans to retire soon.

Child, surname CANFIELD:
   1775. i. Heather[7] Jo, b 20 December 1972 at OK.

714. BETTE[6] EILEEN CANFIELD (d/o Harold[5] M. Canfield #292), b 7 January 1948 at Rome, NY; m 16 May 1967 at Kermit, WV, **Samuel Walter Jonas**, s/o Homer and Bertha (Bowery) Jonas, b 22 July 1946.

Samuel is a mining engineer and they live at Kermit.

Children, surname JONAS:
- 1776. i. Jonathan[7] Robert, b 9 November 1967 at Tinker Air Force Base, OK.
- 1777. ii. David Walter, b 5 May 1969 at OK.
- 1778. iii. Samuel Walter, b 1 January 1975 at Ashland, KN.

715. JIM[6] SCOTT CANFIELD (s/o Harold[5] M. Canfield #292), b 14 August 1950 at Rome, NY; m 17 July 1970 at Elgin, ND, **Sharon Kay Stanley**, d/o Clarence E. Stanley, b 8 March 1949 at Bismark, ND. Jim lives at Saint Joseph, AZ; he teaches at a college nearby. He has charge of a network of computers involved in government work, probably for the state; he is a part-time missionary.

Children, surname CANFIELD:
- 1779. i. Andrew[7] Oliver, b 23 March 1975 at Minneapolis, MN; will be an exchange student at Japan, fall 1992.
- 1780. ii. Adam Earl, b 8 November 1976.

719. LINDA[6] JANE CANFIELD (d/o Oscar[5] W. Canfield #293), b 21 August 1955 at Fulton, NY; m 7 June 1980 at Havre, MT, **Donald Bitterman**, s/o Adolph and Anna Bitterman, b 12 July 1945; he works for Northern Burlington Railroad; Linda was an Administrator of a group home for the handicapped at Havre, until their child was born.

Child, surname BITTERMAN:
- 1781. i. Sandi[7] Lynn, b 16 August 1988 at Havre.

726. BRANT[6] DOW KENNEDY (s/o Sherman[5] W. Kennedy #295), b 10 October 1937 at Oswego, NY; m 14 October 1967, **Wilma Gates**. They are divorced and Brant lives with his parents at Leawood near Kansas City, KS. He is employed by McDonalds.

Children, surname KENNEDY:
- 1782. i. Kenneth[7] Scott, b 23 September 1968.
- 1783. ii. Christine Lee Ann, b 24 August 1971.

730. NEIL[6] CRAIG KENNEDY (s/o Neil[5] D. Kennedy #297), b 30 January 1948 at Syracuse, NY; m 10 June 1972 at Missionary Bible Church, Hanover, PA, **Elaine Joann Myers**, d/o Wilford Leon and Catherine (Landis) Myers, b 20 February 1949 at Hanover. Craig and Elaine both graduated from Baptist Bible College at Clarks Summit, PA.

Craig was ordained to Gospel Baptist ministry 7 September 1975 at First Baptist Church, North Tonawanda, NY; they have served three four year terms in the mission field under the auspices of Association of Baptists for World Evangelism in the Philippine Islands, first on Palawan, and more recently in Manila in an administrative capacity. They returned to the U.S. April 1992, after son Jason's death, and will spend a year with his parents in Camillus, NY.

Children, surname KENNEDY:

1784. i. Jason[7] Neil, b 6 December 1975 at Williamsville, NY; d 5 April 1992 at Tijuana, Mexico where he was undergoing treatment for Hodgkins Disease.
1785. ii. Joyce Elaine, b 19 April 1979 at Manila, Philippine Islands.
1786. iii. Justin Peter, b 25 April 1982 at Syracuse.

731. KAREN[6] JEAN KENNEDY (d/o Neil[5] D. Kennedy #297), b 13 September 1952 at Syracuse, NY; m 31 May 1975 at Memphis, NY Baptist Church, **Eugene Leslie Brock**, s/o Leslie Eugene and Arvena (Hanson) Brock, b 13 May 1947 at Auburn, NY; Gene worked a number of years as a welder at Nine Mile Two Nuclear Plant, Oswego, NY; now is self-employed welder. Karen graduated from Cedarville College [OH] in 1974 and taught at Faith Baptist Academy (1975–76 and 1985–86) and they are active members of Faith Baptist Church in Baldwinsville. They live in Camillus, NY, next to Karen's parents.

Children, surname BROCK:

1787. i. Sarah[7] Jean, b 16 April 1977 at Auburn.
1788. ii. Rachel Elizabeth, b 26 July 1979 at Auburn.
1789. iii. Peter Andrew, b 11 February 1987 at Syracuse.

732. ROGER[6] BRUCE KENNEDY (s/o Roger[5] B. Kennedy #299), b 19 may 1956 at Ithaca, Tompkins Co, NY; m/1 5 October 1974, **Delores Maxine Dean**, d/o John Harold and Lois Maxine (Ross) Dean, b 1 October 1955 at Medina, OH; they were later divorced. Bruce, a graduate of Mapleton High School, was working for Grumman Flexible Bus Company as computer programmer. He m/2, 5 August 1978, **Marilyn Naomi Brown**, d/o Richard and Janice (VanAsdale) Brown, b 19 January 1953 at Bucyrus, OH; they were later divorced.

Bruce m/3, 13 July 1984 at Delaware, OH, **Donna Sue (Howard) Scheeler**, d/o Jarvie and Bernice (Roark) Howard, b 18 May 1954 at

Marysville, OH. Donna makes dolls at home and sells at craft fairs; Bruce is employed by Compuware as a computer programmer analyst. Bruce and Donna are very interested in their family history and do as much research in court houses, libraries, and cemeteries as they have time available; they live in Ashley, OH.

Children, surname KENNEDY:
 1790. i. Tamra[7] Lynn, b 10 May 1975 at Columbus, OH.
 1791. ii. Valerie[7] Nicole, b 14 February 1980 at Delaware, OH.
 1792. iii. Roger Bruce, b 7 July 1982 at Delaware.

Children, surname SCHEELER, from Donna's prior marriage:
 1793. iv. Jennifer Marie, b 11 September 1973 at Delaware.
 1794. v. Aaron Ronald, b 4 February 1977 at Delaware.
 1795. vi. Jeremy Todd, b 16 June 1978 at Delaware.
 1796. vii. Adam Michael, b 17 December 1982 at Columbus, OH.

733. GLORIA[6] DAWN KENNEDY (d/o Roger[5] B. Kennedy #299), b 14 April 1957 at Ithaca, NY; m 25 June 1977 at Pavonia, OH United Methodist Church, **Barry Spangenberg**, s/o John D. and Bernice M. (Freer) Spangenberg, b 1 November 1957 at Carbondale, PA; her father, Rev. Roger Kennedy, officiated at their marriage ceremony. Dawn is a graduate of Mapleton High School in Ashland Co., OH and was as a practical nurse before the birth of their children. Dawn and Barry own and run their own appliance repair service, "North Coast Appliances" and live at Madison, OH.

Children, surname SPANGENBERG:
 1797. i. Julie[7] Ann, b 17 April 1981 at Geneva, OH
 1798. ii. Marc Aaron, b 23 October 1982 at Geneva.
 1799. iii. Ryan Scott, b 30 September 1991 at Painsville, OH.

734. SHARON[6] JOY KENNEDY (d/o Roger[5] B. Kennedy #299), b 20 March 1959 at Syracuse, NY; m/1 26 June 1977 in Greenville, SC, **David Wayne Kendall**, s/o Charles Harry and Rosemary (Farnsworth) Kendall, b 7 April 1960 in Ashland, OH. They were divorced in 1979 before their second child was born.

Sharon m/2 19 April 1980 at Pavonia, OH, **James Earl Heimberger**, s/o James Robert and Alice Virginia (Goff) Heimberger. Sharon divorced James Earl and remarried David Kendall 28 April 1991 at Ashland, OH. Sharon continued her education in data processing and earned her GED from Mapleton High School; they now live in Salem, OR where David found a job in construction.

Children, surname KENDALL, born at Ashland:
- 1800. i. David[7] Charles, b 5 November 1977.
- 1801. ii. Jamie Earl, b 3 February 1980.
- 1802. iii. Ashley Rosemary, b 16 March 1992.

735. STEPHEN[6] SCOTT KENNEDY (s/o Roger[5] B. Kennedy #299), b 17 May 1960 at Cortland, NY; m/1 23 February 1980, **Nora Marie Crossen**, d/o Lawrence A. and Ruth Marie (Sterling) Crossen, b 12 September 1963, at Ashland, OH. Stephen and Nora are divorced.

Stephen m/2 17 December 1988 at Ruggles, OH, **Michelle Grace Fingulin**, d/o Joseph Paul and Carolyn Sue (Campbell) Fingulin, b 26 April 1965. Both of Stephen's parents participated in the ceremony. Stephen is an auto body man; they moved to Angier, NC, near Raleigh in 1991.

Child, surname KENNEDY:
- 1803. i. Jessica[7] Marie, b 21 June 1980 at Ashland.
- 1804. ii. Kayla Renee, b 13 May 1989 at Ashland.

Child, surname Wargo, Michelle's son by a former marriage:
- 1805. iii. Justin James, b 19 June 1983 at Ashland.

736. DAVID[6] MARTIN KENNEDY (s/o Roger[5] B. Kennedy #299), b 15 October 1961 at Cortland, NY. He had his own refrigeration business in Ashland, OH until he enlisted in he US Navy in 1990. He is stationed at Subic Bay, Philippine Islands; to be transferred to Guam in July 1992. David m 18 November 1991 in Philippine Islands, **Francia** —.

Child, surname KENNEDY:
- 1806. i. Benjamin[7] Kevin, b 19 November 1991 in Philippine Islands.

737. MARLA[6] ANN DeSEYN (d/o Martha[5] Kennedy DeSeyn #300), b 20 August 1963 at Bethpage, Nassau Co., NY. She graduated from West Genesee High School in 1981 and trained as a chef at Culinary Institute of America at Hyde Park, NY and worked at several restaurants in the Syracuse area, including Top of the Hill, Hotel Syracuse, and Nikkis. She is residing in Warners, NY in the Kennedy family homestead.

Child, surname SEAMAN:

1807. i. Ronald[7] Seaman II, b 15 February 1990.

742. CYNTHIA[6] KAY KENNEDY (d/o Hugh[5] I. Kennedy #301), b 19 April 1958 at Laramie, WY; m 24 June 1978 at her home near Walden, CO in an outdoor ceremony performed by her uncle, Rev. Roger Kennedy, **William King Biggs**, s/o William King and Patricia (Loring) Biggs, b 30 June 1957 at Chicago, IL. Bill was a mid-westerner, living at Saint Louis, MO when he went to Colorado to work for Cindy's uncle on the Wamsley Ranch. He fell in love with the West and then with Cindy. For a few years they worked together on the nearby Mayring livestock ranch. Since ranch work did not provide financial security they moved to Saint Louis, where Bill's parents lived, for a new start. Bill graduated from the Police Academy in Saint Louis and he is now serving with the police force at Kirkwood, a Saint Louis suburb. Cindy is the manager of a cafeteria. They enjoy their new life, in Saint Louis, and the children are glad for more children to play with.

Children, surname BIGGS:
    1808. i. William[7] Cody, b 17 February 1979 at Laramie, WY.
    1809. ii. Bo James, b 14 November 1980 at Steamboat Springs, CO.

743. GWEN[6] ANN KENNEDY (d/o Hugh[5] I. Kennedy #301), b 20 June 1959 at Denver, CO. She prefers to be called Windi. She graduated from Walden, Colorado, High School in 1977, attended Community College in Cheyenne, WY for one year, while living with her father; then became a Dental Assistant in Walden, then Deputy Town Clerk in Walden, CO. She m 18 June 1988 at Greeley, CO, **Michael John Allnutt**, s/o William Frederick and Dolores Esther (MacDonald) Allnutt, b 7 September 1957. Mike is a rancher and works for Stephens Brothers Ranch, at Rand, CO. He graduated from Colorado State University at Fort Collins, CO, with a degree in accounting; his parents have a mortuary business in Greeley, CO. Windi worked for McGill Professional Law Corp. before her marriage. They live at Rand, CO.

Children, surname ALLNUT:
    1810. i. Michael[7] Wade, b 7 February 1990, at Greeley, CO.
    1811. ii. Karen Danielle, b 15 August 1991, at Greeley.
    1811A. iii. Lara Beth, b 21 September 1992, at Greeley.

744. TAMI[6] LOUISE KENNEDY (d/o Hugh[5] I. Kennedy #301), b 21 December 1960 at Laramie, WY. She graduated from Walden, CO, High

School in 1979, and attended Cheyenne, WY, Community College a few months; m 30 August 1980, **Scott Leslie Mote** at her home on the Wade Ranch, near Walden, CO, s/o Richard Lawrence and Betty Louise (Turner) Johnson, b 27 November 1955 at Denver, CO. Scott trained in Geology at the University of Colorado. Tami divorced Scott and in 1990 received a degree in economics from the University of Colorado at Colorado Springs. She now works for Traveler's Insurance Company in Denver as an assistant account manager; she resides in Denver.

Children, surname MOTE:
- 1812. i. Nathan[7] Scott, b 5 September 1983 at Denver.
- 1813. ii. Sarah Elizabeth, b 25 January 1985 at Denver.

745. JULIE[6] LYNN KENNEDY (d/o Hugh[5] I. Kennedy #301), b 7 February 1963 at Greeley, CO; graduated from Walden, Colorado, High School in 1982. She then joined the US Army 22 September 1982, as a specialists in intelligence work. While stationed at Fort Meade, MD she met and m 2 August 1985 at Annapolis, **Milton Eugene Marshall**, s/o Joseph and Nellie (Taylor) Marshall, b 23 July 1962 at Washington, DC. Julie separated from the army and attended Brookdale Community College for awhile, receiving her Associate Degree in 1989. Milton graduated from High Point High School, Beltsville, MD in 1980. He is in supply work in the army. They have been on a tour of duty in Italy, returned to the US for further training, and returned to Italy again; a few months later Milton was called back in August 1992 and assigned to a base in San Antonio, TX.

Children, surname MARSHALL:
- 1814. i. Milton[7] Eugene, b 20 August 1989.
- 1815. ii. Monica Effie Lou, b 1 August 1991.

Chapter 8

The Seventh Generation

747. DOROTHY[7] CHEESEMAN (d/o Roland[6] G. Cheeseman #302), b 5 October 1920 in Queens, NY; m 1 October 1938, **Gordon Dayton Mattoon**, s/o Harry Dayton and Dorothy May (Peck) Mattoon, b 13 June 1918; d 13 April 1983 at Tuckerton, NJ. Latest address for Dorothy is Whiting, NJ.

Children, surname MATTOON:
- 1816. i. Gordon[8] Dayton, b 14 June 1940 at Newark, NJ.
- 1817. ii. Roland Harry, b 15 October 1942 at Newark; d 20 October 1942.
- 1818. iii. Dorothy Merle, b 21 July 1944 at East Orange, NJ. She was married to Charles Waldo; d September 1978.
- 1819. iv. Karen Lynn, b 21 July 1944 at East Orange.
- 1820. v. Roland Harry, b 12 July 1947 at East Orange.
- 1821. vi. Robert Vaughn, b 29 December 1948 at Newark.
- 1822. vii. Patricia Ann, b 20 June 1950 at Montclair, NJ.

748. JOHN[7] ROYAL CHEESEMAN (s/o Hubert[6] E. Cheeseman #303), b 13 August 1927 at New Haven, CT; m/1 in Hamden, CT on June 1951,**Corrine J. Veglianti**, b New Haven. John m/2 **Joan Boegler**, b about 1932 in Warwick, RI; they lived at Brantford, CT. John graduated from University of Connecticut School of Mechanical Engineering in 1951. Later earned a Masters Degree; worked 10 years at his profession. He now runs a bowling alley and has gone into business for himself.

Children, surname CHEESEMAN, both born at New Haven:
- 1823. i. Valerie[8], b 18 May 1955; saleslady for a jewelry company; expert in diamonds and gold. See addenda.
- 1824. ii. John Royal, b 25 April 1962; he was to graduate from Northwestern College, MA as a mechanical engineer in 1984. Expected to marry March 1986, Nancy Ross from Madison, CT.

749. CAROL[7] EDNA CHEESEMAN (d/o Hubert[6] E. Cheeseman #303), b 17 November 1933 at Brooklyn, NY; m 28 October 1961 at East Haven, CT **Anthony F. Mulone**, s/o Frank and Teresa Mulone, b about 1933 at Mount Kisco, NY. Tony is a roofer for Yale University, and they lived at Branford, CT. Carol d 30 December 1984 at Brantford.

Children, surname MULONE:
- 1825. i. Linda[8], b 17 January 1965, New Haven, CT.
- 1826. ii. Anthony, b 23 April 1968, New Haven.

752. NORMA[7] RUTH WIEDENDORF (d/o Grace[6] Stevens Wiedendorf #308), b 5 October 1922 at Dodge Co., MN; m 16 May 1941 at Austin, MN, **Hans Musolf**, s/o Harry and Clara (Tweton) Musolf, b 26 August 1913 at Dodge Co. Hans was a driver for a Rochester, MN dairy; lives in Kasson, MN.

Children, surname MUSOLF:
- \+ 1827. i. Ronald[8] Richard, b 10 February 1942.

753. GERYL[7] EARL WIEDENDORF (s/o Grace[6] Stevens Wiedendorf #308), b 2 November 1924 at Dodge Co., MN; d 2 February 1978 at Minneapolis, MN; buried at Calvary Cemetery, Anoka, MN; m 4 December 1943 at Duluth, MN, **Lorraine Frances Brow**, d/o Aloyosis and Elsie (Drolet) Brow, b 28 June 1926 at Superior, WI. Geryl drove freight trucks in Minneapolis area.

Child, surname WIEDENDORF:
- \+ 1828. i. Rosean[8] Marie, b 20 April 1947.

754. WAYNE[7] ANDREW WIEDENDORF (s/o Grace[6] Stevens Wiedendorf #308), b 15 September 1939 at Rochester, MN; m 27 February 1960 at Motley, MN, **Betty Konen**, d/o Werner and Margaret (Kraft) Konen, b 2 December 1941 at Hillman, MN. Wayne is a national sales trainer for Schwan Sales Enterprises.

Children, surname WIEDENDORF:
- 1829. i. Tammie[8] Ann, b 5 March 1961 at Minneapolis, MN; unmarried. Tammie is a nurse at Saint Mary's Hospital, Rochester.
- 1830. ii. Timothy Alan, b 8 November 1963 at Minneapolis; m 12 May 1984, Kathy Harriet De Baere at Marshall, MN; d/o Raymond and Margaret De Baere. Timothy is a material handler for Schwan Sales Enterprises, Marshall, MN.

755. LEA[7] ETTA STEVENS (d/o Norman[6] C. Stevens #309), m **Arie Salbro**, since deceased. Lea resides in Anoka, MN.

Children, surname SALBRO:
- 1831. i. Cheryl[8].

The Seventh Generation 311

1832. ii. Sheldon, lives in Minneapolis, MN.

757. KENNETH[7] ROY SCHUFFENHAUER (s/o Thelma[6] Stevens Schuffenhauer #310), b 20 August 1933 at Minneapolis, MN; m 10 April 1965 at Minneapolis, **Jeanette Olson**, d/o Joseph and Lurene (Ellingboe) Olson, b 17 December 1936 at Hastings, MN. Kenneth works for Griggs Cooper at Saint Paul, MN.

Child, surname SCHUFFENHAUER:
    1833. i. Dawn[8] Marie, b 27 January 1978 at Minneapolis.

758. JO[7] ANN SCHUFFENHAUER (d/o Thelma[6] Stevens Schuffenhauer #310), b 9 June 1934 at Minneapolis, MN; m 24 April 1954, **Wallace John Stigsell**, s/o John and Mary (Rolfson) Stigsell. Wallace is a heavy machine operator.

Children, surname STIGSELL, both born at Minneapolis:
    1834. i. Gary[8] Allen, b 13 December 1967.
    1835. ii. Terri Lyn, b 21 February 1969.

761. BETTY[7] JANE SCHUFFENHAUER (d/o Thelma[6] Stevens Schuffenhauer #310), b 8 July 1940 at Minneapolis, MN; m 7 April 1961 at Minneapolis, **Bruce Dennis Hofstad**, b Minneapolis. Bruce works for Minneapolis Water Works.

Children, surname HOFSTAD, all born at Minneapolis:
    1836. i. Randy[8], b 9 October 1961.
    1837. ii. Cheri Lyn, b 2 August 1963.
    1838. iii. David, b 16 August 1964.

762. ROBERT[7] DONALD SCHUFFENHAUER (s/o Thelma[6] Stevens Schuffenhauer #310), b 19 September 1941 at Minneapolis, MN; m 20 October 1962, **Margaret Illene Tuttle**, d/o William and Kathy (Manley) Tuttle, b 19 June 1941 at Minneapolis. Robert is Assistant Manager of Landry Transfer Co.

Children, surname SCHUFFENHAUER, all born at Minneapolis:
    1839. i. Michael[8] Frank, b 27 August 1965.
    1840. ii. Mary Kay, b 5 February 1967.
    1841. iii. Debra Lyn, b October 1970.

763. RONALD[7] DEAN SCHUFFENHAUER (s/o Thelma[6] Stevens Schuffenhauer #310), b 19 September 1941 at Minneapolis, MN; m 4

February 1967, **Sharon Hansen**, d/o Virgil John and Dorothy Elizabeth (Buschenfield) Hansen, b at Council Bluffs, IA. Ronald is Manager at Landry Transfer Co.

Children, surname SCHUFFENHAUER, both born at Minneapolis:
- 1842. i. Ann[8] Elizabeth, b 19 September 1970.
- 1843. ii. Steven John, b 7 March 1974.

764. CLARENE[7] ELMINA CROUCH (d/o Clarence[6] Crouch #311), b 23 June 1926 at Abilene, KS; m **Charles Wesley Rogers**. They live in San Jose, CA.

Children, surname ROGERS:
- 1844. i. Sandra[8] Leigh, b 18 June 1947 at Nampa, ID; m — Curtis.
- 1845. ii. Karen, b 14 June 1950 at Portland, OR; m — Harris.
- 1846. iii. Michel, b 3 September 1958 at Salem, OR; m — Charko.

765. LaVON[7] ELAINE CROUCH (d/o Clarence[6] Crouch #311), b 8 August 1931 at Abilene, KS; m **Larry Crafton**; m/2 **Phillip Stallings**.

Children, surname CRAFTON, all of whom were born at Portland, OR:
- 1847. i. Larry[8] Lynn, b 26 September 1951.
- 1848. ii. Jerry Leon, b 19 November 1952.
- 1849. iii. Debra Jane, b 5 September 1954.
- 1850. iv. Dennice Jean, b 20 May 1956.

766. LYNN[7] MONROE LEE (s/o Mildred[6] Crouch Lee #312), b 20 January 1936 at Oklahoma City, OK; m 29 August 1958 at First Church of Nazarene, Stockton, CA, **Norma Ethel Dean**, d/o Frank and Elvira Dean, b 26 September 1936 at Stockton. Lynn graduated from University of Pacific at Stockton; was Foreign Service Officer on overseas assignments from 1966–1981. Lynn is with the Agency for International Development, and has servied in Vietnam, Panama, Ethiopia, Pakistan, and Philippines. His family was with him except in Vietnam; when last known they were living in Washington, DC.

Children, surname LEE:
- 1851. i. Randall[8] Howard, b 19 May 1962 at Oakland, CA; attended High School in Karachi, Pakestan; in 1984 was a senior at U.S. Military Academy, West Point, NY.
- 1852. ii. Ronald Dean, b 18 April 1964 at Oakland; attended High Schools in Karachi, Pakistan and Manilla, Philippines; in 1984 a sopho-

The Seventh Generation 313

more at Virginia Tech., Blacksburg, VA.

767. BEVERLY[7] **ANN LEE**, (d/o Mildred[6] Crouch Lee #312), b 12 May 1941 at Oklahoma City, OK; m 19 March 1962 at Corvallis, OR, **John Allen Granthom**, s/o John and Verna Granthom, b 3 December 1938 at Blacksburg, VA. John is Superintendent of Paper Machine Dept. of Crown Zellerbach Paper Co. at Wauna, OR, on the Columbia River near Astoria. They live at Clatskinie, OR.

Children, surname GRANTHOM, all born at Vancouver, WA:
- 1853. i. John[8] Lee, b 20 August 1962.
- 1854. ii. James Roy, b 11 February 1965.
- 1855. iii. Thomas Allen, b 7 May 1966.

768. ROBERT[6] **BRAMMER** (s/o Evelyn[5] Crouch Brammer #313), b 9 August 1936; m Jan 1977 at Indianapolis, IN, **Carol Bailey**. Robert is a Farm Bureau Insurance representative.

Children, surname **BRAMMER:**
- 1856. i. Terry Lee, b 4 April 19—.
- 1857. ii. Brenda, b 2 February 19—.
- 1858. iii. Karen.
- 1859. iv. Carol.

769. JANICE[6] **ADELL BRAMMER** (s/o Evelyn[5] Crouch Brammer #313), b 6 December 1939; m/1 **Joe Farrell**; m/2 **Hearn Newby**; m/3 13 March 1988 at Palm Harbor, FL, **Walter Weiss**.

Children, surname FARRELL:
- 1860. i. Timothy, b 23 May 19–.
- 1861. ii. Greg, b 28 May 19–.

Children, surname NEWBY:
- 1862. iii. Kevin.

770. RONALD[6] **ALLEN BRAMMER** (s/o Evelyn[5] Crouch Brammer #313), b 29 November 1947; m 24 November 1971 at Cleveland, OH, **Peggy Moyer**. Ronald is in a landscaping business.

Children, surname **BRAMMER:**
- 1863. i. Ronald, b 23 October 1982.

771. SHARON[7] **LU CROUCH** (d/o Vernon[6] Crouch #314), b 30

October 1942 at Newcastle, IN; m 6 October 1962, at Miltonvale, KS, **Kenneth Elbert Dyer**, b in Iowa, s/o William H. Dyer.

Children, surname DYER:
- 1864. i. Cathy[8] Jo, b 6 July 1963 at Omaha, NE.
- 1865. ii. Mark Jeffrey, b 16 July 1967 at Sacramento, CA.
- 1866. iii. Keron Lene, b 28 September 1968 at Omaha.

772. LINDA[7] KAY CROUCH (d/o Vernon[6] Crouch #314), b 28 March 1947 at Marion, IN; m 18 December 1965, **Gary Gordon Beck**; divorced June 1978; m/2 18 April 1980 at Leesburg, FL, **Thomas Norman Grizzard**, s/o Dana and Beverly Grizzard. Tom is a real estate salesman.

Children, surname BECK:
- 1867. i. Marla[8] Jene, b 22 May 1967.
- 1868. ii. Matthew Gordon, b 21 August 1973.

774. DONALD[7] LLOYD GARRISON (s/o Lloyd[6] H. Garrison #316), b 19 September 1929 at Long Beach, CA; m 9 January 1954 at Yuma, AZ, **Donna More**, b San Diego, CA, d/o Verne and Lucille (Vaughn) More. Donald is a barber.

Children, surname GARRISON, both born at LaMesa, CA:
- 1869. i. Steven[8] Ritchard, b 30 October 1954.
- 1870. ii. Dee Ann Robin, b 16 February 1956.

775. NONA[7] LOU GARRISON (d/o Lloyd[6] H. Garrison #316), b 6 July 1935 at Long Beach, CA; m 29 January 1955 at Long Beach, **William Bryan Byrnes**. Nona and her husband are in the insurance business.

Children, surname BYRNES, all born at Long Beach:
- 1871. i. Terri[8] Lynn, b 5 June 1958.
- 1872. ii. William Bryan, b 12 September 1962.
- 1873. iii. Dannial Lloyd, b 28 March 1964.

776. BETTY[7] JUNE MEEKER (d/o Myrtle[6] Garrison Meeker #318), b 5 July 1929 at Long Beach, CA; m 3 July 1948 at Los Angeles, CA, **Jack B. Trimble**. Jack is a plasterer; they live at Thousand Oaks, CA.

Children, surname TRIMBLE:
- 1874. i. Steven[8] C., b 10 April 1949 at Los Angeles.
- 1875. ii. Martha, b 8 December 1951 at Los Angeles; m — Waller.
- 1876. iii. Becky Ann, b 7 July 1953 at Gardena, CA; m — Cothern.

1877. iv. Mary Colleen, b 1 September 1955 at Lynwood, CA; m — Felt.

780. DONALD[7] GARRISON (s/o Donald[6] Garrison #321), b 26 July 1944 at Long Beach, CA; m **Elizabeth Goss**; later divorced. Donald is a missionary in Children of God Church. He lives in Long Beach.
Child, surname GARRISON:
    1878. i. Josiah[8], b 21 January 1972.

781. DAVID[7] GARRISON (s/o Donald[6] Garrison #321), b 4 November 1946 at Long Beach, CA; m/1 **Lynda Kay Grip**, d/o Ben and Maxine Grip, b 8 April 1949 in ND; divorced. David m/2 **Chrysandra Dell Hudson**, d/o John and Frances (Watson) Hudson, b 12 December 1949 at Shelbyville, TN. Chrysandra has three children from previous marriages. David is an energy consultant, living in Long Beach.
Child, surname GARRISON;
    1879. i. Darion[8] Wayne, b 22 June 1971 at Anaheim, CA.
Children, surname BAKER:
    1880. ii. Mary Margaret, b 20 May 1969.
    1881. iii. David Michael, b 2 April 1972.
Child, surname HERRIN:
    1882. iv. Mark Allen, b 29 January 1975.

782. KATHY[7] LA VONNE GARRISON (d/o Donald[6] Garrison #321), b 22 June 1956 at Alhambra, CA; m 21 June 1980 at Lakeport, CA, **Carl Blane Wilbur**, s/o Mason Kenyon and Tekla Frances (Jessel) Wilbur, b Hayward, CA 17 September 1948. Carl is General Manager of Bruce Fewel Mobil Home Sales; Roofing Co. and Kathy is an optometric assistant. Carl had two children, Patricia and Mason, by a previous marriage; they live with Kathy and Carl.
Children, surname WILBUR:
    1883. i. Patricia[8] Ann, b 6 May 1968.
    1884. ii. Mason Kenyon II, b 19 November 1970.
    1885. iii. Jillian Jacqueline, b 21 May 1981.

784. RICHARD[7] ALLEN EVANS (s/o Juanita[6] Daniels Evans #322), b 21 January 1933 in Minneapolis, MN; m 18 January 1958 at Princeton, MN, **Carol Schmiege**. They later divorced. Richard is a piano salesman, and lives at Golden Valley, MN.

Children, surname EVANS:
- 1886. i. Deborah[8] Lynn, b 3 August 1958; m Lynn Markey.
+ 1887. ii. Michael Allen, b 4 October 1959.

785. DAVID[7] WAYNE EVANS (s/o Juanita[6] Daniels Evans #322), b 11 February 1935 at Minneapolis, MN; m 5 September 1964 in IA, **Shirley Weldon**. David is a cigar Salesman and they live in Cedar Rapids, IA.

Children, surname EVANS, all born at Cedar Rapids:
- 1888. i. Michel[8] Cae, b 29 May 1965.
- 1889. ii. Todd David, b 25 March 1967.
- 1890. iii. Timothy Glen, b 19 June 1969.

786. THOMAS[7] GLENN EVANS (s/o Juanita[6] Daniels Evans #322), b 5 December 1938 at Minneapolis, MN; m 22 August 1959, **Judy O'Konek**, b 4 September 1942; Thomas a printer-lithographer, lives in Blaine, MN.

Children, surname EVANS:
- 1891. i. Steven[8] Wayne, b 30 March 1960.
- 1892. ii. Robert Thomas, b 23 January 1962.
- 1893. iii. Peggy Susan, b 13 September 1964.
- 1894. iv. Patricia Kay, b 7 February 1967.

787. SARAH[7] ADELL EVANS (d/o Juanita[6] Daniels Evans #322), b 7 March 1940 at Minneapolis, MN; m/1 18 August 1962, **Richard Johnson**. Sarah m/2 **Gary Knutson** 3 September 1966; Gary is a pilot for Northwest Airlines.

Children, surname KNUTSON:
- 1895. i. Stacey[8] Christa (Johnson), b 10 July 1963; later adopted by Sarah's 2nd husband, Gary Knutson.
- 1896. i. Cathleen[8] Sarah, b 9 May 1968 at Seattle, WA.
- 1897. ii. Charles Gary, b 19 May 1974 in MN.

788. SHARON[7] ELIZABETH EVANS (d/o Juanita[6] Daniels Evans #322), b 5 October 1943 at Minneapolis, MN; when she was six weeks old her mother had a nervous breakdown and was hospitalized; family was split up among different homes. Sharon was taken in by the Adair family until six years old, when her father brought the children home after remarrying. She m 14 September 1963 at Minneapolis, MN, **William Joseph McDearmon**, s/o Taft and Dorothy (Haney) McDearmon, b 21 October 1942 at Saint Paul, MN. William is a book binder at McGill-Jen-

The Seventh Generation 317

son Co. and Sharon is a bookkeeper. They live in Minneapolis.
Children, surname McDEARMON, all born at Minneapolis:
    1898. i. Julie^8 Marie, b 29 April 1966.
    1899. ii. Kelly Lynn, b 9 February 1969.
    1900. iii. Jeremy Joseph, b 24 October 1976.

789. DAVID^7 WYNOT DANIELS (s/o Wynot^6 B. Daniels #323), b 13 June 1935 at Minneapolis, MN; m 15 July 1955 at Long Beach, CA, **Barbara Jean Goar**, d/o Gordon Mims and Helen Mertie (Cozart) Goar, b 15 July 1938 at Pittsboro, MS.
Child, surname DANIELS:
+   1901. i. David^8 Blake, b 4 February 1958.
+   1902. ii. Julie Kay, b 21 August 1959.
    1903. iii. Eric Christopher, b 5 March 1966 at Santa Ana, CA.

790. CONSTANCE^7 DIANE DANIELS (d/o Wynot^6 B. Daniels #323), b 18 December 1938 at Long Beach, CA; m 28 January 1956 at Long Beach, **William David Brewster**, s/o William Looender and Ella Louise (Koch) Brewster, b 12 April 1914 in Los Angeles, Ozura Co., CA.
Children, surname BREWSTER:
    1904. i. Pamela^8 Jean, b 9 March 1957 at Torrance, CA.
+   1905. ii. James Wyatt, b 2 May 1959.

791. ROBERT^7 BLAKE DANIELS (s/o Wynot^6 B. Daniels #323), b 11 September 1943 at Long Beach, CA; m 21 August 1977 at Keene, TX, **Kay Rose Block**, d/o Cecil Edgar and Betty Carolyn (Geer) Caddis, her natural parents (name of adoptive parents is unknown), b 16 April 1945 in TX. They live at Lakeside, CA.
Children, surname DANIELS:
    1906. i. Benjamin^8 Edward, b 29 September 1978 at Walla Walla, WA.
    1907. ii. Edwin Alec, b 13 June 1982 at San Diego, CA.

792. RICKY^7 REED HUNT (s/o Bethel^6 Daniels Hunt #324), b 2 September 1944 at Long Beach, CA; m February 1983 at Honolulu, HI, **Diane Wilson**, d/o Joe E. and Doreen A. Wilson, b 11 August 1948 at Los Angeles, CA. In 1984 Ricky had just retired after 20 years in the army. He was going back to college to get his degree in business, and was buying a house in Florida.

Children, surname HUNT:
    1908. i. Drusilla[8], b 9 January 1966 in KY.
    1909. ii. Sarah, b 25 June 1969 in KY.

793. GARY[7] DEAN HUNT (s/o Bethel[6] Daniels Hunt #324), b 23 March 1946 at Long Beach, CA; m 12 November 1969 in PA, divorced Aug 1982, **Irene Klebacha**, d/o Henry and Blanche (Zavatsky) Klebacha, b 19 September 1946 at DuBois, PA. Gary has his own surveying company; they lived in Winter Springs, FL.

Children, surname HUNT:
    1910. i. Christopher[8], b 21 March 1970 at DuBois.
    1911. ii. Thadius, b 5 March 1976 at Winter Park, FL.
    1912. iii. Amy, b 18 December 1978 at Winter Park.

794. GARTH[7] CROUCH (s/o Harlie[6] L. Crouch #326), b 13 March 1952 in MN; m **Connie Butterfield**, d/o John and Elaine Butterfield, b 24 July 1951. Garth is running his father's farm at West Concord, MN.

Children, surname CROUCH:
    1913. i. Jennifer[8], b 28 November 1977, Owatonna, MN.
    1914. ii. Erin, b 21 August 1980, Owatonna.

795. ELIZABETH[7] CROUCH (d/o Harlie[6] L. Crouch #326), b 10 September 1953 at Faribault, Rice Co., MN; m **David Vanburkleo**, s/o Francis and Gladys Vanburkleo, b 31 May 1951. In 1984 David was the Police Chief of Dodge Center, MN, where they live.

Child, surname VANBURKLEO:
    1915. i. Natalie[8], b 21 May 1981.

796. KATHRYN[7] CROUCH (d/o Harlie[6] L. Crouch #326), b 5 March 1956; m **Steven O'Connor**, s/o David and Arlene O'Connor, b 26 June 1956. Steven is a professional photographer and Kathy is a police officer. They live in West Concord, MN.

Child, surname O'CONNOR:
    1916. i. Joshua[8], b 17 November 1982.

797. DAVID[7] BURDETTE HART (s/o Leora[6] Crouch Hart #327), b 28 May 1939 at Pine Island, MN; m 1 April 1956 at Columbus Junction, IA, **Sally Jo Ebbesmier**, d/o Lyman and Margaret (Welch) Ebbesmier, b 10 August 1938 at Burlington, IA. David is labor mediator for state of CA;

The Seventh Generation

they live at Carlsbad, CA.

Child, surname HART:

+ 1917. i. David[8] Dean, b 26 November 1956.
   1918. ii. Kevin Bradley, b 17 December 1958 at Mesa, AZ; not married is a landscaper.
   1919. iii. Steven Craig, b 5 December 1962 at Mesa; not married, does pool maintenance.
   1920. iv. Deborah Jo, b 25 March 1965 at Mesa; not married works for Kraft Foods.
   1921. v. Richard Kennedy, b 12 January 1968 at Mesa; when last known was a student.

798. LARRY[7] DUANE HART (s/o Leora[6] Crouch Hart #327), b 22 July 1941 at Pine Island, MN; m 28 November 1962 at Tempe, AZ, **Mary Kay Wampler**, b 23 March 1945 at Springfield, MO; In 1984 Larry was in the Corps of Engineers, Warsaw, MO.

Children, surname HART, all born at Mesa, AZ:
   1922. i. Tami[8] Lea, b 30 June 1963.
   1923. ii. Todd, b 19 November 1965.
   1924. iii. Michael, b 18 May 1969.
   1925. iv. Bobby Jo, b 12 October 1972.

799. CHERELYN[7] LEA HART (d/o Leora[6] Crouch Hart #327), b 31 December 1943 at Rochester, MN; m 12 January 1965, **James Estel Chaney**, b 13 June 1941 at Rolla, MO; Cherelyn owns a trailer park at Apache Junction, AZ; James works on a pipe line as equipment operator. They have no children.

800. NANCY[7] KAY HART (d/o Leora[6] Crouch Hart #327), b 11 February 1948 at Pine Island, MN; m/1 6 May 1966 at Tempe, AZ, **Cruz Alfred Blanco**, s/o Cruz R. and Anita (Guiterrez) Blanco, b 31 October 1944 at Scottsbluff, NB; divorced Cruz at Mesa, AZ, 23 March 1976; m/2 22 May 1982 at Apache Junction, AZ, **Carlos Rael Baldenegro**, s/o Felipe and Sarah (Rael) Baldenegro, b 7 June 1940 at Chandler, AZ. Carlos is supervisor of production. They live at Chandler.

Children, surname BLANCO, all born at Mesa:
   1926. i. Kristine[8] Marie, b 22 November 1966.
   1927. ii. Stephanie Ann, b 7 September 1968.

1928. iii. Brandon Cruz, b 26 October 1970.

801. SUE[7] RANAL HART (d/o Leora[6] Crouch Hart #327), b 18 January 1953 at Burlington, IA; m 16 July 1971 at Florence, AZ, **Albert Joe Trice Bailey**, s/o Norman Jo Trice and Janet May (Lee) Bailey, b 3 October 1953 at Joplin, MO. Albert works at Sahuaro Paving Co., Phoenix, AZ and Sue works at Holmes School, Mesa, AZ, as a cafeteria manager. They live at Mesa.

Children, surname BAILEY, both born at Mesa:
1929. i. April[8] Sue, b 14 February 1972.
1930. ii. Norman Joshua, b 7 October 1975.

803. MARCIA[7] JEAN CROUCH (d/o Quentin[6] Crouch #329), b 16 April 1957 at Peoria, IL; m 21 June 1980, at Rochester, MN, **David Holtorf**, s/o Norman and Lenora (Schmidt) Holtorf, b 30 March 1954 at Hastings, MN. David is air traffic controller at Vermillion, MN.

Child, surname HOLTORF:
1931. i. Renee[8] Marie, b 16 June 1983 at Hastings, MN.

804. BRENDA[7] EILEEN CROUCH (d/o Quentin[6] Crouch #329), b 20 January 1959 at Minneapolis, MN; m 19 June 1982 at Rochester, MN, **Mark Fairchild**, s/o David and Lucille Fairchild, b 13 October 1958 in Japan. Mark is a teacher at Coleraine, MN.

Child, surname FAIRCHILD:
1932. i. Kyle[8] Nathan, b 15 March 1983 at Grand Rapids, MN.

805. VIRGINIA[7] LEE CROUCH (adopted d/o Kermit[6] Crouch #330), b 7 May 1954 at Minneapolis, MN; m 18 June 1976 in Minneapolis, **Larry Saltvedt**. They live in Apple Valley, MN.

Children, surname SALTVEDT:
1933. i. Shara[8] Lee, b 7 July 1977 at Colorado Springs, CO.
1934. ii. Shane Eric, b 6 November 1979 at Minneapolis.
1935. iii. Laura Lynn, b 3 May 1983 at Minneapolis.

806. BYRON[7] ROSS CROUCH (adopted s/o Kermit[6] Crouch #330), b 27 July 1955 at Minneapolis, MN; m **Lois Quick**. Byron works for Sears Roebuck and they live in Minneapolis, MN.

Children, surname CROUCH, all born at Minneapolis:
1936. i. Collin[8] Kermit, b 14 August 1979.

1937. ii. Quentin Vincent, b 4 December 1980.
1938. iii. Troy Lee, b 25 July 1983.

807. VINCENT[7] KEVIN CROUCH (s/o Kermit[6] Crouch #330), b 13 October 1957 at Minneapolis, MN; m 16 July 1977 at Minneapolis, **Kim Weikle**. Vincent is in construction work; they live in Minneapolis.

Children, surname CROUCH, both born at Minneapolis:
1939. i. Chelsea[8] Kaley, b 22 March 1979.
1940. ii. Vincent Joshua, b 31 December 1980.

808. KURT[7] JEFFREY CROUCH (s/o Kermit[6] Crouch #330), b 19 November 1958 at Minneapolis, MN; m/1 10 Feb 1979, **Roni Jo Neppl**; divorced 1983; m/2 29 June 1985 at Minneapolis, **Kathy Lorraine Hall**. Kurt works for Honeywell Co. in Minneapolis, where they live.

Child, surname CROUCH:
1941. i. Lindsey[8] Jo, b 9 February 1980 at Minneapolis.

815. PAMELA[7] RUTH MILLER (d/o Ruth[6] Crouch Miller #334), b 3 April 1950 at Owatonna, MN; m **Gary Wandrey**, s/o Alfred and Theodora (Valentine) Wandrey, he b 9 November 1948 at Owatonna; they were divorced in 1981 and Pam lives in Dodge Center, MN.

Children, surname WANDREY:
1942. i. Tricia[8] Lee Miller, b 20 September 1968 at Owatonna.
1943. ii. Kellie Lynn, b 8 November 1970 at Washington State.
1944. iii. Gary Scott, b 24 April 1971 in Germany.
1945. iv. Regina Ann, b 18 April 1973 in Texas.
1946. v. James Gordon, b 19 October 1974 at Rochester, MN.

816. STEVEN[7] DOUGLAS MILLER (s/o Ruth[6] Crouch Miller #334), b 20 November 1953 at Owatonna, MN; m/1 **Cheryl Jacobson**, d/o Oral and Lorraine Elsie (stepmother) Jacobson; divorced; m/2 3 April 1982 at Austin, TX, **Maureen McFarland**, d/o Dean and Lorraine McFarland; They live in Austin, TX, where Steve is in construction work.

Children, surname MILLER:
1947. i. Christopher[8] Douglas, b 5 September 1971 at Owatonna.
1948. ii. Jasmine Elizabeth, b 21 August 1982 at Austin.
1949. iii. Twin to Jasmine, name unknown, died at an early age.

821. WILLIAM[7] KENNETH GAY (s/o Cheryl[6] Crouch Gay #339), b

10 July 1958 at Tempe, AZ; m 10 July 1980, **Lila Joni Hammaker**.
Child, surname GAY:
    1950.   i. Warren[8] Kenneth, b 12 June 1981 at Tempe.

822. CAROLYN[7] ELAINE GAY (d/o Cheryl[6] Crouch Gay #339), b 3 July 1959 at Tempe, AZ; m 1 December 1978, **Bennett Painter**.
Child, surname PAINTER:
    1951.   i. Matthew[8] Seth, b 15 March 1982 at Phoenix, AZ.

829. PATRICK[7] GERALD SCHOENFELDER (s/o Betty[6] Jane Crouch Schoenfelder #342), b 22 November 1947 at Minneapolis, MN; m 26 August 1968, **Gail Mastenbrook**, b 30 April 1945. Patrick is a doctor, specializing in radiology.
Children, surname SCHOENFELDER:
    1952.   i. John[8] Wilbur, b 17 April 1977 at Saint Paul, MN.
    1953.   ii. Lindsey Ann, b 23 April 1980 at Rochester, MN.

830. DANIEL[7] JOHN SCHOENFELDER (s/o Betty[6] Jane Crouch Schoenfelder #342), b 7 June 1949 at Albert Lea, MN; m 29 December 1973 in Minneapolis, MN, **Marla Joy Bockelman**, d/o William and Eleanor Bockelman, she b 8 February 1949. Daniel manages his father's ranch at Elfrida, AZ.
Children, surname SCHOENFELDER:
    1954.   i. Jason[8] Daniel, b 26 March 1975, at Kansas City, MO.
    1955.   ii. Jeremy John, b 15 July 1977, at Kansas City.

831. TIMOTHY[7] WILLIAM SCHOENFELDER (s/o Betty[6] Jane Crouch Schoenfelder #342), b 9 July 1950 at Albert Lea, MN; m 22 May 1983, **Ellen Kaiser**, b 15 February 1953; Timothy is an anesthesiologist; Ellen is also a doctor, and both are doing their residency at Madison, WI.
Child, surname SCHOENFELDER:
    1956.   i. Michael[8] Kaiser, b 22 February 1984.

832. KEVIN[7] PETER SCHOENFELDER (s/o Betty[6] Jane Crouch Schoenfelder #342), b 28 February 1952 at Mason City, IA; m 1/ 26 June 1972, **Cindy Nelson**; divorced about 1978; m/2 26 March 1983, **Emily Tikton**, at Seattle, WA; Emily b 27 July 1954. She is a psychologist and has her office in her home. Kevin is an orthopedic surgeon in Seattle.

Child, surname SCHOENFELDER:
   1957.   i. Erin[8] Nicole, b 28 March 1984.

833. BRIDGET[7] MARY SCHOENFELDER (d/o Betty[6] Jane Crouch Schoenfelder #342), b 3 September 1953 at Davenport, IA; m 28 December 1974 at Minnetonka, MN, **Rossi Morrone**, b 29 October 1949. Bridget is a respiratory therapist; Rossi has a photography business.

Children, surname MORRONE:
   1958.   i. Sean[8] Rossi, b 1 July 1979 at Minneapolis, MN.
   1959.   ii. Seamus Rosario, b 22 July 1981 at Seattle, WA.

838. LAWRENCE[7] PHELPS (s/o Eva[6] Palmer Phelps #344), b 10 December 1938 at Milton, Dodge Co, MN; m 29 June 1963 at Saint Paul, MN, **Carol Schacht**. Lawrence d 13 January 1981.

Child, surname PHELPS:
   1960.   i. Kelly[8] Jean, b 14 July 1969 at Saint Paul.

839. SHIRLEY[7] PHELPS (d/o Eva[6] Palmer Phelps #344), b 11 August 1941 at Milton, Dodge Co., MN. Shirley was m/1 at Northwood Co, IA, 21 September 1957, **John D. McKeig**. She m/2 at South Saint Paul, MN, 30 June 1973, **Thomas Eisen**.

Child, surname McKEIG:
   1961.   i. James, b 17 April 1958, at Saint Paul.

840. MAXINE[7] PAULA STAFFORD (d/o Marian[6] Palmer Stafford #345), b 23 October 1941 at Dodge Center, MN; m 12 June 1959, **Stanley Craig Salisbury**, b 11 September 1938. Stanley is full time fireman at Owatonna, MN; Maxine is assistant business manager of Owatonna Public Schools.

Children, surname SALISBURY:
   1962.   i. Lisa[8] Ann, b 17 April 1961.
   1963.   ii. Steven Michael, b 16 August 1963.

841. BONITA[7] JEAN STAFFORD (d/o Marian[6] Palmer Stafford #345), b 1 March 1945, Dodge Center, MN; m 30 April 1966, **Joseph Eugene Henkel**, b 24 June 1940. He is an industrial engineer with IBM in Austin, TX; Bonnie is a business manager with IBM.

Children, surname HENKEL:

1963A.   i. Jason[8] Andrew, b 20 Nov 1967.
1963B.   ii. Heidi Jo, b 29 August 1970.

842. BETTY[7] KAY STAFFORD (d/o Marian[6] Palmer Stafford #345), b 21 July 1947 at Dodge Center, MN; m 28 December 1967, **Douglas Calvin Blood**. Betty lives at Springfield, OR. Douglas is in the blacksmith trade.

Children, surname BLOOD:
1964.   i. Michelle[8] Nadine, b 10 July 1974.
1965.   ii. Felicia Ann, b 21 November 1978.

844. MARVIN[7] KYLE STAFFORD (s/o Marian[6] Palmer Stafford #345), b 11 November 1953 at Dodge Center, MN; m 14 April 1979, **Cheryl Jeannine Massey**. Marvin is a graduate of Bemidji State College prepared for teaching and licensed for coaching football & wrestling; when last known a foreman for a construction company in Rochester, MN. They are divorced.

Children, surname STAFFORD:
1966.   i. Michael[8] Ryan, b 26 February 1980.
1967.   ii. Sarah Jeannine, b 28 October 1981.

845. DALE[7] PALMER (s/o Clinton[6] Owen Palmer #346), b 17 January 1958 at Saint Paul, MN; m 22 July 1978 at Concordia Lutheran Church, South Saint Paul, MN, **Linda Marie Kronschnable**. When last known he worked at Villume Industries, a lumber Co.

Children, surname PALMER:
1968.   i. Jason[8] Owen, b 24 October 1978, at South Saint Paul.
1969.   ii. Jeremy Alan, b 8 August 1980, at South Saint Paul.

846. NANCY[7] PALMER (d/o Clinton[6] Owen Palmer #346), b 10 August 1959 at Saint Paul, MN; m 27 October 1979 at Dakota Co., MN, **Clifford O. Hickman**. She works at a photo anodizing plant.

Children, surname HICKMAN:
1970.   i. Cyrus[8], b 4 March 1980 at Ramsey Co.
1971.   ii. Pamela, b 5 October 1981 at Ramsey Co.

847. ROWENA[7] HARLENE LEWIS (d/o Lois[6] Mason #347), b 12 April 1940 at Kasson, MN; m 25 April 1958 at Las Vegas, NV, **Floyd Lokoen**. When last known Rowena was secretary at the Betty Ford Center,

Rancho Mirage, CA; she resides at Bermuda Dunes, CA.

Children, surname LOKOEN:
+ 1972. i. Lida[8] Leigh, b December 1959.
   1973. ii. Lisa Diane, b 1960 at Banning, CA. Still born.
   1974. iii. Lisa Diane, b 11 February 1961; she graduated from Deadwood, [SD] High School and attended a two year college. In 1987 she was a photographer in Deadwood and not married.
   1975. iv. Laura Ann, b 12 March 1964 at Rapid City, SD. She attended San Diego State University, receiving her degree in June 1988. Not married when last known.

848. DARLENE[7] FAYE MASON (d/o Myron[6] Mason #349), b 4 July 1939 at Kasson, MN; m 9 October 1957 at Lemon Grove, CA, **Vincent Breit**, s/o Gene Franklin and Adele (Vendetti) Breit, b 11 February 1939 at Philadelphia, PA. Darlene has a small pool service and Vincent is an electrician. They live at Spring Valley, CA.

Children, surname BREIT:
+ 1976. i. Melody[8] Ann, b 16 July 1957.
+ 1977. ii. Donald Vincent, b 6 August 1958.
+ 1978. iii. Joy Linda, b 30 November 1959.

849. ROBERT[7] MYRON MASON (s/o Myron[6] Mason #349), b 9 April 1943 at Hutchinson, KS; m Fall 1961, **Gerry Ann McCarthy**, b 28 July 1944 at Brooklyn, NY; d/o Jerimah and Mary Ann (McCormick) McCarthy. They were divorced in 1971. Robert m/2 on June 1972, **Karen Ann Kelly**, d/o Leo James and Marie Ann (Fritz) Kelly, b 7 June 1946 at Chula Vista, CA. Robert works at a CO_2 plant, used in oil wells near Dove Creek, CO.

Children, surname MASON:
+ 1979. i. Mary[8] Ann, b 15 November 1962.
   1980. ii. Patricia Lee, b 25 November 1966 at San Deigo.
   1981. iii. Veronica, b 28 December 1973 at Chula Vista, CA.
   1982. iv. Jeremiah James, b 14 April 1978, Chula Vista.
   1983. v. Alicia Marie, b 2 March 1977, Chula Vista.
   1984. vi. Rose Ann, b 19 April 1979, Chula Vista.

850. JOHN[7] GERALD MASON (s/o Myron[6] Mason #349), b 13 March 1947 at Kasson, MN; m June 1965, **Phyllis Marie Nieto**, d/o Simon Cantu and Raymunda (Hernandez) Nieto, b 8 August 1947 at Chula Vista, CA. John owns and runs a wheel and brake service in Imperial Beach, near San Diego, CA.

Children, surname MASON:
+ 1985. i. Deborah[8] Thais, b 27 January 1966.
   1986. ii. Cephas Peter, b 5 April 1974 at San Bernadino, CA.

859. ELIZABETH[7] JO WALENGA (d/o Rilla[6] Franklin Walenga #355), b 17 July 1961 at Chicago, IL; m February 1984, **Brian Kelly Hecht**. When last known she was a student majoring in computer science at Texas State University.

Child, surname HECHT:
   1987. i. Jessica[8] Lynn, b 10 March 1984.

860. LORA[7] MARIE WALENGA (d/o Rilla[6] Franklin Walenga #355), b 6 August 1962 at Chicago, IL; m 26 July 1982, **Kevin Neiliert**; he died 1 November 1983 at Longmont, CO. Lora is a beautician.

Children, surname NEILIERT:
   1988. i. Amber[8] Nicole, b 7 January 1983.

862. VIRGINIA[7] JEAN QUICK, (d/o Eugene James Quick[6] #356) better known as "Virjean," b in the 1930. She reportedly is married and lives in Bonanza, OR.

Children, surname UNKNOWN:
   1989. i. Linda.
   1990. ii. Gina.
   1991. iii. Shane.

863. BETTY[7] MAE QUICK (d/o Georgia[6] Mae Quick #363), b 28 October 1926 at Colorado Springs, CO; m/1 at Modesto, CA, 28 October 1943, **Charles H. Paioni**, b 8 November 1922 at Oakdale, CA, s/o Roe and Rose (Sqhezia) Paioni. He was a dairy farmer, until his death. Betty m/2 27 February 1975 at Santa Cruz, CA, **Wallace E. Boring**, b 9 October 1935 at Santa Cruz, s/o Charles and Ruth (Wilton) Boring. Wallace works at Gallo Glass Co. and Betty is a medical receptionist.

Children, surname PAIONI:
   1992. i. Dwayne[8] Charles, b 4 April 1945.
+ 1993. ii. Darrell Edwin, b 8 September 1950.

867. LOIS[7] JEAN HOUGHTON (d/o Doris[6] Quick Houghton #362), b 30 June 1940 at Taft, CA; m 27 January 1963 at San Francisco, CA, **Terry Link**. Terry is a newspaper writer for Oakland Tribune. He was b 1 May 1941 at Madison, WI, s/o Phillip and Mitzi (Sweet) Link.

Children, surname LINK:
- 1994. i. Phillip[8] J., b 21 November 1963 in San Francisco.
- 1995. ii. Charles J., b 8 June 1965 in San Francisco.
- 1996. iii. Zachary J., b 22 December 1969 in San Francisco
- 1997. iv. Doris J., adopted 31 December 1967.

868. ANN[7] LOUISE HOUGHTON (d/o Doris[6] Quick Houghton #362), b 8 October 1943 at Santa Monica, CA; m December 1964 at Santa Maria, CA, **Dan R. White**, b 22 October 1943 at Los Angeles, s/o Ralph and Eleanor (Olson) White; divorced early 1972; m/2 July 1973 at Carson City, NV, **Tom Keithley**; now divorced. Ann is Director of Programs for Alcoholism and Drugs, Chester, PA.

Children, surname WHITE:
- 1998. i. Derek[8], b 27 March 1965, Santa Barbara, CA.
- 1999. ii. Nathaniel, b 7 August 1968, Santa Barbara.

869. DENNIS[7] LEE QUICK (s/o Calvin[6] Quick #363), b 25 February 1939 at Beaver Dam, WI; m 9 June 1962 at Evanston, IL, **Joan Barbara Holloway**, b 1 May 1940 at Madison, WI; d/o Claude S. and Kathryn (Hensey) Holloway. Dennis is a computer systems analyst and Joan is family counselor at a chemical dependency treatment center. They live in Plymouth, MN.

Children, surname QUICK:
- 2000. i. Kelly[8] Jean, b 1966 at Madison.
- 2001. ii. Susan Marie, b 1967 at Madison.
- 2002. iii. Deborah Lee, b 1974 at Concord, MA.

871. JEANNE[7] ANN QUICK (d/o Elmer[6] Quick #364), b 17 May 1945 at Horicon, WI; m May 1967 at Horicon, **Michael Green**. Jeanne is management consultant for training systems, Inc. at Evanston, IL. Michael works for the Chicago Board of Options.

Children, surname GREEN:
- 2003. i. Shayna[8] Lynn, b 15 April 1970, Chicago, IL.
- 2004. ii. Barrie Jo, b 15 May 1973, Chicago.

872. JAMES[7] RUSSELL QUICK (s/o Russell[6] E. Quick #365), b 20 October 1946; m 16 April 1967, **Georgene "Ginger"Bednarek**, b 25 September 1947. James works for the state at Waupun, WI.

Children, surname QUICK:
 2005. i. Jamie[8] Ann, b 13 October 1967.
 2006. ii. Ginette Kathleen, b 12 August 1969.
 2007. iii. Jesse Russell, b 4 May 1977.

873. ROBERT[7] ALAN QUICK (s/o Russell[6] E. Quick #365), b 1 October 1948; m 6 December 1972, **Nancy Susan Cumming**, b 30 August 1950. Robert is a lineman for Wisconsin Power and Light.

Children, surname QUICK:
 2008. i. Amy[8] Beth, b 9 October 1976.
 2009. ii. Ann Marie, b 23 January 1978.
 2010. iii. Robert Alan, b 18 August 1981.

874. MARY[7] L. QUICK (d/o Leland[6] Quick #366), b 23 August 1946 at Ripon, WI; m 12 December 1968 at Tucson, AZ, **Frank Vegera**. Frank is a salesman for Eccno Lab. and Mary is a nurse.

Child, surname VEGERA:
 2011. i. Ricky[8], b 1968 at Tucson.
 2012. ii. Tony, adopted.

875. DAVID[7] QUICK (s/o Leland[6] Quick #366), b 1 May 1948 at Sturgis, SD; m 3 May 1975 at Baltic, SD, **Barbara Doppenberg**, b 13 November 1943 at Brandon, SD, d/o Garrett Doppenberg. David is a carpenter at Colville, WA.

Children, surname QUICK:
 2013. i. Jennifer[8], b 10 March 1978.
 2014. ii. Benjamin, b 17 August 1980.

876. BRUCE[7] QUICK (s/o Leland[6] Quick #366), b 24 July 1951 at Sturgis, SD; m 17 February 1984, **Robyn Dellon**. Bruce is personnel manager at Lodi Hospital, Lodi, CA.

Child, surname QUICK:
 2015. i. Kylan[8] Michael, b 14 March 1987 at Lodi.

877. THOMAS[7] LEE ILGEN (s/o Irene[6] Quick Ilgen #367), b 13

February 1946 at Ripon, WI; m 23 December 1972, **Christine Littleton**. Tom is Professor of Political Science at Brandeis University.

Children, surname ILGEN:
- 2016. i. Jonathon[8] Seth, b 11 December 1976 at Princeton, NJ.
- 2017. ii. Colin Thomas, b 2 February 1981 at Boston, MA.

878. JANE[7] ELLEN ILGEN (d/o Irene[6] Quick Ilgen #367), b 22 July 1948 at Fond du Lac, WI; m 5 September 1970 at Madison, WI, **Russell William Whitacre**. Russell does personnel work for Oscar Meyer Co. and Jane is a nursery school teacher.

Child, surname WHITACRE:
- 2018. i. Adam[8] Thomas, b 20 December 1980 at Chowa, IL.

879. GARY[7] GRAHN (s/o Evelyn[6] Quick Grahn #368), b 7 February 1942 at Ripon, WI; m 30 September 1961, **Patricia Dorseh**, b 19 April 1942. Gary farmed a long time in West Rosendale area where the Grahns first settled; now works in the woods lumbering. They live at Fence, WI.

Children, surname GRAHN, all born at Fond du Lac, WI:
- 2019. i. Robert[8], b 12 August 1962; m Jayne Sanderson 20 June 1987, b 3 March 1963 at Cambria, WI area, d/o James & Joanne Sanderson.
- 2020. ii. Michael, b 15 April 1964.
- 2021. iii. Brian, b 11 December 1965.

881. PHYLLIS[7] QUICK (d/o Lyle[6] James Quick #369), b 8 November 1945 at Ripon, WI; m 4 December 1965, **Gary Martin Schoening**, s/o Cecil Martin and Ruth Elaine (Douglass) Schoening, b 11 August 1943. They have a farm, raising cattle, sheep, and hogs; Gary also works at the Fulton State Hospital power plant.

Children, surname SCHOENING:
- 2022. i. Dean Martin, b 12 August 1971.
- 2023. ii. Chad Austin, b 12 July 1979.

882. SHARON[7] MAE HECKES (d/o Naomi[6] Quick Heckes #370), b 19 March 1938 at Ripon, WI; m **Duane Christianson**, s/o Bud and Dorothy Christianson. Sharon and Duane are now divorced.

Children, surname CHRISTIANSON:
- 2024. i. Lee[8] Duane, b 16 October 1958.

2025. ii. Pamela, b 22 June 1960 at Wausau, WI.

2026. iii. Kay Lynn, b 17 September 1965 at Wausau.

883. RONALD[7] GORDON HECKES (s/o Naomi[6] Quick Heckes #370), b 26 November 1941 at Ripon, WI; m 7 May 1967 at Marquette, WI, **Shirley Cluppert**, b 14 September 1942 at Marquette, d/o Irvin and Bonita (Klawitter) Cluppert. Ronald lives at Avon Lake, OH and is Quality Control Manager for Kirby Cleaners.

Children, surname HECKES, both born at Ripon, WI:

2027. i. Melody[8], b 25 March 1972.

2028. ii. Jennifer, b 10 May 1973.

884. CAROLINE[7] DOROTHY BADTKE (d/o Dorothy[6] Quick Badtke #371), b 8 August 1938 at Ripon, WI; m 14 September 1956, **Donald Retzlaff**, s/o Otto and Dora (Slotffus) Retzlaff.

Child, surname RETZLAFF:

+ 2029. i. Susan[8], b 16 April 1958.
+ 2030. ii. Dianna Marie, b 10 December 1959.

2031. iii. Christopher Donald, b 1 September 1967; not married.

885. JAMES[7] ARNOLD ALBERT BADTKE (s/o Dorothy[6] Quick Badtke #371), b 12 June 1940 at Ripon, WI; m **Sandra Lipton**, d/o Ralph and Arlene (Weise) Lipton.

Children, surname BADTKE:

2032. i. Debra[8] May, b 22 February 1963; m David Ehler 7 December 1985.

2033. ii. Wayne James, b 24 November 1965; not married.

2034. iii. Brian Arnold, b 23 October 1966; not married.

2035. iv. Peter William, b 22 November 1969; not married.

886. TOM[7] NORBERT BADTKE (s/o Dorothy[6] Quick Badtke #371), b 20 February 1945 at Ripon, WI; m 16 September 1966, **Dorreen Rupnow**, d/o Robert and Doris Rupnow.

Children, surname BADTKE:

2036. i. Jeffrey[8] Tom, b 27 November 1967.

2037. ii. Matthew Robert, b 19 April 1971.

2038. iii. Kimberly May, b September 1973.

2039. iv. Cory, b 11 August 1980.

887. JON[7] DENNIS BADTKE (s/o Dorothy[6] Quick Badtke #371), b 16 April 1946 at Ripon, WI; m **Shirley Ann Faust**, d/o William and Elsie (Wolcholz) Faust 30 September 1967.

Children, surname BADTKE:
- 2040. i. Jon[8] Dennis, b 22 January 1969.
- 2041. ii. Sherry Lynn, b 21 June 1971.
- 2042. iii. Tracy Lynn, b 21 August 1975.
- 2043. iv. William, b 1 May 1978.

888. BEVERLY[7] JEANETTE SHIPTON (d/o Beatrice[6] Peckham Shipton #378), b 8 October 1919 at Mitchell, SD; m 10 August 1940, **Kenneth Guenchner**, b 17 June 1912 at Bridgewater, SD, s/o Otto Guenchner (mother died years ago). They live at Rapid City, SD.

Children, surname GUENCHNER:
- + 2044. i. Sue[8] Ellen, b 26 August 1942.

889. VIRGINIA[7] LOLA SHIPTON (d/o Beatrice[6] Peckham Shipton #378), b 25 September 1922 at Alexandria, SD; m 26 January 1944 at Sioux Falls, SD, **Roland Bauer**, b 14 June 1921, s/o Martin Richard and Clara (Phillips) Bauer. They live in Sioux Falls; James works for American Freight System, a trucking firm.

Children, surname BAUER:
- + 2045. i. Shari[8] Bea, b 5 January 1945.
- 2046. ii. Thomas Arthur, b 16 May 1947 at Sioux Falls. He is manager for American Freight at Nashville, TN; not married.
- + 2047. iii. James Kenneth, b 3 May 1951.

890. ARTHA[7] JANE SHIPTON (d/o Beatrice[6] Peckham Shipton #378), b 16 February 1932 at Sioux Falls, SD, m November 1953, **Glenn Dennis Rognrud**, b 22 May 1921 at Minneapolis, MN, s/o Walter and Evelyn Rognrud. Glenn is a salesman.

Children, surname ROGNRUD:
- + 2048. i. Steven[8] Dennis, b 18 September 1954.
- 2049. ii. Mark Shipton, b 21 July 1956; m Pamela McDonald, June 1977. First child due 1 October 1984. Mark works for his father in real estate.
- 2050. iii. Bradley Thomas, b 16 November 1957. He m Mary Ann — 15 October 1983. Both are registered pharmacists and live in

Minneapolis.

2051. iv. Susan Kay, b 3 January 1961. She works for a travel agency.

891. BETTY[7] JEAN HATHORN (d/o Harriet[6] Peckham Hathorn #379), b 15 April 1921 at Des Moines, IA; m 1942, **Lowell Baal,** s/o John and Genevieve (Wheat) Baal, b 1920 at Des Moines IA. Betty divorced 1944. Died 17 December 1969 at Wilmington, DE. Betty Jean m/2 1945 at Louisville, KY, **W. H. Nesbitt** of Eugene, OR.

Child, surname BAAL:
- 2052. i. Marriann[8] H., b 19 August 1943. Died 14 November 1958 in Wilmington.

893. PHILLIP[7] DURWARD PECKHAM (s/o Ellsworth[6] Peckham #380), b 6 March 1927 at Minneapolis, MN; m 28 January 1950, **Jean Elizabeth Ross,** b 25 November 1928 at Madison, WI, d/o Joseph Ambrose and Adeline Mary (Pschorr) Ross. He is a professional engineer.

Children, surname PECKHAM:
- + 2053. i. Timothy[8] Joseph, b 6 June 1950.
- 2054. ii. Daniel Phillip, b 11 October 1951 at Milwaukee.
- 2055. iii. David Ellsworth, b 28 February 1958 at Milwaukee.
- 2056. iv. Steven Louis, b 2 January 1960 at Milwaukee; m 7 September 1982, Paula Eileen Neumann at Glen Ellyn, IL; she b 24 February 1959 at Glen Ellyn, d/o William and Carol Neumann.
- 2057. v. James John, b 4 September 1964 at Milwaukee.

894. JOHN[7] RICHARD PECKHAM (s/o Ellsworth[6] Peckham #380), b 14 April 1930 at Madison, WI; m 4 June 1955 at Sheboygan, WI, **Clarabelle Margaret Goebel,** b 9 September 1933, d/o Adam and Cecilia (Stahl) Goebel.

Children, surname PECKHAM:
- 2058. i. Marcus[8] John, b 30 August 1956 at Tucson, AZ; m 8 October 1983, Sandra Lee Gutzmann. Marcus is an insurance agent.
- 2059. ii. Michelle Cecile, b 7 September 1958 at Fond du Lac, WI; m 30 June 1984, David Waldoch, s/o Robert and Betty Waldoch. Michelle is a computer technician.
- 2060. iii. Jennifer Maytum, b 27 October 1963 at Watertown, WI, m 4 September 1982, Todd Leslie Melby, s/o Tom and Ruth Melby. Jennifer is a nurse.
- 2061. iv. Dean Aaron, b 6 February 1965 at Madison.

2062. v. Adam Paul, b 1 September 1967 at Minneapolis, WI.

895. DONALD[7] DEAN PECKHAM (s/o Donald[6] Seth Peckham #381), b 8 February 1932; m/1 August 1952, **Dolores Pedersen**; divorced; m/2 January 1955, **Shirley** —.

Children, surname PECKAHAM:
- 2063. i. Dean[8].
- 2064. ii. Deanna.

896. JANET[7] MAY PECKHAM (d/o Donald[6] Seth Peckham #381), b 30 July 1934; m 30 June 1956, **Verne Billings**.

Children, surname BILLINGS:
- 2065. i. Caroly[8] Denise, b 22 September 1958.
- 2066. ii. Bryon Wayne, b 1 November 1959.

898. JAMES[7] MAYTUM PECKHAM (s/o Donald[6] Seth Peckham #381), b 13 December 1938; m **Hilda Schumacher**.

Children, surname PECKHAM:
- 2067. i. Scott[8] Allen.
- 2068. ii. Steve.
- 2069. iii. Beth Ann.

899. HOWARD[7] JOHN PECKHAM (s/o Howard[6] John Peckham #382), b 25 March 1934, at Sioux Falls, SD; m 24 July 1955 at Sioux Falls, SD, **Gertrude "Trudy" Anne Aker**, d/o Edwin and Dora (Anderson) Aker, b 2 November 1934 at Sioux Falls. He is business manager for medical buildings I and II at 1200-1201 South Euclid in Sioux Falls.

Children, surname PECKHAM:
- + 2070. i. Anne[8] Christine, b 29 November 1956.
- 2071. ii. Mary Kathryn, b 18 April 1959 at Bolling Air Force Base, Maryland. She is a Rhodes Scholar at Oxford University, England.
- 2072. iii. Thomas John, b 21 September 1964 at Sioux Falls.

900. MARY[7] ELIA PECKHAM (d/o Howard[6] John Peckham #382), b 16 March 1938; m 26 June 1965 at Seattle, WA, **John Galgoczy**, s/o Kalman and Terez Galgoczy, b 23 February 1926 in Hungary, near Budapest. Mary is a teacher; John is a design engineer, partner in Trigon Co.

Children, surname GALGOCZY, both born at Seattle, WA:
 2073. i. Stephan[8] Kalman, b 13 October 1969.
 2074. ii. David John, b 2 February 1973.

902. DEAN[7] STANTON OLSEN (s/o Norma[6] Peckham Olsen #383), b 22 April 1935 at Sioux Falls, SD; m 6 May 1960, Dallas, TX, **Judy Thompson**. Dean is activities director at Katelli Real Estate Co.; lives at Anaheim, CA.

Children, surname OLSEN:
 2075. i. Christopher[8] Reed, b 28 March 1961 in IA.
 2076. ii. Wendy Elizabeth, b 7 November 1964 at Anaheim.

903. DAVID[7] PECKHAM OLSEN (s/o Norma[6] Peckham Olsen #383), b 27 May 1939 at Sioux Falls, SD; m 8 August 1958, **Lynda Larson**, b near Egan, SD, 19 January 1939. He has a doctor's degree in physics and teaches at Metropolitan University at Denver, CO.

Children, surname OLSEN:
 2077. i. Jeffrey[8] David, b 21 February 1959 at Sioux Falls.
 2078. ii. Jennifer Lyn, b 18 April 1961 at Sioux Falls.
 2079. iii. Rebecca Ann, b 20 December 1964 at Norman, OK.

904. BARBARA[7] JOANNE OLSEN (d/o Norma[6] Peckham Olsen #383), b 21 August 1940 at Sioux Falls, SD; m 19 September 1961, **Erwin L. Williams**, b 15 August 1938 at CO. Erwin is vice-president of an architectural firm in San Francisco, CA. Barbara is a teacher's helper in San Rafael, CA, where they live.

Children, surname WILLIAMS:
 2080. i. Mark[8] Talbot, b 4 April 1963 at Champaign, IL.
 2081. ii. Laurie Lee, b 21 October 1964 at Moline, IL.
 2082. iii. Elizabeth Lynn, b 6 August 1968 at Mill Valley, CA.

907. CAROLE[7] JANE PECKHAM (d/o Francis[6] Herbert Peckham #384), b 6 February 1943 at Sioux Falls, SD; m 5 July 1963 at Sioux Falls, **Donald Katzenmeyer**, s/o Jason Curtis and Katherine (Caspers) Katzenmeyer, b 14 March 1942 at Minneapolis, MN. Donald works for American Breeders Service. Carole owns The Cheddar Wheel, a cheese shop.

Children, surname KATZENMEYER, all born at Sioux Falls:

2083. i. Kim[8] Elizabeth, b 2 April 1964.
2084. ii. Kelly Elaine, b 26 June 1967.
2085. iii. Robert Peckham, b 5 January 1969.

914. WILMA[7] MAXINE JELMELAND (d/o Nettie[6] Palmer Jelmeland #390), b 2 November 1921 at Mitchell, SD; m/1 15 March 1947 at Huron SD, **Vern Charles Erickson**; divorced September 1950; m/2 4 February 1956 at Huron, SD, **Maynard William McDonnell**, s/o James M. and Sarah (Keegan) McDonnell, b 20 October 1919. He was a civil engineer and worked for Amco Steel, Sioux Falls, SD. Maynard d 20 December 1966; m/3 29 February 1968 at Des Moines, IA, **Bob Ray Holdren**. Bob was a Professor of Economics, Iowa State University; d 1 January 1980; m/4 9 July 1983 at Nevada, IA, **Ralph Marvin Brugger** a Doctor of Internal Medicine, McFarland Clinic, Ames, IA. Ralph b 25 February 1928 in Erie, PA, s/o Edward and Dorothy (Demuling) Brugger.

Child, surname McDONNELL:
    2086. i. Michaela[8] Wynne, b 27 December 1956 at Huron, SD; m Bruce Howard Kolberg, 16 June 1984 Iowa City, IA. No children. Both are doctors: Bruce in OB-GYN and Michaela in Dermatology.

915. DONALD[7] KENNETH JELMELAND (s/o Nettie[6] Palmer Jelmeland #390), b 12 January 1924 at Mitchell, SD; m April 1946, **Vera June Foster**, d/o George Earl and Karen (Stamstad) Foster, she b 16 June 1924 at Devil's Lake, ND. Donald is retired from Marathon Corp., Wausau, WI. They live at Lake Lokomis in summer and spend the winters at Fort Myers, FL.

Child, surname JELMELAND:
+ 2087. i. Richard[8] Kenneth, b 13 March 1947.
+ 2088. ii. David, b 4 October 1948.

916. HARVEY[7] VINCENT JELMELAND (s/o Nettie[6] Palmer Jelmeland #390), b 9 November 1925 at Miller, SD; m **Ethel Jennings**, b at Del Norte, CO, m 31 January 1956, Colorado Springs, d/o William and Marie (Hardin) Jennings. He is retired from the Denver Post and spends summers at Lake Lokomis, near Lake Tomahawk, WI and winters at Fort Myers, FL. They were divorced June 1971 at Denver, CO. No children.

918. DONALD[7] GORDON PETERSON (s/o Laura[6] Vining Peterson

#392), b 11 June 1924; m September 1948/49, **Bonnie Foss**, b 20 March 1927 at Canby, MN, d/o Oscar and Esther Foss. They live at Brooklyn Center, MN.

Children, surname PETERSON:
    2089.   i.   Steven[8], b 12 July 1949, Minneapolis, MN.
    2090.   ii.   Tim, b 7 October 1951, Minneapolis.
    2091.   iii.   Mark, b 29 June 1954, Minneapolis.

919. DONA[7] JANE PETERSON (d/o Laura[6] Vining Peterson #392), b 15 December 1925; m 29 June 1945 at Minneapolis, MN, **Paul Allen Curtis**, b 28 February 1924 at Hopkins, MN, s/o William and Gladys Curtis. Dona & Paul live at Anchorage, AK.

Children, surname CURTIS:
    2092.   i.   Paul[8] Rocky, b 17 November 1946, Minneapolis.
    2093.   ii.   Allen, b 14 February 1950, Minneapolis.

920. BEVERLY[7] ANN PETERSON (d/o Laura[6] Vining Peterson #392), b 17 January 1932; m 5 December 1951 at Abilene, TX, **Duane Leon Gates**, b 25 July 1929 s/o Leon and Harriet Gates. Duane was in theater business; they live at Azle, TX.

Child, surname GATES:
    2094.   i.   Michael[8], b 14 March 1955 at Abilene, TX.

921. WAYNE[7] FORBES (s/o Ralph[6] Jess Forbes #393), b 16 January 1933 at Wisconsin Rapids, WI.

Child, surname FORBES:
    2095.   i.   Darcy[8], m Keith Krupinski.

922. DANNY[7] FORBES (s/o Ralph[6] Jess Forbes #393), b 9 October 1946; m 16 October 1965, in Wisconsin Rapids, WI, **Terre Arndt**. Danny is employed by Nekoosa Paper Co., also owns a mobil home park.

Child, surname FORBES:
    2096.   i.   Angela[8] Vonn, b 18 May 1966 at Wisconsin Rapids.

923. DAVID[7] ADAMS (s/o Mabel[6] Vining Adams #394), b 28 February 1934; m/1 **Jeanette Harris**. David m/2 **Madeline Hewen**. No children. David works at Abbott Laboratories, Chicago, IL.

Children, surname ADAMS:

2097. i. Fred, b 21 November 1958.
2098. ii. Barbara, b 13 October 1959.
2099. iii. John, b 5 March 1962.
2100. iv. Audrey, b 5 June 1964.

924. ALVIN[7] ADAMS (s/o Mabel[6] Vining Adams #394), b 17 October 1936; m **Frances Ann** —. He works for Huntington Beach, CA Water Dept.

Children, surname ADAMS:
2101. i. Dawn, b 17 November 1960.
2102. ii. Scott Edward, b 6 March 1962.
2103. iii. Mark, b 19 June 1963.

925. LARRY[7] ADAMS (s/o Mabel[6] Vining Adams #394), b 22 December 1947; m **Carol** —. Larry works for water department at Gurnee, IL.

Child, surname ADAMS:
2104. i. Andrea[9] Lynn, b 13 April 1971.

926. SHIRLEY[7] ANN VINING (d/o Raymond[6] Hans Vining #395), b 2 June 1936 at Farmer, SD; m/1 26 November 1954 at Ethan, SD, **David Fogner**. Shirley Ann m/2 22 November 1967 at Colorado Springs, **Ronald Jackson**. Ronald is and executive for National Farmers Union Insurance Co., Denver.

Children, surname FOGNER:
+ 2105. i. Davida[8] Marie, b 5 September 1956.
  2106. ii. Gwendolyn, b 31 October 1958 at Ottawa; m 22 November 1983 at Denver, CO, Paul Nappo.
  2107. iii. Douglas, b 27 May 1960.
  2108. iv. Daniel, b 27 May 1960, (twin).

Child, surname JACKSON:
2109. v. Heather[8] Lee, b 17 February 1971 at Colorado Springs.

927. CAROLYN[7] RAE VINING (d/o Raymond[6] Hans Vining #395), b 23 March 1939 at Farmer, SD; m 5 June 1961, **Robert Greenfield**. They run "Lookout Mountain Realty" in Spearfish, SD. Carolyn is a registered nurse and Robert was vice-principal of a school.

Children, surname GREENFIELD:
2110. i. Roberta[8] Rae, b 15 April 1962 at Lawton, OK.

2111. ii. Rene Lynn, b 26 June 1963 Sioux Falls, SD.
2112. iii. Paula Marie, b 10 July 1967.

928. HELEN[7] MARIE VINING (d/o Edward[6] Harrison Vining #396), b 26 April 1940 at Ethan, SD; m 30 November 1958 at Mitchell, SD, **Donald Glen Ewing**. They live at Sedalia, MO.

Children, surname EWING:
    2113. i. Glenda[8], b 31 July 1960 at Mitchell, SD; m Thomas Caniglia, 7 April 1984 at Omaha, NB; they live at Rapid City, SD. Thomas is Chef at Covered Wagon in Rapid City. No children.
+ 2114. ii. Janet Marie, b 23 May 1962.
    2115. iii. Karen Sue, b 16 February 1966.
    2116. iv. Kurtis Glen, b 27 May 1971.

929. THOMAS[7] WILLIAM VINING (s/o Edward[6] Harrison Vining #396), b 25 January 1943 at Parkston, SD; m 2 January 1966 at Reading, PA, **Barbara DiLullo**; m/2 about 1981, **Lena —**, no children.

Child, surname VINING:
    2117. i. Holly Jo, b 1 February 1969 at Mitchell, SD.

930. EDWARD[7] WARREN VINING (s/o Edward[6] Harrison Vining #396), b 21 April 1944 at Parkston, SD; m 9 June 1967 at Mitchell, SD, **Janet Lee Washburn**. Edward lives at Carlsbad, NM; Edward has the children and is manager of hardwood lumber yard.

Children, surname VINING, both born at Mitchell:
    2118. i. Vickie[8] Lee, b 9 July 1969.
    2119. ii. Jason Edward, b 27 June 1970.

931. MARY[7] MARGARET VINING (d/o Edward[6] Harrison Vining #396), b 21 May 1947 at Parkston, SD; m/1 11 November 1967, **Leonard White** at Worthington, MN. Leonard, a telephone repairman, left Mary when Krista was nearly 3 years old. Mary m/2 20 Nov 1983, **Myril Ferguson** of Worthington, MN, where they live; he drives a gas transport.

Children, surname WHITE:
    2120. i. Linette[8] Marie, b 24 January 1968 at Mitchell, SD.
    2121. ii. Leslie Michelle, b 27 October 1970.
    2122. iii. Krista Anne, b 15 June 1973.

932. JUDY[7] VINING (d/o Charles[6] Lester Vining #397), b 31 July 1941;

m **Duane Schroeder**. They live at Cambridge.

Children, surname SCHROEDER:
- 2123. i. Steven[8].
- 2124. ii. Jeffery.

933. JOANNE[7] **VINING** (d/o Charles[6] Lester Vining #397), married several times.

Children, surname unknown:
- 2125. i. Wendy[8].
- 2126. ii. Eddie.
- 2127. iii. Cory.

934. LINDA[7] **VINING** (d/o Charles[6] Lester Vining #397), m **Glen Nelson**.

Children, surname NELSON:
- 2128. i. Cory[8].
- 2129. ii. Jamie.
- 2130. iii. Matthew.

936. BARBARA[7] **JOYCE WILSON** (d/o Joyce[6] Vining Wilson #398), b 26 January 1944 at Lakewood, OH; m 10 June 1967 at Minneapolis, MN, **Ernest Leon Surprenant**, b 3 January 1934 at East Grand Forks, MN, s/o Ernest James and Angeline (Vigen) Surprenant. Ernest is customer engineer for Control Data Corp. They live at Washington, IL.

Children, surname SURPRENANT:
- 2131. i. Glenn[8] James, b 25 March 1971 at Hinsdale, IL.
- 2132. ii. Lee Ray, b 28 February 1976 at Joliet, Il.

937. JOHN[7] **DAVID WILSON** (s/o Joyce[6] Vining Wilson #398), b 4 December 1946 at Minneapolis, MN; m/1 9 March 1968 at Minneapolis, **Joan Stout**, b 5 January 1946 at Des Moines, IA, d/o James Martin & Barbara Louise (Langland) Stout. John is a metal sculptor and lives at Houston, MN. John and Joan divorced in 197–; they had three children. John m/2 29 December 1982, **Linda Louise Riddle**.

Children, surname WILSON:
- 2133. i. Krishna[8] Robert, b 11 June 1971 at Long Beach, CA.
- 2134. ii. David Christopher, b 7 February 1974 at Minneapolis.
- 2135. iii. Cecelia Sunshine, b 30 May 1976 at Minneapolis.

2136. iv. Celeste[8] Rose, b 28 December 1981 at Winona Co., MN.

938. JAMES[7] RICHARD WILSON (s/o Joyce[6] Vining Wilson #398), b 12 March 1948 at Minneapolis, MN; m 29 March 1973 at Tustin, CA, **Lashelli Sue Mitchell**, b 1 Oct 1951 at Beach Grove, IN, d/o William L'Dell and Sonya Ann (Lawyer) Mitchell. When last known James was manager of Rapid Oil Change. He and Lashelli are divorced. He and the two boys went back to Kentucky to live.

Children, surname WILSON:
    2137. i. Nicolette[8] Sunshine, b 15 May 1975 at Honolulu, HI.
    2138. ii. Justin Teria, b 18 July 1976 at Honolulu.
    2139. iii. John Vining, b 16 September 1980 at Bowling Green, KY.

939. SHERYL[7] ANN KOCH (d/o Lilas[6] Vining Koch #399), b 15 January 1949 at Blue Earth, MN; m at Blue Earth, 20 June 1970, **James Alvin Richardson**. Sheryl is a legal secretary in County Attorney's office at Glencoe, MN. James is an engineering aide for Eden Prairie, MN as a draftsman.

Child, surname RICHARDSON:
    2140. i. Jason[8] James, b 4 October 1978 at Cloquet, MN. He was adopted in November 1978.

940. JOYCE[7] CAROL KOCH (d/o Lilas[6] Vining Koch #399), b 20 April 1952 at Blue Earth, MN; m 23 June 1973 at Blue Earth, **Charles Robert More**. Joyce is a licensed child caregiver for Fairbault Co., Blue Earth. Charles is in the Fertilizer business at Blue Earth.

Children, surname MORE:
    2141. i. Kelly[8] Rae, b 11 March 1977, Blue Earth.
    2142. ii. Angela Joy, b 10 September 1978, Blue Earth.
    2143. iii. Thomas Charles, b 27 November 1989, Blue Earth.

942. MARY[7] CURTIS VINING (d/o Curtis[6] Harry Vining #400), b 24 April 1955 at Minneapolis, MN; m 24 March 1979, **James Radomski**.

Children, surname RADOMSKI:
    2144. i. Lauren[8], b 31 July 1985, Minneapolis.
    2145. ii. Allison, b 7 September 1989, Minneapolis.

943. NANCY[7] DALE VINING (d/o Curtis[6] Harry Vining #400), b 18 June 1957; m **Bradley Allan Holmberg**.

The Seventh Generation 341

Children, surname HOLMBERG:
   2146. i. Kyle[8] Vining, b 25 September 1986, Mankato, MN.
   2147. ii. David Vining, b 24 November 1988, Mankato.
   2148. iii. Kristi Vining, b 30 April 1990, Mankato.

945. VERNON[7] EVERETT POGUE (s/o Beulah[6] Roberts Pogue #401), b 20 October 1931, Town of Scott, Columbia Co., WI; m 17 October 1953 at Marshall, WI, **Delores A. Scheel**, b 17 July 1934 at Pleasant Springs, WI.

Children, surname POGUE, all born at Columbia Co:
+ 2149. i. Steven[8] V., b 26 March 1957; m 23 June 1984, Darcy Suprise at Sun Prairie, WI.
   2150. ii. Kathleen R., b 31 May 1960; d 12 September 1960.
   2151. iii. Sharon A., b 19 June 1961; m 20 June 1988 at Sun Prairie, WI, Alan Frank.
   2152. iv. Susan R., b 15 January 1968; m 28 October 1989, Todd Kubly.

946. ROY[7] ROGER POGUE (s/o Beulah[6] Roberts Pogue #401), b 21 May 1933 in Town of Scott, Columbia Co., WI; m 8 December 1957, **Ruth Shaben**, b 12 May 1938. Retired.

Children, surname POGUE:
+ 2153. i. Barbara[8] J., b 20 November 1958.
+ 2154. ii. Bonnie J., b 22 June 1960.
   2155. iii. Daniel J., b 5 April 1962 at Portage.
   2156. iv. Juanita P., b 20 April 1964 at Portage, married and lives in MI.
   2157. v. Dale E., b 14 April 1967 at Portage; d 18 April 1984.
   2158. vi. Fay F., b 25 October 1969 at Fort Atkinson, WI.
   2159. vii. John O., b 20 May 1973 at Fort Atkinson.
   2160. viii. Paul D., b 4 December 1978.

948. IONE[7] PEARL POGUE (d/o Beulah[6] Roberts Pogue #401), b 23 October 1938, Town of Scott at Columbia Co., WI; m 4 June 1960, **Floyd H. Gustrowsky**, b 26 January 1939 at Dane Co., WI.

Children, surname GUSTROWSKY, all born at Dane Co:
+ 2161. i. Wanda[8] P., b 2 September 1961.
+ 2162. ii. Ramona M., b 1 August 1963.
+ 2163. iii. Linda G., b 26 February 1965.
   2164. iv. Lloyd H., 4 March 1969.

2165. v. Verna G., b 3 August 1971.

949. IRENE[7] POGUE (d/o Beulah[6] Roberts Pogue #401), b 23 October 1938, Town of Scott Columbia Co., WI, twin of Ione; m 2 August 1958 at Sun Prairie, WI, **George B. Weisensel**, b 30 August 1927 at Sun Prairie. George works for John Deere and they live in rural Sun Prairie.

Children, surname WEISENSEL, all born at Dane Co, WI:
+ 2166. i. Margaret[8] R., b 26 April 1959.
+ 2167. ii. Rebecca G., b 23 August 1960.
   2168. iii. Phyllis E., b 21 October 1961.
   2169. iv. Bruce L., b 6 January 1963.
   2170. v. Natalie C., b 24 May 1964.
   2171. vi. Arlene P., b 21 July 1966; was to m 16 March 1991, Brent Danz.
   2172. vii. Lisa M., b 11 April 1968.
   2173. viii. Joseph M., b 19 March 1972.
   2174. ix. David C, b 25 June 1974.
   2175. x. Jill E., b 9 November 1976.
   2176. xi. Tina E., b 13 February 1979.

950. JANICE[7] ROBERTS (d/o Roger[6] Wayman Roberts #402), b 7 September 1940 at Portage, WI; m 16 June 1962, **Charles E. Miller**. Charles and Janice are teachers at Glen Ellyn, IL.

Children, surname MILLER, both born at Glen Ellyn:
   2177. i. Heidi[8], b 24 August 1966.
   2178. ii. Jeffery, b 19 April 1969.

951. ROGER[7] WILLIAM ROBERTS (s/o Roger[6] Wayman Roberts #402), b 11 January 1943 at Milwaukee, WI; m 11 August 1979 at Palos Verdes Estates, CA, **Melinda Ann Rapp**. Roger served in the U.S. Navy and later was employed by Continental Airlines.

Children, surname ROBERTS:
   2179. i. Dustin[8] William, b 5 March 1981 at Redondo Beach, CA.
   2180. ii. Jessica.

952. DOLORES[7] JANETTE DALTON (d/o Ruth[6] Roberts Dalton #403), b 23 December 1933 at Pardeeville, Columbia Co., WI; m 2 May 1953 at Portage, WI, **Wayne Meiller**, b 18 January 1931 at Madison, WI, s/o Arthur and Lillian (Bruce) Meiller.

Children, surname MEILLER:
- 2181. i. Ricky[8] L., b 26 July 1954; m 14 August 1976, Mary Galer. He is a music teacher at Baraboo, WI.
- 2182. ii. Brian, b 28 April 1961; m 30 July 1988, April Johnson. They live and work in Madison, WI.

953. MONNA[7] ELAINE DALTON (d/o Ruth[6] Roberts Dalton #403), b 4 October 1937 at Dalton, WI; m 21 April 1956 at Dalton, Green Lake Co., **Billy R. Aldrich**, b 18 April 1935 at Town of Kingston, Green Lake Co., WI, s/o Raymond and Myrtle (Bremner) Aldrich. Billy was a truck driver; now retired.

Children, surname ALDRICH, both born at Madison, WI:
- 2183. i. Julie[8] Elaine, b 7 December 1960.
- 2184. ii. Amy Elizabeth, b 7 December 1962; m/1 4 Feb 1984, Patrick McBride; m/2 Michael McGettigan, 11 August 1989 for the second time; they live in DeForest, WI.

954. RICHARD[7] ORIN DALTON (s/o Ruth[6] Roberts Dalton #403), b 15 March 1940 at Portage, WI; m 25 June 1966 at Kendall, WI, **Mildred Bunk**, b 4 May 1947 at Kendall, the d/o Francis and Gertrude (Huschka) Bunk. Richard is a Major in the U.S. Army; they live at Elk Grove Village, IL; retired.

Children, surname DALTON:
- 2185. i. Richard[8] O., b 8 July 1968 at Fort Polk, LA; m 3 September 1988 at Fort Huachuca, AZ, Laura Ann Ferguson.
- 2186. ii. Jeffery S., b 24 June 1969 at Lawton, OK. Richard and Jeff live at Tucson, AZ, and going to college.

955. RUSSELL[7] CHARLES DALTON (s/o Ruth[6] Roberts Dalton #403), b 5 February 1946 at Portage, WI; m 9 December 1972 at Adams, WI, **Nola Moore**, d/o Dale and Beulah (Lincicum) Moore, b 10 March 1947. Russell served in the U.S. Army; is employed by General Telephone Co., at Reedsville, WI.

Children, surname DALTON:
- 2187. i. Darcy[8] D., b 7 June 1973 at Sauk Co., WI.
- 2188. ii. Darin D., b 22 September 1974.
- 2189. iii. Danny D., b 6 December 1975.

956. MARILYN[7] STOLLFUS (d/o Amber[6] Roberts Stollfus #404), b

22 October 1937 at Columbia Co., WI; m 12 July 1958 at Madison, WI, **James Hopper**. Now divorced; Marilyn works in an insurance office and lives in Madison WI.

Children, surname HOPPER:
- 2190. i. Kim[8] Renee, b 7 July 1959 at Fairbanks, AK; m 18 December 1982 at New Baltimore, MI, Mark Berland; live in CA.
- 2191. ii. James D., b 28 February 1962 at New Baltimore, MI.

957. WAYNE[7] GEORGE STOLLFUS (s/o Amber[6] Roberts Stollfus #404), b 15 May 1944 in Columbia Co., WI; m 20 December 1965, **Carol Sommers**. Wayne served in the U.S. Army Air Force. He is now employed in real estate; Carol is an elementary school teacher at Boise, ID, where they live.

Children, surname STOLLFUS:
- 2192. i. Brennen[8], b 1 December 1970.
- 2193. ii. Nathan, b 8 September 1976.

961. GORDON[7] LYLE JENKINS (s/o Ronald[6] Ralph Jenkins #406), b 6 September 1945 at Dalton, WI; m 14 August 1976, **Mary M. Redeker**.

Children, surname JENKINS:
- 2194. i. Pamela[8], b 3 October 1979.
- 2195. ii. Jeffery, b 8 May 1981.
- 2196. iii. Gregory, b 22 October 1982.

963. NEAL[7] EDWARD JENKINS (s/o Ronald[6] Ralph Jenkins #406), b at Portage, WI; m 23 August 1980, **Alyson Tasch**.

Children surname JENKINS:
- 2197. i. Benjamin[8] Neal, b 9 October 1981.
- 2198. ii. Joshua Lee, b 19 January 1984.

964. JAMES[7] ORRIS JENKINS (s/o Orris[6] Durwood Jenkins #407), b 10 January 1942 at Waupun, WI, m 7 July 1962 at Markesan, **Barbara Walker**, b Kingston, WI; divorced 7 July 1982 at Markesan, WI.

Children, surname JENKINS:
- 2199. i. Kenneth[8] James, b 11 May 1963.
- 2200. ii. Laura Lorraine, b 19 April 1966.
- 2201. iii. Rustin James, b 14 February 1970.
- 2202. iv. Tricia Cherie, b 30 May 1971.

965. STEPHEN[7] ROY JENKINS (s/o Orris[6] Durwood Jenkins #407), b 15 April 1948 at Waupun, WI; m 28 January 1967, **Sharon Terbeest**.
Children, surname JENKINS:
- 2203. i. Sheila[8] Sue, b 30 September 1968.
- 2204. ii. Scott Stephen, b 19 July 1971.
- 2205. iii. Shannon Carol, b 5 January 1973.
- 2206. iv. Shane Roy, b 30 June 1975.
- 2207. v. Shawn Ray, b 30 June 1978.
- 2208. vi. Sarah Ann, b 28 January 1981.

966. LINDA[7] RAE JENKINS (d/o Orris[6] Durwood Jenkins #407), b 18 August 1949 at Waupun, WI; m 7 September 1968, **Norman Penke**.
Children, surname PENKE:
- 2209. i. Michael[8] Ray, b 27 February 1970.
- 2210. ii. Sandra Rae, b 4 September 1982.

967. DOUGLAS[7] LEE JENKINS (s/o Orris[6] Durwood Jenkins #407), b 5 June 1952 at Waupun, WI; m 28 December 1972, **Kathleen Meyer**.
Children, surname JENKINS:
- 2211. i. Valorie[8] Louise, b 8 August 1975.
- 2212. ii. Jason Lee, b 11 December 1979.

968. VIVIAN[7] CAROL JENKINS (d/o Orris[6] Durwood Jenkins #407), b 11 April 1954 at Waupun, WI; m 6 September 1975, **Michael Geoffrion**.
Children, surname GEOFFRION:
- 2213. i. Joseph[8] Paul, b 12 February 1978.
- 2214. ii. Lucas Michael, b 1 July 1981.

971. CAROLINE[7] MAY HAYNES (d/o Lucille[6] Jenkins Haynes #408), b 23 March 1948 at Portage, WI; m 9 August 1969, **Michael Bolghrin**.
Children, surname BOLGHRIN:
- 2215. i. Josephine[8] Elizabeth, b 2 December 1977.
- 2216. ii. Jessica May, b 5 September 1981.

972. COLLEEN[7] JOYCE HAYNES (d/o Lucille[6] Jenkins Haynes #408), b 26 July 1952 at Portage, WI; m **Paul Comacho**; later divorced.
Children, surname COMACHO:

2217. i. Dawn[8] Marie, b 14 March 1972.
2218. ii. Angela Louise, b 15 October 1975.

974. KENNETH[7] **DUANE JENKINS** (s/o Stanley[6] William Jenkins #409), b 1 April 1946 at Sheboygan Falls, WI; m 6 November 1965, **Judith Morrison**.

Children, surname JENKINS:
2219. i. Theresa[8] Rene, b 5 September 1966.
2220. ii. Karen Jean, b 14 October 1967.
2221. iii. Richard Carl, b 2 March 1970.
2222. iv. Daniel Lee, b 22 August 1978.

975. BEVERLY[7] **JEAN JENKINS** (d/o Stanley[6] William Jenkins #409), b 27 August 1948 at Sheboygan Falls, WI; m 20 March 1970, **Ronald Haag**.

Children, surname HAAG:
2223. i. Randall[8] Alan, b 20 March 1970.
2224. ii. Gerald David, b 13 April 1971.
2225. iii. William Richard, b 6 July 1973.
2226. iv. Victoria Lynn, b 27 November 1975.
2227. v. Paul Michael, b 2 February 1977.

976. ALAN[7] **RAY JENKINS** (s/o Stanley[6] William Jenkins #409), b 30 April 1951 at Sheboygan Falls, WI; m 12 April 1980, **Patricia Wehrmann**.

Children, surname JENKINS:
2228. i. Monica[8] Marie, b 15 April 1982.
2229. ii. Joseph Alan, b 29 August 1983.

977. DENNIS[7] **LEE JENKINS** (s/o Stanley[6] William Jenkins #409), b 26 March 1954 at Sheboygan Falls, WI; m 2 November 1974, **Kathy Meyer**. Dennis d 6 July 1977.

Child, surname JENKINS:
2230. i. Brian[8] James, b 21 January 1976.

981. RUSSELL[7] **EARL JENKINS** (s/o Donald[6] Earl Jenkins #410), b 11 December 1956 at Madison, WI; m 3 May 1980, **Paula Stier**.

Child, surname JENKINS:

2231. i. Nathaniel[8] Michael, b 15 September 1981.

984. GARY[7] LEE JENKINS (s/o Vernon[6] Jess Jenkins #411), b 6 August 1956 at Waupun, WI; m 12 February 1977, **Louise Dickerson**.

Children, surname JENKINS:
    2232. i. Amie[8] Elizabeth, b 15 July 1977.
    2233. ii. Carrie Marie, b 7 October 1980.
    2234. iii. Amber Louise, b 4 June 1982.

985. LARRY[7] LYNN JENKINS (s/o Vernon[6] Jess Jenkins #411), b 7 August 1958 at Waupun, WI; m 14 May 1977.

Children, surname JENKINS:
    2235. i. Jessica[8] Lynn, b 14 June 1979.
    2236. ii. Joshua Donald, b 22 September 1980.
    2237. iii. Justin Lyle, b 31 August 1982.

992. DOUGLAS[7] BRENEMAN (s/o Floy[6] Gorsuch Breneman #416), b 7 October 1942 at Portage, WI; m 5 September 1964 at Pardeeville, Marcellon Co., WI, **Rosalind Gail Sundsmo**, d/o John and Hilda Sundsmo, b 26 December 1945 at Chicago, IL. They live on a farm near his parents.

Children, surname BRENEMAN, all born at Portage:
    2238. i. Gregory[8] Douglas, b 23 March 1965.
    2239. ii. Timothy Douglas, b 24 February 1968.
    2240. iii. Valori Rose, b 22 May 1970.
    2241. iv. Blakely Douglas, b 31 August 1973.

993. RICHARD[7] BRENEMAN (s/o Floy[6] Gorsuch Breneman #416), b 9 February 1950 at Portage, WI; m 11 November 1972 at Portage, **Sandra Jean Mohr**, d/o Merlyn and Helen Mohr, b 27 September 1952 at Portage. They live on Richard's parent's farm at Dalton, WI.

Children, surname BRENEMAN, both born at Portage:
    2242. i. Matthew[8] James, b 11 February 1975.
    2243. ii. Wendy Lynn, b 12 August 1976.

994. BETH[7] BRENEMAN (d/o Floy[6] Gorsuch Breneman #416), b 22 July 1955 at Portage, WI; m 2 April 1977 at Dalton, WI, **Keith Marshall Hines**, s/o Clarence and Marilyn Hines, b 4 April 1954 at Northfield, MN. Keith works for Northrup Seed Co. at Stanton, MN.

Children, surname HINES, both born at Faribault, MN:
  2244.   i. Rebecca[8] Jo, b 10 June 1979.
  2245. ii. Brian Zachary, b 10 June 1981.

1012. CLIFFORD[7] CARLYLE WILLIAMSON (s/o Luvia[6] Chowen Williamson #423), b 10 June 1930 at Berwyn, Alberta, Canada; m 18 June 1955 in Berwyn, **Annie Trochanowski**, b 16 April 1933 at LacCardinal, Alberta, d/o Alexander and Mary (Palochuk) Trochanowski, both born in Poland. Clifford is municipal accountant and holds the position of Treasurer for Town of Spruce Grove, Alberta.

Children, surname WILLIAMSON:
+ 2246.   i. Deborah[8] Lynn, b 17 August 1956.
  2247. ii. Craig Alexander Clifford, b 14 March 1958 at Berwyn. He lives in Fernie, BC and works in the mining and forestry industry. Not married.
  2248. iii. Teri-Ann Theresa, b 8 April 1968 at Edmonton, Alberta. Was scheduled to attend University of Edmonton, Alberta when last known.

1013. CAROLE[7] MAVIS WILLIAMSON (d/o Luvia[6] Chowen Williamson #423), b 9 December 1939 at Berwyn, Alberta, Canada; m 4 July 1964, at Dawson City, Yukon Territory, Canada, **Norman Alexander Ross**, s/o James Alexander and Marjorie Jean (MacDonald) Ross, b 20 October 1939 at Dawson Creek, BC. Carole's brother reported in 1984 that she is legally separated from her husband. She attended University of El Paso, TX. She was to be qualified to work in Town Planning. Norman is a qualified mining engineer and has operated his own mining site in the Yukon for several years.

Child, surname ROSS:
  2249.   i. James[8] Carlyle, b 28 May 1970 at Penticton, BC.

1014. NANCY[7] BATES (d/o Arlo[6] Wayne Bates #427), b 23 December 1945 at Burbank, CA; m 12 June 1965 at Webster, SD, **Charles Koenig**. Charles is an engineer for Thompson Pipe and Steel Co.

Children, surname KOENIG:
  2250.   i. David[8], b April 1966 at Los Angeles, CA.
  2251. ii. Krissy, b April 1967 at Watertown, SD.
  2252. iii. Barbara, b November 1972 at Denver, CO.

The Seventh Generation 349

1015. JUDY[7] BATES (d/o Arlo[6] Wayne Bates #427), b 10 May 1947 at Burbank, CA; m 30 May 1969 at Webster, **Jim Koenig**. Both teach in Iowa; he teaches wrestling and Industrial Arts at Charles City; she teaches 4th grade.

Children, surname KOENIG:
    2253.   i. Daniel[8], b 13 August 1972, Charles City, IA.
    2254.   ii. Julie, b 17 August 1974, Charles City.

1016. SUSAN[7] BATES (d/o Arlo[6] Wayne Bates #427), b 19 March 1949 at Los Angeles, CA; m 31 May 1971, **Kerry Johnston** at Aberdeen, SD. Kerry is an insurance man and Susan is a librarian at Central High School, Aberdeen.

Children, surname JOHNSTON:
    2255.   i. Robert[8], b 27 February 1978, Aberdeen.
    2256.   ii. Scott James, b 3 June 1981, Aberdeen.
    2257.   iii. Micah, b 28 January 1983, Aberdeen.

1017. SONJA[7] BATES (d/o Arlo[6] Wayne Bates #427), b 24 August 1953 at Los Angeles, CA; m 15 June 1973 at Waubay, SD, **John Holme**. John works for an oil company in Waubay.

Child, surname HOLME:
    2258.   i. Andrea[8] Marie, b 7 October 1981.

1018. KATHY[7] BATES (d/o Arlo[6] Wayne Bates #427), b 16 December 1955 at Watertown, SD; m 9 October 1974, **Tim Tracey**. They live at Lincoln, NB. Kathy is a dental hygienist and Tim works for Federal Land Bank.

Child, surname TRACEY:
    2259.   i. Elizabeth[8] Ann, b 13 March 1984 at Lincoln.

1020. DELORES[7] HELEN PECKHAM (d/o Orville[6] Charles Peckham #428), b 16 February 1933 at Wilmot, SD; m 6 October 1951 at rural Butler, SD, **Lester Holland**, s/o Martin and Myrtle (Birget) Holland, b 2 August 1928 at Pierpont, SD. Delores is part time nurse's aide and Lester is an electrical lineman; they live in Webster, SD.

Children, surname HOLLAND, all born at Webster:
+   2260.   i. Patsy[8] Lynne, b 14 November 1955.
    2261.   ii. Janet Kay, b 24 May 1958; m Eureka, about 1980, Gordon

Bertsch.
2262. iii. Diane Laurel, b 3 October 1960.
+ 2263. iv. David Leslie, b 3 October 1960 (twin).

1021. JEAN[7] CAROLYN PECKHAM (d/o Orville[6] Charles Peckham #428), b 25 March 1934 at Wilmot, SD; m 16 August 1953 at Bristol, SD, **John Leo Irving Skaare**, s/o John Richard and Bertha Augusta (Langeland) Skaare, b 3 April 1926 at Webster, SD. John is a farmer. They live at Bristol.

Children, surname SKAARE, all born at Webster:
+ 2264. i. Jeffery[8] Lee, b 30 August 1956.
+ 2265. ii. Jerald Wayne, b 21 June 1958.
   2266. iii. Joan Elaine, b 30 December 1959.
   2267. iv. Julie Ann, b 19 June 1964.
   2268. v. Joy Kathleen, b 20 December 1969.

1022. DONALD[7] ORVILLE PECKHAM (s/o Orville[6] Charles Peckham #428), b 5 September 1936 at Bristol, SD; m 26 July 1956 at Bath, SD, **Bette Lorraine Graves**, d/o Harold and Ruth (Smith) Graves, b 23 November 1936 at Aberdeen, SD. Donald is Rural Letter Carrier for US Postal Service. They live at Barth, SD

Children, surname PECKHAM, all born at Aberdeen:
+ 2269. i. Vicki[8] Lee, b 18 January 1958.
   2270. ii. Vance Lester, b 29 May 1959.
+ 2271. iii. Cheryl Lynn, b 2 March 1961.
   2272. iv. Kristi Kae, b 28 July 1964.

1023. REX[7] MAYNARD PECKHAM (s/o Orville[6] Charles Peckham #428), b 22 October 1939 at Butler or Bristol, SD; m 26 July 1957 at Groton, SD, **Sandra Thompson**, d/o Chester and Florence (Wagner) Thompson. They live at Buckley, WA.

Children, surname PECKHAM:
   2273. i. Bradley[8] Rex, b 13 January 1958 at Aberdeen, SD.
   2274. ii. Lane Ray, b 4 July 1959 at Aberdeen.
   2275. iii. Brett Michael, b 17 August 1960 at Aberdeen.
+ 2276. iv. Lisa Kay, b 27 December 1961.
   2277. v. Wendy Jeanne, b 15 February 1962 at Webster, SD; m Paul Plewnarz.

2278. vi. Leigh Anna, b 2 August 1963 at Webster.

1024. WAYNE[7] **RUSSELL PECKHAM** (s/o Orville[6] Charles Peckham #428),b 9 November 1943 at Webster, SD; m **Marlene Carole Blow**, d/o Clyde and Mattie (Kramer) Blow, b 3 March 1943 at Livermore, CA,. Wayne is an electrician. They live at White Bear Lake, MN.

Children, surname PECKHAM:
    2279. i. Janelle[8] Marie, b 9 February 1965, in Minnesota.
    2280. ii. Steven Wayne, b 4 March 1967, in Minnesota.

1025. WILLIAM[7] **DONALD SPARROW** (s/o Grace[6] Peckham Sparrow #429), b 24 February 1934 at Webster, SD; m 6 June 1956 at Carrington, ND, **Gloria Pederson**, d/o Henry and Mabel (Anderson) Pederson, b 21 March 1935 at Juanita, ND.

Children, surname SPARROW:
    2281. i. Len[8], b 6 July 1957 at Dallas, TX. He is a logger at Spearfish, SD.
    2282. ii. Craig, b 3 March 1961 at Santa Monica, CA.
    2283. iii. Julie, b 6 December 1962 at Santa Monica.
    2284. iv. Monica, b 5 May 1964 at Santa Monica.
    2285. v. Sara, b 2 December 1966 at Santa Monica.

1031. RALPH[7] **SHELP** (s/o Anne[6] Peckham Shelp #431), b 30 September 1939 at Bristol or Webster, SD; m **Carol Koslowski**; divorced. He lives in Dallas, TX on a ranch and is a teacher in a community college.

Children, surname SHELP:
    2286. i. Ann[8].
    2287. ii. Kristi.

1032. JOHN[7] **SHELP** (s/o Anne[6] Peckham Shelp #431), b 25 June 1942; m **Wanda Fredenthal**. He operates a True-Value Davis Lumber Co., in Worland, WY. He speculates on land in the area.

Child, surname SHELP:
    2288. i. Cheri[8].
    2289. ii. Darron (adopted)
    2290. iii. Roger (adopted; died)
    2291. iv. Jack (adopted)

1034. DAVID[7] **SCOTT SHELP** (s/o Anne[6] Peckham Shelp #431), b 12

March 1948; m **Pat Wiswell**; they divorced in 1983. When last known David was in Juneau, AK, working in a factory making trusses for construction.

Child, surname SHELP:

2292. i. Tricia[8], b about 1972 in Pierre, SD.

1035. JEAN[7] SHELP (d/o Anne[6] Peckham Shelp #431), b 10 November 1951 at Thermopolis, WY; m 20 July 1974 at Spearfish, SD, **Terry Padgett**, s/o Clarence and Neta (Westendorf) Padgett, b 31 July 1953 at Sioux Falls, SD. She graduated in 1974 from Black Hills State College, Spearfish, with a major in music. Terry completed his degree in 1980 and is in respiration therapy at McKennan Hospital, when last known.

Children, surname PADGETT:

2293. i. Timothy[8], b 7 November 1980.
2294. ii. Andrea Lynn, b 29 September 1984.

1036. MARY[7] SUE DAY (d/o Hazel[6] Peckham Day #432), b 28 August 1948 at Norfolk, NE; m 27 June 1970 at Bethesda Lutheran Church, Belle Fourche, SD, **Verne Hartwick Leverson**, s/o Hartwick Nicholai and Gudrun Borghild (Hilmoe) Leverson, b 15 May 1948. They live in Lakewood, CO. Mary is a nurse and Verne is a meteorologist with the U.S. Government.

Children, surname LEVERSON, both born at Denver, CO:

2295. i. Eric[8] Day, b 7 April 1977, (adopted).
2296. ii. Sarah Christine, b 17 November 1981, (adopted).

1037. BARBARA[7] JUNE DAY (d/o Hazel[6] Peckham Day #432), b 24 May 1951 at Huron, SD; m 15 July 1978 at Saint James Lutheran Church, Belle Fourche, SD, **Tom Wayne Thomsen**, s/o Richard N. and Eli (Zapek) Thomsen, b June 1950. Barbara is a teacher for the hearing impaired and Tom is a Lutheran Pastor, on the staff of Wartburg Lutheran College, when last known.

Child, surname THOMSEN:

2297. i. Hans[8] Day, b 10 January 1979 at Joliet, IL.

1038. MARTHA[7] JOAN DAY (d/o Hazel[6] Peckham Day #432), b 19 August 1954 at Huron, SD; m at the church in Spearfish Canyon, **Mark David Wenzel**, s/o Stirling Albert and Esther Wenzel. They live in Phoenix, AZ and both are registered nurses, Mark is employed at

The Seventh Generation 353

Veteran's Hospital. They are medical missionaries.
Child, surname WENZEL:
    2298. i. Katie[8] Day, b 23 August 1983 at Nyankundi, Zaire, Africa.

1044. MATTHEW[7] **PECKHAM** (s/o Percy[6] Donald Peckham #434), b 28 July 1955 at Denver, CO; m 4 April 1976 at Seattle, WA, **Mary Ann Hall**. Matthew is a computer operator at Pacific North West Bell. They live at Snohomish, WA.
Children, surname PECKHAM, both born at Seattle:
    2299. i. Christopher[8] Reed, b 26 May 1979.
    2300. ii. Melinda Ann, b 10 September 1982.

1048. KRISTIN[7] **AMY RONNING** (d/o Ruth[6] Peckham Ronning #435), b 6 May 1949 at Brookings, SD; m **Stan Schwarzkopf**, s/o Erwin and Marie Schwarzkopf. Kris and Stan live in Lincoln, NB. She is a nurse in the Neo-Natal intensive care unit in a local hospital, in Lincoln, NB.
Children, surname SCHWARZKOPF:
    2301. i. Seth[8] David, b 29 October 1978.
    2302. ii. Lisel Marie, b 17 October 1981.

1049. KARI[7] **ANN RONNING** (d/o Ruth[6] Peckham Ronning #435), b 6 May 1949, twin to Kristin, at Brookings, SD; m **Curt Donaldson**, s/o Glen and Bea Donaldson, b Danville, IL. Kari has retained her maiden name. Kari has a PHD in English and was instructor in University of Nebraska before the birth of their child. They live in Lincoln, NB.
Children, surname DONALDSON:
    2303. i. Gavin[8] Douglas, b 20 July 1981.
    2304. ii. Nicholas, b 1985.

1050. RICHARD[7] **ROYCE RONNING** (s/o Ruth[6] Peckahm Ronning #435), b 19 December 1950; m **Laura Ulrich**, d/o Walter and Martha Ulrich. Rich and Laura served in the Peace Corps two years, taught school, and when last known Rich was getting a degree in electrical engineering. They live in Lincoln, NB.
Child, surname RONNING:
    2305. i. Rachel[8] Ulricka, b 23 May 1980.

1051. DARWIN[7] **DENNIS PECKHAM** (s/o Clayton[6] Maurice Peckham #436), b 20 September 1947 at Britton, SD; m **Marsha Meyer**.

Children, surname PECKHAM, both born at Aberdeen, SD:
>   2306.   i.   Darla[8] Dean, b 31 October 1971.
>   2307.   ii. Dennis James, b 19 October 1972.

1058. VICKI[7] RENEE PECKHAM (d/o Jesse[6] Vernon Peckham #439), b 2 March 1952 at Aberdeen, SD; m 6 October 1973, **Brent Zimmerman**. They are farming, raising pigs and cattle.

Children, surname ZIMMERMAN:
>   2308.   i.   Kara[8], b 22 October 1975, Aberdeen.
>   2309.   ii. Tiffany, b 2 December 1977, Aberdeen.
>   2310.   iii. Jacob, b 5 January 1982, Aberdeen.

1059. REBECCA[7] LYNN PECKHAM (d/o Jess[6] Vernon Peckham #439), b 2 April 1956 at Aberdeen, SD; m 27 September 1981 at Eagle River, WI, **Daniel Jefferson**. Daniel is in the lumber business in northern WI. Live at Eagle River, WI.

Child, surname JEFFERSON:
>   2311.   i.   Jesse[8], b 20 February 1984 at Eagle River, WI.

1061. KAREN[7] JOY ARNTZ (d/o Virginia[6] Cleone Peckham Arntz #440), b 13 May 1954 at Hoven, SD; m 11 January 1975, **Douglas Lundy**.

Child, surname LUNDY:
>   2312.   i.   Matthew[8] Douglas, b 24 January 1985.

1064. DIANA[7] PECKHAM (d/o James[6] Peckham #441), b 23 January 1961 at Oakes, SD; m 9 August 1980, **Monte White**.

Children, surname WHITE:
>   2313.   i.   Lindsey[8], b 29 August 1981.
>   2314.   ii. Nicholas, b 8 March 1984.

1067. MARIE[7] PECKHAM (d/o Robert[6] Peckham #442), b 15 June 1953 at Watertown, SD; m 17 December 1971 at Watertown, SD, **Tony Palluck**.

Children, surnaame PALLUCK:
>   2315.   i.   Bernie[8], b 22 June 1972 at Rantoul, IL.
>   2316.   ii. Samantha, b 14 April 1982, at Minot, ND.

1068. CINDY[7] PECKHAM (d/o Robert[6] Peckham #442), b 8 November 1955 at Watertown, SD; m 25 November 1978 at Clarke, SD, **Jeff White**.

Children, surname WHITE:
- 2317. i. Mike[8], b 14 June 1977 at Watertown.
- 2318. ii. Jon, b 5 March 1980 at Webster, SD.

1069. LINDA[7] PECKHAM (d/o Robert[6] Peckham #442), b 3 May 1962 at Watertown, SD; m 7 June 1980 at Clarke, SD, **Joe Beving**.

Child, surname BEVING:
- 2319. i. Alisa[8], b 2 December 1981 at Watertown, SD.

1073. MARVEL[7] KEITH KRUSE (s/o Orel[6] Roseth Kruse #443), b 10 August 1938 at Webster, SD; m 26 September 1958 at Miami, OK, **Beverly Beardsley**, b 9 April 1939. Marvel lives in Luquillo, Puerto Rico and is an air traffic controller.

Children, surname KRUSE:
- 2320. i. Debra[8] Kay, b 6 January 1961, Olathe, KS; m 19 August 1979, Michael Garcia, b Columbia, South America.
- 2321. ii. Scott Alan, b 26 August 1962, Olathe.
- + 2322. iii. Kevin Lee, b 3 April 1964, Olathe.

1074. JAMES[7] WESLEY KRUSE (s/o Orel[6] Roseth Kruse #443), b 13 April 1942 at Webster, SD; m 4 February 1961, **Janice Marie Marx**, d/o Edward and Elizabeth Marx, b 1 December 1944 at Bristol, SD. James works for Texaco Oil Co., live in Hurst, TX.

Children, surname KRUSE:
- + 2323. i. Kristel[8] Ann, b 16 March 1961.
- 2324. i. Michele Dawn, b 18 October 1962 at Webster.
- 2325. ii. Lisa, b 25 May 1964 at Webster; m 2 November 1986, David Burkel.
- 2326. iii. Mark James, b 25 January 1970 at Albuquerqe, NM.

1076. LESLIE[7] WILLIAM KRUSE (s/o Orel[6] Roseth Kruse #443), b 17 January 1952 at Webster, SD; m 24 November 1973 at Aurora, CO, **Roxanne Barnes**, d/o Robert and Betty Barnes, b 27 December 1948. Leslie lives in Rosenberg, TX, where he is a house painter.

Children, surname KRUSE:
- 2327. i. Kurt[8] William, b 13 February 1974 at Denver, CO.
- 2328. ii. Alicia Orel, b 9 July 1977 at Houston, TX.
- 2329. iii. Shane Franklin, b 1 April 1982 at Wharton, TX.

1078. WALTER[7] THEODORE SIGMONT, (s/o Beryl[6] Roseth Sigmont #446), b 9 January 1939 at Downey, CA; m 29 May 1961, **Ruth Ann Beckert**, d/o Raymond Orville and Doris June (Pruitt) Beckert, b 9 May 1942 at Denver, CO. Walter an electrical contractor.

Children, surname SIGMONT:
    2330. i. Nikki[8] Lynn, b 2 September 1967 at Englewood, CO.
    2331. ii. Jodi Ann, b 16 May 1972 at Denver.

1079. WILLIAM[7] CHARLES SIGMONT (s/o Beryl[6] Roseth Sigmont #446), b 23 June 1940 at Downey, CA; m 21 June 1961, **Carol Jean Fisher**, d/o Henry and Lydia (Wagner) Fisher, b 29 January 1942 in Denver. William is a retired heating and air conditioning contractor.

Children, surname SIGMONT, all born at Denver:
    2332. i. Dawn[8] Marie, b 21 July 1962.
    2333. ii. Wendy Rhena, b 6 June 1963.
    2334. iii. Lori Jean, b 27 July 1965.

1080. JO[7] ANN SIGMONT (d/o Beryl[6] Roseth Sigmont #446), b 21 December 1942 at Downey, CA; m 4 June 1961, **Douglas John Dale**, s/o Ronald Everet and Esther (Schekel) Dale, b 16 September 1939 at Denver.

Children, surname DALE, all born at Denver:
    2335. i. Richard[8] Ryan, b 12 January 1963.
    2336. ii. Michael Scott, b 26 June 1966.
    2337. iii. Jennifer Lynn, b 24 March 1974.

1081. BERYL[7] JO SIGMONT (d/o Beryl[6] Roseth Sigmont #446), b 25 March 1949 at Los Angeles, CA; m 17 June 1967 at Littleton, CO, **Richard Harden**. Beryl is an artist and writer. They were divorced in August 1976 at Littleton, CO. She lives at Aurora, CO.

Child, surname HARDEN:
    2338. i. Jeffrey[8] Todd, b 30 April 1968.

1083. LAURIE[7] WAITE (d/o Beverly[6] Roseth Waite #447), b 18 January 1952 at Huntington Park, CA; m in 1973, at Culver City, CA, **Marc Florio**; divorced June 1983. She is a secretary for the State of California Housing Finance agency at Culver City. Moved to Marceline, MO at urging of friends, and for space for her horses, which she trains, rides and shows; and her dogs, breeding Labs and Cairn Terriers, which she trains and shows.

Child, surname FLORIO:
> 2339. i. Serena[8] Marie, b 30 August 1977.

1084. JAMES[7] HAROLD ROSETH (s/o Harold[6] Merwyn Roseth #499), b 18 January 1949 at Maywood, CA; m 9 September 1978 at Lake Tahoe, NV, **Judy Lilith Hockenberry,** d/o John E. and Doris A. (Buchanan) Hockenberry, b 24 January 1955 at Grove City, PA. Jim works for a Masonry and building supply company in Apple Valley, CA.

Children, surname ROSETH:
> 2340. i. Jon[8] Harold, b 5 April 1979.
> 2341. ii. Jessica Aileen, b 5 November 1982.

1085. KATHLEEN[7] DAWN ROSETH (d/o Harold[6] Merwyn Roseth #499), b 19 February 1952 at Huntington Park, CA; m 31 July 1971 at Corona, CA, **Anthony Paul Cardoza,** b 15 November 1949 at Torrance, CA, s/o Antonio and Florence (Fagundes) Cardoza. They are in the dairy business.

Children, surname CARDOZA:
> 2342. i. Nicole[8] Michelle, b 17 April 1972.
> 2343. ii. Natal Dawn, b 31 September 1974.
> 2344. iii. Noel Muriel, b 17 August 1981.
> 2345. iv. Marissa Kathleen, b 12 September 1983.

1086. DEBRA[7] LYNN ROSETH (d/o Harold[6] Merwyn Roseth #499), b 5 January 1954 at Lynwood, CA; m 16 March 1974 at Norco, CA, **David Laurence Cardoza,** s/o Antonio and Florence (Fagundes) Cardoza, b 19 October 1951 at Torrance, CA. They are in the dairy business.

Children, surname CARDOZA:
> 2346. i. David[8] Ryan, b 20 November 1976.
> 2347. ii. Dustin Anthony, b 10 April 1979.
> 2348. iii. Deana Lynette, b 19 September 1983.

1087. THOMAS[7] WILLIAM ROSETH (s/o Harold[6] Merwyn Roseth #499), b 12 September 1956 at Corona, CA; m 31 December 1978 at Big Fork, MT, **Kim Russo,** d/o Jim and Jean (Vaughn) Russo, b 2 November 1954 at Wyandotte, MI. Jim is a building contractor; they live in Apple Valley, CA.

Children, surname ROSETH:
2349. i. Summer[8] Gabriel, b 7 August 1979.
2350. ii. Holly Breeze, b 14 July 1982.

1088. INEZ[7] ROSETH (d/o Jon[6] Henry Roseth #451), b 1 June 1957 at Torrance, CA; m 22 June 1974 at First Lutheran Church, Lake Elsinore, CA, **Charles Richard Connor**. Inez is a secretary in Lloyd's Bank; when last known Charles was a student at Christ College, Erbini.

Children, surname CONNOR:
2351. i. Nicole[8] Elizabeth, b 7 August 1977 at Spokane, WA.
2352. ii. Michelle Inez, b 9 August 1979 at Corona, CA.

1089. ANNETTE[7] ROSETH (d/o Jon[6] Henry Roseth #451), b 11 September 1959 at Long Beach, CA; m 26 May 1979 at San Luis Obispo, CA, **George Kenneth Chatham**. Ken is a carpenter.

Children, surname CHATHAM:
2353. i. Peter[8] Joshua, b 15 January 1982 at Kennewick, WA.
2354. ii. Matthew Jeremiah, b 30 March 1983 at Elk City, OK.

1090. GREGORY[7] LYNN CASEY (s/o Elizabeth[6] Roseth Casey #452), b 18 November 1956 at Englewood, CA; m/1 **Cynthia Jean Sherman**, b 21 May 1957, d/o Richard and Jean (Toole) Sherman. Gregory m/2, 31 January 1987 at Las Vegas, NV, **Kathrine Jean Heard**, b 2 October 1949. Greg builds houses to sell.

Child, surname CASEY:
2355. i. Shane[8] Lynn, b 4 December 1978 at Kalispell, MT. Lives at Bigfork, MT.

1091. CAREN[7] ELIZABETH CASEY (d/o Elizabeth[6] Roseth Casey #452), b 28 May 1959 at Englewood, CA; m 12 May 1979, **Lawrence Trent Carson**, s/o Kenneth and Barbara (Jenkins) Carson, b 30 July 1955. Caren and Lawrence work for National Processing Equipment Co.

Children, surname CARSON:
2356. i. Jannela[8] Elizabeth, b 29 August 1982 at Montclair, CA.
2357. ii. Blake Ryan, b 2 June 1984 at San Bernadino, CA.

1097. ANTHONY[7] JAMES O'DONNELL (s/o Elwyn[6] Peckham #455), b to Dianne O'Donnell 1 February 1950 in San Francisco; he was brought up by Elwyn and Dianne; m 22 January 1977 at French Gulch,

The Seventh Generation

CA, **Carolyn Jeanne Wiley**. Tony does leather work, upholsters house boats. Now divorced.

Child, surname O'DONNELL:
    2358.   i.   Vashti[8] Rose, b 10 May 1979, in Redding, CA.

1098. SAMUEL[7] **CHARLES PECKHAM** (s/o Elwyn[6] Peckham #455), b 6 October 1953 at Oakland, CA; m 11 October 1980 at Santa Monica, CA, **Teresa Ann Dominquez**. He is now a contractor; previously he was a forester at Sea Side, OR. Becuase of his wife's health, they moved to Bear Lake, near San Diego, CA.

Child, surname PECKHAM:
    2359.   i.   Erin[8] Christine, b 20 October 1985.

1106. KIMBERLY[7] **LAYNE DAWSON** (d/o Donna[6] Peckham Dawson #456), b 23 January 1958 at San Francisco, CA; m **Vasile Kurnizki**.

Children, surname KURNIZKI:
    2360.   i.   Andrew[8] Paul Dawson, b 6 February 1989.
    2361.   ii. Anna Sophia, b 18 September 1990.

1107. PAMELA[7] **ANN MITCHELL** (d/o Elizabeth[6] Peckham Mitchell #457), b 7 May 1953 at Berkeley, CA; m 21 September 1974, at Stanford, CA, **Gery Will Groslimond**. He teaches tennis at University of Atlanta, GA.

Children, surname GROSLIMOND:
    2362.   i.   Andrew[8] Mitchell, b 3 November 1980, Atlanta.
    2363.   ii. Jeffrey Paul, b 4 February 1983, Atlanta.

1108. MARK[7] **STEVEN MITCHELL** (s/o Elizabeth[6] Peckham Mitchell #457), b 5 June 1954 at Berkeley, CA; m 7 June 1977 at Orinda, CA, **Susan Sanborn Paddock**. Mark is buying his father's business; lives and works at Menlo Park, CA.

Children, surname MITCHELL:
    2364.   i.   Cameron[8] Paddock, b 27 April 1982.
    2365.   ii. Caitlin Patricia, b 9 August 1985.

1111. PERI[7] **ANNE PECKHAM** (adopted d/o Charles[6] Wesley Peckham #458), b 16 January 1960 at Berkeley, CA; m 5 September 1981 at Corvallis, OR, **Lee William Kuhl**. Lee with electric company in Portland, OR; Peri is a teacher.

Children, surname KUHL:
 2366. i. Brett[8] Lee, b 1 November 1986.
 2367. ii. Flynn James, b 1 May 1988.

1114. CALVIN[7] ROGER DEWSNAP (s/o Carol[6] Clark Dewsnap #459), b 31 January 1940 at Portage, WI; m 25 October 1976 at Worthington, MN, **Linda Friedly**, b 6 February 1948 at Fulda, MN. Calvin works for Armour Co. in Louisville, KY, as a supervisor of the buying and selling of their meat.

Children, surname DEWSNAP; Linda's first three children were adopted by Calvin:
 2368. i. Tammy[8] Sue, b 11 May 1966.
 2369. ii. Cory Allan, b 14 March 1969.
 2370. iii. Amy Leigh, b 30 March 1972.
 2371. iv. Daniel Ryan, b 7 December 1977.

1115. DOUGLAS[7] WAYNE DEWSNAP (s/o Carol[6] Clark Dewsnap #459), b 20 August 1941 at Portage, WI; m 1 June 1963 at Summit, IL, **Lucy Jean Duell**, b 20 September 1940 at Summit, IL, d/o Sidney and Alice Duell. Douglas is a carpenter for Madsen Construction in Ft. Collins, Co. headquartered are in Madison WI. He has worked for them 20 years.

Children, surname DEWSNAP:
 2372. i. Douglas[8] Wayne, b 29 December 1964.
 2373. ii. Steven Clark, b 2 March 1968.

1117. DENNIS[7] DEAN DEWSNAP (s/o Carol[6] Clark Dewsnap #459), b 7 April 1947 at Endeavor, WI; m 5 February 1977 in Coon Valley, WI; **Susan Nelson**, b 13 May 1952 at Coon Valley, WI; d/o Layton and Betty Nelson. Dennis is in partnership with an insurance firm in Green Bay, WI. They live at DePere, WI.

Children, surname DEWSNAP:
 2374. i. Christopher[8] Adam, b 25 May 1978.
 2375. ii. Nickolas Jon, b 12 May 1980.

1119. STEWART[7] HAROLD DEWSNAP (s/o Carol[6] Clark Dewsnap #459), b 15 December 1958 at Portage, WI; m 31 March 1979, **Dawn Anacker**, b 18 October 1957; d/o Art and Carol Anacker. Stewart is employed at a large potato growing farm in Grand Marsh, WI. They live

The Seventh Generation　　361

at Endeavor, WI.

Child, surname DEWSNAP:
    2376.　i. Michael[8] Stewart, b October 1981.

1120. NANCY[7] MARIE AUDISS (d/o Norma[6] Clark Audiss #460), b 4 November 1944; m 8 September 1962, **Richard Meyer**, b 16 February 1943, s/o Herbert and Viva Meyer. They live at Stoughton, WI.

Children, surname MEYER:
    2377.　i. Derek[8], b 16 June 1972.
    2378.　ii. Andrea, b August 1969.

1121. JEFFREY[7] CLARK AUDISS (s/o Norma[6] Clark Audiss #460), b 6 December 1949; m 17 August 1968, **Wendy Houston**; Divorced. Jeffery m/2 **Faith —**, b 18 September 1976.

Child, surname AUDISS:
    2379.　i. Todd[8], b 3 March 1969.
    2380.　ii. Joshua Eldon, b 15 August 1978.

1122. SALLY[7] JANE AUDISS (d/o Norma[6] Clark Audiss #460), b 27 July 1956; m 18 December 1982, **Gary Terry**.

Child, surname TERRY:
    2381.　i. Brian[8] Lee, b 15 May 1984 in Michigan.

1123. LORENCE[7] ORVILLE KAROW (s/o Beverly[6] Clark Karow #461), b 17 June 1952; m **Ellen Schultz**; they live at Beaver Dam, WI.

Child, surname KAROW:
    2382.　i. Joshua[8] Lorence, b 4 September 1981.

1127. BETTY[7] JEAN HARTWELL (d/o Mary[6] Ann Spratt Hartwell #464), b 18 August 1940 at Eau Claire, WI; m 7 October 1961 at Christ Church Cathedral (Episcopal), Eau Claire, **John Tronsdall**. Betty Jean was killed in an automobile accident 23 April 1965.

Children, surname TRONSDALL:
    2383.　i. Mary[8] Louise, b 9 August 1962.
    2384.　ii. Peggy Ann, b 27 July 1963.

1129. PAMELA[7] LOUISE SPRATT (d/o William[6] Spratt #465), b 21 March 1948 at Eau Claire, WI; m 18 July 1970 at Christ Church, Eau Claire, **John Donald Hansen Lee**, s/o John and Bessie (Hansen) Lee, b

2 May 1943 at Eau Claire. Pam is a substitute teacher and John is Office Manager and Accountant.

Children, surname LEE:
- 2385. i. Kristin[8] Marie, b 28 January 1973, at Eau Claire.
- 2386. ii. John William, b 16 July 1975, at Eau Claire.

1130. PHILIP[7] REECE SPRATT (s/o William[6] Spratt #465), b 18 January 1954 at Santa Monica, CA. In 1984, Phillip m/1 briefly to **Sharon Mercer** and divorced; m/2 in Spring of 1985, **Sharon Kay Kopp**, b 30 May 1954 at Eau Claire, d/o Edward Dewey and Kathryn May (Simonson) Kopp. Phillip works for a private ambulance service in Eau Claire and is called an Emergency Medical Technician.

Child, surname MERCER:
- 2387. i. Olga[8] Marie, b 17 February 1978 at Eau Claire.

1131. WANETA[7] BETH MEEKER (d/o Edna[6] Kroeplin Meeker #466), b 14 March 1932 at Taylor Co., WI; m 2 August 1949 at Medford, WI, **Walter Gwiazda**, s/o Nicholas and Mary Gwiazda. He died 8 February 1985 and is buried in the Ukranian Cemetery at Thorp, WI.

Children, surname GWIAZDA:
- + 2388. i. Cheryle[8] Ann, b 27 June 1949.
- + 2389. ii. Irene Mary, b 16 November 1950.
- + 2390. iii. Gregory Gene, b 22 March 1955.
- + 2391. iv. Duane Walter, b 1 January 1957.

1132. ROSE[7] BLANCHE MEEKER (d/o Edna[6] Kroeplin Meeker #466), b 15 December 1933 at Taylor Co., WI; m 24 July 1952, **Theodus Zaszczurynski**, b 20 October 1920 at Thorp, WI. Theodus is a factory maintenance man in Chicago, IL.

Children, surname ZASZCZURYNSKI, all born at Chicago, IL:
- 2392. i. Theodore[8] Eugene, b 13 October 1952; m 16 August 1984 Sharon Goebel, at Chicago, IL.
- 2393. ii. Geraldine Edna, b 20 October 1954; m Dennis Goebel.
- + 2394. iii. Gail Marie, b 5 January 1956.
- + 2395. iv. Terrance Emmet, b 28 February 1957.
- 2396. v. Glenda Emma, b 5 July 1960.
- + 2397. vi. Gabrielle Michelle, b 29 July 1962.
- + 2398. vii. Gwen Rose, b 30 December 1964.

1133. MARVIN[7] CECIL MEEKER (s/o Edna[6] Kroeplin Meeker #466), b 18 October 1935 at Taylor Co., WI; m/1 1 July 1954, **Irene Anne Fate** (#1218), b 2 March 1939 at Clairmont, MN, d/o Ray and Beatrice (Baker) Fate. Irene d 30 May 1961 when she accidentally set fire to herself while starting the furnace. Marvin m/2 19 October 1963, **Alice Lois McCartny**, b 6 December 1930 at Stanley, d/o Merl and Dorothy (Westaky) McCartny. Marvin a Minister at Dubuque, IA.

Children, surname MEEKER:
+   2399.   i.   LaDonna[8] Bea, b 22 January 1955.
+   2400.   ii.   Debbie Ann, b 3 December 1960.
      2401.   iii.   Samuel Marvin, b 21 November 1967 at DuBuque.

1134. GEORGE[7] HENRY MEEKER (s/o Edna[6] Kroeplin Meeker #466), b 2 December 1937 at Taylor Co., WI; m 3 August 1960 at Stanley, WI, **Ethel Ann Draeger**, b 5 September 1944, d/o Ervin and Irene (Matthews) Draeger. George is a truck driver and does general farm work.

Children, surname MEEKER, all born at Stanley:
      2402.   i.   George[8] Allen, b 23 November 1960.
+   2403.   ii.   Susan Kay, b 19 January 1962.
      2404.   iii.   Deanne Marie, b 26 February 1963; m 5 May 1984, Don Bauer at Eau Claire, WI.

1135. CHESTER[7] EUGENE MEEKER (s/o Edna[6] Kroeplin Meeker #466), b 7 February 1940 at Taylor Co., WI; m 24 March 1961 at Stanley, WI, **Sandra Louise Turner**, b 17 April 1944 at Waukegan, IL, d/o John and Amelia Turner. Stanley is a laborer in a factory in Stanley.

Children, surname MEEKER, all born at Stanley:
      2405.   i.   Jeffrey[8] John, b 7 September 1961; m 16 January 1982, Candy Biddle, d/o Brandon and Marvel Biddle.
      2406.   ii.   Joseph Michael, b 7 January 1964; d February 1964.
      2407.   iii.   Josephine Penny, b April 1965; d April 1965.
      2408.   iv.   Sabrina Louise, b 16 November 1967; m 24 July 1987, Mark Cheevers, s/o Clarence and Janet Cheevers.
      2409.   v.   Trinity Eric, b 4 November 1975.

1136. LESTER[7] DAVID MEEKER (s/o Edna[6] Kroeplin Meeker #466), b 9 January 1942 at Taylor Co., WI; m/1 23 February 1966 at Chicago IL, **Sharon Lee Myers**; they were divorced and he m/2 24 February 1980 at Milwaukee, WI, **Darlene Ruth Gerky**. Lester is a truck driver.

Children, surname MEEKER, both born at Chicago:
    2410. i. Lester[8] David, b 27 July 1969.
    2411. ii. Nancy Elizabeth, b 4 August 1974.

1137. JUDITH[7] ANN MEEKER (d/o Edna[6] Kroeplin Meeker #466), b 14 January 1944 at Stanley, WI; m 5 September 1964 at Stanley, **Raymond Eugene Saunders**, b 26 April 1938 at Saint Paul, MN, s/o Floyd and Clara (Westaky) Saunders. Judith is an aide to dependent children; Judith and Raymond were divorced 14 April 1980.

Children, surname SAUNDERS, both born at Saint Paul:
+ 2412. i. Lisa[8] Lynn, b 26 June 1965.
    2413. ii. Sheila Ann, b 6 June 1967.

1138. SHARON[7] ALICE MEEKER (d/o Edna[6] Kroeplin Meeker #466), b 22 April 1951 at Stanley, WI; m 13 June 1970 at Stanley, **Dale Arthur Kocherer**, s/o Clarence and Myrtle (White) Kocherer, b 18 June 1951 at Stanley. They live in Cornell, WI. Dale works in a factory.

Children, surname KOCHERER:
    2414. i. Angela[8] Michelle, b 1 January 1971 at Stanley.
    2415. ii. Crystal Lynn, b 18 October 1976 at Chippewa Falls, WI.

1139. BESSIE[7] MAY KROEPLIN (d/o Elmer[6] Thomas John Kroeplin #467), b 26 December 1952 at Minneapolis, MN; m/1 August 1978, **Juff Christeson**; divorced August 1982; m/2 5 October 1984 at Hastings, MN, **Michael H. Fortier**. Michael is a singer in a rock and roll band; live in Eagan, MN.

Child, surname CHRISTESON:
    2416. i. Cory[8], b 2 August 1975 at Minneapolis.

1150. MARY[7] ELIZABETH KROEPLIN (d/o Henry[6] Albert Neil Kroeplin #469), b 8 March 1947 at Cleveland, OH; m 30 October 1966 at Cleveland, OH, **Earl Darl McCloy**. Mary is an LPN; Earl is jack of all trades; lives at Coshocton, OH.

Children, surname McCloy:
    2417. i. Lena[8] Ruth Anne, b 21 April 1967 at Chicago, IL.
    2418. ii. Earl Darl, b 8 March 1968 at Coshocton, OH.
    2419. iii. James William, b 5 February 1969 at Cleveland, OH.
    2420. iv. Audra Lynn, b 2 January 1967 at Cleveland.

1151. THOMAS[7] WILLIAM KROEPLIN (s/o Henry[6] Albert Kroeplin #469), b 20 December 1949 at Stanley, WI; m 29 June 1970 at Winter, WI, **Wendy Shadis**, b 29 September 1929 at Cleveland, OH. Tom is a game warden for state of Wisconsin in upper part of state; they live in Minoqua, WI.

Children, surname KROEPLIN, both born at Chippewa Falls, WI:
    2421.   i.   Roxanne[8], b 24 March 1973.
    2422.   ii.   Nathan, b 5 September 1976.

1152. TIMOTHY[7] WARREN KROEPLIN (s/o Henry[6] Albert Kroeplin #469), b 20 November 1952 at Stanley, WI; m 5 August 1978 at Stanley, **Cindy Schneider**. Tim is a dairy farmer; they live at Stanley.

Children, surname KROEPLIN, both born at Chippewa Falls, WI:
    2423.   i.   Noel[8] Elizabeth, b 15 December 1980.
    2424.   ii.   Benjamin Jacob, b 26 June 1983.

1153. MARGARET[7] ELAINE KROEPLIN (d/o Henry[6] Albert Kroeplin #469), b 1 February 1953 at Stanley, WI; m 25 January 1974 at Chicago, IL, **Talal Dajani**; divorced 1 April 1979. Marge is an office worker in Chicago.

Child, surname DAJANI:
    2425.   i.   Heather[8] Ann, b 2 January 1977 at Chicago.

1154. KAREN[7] JOYCE RICHARDSON (d/o Ilene[6] Joyce Richardson, w/o Palmer Kroeplin #471), Karen b 6 June 1950 at Stanley, WI; adopted by Palmer Kroeplin; m 6 April 1974 at Stanley, **Edward L. Shilts**. Edward works at Phoenix Steel in Eau Claire, WI.

Children, surname SHILTS:
    2426.   i.   Rodney[8], b 26 November 1976, at Eau Claire.
    2427.   ii.   Samuel, b 13 April 1978, at Eau Claire.
    2428.   iii.   Tracy, b 6 July 1983, at Eau Claire.

1155. CHARLES[7] LEE CULBERT (s/o Bessie[6] French Culbert #473), b 12 October 1931 at Pine Island, MN; m 5 February 1952 at Norfolk, VA, **Bonnie Lou McKnight**, b 31 December 1931 at Moreland, Bingham Co., ID. Lee manages Red Gate Inc. a family corporation.

Children, surname CULBERT:
+   2429.   i.   Douglas[8] Lee, b 28 October 1953.

+   2430.   ii. David Lyle, b 14 January 1955.
+   2431.   iii. Daryl Lynn, b 11 December 1956.
    2432.   iv. Dale Leslie, b 21 January 1958 at Missoula, MT.
+   2433.   v.   Shari Lynette, b 14 November 1961, Missoula.

1156. JERALD[7] LANCE CULBERT (s/o Bessie[6] French Culbert #473), b 4 August 1933 at Dodge Center, Dodge Co., MN; m 30 June 1956 at Hibbing, MN, **Judith Mabel Halbom**, d/o John and Johanna Halbom, b 12 September 1938 at Saint Louis Co., MN. Jerald is a contractor.

Children, surname CULBERT:
    2434.   i.   Jeffrey[8], b 31 August 1958 at Kalispell, MT; bar tender in Missoula.
+   2435.   ii. Brian, b 5 October 1959.
    2436.   iii. Kim, b 24 January 1964 at Missoula; m 25 August 1984, John Franklin Peterson at Missoula. Kim is a waitress and John is a drywaller.

1157. MARY[7] LAYNE CULBERT (d/o Bessie[6] French Culbert #473), b 27 July 1940; m/1 **Lee Hyslop**. Mary m/2 **Ken Fitzgerald**.

Children, surname HYSLOP:
    2437.   i.   Barbara[8].
+   2438.   ii. Brenda.
    2439.   iii. Pamela.

Children, surname FITZGERALD:
    2440.   iv. Terri[8].
    2441.   v.   Colleen.

1159. DENNIS[7] ALLEN FRENCH (s/o Allen[6] Flavel French #474), b 13 June 1936 at West Concord, MN; m **Margaret Rasmussen**.

Children, surname FRENCH:
+   2442.   i.   Denise[8] Margaret.
    2443.   ii. Kelly Lynn; m Bill — in 1984.

1160. BEVERLY[7] ANN FRENCH (d/o Allen[6] Flavel French #474), b 5 May 1938; m **Ronyle Kreft**.

Children, surname KREFT:
    2444.   i.   David[8].

2445. ii. Sarah.

1161. DANAL[7] CHARLES FRENCH (s/o Allen[6] Flavel French #474), b 25 July 1947; m **Muriel Loguia**; live in Dodge Center; he is a farmer.

Children, surname FRENCH:
    2446. i. Anthony[8] Raymond.
    2447. ii. Jason.

1162. RONALD[7] RICHARD FRENCH (s/o Allen[6] Flavel French #474), b 3 May 1950; m/1 **Cheryl Finstune**; divorced; m/2 **Jane** —.

Children, surname FRENCH:
    2448. i. Lara[8].
    2449. ii. Nathan.

1164. LARRY[7] KAY HANSON (s/o Clara[6] French Hanson #475), b 15 October 1935 Dodge Co., MN; m 19 December 1959 in CA, **E. Joyce Ferguson**, b 6 March 1952 in Oklahoma. Larry was in the Marine Corp. for four years and lives in Mount Pleasant, AZ; had a retail bread route until 1981 when he was injured.

Children, surname HANSON:
+ 2450. i. Michael[8] C., b 1 December 1960.
    2451. ii. Pamela R., b 30 December 1962.
    2452. iii. Patricia G., b 19 March 1964; m 30 June 1984, Michael Deyoung.
    2453. iv. Penny L., b 27 February 1968.
    2454. v. Andrew L., b 9 November 1973 at Izzard Co., AR.

1165. GLENN[7] ELDON HANSON (s/o Clara[6] French Hanson #475), b 18 December 1938 Dodge Co., MN; m 27 April 1960 at West Concord, MN, **Mary Lou Urch**, b 11 July 1942 at Kasson, Dodge Co., MN. They live in Old Concord, MN. Glenn works at IBM in Rochester, MN, after two years in the army at Dugway, UT.

Children, surname HANSON, both born at Owatonna, MN:
    2455. i. Jill[8] G., b 14 April 1966.
    2456. ii. Leslie E., b 6 November 1967.

1166. LOREN[7] RICHARD HANSON (s/o Clara[6] French Hanson #475), b 26 March 1942 in Dodge Co., MN; m 3 October 1965 in Illinois, **Mary Sue Grimes**, b 4 December 1946 in MS. Loren d 11 September 1971 at Zion, IL. He worked for an air conditioning and plumbing company. Mary Sue m/2 20 April 1974, **Leo Reindl**, b 21 February 1944; Leo adopted the two girls in 1974.

Children, surname HANSON, both born in IL:
- 2457. i. Laura[8] Lynn, b 31 October 1967.
- 2458. ii. Tina Marie, b 17 October 1969.

Child, surname REINDL:
- 2459. iii. Tim[8] L., b 13 May 1975.

1167. ROGER[7] **ARLEN HANSON** (s/o Clara[6] French Hanson #475), b 5 March 1944 at Owatonna, MN; m 27 March 1965 at West Concord, MN, **Sharon Reynolds**, b 13 May 1943. They live in rural Kenyon area. Roger works for Wenger Corp. in Owatonna. Sharon is secretary at First Baptist Church in West Concord.

Children, surname HANSON, all born at Owatonna:
- 2460. i. Denise[8] K., b 25 April 1966.
- 2461. ii. Douglas A., b 2 February 1968.
- 2462. iii. Darla R., b 15 May 1970.

1168. PHILIP[7] **HANSON** (s/o Clara[6] French Hanson #475), b 25 July 1945 at Owatonna, MN; m 21 May 1965 at West Concord, MN, **Barbara A. Vangness**, b 28 July 1945 in WI. They live in Dodge Center, MN and Phil works for Wenger Music Corp. in Owatonna.

Children, surname HANSON, all born at Owatonna:
- 2463. i. Teri[8] L., b 4 December 1965.
- 2464. ii. Todd P., b 12 January 1967.
- 2465. iii. Carla S., b 7 July 1968.
- 2466. iv. Curt D., b 24 April 1970.

1169. ANNA[7] **LOUISE HANSON** (d/o Clara[6] French Hanson #475), b 2 November 1946 at Owatonna, MN; m 28 August 1970 at West Concord, MN, **Todd M. Severud**, b 14 April 1947 at Minneapolis, MN. Todd works at Methodist Hospital in Rochester, MN; Anna taught school several years; they live in Rochester.

Children, surname SEVERUD:
- 2467. i. Kristin[8] E., b 4 July 1977 at Saint Paul, MN.
- 2468. ii. Joshua A., b 2 August 1981 at Rochester.
- 2469. iii. Shawn M., b 29 March 1985 at Rochester.

1170. ANOLA[7] **GAYLE HANSON** (d/o Clara[6] French Hanson #475), b 11 September 1949 at Owatonna, MN; m 23 June 1973 at West Concord, MN, **William G. Lakemacher**, b 23 March 1949. William works for Hinkley & Schmidt Bottled Water Co., Chicago, IL. They live in Rolling Meadows, IL.

Children, surname LAKEMACHER, all born at Cook Co., IL.
    2470.   i.   Jeffrey[8] J., b 9 March 1981.
    2471.   ii. Jeremy W., b 22 November 1982.
    2472.   iii. Justin S., b 25 January 1985.

1171. DAVID[7] **BRUCE HANSON** (s/o Clara[6] French Hanson #475), b 11 April 1951 at Owatonna, MN; m 15 March 1974 at Owatonna, MN, **Brenda K. Johnson**, b 27 September 1953 at Austin, Mower Co., MN. David works for Owatonna Tool Co., and they live in Owatonna, MN.

Children, surname HANSON:
    2473.   i.   Aaron[8] J., b 15 December 1974, at Owatonna.
    2474.   ii. Rebekah J., b 29 May 1977, at Owatonna.
    2475.   iii. Levi D., b 19 September 1981, at Owatonna.

1174. TIMOTHY[7] **CLAYTON HANSON** (s/o Clara[6] French Hanson #475), b 14 October 1959 at Owatonna, MN; m 21 August 1981 at West Concord, MN, **Laurie Ann Conwell**, b 2 January 1964 at Minneapolis, MN. Timothy works for McNeelus Manufacturing Co. in Dodge Center. They live in West Concord, MN.

Children, surname HANSON:
    2476.   i.   Mark[8] J., b 2 March 1982, at Zumbrota, MN.
    2477.   ii. Brittany Lynn, b 6 August 1984, at Zumbrota.

1175. DARRELL[7] **FREDERICK PHELPS** (s/o Dorothy[6] French Phelps #476), b 7 February 1937; m 7 December 1959 at First Baptist Church, West Concord, MN, **Laurel Flaven**.

Children, surname PHELPS:
    2478.   i.   Steven[8] Darrell, b 10 September 1966, at Owatonna, MN.
    2479.   ii. Corey Lynn, b 31 August 1968, at Owatonna.
    2480.   iii. Kent David, b 26 August 1971, at Owatonna.

1176. DALE[7] **LOREN PHELPS** (s/o Dorothy[6] French Phelps #476), b 27 July 1938; m 7 June 1960 at West Concord, MN, **Karen Renner**. He is Pastor at Luverne, MN.

Children, surname PHELPS:
- 2481. i. Barbara[8] Jean, b 6 February 1962 at Columbia CIty, IN.
- 2482. ii. Keith Dale, b 22 April 1964 at Albion, MI.
- 2483. iii. Shirley Ann, b 24 February 1971 at Cedar Rapids, IA.

1177. CONSTANCE[7] FAYE PHELPS (d/o Dorothy[6] French Phelps #476), b 12 November 1943; m 22 March 1963 at West Concord, MN, **Charles Harold Avery.**

Children, surname AVERY, all born at Owatonna, MN:
- 2484. i. Leland[8] Charles, b 8 August 1964.
- 2485. ii. Kevin Mark, b 11 August 1966.
- 2486. iii. Jodee Faye, b 7 September 1967.
- 2487. iv. Renae Ruth, b 19 August 1970.

1178. RUTH[7] LILYAN FRENCH (d/o Richard[6] Andrew French #477), b 15 March 1945; m **Jim Borgan**; live in Washington State.

Children, surname BORGAN:
- 2488. i. Jessica[8].
- 2489. ii. Jamie.

1180. EVON[7] LYNETTE FRENCH (d/o Richard[6] Andrew French #477), b 12 October 1956; m **Brett Naylor**; live in Hayfield, MN.

Child, surname Naylor:
- 2490. i. Justina[8].

1181. DAWN[7] RENEE FRENCH (d/o Richard[6] Andrew French #477), b 21 January 1958 at Saint Paul, MN; not married. She works with mentally retarded children at a Group Home in Rochester, MN; lives in Dodge Center, MN.

Child, surname FRENCH:
- 2491. i. Joshua[8] Curtis, b 8 November 1982 at Rochester.

1183. SCOTT[7] BENJAMIN FRENCH (s/o Richard[6] Andrew French #477), b 14 February 1961 at Owatonna, MN; m 12 September 1981 at Dodge Center MN, **Julie Weitzenkemp.** They live at Wasioja, MN and Scott works for Brad Ragan Commercial Tire Service at Rochester, MN as a service man.

Child, surname FRENCH:
2492.   i.   Michelle[8] Jean, b 13 December 1982.

1185. CAROL[7] **ANN URCH** (d/o Evelyn[6] French Urch #478), b 25 January 1946 at Owatonna, MN; m 2 May 1970 at West Concord, MN, **Richard Hochreiter**. Lived 5 years in CA; own business-Wildex-clothes for motorcycle racing.

Children, surname HOCHREITER, both born at Minneapolis, MN:
2493.   i.   Wendi[8] Ann, b 28 January 1971.
2494.   ii. Dustin Richard, b 5 December 1975.

1186. LOWELL[7] **EARL URCH** (s/o Evelyn[6] French Urch #478), b 28 April 1947 at Owatonna, MN; m 9 December 1967 at Solway, MN, **Mavis Bender**. They live in Concord, MN and Lowell is a salesman for Agri-King Co.

Children, surname URCH, all born at Owatonna, MN:
2495.   i.   Laurelie[8] Mae, b 10 November 1969.
2496.   ii.   Suzan Marie, b 31 January 1970.
2497.   iii. Rachel Lynn, b 1 June 1975.
2498.   iv.   Jared Michael, b 29 June 1976.

1187. VICKI[7] **LEA URCH** (d/o Evelyn[6] French Urch #478), b 9 October 1953 at Owatonna, MN; m 17 March 1973 at West Concord, **Mark Gustafson**. They live in Winona, MN; Mark is manager of furniture store.

Children, surname GUSTAFSON:
2499.   i.   Lezlie[8] Marie, b 5 April 1975 at Wausau, WI.
2500.   ii.   Theodore Charles, b 19 May 1981 at Winona, MN.
2501.   iii. Lizbeth, b 1 June 1983 at Winona.

1194. FORREST[7] **EDWARD ABEL** (s/o Forrest[6] Edward Abel #480), b 21 October 1946 at McMinnville, OR; m April 1966 at Mobile, AL, **Janice Diane Lasher**. He was an airport fireman and part of the emergency crew for four years. He spent four years in U.S. Navy and now is a policeman.

Children, surname ABEL:
2502.   i.   Monica[8] Beth, b 29 January 1967 at Pensicola, FL.
2503.   ii. Naomi Christine, b 4 September 1969 at Portland, OR.

1195. SHARON[7] NADINE ABEL (d/o Forrest[6] Edward Abel #480), b 19 July 1950 at McMinnville, OR; m 1 October 1973 at Vancouver, WA, **Norman Erickson.**

Children, surname ERICKSON, all born at McMinnville:
- 2504. i. Melinda[8] Ann, b 11 January 1974.
- 2505. ii. Norman Aaron, b 3 March 1978.
- 2506. iii. Christel Lynn, b 27 April 1981.

1196. LORETTA[7] ALICE GOUTERMONT (d/o Helen[6] Abel Goutermont #481), b 22 July 1948 at Scotia, CA; m 20 July 1968 at Santa Rosa, CA, **Robert E. Brattain.**

Children, surname BRATTAIN:
- 2507. i. Renee[8] Elaine, b 1 December 1973 at Manassas, VA.
- 2508. ii. Raymond Eugene, b 8 May 1978 at Edgewood, MD.

1197. ROY[7] LUVERNE GOUTERMONT (s/o Helen[6] Abel Goutermont #481), b 17 January 1951 at Scotia, CA; m 7 April 1972, **Lynne White.** Divorced in 1983.

Children, surname GOUTERMONT:
- 2509. i. Shawn[8] Aaron, b 2 September 1974 at Sacramento, CA.
- 2510. ii. Heather, b 19 July 1971 Lynne's daughter by a previous marriage and adopted by Roy

1198. KATHY[7] LYNN PARDINI (d/o Alice[6] Abel Pardini #482), b 3 December 1953 at Santa Rosa, CA; m 7 July 1973 at Santa Rosa, **Darrell Johnson.** Darrell works at National Controls Inc. They live in Santa Rosa.

Children, surname JOHNSON:
- 2511. i. Joshua[8] Wade, b 24 March 1976.
- 2512. ii. Wendy Marie, b 24 June 1974.

1199. KEITH[7] THOMAS PARDINI (s/o Alice[6] Abel Pardini #482), b 20 October 1954 at Santa Rosa, CA; m 4 September 1981 at Reno, NV, **Debbie Haggerman Turner.** Keith works at a feed mill at Santa Rosa.

Child, surname PARDINI:
- 2513. i. Amanda Rose, b 1 August 1983.
- 2513A. i. Phillip[8] Haggerman, b 11 March 1979. (step-son)

1200. KAREN[7] MARIE PARDINI (d/o Alice[6] Abel Pardini #482), b

21 June 1958 at Santa Rosa, CA; m 30 June 1979 at Santa Rosa, **Wayne Guillory**. They live in Santa Rosa; Wayne works for United Parcel Service.

Children, surname GUILLORY:
- 2514. i. Denver[8] Imo, b 19 January 1981.
- 2515. ii. Tyler Wayne, b 16 November 1983.

1201. ROSS[7] ABEL (s/o James[6] Daniel Abel #484), b 20 January 1955 at Rochester, MN; m 14 August 1976 at Dodge Center, MN, **Rosanne Wood**. They live at Kasson, MN.

Children, surname ABEL:
- 2516. i. James[8], b 25 May 1979.
- 2517. ii. Ryan, b 6 January 1981.

1202. KIM[7] ABEL (d/o James[6] Daniel Abel #484), b 13 July 1960 at Rochester, MN; m 16 August 1978 at Dodge Center, **Russell Bond**, b at Dodge Center, MN.

Children, surname BOND:
- 2518. i. Michael[8], b 2 February 1980.
- 2519. ii. Jennifer, b 26 July 1982.

1205. DANIEL[7] JAMES ABEL (s/o Leonard[6] Orlow Abel #485), b 14 January 1952, Owatonna, MN; m 15 April 1972 at Christ Lutheran Church, Zumbrota, MN, **Susan Margaret Tangen**, b 28 Nov 1951. Daniel is a nursing student, working on his RN degree, at University of Iowa Hospital. Susan is a bookkeeper at large lumber company in Cedar Rapids, IA. They live in Cedar Rapids. See Addenda.

Children, surname ABEL:
- 2520. i. Yon[8] Aron, b 3 October 1972 at Aviono, Italy.
- 2521. ii. Hans August, b 27 August 1974 at Ellsworth Air Force Base, Rapid City, SD. Died at Rochester, MN 7 October 1974.
- 2522. iii. Kirsten Caron, b 20 December 1975 at Ellsworth Air Base.
- 2523. iv. Heide Hannah, b 23 February 1978 at Peterson Field, Colorado Springs, CO.
- 2524. v. Rebecca Rae, b 19 May 1983 at Sheppard Air Force Base, Whichita Falls, TX.

1206. MARY[7] JANE ABEL (d/o Leonard[6] Orlow Abel #485), b 16 April 1953 at Owatonna, MN; m 18 August 1973 at Saint Francis Catholic Church, Rochester, MN, **Thomas Earl Crowe**. Tom is a carpenter for

Forest Home Builders Stewartville, MN. Mary is secretary/receptionist at Hiawatha Children's Home for profoundly retarded children.

Children, surname CROWE, all born at Rochester:
- 2525. i. Todd[8] Brian, b 13 April 1970.
- 2526. ii. Heather Lyn, b 18 April 1975.
- 2527. iii. Jennifer Lyn, b 16 August 1977.

1207. MELINDA[7] JO ABEL (d/o Leonard[6] Orlow Abel #485), b 1 March 1955 at Rochester, MN; m 28 July 1973 at Saint Clemmets Catholic Church, Hammond, MN, **Thomas Charles Kelley**. Melinda does laundry and maintenance at Hiawatha Children's Home. Tom works for Ajustable Joist out of Saint Paul.

Children, surname KELLY, both born at Rochester:
- 2528. i. Matthew[8] Gregory, b 24 December 1977.
- 2529. ii. Nicholas Leonard, b 10 April 1982.

1210. THOMAS[7] EDWARD BAKER (s/o Chester[6] Lamont Baker #486), b 20 April 1942 at Saint Paul, MN; m 24 October 1965 at Denver, CO, **Mary Sheridan Simpkovitz**.

Child, surname BAKER:
- 2530. i. Thomas[8] Sheridan, b 21 July 1967 at Denver.

1211. EUGENE[7] ARTHUR BAKER (s/o Chester[6] Lamont Baker #486), b 2 June 1944 at Rhinelander, WI; m 18 November 1969 at Wausau, WI, **Jane Teetz**.

Children, surname BAKER, all born at Wausau:
- 2531. i. Nicole[8] Renee, b 24 April 1973.
- 2532. ii. Kimberly Anne, b 18 November 1976.
- 2533. iii. Mathew Allen, b 14 April 1981.

1212. FAYE[7] ETTA BAKER (d/o Chester[6] Lamont Baker #486), b 17 May 1946 at Medford, WI; m 3 January 1970 at Antigo, WI, **Gary Robert Merwyn**.

Children, surname MERWYN:
- 2534. i. Gary[8] Robert, b 10 December 1970, at Antigo.
- 2535. ii. David, b 1 January 1977, at Antigo.
- 2536. iii. Robert, b 15 October 1982, at Antigo.

1213. RUTH[7] LUCILLE BAKER (d/o Chester[6] Lamont Baker #486), b 10 August 1947 at Medford, WI; m 21 January 1967, **Armin Kindschy**.

Children, surname KINDSCHY:
- 2537. i. Chester[8] Armin, b 11 August 1967; m 11 August 1986, Lorie Garten at Mountain Lake, MN.
- 2538. ii. Curtis Allen, b 24 November 1968 at Owatonna, MN.
- 2539. iii. Christopher Aris, b 23 June 1971.
- 2540. iv. Roger Lee, b 11 December 1972.
- 2541. v. Donna Marie, b 28 January 1986 at Austin, MN.
- 2542. vi. Ona Marie, b 28 January 1986.

1215. GLADYS[7] IRENE BAKER (d/o Chester[6] Lamont Baker #486), b 23 August 1952 at Owatonna, MN; m 7 October 1972 at Dodge Center, MN, **John Wesley Schroeder**.

Children, surname SCHROEDER:
- 2543. i. Charity[8] Ann, b 13 May 1974 at Dallas, TX.
- 2544. ii. Melissa Joy, b 19 March 1978 at Minneapolis, MN.
- 2545. iii. Jason, b 3 August 1983 at Minneapolis.

1216. ROSE[7] ALVERETTA BAKER (d/o Chester[6] Lamont Baker #486), b 30 September 1953 at Owatonna, MN; m 5 June 1976 at Dodge Center, MN, **Robert Hunn**.

Children, surname HUNN:
- 2546. i. Robert[8] Leroy, b 16 September 1980 at Owatonna, MN.
- 2547. ii. Brian, b 15 July 1984, Owatonna.
- 2548. iii. Laura Lucille, b 28 February 1987.
- 2549. iv. Joel, b 17 July 1989 at Rochester, MN.

1218. CHAN[7] FATE (s/o Beatrice[6] Baker Fate #487), b 19 November 1940 at Claremont, MN; m 7 April 1962, **Jean Wilke**. Chan is a laborer and they live at West Concord, MN.

Children, surname FATE:
- 2550. i. Denise[8] Jean, b 22 January 1963 at Rochester, MN. Was attending North Central Bible College in Minneapolis.
- 2551. ii. Martin James, b 10 February 1964 at Dodge Center, MN. Was working in a canning factory.
- 2552. iii. Thomas Daniel, b 1 April 1965 at Dodge Center. Was working in a canning factory.

2553. iv. Michael Todd, b 21 December 1967 at Dodge Center.
2554. v. Melody Ann, b 16 April 1968 at West Concord.
2555. vi. Dayton Andrew, b 3 April 1971 at West Concord.

1220. TROY[7] FATE (s/o Beatrice[6] Baker Fate #487), b 3 January 1962 at Rochester, MN; m 15 June 1984, **Randy Urkmann**. They live at Kasson, MN and Troy works for Greenway Fertilizer Co., Dodge Center, MN.

Children, surname FATE:
2556. i. Erin[8] Nicole, b 10 March 1984.
2557. ii. Nathan.

1235. DEBORAH[7] KAY WESTER (d/o Donald[6] Wester #490), b 25 September 1958 in Spain; m **David Anderson** in OH.

Child, surname ANDERSON:
2558. i. Jennifer[8] Marie, b 23 September 1980 in Durango, CO.

1238. MITCHELL[7] ALLEN WESTER (s/o Phillip[6] Wester #491), b 28 June 1955 at Portsmouth, VA; m 28 July 1980/81 at Black River Falls, WI, **Susan Emerson Smith**.

Children, surname WESTER:
2559. i. Marcus[8] Allen, b 8 April 1982 at Black River Falls.
2560. ii. Melissa, (step-daughter).

1239. MICHAEL[7] LEE WESTER (s/o Phillip[6] Wester #491), b 12 February 1957 at Superior, WI; m in California, 7 May 1983, **Anna Callahan**. Michael is stationed at the USAF base in California.

1240. VICTORIA[7] LYNN WESTER (d/o Philip[6] Wester #491), b 19 August 1958 at Superior, WI; m 29 October 1977 at Solon Springs, WI, **Tom Evans**.

Child, surname EVANS:
2562. i. Jennifer[8] Lynn, b 2 September 1979 in CA.

1245. GAIL[7] MARIE THEIEN (d/o Linda[6] Wester Theien #493), b 27 April 1958 at Minneapolis, MN; m 26 August 1978 at Peoria, IL, **Mike Patton**.

Child, surname THEIEN:
    2563. i. Erin[8] Marie, b 16 May 1981.

1249. TAMMARA[7] **KAY WESTER** (d/o Victor[6] Wester #494), b 26 September 1962 at Superior, WI; m 27 December 1980 at Lake Nebagamon, WI, **Ronald Johnson**.

Child, surname JOHNSON:
    2564. i. Matthew[8] Ronald, b 5 March 1983 at Superior, WI.

1255. DENNIS[7] **JAMES SCHMIDT** (s/o Ruth[6] Johnson Schmidt #496), b 15 July 1958 at Superior, WI; m 8 October 1984 at Rochester, MN, **Joan DuBuque**. Dennis is a computer programmer, analyst, researcher for IBM in Rochester where they live.

Child, surname SCHMIDT:
    2565. i. Daniel[8] Ryan, b 11 May 1985.

1257. NANCY[7] **KAYE INGERSOLL** (d/o Alice[6] White Ingersoll #497), b 31 July 1948; m/1 18 February 1967, **Ray Stennett**; marriage annulled. Nancy m/2 **Rodney Delose Bacon**. They live at Eldon, MO.

Children, surname STENNETT:
    2566. i. Michelle[8] Ivena, b 2 December 1968 at Austin, MN.
    2567. ii. Shane Ray, b 30 June 1969 at Perry, IA.

Child, surname Bacon:
    2568. iii. Danelle[8] Dorothy, b 9 September 1972 at Rochester, MN.

1258. JOYCE[7] **ANN INGERSOLL** (d/o Alice[6] White Ingersoll #497), b 21 August 1951 at Owatonna, MN; m 10 July 1972, **James McNatt**. They reside in Madison, AL.

Children, surname McNATT:
    2569. i. Jamie[8] Marvin, b 19 April 1970 at Bartow, FL.
    2570. ii. Jason Lee, b 10 November 1972 at Austin, MN.
    2571. iii. Joshua Andrew, b 29 July 1976 at Mora, MN.
    2572. iv. Jodie Ilene, b 9 October 1979 at Athens, AL.

1261. CINDY[7] **LOU INGERSOLL** (d/o Alice[6] White Ingersoll #497), b 22 August 1961 Rochester, MN, m **Edward Nold**. Later divorced.

Child, surname NOLD:
    2573. i. John Edward, b June 1979.

1263. DONALD[7] KEITH EISENHAUER (s/o Donald[6] Leslie Eisenhauer #498), b 20 April 1954 at Glendale, CA; m 1 December 1973 at Santa Barbara, CA, **Peggy Light**.

Children, surname EISENHAUER:
    2574.   i.   Donald[8], b 2 March 1976, at Tarzana, Los Angeles Co., CA.
    2575.   ii. Garry, b 12 September 1979, at Tarzana.

1264. TERRI[7] ANN EISENHAUER (d/o Donald[6] Leslie Eisenhauer #498), b 12 November 1957 at Northridge, CA; m 21 April 1979 at Glendale, CA, **Ralph Helm Johonnot**.

Children, surname JOHONNOT:
    2576.   i.   Ralph[8], b 9 January 1980, at Ridgecrest, CA.
    2577.   ii. Samantha, b 21 September 1982, at Ridgecrest.

1265. DENA[7] HAUGEN (d/o Patricia[6] Eisenhauer Haugen #499), b 1 February 1959 at Los Angeles, CA; m 5 September 1976 at Las Vegas, NV, **Timothy James Burke**.

Children, surname BURKE:
    2578.   i.   Jennifer[8], b 8 October 1976 at Tarzana, CA.
    2579.   ii. Christie, b 4 April 1978 at Van Nuys, CA.

1269. MARK[7] DANIEL McATEE (s/o Anne[6] Goodrich McAtee #500), b 31 January 1957; m 12 June 1977, **Kimberley Anne Lemon**.

Child, surname McATEE:
    2580.   i.   Christopher[8] Mark, b 5 February 1983 in Laramie, WY.

1274. LILA[7] JEAN NOBLE (d/o Frances[6] McDaniel Nobel #502), b 11 May 1947 at Laramie, WY; m 22 January 1983 at Port Angeles, WA, **Ronald J. Owes**, b 5 July 1943. Ron is a civil engineer and Lila ia a day care center owner/operator.

Child, surname OWES:
    2581.   i.   Erin[8] Elizabeth, b 21 June 1983 at Seattle, WA.

1276. GRANT[7] LEE NOBLE (s/o Frances[6] McDaniel Noble #502), b 18 January 1962 at Saint Charles, IL; m 22 August 1983 in Vancouver, WA, **Rhonda Lynn Denny**, b 16 July 1963. They were divorced in 1986.

Child, surname NOBLE:
    2582.   i.   Christopher[8] Scott, b 31 January 1985.

The Seventh Generation 379

1277. LORA[7] **NOBLE** (d/o Frances[6] McDaniel Noble #502), b 19 January 1964 at Geneva, IL; m 24 November 1984, **Talbert Lloyd Looking Elk** of the Fort Peck Indian Reservation, b 18 March 1962 in Phoenix, AZ. His mother's maiden name: Lavonne Big Horn.

Child, surname LOOKING ELK:
- 2583. i. Paula[8] Victoria, b 18 June 1986 in Glasgow, MT.

1278. THOMAS[7] **LANE McDANIEL** (s/o Ward[6] Emery McDaniel #504), b 1 June 1952 at Rugby, ND; m 4 May 1974 in Casper, WY, **Deborah Jean Moore**, b 6 April 1952 in Denver, CO, d/o Harold and Shirley Moore of Casper, WY. Tom is a building contractor. Debbie is a teacher.

Children, surname McDANIEL, all born at Farmington, NM:
- 2584. i. Jennifer[8] Lynn, b 24 October 1979.
- 2585. ii. Jeffery Lane, b 9 May 1981.
- 2586. iii. Jamie Lee, b 30 October 1983.
- 2587. iv. Lynsey Jean, b 17 November 1986.
- 2588. v. Robert Thomas, b 13 April 1988.

1279. LUCINDA[7] **JEAN McDANIEL** (d/o Ward[6] Emery McDaniel #504), b 14 July 1954 at Belleville, IL; m 22 December 1979, **Kenneth Alan Griffith**, b 8 August 1949 at Bridgeport, NE, s/o Ivan and Dorothy Griffith. Kenneth is a guidance counsellor; Cindy is a teacher.

Children, surname GRIFFITH:
- 2589. i. Austin[8] Thomas, b 16 August 1982 at Sidney, NE.
- 2590. ii. Zachery Eugene, b 15 February 1984 at Chadron, NE.

1283. DEAN[7] **BRENT HERTZLER** (s/o Betty[6] Jo McDaniel Hertzler #505), b 21 November 1955 at Torrington, WY; m 25 July 1976, **Pamela Michael**, b 29 June 1957 at Cheyenne, WY, d/o Chris and Sharon (Beede) Michael. Dean is a farmer with his father near Veteran, WY. Pam is a nurse.

Child, surname HERTZLER:
- 2591. i. Joshua[8] Brent Zacharia, b 22 February 1986; he was adopted as an infant.

1284. CYNTHIA[7] **LUCILLE ROBERTSON** (d/o Thomas[6] Earl Robertson #507), b 9 July 1955; m 20 September 1980, **Rodney C. Street**, b 5 September 1950, s/o Don and Lorene Street.

Child, surname STREET:
  2592. i. Marcia[8] Lu, b 20 January 1986.

1288. DEBORAH[7] ANN COURTNEY (d/o Mary[6] Robertson Courtney #508), b 9 April 1956 at Denver, CO; m 30 October 1982, **Robert J. Pretz**, b 1 April 1956, s/o John and Rosemarie Pretz of Denver.

Children, surname PRETZ:
  2593. i. Stacey[8] Lynn, b 20 November 1983.
  2594. ii. Lisa Marie, b 20 November 1983, an identical twin.

1291. KAREN[7] LYNN LINDBURG (d/o Joyce[6] Austin Lindburg #509), b 13 February 1966 in Cheyenne, WY; m 12 November 1989 at Lake Tahoe, **Matthew Thomas Person**. Karen is a legal secretary; Matthew works in the parts department of the local Ford dealership; they live in Cheyenne.

Child, surname PERSON:
  2595. i. Valan[8] Nicole (Lindburg), b 1 June 1985 at Cheyenne; she was adopted by Matthew in August 1991.
  2596. i. Matthew Shane, b 13 March 1990.

1296. CHADRICK[7] ARTHUR ROOTS (s/o Gladys[6] Rogers Roots #513), b 21 May 1932 at Eureka, NV; m in 1961, **Loretta Mary Yank**, b 25 March 1935. Chadwick is a "Pug Mill" operator in the Ione, CA Buick Plant.

Children, surname ROOTS:
+ 2597. i. Chadrick[8] Arthur Joseph, b 15 January 1961.
  2598. ii. Crystal Maria, b 24 April 1965 at Truckee, CA; works for a hospital in Sacramento for troubled children.
  2599. iii. Amber Adora, b 24 April 1965 (twin) at Truckee. Works at a convalescent hospital at Sacramento.
  2600. iv. Nicholas Anthony, b 3 June 1969 at Fortuna, CA.

1297. BEAUFORD[7] ALBA ROOTS (s/o Gladys[6] Rogers Roots #513), m in 1955, **Dolores Layer**.

Children, surname ROOTS:
  2601. i. Jeffery[8].
  2602. ii. Mike.

1298. WILFORD[7] ACCORD ROOTS (s/o Gladys[6] Rogers Root #513),

The Seventh Generation 381

m about 1954, **Patricia** —.

Children, surname ROOTS:
- 2603. i. Joe[8], d 1984/85 in a car accident.
- 2604. ii. William.
- 2605. iii. Paula.

1305. JOAN[7] **GAYLE PERCHETTI** (d/o Lucy[6] Cates Perchetti #519), b 8 May 1936 at Tonopah, NV; m 17 April 1955 at Tonopah, **William George Kretschmer**, b 14 August 1936, s/o William Harvey and Jessie Irene (Baker) Kretschmer. William is a teamster.

Children, surname KRETSCHMER:
- 2606. i. William[8] Dean, b 23 February 1957 at Tonopah; m 29/30 June 1983, Larci April Yates at Reno, NV; he has Christmas Disease, a bleeding disorder, where they are missing the factor nine in their blood, inherited from his mother. Also has a bad heart. Was an assessor before he got sick. No children.
- + 2607. ii. Tamra Gaye, b 19 April 1958.
- 2608. iii. Kenneth Lee, b 26 November 1962 at Carson City, NV, also has Christmas disease.
- 2609. iv. Roy Allen, b 2 March 1968 at Seattle, WA.

1314. DAVID[7] **OLIVER HARDT** (s/o Aroline[6] Cates Hardt #521), b 14 April 1940 at Bisbee, AZ; m 25 August 1956 at Silver City, NM, **Louise Fay Fultz**, b 4 May 1938 at Douglas, AZ, d/o Carl Buck and Cloma (Ratliff) Fultz. David works as control room dispatcher for Phelps Dodge Corp., Tyrone, NM. Louise is a bookkeeper at J.C. Penney.

Children, surname HARDT, all born at Bisbie, AZ:
- + 2610. i. Darrell[8] Oliver, b 14 January 1957.
- + 2611. ii. Nina Louise, b 18 December 1957.
- + 2612. iii. Gay Jeanette, b 6 July 1960.
- + 2613. iv. Ivan Thomas, b 15 October 1962.

1315. VERNALINE[7] **MARIE HARDT** (d/o Aroline[6] Cates Hardt #521), b 9 May 1941 at Bisbee, AZ; m 8 June 1957, **Roger Koy Haynie**, b 18 April 1938 at Douglas, AZ, s/o Robert and Mary Eileen (Udell) Haynie; m Naco, Mexico. Vernaline is a talented seamstress and cook; Roger manages a junk yard and has strong mechanical abilities.

Children, surname HAYNIE:

+ 2614. i. Roger[8] Koy, b 11 May 1958.
+ 2615. ii. Walter Lyn, b 10 May 1959.
+ 2616. iii. Dee Ann, b 4 August 1960.
+ 2617. iv. Dorene Marie, b 5 December 1961.
+ 2618. v. Clinton Dewayne, b 8 March 1963.
   2619. vi. Byron Jerome, b 2 April 1964 at Douglas, AZ.
   2620. vii. Kelly Jeanette, b 3 March 1966 at Douglas.

1317. RONALD[7] MICHAEL HARDT (s/o Aroline[6] Cates Hardt #521), "Mickey" was b 1 January 1946 at Bisbee, AZ; m 16 November 1964, **Winnie Mae Alexander**, b 23 June 1946 at Bisbee, d/o George Alfred and Helen Marie (Smith) Alexander. Ronald retired from the U.S. Navy in 1990.

Children, surname HARDT:
   2621. i. Timothy[8] V., b 9 May 1975 at Bisbee.
   2622. ii. Andrew E., b 5 October 1976 at Silver City, NM.
   2623. iii. Bradley W., b 27 December 1977 at Silver City.

1318. LINDA[7] SUSAN HARDT (d/o Aroline[6] Cates Hardt #521), b 2 May 1948 at Bisbee, AZ; m 3 March 1972 at Saint Patrick Catholic Church, Bisbee, **Ronald Lee Hughes**, b 17 February 1943 at Greenville, KY, s/o John and Edith Evelyn (Foster) Hughes. Linda works as a Financial Assistant/Secretary of Greenlee Co. Probation Dept. Ronald is shift foreman at Metcalf Concentrator, Phelps Dodge. Ronald m/1 14 September 1963, **Edna Marie Vaughn**, d/o Jessie Lawrence and Myrtle Vaughn; divorced 1 June 1967 at Bisbee;

Children, surname HUGHES:
   2624. i. Christopher[8] Shawn, b 28 September 1969, at Bisbee; m 30 September 1988, Barbara Ann Layton, d/o Delbert Scott and Joy Lynn (Johnson) Layton, b 28 October 1968 at Wickenburg, AZ.
   2625. ii. Amber Michelle, b 25 September 1972, at Bisbee.

1320. PHILLIP[7] JOEL HARDT (s/o Aroline[6] Cates Hardt #521), b 3 March 1956 at Bisbee, AZ; m 28 June 1975 at Saint Luke's Parish, Douglas, AZ, **Laura Ann Bohmfalk**, b 19 October 1955 at Honolulu, HI (army hospital), d/o Thomas LeRoy and Rita Ann (Contreras) Bohmfalk. Phillip has Hemophilia (lacks factor 9); has masters degree in English, a great piano player and singer. Works as purchaser for Bendel (they make seat belts) and teaches English & computers part time at Cochise Jr.

College in Douglas; Laura teaches business courses at state prison in Douglas and has degree in business administration.

Children, surname HARDT:
    2626. i. Joeline[8] Nicole, b 23 January 1976 at Tucson, AZ.
    2627. ii. Michelle Elizabeth, b 16 March 1978 at Silver City, NM.
    2628. iii. Jenifer Ann, b 13 October 1979 at Silver City; d 13 March 1979.
    2629. iv. Phillip Thomas, b 4 September 1980 at Silver City.
    2630. v. Meredith Angelee, b 5 January 1989 at Fort Huachuca, Cochise City, AZ. (adopted 24 July 1989)

1326. GLORIA[7] JEAN MILLER (d/o Sylvia[6] Cates Miller #524), b 30 May 1942 at Waterloo, IA; m/1 1959, **Richard Beckwith**; m/2 1961, **Jack Paul Roberts**; m/3 1971, **Rudy Montoya**.

Children, surname ROBERTS, Gloria's first two children were adopted by Roberts:
+   2631. i. Richard[8] L. (Beckwith).
+   2632. ii. Kevin Gene (Beckwith).
    2633. iii. Stanley Paul.

1327. JUDY[7] KAY MILLER (d/o Sylvia[6] Cates Miller #524), b 15 August 1944 at Waterloo, IA; m 1963, **John Proutsos**.

Children, surname PROUTSOS:
    2634. i. Johanna[8] Lin, b 1964.
    2635. ii. Georgene, b 1966.
    2636. iii. Crintina Maria, b 1969.

1328. DORIS[7] GENEIL MILLER (d/o Sylvia[6] Cates Miller #524), b 29 June 1947 at Ely, NV; m 1965, **Ronald Niman**.

Children, surname NIMAN:
    2637. i. Duane[8] Lee, b 1965.
    2638. i. Nicci Lin, b 1972.

1339. PAULINE[7] YVETTE BASS (d/o Geneil[6] Cates Bass #527), b 13 February 1950 at Ely, NV; m 20 September 1969 at Ruth, NV, **William Dee Rollins**. He is a laborer for Kennicott Copper; they live in West Jordan, UT.

Children, surname ROLLINS:
    2639. i. John[8] Dee, b 17 July 1970 at Darnell Army Hospital, Fort Hood,

TX.
2640. ii. Kami Jo, b 15 September 1974 at Ely, NV.
2641. iii. Todd James, b 12 February 1981 at Salt Lake City, UT.

1340. BARBARA[7] LYDIA CARLING (d/o Geneil[6] Cates Bass Carling #527), b 14 February 1951 at Ely, NV; m 14 June 1968 at Wichita Falls, TX, **Jerry Dee Bettridge**. He took his life in Elka, NV, 8 November 1982. Barbara works for Dee Mining Co, a gold mine.

Children, surname BETTRIDGE, both born at Ely:
2642. i. Troy[8] Dee, b 14 November 1968.
2643. ii. Tauna, b 24 February 1972.

1341. MARY[7] ELLEN CARLING (d/o Geneil[6] Cates Bass Carling #527), b 18 October 1954 at Ely, NV; m 29 June 1974, **Daniel Gault** at Ruth, NV. Daniel works for a chemical company in Henderson, NV; Mary is a cosmotologist.

Child, surname GAULT:
2644. i. Lisa[8] Karen, b 29 October 1980 at Henderson, NV.

1342. KAREN[7] GENEIL CARLING (d/o Geneil[6] Cates Bass Carling #527), b 10 August 1956 at Ely, NV; m 15 September 1979, **Harold Wayne Wabbel** at Stateline, NV.

Child, surname WABBEL:
2645. i. Geneil[8] Naomi, b 9 November 1979 at Carson, City, NV.

1343. LOUIS[7] CHRISTOPHER TOGNONI (s/o Nye[6] Woodrow Tognoni #530), b 16 August 1945 at Kimberly, NV; m 21 November 1966 at the Methodist Church at Ruth, NV, **Caroline Joyce Rasmussen**, b 22 October 1948 at Park Rapids, MN, d/o Anker Conrad and Mildred Marie (Meligan) Rasmussen. A retired navy man; enlisted 25 March 1965. When last known he planned on attending Reno State to become a teacher; living at San Jose, CA.

Children, surname TOGNONI:
2646. i. Marie[8] Faye, b 30 August 1968 at Jacksonville, FL.
2647. ii. Christine Joyce, b 21 March 1970 at Ely, NV.
2648. ii. Nye Woodrow III, b 15 January 1976 at Mount View, CA.

1346. PATRICIA[7] LINDA TOGNONI (d/o Nye[6] Woodrow Tognoni #530), b 13 May 1950 at Chelan, WA; m 22 November 1969 at Carson

The Seventh Generation 385

City, NV, **Ronald Sidney McQueen**, b 22 January 1951 in CO, s/o Sidney Clifford and Ruth Esther (Ranch) McQueen; Ronald d 19 July 1974 at Yerington, NV. He was a driller for different companies; also was a self-employed carpenter and truck driver for Valley Dairy. Patricia is a special education teacher.

Children, surname McQUEEN, all born at Yerington:
    2649. i. Bonnie[8] Ester, b 4 June 1970.
    2650. ii. Rebecca Renee, b 17 February 1973.
    2651. iii. Joseph Sidney, b 29 January 1975.

1348. JOEY[7] ANN MENDEZ (d/o Neva[6] Tognoni Mendez #531), b 12 May 1939 at Eureka, NV; m 8 February 1958 Tacoma, WA, **Marvin Arnold Percha**, b 7 February 1938 at Detroit, MI, s/o Frank and Irene Percha. Joey was sergeant on the campus police force at Maricopa Co, AZ; wants to study criminal justice. They are divorced and Joey lives at Phoenix, AZ.

Children, surname PERCHA:
    2652. i. Julie[8] Irene, b 8 May 1959 at Tacoma; was studying to be marine biologist.
    2653. ii. Laurie Neva, b 28 April 1960 at Tacoma; was studying for business career.
    2654. iii. Marvin Arnold, b 30 June 1961 at Englewood, CA, was studying to be a meteorologist.
    2655. iv. Michelle Marie, b 27 March 1963 at Englewood, was preparing for law career.
    2656. v. Claudine Lee, b 28 December 1969 at Mesa, AZ.
    2657. vi. Perfidia Loretta, b 28 December 1969 at Mesa.

1349. ANTONIO[7] JOSEPH MENDEZ (s/o Neva[6] Tognoni Mendez #531), b 15 November 1940 at Eureka, NV; m at Englewood, CO, **Karen Smith** b 5 Oct 1943. Antonio has 45 acres, a home and art studio in the Appalachians in Maryland.

Children, surname MENDEZ:
    2658. i. Amanda[8] Lynn, b 24 January 1961 at Denver, CO; a travel agent in Dallas.
    2659. ii. Anthony Tobias, b 28 September 1963 at Denver; gifted in art.
    2660. iii. Ian Archer, b 12 June 1965 at Littleton, CO.

1350. JOHN[7] FRANK MENDEZ (s/o Neva[6] Tognoni Mendez #531), b 12 September 1942 at Eureka, NV; m 20 January 1966 at San Francisco, CA, **Edith Holmes Prentice**, b 5 August 1942 at Boston, MA, d/o William Hardy and Eleanor Louise (Holmes) Prentice. Hale says they later divorced. John has Masters Degree in business from Harvard School of Business; is Divisional President of Amfax Corp.

Children, surname MENDEZ:
    2661.   i.   Damon^8 Miguel, b 11 August 1971 at San Francisco, CA.
    2662.   ii. Derek Jonathan, b 11 October 1973 at San Rafael, CA.

1351. CINDY^7 JILL MENDEZ (d/o Neva^6 Tognoni Mendez #531), b 31 March 1944 at Eureka, NV; m 23 August 1965 at Reno, NV, **Michael Violante**, b July 1943 at San Francisco, CA. It is reported that they are divorced. She was a playboy bunny in San Francisco and became assisstant manager of a playboy club. Now doing public relations for Holiday Inn.

Children, surname VIOLANTE:
    2663.   i.   Monica^8 Michelle, b 31 October 1966, at San Francisco.
    2664.   ii. Adam Joseph, b 28 March 1969, San Francisco.

1352. MAUREEN^7 PATRICIA RICHEY (d/o Neva^6 Tognoni Mendez Richey #531), b 7 May 1946 at Eureka, NV; m 11 April 1964, **Loren Kenneth Bybee**, b 22 June 1944 at Denver, CO., s/o Leslie Eugene and Frances (Rosenstengle) Bybee; manager in a stained glass factory and produces her own creations.

Children, surname BYBEE:
    2665.   i.   Dagny^8 Soubrette, b 25 January 1965 at Honolulu, HI.
    2666.   ii.   Tonia, b 13 December 1966 at Denver.
    2667.   iii. Raquel, b 6 May 1969 at Denver.
    2668.   iv. Natalie Marie, b 31 December 1973 at Mundelein, IL.

1353. NANCY^7 LYNN RICHEY (d/o Neva^6 Tognoni Mendez Richey #531), b 14 February 1948 at Eureka, NV; m August 1965 at Reno, NV, **Steven Eric Wilson**, b 12 January 1947 at Grand Junction, CO. Both are active in Rodeo's, riding and managing. Steve operates big equiptment for Union Oil. Nancy writes for several newspapers and magazines and is a published poet.

Children, surname WILSON:
    2669.   i.   Brandy^8 Lynn, b 10 July 1966 at Denver, CO; wants to be a horse trainer.

2670. ii. Shawn Eric, b 8 August 1969 at Denver.
2671. iii. Jodie Jacqueline, b 25 August 1971 at Salida, CO.

1354. BECKY[7] LOU TOGNONI (d/o Hale[6] Christopher Tognoni #532), b 3 January 1949 at Butte, MT; m 12 July 1974 at Heber, AZ, **Edward White Boudway**, b 17 July 1945 at Northampton, MA, s/o Edward White Sr., and Mary Jane (Kennedy) Boudway. They live at Oracle, AZ. Becky wrote several accounts about mining history and the part her grandfather Tognoni played in it for *Western Prospector and Miner* newspaper.

Children, surname BOUDWAY, all born at Tucson, AZ:
    2672. i. Matthew[8] Flannery, b 7 January 1976.
    2673. ii. Ira Martin, b 1 May 1978.
    2674. iii. Wallace Jeremy, b 27 January 1986.

1355. BRIAN[7] HALE TOGNONI (s/o Hale[6] Christopher Tognoni #532), b 18 November 1950 at Arlington, VA; m/1 **Mickey Howzdy**; divorced her; m/2 **Mary Finster**, b 15 May 1951 at San Francisco, d/o George and Loretta Finster; she d 18 September 1976. When last known he was planning a third marriage. He had a child by his first wife. He lives in Phoenix, AZ. Brian is landman for Mineral Services Corperation's.

Child, surname TOGNONI:
    2675. i. Sean Bradley, b 14 April 1970; stepson.
    2676. ii. Nathan[8], b 25 June 1970 at Phoenix.

1356. DAVID[7] QUENTIN TOGNONI (s/o Hale[6] Christopher Tognoni #532), b 4 March 1952 at Moscow, ID; m **Patricia Severn**, b 9 December 1953. David is a consulting geological engineer. His wife is an agricultural engineer. Now divorced. He lives at Savory, WY.

Children, surname TOGNONI:
    2677. i. Dayle[8] Christine, b 17 February 1979 at Phoenix, AZ.
    2678. ii. Gary, b 18 December 1980 at Craig, CO.
    2679. iii. Wesley, b 4 May 1984 at Craig.

1357. SANDRA[7] ANN TOGNONI (d/o Hale[6] Christopher Tognoni #532), b 21 July 1953 at Superior, AZ; m 26 May 1982 at Phoenix, AZ, **William Nelson Hewitt**, b 15 August 1933 at Oklahoma City, OK, s/o John and Elizabeth Hewitt; Sandra is a graphic artist and William is a consultant in business management with Transportation and Communication. They live in Phoenix.

Child, surname HEWITT:
    2680. i. Winston[8] Jonathan, b 15 August 1986.

1358. JEFFERY[7] R. TOGNONI (s/o Hale[6] Christopher Tognoni #532), b 24 January 1957 at Phoenix, AZ; m 26 June 1981 at Phoenix, **Cathy Murphy**, b 3 December 1957. Jeffery is a geological engineer, but thinking of a career in investment banking. Cathy is a structural engineer working for a consulting firm.

Children, surname TOGNONI:
    2681. i. Nicholas[8] Ford, b 26 May 1985.
    2682. ii. Cassandra, b 21 July 1987.

1359. LYNNE[7] MARIE TOGNONI (d/o Robert[6] Louis Tognoni #533), b 28 July 1958 at Denver, CO; m 4 March 1979 at Denver, **Bruce Keating**, b 11 November 1954 at Oakcliffe, TX, a suburb of Dallas, TX, s/o Leonard and Margaret Theresa (Ekwinski) Keating. She studied aerial photography.

Children, surname KEATING:
    2683. i. Anjelina[8] Michelle, b 26 August 1979 in Aurora, CO.
    2684. ii. Xandon Xaviree, b 30 October 1981 in Denver.

1361. KENNETH[7] ALLEN COX (s/o Gertrude[6] Reed Cox #535), b 19 April 1947 at Shawano, WI; d 1 July 1990 at Peoria, IL of aneurism, m 22 May 1970 at Carlsbad, NM, **Marilyn Palmer**, b 3 November 1945 at Midland, TX, d/o Howard and Leola (Duke) Palmer. Kenneth was a production foreman for Texas Oil Co.

Child, surname COX:
    2685. i. Brian[8] Howard, b 23 October 1980 at Kermit.

1362. ALAN[7] WAYNE COX (s/o Gertrude[6] Reed Cox #535), b 18 January 1949 at Oconto Falls, WI; m 26 August 1978 at Gillett, WI, **Katherine Hearley**, b 4 November 1954 at Oconto Falls, WI, d/o Harold and Bonnie (Dunk) Hearley. They live in suburban Lena, WI. Alan is employed by Our Own Construction.

Children, surname COX, both born at Oconto Falls:
    2686. i. Tirrell[8] Jason, b 5 December 1981.
    2687. ii. Jason Alan, b 29 May 1985.

The Seventh Generation 389

1363. CAROL[7] **JEAN COX** (d/o Gertrude[6] Reed Cox #535), b 30 July 1950 at Oconto Falls, WI; m 14 August 1971 at Gillett, WI, Methodist Church, **Bruce Jensen**, b 24 April 1950 at Oconto Falls, WI, s/o Arnold and Edna (Bahrke) Jensen. They live at Oconto Falls and Bruce is American Family Insurance agent. Carol is head of O.B. Dept. in Oconto Falls Hospital.

Children, surname JENSEN:
    2688. i. Jens[8] Paeter, b 13 January 1972, Oconto Falls.
    2689. ii. Kara Krista, b 17 April 1975, Oconto Falls.
    2690. iii. Kristina Matia, b 29 August 1980, Oconto Falls.

1364. GLORIA[7] **MAE COX** (d/o Gertrude[6] Reed Cox #535), b 31 May 1952 at Oconto Falls, WI; m 15 June 1974 at Gillett, WI, Methodist Church, **Lee Allen Witter**, b 25 April 1945 at Appleton, WI, s/o Harry and Ernice (Loeper) Witter. They live at Neenah, WI and Lee works for Gilbert Paper Co., and Gloria works for Aid Association for Lutherans.

Children, surname WITTER:
    2691. i. Corey[8] Lee, b 22 July 1977 at Neehah.
    2692. ii. Paul Robert, b 12 March 1983 at Neehah.

1366. SHARON[7] **LYNN REED** (d/o Gordon[6] Elmer Reed #536), b 25 January 1959 at Tacoma Park, MD; m 31 December 1980, **Thorne Bertrand**, b 15 January 1957 at Evergreen Park, IL, s/o Neal and Barbara (Hagreen) Bertrand. Live at Sonoma, CA; Thorne is a computer salesman.

Children, surname BERTRAND:
    2693. i. Kirsten[8] Lynn, b 14 June 1981 at San Jose, CA.
    2694. ii. Chandra Pearl, b 29 January 1983 at San Jose.
    2695. iii. Michelle Anne, b 29 June 1984 at San Jose.
    2696. iv. Gillion Neal, b 5 December 1986 at Sonoma, CA.

1370. LORAINE[7] **LESTER** (d/o Geneva[6] Beekman Lester #540), b 9 January 1939 at Philipsburg, MT; m 14 March 1955 at Anaconda, MT, **William Alvin Spaun**, b 12 March 1937 at Helena, MT, s/o William and Kathryn (Maddox) Spaun. William d 15 August 1988.

Children, surname SPAUN:
+   2697. i. Deborah[8] Kay, b 12 September 1955.
+   2698. ii. Rhonda Lee, b 20 October 1956.
    2699. iii. Lois Marie, b 17 September 1957 at Anaconda. Was working for

forest service and a school bus driver.
+ 2700. iv. Billie Jean, b 25 August 1958.

1371. LAWRENCE[7] ARTHUR LESTER (s/o Geneva[6] Beekman Lester #540), b 31 October 1942 at Anaconda, MT; m 24 July 1965 at Anaconda, **Barbara Harrington**, b 28 May 1949 at Anaconda, d/o Francis and Doris (Larivee) Harrington. They are divorced. Lawrence m/2 10 June 1979 at Anaconda, **Joanne Hanson**, b 26 February 1941, d/o Lyle Hanson. Later divorced. Lawrence d 23 November 1988.

Children, surname LESTER, both born at Anaconda:
 2701. i. Terry[8], b 22 July 1966.
 2702. ii. Robin, b 31 May 1969.

1372. CHARLES[7] ANTHONY MUSGRAVE (s/o Mary[6] Wennell Musgrave #541), b 13 April 1947 at Evanston, IL; m 26 May 1969 at Kansas City, MO, **Robbin Scharhag**, d/o Herman and Phyllis (MacKay) Scharhag. Charles works for *Kansas City Star* newspaper in circulation dept.

Children, surname MUSGRAVE, both born at Kansas City:
 2703. i. Brady[8] Alexander, b 30 April 1977.
 2704. ii. Christopher, b 15 March 1979.

1373. DIANE[7] LEE MUSGRAVE (d/o Mary[6] Wennell Musgrave #541), b 1 April 1944 at Evanston, IL; m 19 November 1961 at Acuna, Mexico, **Ronald Holland**, b 4 May 1943 at Big Springs, TX, s/o Wilford and Johnny (Townsend) Holland. They were divorced. Diane is now a single mother; she is a reading specialist at Hazlewood School Dist., Hazelwood, MO. Her last name is now Lee.

Children, surname HOLLAND, both born at Odessa, TX:
 2705. i. Michael[8] Douglas, b 24 October 1962.
 2706. ii. Kenneth Paul, b 6 May 1965.

1374. CAROL[7] LYNN BRANDENHOFF (d/o Hazel[6] Wennell Brandenhoff #542), b 30 June 1943 at Evanston, IL; m 31 July 1965 at Prairie Grove, AR, **Michael Fidler**, b 27 September 1943 at Prairie Grove, s/o Howard and Marit (Carter) Fidler. Carol teaches in Prairie Grove schools.

Children, surname FIDLER:
 2707. i. Shawn[8] Gregory, b 23 September 1970, Fayetteville, AR.
 2708. ii. Shannon Leanne, b 24 April 1972, Fayetteville.

The Seventh Generation 391

1375. DONNA[7] **JEAN BRANDENHOFF** (d/o Hazel[6] Wennell Brandenhoff #542), b 23 January 1947 at Evanston, IL; m 23 December 1970 at Wahoo, NB, **Lawrence Eads**, b 8 December 1943 at Nebraska City, NE, s/o Eli and Frances (Hartley) Eads. Donna teaches in the Omaha, Nebraska schools.

Children, surname EADS:
- 2709. i. Kerry[8] Rae, b 4 July 1972, at Omaha.
- 2710. ii. Torey, b 21 March 1974, at Omaha.

1380. OLYMPIA[7] **LAURA JAMES** (d/o June[6] Carey James #544), b 1 December 1952 at Cutbank, MT; m 3 July 1969, **Charles C. Whatley**, b 21 August 1944 at Houston, TX, s/o Brayton and Roxie Whatley. Laura lives in Houston and is a Mary Kay representative.

Children, surname WHATLEY:
- 2711. i. Blair[8] Ann, b 21 February 1970.
- 2712. ii. Clifton Alan, b 2 February 1972.

1381. JESSE[7] **FRANKLIN JAMES** (s/o June[6] Carey James #544), b 21 April 1955 at Colorado Springs, CO; m **Dava E. Gibson**, b 13 October 1955 at Houston, TX, s/o David Gibson. Jesse is a machinist.

Children, surname JAMES:
- 2713. i. Zachara[8] Nathan, b 5 September 1974.
- 2714. ii. Shilo Christopher, b 13 November 1978.

1382. WOODSON[7] **LEE JAMES** (s/o June[6] Carey James #544), b 29 April 1956 at Colorado Springs, CO; m 29 July 1975, **Elizabeth Jo Peters**, b 23 March 1960 at Dallas, TX, d/o Joe Peters.

Child, surname JAMES:
- 2715. i. Jesse[8] Curtis Ray, b 3 February 1976.

1385. JOHN[7] **CALVIN THOMPSON** (s/o John[6] Norman Thompson, #545), b 2 September 1953; m 31 October 1975, **Pamela Renea Dixon**.

Child, surname THOMPSON:
- 2716. i. Cassie Elizabeth.

1387. LOIS[7] **ANN MISSALL** (d/o Clarice[6] Wright Missall #548), b 9 October 1948 at Suring, WI; m 23 August 1969, **John David Kumhala**. Lois m/2 30 July 1977 **Andrew Bernard Gallenberger**, s/o Bernard and Mary Ann (Shwanke) Gallenberger.

Children, surname KUMHALA:
  2717. i. James[8] Clifford, b 7 November 1970, Oconto, WI.
  2718. ii. Richard Jon, b 31 October 1972, Oconto.
Children, surname MISSALL:
  2719. iii. Dion John, b 22 February 1976.
  2720. iv. Kristi Lynn, b 2 August 1978 at Green Bay, WI.
Child, surname GALLENBERGER:
  2721. v. Nicholas[8] Andrew, b 4 July 1979 at Oconto.

1390. DONALD[7] RAYMOND VANCASTER (s/o Delores[6] Wright Vancaster #550), b 7 August 1948 at Oconto Falls, WI; m 26 October 1973, **Susan Kozar**.
Children, surname VANCASTER, both born at Green Bay, WI:
  2722. i. Jolene[8], b 23 September 1977.
  2723. ii. Aaron, b 22 February 1980.

1391. ELLEN[7] MARIE VANCASTER (d/o Delores[6] Wright Vancaster #550), b 10 July 1952 at Green Bay, WI; m 14 June 1980, **Steven Kosmoski**.
Children, surname KOSMOSKI, both born at Green Bay:
  2724. i. Jack[8], b 17 April 1969. (step-child)
  2725. ii. Ben, b 21 September 1971. (step-child)

1403. JOSEPH[7] CLYDE VALENTA (s/o Wilma[6] Johnson Valenta #557), b 25 November 1942 at Oconto Falls, WI; m 27 November 1965 at Saint Paul, MN, Gustavus Adolphus Lutheran Church, **Margaret Schoewe**, b 23 February 1942, d/o Walter and Agnes (Kiesner) Schoewe. Joseph is a veterinarian in Middleton, WI.
Children, surname VALENTA, both born at Madison, WI:
  2726. i. Adam[8], b 18 December 1975.
  2727. ii. Paige, b 3 August 1976.

1404. LAUREL[7] FERN VALENTA (d/o Wilma[6] Johnson Valenta #557), b 5 January 1946 at Oconto Falls, WI; m 26 June 1971 at Bethel Lutheran Church, Green Valley, WI, **Joseph Abboud**, b 28 October 1947 at Bagdad, Iraq, s/o Joseph and Paula (Sokol) Abboud. Laurel graduated from Wisconsin State College in 1968; she was a physical education teacher. Joseph is the vice-president of Shankers, Inc., an import-export business. They live at Hoffman Estates, IL.

Children, surname ABBOUD:
- 2728. i. Amir[8] Abraham, b 4 January 1975 at Amboy, NJ.
- 2729. ii. Yasmin Fern, b 27 November 1979 at Hoffman Estates, IL.

1406. LARRY[7] LARS JOHNSON (s/o Lars[6] Christian Johnson #558), b 18 July 1950 at Oconto, WI; m 24 May 1969 at Hickory, WI, Church of Christ, **Bonnie Sue Colson**, b 1 October 1957 at Oconto Falls, d/o Vernon and Cleo (Longard) Colson. Larry is a farmer; they live in Hayes, WI.

Children, surname JOHNSON, all born at Oconto Falls:
- 2730. i. Sara[8] Ann, b 20 November 1969.
- 2731. ii. Julie Mae, b 1 January 1971.
- 2732. iii. Timothy James, b 5 June 1973.

1407. MARLENE[7] JOSEPHINE JOHNSON (d/o Ronald[6] Eugene Johnson #559), b 22 July 1941 at Plymouth, WI; m 12 October 1968 at Saint Gabriel's Catholic Church, Prairie du Chen, WI, **Johannes "John" Maass**, b 9 March 1935 in Holland.

Children, surname MAASS:
- 2733. i. Sean[8] Bradley, b 8 March 1973, Wilmington, DE.
- 2734. ii. Brian Michael, b 21 January 1977, Wilmington.

1408. BONNIE[7] LOUISE JOHNSON (d/o Ronald[6] Eugene Johnson #559), b 20 January 1945 at Plymouth, WI; m 29 August 1964 at Prairie du Chen, WI, **Dennis Fuller**, b 1 October 1943, s/o Earl and Doris (Hamilton) Fuller.

Children, surname FULLER, born at Prairie du Chen:
- 2735. i. Kelly[8] Lynn, b 13 May 1965.
- 2736. ii. Micheal Ann, b 29 March 1966.
- 2737. iii. Barron Bradley, b 4 August 1968.

1409. MERLYNN[7] JOHN JOHNSON (s/o Ronald[6] Eugene Johnson #559), b 23 November 1949 at Richland Center, WI; m 5 September 1980 at Orlando, FL, **Connie McCoy Andersen**.

Child, surname JOHNSON:
- 2738. i. Kara[8] Ann, b 14 September 1981 at LaCrosse, WI.

1410. KAREN[7] KATHRYN JOHNSON (d/o Ronald[6] Eugene Johnson #559), b 14 August 1953 at Richland Center, WI; m 7 May 1977 at Prairie du Chen, WI, **Bruce Renile Bowles**, b 26 September 1949 at Janesville, WI, s/o Renile Edgar and Shirley (Conkling) Bowles. Bruce is sales manager of a corrugated container plant. Bruce's great-grand-parents on his father's side were from Belgium.

Child, surname BOWLES:
    2739.   i. Reid[8] Hunter, b 1 December 1980 at Nashville, ID.

1411. CECILIA[7] JEAN JOHNSON (d/o Kenneth[6] LeRoy Johnson #560), b 6 March 1944 at Green Bay, WI; m 12 July 1964 at Green Bay, WI, **Patrick William Walker**, s/o Roger Walker.

Children, surname WALKER, all born at Green Bay, WI:
    2740.   i. James[8], b 16 February 1965.
    2741.   ii. Dawn, b 19 February 1967.
    2742.   iii. Patrick, b 2 September 1973.

1412. PATRICIA[7] JOHNSON (d/o Kenneth[6] LeRoy Johnson #560), b 12 November 1947 at Green Bay, WI; m 8 April 1967 at Green Bay, WI, **Ernest Kimball**, b 25 October 1946 at Leona, WI, s/o Ward and Ruth (Schemmel) Kimball.

Children, surname KIMBALL, all born at Green Bay:
    2743.   i. Kenneth[8], b 1 January 1968.
    2744.   ii. Todd, b 27 November 1970.

1414. FAY[7] ANN JOHNSON (d/o Clyde[6] Lyle Johnson #561), b 2 August 1946 at Oconto, WI; m 7 August 1949 at Prairie du Chen, WI, Saint Gabriel's Church, **Raymond Lee Sporleder**, b 7 August 1946, s/o Raymond John and Alyce Mae (Honzu) Sporleder. Ray is a construction worker and they live at Morrison, CO.

Children, surname SPORLEDER, both born at Greeley, CO:
    2745.   i. Andrea[8], b 13 November 1972.
    2746.   ii. Lea, b 13 July 1975.

1415. GARY[7] JOHNSON (s/o Clyde[6] Lyle Johnson #561), b 9 October 1948 at Prairie du Chen, WI; m 31 July 1971 at Oakland, CA, **Karin Marlis Wackenagel**, b 26 January 1951 in Germany, d/o Fritz and Inge Wackenagel. Gary is a carpenter and an artist. Divorced in 1982.

The Seventh Generation

Children, surname WACKENAGEL:
    2747.   i.   Erick[8], b 11 October 1972.
    2748.   ii.   Keith, b 8 September 1975.
    2749.   iii.   Heika, b 10 February 1978.

1416. LINDA[7] **JOHNSON** (d/o Clyde[6] Lyle Johnson #561), b 25 January 1949 at Prairie du Chen, WI; m 8 March 1969 at Seneca, WI, **Glenn Wisdom Eldon McCullick**, b 28 August 1946 at Prairie du Chen, s/o Max Eldon and Betty Lillian (Martin) McCullick. Glenn and Linda own a TV shop.

Children, surname McCULLICK:
    2750.   i.   Melanie[8] Mae, b 24 April 1971.
    2751.   ii.   Jason Glenn, b 12 May 1975.

1421. PAMELA[7] **OLICK** (d/o Mae[6] Johnson Olick #563), b 17 May 1955 at Milwaukee, WI; m 10 July 1976 at Our Redeemer Lutheran Church, Suring, WI, **Ronald Raddant**, b 20 April 1951 at Shawano, WI. Ronald is a farmer.

Children, surname RADDANT:
    2752.   i.   Jason[8] David, b 29 October 1979.
    2753.   ii.   Alicia Mae, b 11 January 1983 at Shawano.

1422. JEANETTE[7] **CAROL SLANG** (d/o Dora[6] Johnson Slang #564), b 24 June 1945 at Shawano, WI; m 22 December 1979, **Sam Kootaka**, an Hawaiian. Jeanette is a nurse in HI.

Children, surname KOOTAKA:
    2754.   i.   Sajen[8] Lo'iki (Lo'ki) Mei Ling Jo Slan, ("Our baby's first name Samuel (SA) and Jeanette (JEN). Her Hawaiian name Lo'iki represents my family of Polynesian descent. The Chinese name Mei Ling was chosen on behalf of my grandfather, who was of Chinese descent. Jo Slan is from the last names of Jen's parents which were combined by using Jo from her mother's maiden name Johnson and Slan from her father's name Slang. Kootaka Represents my grandfather who migrated to Hawaii from Japan. Thus the bloodlines Sajen is Danish, Norwegian, Chinese, Japanese and Hawaiian.)

1423. CAROL[7] **LEA SLANG** (d/o Dora[6] Johnson Slang #564), b 6 June 1948 at Oconto Falls WI; m 29 August 1970 at Our Redeemer Lutheran Church at Suring, WI, **Lowell Howard Suring**, b 18 July 1948 at Oconto

Falls, s/o Louis and Martha (Schuettpelz) Suring; Lowell works for Dept. of Environmental Conservation. Lowell's great grandfather Louis is brother of the one who started a saw mill in Suring; giving the town it's name. Carol worked as a medical technician before having children.

Children, surname SURING:
- 2755. i. Erik[8] John, b 23 February 1977 at Albany, NY.
- 2756. ii. Aaron James, b 23 June 1978 at Albuquerque, NM.

1424. LORA[7] JEAN SLANG (d/o Dora[6] Johnson Slang #564), b 10 February 1952 at Oconto Falls, WI; m 28 June 1975 at Our Redeemer Lutheran Church, Suring, WI, **Darryl Daniel Houska**, b 2 May 1945 at Lena, WI, s/o Frank and Rose A. (Nemacheck) Houska. Darryl had 3 sons by a first marriage to Patricia Vanden Elzen.

Children, surname HOUSKA:
- 2757. i. Scott[8] Daniel, b 2 May 1963, Green Bay, WI.
- 2758. ii. Darryl Daniel, b 13 May 1964, Green Bay.
- 2759. iii. Sean James, b 21 April 1970, Green Bay.
- 2760. iv. Megan[8] Jean, b 6 September 1980, at Shawano, WI.
- 2761. v. Isaiah Franklin John, b 17 September 1983, at Shawano.

1426. DAVID[7] VIRGIL JOHNSON (s/o Virgil[6] Arling Johnson #566), b 6 December 1947 at Oconto Falls, WI; m **Cheryl Rae Copus**, b 11 December 1947 at Madison, WI, d/o Hank and Harriet Christina (Boch) Copus. Cheryl's great grandfather on her mothers side, Halvor Bakken, came from Norway; David is a Logger and a hunter.

Child, surname JOHNSON:
- 2762. i. David[8] Erik, b 29 December 1977.

1428. CYNTHIA[7] MARIE JOHNSON (d/o Virgil[6] Arling Johnson #566), b 2 August 1955 Lancaster, WI; m **Lane Gene Landenberger**, b 7 October 1955 at Bismark, ND, s/o Leonard Walter and Doris Elaine (Merkel) Landenberger. Leonard's grandparents, John and Rosina Landenberger, on his father's side came from Neudorf, Russia in 1903; Leonard's great-grandparents on his mother's side came from Worms, Russia..

Child, surname LANDENBERGER:
- 2763. i. Lisa[8] Marie, b 4 December 1980 at Lancaster, WI.

1431. TYRONE[7] ERLING ARNESON (s/o Beverly[6] Johnson Arneson #567), b 23 May 1952 at Oconto Falls, WI; m 31 July 1971 at Saint John's Lutheran Church at Oconto Falls, WI, **Audrey Carol Birr**, b 22 May 1954 at Oconto Falls, d/o Alvin and Florence (April) Birr. Tyrone is head cheesemaker of Morgan Coop Dairy, Oconto Falls.

Children, surname ARNESON:
- 2764. i. Tyrone[8] Erling, b 22 December 1971 at Oconto Falls.
- 2765. ii. Jennifer Lynn, b 21 March 1974 at Oconto Falls.
- 2766. iii. Charlene Beverly, b 7 July 1977 at Krakow,WI.
- 2767. iv. Aaron Richard, b 2 September 1978 at Krakow.

1433. KEITH[7] DALE ARNESON (s/o Beverly[6] Johnson Arneson #567), b 21 February 1957 at Prairie du Chen, WI; m 18 June 1975, **Wendy Marie Bastien**. Keith works at Kohler Co, Kohler, WI.

Children, surname ARNESON:
- 2768. i. Keith[8] Erling, b 21 September 1975.
- 2769. ii. Shane George, b 19 September 1976.
- 2770. iii. Mandy Marie, b 19 February 1978; deceased.
- 2771. iv. Jackie Marie, b 8 May 1979.

1434. KIM[7] DONALD ARNESON (s/o Beverly[6] Johnson Arneson #567), b 5 September 1958 at Oconto Falls, WI; m 12 August 1978, **Shirley Ann Birr** of Oconowoc, WI, b 15 March 1963 at Oconto Falls. He is a farmer mechanic; live at Krakow, WI.

Child, surname ARNESON:
- 2772. i. Lance[8] Kim, b 11 March 1981.

1444. SHARON[7] LYNN VANDEN BOOGART (d/o Gloria[6] Verwey Vanden Boogart #570), b 30 October 1950 at Appleton, WI; m 7 February 1970 at Little Chute, WI, **James Vissers**, b 25 November 1949, s/o Gregory George and Frances Catherine (LeNoble) Vissers. James is a finishing room supervisor at Appleton Paper Co.

Child, surname VISSERS:
- 2773. i. Adam[8] Ryan, b 3 January 1976 at Appleton.

1445. RICK[7] CHARLES VANDEN BOOGART (s/o Gloria[6] Verwey Vanden Boogart #570), b 15 May 1953 at Appleton, WI; m 29 October 1977 at Holy Name Church, Kaukauna, WI, **Jane Nelessen**, b 13

December 1956, d/o Robert and Marion (Hendricks) Nelessen. Rick graduated from Illinois Institute of Technology and is underwriter and safety engineer at Integrity Mutual Insurance Co., Kaukauna.

Child, surname VANDEN BOOGART:
    2774. i. Amy[8] Lynn, b 29 May 1982.

1446. JAY[7] MARTIN VANDEN BOOGART (s/o Gloria[6] Verwey Vanden Boogart #570), b 16 May 1958 at Appleton, WI; m 12 July 1980 at Trinity Lutheran Church, Appleton, **Sally Strutz**, b 4 September 1958 at Appleton, d/o Donald and Natalie (Dohlmon) Strutz. Jay is Operations Supervisor at First National Bank in Appleton.

Child, surname VANDEN BOOGART:
    2775. i. Matthew[8] Robert, b 11 August 1981 at Appleton.

1451. RANDALL[7] ROY PAULSEN (s/o Harold[6] Paulsen #571), b 4 April 1951 at Green Bay, WI; m 14 September 1974, **Marla Martell**, b 19 August 1954 at Green Bay, WI, d/o Eugene and Beverly (Petrie) Paulsen. They are divorced.

Child, surname PAULSEN:
    2776. i. Jed[8] Roy, b 2 July 1976.

1452. SCOTT[7] PAULSEN (s/o Harold[6] Paulsen #571), b 19 July 1953 at Green Bay, WI; m 5 October 1974, **Janet Marie Ver Vooren**, b 8 July 1954 at Milwaukee Co., WI, d/o Richard and Constance (Buchanan) Ver Vooren.

Child, surname PAULSEN:
    2777. i. Carrie[8] Lynn, b 22 August 1980 at Green Bay.

1454. BARBARA[7] JEAN VERRIDEN (d/o June[6] Paulsen Verriden #572), b 18 April 1949 at Green Bay, WI; m 10 October 1981 at Spokane, WA, **Fred Grubb**, b 31 July 1948 at Denver, CO, s/o John Hiram and Mary Ann (Mazanec) Grubb. When last known, Fred was a camp counselor at a ranch for boys.

Child, surname GRUBB:
    2778. i. Joshua[8], b 12 May 1981 at Spokane.

1455. ALLAN[7] ROY VERRIDEN (s/o June[6] Paulsen Verriden #572), b 8 June 1951 at Green Bay, WI; m 16 August 1975 at Green Bay, **Susan Lampereur**, b 27 January 1953 at Green Bay, d/o Clifford and Doris

(Amenson) Lampereur. Allen is office manager of a trailer sales company.
Children, surname VERRIDEN, both born at Green Bay:
   2779.   i.   Leah[8], b 2 January 1979.
   2780.   ii. Trisha, b 17 July 1981.

1456. KAREN[7] MARIE VERRIDEN (d/o June[6] Paulsen Verriden #572), b 8 August 1952 at Green Bay, WI; m 28 July 1973 at Green Bay, **John Devlin Mefford**, b 1 September 1951 at Springfield, IL, s/o Donald and Mary (Devlin) Mefford.
Child, surname MEFFORD:
   2781.   i.   Dawn[8], b 21 October 1980 at Morton, IL.

1459. DIANA[7] LYNN HYSKA (d/o Lois[6] Paulsen Hyska #573), b 4 December 1953 at Green Bay, WI; m 15 July 1973 at Tucson, AZ, **James Eugene Ramsey II**, b 14 May 1951 at Erie, PA, s/o James Eugene and Elenore (Bauder) Ramsey. James is a career officer in U.S. Air Force. He got his degree in Electrical Engineering while in the service.
Child, surname RAMSEY:
   2782.   i.   James[8] Eugene III, b 25 March 1981 at Tucson.

1471. BRUCE[7] ALLAN MILLER (s/o Norma[6] Reed Miller #580), b 5 December 1964 at Two Rivers, WI; m 10 January 1988, **Brenda Riehl**, in CO.
Children, surname MILLER:
   2783.   i.   Nathan[8] James, b 6 April 1987.
   2784.   ii. Cameron Scott, b 19 August 1988.

1496. KYM[7] MARIE REED (d/o Wallace[6] James Reed #588), b 21 December 1959 at Oconto Falls, WI; m **Dennis Helgeland** from Mason City, IA, on 3 October 1980.
Child, surname HELGELAND:
   2785.   iii. Dennis[8] Troy, b 9 June 1979 at Iowa City.

1525. LAURIE[7] JUNE CORN (d/o Donna[6] Schroeder Corn #599), b 7 January 1956 at Oconto Falls, WI; m 28 July 1973 at Gillett, WI, Lutheran Church, **Irvin Mueller**, b 7 September 1953 at Oconto Falls, s/o Walter and Doris (Buhrandt) Mueller; divorced 1958.
Children, surname MUELLER:

2786.   i. Amy[8] Lynn, b 27 August 1973 at Oconto Falls.
2787.   ii. Blake Irwin, b 24 March 1981 at Shawano, WI.

1526. CHERYL[7] LYNN CORN (d/o Donna[6] Schroeder Corn #599), b 2 September 1958 at Kashena, WI; m 24 September 1982 at Shawano, WI, **Curt Lachapelle.**

Child, surname LACHAPELLE:
2788.   i. Teir[8] Rae, b 12 September 1986 at Shawano.

1527. SELENA[7] GRIGNON (d/o Donna[6] Schroeder Corn Grignon #599), b 25 September 1961 at Chicago, IL; m 27 March 1981 at Racine, WI, **Paul Lueckfeld,** b 1957, s/o Kenneth and Renata (Priez) Lueckfeld.

Children, surname LUECKFELD:
2789.   i. Raven[8] Star, b 5 July 1980.
2790.   ii. Erick Paul, b 4 May 1981.

1528. TAMMY[7] GRIGNON (d/o Donna[6] Schroeder Corn Grignon #599), b 6 October 1963 at Chicago, IL; m 19 May 1984 at Gillett, WI, **Gary De Bauch,** b at Oconto Falls, WI, s/o Vincent and Joyce (Operman) De Bauch.

Children, surname DeBAUCH:
2791.   i. Aaron[8] Clyde Joseph, b 13 February 1984.
2792.   ii. Shiloh David Lee, b 6 July 1988.

1529. DARLA[7] GRIGNON (d/o Donna[6] Schroeder Corn Grignon #599), b 4 July 1965 at Chicago, IL; m 7 June 1985 at Green Valley, Shawano Co., WI, **Regan Wolske.**

Children, surname WOLSKE:
2793.   i. Logan[8] Lane, b 10 September 1986.
2794.   ii. Seth Taylor, b 3 June 1989.

1531. BANNON[7] JAMES SCHROEDER (s/o Vernon[6] Clyde Schroeder #600), b 17 September 1958 at Oconto Falls, WI, m 24 February 1979 at Methodist Church, Suring, WI, **Bettina Kunz,** b March 1961 at Idar-Oberstein, West Germany, d/o Richard and Crystal Kunz. Bannon met Bettina while in the service in Germany. They are divorced and Bettina and child live in the town where she was born. Bannon has worked some for his father.

Child, surname SCHROEDER:

2795. i. Bjorn[8] Torben, b 7 November 1980 at Idar-Oberstein, West Germany.

1532. DURAN[7] VERNON SCHROEDER (s/o Vernon[6] Clyde Schroeder #600), b 13 January 1960 at Oconto Falls, WI; m 24 September 1977 at Methodist Church, Suring, WI, **Jackie Carol Johnson**, b 17 July 1965 at Green Bay, WI, d/o Richard and Viola (Charles) Johnson. Duran is a logger and works with his father. Jackie's father drove truck for Vernon 2 or 3 years before he died in 1982 at 45 years of age.

Children, surname SCHROEDER:
   2796. i. Clint[8] Duran, b 27 June 1978 at Green Bay.
   2797. ii. Bobbi Lee, b 29 December 1980 at Neilsville, WI.

1533. SHANE[7] SHELDON SCHROEDER (s/o Vernon[6] Clyde Schroeder #600), b 24 June 1965 at Oconto Falls, WI; m **Beth** —.

Child, surname SCHROEDER:
   2798. i. Zackery[8] Shane, b 22 October 1989.

1535. CAROLINE[7] SIEGEL (d/o Raymond[6] Cecil Siegel #601), b 7 August 1962 at Milwaukee, WI; m —.

Children, surname unknown:
   2799. i. Gerett[8], b 11 December 1981.

Caroline divorced and m/2 **John Gunderson**, 23 January 1988, at Watertown, WI.

1538. JEFFERY[7] SIEGEL (s/o Jorden[6] Lee Siegel #602), b 15 March 1961 at Milwaukee, WI; m **Patti Renee Clark**, 19 July 1980 at Wautona, WI.

Children, surname SIEGEL:
   2800. i. Son[8].
   2801. ii. Daughter.

1540. JON[7] SIEGEL (s/o Jorden[6] Lee Siegel #602), b 17 December 1963 at Milwaukee, WI; m 27 June 1981 at Gillett, WI, **Mary Katherine Montgomery**.

Child, surname SIEGEL:
   2802. i. Daughter[8].

1548. SHERYL[7] LYNN HAWKINS (d/o Ralph[6] George Hawkins

#604), b 18 May 1968 at Shawano, WI; m 27 February 1987, **Brian Alan Fink**.

Child, surname FINK:

    2803.   i.   Beau[8], b 23 July 1987.

1565. MELINDA[7] SUE PROTHERO (d/o Ruth[6] Reed Prothero #615), b 16 April 1950 at Racine, WI; m 19 May 1969 at Saint Joseph's Church, Racine, WI, **Jeffrey J. DeGuire**, b 26 April 1948 at Racine, WI, s/o Marvin and Anna Maria Irene (Gillis) DeGuire. Jeffrey is foreman at J. I. Case Co., Racine, WI. They live in Sturtevant, WI.

Children, surname DeGUIRE:

    2804.   i.   Barbara[8] Ann, b 24 March 1971, at Racine.
    2805.   i.   Michael John, b 10 August 1973, at Racine.

1566. RUSSELL[7] LeROY PROTHERO (s/o Ruth[6] Reed Prothero #615), b 24 February 1951 at Racine, WI; m 4 July 1970 at Messiah Lutheran Church, Racine, **Debra Diane Hotchkiss**, b 25 January 1952, d/o Gut and Marguerite (Purkey) Hotchkiss.

Children, surname PROTHERO:

    2806.   i.   Russell[8] David, b 15 November 1971 at Lincoln, NB.
    2807.   ii. Tabitha Renee, b 25 February 1975 at Racine.
    2808.   iii. Leah Ruth, b 9 November 1981 at Honolulu, HI.

1567. RUBY[7] LYNN PROTHERO (d/o Ruth[6] Reed Prothero #615), b 21 January 1954 at Racine, WI; m 18 July 1970 at Grace Lutheran Church, Racine, **Robert James Ferg**, b 2 November 1951 at Racine, s/o Elmer and Marie (LaFave) Ferg.

Children, surname FERG, all born at Racine:

    2809.   i.   Robert[8] James, b 18 November 1970.
    2810.   ii. Tracy Marie, b 25 October 1971.
    2811.   iii. Adrienne Ann, b 14 January 1975.

1568. BONNIE[7] ANN REED (d/o Russell[6] Sadell Reed #616), b 13 October 1956 at Racine, WI; m 1/ 30 August 1975 at Saint Joseph's Church, Racine, WI, **Joseph John Rudelich, Jr.**, b 15 April 1949, s/o Joseph and Lucille (Catapano) Rudelich; divorced 20 February 1981; m 2/ 2 August 1981 at Saint Luke's Episcopal Church, Racine, **Danim Hagopian**, b 15 February 1954, s/o Milton and Mary (Chardukian)

Hagopian. Danny owns Eitel's Coats Store in Racine.

Child, surname RUDELICH:
    2812.   i. Lisa[8] Marie, b 10 July 1977 at Racine.

1569. JEFFREY[7] ALLEN REED (s/o Russell[6] Sadell Reed #616), b 1 April 1958 at Racine, WI; m 18 November 1978 in Saint Paul the Apostle Church in Racine, WI, **Donna Rae Jarstad**, b 23 October 1958, d/o Ardell and Caroline (Cibourski) Jarstad. Jeff worked for Twin Disc Co., before being laid off.

Children, surname REED:
    2813.   i. Anthony[8] Alan, b 14 April 1979, at Racine.
    2814.   ii. Jenifer Nicole, b 23 March 1980, at Racine.

1570. CHARLES[7] ANTHONY REED (s/o Russell[6] Sadell Reed #616), b 4 September 1961 at Racine, WI; m 26 December 1981 at Aurora, IL, **Barbara Jacobi**, b 29 August 1962, d/o Robert and Muriel Jacobi. Charles and Barbara were both in the Marine Corps.

Child, surname REED:
    2815.   i. —[8], b March 1984.

1571. PATRICK[7] ROCK (s/o Jacqueline[6] Reed Rock #618), b 25 march 1957 at Kenosha, WI; m 23 February 1980 at Saint Patrick's Church, North Hollywood, CA, **Sue Baele**. Patrick is night supervisor at Ralph's Supermarket.

Child, surname ROCK:
    2816.   i. Jennifer[8] Anne, b 2 February 1981, Hollywood.

1573. ERIN[7] ROCK (s/o Jacqueline[6] Reed Rock #618), b 10 July 1960 at Kenosha, WI; m —.

Child, surname ROCK:
    2817.   i. Cortney[8] Crystal, b 23 June 1981, Tustin, CA.

1576. SHARON[7] BEYER (d/o Darla[6] Reed Beyer #619), b 21 June 1958 at Racine WI; m 31 January 1976, **Ronald Dixon**, b 17 November 1955 at Racine, s/o Raymond and Ruth Ann (Andekain) Dixon.

Children, surname DIXON:
    2818.   i. Shane[8], b 11 April 1976.
    2819.   ii. Rhonda, b 25 July 1978.

1582. TERRY[7] SCHAUMAN (s/o Delores[6] Nygard Schauman #621), b 16 October 1955 at Neenah, WI; m 18 March 1978 at Little Chute, WI, **Julie A. Hassell**, d/o Russell Hassell; now divorced.

Child, surname SCHAUMAN:
    2820. i. Eric[8], b 12 September 1978 at Neenah.

1586. THEODORE[7] BURGER (s/o Jean[6] Erickson Burger #622), b 7 July 1952 at Wausau, WI; m 10 September 1976, **Jerry Prahl**, s/o Mr. & Mrs. Warren Prahl.

Child, surname BURGER:
    2821. i. Nicholas[8], b 7 February 1979.

1591. CYNTHIA[7] LEE ERICKSON (d/o William[6] Charles Erickson #623), b 22 May 1955 at Wausau, WI; m 4 September 1976, **Rodney Schroeder**, s/o Ralph Schroeder.

Children, surname SCHROEDER:
    2822. i. Shane[8], b 7 May 1978.
    2823. ii. Shannon, b 9 May 1980.

1609. LINDA[7] LORD-SIMMONS (d/o Audrey[6] Everitt Lord-Simmon #640), m **Gary Wagner** .

Children, surname WAGNER:
    2824. i. Christine[8].
    2825. ii. Darrell.
    2826. iii. Marylu.

1617. STEVEN[7] WILLIAM TICKNOR (s/o William[6] Alan Ticknor #644), b 29 November 1962, Portland, OR; m 23 February 1985 at Beaverton, OR, **Jodenne Kay Ness**, b 19 September 1964, d/o John and Barbara (Schroeder) Ness. Steven is a self-employed newspaperman at *The Oregonian*; Jodenne is a cash management supervisor for a restaurant chain, The Shari; they live at Beaverton.

Children, surname TICKNOR:
    2827. i. Ashley[8] Rae, b 14 December 1986.
    2828. ii. Cole Thomas, b 16 August 1991.

1630. THOMAS[7] ALEXANDER PACK (s/o Harold Lloyd Pack #649), b 12 December 1957 at Flint, MI; m **Kathy O'Neil**; divorced

Child, surname PACK:
  2829. i. Karen

1633. MARY[7] MENTZ (d/o Ruth[6] Reed Mentz #650), b 10 March 1943 at Minacqua, WI; m 24 February 1962 at Calvary Lutheran Church, Minacqua, **John Duranso**, b 27 October 1940 at Wausau, WI, s/o Orville and Esther (Thompson) Duranso. John had a large body shop and wrecking service. John d 28 June 1987. Mary m 2/ 15 August 1989 at Las Vegas, NV, **Kerry Brent Woodruff**, s/o William and Wilma (Heidamann) Woodruff, b 6 November 1942 at Waterloo, WI.

Children, surname DURANSO:
  2830. i. Jeffrey[8] Allen, b 4 June 1963; m 11 August 1990 at Saint Michael's Church, Wausau, Lori Baierl, b 20 December 1966 at Marshfield, WI, d/o Eugene Arthur and Rosalie Luella (Gamble) Baierl. Jeffery owns and operates Pat's Body Shop.
+ 2831. ii. Jacqueline Ann, b 2 October 1964.

1634. BRIAN[7] M. REED (s/o Richard[6] Morris Reed #652), b 3 June 1954 at Pomona, CA; m 4 June 1977 at Our Lady, Queen of the Universe Catholic Church at Woodruff, WI, **Cleo Seipel**, d/o Richard James and Beulah Helen (Yourell) Seipel, b 6 June 1955 at Plum City, Pepin Co., WI.

Children, surname REED:
  2832. i. McKenzie[8] Kathryn, b 27 October 1981 at Woodruff.
  2833. ii. Brigham Ryan Lowell, b 16 November 1984.
  2834. iii. Bailey Yourell, b 22 August 1988.

1637. SHERRY[7] LYNN REED (d/o Roland[6] Lowell Reed #654), b 1 May 1956 at Waukesha Co., WI; m 2 November 1974 at New Berlin, WI, **Gregory Bernard Jezak**, b 21 June 1953. Gregory works for the electric co., Waukesha, WI. They live at Allis, WI.

Children, surname JEZAK, both born at Waukesha Co:
  2835. i. Stephanie[8] Lynn, b 4 February 1977.
  2836. ii. Kevin Gregory, b 11 February 1980.

1638. DAVID[7] ROLAND REED (s/o Roland[6] Lowell Reed #654), b 27 May 1954 at Waukesha Co., WI; m 17 May 1975 at New Berlin, WI, **Luanne Marie Carey**, b 26 June 1954 at Waukesha. David works for Hines Warner and they live at New Berlin.

Child, surname REED:
2837. i. Michelle[8] Lynette, b 18 December 1980.

1640. JO[7] LYNN ELKINS (d/o Joyce[6] Reed Elkins #656), b 18 November 1943 at Orlando, FL; m 9 March 1963 at Gelnhausen, Germany, **James Hamilton,** b 3 September 1943 at Humphrey, AR, s/o Halsey Hobert and Dora Alice (Hudson) Hamilton. Jo and James were high school sweethearts; after James was inducted into the army Jo went to Germany where he was stationed; she stayed and they were married. They later divorced in 1964.

Jo Lynn m/2 28 May 1969 at Fairfax, VA, **Linden Harris Fenety,** b 16 June 1928, at Frederickton, New Brunswick, s/o John and Beatrice Fenety. Linden was Purchasing Agent for Stone & Webster Engineering Co., Frederickton. Jo was in the real estate business; they were divorced in 1976 and had no children.

Jo Lynn's real estate business became "rocky" in 1974, and her savings were giving out. She decided to moved to Alaska to earn some money, and ended up staying there. Jo Lynn kept the name Fenety when she m/3 15 April 1977 at Juneau, AK, **Donald McClenaghan,** b 11 January 1932 at Indianapolis, IN, s/o Robert S. and Gertrude Joy (Seabrook) McClenaghan. Donald is a self-employed accountant. She is a leasing officer for airports for the State of Alaska; she manages a leasing unit for Alaska's two international airports: Anchorage and Fairbanks. They have no children.

Children, surname HAMILTON:
2838. i. Sara[8] Celeste, b 12 March 1963 at Frankfort, Germany.
2839. ii. Annette Dora, b 4 August 1964 at Tampa, FL.

1642. THOMAS[7] JOHN MINOR (s/o Virginia[6] Reed Minor #657), b 21 September 1945 at Jersey City, NJ; m 1 August 1964 at Kansasville, WI, **Frances Jozwiak,** b 10 September 1945 at Chicago, IL, d/o Frank and Margaret (Poe) Jozwiak. Thomas is Lieutenant in the Navy, stationed at Groton, CT.

Children, surname MINOR:
2840. i. Timothy[8] James, b 17 September 1965.
2841. ii. Tammy Ann, b 28 April 1969 at HI.

1644. GERALD[7] ANTHONY MINOR (s/o Virginia[6] Reed Minor

#657), b 9 August 1948 at Racine, WI; m 9 January 1971, Saint Roberts Church, Union Grove, WI, **Roxanne Louise Blackstone**, d/o Silwin and Gertrude (Rutgowski) Blackstone. They were divorced 5 March 1976 at Racine.

Gerald m/2 on 7 July 1979, **Katherine Marie Madden**, b 19 August 1958, d/o Donald and June (Schooltz) Madden. Gerald is a tool and die maker for American Motors.

Children, surname MINOR, both born at Racine:
    2842.   i.   Gerald^8 II, b 28 January 1971 at Racine.
    2843.   ii. Justin^8 Thomas, b 8 November 1979.
    2844.   iii. Jessica Marie, b 19 February 1982.

1645. MICHAEL^7 HERBERT MINOR (s/o Virginia^6 Reed Minor #657), b 8 February 1950 at Racine, WI; m 14 July 1970, **Marilyn White**, b 28 August 1951, d/o Norman and Mary White from Boise, ID. Michael is a Navy career man, on an aircraft carrier.

Children, surname MINOR:
    2845.   i.   Anthony^8 Lee, b 16 February 1971 at Brunswick, GA.
    2846.   ii. Joseph Michael, b 1 November 1972 at Burlington, WI.

1646. MARY^7 ANN MINOR (d/o Virginia^6 Reed Minor #657), b 29 October 1951 at Racine, WI; m 22 March 1973, **Geoffrey Thomas Downey**, at Waukegan, WI, b 28 July 1951 at Rockford, IL. Geoffrey is a chemical test coordinator for the state police and they live at Fox Lake, WI. Geofrey has a private pilot's license and has his own plane.

Child, surname DOWNEY:
    2847.   i.   Geoffrey^8 Thomas, b 12 December 1972.

1647. WILLIAM^7 DAVID MINOR (s/o Virginia^6 Reed Minor #657), b 4 February 1953 at Racine, WI; m 16 October 1976, **Pamela Ann Day**, at Burlington, WI, b 23 September 1955 at Chicago, IL, d/o Leo and Helen Day. William is a career Navy man, stationed at Great Lakes; they live at Waukegan, IL.

Children, surname MINOR:
    2848.   i.   Christopher^8, b 14 August 1979 at Norfolk, VA.
    2849.   ii. Jennifer, b 12 January 1981 at Norfolk.
    2850.   iii. Michael, b 2 October 1982.

1648. DOUGLAS[7] ALLEN MINOR (s/o Virginia[6] Reed Minor #657), b 20 August 1954 at Racine, WI; m 12 October 1976, **Cindy Castle** at Sturtevant, WI. Douglas works at American Motors in Quality Control; live in Kenosha.

Children, surname MINOR, both born at Racine:
    2851.   i.   Robert[8], b 3 January 1977.
    2852.   ii. Spring Marie, b 27 September 1978.

1649. DYANNE[7] PATRICIA MINOR (d/o Virginia[6] Reed Minor #657), b 1 May 1956 at Racine, WI; m 17 July 1976, **Karl Regall**, b 3 March 1953 at Truman, MN, s/o Helmet and Ella (Westphal) Regall. Karl works at J. I. Case Co. foundry at Racine.

Children, surname REGALL:
    2853.   i.   Gregory[8] Scott, b 31 October 1975 at Burlington, WI.
    2854.   ii.   Renee Dyanne, b 20 March 1979.
    2855.   iii. Kevin Karl, b 21 November 1982.

1650. DONNA[7] MARIE MINOR (d/o Virginia[6] Reed Minor #657), b 1 May 1956 at Racine, WI; m 8 June 1973, **Joseph Myszkewicz**, s/o Arthur and Julia (Hockman) Myszkewicz, b 4 May 1954. Donna is a computer operator. They were divorced in 1982.

Children, surname MYSZKEWICZ:
    2856.   i.   Kenneth[8] Joseph, b 6 August 1973, Burlington, WI.
    2857.   ii. Mark Philip, b 5 March 1975, Burlington.

1651. DARLENE[7] MARGARET MINOR (d/o Virginia[6] Reed Minor #657), b 26 March 1958 at Racine, WI; m 6 March 1976, **Kenneth Bower**, b 28 July 1955 at Racine, s/o Leslie and Ruth (Monty) Bower. Divorced 5 August 1980. Katherine remarried 5 August 1980, Kenneth Bower, live at LaFargeville, NY. Kenneth is in the Army.

Children, surname BOWER:
    2858.   i.   Karrie[8] Jean, b 16 July 1976, Burlington, WI.
    2859.   ii.   Tina Marie, b 10 February 1980, Burlington.
    2860.   iii. Daniel Thomas, b 22 March 1981, Burlington.

1652. DONALD[7] GERARD MINOR (s/o Virginia[6] Reed Minor #657), b 19 January 1960 at Racine, WI; m 18 December 1982, **Linda —**, b 26 November 1961 in CO. Donald is a airman with the U.S. Navy stationed at Key West, FL.

Child, surname MINOR:
- 2861. i. Julie[8] Kristin, b 26 April 1983.

1653. JOHN[7] THOMAS MINOR (s/o Virginia[6] Reed Minor #657), b 11 May 1961 at Racine, WI; m 23 May 1981, **Carla Marie Willoughby**, d/o Eugene and Margaret (Lyons) Willoughby, b 12 September 1959. John drives a bakery truck.

Child, surname MINOR:
- 2862. i. Corrie[8] Ann, b 4 March 1982 at Racine.

1656. CHERYL[7] LYNN PRYOR (d/o Patricia[6] Reed Pryor #659), b 25 December 1950 at Racine, WI; m 10 December 1967, **Thomas Villwock**, b 30 May 1946 at Milwaukee, WI, s/o Henry Villwock. Thomas is an independent truck driver. Live at Zillah, WA, in the Yakima Valley.

Children, surname VILLWOCK:
- 2863. i. Tammy[8], b 18 May 1969 at Kenosha, WI.
- 2864. ii. Scott, b 12 February 1971 at Burlington, WI.
- 2865. iii. Diana, b 30 March 1972 at BurlingtonI.
- 2866. iv. Edward, b 4 December 1974 at Burlington.

1657. JAMES[7] ROBERT PRYOR (s/o Patricia[6] Reed Pryor #659), b 19 November 1951 at Racine, WI; m 5 April 1977, **Kathleen Krielcamp**, b 14 October 1952 at Milwaukee, WI, d/o Robert and Ruth (Wolf) Krielcamp. James is a journeyman machine repairman at American Motors Corp. at Kenosha, WI. They live in Paddock Lake, Salem, WI. James gave Kathleen a valentine when she was in the third grade and he in the fourth grade. Just before she boarded the bus he ran up to her and said "This is for you. I love you, but don't tell anybody." She was so excited she told her mother as soon as she was home.

Children, surname PRYOR:
- 2867. i. Christopher[8] James, b 10 November 1978 at Kenosha.
- 2868. ii. Paula, b 26 February 1980 at Burlington, WI.

1659. MARCIA[7] JOAN PRYOR (d/o Patricia[6] Reed Pryor #659), b 18 March 1958 at Racine, WI; m 23 April 1976, **Michael Ray English**, b 24 March 1956 in CA; very talented musically.

Children, surname ENGLISH:

2869. i. Angela[8], b 5 October 1976, at Pomona, CA.
2870. ii. Michelle, b 25 October 1977, at Pomona.

1661. JUDITH[7] LORRAINE PRYOR (d/o Patricia[6] Reed Pryor #659), b 13 September 1962 at Racine, WI; m 8 July 1981 at Racine, WI, **Cardell Briggs**, b 28 September 1960, s/o Cleveland and Dorothy Briggs.

Child, surname BRIGGS:
 2871. i. Joshua[8] James Cleveland, b 9 December 1981.

1662. CLIFFORD[7] "BUDDY" HENRY KUTZNER (s/o June[6] Reed Kutzner #660), b 30 June 1949 at Chicago, IL; m 5 July 1967 at County Court House, Racine, WI, **Jo-Lynn Gustavson**, b 21 August 1949, d/o Robert and Mildred (Hedstron) Gustavson. On marriage record it says he was a manager trainee of a discount store.

Child, surname KUTZNER:
 2872. i. Clifford[8] Henry, b 9 July 1967 at Racine.

1663. KATHERINE[7] SUE KUTZNER (d/o June[6] Reed Kutzner #660, b 15 October 1950 at Chicago, IL; m 1 November 1969 at County Court House, Racine, WI, **Delos Michael Bixby**, b 2 June 1948 at Stuttgart, Germany, s/o Lewis and Cecilia (Iglinski) Bixby. They live in Yorkville, Racine Co.

Child, surname BIXBY:
 2873. i. Aaron[8], b 4 June 1971 at Racine.

1665. ELIZABETH[7] ANN KUTZNER (d/o June[6] Reed Kutzner #660), b 30 November 1956 at Chicago, IL; m 9 February 1977, **Eugene Gonzales**. Eugene is half Oneida Indian and half Mexican.

Children, surname GONZALES:
 2874. i. Jacob[8] Eugene, b 16 February 1977 at Racine, WI.
 2875. ii. Gabriel Adam, b 28 November 1979.

1686. MICHAEL[7] DAVID WEBB (s/o Shirley[6] Simmons Webb #667), b 31 August 1956 at Gainsville, FL; m 27 September 1974, **Debora Fischer**, at Deerfield Beach, FL.

Children, surname WEBB, both born at Deerfield Beach:
 2876. i. Jason[8], b 27 December 1980.
 2877. ii. Jerod, b 12 May 1981.

1697. COLENE[7] ANN McMANNIS (d/o Pearl[6] Jorgensen McMannis #675), b 8 October 1947 at Battle Creek, MI; m 26 June 1965, **Lewis William Gaw**, b 30 June 1945, s/o William and Betty (Weaver) Gaw. Lewis has a trucking company.

Child, surname GAW:
    2878. i. Rodney[8], b 15 August 1966 at Battle Creek.

1698. BRYAN[7] WAYNE JORGENSEN (s/o Robert[6] Stanley Jorgensen #676), b 17 August 1945 at Seattle, WA; m 28 October 1967, **Karen Nichols**, b 2 September 1950 at Saratoga, NY.

Children, surname JORGENSEN:
    2879. i. Danielle[8], b 18 May 1968 in CT.
    2880. ii. Eric, b 6 May 1975 at Muskegan, MI.

1699. JOHN[7] REED JORGENSEN (s/o Robert[6] Stanley Jorgensen #676), b 6 May 1947 at Greenville, MI; m 11 December 1965, **Audrey Harkness**, b 28 May 1947, d/o Emerson and Ellen Harkness.

Children, surname JORGENSEN:
    2881. i. Scott[8], b 29 May 1966.
    2882. ii. Mary, b 27 May 1968.
    2883. iii. John Reed, b 6 May —, at Grand Rapids, MI.
    2884. iv. Mindy, b 3 October 1974 at Alma, MI.

1700. SHERRY[7] RAE JORGENSEN (d/o Robert[6] Stanley Jorgensen #676), b 25 December 1948 at Alma, MI; m 10 February 1967 at Wichita Falls, TX, **Robert Christensen**, b 17 December 1947 at Saint Louis, MO, s/o Arthur and Frances (Spradling) Christensen. Robert works for the Coca Cola Co. They live at Elizabethtown, KY.

Children, surname CHRISTENSEN:
    2885. i. Jeffrey[8], b 13 September 1967 at Sheridan, MI.
    2886. ii. Scarlet Louisa, b 18 June 1977 at Elizabethtown.

1702. CURTIS[7] JORGENSEN (s/o Reed[6] Carlyle Jorgensen #677), b 12 May 1948 at Carson City, MI; m 27 July 1978 at Reading, PA, **Patricia Hosche**, b 10 October 1958 at Sheboygan, WI, d/o Frederick Elmer and Rosemary (Spencer) Hosche. Curtis works for Brown and Root out of Houston, TX.

Child, surname JORGENSEN:

2887. i. Joshua[8] Reed, b 16 December 1980 at Alma, MI.

1703. CHERYL[7] JORGENSEN (d/o Reed[6] Carsyle Jorgensen #677), b 1 April 1953 at Carson City, MI; m 13 November 1971 at Edmore, MI, **Clifford Doberstine**, b 22 January 1952 at Edmore, s/o Clifford and Rose (LaGuire) Doberstine. Clifford does telephone repair work for General Telephone Co. They live in Edmore, MI.

Children, surname DOBERSTINE, both born at Carson City, MI.
    2888. i. Candace[8], b 30 January 1975.
    2889. ii. Marcie Ann, b 22 May 1972.

1704. CONSTANCE[7] ELLEN NESTLE (d/o Betty[6] Jorgensen Nestle #678), b 2 October 1945 at Battle Creek, MI; m 2 July 1977, **Harry Schultz**, b 8 May 1928 at Alpena, MI, s/o Albert and Emma (Kolisch) Schultz. They live in Alpena.

Child, surname SCHULTZ:
    2890. i. Kimberly[8] Sue, b 7 September 1978 at Alpena.

1705. CARL[7] NESTLE (s/o Betty[6] Jorgensen Nestle #678), b 16 June 1947; m 30 June 1972, **June Morey**, b 3 May 1953 at Vestaburg, MI, d/o Harry and Wilma (Bilsby) Morey.

Children, surname NESTLE, both born at Alma, MI:
    2891. i. Heather[8] Rae, b 3 October 1975.
    2892. ii. Ben Heath, b 8 September 1973.

1706. DAVID[7] McCORMICK (s/o Donald[6] Albert McCormick #681), b 28 October 1947 at Bremerton, WA; m June 1970, **Sarah Bruns**.

Children, surname MCCORMICK:
    2893. i. Ann[8] Elizabeth, b 29 October 1974.
    2894. ii. Paul William, b 23 May 1977.

1709. ROXANNE[7] LEE RALEIGH (d/o Lois[6] Archibald Raleigh #682), b 11 October 1951 at Seattle, WA; m/1 **Gerald Wayne Thomas**, 6 February 1971, b 2 September 1951 at Grapevine, TX, s/o Billy Jo and Doris Elaine (Woodruff) Thomas; they had two children. Roxanne m/2 18 February 1977, **Steven Earl Thomas**, Gerald's younger brother, b 2 February 1956 at Inglewood, CA, s/o Billy Joe and Doris Elaine (Woodruff) Thomas. Roxanne m/3 at Chillicoth, MO, **Arthur Wayne Rolls**, on 1 April 1984, b 14 July 1949 at Chillicoth, MO, s/o Opal and Frances

The Seventh Generation 413

(McNally) Rolls. No children.

Children, surname THOMAS:
    2895. i. Jeffrey[8] Paul, b 1 July 1972 at Las Vegas, NV.
    2896. ii. Deanna Charlene, b 13 December 1973 at Columbia, SC.
    2897. iii. Kainen[8] Braun, b 24 August 1979 at Yakima, WA.

1711. DOUGLAS[7] LOY GIBSON (s/o Donna[6] Archibald Gibson #683), b 22 September 1952 at Seattle, WA; m 26 August 1978, **Susan Stultz**, b 13 October 1951 at Terre Haute, IN, d/o Charles and Donna (Stilwell) Stultz. Douglas works at University of Washington Hospital, Pharmacist Dept. They live at Woodinville, WA.

Child, surname GIBSON:
    2898. i. Kaylin[8] Ashley, b 27 March 1982.

1712. SHARILYN[7] AUTUMN GIBSON (d/o Donna[6] Archibald Gibson #683), b 10 October 1955 at Everett, WA; m/1 1 June 1973 at Sulton, WA, **Richard Carl Shepardson**, s/o Donald and Naida (Lindley) Shepardson. Richard is a truck driver for King County Road Works. Sharilyn m/2 **Kenneth Webster**, 22 September 1979, b 9 July 1947 at Snohomish, WA, s/o Floyd Stanley and Sylvia (Hunziker) Webster. Kenneth works for General Telephone Co; they live at Monroe, WA.

Children, surname SHEPARDSON:
    2899. i. Tawnya[8] Ann, b 1 September 1973 at Everett, WA.

Children, surname WEBSTER, both born at Everett:
    2900. ii. Travis[8], b 1 July 1980.
    2901. iii. Troy Douglas, b 12 January 1984.

1718. GARY[7] BEAVERT (s/o Frank[6] Beavert #686), b 19 August 1952 at Seattle, WA; m 27 July 1974 at Seattle, **Madeline Crotty**, b 19 January 1952 at Jersey City, NJ, d/o Michael and Irene (Oros) Crotty. Gary is a truck driver for Associated Grocers in Seattle, WA. They live at Kent, WA.

Children, surname BEAVERT, all born at Seattle:
    2902. i. Kelley[8], b 30 January 1976.
    2903. ii. Kimberley, b 22 August 1978.
    2904. iii. Kyle Patrick, b 23 July 1980.

1719. GAIL[7] BEAVERT (d/o Frank[6] Beavert #686), b 5 June 1955 at

Seattle, WA; m/1 **Scott Defazio** on 30 May 1982 at Walnut Creek, CA, b 27 August 1944 at Dallas, TX; m/2 **Jeffery Raymond Ganzer**, b 13 October 1955 at Cleveland, OH. Jeffery is an air balance technician at Air Metrics at Alameda, CA. Gail is Sales Representative in the Bay Area for Perrigo Co., manufacturer of beauty aids. Live at Walnut Creek, CA.

Child, surname GANZER:

    2905. i. Morgan[8] Elizabeth, b 17 April 1988 at Vallejo, CA.

1722. JUDY[7] DUNN (d/o Betty[6] Beavert Dunn #687), b 30 June 1965 at Seattle, WA; m 7 May 1988 **Daniel Lee Seth**, s/o Richard Lee and Katherine Christina (Johnson) Seth, b 21 September 1965 at Seattle.

Children, surname SETH:

    2906. i. Tyler Lee, b 27 December 1989 at Renton, WA.
    2907. ii. Jordan Michael, b 18 June 1992 at Renton.

1734. PATRICIA[7] ANN CLARKE (d/o Leonard[6] Robert Clarke #694), b 1 April 1957 at Syracuse, NY. She is a professional glass blower, sells at craft shows, lives in North Syracuse.

Child, surname CLARKE:

    2908. i. Evan Taylor[8], b 25 August 1990 at Syracuse.

1735. ELIZABETH[7] JANE CLARKE (d/o Leonard[6] Robert Clarke #694), b 13 October 1959 at Syracuse, NY; m 29 October 1984 at Tampa, FL, **Joseph Lamb**, b 27 April 1956, s/o Donald and Evelyn Lamb.

Child, surname LAMB:

    2909. i. April[8] McCall, b 15 April 1985 at Brandon, FL.

1749. ROBERT[7] THOMAS CANFIELD (s/o Robert[6] Gene Canfield #701), b 3 April 1953 at Portsmouth, VA; m **Anna Heiser**. He is employeed by the US Postal Service.

Children, surname CANFIELD:

    2910. i. Michelle[8].

1750. MARK[7] FRANCIS CANFIELD (s/o Robert[6] Gene Canfield #701), b 19 June 1956 at Syracuse, NY; m **Cathy Carver**. Mark is a carpenter; they live in Payson, AZ.

Children, surname CANFIELD:

    2911. i. Jody[8] May.

The Seventh Generation 415

1752. DAVID[7] **JOSEPH CANFIELD** (s/o Robert[6] Gene Canfield #701), b 9 June 1960 at Syracuse, NY; lives in Arizona and is a cabinet maker and an artist; he sells his paintings on Indians and nature.

Children, surname CANFIELD:
    2912. i. Natasha[8] Eve.

1762. LEONA[7] **NORENE CHASE** (d/o Thelma[6] Canfield Chase #707), b 13 February 1957 at Oneida, NY; m 7 July 1984, **James Harold Woodcock**, at Camden, NY, s/o Eugene and Joyce (Debrucque) Woodcock, b 4 November 1962 at Oneida, NY.

Children, surname WOODCOCK:
    2913. ii. Jamie[8] Marie, b 6 April 1985 at Oneida, NY.
    2914. iii. Norene Cora, b 18 November 1987 at Rome, NY.

1763. RICHARD[7] **DONALD CHASE** (s/o Thelma[6] Canfield Chase #707), b 30 June 1958 at Rome, NY; m 2 November 1985 at Camden, NY, **Tammy Marie Turk**, d/o Stanley and Dorcus Marie (Kirk) Turk, b 30 December 1961 at Rome. Richard is an auto mechanic, works for Jay Ford in Blossvale, NY.

Children, surname CHASE, both born at Rome:
    2915. i. Rachel[8] Lynne, b 17 May 1986.
    2916. ii. Richard Donald III, b 23 June 1987.

1764. DANIEL[7] **EDWARD CHASE** (s/o Thelma[6] Canfield Chase #707), b 20 August 1960 at Rome, NY; m 18 August 1985 at Chittenango, NY, **Daphne Marie Hammond**, d/o Walter Joseph and Lucille Katherine (Smith) Hammond. Daniel is custodian of Oneida City Schools. Daphne had three children by a previous marriage.

Children, surname ALLEN, all born at Syracuse, NY, all adopted by Dan:
    2917. i. Robert[8] Jay, b 22 November 1976.
    2918. ii. Lisa Marie, b 21 October 1979.
    2919. iii. Liza Marie, b 21 October 1979 (twin).

1765. MATHEW[7] **RONALD CHASE** (s/o Thelma[6] Canfield Chase #707), b 23 December 1962 at Rome, NY; m 17 July 1982, **Kathleen Louella Chaires**, d/o Floyde Irving and Rita Irene (Kilbourn) Chaires, b 14 April 1963 at Vernon, NY. Mathew is a mailman for BOCES and lead guitarist and vocalist for Blue River Band.

Children, surname CHASE:
    2920. i. Danielle[8] Rita, b 14 November 1983.
    2921. ii. Bryan Matthew, b 10 August 1988.

1767. DAWN[7] PAULETTE CHASE (d/o Thelma[6] Canfield Chase #707), b 29 May 1964 at Rome, NY; she works at Oneida Molded Plastics as a machiner operator.

Children, surname CHASE:
    2922. i. Loretta[8] Sue, b 29 June 1980 at Utica, NY, she had a stroke when she was four years old; is learning to speak, and is being raised by her grandmother Thelma Grace Chase.

1770. SHARON[7] BETH KENT (d/o Carol[6] Canfield Kent #711), b 12 July 1965 at Rome, NY; m 17 July 1983 at Williamstown, NY, **Shawn Wesley Johnson**, s/o Wesley and Clara (Wilson) Johnson, b 19 March 1962 at Rome, NY. Shawn is a farmer at Marcy, NY.

Children, surname JOHNSON, all born at Rome:
    2923. i. Michael[8] Shawn, b 12 May 1981.
    2924. ii. William Hayes, b 15 August 1983.
    2925. iii. Andrew Edward, b 21 June 1987.
    2926. iv. Jessica Ann, b 22 November 1988.

1772. BRENDA[7] LEE MARSHALL (d/o Jean[6] Canfield Marshall #712), b 22 January 1960 at Rome, NY; m 2 October 1977, **Robert David Wines**, s/o Raymond John and Elizabeth Nette (Brockway) Wines. Robert is wire strander at Camden Wire Co.

Children, surname WINES:
    2927. i. Raymond[8] Robert, b 1 April 1978 at Oneida, NY.
    2928. ii. Elizabeth Jean, b 27 July 1980 at Oneida.
    2929. iii. Robyn Lee, b 14 June 1983 at Rome.

1773. PATTI[7] SUE MARSHALL (d/o Jean[6] Canfield Marshall #712), b 1 September 1964 at Rome, NY; m 16 October 1982 at Oneida, NY, **Scott Douglas Moyer**, s/o Norman and Mary Moyer, b 1 September 1960 at Oneida, NY. Scott is a strander at Camden Wire.

Children, surname MOYER, all born at Oneida:
    2930. i. Melissa[8] Sue, b 11 September 1983.
    2931. ii. Susan Elizabeth, b 8 June 1985.

2932. iii. Daniel Norman, b 15 May 1987.
2933. iv. Tamera Myra, b 16 March 1990.

1774. ROBERT[7] **FRED MARSHALL** (s/o Jean[6] Canfield Marshall #712), b 1 August 1970; m 17 February 1990, **Sharleen Rae Rodgers**. Child, surname MARSHALL:
2934. i. Carissa[8] LeRay, b 19 August 1990.

Chapter 9

Eighth Generation

1827. RONALD[8] **RICHARD MUSOLF** (s/o Norma[7] Wiedendorf Musolf #752), b 10 February 1942 at Dodge Co., MN; m 12 December 1964 **Sandra Yentsch**, d/o Wayne and Benita Yentsch, b 7 September 1944. Ronald is a truck driver.

Children, surname MUSOLF, both born at Olmstead, Co., MN:
    2937. i. Kimberly[9], b 10 April 1966.
    2938. ii. Karlene, b 14 August 1969.

1828. ROSEAN[8] **MARIE WIEDENDORF** (d/o Geryl Earl Wiedendorf #753), b 20 April 1947 at Minneapolis, MN; m/1 3 July 1965, **Glenn Parks** at Anoka, MN, d 7 October 1967; m/2 27 June 1970 at Anoka, **James Hays**; divorced him 17 July 1978; m/3 at Gethsemanie Lutheran Church, Hopkins, MN, 28 July 1979, **Carl Rendahl**, s/o Earl and Marian (Donnelly) Rendahl. Carl is a safety inspector at Liberty Carton.

Children, surname HAYS, born at Minneapolis:
    2939. i. Scott[9] Alan, b 23 June 1969.
    2940. ii. Corrie Ann, b 16 September 1972.
    2941. iii. Kelly Thomas, b 17 July 1974.

1887. MICHAEL[8] **ALLEN EVANS** (s/o Richard[7] Allen Evans #784), b 4 October 1959; m **Nancy Seehusen**.

Child, surname EVANS:
    2942. i. Matthew[9], b July 1983.

1901. DAVID[8] **BLAKE DANIELS** (s/o David[7] Wynot Daniels #789), b 4 February 1958 at Long Beach, CA; m —.

Children, surname DANIELS:
    2943. i. Ashlie[9] Noelle, b 6 January 1981 at Orange, CA.
    2944. ii. Whittnie Nicolle, b 22 December 1982 at Orange.

1902. JULIE[8] **KAY DANIELS** (d/o David[7] Wynot Daniels #789), b 21 August 1959 at Long Beach, CA; m — **Webster**.

Children, surname WEBSTER:
- 2945. i. Micah[9] Daniel, b 12 March 1980 at Orange, CA.
- 2946. ii. Bryan David, b 21 June 1983 at Richmond, VA.

1905. JAMES[8] WYATT BREWSTER (s/o Constance[7] Daniels Brewster #790), b 2 May 1959 at Long Beach, CA; m/1 in 1976, **Karen Cox**; divorced 1978. James m/2 17 March 1984 at Santa Ana, CA.

Children, surname BREWSTER:
- 2947. i. Jennifer[9], b 5 June 1977.

1917. DAVID[8] DEAN HART (s/o David[7] Burdette Hart #797), b 26 November 1956 at Burlington, IA; m 30 October 1976 at Laguna Niguel, CA, **Lisa Marie Daniele**, d/o Bob and Mary Daniele, b 5 April 1958 at Pasadena, CA. David is a writer.

Children, surname HART:
- 2948. i. Harmony[9] Lee, b 6 May 1977 at San Clemente, CA.
- 2949. ii. Jason David, b 8 April 1980 at Oceanside, CA.

1972. LIDA[8] LEIGH LOKOEN (d/o Rowena[7] Lewis Lokoen #847), b December 1959 Indio, CA; m **Robert Jensen** February 1977 at Deadwood, SD.

Children, surname JENSEN:
- 2950. i. Lee[9] Harlene, b 28 April 1978 at Deadwood.
- 2951. ii. Phadrah Rae, b 26 June 1979.
- 2952. iii. Daman, b 11 August 1980.

1976. MELODY[8] ANN BREIT (d/o Darlene[7] Mason Breit #848), b 16 July 1957 at LaMesa, CA; m/1 **Robert Brunswick**, June 1975. Melody is department manager in large health store. Divorced about 1980. Melody m/2 23 November 1984 at Lake Tahoe, NV, **Steve Lee Merker**, b 26 February 1955 at Chicago, IL the s/o Bernard and Audrey Lenore (Becker) Merker. They live in San Diego, CA. Steve is a lawyer.

Child, surname BRUNSWICK:
- 2953. i. Crystal[9] Marie, b 13 May 1977 at San Diego.

1977. DONALD[8] VINCENT BREIT (s/o Darlene[7] Mason Breit #848), b 6 August 1958 at San Diego, CA; m **1 July 1977, Teresa Hebb Smith**, b 17 November 1953 at Topeka, KS, d/o Ivan Glenn and Donna (Gaerger) Hebb. They live at Spring Valley, CA. Donald works for a large wholesale

The Eighth Generation 421

liquor company as a salesman and delivery man.

Children, surname SMITH:
    2954. i. Shawn^9, b 1976 (step child).
    2955. ii. Angela, b 1975 (step child).

Child, surname BREIT:
    2956. iii. Ivan Gene, b 20 September 1979 at La Jolla, CA.

1978. JOY^8 LINDA BREIT (d/o Darlene^7 Mason Breit #848), b 30 November 1959 at San Diego, CA; m **John Frederick Brock II**, 13 May 1977; b 23 October 1958, s/o John Frederick & Michico (Araki) Brock; b Manchuria. Fred a finish carpenter; live at Spring Valley, CA.

Children, surname BROCK:
    2957. i. Wendy Marie, b 1 June 1979 at Tiajuana, Mexico.
    2958. ii. John Frederick, III, b 21 May 1980 at San Diego.

1979. MARY^8 ANN MASON (d/o Robert^7 Myron Mason #849), b 15 November 1962 at San Deigo, CA; m 19 February 1982 **Steven Hammond**. He is physical therapist and they live in Kelseyville, CA.

Child, surname HAMMOND:
    2959. i. Stephanie^9 Ann, 20 July 1983 at Albuquerque, NM.

1985. DEBORAH^8 THAIS MASON (d/o John Gerald Mason #850), b 27 January 1966 at San Deigo; m 1982, **Bryan Judd Peyton**; b 20 October 1964 in Flagstaff, AZ, s/o Bruce Almy and Mary Elaine (Abdoo) Peyton. They live in Indio, CA

Child, surname PEYTON:
    2960. i. Stacy^9, b 19 January 1983 at Indio, CA.

1993. DARRELL^8 EDWIN PAIONI (s/o Betty^7 Quick Paioni #863), b 8 September 1950 at Modesto, CA; m **Denise Salo**, 12 November 1968 at Carson City, NV.

Children, surname PAIONI:
    2961. i. Brandon^9, b 31 October 1974 at Modesto.
    2962. ii. Jessica Ann, b 6 May 1982 Modesto.

2029. SUSAN^8 RETZLAFF (d/o Caroline Badtke Retzlaff #884), b 16 April 1958; m **Dennis Jahns**, s/o Raymond and Lorene Jahns.

Children, surname JAHNS:

2963. i. Ryan[9].
2964. ii. Kiel.

2030. DIANNA[8] MARIE RETZLAFF (d/o Caroline[7] Badtke Retzlaff #884), b 10 December 1959; m **Steve Olm**, s/o Bill and Kay Olm.

Child, surname OLM:
2965. i. William[9].

2044. SUE[8] ELLEN GUENCHNER (d/o Beverly[7] Shipton Guenchner #888), b 26 August 1942 at Sioux Falls, SD; m/1 20 November 1965 at Madras, India, **Harry Lawrence Lack, III**, b 30 September 1942 at Harrisburg, PA, s/o H. Lawrence II and Mildred (Sur) Lack. They were divorced in 1973, at Huntington, WV. Sue m/2 at Rapid City, SD, 31 March 1975, **Tony Norris**, b 14 April 1950 at Aledo, TX, s/o Henry Brantley and Alice (Kinser) Norris. They live at Flagstatt, AZ. Tony is a telephone technician.

Child, surname LACK:
2966. i. Aaron Isaac, b 14 October 1969 at Freeland, MD.

Child, surname NORRIS:
2967. ii. Jacob, b 23 September 1973.
2968. iii. Leah Beth, b 21 September 1976.
2969. iv. Ruth Ellen, b 25 July 1978.
2970. v. Charity Grace, b 16 October 1982.

2045. SHARI[8] BEA BAUER (d/o Virginia[7] Shipton Bauer #889), b 5 January 1945 at Sioux Falls, SD; m **Lloyd Tarter** from Casper, WY, 21 August 1965. They live in Marietta, GA. Lloyd works for IBM in Atlanta.

Children, surname TARTER, both born at Rochester, MN:
2971. i. Michael[9], b 17 May 1971.
2972. ii. Amy, b 21 July 1973.

2047. JAMES[8] KENNETH BAUER (s/o Virginia[7] Shipton Bauer #889), b 3 May 1951; m **Andrea Heath** from Gettysburg, SD. They live in Sioux Falls, SD; James works for a trucking firm, American Freight Systems.

Children, surname BAUER:
2973. i. Brooke[9] Marguerite, b 23 June 1981, at Sioux Falls, SD.
2974. ii. Christopher Thomas, b 8 December 1983, Sioux Falls.

The Eighth Generation 423

2048. STEVEN[8] DENNIS ROGNRUD (s/o Artha[7] Shipton Roognrud #890), b 18 September 1954; m **Karen Fischer** from Saint Louis, MO.

Children, surname ROGNRUD:
    2975. i. Jason[9].
    2976. ii. Christopher Brian.

2053. TIMOTHY[8] JOSEPH PECKHAM (s/o Phillip[7] Durward Peckham #893), b 6 June 1950 at Big Bend, WI; m 21 August 1971, **Mary Louise Galewski** at Milwaukee, WI, b 26 August 1951 at Milwaukee, d/o Edward and Grace Galewski. He is a project engineer for Flad Associates.

Children, surname PECKHAM:
    2977. i. Scott[9] David, b 5 January 1978, at Madison, WI.
    2978. ii. David Andrew, b 9 January 1980, at Madison.

2070. ANNE[8] CHRISTINE PECKHAM (d/o Howard[7] John Peckham #899), b 29 November 1956 at Sioux Falls; m 25 November 1978, **Robert Scheffel Wright**, s/o Jack and Berl Wright.

Child, surname WRIGHT:
    2979. i. Austin Scheffel, b 20 May 1981 at Tallahassee, FL.

2087. RICHARD[8] KENNETH JELMELAND (s/o Donald[7] Kenneth Jelmeland #915), b 13 March 1947 at Wausau, WI; m **Lennis Ann Neinast**, 6 June 1970, b 8 March 1948 at Sparta, WI; d/o Harold and Marie (Woombill) Neinast. Richard is assistant administrator of Beloit Clinic. They live at Beloit, WI.

Children, surname JELMELAND, both born at West Bend, WI:
    2980. i. Coy[9], b 1 August 1973.
    2981. ii. Carie, b 17 October 1976.

2088. DAVID[8] JELMELAND (s/o Donald[7] Kenneth Jelmeland #915), b 4 October 1948 at Wausau, WI; m **La Rae Rainville** 14 May 1977; b 11 March 1955 at Wausau, d/o Lloyd and Elizabeth (Frank) Rainville. He is President of Mosinee Paper Credit Union; they live in Schofield, WI.

Children, surname JELMELAND:
    2982. i. Amy[9], b 6 September 1978 at Wausau.
    2983. i. Jenny, b 18 September 1980 at Wausau.

2105. DAVIDA[8] MARIE FOGNER (d/o Shirley[7] Vining Fogner #926), b 5 September 1956 at Ottawa, IL; m/1 12 October 1974 at Colorado Springs, CO, **John Montoya**; m/2 8 November 1978 at Denver, CO, **Greg Olinyk**. Shirley was a model for several years at a Denver department store and other locations; lives at Castle Rock, CO.

Child, surname OLINYK:
    2984. i. Oliver^9 Z., b 12 July 1984.

2114. JANET^8 MARIE EWING (d/o Helen^7 Vining Ewing #928), b 23 May 1962 at Mitchell, SD; m **Wayne Phillips**, 30 May 1980 at Mitchell. Wayne is a welder.

Child, surname PHILLIPS:
    2985. i. Brandon^9 Wayne, b 28 April 1981 at Fort Hood, TX.

2149. STEVEN^8 V. POGUE (s/o Vernon^7 Everett Pogue #945), b 26 March 1957; m 23 June 1984 at Sun Prairie, WI, **Darcy Surprise**.

Child, surname POGUE:
    2986. i. Michael Steven, b 4 May 1987.

2153. BARBARA^8 J. POGUE (d/o Roy^7 Roger Pogue #946), b 20 November 1958 at Portage, WI; m **Richard Tallent**; they live at Clear Lake, WI.

Child, surname TALLENT:
    2987. i. Richard^9.

2154. BONNIE^8 J. POGUE (d/o Roy^7 Roger Pogue #946), b 22 June 1960 at Portage, WI; m 24 August 1980, **Stephen Guiney** at Paris Island, NC. They live at Groton, CT.

Children, surname GUINEY:
    2988. i. Christy^9 Lynn, b 10 June 1981.
    2989. ii. Shawn.

2161. WANDA^8 P. GUSTROWSKY (d/o Ione^7 Pogue Gustrowsky #948), b 2 September 1961, Dane Co., WI; m 27 June 1987, **James Carpenter**.

Child, surname CARPENTER:
    2990. i. Lacy^9, b 4 June 1989.

2162. RAMONA^8 M. GUSTROWSKY (d/o Ione^7 Pogue Gustrowsky #948), b 1 August 1963, Dane Co., WI; m 6 December 1986, **Kurt**

The Eighth Generation

Holland, Garden Valley, TX.

Child, surname HOLLAND:
    2991.   i.   Amanda[9], b 19 January 1990.

2163. LINDA[8] G. GUSTROWSKY (d/o Ione[7] Pogue Gustrowsky #948), b 26 February 1965, Dane Co., WI; m 21 July 1986, **Russell Black**.

Child, surname BLACK:
    2992.   i.   Melinda[9] Mae, b 9 November 1986.
    2993.   ii. Scott Russell, b 8 December 1988.

2166. MARGARET[8] R. WEISENSEL (d/o Irene[7] Pogue Weisensel #949), b 26 April 1959, Dane Co., WI; m 4 June 1983, **Darrah Chavey**. Margaret changed her name to Peggy.

Children, surname CHAVEY:
    2994.   i.   Rhiannon[9] Christine, b 15 January 1986.
    2995.   ii. Peter Russell, b 10 February 1988.

2167. REBECCA[8] G. WEISENSEL (d/o Irene[7] Pogue Weisensel #949), b 23 August 1960, Dane Co., WI; m 27 February 1982, **Brian Strang**.

Children, surname STRANG:
    2996.   i.   Anthony[9] Joseph, b 17 December 1984.
    2997.   ii. Cory Alan, b 10 June 1987.

2246. DEBORAH[8] LYNN WILLIAMSON (d/o Clifford[7] Carlyle Williamson #1012), b 17 August 1956 at Berwyn, Alberta. She is a qualified property appraiser and works for the Alberta Government Assessment Dept.

Child, surname WILLIAMSON:
    2998.   i.   Kyle[9] Thomas, b 8 October 1988 at Edmonton, Alberta.

2260. PATSY[8] LYNN HOLLAND (d/o Delores[7] Helen Peckham Holland #1020), b 14 November 1955 at Webster, SD; m **Victor Rodriguez**; now divorced.

Child, surname RODRIGUEZ:
    2999.   i.   Victor, b 27 March 1982.

2263. DAVID[8] LESLIE HOLLAND (s/o Delores[7] Peckham Holland

#1020), b 3 October 1960 at Webster, SD. He is divorced.

Children, surname HOLLAND:
    3000. i. Amy[9], b 27 December 1980.
    3001. ii. Brandon, b 2 March 1982.

2264. JEFFREY[8] LEE SKAARE (s/o Jean[7] Peckham Skaare #1021), b 30 August 1956; m 10 June 1974 at Bristol, **Mary Jo Moxness**. They live at Coon Rapid, MN and he works in Roseville, MN where he tests computers at Sperry-Rand Co.

Children, surname SKAARE:
    3002. i. Eric[9] David, b 22 December 1974.
    3003. ii. Angela Marie, b 29 August 1978.

2265. JERALD[8] WAYNE SKAARE (s/o Jean[7] Peckham Skaare #1021), b 21 June 1958; m 25 August 1979 at Aberdeen, SD, **Carol Doreen Webb**. Jerry lives at Brooklyn Park, MN. He works in Plymouth, he is systems analyst on computers at L.S.I. Corp.

Children, surname SKAARE:
    3004. i. Tiffany[9] Jeanne, b 15 March 1980.
    3005. ii. Joshua Jerald, b 1 April 1984.

2269. VICKI[8] LEE PECKHAM (d/o Donald[7] Orville Peckham #1022), b 18 January 1958; m — **Charron**. Later divorced.

Children, surname CHARRON:
    3006. i. Heather[9] Marie, b 2 September 1977, at Aberdeen, SD.
    3007. ii. Joey Donald, b 5 December 1980.

2271. CHERYL[8] LYNN PECKHAM (d/o Donald[7] Orville Peckham #1022), b 2 March 1961; m 26 June 1982 at Bath, SD, **Bernard Hermans**.

Child, surname HERMANS:
    3008. i. Candase Marie, b 27 December 1982.

2276. LISA[8] KAY PECKHAM (d/o Rex[7] Maynard Peckham #1023), b 27 December 1961 at Aberdeen, SD; m — **Gallagher**.

Child, surname GALLAGHER:
    3009. i. Jenni[9] Kay, b 7 October 1983.

2322. KEVIN[8] LEE KRUSE (s/o Marvel[7] Keith Kruse #1073), b 3 April

1964 at Olathe, KS; m 15 February 1983 in Puerto Rico, **Cynthia Chico**, b 29 January 1965.

Child, surname KRUSE:
    3010.   i. Samantha^9 Lee, b 14 April 1983 in Puerto Rico.

2323. KRISTEL^8 ANN KRUSE (d/o James^7 Wesley Kruse #1074), b 16 March 1961 at Webster, SD; m 9 January 1981 at Mercedes, TX, **Ronald Rowe**.

Child, surname ROWE:
    3011.   i. Kody^9 Alan, b 21 May 1981 in TX.

2378. CHERYLE^8 ANN GWIAZDA (d/o Waneta^7 Meeker Gwiazda #1131), b 27 June 1949 at Stanley, WI; m 3 April 1971, **James Malecki** at Dubuque, IA.

Children, surname MALECKI:
    3012.   i. Corey^9 James, b 26 March 1972 at Stanley.
    3013.   ii. Russell Louis, b 17 August 1978 at Marshfield, WI.

2389. IRENE^8 MARY GWIAZDA (d/o Waneta^7 Meeker Gwiazda #1131), b 16 November 1950 at Stanley, WI; m 9 June 1973 at Thorp, WI, **Bernard Przybylski**.

Children, surname PRZYBYKSKI:
    3014.   i. Jessica^9 Mary, b 16 March 1974 at Stanley.
    3015.   ii. Dustin Bernard, b 5 January 1978 at Chippewa Falls, WI.

2390. GREGORY^8 GENE GWIAZDA (s/o Waneta^7 Meeker Gwiazda #1131), b 22 March 1955 at Stanley, WI; m 30 June 1976, **Beatta Huth** at Kern, Germany.

Children, surname GWIAZDA:
    3016.   i. Nicholas^9 Walter, b 2 October 1976 at Stanley.
    3017.   ii. Eric Daniel, b 27 July 1978 at Marshfield, WI.
    3018.   iii. Jeanine Lynn, b 16 September 1979 at Marshfield.

2391. DUANE^8 WALTER GWIAZDA (s/o Waneta^7 Meeker Gwiazda #1131), b 1 January 1957 at Stanley, WI; m 7 April 1978, **Gloria Welner** at Thorp.

Child, surname GWIAZDA:
    3019.   i. Regina^9 Camille, b 4 March 1979 in Maryland.

2394. GAIL[8] **MARIE ZASZCZURYNSKI** (d/o Rose[7] Meeker Zaszczurynski #1132), b 5 January 1956, Chicago, IL; m 24 March 1974, at Chicago, **Richard Teschke**.

Children, surname TESCHKE:
- 3020. i. Lena[9] Marie, b 28 May 1976 at Chicago.
- 3021. ii. Michelle Ann, b 23 October 1980 in California.

2395. TERRANCE[8] **EMMET ZASZCZURYNSKI** (s/o Rose[7] Meeker Zaszczurynski #1132), b 28 February 1957, Chicago, IL; m May 1983, **Patricia Green** in Tennessee.

Child, surname ZASZCZURYNSKI:
- 3022. i. Cecil[9] Joseph, b 28 January 1984 in Chicago.

2397. GABRIELLE[8] **MICHELLE ZASZCZURYNSKI** (d/o Rose[7] Meeker Zaszczurynski #1132), b 29 July 1962, Chicago, IL; m 15 December 1979, **Efran Trinidad**; divorced September 1984.

Child, surname TRINIDAD:
- 3023. i. Roselenna[9] Michelle, b 24 February 1983, Chicago.

2398. GWEN[8] **ROSE ZASZCZURYNSKI** (d/o Rose[7] Meeker Zaszczurynski #1132), b 30 December 1964, Chicago, IL.

Child, surname ZASZCZURYNSKI:
- 3024. i. Yaritza[9] Iris, b 28 September 1982 in Chicago.

2399. LaDONNA[8] **BEA MEEKER** (d/o Marvin[7] Cecil Meeker #1133 and Irene[7] Fate Meeker #1218), b 22 January 1955 at Stanley, WI; m 29 November 1975, **Don Brauhn** at Dubuque, IA. Don is a teacher and they live in Dubuque.

Children, surname BRAUHN:
- 3025. i. Molly[9] Irene, b 21 February 1979 at Dubuque.
- 3026. ii. Meghen Marie, b 29 May 1980.

2400. DEBBIE[8] **ANN MEEKER** (d/o Marvin[7] Cecil Meeker #1133 and Irene[7] Fate Meeker #1218), b 3 December 1960 at Stanley, WI; m 4 December 1979, **Tory Blomberg** at Windom, MN. They live in Rochester, MN; when last known Tory was looking for new employment and Debbie was training as a dental assistant.

Children, surname BLOMBERG:

3027. i. Jennifer[9] Irene, b 14 November 1979 at Rochester.
3028. ii. April Ann, b 1 October 1981 at Rochester.

2403. SUSAN[8] KAY MEEKER (d/o George[7] Henry Meeker 1134), b 19 January 1962, Stanley, WI; m 25 September 1982, **Eric Mentink** at Stanley.

Child, surname MENTINK:
3029. i. Travis[9] Eric, b 9 February 1984 at Stanley.

2412. LISA[8] LYNN SAUNDERS (d/o Judith[7] Meeker Saunders #1137), b 26 June 1965, Saint Paul, MN; m 19 May 1987 **Michael Sitter**.

Child, surname SITTER:
3030. i. Renee[9] Marie, b 21 April 1982 at Stanley, WI.

2429. DOUGLAS[8] LEE CULBERT (s/o Charles[7] Lee Culbert #1155), b 28 October 1953 at Oakland, CA; m 17 May 1980, **Celeste Joy Ropelt** at Mundelein, IL. Douglas is in the repair department of NW Telephone.

Child, surname CULBERT:
3031. i. Kristin[9] Tara, b 22 April 1983 at Kalispell, MT; stillborn, buried at Lone Pine Cemetery, Big Forks, MT.

2430. DAVID[8] LYLE CULBERT (s/o Charles[7] Lee Culbert #1155), b 14 January 1955 at Kalispell, MT; m 1 June 1974, **Carolyn Lisa Rogers** at Swan Lake, MT. Carolyn works at NW Telephone.

Children, surname CULBERT, both born at Kalispell, MT:
3032. i. Aaron[9] Lee, b 5 January 1977.
3033. ii. Adrienne Leanna, b 24 October 1980.

2431. DARYL[8] LYNN CULBERT (s/o Charles[7] Lee Culbert #1155), b 11 December 1956 at Missoula, MT; m/1 3 November 1977, **Lydia Ann Cagle**: marriage annulled February 1978 at Polson, MT, m/2 7 January 1979 at San Diego, CA, **Sheila Ann Holbrook**; divorced 10 February 1981 at Kalispell. Daryl is a sawyer in the Plymouth plant.

Child, surname CULBERT:
3034. i. Daniel[9] William, b 25 October 1979 at Seattle, WA.

2433. SHARI[8] LYNETTE CULBERT (d/o Charles Lee Culbert #1155), b 14 November 1961 at Missoula, MT; m 12 April 1980, **Martin Willus Kitzmiller** at Swan Lake, MT. Martin is a mechanic.

Children, surname KITZMILLER, Kalispell:
- 3035. i. Andi[9] Bruce, b 18 September 1981.
- 3036. ii. Jesse Allyn, b 31 October 1983.

2435. BRIAN[8] CULBERT (s/o Jerald[7] Lance Culbert #1156), b 5 October 1959 at Missoula, MT; m 28 August 1982, **June Froelich**. He is a diesel mechanic.

Children, surname CULBERT, both born at Missoula:
- 3037. i. Gary[9] Allen, b 13 January 1983.
- 3038. i. Jennifer Lacy, b 13 January 1983 (twin).

2438. BRENDA[8] HYSLOP (d/o Mary[7] Culbert Hyslop #1157), married —.

Child, surname UNKNOWN:
- 3039. i. Brandie[9].

2442. DENISE[8] MARGARET FRENCH (d/o Dennis[7] Allen French #1159), m **Dale Michelson** in 1983.

Child, surname MICHELSON:
- 3040. i. Curtis[9] Allen.

2450. MICHAEL[8] C. HANSON (s/o Larry Kay Hanson #1164), b 1 December 1960 at Owatonna, MN; m 19 October 1981, **Debbie Speaks**, b 1 October 1962.

Children, surname HANSON, both born at Izzard Co., AR:
- 3041. i. Matthew[9], b 23 February 1983.
- 3042. ii. Michael, b 28 May 1984.

2597. CHADRICK[8] ARTHUR JOSEPH ROOTS (s/o Chadrick[7] Arthur Roots #1296), b 15 January 1961 at Tucson, AZ; m **Erin Lee Appleton**, 9 October 1981 at Mokelumne Hills, CA, b 20 August 1960, d/o Donn Michael and Anne Sheridan (Hicks) Appleton. Chad is head jailer at Calaveras Co. Sheriff's Dept.; Erin operates her own day care center.

Child, surname ROOTS:
- 3043. i. Jesse[9] Joseph, b 21 January 1987 at Jackson, CA.

2606. TAMRA[8] GAYE KRETCHMER (d/o Joan[7] Perchetti Kretschmer #1305), b 19 April 1958 at Las Vegas, NV; m 18 August

1978, **Richard Harold Boone**. They are divorced.

Child, surname BOONE:

3044. i. Justin^9 Richard, b 7 September 1979 at Reno, NV.

2609. DARRELL^8 OLIVER HARDT (s/o David^7 Oliver Hardt #1314), b 14 January 1957 at Bisbee, AZ; m 1 August 1974 at Silver City, NM, **Dorothy Ellen Cooper**, b 12 November 1955, d/o Howard Marvin and Alvie (Roseberry) Cooper.

Children, surname HARDT, both born at Silver City:

3045. i. Barbara^9 April Rachael, b 2 March 1975.
3046. ii. Daniel Oliver, b 11 October 1976.

2610. NINA^8 LOUISE HARDT (d/o David^7 Oliver Hardt #1314), b 18 December 1957 at Bisbee, AZ; m 22 June 1974, **Thomas Joseph Herbert** at Tyrone, NM, b 28 January 1958 at Orange Grove, CA, s/o Milton and Elizabeth (Cunningham) Herbert.

Children, surname HERBERT, all born at Silver City, NM:

3047. i. Brandi^9 Lynn, b 25 January 1975.
3048. ii. Christin Louise, b 18 December 1975.
3049. iii. Amy Elizabeth, b 20 March 1978.

2611. GAY^8 JEANETTE HARDT (d/o David^7 Oliver Hardt #1314), b 6 July 1960 at Bisbee, AZ; m 2 April 1982, **Glen Thomas Cole**, b 19 July 1960 at Silver City, NM, s/o Thomas LaMar and Fannie Mayrice (Steele) Cole. Thomas was previously married to Laurie Dawn Warren Upton; divorced 21 July 1981.

Children, surname COLE:

3050. i. Amanda^9 Dawn, b 1 December 1978 at Silver City.
3051. ii. Tanya Gay, b 16 February 1984 at Safford, AZ.
3052. iii. Levi Thomas, b 24 April 1987 at Tucson, AZ.

2612. IVAN^8 THOMAS HARDT (s/o David^7 Oliver Hardt #1314), b 15 October 1962 at Bisbee, AZ; m 27 June 1981, **Shannon Gale Dunn**, b 20 August 1962, d/o Eddie L. and Frances Dunn.

Child, surname HARDT:

3053. i. Tyler^9 Thomas, b 29 November 1984 at Silver City, NM.

2613. ROGER^8 KOY HAYNIE (s/o Vernaline^7 Hardt Haynie #1315), b 11 May 1958 at Bisbee, AZ; m 14 August 1981, **Angela Guerrero**, b 1 December 1962.

Children, surname HAYNIE:
    3054.   i.   Jessica[9] Dalene, b 11 August 1983.
    3055.   ii. Roger Koy III, b 25 July 1985.

2614. WALTER[8] LYN HAYNIE (s/o Vernaline[7] Hardt Haynie #1315), b 10 May 1958 at Mesa, AZ; m 22 September 1979, **Bonnie Ann (Clark) Carter** at Belmont, CA, b 21 September 1952 at San Francisco, CA, d/o Glenn Walter and Jean Helene (Hatch) Clark. Bonnie has two children from a previous marriage: Adam Craig Carter, b 31 July 1973 in San Jose and Nicole Helene Clark, b 4 December 1977 in Albuquerque.

Children, surname HAYNIE:
    3056.   i.   Joseph[9] Lyn, b 2 June 1980 at Burlingame, CA.
    3057.   ii. Cara Ann Marie, b 23 December 1981 at Reno, NV.
    3058.   iii. Talen Eric, b 25 June 1984 at Reno.
    3059.   iv. Thomas Glenn Stan, b 28 August 1987 at Monteray, CA.

2615. DEE[8] ANN HAYNIE (d/o Vernaline[7] Hardt Haynie #1315), b 4 August 1960 at Superior, AZ; m 11 April 1984, **Alan Matthew Homer** at Tucson, AZ, b 9 December 1956 at Augusta, GA, s/o Richard Leslie and Patricia Ann (Page) Homer.

Child, surname HOMER:
    3060.   i.   Matthew[9] Alan, b 14 May 1987 at Tucson, AZ.

2616. DORENE[8] MARIE HAYNIE (d/o Vernaline[7] Hardt Haynie #1315), b 5 December 1961 at Superior. She has a child by a Ambrosio Saldana Lopez; Ambrosio Lopez b 24 April 1959 at Guanajuata, Mexico.

Child, surname LOPEZ:
    3061.   i.   Julio[9] James, b 14 August 1986.

2617. CLINTON[8] DEWAYNE HAYNIE (s/o Vernaline[7] Hardt Haynie #1315), b 8 March 1963 at Douglas, AZ; m/1 5 December 1981 at Douglas, **Katherine Marie Jackson**, b 1 June 1962 in CA; they had one child. Clinton m/2 **Barbara "Bobby Jo" Connor**.

Children, surname HAYNIE:
    3062.   i.   Jessie[9] Dewayne, b 3 May 1983.
    3063.   ii. Roberta[9] Joleen, b 21 April 1985 at Douglas.

The Eighth Generation

2630. RICHARD[8] L. ROBERTS (s/o Gloria[7] Miller Roberts #1326), m —.

Children, surname ROBERTS:
- 3064. i. Jennie Roberts.
- 3065. ii. Rickie Roberts.

2631. KEVIN[7] GENE ROBERTS (s/o Gloria[7] Miller Roberts #1326), m —.

Child, surname ROBERTS:
- 3066. i. Felicia Mae.

2696. DEBORAH[8] KAY SPAUN (d/o Loraine[7] Lester Spaun #1370), b 12 September 1955 at Anaconda, MT; m 7 June 1973 at Smelterville, ID, **Allen Bauer**, s/o Elwood and LaVonne (Windedall) Bauer, b 17 July 1953 at Madison, SD. Allen is a miner at the Arco Mine, Osborn. They live at Kellogg, ID.

Children, surname BAUER:
- 3067. i. Christine[9] Marie, b 11 December 1974 at Kellogg, ID.
- 3068. ii. James Elwood, b 3 June 1977 at Kellogg.
- 3069. iii. Wayne Allen, b 12 July 1980 at Coeur D'Alene, ID.

2697. RHONDA[8] LEE SPAUN (d/o Loraine[7] Lester Spaun #1370), b 20 October 1956 at Anaconda, MT; m 22 October 1974, **Ralph LaClair**, b 22 April 1954 at Tacoma, WA, s/o Loren and Marilyn (Bliner) LaClair. Ralph was a smelterman at Bunker Hill Mine (now closed), Kellogg, ID. He has Multiple Sclerosis and cannot work; lives in Alberton, MT.

Children, surname LaCLAIR, born at Kellogg:
- 3070. i. Robert[9] Michele, b 26 May 1975.
- 3071. ii. William Loren, b 13 March 1977.

2699. BILLIE[8] JEAN SPAUN (d/o Loraine[7] Lester Spaun #1370), b 25 August 1958 at Red Lodge, MT; m 14 June 1975, **Donald Siegfried**, b 25 August 1955 at Silverton, ID, s/o Paul and Doris Siegfried. Donald was a smelterman at the now closed Bunker Hill Mine at Kellogg. Reportedly, they are divorced.

Children, surname SIEGFRIED:
- 3072. i. Dusty[9] Jean, b 21 May 1976 at Wallace, ID.
- 3073. ii. Ammie Dawn, b 23 March 1979 at Kellogg.

2830. JACQUELINE[8] **ANN DURANSO** (d/o Mary[7] Mentz Duranso #1633), b 2 October 1964; m 29 June 1985, **Steven Benjamin Landwehr**, at Wausau, WI. They live in Detroit, MI.

Child, surname LANDWEHR:

    3074.   i. Stephanie[9] Ann, b 29 August 1990.

Appendix

Joshua Wadley's First Family

1. JOSHUA^1 WADLEY (s/o Moses and Beda (Glass) Wadley), b April 1816 at Watertown, NY; d 10 October 1900 at Mexico, Oswego Co., NY of tuberculosis, age 84, as given on his death certificate; m/1 about 1835, **Elizabeth —**, b 1815; d 28 December 1862 in Mexico, and is buried with Joshua in Mexico Village Cemetery (gravestone). Joshua appeared in the 1840 and 1850 Oswego Co. Census in Town of Palermo; in 1860 Census and until his death in Mexico. He was several times listed as a lawyer. They had one child

Joshua m/2 **Martha Reed** (#27) (d/o John^2 Reed #7; see page 47). Child, surname WADLEY:

+   2.   i. Joshua L., b 16 July 1873 in Oswego Co., NY.

Second Generation

2. JOSHUA^2 L. WADLEY (s/o Joshua^1 Wadley #1), b 16 July 1837 in Oswego Co., NY, probably in Town of Palermo. He appeared in 1850 Census at 12 years of age; 1860 Census, at 23 years of age, he was with his father. He enlisted 11 August 1862, age 25, in Co E., 110th Volunteer Infantry in Mexico to serve 3 years in the Civil War. He was discharged 15 March 1864 for disability, at New Orleans, LA, according to his Civil War Record. He m/1 about 1858 at Mexico, **Rosa Reiley (Riley)** d/o John and Elizabeth Reiley; she d 22 January 1881, according to a record of Eluoda Fetcha, Mexico Town Historian. According to a document in Joshua's Civil War Pension file he worked as cabinet maker and foreman in a carpenter shop of the New York Ontario Railroad in Oswego, NY, dated April 12 1882.

Joshua L. Wadley appeared in the 1882 Oswego City Directory as a railroad car builder, living with Seymour and Dora. In 1884 Oswego Directory he appeared, listed as a grocer, probably working for his son-in-law Charles Donohue, According to his Civil War Pension file he was in Buffalo, NY for awhile before proceeding to Christian County, MO. He registered 22 October 1889 at Garrison, MO, applying for a Civil War Pension. On 16 June 1894 Joshua L. Wadley bought 40 acres in Garrison. (Book 32, p. 367) and 12 May 1910 he bought more land (Book 64, p. 215), for a total of 200 acres. Then 14 February 1900 he bought 160 acres of homestead land from the government (Book 57, p. 621). Total acreage was sold 12 May 1910 for $1,000. Joshua m/2 15 April 1897 at Garrison, Christian Co., MO, **Jennie Parks**, b July 1874 in Ozark, MO, d/o Warren and Rowena (Rugh) Parks. The family of Jennie moved to a nearby farm after Jennie gave birth to an illegitimate child in Ozark in 1895. Her family arranged the marriage between Jennie and Joshua as reported by Effie Bradley, a contemporary of daughter Helen, living in Springfield, MO. Joshua and Jennie worked very hard to make a living out of the poor soil, primarily raising sheep. According to Mark Roberts at Century Pines Nursing Home, Ozark, who owned land next to Joshua, he was a close-mouthed man who revealed nothing of his past life. The Wadley land in Garrison is now part of the Mark Twain National Park. About 1909, Joshua and Jennie moved to Kiefer, OK where they ran a store and lived behind the store. Jennie choked on something in her throat, perhaps a goiter. Helen called her aunt Madge Tunnell in Ozark when her mother became ill, but Jennie was dead when Madge arrived, according to Helen, her son Rex's wife. Madge brought Helen and Rex back to Ozark with her and Jennie's body, and buried Jennie in Ozark City Cemetery, 18 January 1911, at 37 years of age. Joshua moved on to Palacious, TX with plans for starting a citrus grove. Joshua, while living at Garrison was known as a skilled cabinet maker.

On 21 December 1911 Joshua was admitted to the National Military Home, at Leavenworth, KS, where he died 2 June 1917; he is buried in the military cemetery there.

Children, surname WADLEY:

3.   i. Dora^3, b about 1859 in Mexico, NY; m 22 August 1882 in Oswego, Charles Donohue, s/o John and Margaret (Williams) Donohue; Charles listed as butcher, as given in a marriage record, office of City Clerk, Oswego. In Oswego City Directories for 1884 and 1886 and 1890/91 Charles is listed as a grocer; in 1892/93 as a RR car inspector; 1895 as RR car inspector and Dora as grocer at 133 E. Seneca St.; 1897 Charles, machinist, boards at 145 E. Seneca and Dora is grocer at 133 E. Seneca St. This is based on the last record we have; land transaction records of 1911

Appendix 437

        in Oswego mentions Charles H. Donahue and Dora, his wife, and *Dennis J. Donahue of New Brunswick, NJ, formerly of Oswego.*
- 4. ii. Seymour, b about 1865 at Mexico, NY, according to the City of Oswego 1880 Federal Census, aged 15 years with father, mother and sister; was living in Oswego, NY with father and sister in 1882 City Directory; in 1884/85 Syracuse City Directory he was there on North Salina St., a laborer; in 1886 Oswego City Directory he was boarding at E. Seneca St., corner of 10th St., a carpenter; the last record we have of him.
- + 5. iii. Helen (Jennie's daughter), b 29 January 1895.
- + 6. iv. Lester, b 25 January 1898.
- + 7. v. Rex, 3rd child of Joshua and Jennie, b 18 July 1901.

Third Generation

5. HELEN^3 WADLEY (d/o Jennie^2 Parks Wadley), b 29 January 1895 at Ozark, MO. Effie Bradley said Helen lived in Ozark with her Aunt Gladys Johnson while going to school and her Aunt Madge Tunnell helped her through college and she became a registered nurse. Helen m/1 **John A. Blake** of Kiefer, Creek Co., OK, 25 April 1914. She only lived with him a few months and had no children by him, divorcing him in Tulsa, OK. In a conversation with her, by telephone, in Anaheim, CA, she said she worked her way through nursing school 1915–1918 and worked four years in the same hospital in Tulsa, OK. She met Clarence Barone as a patient in the hospital; he had injured his foot in the oil fields where he worked. Helen m/2 24 September 1923 at Tulsa, OK, **Clarence Barone**, s/o Franklin and Emma Barone, b 15 April 1893 at Ashland, OH; d 1959. They were in Seminole, OK, 8 years, later were located in Borger, TX; Clarence was a restless man and they moved frequently.

Helen Wadley Barone and her brother Lester moved to CA, after Clarence's death; while back in Ozark visiting her Aunt Madge Tunnell, she met **Edward Harrison Powell**, who was visiting relatives across the street from her aunt's. She returned to CA and he followed he there. They were married at her younger daughter's home. They returned to MO because her husband didn't like CA. They lived at Nixa, MO from 1968–1977; Edward d 15 January 1977 and is buried outside of Ozark. She remained in Nixa about a year after his death, then moved back to CA, April 1978. She lived in a mobile home in Anaheim, CA, when last known.

Children, surname BARONE:
+   8.   i.   Clarence[4] Vernon, b 21 July 1927.
+   9.   ii.   Helen Margaret, b 18 July 1930.
+   10.   iii.   Bonnie Jane, b 13 April 1932.

6. LESTER[3] P. WADLEIGH (s/o Joshua[2] L. Wadley #2), b 25 January 1898 at Ozark, MO; d 10 June 1971 at Yucaipa, CA. He was about 13 when his mother died in OK; he was sent to live with Ellen Wadley an aunt of Jennie's in KS. He m/1 **Marguerite Cecilia Gallaglier**, d/o Bernard and Margaret (Muldowney) Gallaglier, b 2 July 1896 in PA; d 7 April 1960 at Los Angeles, CA. Lester always spelled his last name differently than the rest of the family. He m/2 **Margaret Walker**; she lived, when last known, at 510 Central Ave., Fillmore, CA. Marguerite and Lester both buried at Rose Hills Memorial Park, Whittier, CA. He was a truck driver in later years.

Children, surname WADLEIGH:
     11.   i.   Lorraine[4], m Robert Reeder, now deceased; lives in Whittier.
     12.   ii.   Lester Parks, lives in Orange, CA. He was in the Marines in WW I and reportedly has three children.
     13.   iii.   Marguerite, m — Weber.

7. REX[3] WADLEY (s/o Joshua[2] Wadley #2), b 18 July 1901 at Ozark, MO. He was 10 or 11 when his mother died and the family was split up; he was brought up by one of the Parks families in Ozark; as a young man he worked on the Pennsylvania Railroad; served in the Navy in WW I, working in shipyards running big cranes; m/1 in 1922, **Stella Kopalecki**, b 1899 in Poland near Gadansk; d 11 October 1960. Rex m/2 20 April 1963 at Newark, NJ, **Ellen Twohig**; she b 11 February 1908 at Peapack, NJ, d/o John and Abigail (Young) Twohig who were both born in Ireland; they had no children. Rex d 22 February 1968 and is buried at Mahwah, NJ. Ellen lives at Paramus, NJ. Rex was a truck driver.

Children, surname WADLEY, both born at Jersey City, NJ:
+   14.   i.   Lillian[4], b 17 July 1918.
+   15.   ii.   Jerry Arthur, b 9 October 1927.

Fourth Generation

8. CLARENCE[4] **VERNON BARONE** (s/o Helen[3] Wadley Barone #5), b 21 July 1927 at Seminole, OK; m/1 about 1948 at Lorain, OH, **Julia Holley**, d/o Francis and Margaret (Rado) Holley, b 24 June 1925 at Lorain. He lives in Hawaii and Julia lives at Inglewood, CA. He m/2 **Betty Robinson**; no children. He is an airplane mechanic and works for United Air Lines.

Children, surname BARONE, both born at Los Angeles, CA:
+   16.   i.   Stephanie[5] Marie, b 16 December 1949.
       17.   ii.   Richard, b 2 April 1955 at Los Angeles, CA. He is a machinist and lives at Modesto, CA and is not married.

9. HELEN[4] **MARGARET BARONE** (d/o Helen[3] Wadley Barone #5), b 18 July 1930 at Ozark, MO; m 6 July 1957 at Las Vegas, NV, **Edward Paul O'Neal**, s/o Edward Kyle and Helen Beatrice (O'Downally) O'Neal; d 30 July 1980. Edward was a long haul truck driver. They were divorced in 1979; he remarried 3 months before being killed in an automobile accident. Helen lives at Garden Grove, CA.

Children, surname O'NEAL, both born at Westchester, CA:
+   18.   i.   Kathleen[5], b 30 August 1960.
       19.   ii.   Karleen, b 6 September 1961; not married as of 1982.

10. BONNIE[4] **JANE BARONE** (d/o Helen[3] Wadley Barone #5), b 13 April 1932 at Henderson, TX; m in 1952 at Las Vegas, **Stewart Melvin Louis**, s/o Luelle (Avery) Louis, b 3 December 1929 at Los Angeles, CA. Bonnie lives at Huntington Beach, CA; she is divorced.

Children, surname LOUIS, all born at Los Angeles:
       20.   i.   William[5], b 28 June 1953; is a car salesman; unmarried.
       21.   ii.   Robert, b 27 June 1956; lives at home; unmarried.
       22.   i.   Laura, b 31 August 1960; is a secretary; lives at home; unmarried.

14. LILLIAN[4] **WADLEY** (d/o Rex[3] Wadley #7), b 17 July 1918 at Jersey City, NJ; m in 1945, **James Kilroy**, b 1911; he is a lawyer. They live at North Falmouth, MA.

Children, surname KILROY:
       23.   i.   Maureen[5], b 1946.
       24.   ii.   Gerald, b 1947.

25. iii. Lynn.
26. iv. Joyce.
27. v. James.

15. JERRY[4] ARTHUR WADLEY (s/o Rex[3] Wadley #7), b 9 October 1927 at Jersey City, NJ; m 8 February 1947 at Union, NJ, **Beatrice Ann Ryan**, d/o Martin Francis and Beatrice (Keenan-O'Keefe) Ryan, b 7 April 1927 at Scranton, PA. Jerry is sales representative for Cochran and Cribby, who sell aluminum products; Beatrice is in the accounting department of Gulfstream Bank in Boca Raton, where they live.

Children, surname WADLEY:

+ 28. i. Judith[5] Gloria, b 31 August 1949, at Jersey City.
+ 29. ii. Geraldine Dolores, b 12 October 1952, at Paramus, NJ.
   30. iii. Pamela Jane, b 1 June 1961 at Paramus. She lived when last known with her sister Judy and was a secretary and model.

Fifth Generation

16. STEPHANIE[5] MARIE BARONE (d/o Clarence[4] Vernon Barone #8), b 16 December 1949 at Los Angeles, CA; m **Michael Smith**.

Child, surname SMITH:

   30. i. Amy-Lynn[6] Marie, b 7 March 1979.

18. KATHLEEN[5] O'NEAL (d/o Helen[4] Margaret Barone O'Neal #9), b 30 August 1960 at Westchester, CA. She m 27 December 1980, **Lennie Dale Martin** (in army in Germany in 1982).

Child, surname MARTIN:

   31. i. Derick[6] Edward.

28. JUDITH[5] GLORIA WADLEY (d/o Jerry[4] Arthur Wadley #15) b 31 August 1949 at Jersey City, NJ; m 18 September 1971, **James Hedgecock**, s/o Fred and Virginia (Martin) Hedgecock, b 27 December 1945 at Brooklyn, NY. James has his own business delivering art supplies at West Milford, NJ.

Child, surname HEDGECOCK:

   32. i. Jamie, b 8 March 1979 (adopted).

29. GERALDINE[5] DOLORES WADLEY (d/o Jerry[4] Arthur Wadley

#15), b 12 October 1952 at Paramus, NJ; m 20 May 1972, **Fred Reardon**, s/o Francis and Josephine (Amerelli) Reardon, b 17 August 1951 at Butler, NJ. Fred drives an oil truck for Florida General Company.

Children, surname REARDON:
    33. i. David[6] James, b 21 January 1978.
    34. ii. Ryan, b 14 April 1979.

The Second Family of Lyman L. Austin

1. LYMAN[1] **L. AUSTIN**, husband of **Pauline Reed (#5)**, m/2 in Town of Harden, Green Lake Co., WI, **Cornelia (Cooper) Smith** 31 March 1855, b about 1825 according to the 1860 Census. She had two children from a previous marriage: William, b about 1846 and John, b about 1850.

Children, surname AUSTIN:
+   2. i. Emmett[2] D., b 3 June 1855.
+   3. ii. Nelson C., b in 1860.

Second Generation

2. EMMETT[2] **D. AUSTIN** (s/o Lyman[1] L. Austin #1), b 3 June 1855 at Mackford, Green Lake Co., WI; m/1 6 October 1876 at Kingston, Green Lake Co., WI, **Roccina/Rocinna M. Austin**, d/o Horace E. and Susan M. Austin, residence of the groom in Montello, Marquette Co., WI; they were divorced; m/2 19 May 1886 at Columbia Co, **Anna Bunn**, d/o James and Emma Bunn, res. of groom Portage, Columbia Co; they were divorced; m/3 20 May 1894 at Portage, **Bertha Pieper**, d/o Fred and Augusta (Riemes) Pieper, b 30 October 1874; d 12 August 1959 at Rio, WI; they were divorced. Emmett d 10 May 1920 at Portage; buried at Oak Grove Cemetery, Portage.

Children, surname AUSTIN:
    4. i. Louise[3], b 1878.
    5. ii. Bertha, b 1880.
+   6. iii. Ella May "Annie," b 13 February 1887.
+   7. iv. Zella.
    8. v. Myrtle, b 30 July 1895 at Columbia Co; m 19 May 1913, Elias

+ 9. vi. Roy Young in Columbia, CO; they were divorced; Roy d 1976.
Roy Elfred, b 13 September 1897.
10. vii. Ray William, b 31 March 1889 at Columbia Co; m 31 March 1909, Meta Manteufel (who later married her brother-in-law Roy). Ray d 28 July 1918, age 29, by lightning strike.

3. NELSON[2] C. AUSTIN (s/o Lyman[1] L. Austin #1), b in 1860 in WI; m 12 October 1883 at Portage, Columbia Co., WI, **Anna Bunn**, d/o James and Emma Bunn, b OH, witnesses: Emmett D. and Roccina Austin; they were divorced; m/2 **Elisea J. Van Schoch**, d/o Frederick and Elizabeth Van Schoch, b in AZ; (marriage record says Nelson's mother is Susan Austin) they were divorced; Nelson had no children (Lyman L. Austin's will lists as an heir, his grandson, Nelson). Nelson d 17 March 1931 at Marcellon, Columbia Co., WI and he is buried in the Cemetery at Marcellon.

Child, surname AUSTIN:
11. i. Nelson[3].

Third Generation

6. ANNIE[3] AUSTIN (d/o Emmett[2] Austin #2), b 13 February 1887, in Columbia Co., WI (some confusion with the name Ella May) m/1 **Fred Kefer**; m/2 **William Vivian**; m/3 **Henry Hommen**. There were several children; only two names known:

Children, surname unknown:
12. i. Clyde[4].
13. ii. Jack.

7. ZELLA[3] AUSTIN (d/o Emmett[2] Austin #2), had two "partners" 1/ Kegler; 2/ Kaiser; reportedly had two children, unmarried.

Children, surname AUSTIN (?):
14. i. Myrtle[4].
15. ii. unknown.

9. ROY[3] ELFRED AUSTIN, b 13 September 1897; m 23 May 1920 in Columbia Co., WI, **Meta (Manteufel) Austin**, who had m/1 Roy's younger brother Ray. She d 30 August 1972 at Rio, Columbia Co, WI; Roy d 11 November 1976 in Madison, WI Hospital from burns he received while burning leaves. He was employed over 40 years by the Columbia County Highway Department. The list of children is based on the obituary.

Children, surname AUSTIN:

- 16. i. Dorothy[4], of Rio; m Ronald Daugherty.
- 17. ii. William, of Rio.
- 18. iii. Mrs. Ormul Conford, of Cambria.
- 19. iv. Orville, of Elko, NV.
- 20. v. Lowell, of Pardeeville, WI.
- 21. vi. Sylvia, of Rio; m Delbert Tomlinson 29 April 1972.

Emmett Austin's Obituary

Emmett Austin, resident of Portage. Born at Lake Maria (Mackford) June 13, 1854. Leaves four children: Mrs. Fred Kiefer of Madison, Miss Zella of Rio, WI, E.R. Young of Portage, Roy of Portage. One son, Ray killed by lightening July 1918. Funeral from E.R. Young's 121 E. Burns St., Portage. Mr. Austin was in the wood sawing business.

Pardeeville Times, 1920

Addenda

27. Martha Reed, wife of Joshua Wadley. Mr. Castle found in *Mexico Independent* of March 25, 1885 "Lera Wadley of New York, brother of Joshua Wadley of Mexico, was buried today in Mexico."

96. Pearl Lera Wadley's grandfather, Moses Wadley, d at Woodland MI in 1848 and his wife Beda d there in 1874. Moses' daughter Mary Eggleston lived there and died in 1905. It was also reported that Blanche Wadley was first cousin of Pearl's second wife, Ruby Farnsworth.

503. Thomas Runyan was an engineering specialists for General Dynamics Corporation in San Diego, CA; they lived in Spring Valley, CA, until their retirement when they moved to Loveland Co. Vena's book, *And Now the Golden Years*, is about the Austin family.

721. Douglas Canfield m 21 October 1989 at Gratz, PA, Ethel Hoftetter, d/o Glenn and Anna (Heff) Hoftetter. He has an antique business in Bouckville, NY. They have identical twin daughters, Evangeline Joy and Elizabeth Ann, b 21 March 1991.

864. Paul Brown has been married twice and currently lives with Ellen at Turlock, CA. He has seven children and eight grandchildren.

929. Thomas Vining and family live in Carlsbad, NM.

1205. Daniel Abel is an Eagle Scout and attended the World Jamboree in 1967 at Faragutt, ID. He was also one of 29 Eagle Scouts who attended the 1968 Olympics in Mexico City; in 1969 he served on the staff. His two brothers are also Eagle Scout.

1206. Thomas Crowe was born 4 May 1954 at Mankato, MN.

1257. Nancy's husband Rodney Bacon was born 17 July 1971.

1288. Deborah Ann Courtney is a land lease supervisor for Amoco Oil Company and Bob is in construction. They live in Wheat Ridge, CO.

1433. Keith Arneson wife Wendy is the daughter of George Bastien.

1729. Jan Weston m 11 Sept 1982 Leann Marie Russell; they have a son, Joshua Michiel, b 14 June 1984.

1823. Valerie Cheeseman was engaged to David Pepe of North Haven, CT with a planned marriage date of 13 July 1985.

Index

A

Abboud, Amir Abraham, 393
  Joseph, 392
  Laurel Fern (Valenta), 392
  Paula (Sokol), 392
  Yasmin Fern, 393
Abdoo, Mary Elaine, 421
Abel, Alice, 156, 241
  Andrew Luverne, 106
  Ann (Boyum), 242
  Bertha Irene (Bennett), 157
  Beth, 157
  Daniel James, 242, 373, 445
  Delia Ann, 106, 155, 243
  Dulsie Mae (House) (Taylor), 157
  Edith Velma (Trueax), 241
  Elsie (Hinz), 242
  Estina May, 106, 155
  Ethel (—), 106
  Ethel Lorilla, 106, 158
  Etta Matilda, 106, 157, 237
  Forrest Edward, 156, 241, 371
  Hans August, 373
  Heide Hannah, 373
  Helen May, 156, 241
  James, 43, 373
  James Andrew, 106
  James Daniel, 157, 242
  Janice Diane (Lasher), 371
  John, 242
  Katherine O. (Hayes) (Culbert), 156
  Kim, 242, 373
  Kirsten Caron, 373
  Leonard Orlow, 157, 242
  Lester Ross, 106, 156
  Mabel (Cartwright), 156
  Malinda Alvaretta, 107
  Malinda Alvaretta (Phillips), 106
  Marilyn Dorothy (Stucky), 242
  Mark Leonard, 242
  Mary (Eastman), 106
  Mary Jane, 242, 373
  Melinda Jo, 242, 374
  Monica Beth, 371
  Morgan, 106
  Naomi Christine, 371
  Paul Eric, 242
  Rebecca Rae, 373
  Rosanne (Wood), 373
  Ross, 242, 373
  Ryan, 373
  Sharon Amanda (Briggs), 242
  Sharon Nadine, 241, 372
  Susan Margaret (Tangen), 373
  Thomas, 157
  Thomas Morgan, 106, 156
  Yon Aron, 373
Abernathy, Janet Carlaw, 98
Abney, Iola Gladys, 255
Acker, Carole Jane, 229
  Fern Isabelle (Peckham), 229
  Pansy (—), 229
  Robert, 229
  Robert Charles, 229
Adams, Alvin, 219, 337
  Andrea Lynn, 337
  Audrey, 337
  Barbara, 337
  Carol (—), 337
  David, 219, 336
  Dawn, 337
  Edward, 219
  Frances Ann (—), 337
  Fred, 337
  Inez, 274
  Jeanette (Harris), 336
  Jennie (Brink), 219
  John, 337
  Larry, 219, 337
  Mabel Caroline (Vining), 219
  Madeline (Hewen), 336
  Mark, 337
  Scott Edward, 337
  William, 219
Adel, —, 174
  Verna (Bullock), 174
Agee, Ada Carol, 249
  Helen Agnes (Harper), 249
  Richard Spriggs, 249
Ainsworth, A. Franklin, 101
  Ida Maude (Peckham), 101

Aker, Dora (Anderson), 333
    Edwin, 333
    Gertrude Anne, 333
Albert, Minnie Mary, 211
Alberts, Frances, 241
Aldrich, Amy Elizabeth, 343
    Billy R., 343
    Julie Elaine, 343
    Monna Elaine (Dalton), 343
    Myrtle (Bremner), 343
    Raymond, 343
Alexander, George Alfred, 382
    Helen Marie (Smith), 382
    Winnie Mae, 382
Allan, Esther B., 38
    Ranger, 38
    Sunny, 41
Allcox, Mary Ann, 166
Allen, Jim, 66
    Lisa Marie, 415
    Liza Marie, 415
    Millie, 202
    Robert Jay, 415
    Thomas P., 59
Allman, Annette (Johns), 182
    George, 182
    Gladys Lastrella, 182
Allnut, Dolores Esther (MacDonald), 306
    Gwen Ann (Kennedy), 306
    Karen Danielle, 306
    Lara Beth, 306
    Michael John, 306
    Michael Wade, 306
    William Frederick, 306
Amenson, Doris, 399
Amerelli, Josephine, 441
Ames, Amy Elizabeth, 42
    Edward, 42
    Edward M., 42
    Elizabeth (Austin), 42
    Hannah, 43
    Hannah (Leonard), 42
    Harlow, 79
    Mary Ann, 42, 105
    Phineas, 42
    Rhoda, 42
Anacker, Art, 360
    Carol (—), 360
    Dawn, 360
Andekain, Ruth Ann, 403

Anderson, Aletta Sophia, 203
    Connie McCoy, 393
    David, 376
    Deborah Kay (Wester), 376
    Dora, 333
    Hilma, 174
    Jennifer Marie, 376
    Mabel, 351
    Maren Oline, 147
    Ragna Antine, 129
Andrus, Amy Rosina, 180
    Herbert Mortimer, 180
    Mary Jane (Maier), 180
Antognini, Cindy, 229
    Fern Isabelle (Peckham) (Acker), 229
    Keith, 229
    Kent, 229
    Kim (—), 229
    William, 229
Appleton, Anne Sheridan (Hicks), 430
    Donn Michael, 430
    Erin Lee, 430
April, Florence, 397
Araki, Michico, 421
Archibald, Bertha Beatrice (Beavert), 185
    Donna Jean, 186, 293
    Elizabeth (Winklesky) (Titus), 186
    Lois, 186, 293
    Orin Louis, 185
    William, 185
Argus, Laura, 8
Arhcibald, Elizabeth (Ryan), 185
Arndt, Terre, 336
Arneson, Aaron Richard, 397
    Albert O., 217
    Antoinette Marie (Foral), 265
    Audrey Carol (Birr), 397
    Berthanna (Gudahl), 217
    Beulah M., 217
    Beverly June (Johnson), 265
    CharleneBeverly, 397
    Darryl Ronald, 265
    Delra Lenice, 265
    Elmer Wesley, 265
    Erling Donald, 265
    Jackie Marie, 397
    JenniferLynn, 397
    Kathleen Marie (Hunt), 265
    Keith Dale, 265, 397, 455
    Keith Erling, 397

Index 449

Kim Donald, 265, 397
Lance Kim, 397
Lenice Margaret (Torgerson), 265
Lisa Angeline, 265
Mandy Marie, 397
Shane George, 397
Shirley Ann (Birr), 397
Steven Neal, 265
Tyrone Erling, 265, 397
Wendy Marie (Bastien), 397, 445
Arntz, Charles Ray, 230
   James F., 230
   Karen Joy, 230, 354
   Leo, 230
   Olga Gamena (Lee), 230
   Susan J., 230
   Virginia Cleone (Peckham), 230
Ash, Eva, 153
   Peggy (Bullock), 280
   William, 280
Ashley, Arthur, 219
   Emma (Oatman), 219
   Velma Ruth, 219
Atkins, Ruby Louise, 289
Audiss, Anna (Hanson), 235
   Eldon, 235
   Faith (—), 361
   Jeffrey Clark, 235, 361
   Joshua Eldon, 361
   Nancy Marie, 235, 361
   Norma Elaine (Clark), 235
   Sally Jane, 235, 361
   Todd, 361
   Wendy (Houston), 361
   William, 235
Aune, Kathryn Leigh (Peckham), 216
   Marc Steven, 216
Ausborune, Tom, 75, 76
Austin, —, 161
   Abigail, 26
   Ada Carol (Agee), 249
   Al, 39, 40, 41
   Alfred, 108
   Alice (Guthrie), 162
   Alice Melinda, 38
   Allen M., 38
   Alta (Bright) (Gardner), 107
   Amanda Melissa, 27, 36
   Andrew Harper, 249
   Andrew J., 43

   Andrew Jackson, 27, 35, 38
   Angeline, 27, 35, 42
   Ann Janette, 38, 104
   Anna (Bunn), 441, 442
   Annie, 442
   Bertha, 441
   Bertha (Pieper), 441
   Cornelia (Cooper) (Smith), 26, 441
   Dorothy, 443
   Ebenezer, 26
   Edna, 99
   Edna (Brown), 38
   Edson L., 38
   Elihu, 26
   Elisea J. (VanSchoch), 442
   Eliza (Austin), 26
   Elizabeth, 27, 42
   Ella May, 441
   Emma, 36, 99
   Emmett, 26, 443
   Emmett D., 441, 442
   Ernest, 99
   Florence Anne (Robinson), 107
   Frances Jane (Leach), 37
   Gertrude P., 44
   Gertrude Pauline, 108
   Grace, 107, 159
   Halley Agee, 249
   Hannah Marie (Currie), 44
   Harry Ames, 112, 162
   Horace E, 441
   Irvin Hugh, 107
   J., 121
   Jack, 22, 29
   Joyce, 163, 249
   Kate (Kepley), 37
   Laura Gertrude (Mason), 107
   Llewelyn Edward, 44, 107
   Lorilla (Mershom), 37
   Lou Emma (Church), 35
   Louise, 441
   Lowell, 443
   Lucinda (Hooper) (Peterson), 26
   Lyman, 26, 27, 35
   Lyman L., 26, 29, 441
   Mabel D., 44
   Marjorie Ruth, 112, 163
   Mary (Bickford), 26
   Matilda, 27, 35, 42
   Maud, 161

Melinda, 27
Melvin M., 38
Meta (Manteufel), 442
Minerva, 27, 36
Minnie, 44
Myron, 37
Myrtle, 99, 441, 442
Nelson, 27, 442
Nelson C., 26, 441, 442
Nettie, 38
Nina Noel, 249
Orville, 443
Pauline, 7
Pauline (Reed), 26, 29, 441
R. M. (Austin), 441
Ray, 442, 443
Ray William, 442
Richard Ames, 249
Robert Ames, 163, 249
Roccina (—), 442
Roccina M., 441
Rocinna M., 441
Roy, 443
Roy Elfred, 442
Sarah (Petty), 111
Susan, 442
Susan M. (—), 441
Sylvia, 443
Theron, 37
Theron S., 27
William, 44, 443
William Harrison, 27, 43
Willie, 44
Willis, 108
Willis Wilbur, 44, 111
Zella, 441, 442, 443
Avery, Charles Harold, 370
  Constance Fay (Phelps), 370
  Jodee Faye, 370
  Kevin Mark, 370
  Leland Charles, 370
  Luelle, 439
  Maud, 160
  Renae Ruth, 370
Azevedo, Carole Jane (Acker), 229
  Joaquin, 229

B

Baal, Betty Jean (Hathorn), 332
  Genevieve (Wheat), 332
  John, 332
  Lowell, 332
  Marriann H., 332
Babicky, Deven, 26
  Jacqueline, 268
  Kenneth, 268
  Rosalie (Reed), 268
  Walter, 268
Babikian, Haig M., 192
  Helen H., 192
  Nevart (Shahinian), 192
Bacon, Danelle Dorothy, 377
  Nancy Kay (Ingersoll) (Stennett), 377
  Rodney Delose, 377, 445
Badtke, Albert, 214
  Arnold Garhard Valentine, 214
  Brian Arnold, 330
  Caroline Dorothy, 214, 330
  Cory, 330
  Debra May, 330
  Dorothy (Quick), 330
  Dorothy Mary Ellen (Quick), 214
  Dorreen (Rupnow), 330
  James Arnold Albert, 214, 330
  Jeffrey Tom, 330
  Jon Dennis, 214, 331
  Kimberly May, 330
  Marie (Bolter), 214
  Matthew Robert, 330
  Peter William, 330
  Sandra (Lipton), 330
  Sherry Lynn, 331
  Shirley Ann (Faust), 331
  Tom Norbert, 214, 330
  Tracy Lynn, 331
  Wayne James, 330
  William, 331
Baele, Sue, 403
Bahari, Elizabeth, 183
Bahn, Louise, 114
Bahrke, Edna, 389
Baierl, Eugene Arthur, 405
  Lori, 405
  Rosalie Luella (Gamble), 405
Bailey, Albert Joe Trice, 320
  April Sue, 320

Carol, 313
Janet May (Lee), 320
Norman Jo Trice, 320
Norman Joshua, 320
Phoebe, 298
Sue Ranal (Hart), 320
Baker, Adelbert, 157
   Amanda E. (Oftedall), 243
   Beatrice, 243, 363
   Beatrice I., 157
   Benjamin F., 27
   Chester L., 157
   Chester Lamont, 242
   Claudia L., 157, 244
   David Michael, 315
   Emma (Gay), 157
   Esther (Meeks), 242
   Etta Matilda (Abel), 157, 237
   Eugene Arthur, 243, 374
   Faye Etta, 243, 374
   Florence Elizabeth Minnie, 192
   Gladys Irene, 243, 375
   Jane (Teetz), 374
   Jennie (McBain), 192
   Jessie Irene, 381
   Kimberly Anne, 374
   Lamont Adelbert, 157, 237
   Lorraine, 237, 243
   Lorraine A., 157
   Mary Margaret, 315
   Mary Sheridan (Simpkovitz), 374
   Matthew Allen, 374
   Melinda (Austin), 27
   Nicole Renee, 374
   Rachel Minerva (Dougherty), 27
   Roger Lamont, 243
   Rose Alveretta, 243, 375
   Ruth Lucille, 243, 375
   Sandra Lee (Larson), 243
   Thomas Edward, 243, 374
   Thomas Sheridan, 374
   Walter, 192
Bakken, Ann (Ellinson), 151
   Marie Caroline, 151
   Ole, 151
Baldenegro, Carlos Rael, 319
   Felipe, 319
   Nancy Kay (Hart) (Blanco), 319
   Sarah (Rael), 319
Ball, Iris, 294

Ballinger, Nancy, 254
Bamberg, Evelyn, 297
Banks, —, 45
Barber, Nettie, 241
Barden, David William, 225
   Joan Marie, 225
   Judith Ann, 225
   Reginald, 225
   Richard Ralph, 225
   Ronald, 225
   Sandra Lee, 225
   Wanda Elaine (McElroy), 225
Barker, Sarah, 11
   Versa, 258
Barnes, Betty (—), 355
   Margaret Amanda, 108
   Robert, 355
   Roxanne, 355
Barnett, Jacqueline (Babicky), 268
   Kevin, 268
Barnum, —, 12
Barone, Betty (Robinson), 439
   Bonnie Jane, 438, 439
   Clarence, 437
   Clarence Vernon, 438, 439
   Emma (—), 437
   Franklin, 437
   Helen (Wadley) (Blake), 437
   Helen Margaret, 438, 439
   Julia (Holley), 439
   Richard, 439
   Stephanie Marie, 439, 440
Barthelow, Mary, 209
Bartholomew, Isabelle, 209
Bartlett, Edward, 206
   Susan Cornelia (Romano), 206
Barton, Charles, 80, 92
Bartz, Carolyn (Prausa), 262
   Henry, 262
   Verna, 262
Bashina, Bertha (Schiding), 170
   Frank, 170
   Leona, 170
Bass, Avery Ferdnand, 253
   Geneil (Cates), 253
   Pauline Yvette, 253, 383
Bastien, George, 397
   Wendy Marie, 397
Bates, Anna S. (Grinley), 226
   Arlo Wayne, 151, 226

Darville Delos, 151
Edward H., 151
Frances Mabel, 134
Goldie, 151
Greta, 151
Judy, 226, 349
Kathy, 226, 349
Maude Susan (Peckham), 151
Nancy, 226, 348
Nancy Ann (Hull), 151
Scott, 226
Scott Merrell, 151
Sonja, 226, 349
Susan, 226, 349
Bauder, Elenore, 399
Bauer, Allen, 433
   Andrea (Heath), 422
   Brooke Marguerite, 422
   Christine Marie, 433
   Christopher Thomas, 422
   Clara (Phillips), 331
   Deanne Marie (Meeker), 363
   Deborah Kay (Spaun), 433
   Don, 363
   Elwood, 433
   James Elwood, 433
   James Kenneth, 331, 422
   LaVonne (Windedall), 433
   Martin Richard, 331
   Roland, 331
   Shari Bea, 331, 422
   Thomas Arthur, 331
   Virginia Lola (Shipton), 331
   Wayne Allen, 433
Baumgartner, Mary, 223
Baurer, Fred George, 187
   Gladys Pauline, 187
   Martha Josephine (Dick), 187
Bazeley, Amy, 228
Beach, Lillian, 195
Beaman, Edna, 256
Beardsley, Beverly, 355
Beavert, Bertha Beatrice, 124, 185
   Betty Jane (O'Connor), 294
   Betty May, 187, 294
   Beverly Anne, 186, 294
   Cyrus, 184
   Cyrus John, 124
   Edna Belle, 124
   Elizabeth (McDonald), 187

   Ethel, 124, 184
   Frank, 124, 184, 186, 187, 294
   Gail, 294, 413
   Gary, 294, 413
   John, 294
   Kelley, 413
   Kimberley, 413
   Kyle Patrick, 413
   Madeline (Crotty), 413
   Maud Edna (Reed), 123
   May, 124, 184, 185
   Pearl, 294
   Ruby (Clark), 186
   Sarah, 124
   Warren, 184
   Warren William, 124, 186, 294
   Will, 124
   William, 185
   William Nathan, 123
   Worth Laverne, 124
Beck, Gary Gordon, 314
   Linda Kay (Crouch), 314
   Marla Jene, 314
   Matthew Gordon, 314
   Vivian, 218
Becker, Alfred Fredric John, 173
   Audrey Ethel, 173
   Audrey Lenore, 420
   Margaret Emma (Keipper), 173
Beckert, Doris June (Pruitt), 356
   Raymond Orville, 356
   Ruth Ann, 356
Beckwith, Gloria Jean (Miller), 383
   Richard, 383
Bednarek, Georgene, 328
Beede, Sharon, 379
Beekman, Beatrice, 167
   Elizabeth (DeLowe), 167
   Elmer Dewey, 167
   Geneva Viola, 167, 258
   Gertrude Mary Etta (Wright), 167
   Henry, 167
   Jacob, 167
   Royal Buhel, 167
Bell, Cynthia Diane, 233
   Earl Horace, 233
   Jane (Burkett), 233
   John Wesley, 233
   Maxine (Robertson), 233
   Robert Earl, 233

Wynnie (Swage), 233
Belle, Susan, 80
Bellenbaum, Dolores Anna, 232
    Elizabeth Mary (Pilon), 232
    William Frederick, 232
Bender, Mavis, 371
Benhke, Emma, 287
Bennett, Bertha Irene, 157
    Daniel, 157
    Lottie Irene (Dudley), 157
Benson, Emma Florence, 116
    Jenny (Johnson), 116
    John, 116
Berendsen, Howard, 224
    Jerome, 224
    Maysel Elizabeth (Gorsuch), 224
    Robin Maysel, 224
    Vicki Lou, 224
Berland, Kim Renee (Hopper), 344
    Mark, 344
Bertrand, Barbara (Hagreen), 389
    Chandra Pearl, 389
    Gillion Neal, 389
    Kirsten Lynn, 389
    Michelle Anne, 389
    Neal, 389
    Sharon Lynn (Reed), 389
    Thorne, 389
Bertsch, Gordon, 350
    Janet Kay (Holland), 350
Bettridge, Barbara Lydia (Carling), 384
    Jerry Dee, 384
    Tauna, 384
    Troy Dee, 384
Beving, Alisa, 355
    Joe, 355
    Linda (Peckham), 355
Beyer, Darla (Reed), 278
    Edmund, 278
    John, 278
    Leona (Frey), 278
    Pamela, 278
    Sharon, 278, 403
    Steven, 278
Beyers, Ethel (Beavert) (Colby), 184
    Henry, 184
    Henry Carl, 184
    Patsy, 185
    Pauline, 184
Bickford, Mary, 26

Bida, Neva Faye (Gergen) (Tognoni), 254
    Sam, 253
Biddle, Brandon, 363
    Candy, 363
    Marvel (—), 363
Biddlecome, —, 50
    Harvey, 52
    Harvey N., 54
Biggs, Bo James, 306
    Cynthia Kay (Kennedy), 306
    Patricia (Loring), 306
    William Cody, 306
    William King, 306
Big Horn, Lavonne, 379
Billings, Bryon Wayne, 333
    Caroly Denise, 333
    Janet May (Peckham), 333
    Verne, 333
Bilsby, Wilma, 412
Binion, Helga, 289
    Heidi Marie, 289
    Travis, 289
Birget, Myrtle, 349
Birr, Alvin, 397
    Audrey Carol, 397
    Bernice (Schliep), 273
    Betty (Casper), 397
    Brian Larry, 273
    Colleen Kay (Reed), 273
    Florence (April), 397
    Landon Dale, 273
    Monica Ann, 273
    Nathan, 273
    Otis, 397
    Owen Rinehart, 273
    Shirley Ann, 397
Bissick, Millie, 267
Bitterman, Adolph, 302
    Anna, 302
    Donald, 302
    Linda Jane (Canfield), 302
    Sandi Lynn, 302
Bixby, Aaron, 410
    Cecilia (Iglinski), 410
    Delos Michael, 410
    Katherine Sue (Kutzner), 410
    Lewis, 410
Black, Linda G. (Gustrowsky), 425
    Melinda Mae, 425
    Russell, 425

Scott Russell, 425
Blackstone, Gertrude (Rutgowski), 407
    Roxanne Louise, 407
    Silwin, 407
Blair, Joseph, 117
    Josephine (Burley), 117
    Myrna (Schlais), 117
Blake, Helen (Wadley), 437
    John A., 437
    Lula, 288
Blanco, Anita (Guiterrez), 319
    Brandon Cruz, 320
    Cruz Alfred, 319
    Cruz R., 319
    Kristine Marie, 319
    Nancy Kay (Hart), 319
    Stephanie Ann, 319
Blaschaka, Donald, 244
    Karen (Pepin), 244
Bliner, Marilyn, 433
Block, Kay Rose, 317
Blomberg, April Ann, 429
    Debbie Ann (Meeker), 428
    Jennifer Irene, 429
    Tory, 428
Blood, Betty Kay (Stafford), 324
    Douglas Calvin, 324
    Felicia Ann, 324
    Michelle Nadine, 324
Blow, Clyde, 351
    Marlene Carole, 351
    Mattie (Kramer), 351
Boch, Harriet Christina, 396
Bockelman, Eleanor (—), 322
    Marla Joy, 322
    William, 322
Boderstein, Edwin, 181
Boegler, Joan, 309
Boehm, Alice, 260
Boelk, Amelia (Hackbarth), 224
    Henry, 224
Bohmfalk, Laura Ann, 382
    Rita Ann (Contreras), 382
Bohnfalk, Thomas LeRoy, 382
Bolghrin, Caroline May (Haynes), 345
    Jessica May, 345
    Josephine Elizabeth, 345
    Michael, 345
Bolter, Marie, 214
Bond, Alice May, 106, 158

    Anna Laura, 106, 158
    Fred A., 102
    George, 106
    Jennifer, 373
    Judy, 283
    Kim (Abel), 373
    Lorilla Ann (Phillips), 106
    Michael, 373
    Myrtle Ann (Peckham), 102
    Russell, 373
Boogart, Gloria Ann (Verwey), 266
Boone, Daniel, 76
    Justin Richard, 431
    Richard Harold, 431
    Tamra Gaye (Kretschmer), 430
Boot, Mary Louise, 250
Borgan, Jamie, 370
    Jessica, 370
    Jim, 370
    Ruth Lilyan (French), 370
Boring, Betty Mae (Quick) (Paioni), 326
    Charles, 326
    Ruth (Wilton), 326
    Wallace E., 326
Botton, Mary Edith, 244
Boudway, Becky, 256
    Becky Lou (Tognoni), 387
    Edward White, 387
    Ira Martin, 387
    Mary Jane (Kennedy), 387
    Matthew Flannery, 387
    Wallace Jeremy, 387
Boulanger, Rosalie, 267
Bouressa, Maxine, 276
Bower, Daniel Thomas, 408
    Darlene Margaret (Minor), 408
    Karrie Jean, 408
    Kenneth, 408
    Leslie, 408
    Ruth (Monty), 408
    Tina Marie, 408
Bowery, Bertha, 301
Bowles, Bruce Renile, 394
    Karen Kathryn (Johnson), 394
    Reid Hunter, 394
    Renile Edgar, 394
    Shirley (Conkling), 394
Boyum, Ann, 242
Bracken, Tom, 161
Brackett, Brenda Lee (Theien), 245

Index 455

Greg, 245
Bradley, Effie, 436, 437
   Lucy Martha, 164
Brammer, Bessie (Jones), 201
   Brenda, 313
   Carol, 313
   Carol (Bailey), 313
   Clayton, 201
   Evelyn (Crouch), 201
   Janice Adell, 201, 313
   Karen, 313
   Peggy (Moyer), 313
   Robert, 201, 313
   Ronald Allen, 201, 313
   Ronald, 313
   Terry Lee, 313
Brandenhoff, Anton, 258
   Carol Lynn, 259, 390
   Christene (Nissen), 258
   Donna Jean, 259, 391
   Hazel Jennie (Wennell), 258
   Robert Anton, 258
Brattain, Loretta Alice (Goutermont), 372
   Raymond Eugene, 372
   Renee Elaine, 372
   Robert E., 372
Brauer, Clarence E., 275
   Leona (Wilke), 275
   Sharon Lou, 275
Brauhn, Don, 428
   LaDonna Bea (Meeker), 428
   Meghen Marie, 428
   Molly Irene, 428
Bray, —, 100
Brazeau, Melvine, 261
Breit, Adele (Vendetti), 325
   Darlene Faye (Mason), 325
   Donald Vincent, 325, 420
   Gene Franklin, 325
   Ivan Gene, 421
   Joy Linda, 325, 421
   Melody Ann, 325, 420
   Teresa Hebb (Smith), 420
   Vincent, 325
Bremner, Myrtle, 343
Breneman, Beth, 224, 347
   Blakely Douglas, 347
   Douglas, 224, 347
   Floy Beatrice (Gorsuch), 224
   Gregory Douglas, 347

   Mary Jane (Whirry), 224
   Matthew James, 347
   Richard, 224, 347
   Rosaline Gail (Sundsmo), 347
   Roy, 224
   Sandra Jean (Mohr), 347
   Sharon, 224
   Timothy Douglas, 347
   Valori Rose, 347
   Walter, 224
   Wendy Lynn, 347
Brewer, Violette Marie, 282
Brewster, Constance Diane (Daniels), 317
   Ella Louise (Koch), 317
   James Wyatt, 317, 420
   Jennifer, 420
   Karen (Cox), 420
   Pamela Jean, 317
   William David, 317
   William Looender, 317
Bricco, Mary Elizabeth, 271
Bridger, Jim, 89
Briggs, Abby E. (Cook), 98
   Agnes Abbie, 98
   Cardell, 410
   Cleveland, 410
   Dorothy, 410
   John G., 98
   Joshua James Cleveland, 410
   Judith Lorraine (Pryor), 410
   Sharon Amanda, 242
Bright, Alta (Gardner), 107
   Emery Ulysses, 160
   Harry, 160
   Maud, 107
   Maud (Avery), 160
   Vena (Kuhnast), 160
Brink, Jennie, 219
Brock, Arvena (Hanson), 303
   Eugene Leslie, 303
   John Frederick, 421
   Joy Linda (Breit), 421
   Karen Jean (Kennedy), 303
   Leslie Eugene, 303
   Michico (Araki), 421
   Peter Andrew, 303
   Rachel Elizabeth, 303
   Sara Jean, 303
   Wendy Marie, 421
Brockway, Elizabeth Nette, 416

Brooks, Ace Carl, 174
    Verna (Bullock) (Adel) (Snyder), 174
Brouillette, Lillie, 107
Brow, Aloyosis, 310
    Elsie (Drolet), 310
    Lorraine Frances, 310
Brown, —, 64
    Ann (Whitcomb), 38
    Blanche, 238
    David Gary, 197
    Dwayne, 197
    Edna, 38
    Ellen Elizabeth (Quick), 212
    Florence T. (Moen) (Kennedy), 197
    Janice (VanAsdale), 303
    Lucian, 38
    Marilyn Naomi, 303
    Neva, 113
    Neva June (Tognoni), 254
    Paul, 212
    Paul Shryer, 212, 445
    Richard, 303
    Steven Dwayne, 197
    Victor Raymond, 254
    Wanda Faith, 197
Bruce, Lillian, 342
Brugger, Dorothy (Demuling), 335
    Edward, 335
    Ralph Marvin, 335
    Wilma Maxine (Jelmeland) (Holdren) (Erickson) (McDonnell), 335
Bruno, Anthony, 164
    Lucy Martha (Bradley), 164
    Lydia, 164
Bruns, Sarah, 412
Brunswick, Crystal Marie, 420
    Melody Ann (Breit), 420
    Robert, 420
Buchanan, Constance, 398
    Doris A., 357
    Lizzie, 225
Bucklew, Elizabeth, 273
Buhrandt, Doris, 270, 399
Bullock, Betty (Carpenter), 176
    Bonnie, 175, 280
    Carrie F. (Cottrell), 118
    Chester Jesse, 120, 176
    Christopher Lance, 281
    Della Elsie, 120
    Della Elsie Berdine, 174
    Earlyne (Moore), 281
    Effie, 119, 120
    Effie Maud (Reed), 118
    Eldred, 118, 119, 120
    Eldred Jacob, 118
    Elmer Oscar, 118, 120, 175
    Gail, 176
    Gary, 176, 281
    Jacqueline (Cole), 281
    Mae (Martin), 175
    Marietta Eleanore, 120, 175
    Peggy, 175, 280
    Richard, 175
    Robin Slade, 281
    Ronald, 176, 281
    Steven, 176
    Tammie, 281
    Verna, 120, 174
Bunk, Francis, 343
    Gertrude (Huschka), 343
    Mildred, 343
Bunn, Anna, 441, 442
    Emma (—), 441, 442
    James, 441, 442
Burch, Emma, 97
Burdeau, Irma Jean, 171
Burger, —, 85
    Barbara Ann, 279
    Jean Mildred (Erickson), 279
    Jerry (Prahl), 404
    John, 279
    Marie L., 279
    Nicholas, 404
    Patrick, 279
    Sandra Jean, 279
    Theodore, 279, 404
Burk, Hattie A., 208
Burke, Christie, 378
    Dena (Haugen), 378
    Jennifer, 378
    Timothy James, 378
Burkel, David, 355
    Lisa (Kruse), 355
Burkett, Jane, 233
Burley, Josephine, 117
Burton, Francis, 243
    Starr (Fate), 243
Busch, Florence M, 118
    Frank Raeber, 118
    Minnie, 118

Buschenfield, Dorothy Elizabeth, 312
Bush, Gladys Vivian, 142
    Robert, 142
Butler, Rhoda (Ames), 42
Butterfield, Connie, 318
    Elaine (—), 318
    John, 318
Bybee, Dagny Soubrette, 386
    Frances (Rosenstengle), 386
    Leslie Eugene, 386
    Loren Kenneth, 386
    Maureen Patricia (Richey), 386
    Natalie Marie, 386
    Raquel, 386
    Tonia, 386
Byers, Jean, 135
    John, 135
    Lorena A. (Garloch), 135
    Paul, 135
Byrnes, Dannial Lloyd, 314
    Nona Lou (Garrison), 314
    Terri Lynn, 314
    William Bryan, 314

C

Cabot, Susanna, 10
Caddis, Betty Carolyn (Geer), 317
    Cecil Edgar, 317
Cagle, Lydia Ann, 429
Caldwell, Areta Virginia, 228
Calkins, Irene Minnie, 276
    Maggie, 121, 122
Callahan, Anna, 376
Campbell, Bonnie (Bullock) (Pietsch), 280
    Carolyn, 259
    Carolyn Sue, 305
    H. E., 87
    Lee Harrison, 259
    Maxine (Collier), 259
    William, 280
Campolo, Jennie, 296
Canfield, Adam Earl, 302
    Agnes Martha (Hurlbut), 191
    Alan Kent, 300
    Alta, 94
    Alta May, 94, 132
    Andrew Oliver, 302
    Anna (Heiser), 414
    Anna Marie (Salvaggio), 190
    Anna May (Schwartz), 298
    Arthur, 94
    Bette Eileen, 191, 301
    Caren Alice, 191
    Carol Ann, 191, 301
    Carrie Light, 191
    Cathy (Carver), 414
    Christopher Dwight, 192
    Christopher Jude, 299
    Clinton Arthur, 94
    David Joseph, 299, 415
    David Liston, 192
    Debra Beth (McKay), 192
    Donald Fenton, 191, 300
    Doreatha Ruth, 131, 188
    Dorothy Ellen (Mead), 191
    Douglas Jonathan, 192, 445
    Douglas Liston, 132, 192
    Elmira M., 99
    Elton Fay, 131, 189
    Esther (Turchiarulo), 190
    Fenton Emil, 132, 190
    Floyd Beecher, 94, 132
    Gertrude Estelle (Crump), 131
    Gladys (Kent), 190
    Grace Naomi (Rowell), 131
    Harold Milburn, 132, 191
    Heather Jo, 301
    Helen H. (Babikian), 192
    Herbert Clinton, 132, 190
    Herbert Edward, 190, 300
    Hulda Oella (March), 132
    Ida, 32, 82, 94
    Ida Adella (Reed), 93
    Ida Reed, 7, 28
    Jean Kitty, 191, 301
    Jean Martha, 191
    Jim Scott, 191, 302
    Jody May, 414
    John Harold, 191, 301
    John Paul, 192
    Joseph Francis, 299
    Joyce Marilyn, 131
    Linda Eileen (Esker), 300
    Linda Jane, 192, 302
    Linda Jean (Collins), 301
    Loretta Marie (Wynn), 189
    Lucius Leroy, 94, 131, 132
    Lynette Joan (Mathers), 190

Mabel Sarah (Light), 191
Margaret Isabell (Shubert), 190
Mark Francis, 299, 414
Mary Ann (House), 93
Mary Jane (Cole), 300
Michelle, 414
Natasha Eve, 415
Oscar Willard, 132, 191
Patrick Sean, 299
Piper Lynn, 301
Richard Lucius, 190
Robert Gene, 189, 298
Robert Thomas, 299, 414
Ruth (Portner), 190
Sandra Joyce, 192
Scott, 93, 94
Scott Thomas, 299
Sharon Kay (Stanley), 302
Susan Alta, 300
Syotha Jean (Driggs), 301
Thelma Ann, 132, 189
Thelma Grace, 190, 300
Toni Lynn (Watherm), 301
William, 93
William James, 192
Willis Burton, 94, 131
Caniglia, Glenda (Ewing), 338
  Thomas, 338
Cardoza, Anthony Paul, 357
  Antonio, 357
  David Laurence, 357
  David Ryan, 357
  Deana Lynette, 357
  Debra Lynn (Roseth), 357
  Dustin Anthony, 357
  Florence (Fagundes), 357
  Kathleen Dawn (Roseth), 357
  Marissa Kathleen, 357
  Natal Dawn, 357
  Nicole Michelle, 357
  Noel Muriel, 357
Carey, Bruce Richard, 259
  Carolyn (Campbell), 259
  Eva, 254
  Gayle Nancy, 259
  Irene Orpha (Wright), 168
  James, 168
  June Adeline, 168, 259
  Luanne Marie, 405
  Robbin Lee James, 259

  Tony James, 168, 259
  Tony Steven Ray, 259
Carling, Anna Louise, 253
  Arthur Eugene, 253
  Arthur William, 253
  Barbara Lydia, 253, 384
  Florence Evelyn (Farnsworth), 253
  Geneil (Cates) (Bass), 253
  Karen Geneil, 253, 384
  Kathleen Jeanette, 253
  Mary Ellen, 253, 384
  Norval, 253
Carlson, Fern, 203
  George, 249
  Gladys (Rogers) (Roots), 249
  Juanita Mae (Daniels) (Evans), 203
Carmody, Aloisius, 297
  Charles Aloisius, 297
  Clarke Christopher, 298
  Drew Charles, 298
  Jennifer (—), 298
  Prudence Penelope (Clarke), 297
Carpenter, Betty, 176
  Huldah, 34
  James, 424
  Lacy, 424
  Paul, 176
  Virgie (Robinson), 176
  Wanda P. (Gustrowsky), 424
Carrie, Alvin E., 116
  David, 116
  Elmer H., 117
  Ida May (Reed), 116
  Oliver, 117
  Orpha, 116
Carroll, George Francis, 168
  Judith Ann, 168
  Lillian May (Handlin), 168
Carson, Barbara (Jenkins), 358
  Blake Ryan, 358
  Caren Elizabeth (Casey), 358
  Jannela Elizabeth, 358
  Kenneth, 358
  Lawrence Trent, 358
Carter, Adam Craig, 432
  Bonnie Ann (Clark), 432
  Marit, 390
  Sarah, 11
Cartwright, Aaron, 156
  Arron, 138

Elsie Belle, 138
Mabel, 156
Rosabell (Kramer), 156
Rosilian (Kramer), 138
Carver, Cathy, 414
Case, Naomi Esther, 271
Casey, Alice (Whiteside), 232
Caren Elizabeth, 232, 358
Charles A., 232
Charles Allen, 232
Cynthia Jean (Sherman), 358
Elizabeth Jane (Roseth), 232
Gregory Lynn, 232, 358
Kathrine Jean (Heard), 358
Shane Lynn, 358
Casper, Betty, 397
Caspers, Katherine, 334
Cassutt, Cecilia, 98
Castle, Cindy, 408
Eliza Jane, 97
John, 8, 47
Sarah (Shoemaker), 97
Sydney, 97
Caswell, Eli, 78
Sophina, 78
Catapano, Lucille, 402
Cates, Arlina (Aroline) Bell, 165
Arlina or Aroline Bell, 251
Deloris Jane, 165, 252
Donald Alan, 253
Emma, 113
Emma Augusta (Donnelly), 112
Emma Esther, 164, 251
Emma Reed, 165
Ethan, 113
Geneil, 165, 253
Gordon Anthony, 253
Gordon Bruno, 165, 253
Ina Belle, 113, 165
Jerry Ray, 253
Jessie Anna, 113, 165
Julia Mae, 113, 164
June, 165, 252
Leslie, 253
Lucy Margaret, 164, 250
Lydia (Bruno), 164
Martha Jane (Thrasher), 253
Nelson, 112, 254
Sylvia Joy, 165, 252
Willetta, 165, 252

William H., 112
William Henry, 113, 164
Caukins, —, 99
Chaires, Floyde Irving, 416
Kathleen Louella, 416
Rita Irene (Kilbourn), 416
Chandler, Sarah Higgins, 80
Chaney, Cherelyn Lea (Hart), 319
James Estel, 319
Chapin, Joseph, 274
Laurel, 274
Leo Glen, 271
Mary Gertrude (Jackling), 274
Naomi Esther (Case), 271
Ruth Ann, 271
Chapman, Frances Mabel (Bates), 134
Glenn Maurice, 134
Laurel (Kennedy), 8
Laurel Nadeen (Kennedy), 134
Chardukian, Mary, 403
Charko, —, 312
Michel (Rogers), 312
Charles, Viola, 401
Charron, —, 426
Heather Marie, 426
Joey Donald, 426
Vicki Lee (Peckham), 426
Chase, Bryan Matthew, 416
Daniel Edward, 300, 415
Danielle Rita, 416
Daphne Marie (Hammond), 415
Dawn Paulette, 300, 416
Donald Paul, 300
Elizabeth Thelma, 300
Kathleen Louella (Chaires), 416
Leona Norene, 300, 415
Loretta Sue, 416
Lula-Mae (Trudell), 300
Marilyn (Johnson), 300
Mathew Ronald, 300, 415
Rachel Lynne, 415
Richard Donald, 300, 415
Tammy Marie (Turk), 415
Thelma Grace (Canfield), 300
Chatham, Annette (Roseth), 358
George Kenneth, 358
Matthew Jeremiah, 358
Peter Joshua, 358
Chavey, Darrah, 425
Margaret R. (Weisensel), 425

Peggy (Weisensel), 425
Peter Russell, 425
Rhiannon Christine, 425
Cheeseman, Adelaide Marion (Sargent), 95
  Alburtus, 34
  Alice Juliet, 34
  Benjamin, 25
  Calvin Allen, 26
  Carol Edna, 199, 309
  Carrie, 95, 96
  Carrie I., 33
  Carrie M. (Webster), 135
  Corine J. (Veglianti), 309
  Deborah Elizabeth (Sherman), 34
  Dorothy, 199, 309
  Duran, 17, 19, 25, 26
  Elda E., 33
  Eleanor Merle (Hamilton), 199
  Elizabeth E. (Sherman), 34
  Ella Fear, 7, 26
  Ella Fear (Reed), 25
  Emy D. (Ricky), 33
  Eva M., 33
  Fear, 30
  Genevieve (Stephans), 135
  George, 25
  Hubert, 96
  Hubert Edmond, 135, 199
  Ina E., 95, 135
  Isaac Dwight, 25
  James D., 34
  Jane (Duran), 25
  Jennie, 95
  Jennie C., 33
  Joan (Boegler), 309
  John Royal, 199, 309
  John Smith, 25, 33
  Lenna Sherman, 35, 97
  Lizzie, 34
  Lorina Emeline (Jackson), 33
  Lucien Duran, 26, 34
  Marion Edna (Reynolds), 199
  Mary Adella, 33
  Mary Etta, 25
  Nancy (Ross), 309
  Nellie Louise, 34
  Pauline L., 33
  Roland George, 135, 199
  Royal D., 33
  Royal Duran, 95
  Sarah Ann, 26
  Valerie, 309
  Valnette Miriam (Durkee), 34
  William, 26
  William Alfred, 95, 135
  William B., 25, 33
  Willis Hiram, 25, 34
Cheevers, Clarence, 363
  Janet (—), 363
  Mark, 363
  Sabrina Louise (Meeker), 363
Chico, Cynthia, 427
Chitwood, Donald E., 295
  Lori M., 295
  Marvys Jane (Weston), 295
  Rick E., 295
Chowen, Annie (Long), 150
  Edna Pearl (Peckham), 150
  James Arthur, 150
  Luvia Imogene, 150, 225
  Mickey, 150
  William, 150
  William Wesley, 150
Christensen, Arthur, 411
  Frances (Spradling), 411
  Jeffrey, 411
  Robert, 411
  Scarlet Louisa, 411
  Sherry Rae (Jorgensen), 411
Christeson, Bessie May (Kroeplin), 364
  Cory, 364
  Juff, 364
Christian, Barbara, 175
  Carolee, 175
  Robert, 175
Christiansen, Lena, 170
Christianson, Bud, 329
  Dorothy, 329
  Duane, 329
  Kay Lynn, 330
  Lee Duane, 329
  Pamela, 330
  Sharon Mae (Heckes), 329
Christopherson, Johanna (Jensen), 178
  John, 177
  Nels, 178
  Pearl Eunice (Reed), 177
Church, Joshua, 35
  Lou Emma, 35

Sophronia (Shurtleff), 35
Cibourski, Caroline, 403
Clark, Agnes (Rodger), 154
   Alice (Patchett), 100
   Amanda Elizabeth (Martin), 100
   Amanda Maude, 100, 143
   Anna Marie (Knapp), 186
   Beverly May, 235
   Bonnie Ann, 432
   Carol Ann, 234
   Charles, 154
   George Jay, 100, 143
   George William, 100
   Glenn Walter, 432
   Harold Roberts, 1545
   Jean Helene (Hatch), 432
   Lela Eldora (Peckham), 154
   Leona (Ziellow), 100
   Mary A., 124
   Nicole Helene, 432
   Norma Elaine, 235
   Patti Renee, 401
   Ruby, 186
   Ruth Mae, 143
   Ruth May, 100
   Silas, 20
   Starr, 20
   Steven, 100
   Susan (Popal), 100
   Theodore, 186
Clarke, Ava (—), 298
   Brent, 298
   Bruce Bailey, 189, 297
   Christopher Bruce, 297
   Diane Elyse, 189, 296
   Doreatha Ruth (Canfield), 188
   Elizabeth Jane, 296, 414
   Evan Taylor, 414
   Gary Scott, 189, 298
   Jeremy, 298
   Jill (Misher), 297
   Kamela Kar, 298
   Keith, 298
   Kevin William, 297
   Leonard Robert, 188, 296, 298
   Leonard Robert, 189
   Louise (St. Pierre), 298
   Louise (Taft), 188
   Mara Michelle, 298
   Marcia Louise (Young), 297
   Natalie (Squadrito), 296
   Patricia Ann, 296, 414
   Pheobe (Bailey), 298
   Phyllis (Kawanabe), 296
   Prudence Penelope, 189, 297
   Richard David, 296
   Richard Winston, 189
   Roger Walter, 189, 298
   Ryan Shea, 298
   Silas, 19
   Stacia, 298
   Starr, 19
   Sylvia (Morris), 298
   Wendy Lou, 189
Clausen, Eugene Roger, 210
   Roberta Lois (Franklin), 210
Clauss, Fred, 290
   Judith Lee (Simmons), 290
   Larry Eugene, 290
   Mildred (Huguelet), 290
   Tonya Michelle, 290
Cleeman, —, 54
Clemenson, Ruth L., 192
Clemmons, Bradley, 247
   Jane (Goodrich), 247
   Thomas Powell, 247
Clowen, Laura, 155
Cluppert, Bonita (Klawitter), 330
   Irvin, 330
   Shirley, 330
Cobb, Clara, 96
Cody, Buffalo Bill, 19, 80, 89
   William "Buffalo Bill", 19
Cofern, Hannah (Lowell), 12
   William, 12
Coker, Mary, 207
Colby, Ethel (Beavert), 184
   Ray, 184
Cole, Amanda Dawn, 431
   Dan, 58
   Fannie Mayrice (Steele), 431
   Gay Jeanette (Hardt), 431
   Glen Thomas, 431
   Jacqueline, 281
   Laurie Dawn Warren (Upton), 431
   Levi Thomas, 431
   Mary Jane, 300
   Tanya Gay, 431
   Thomas LaMar, 431
Coleman, Austin, 251

Emma Esther (Cates), 251
Howard Alan, 251
John, 251
Marcus Anthony, 251
Merle, 251
Michael, 251
Miriam, 251
Raleigh O'Key, 251
Willard Enoch, 251
Coles, —, 54
Coley, Calvin, 250
　Elizabeth Jane (Rogers), 250
　Frank, 250
　Frank Virgil, 250
　Minnie (Vaughn), 250
　Robert, 250
Collier, Maxine, 259
Collins, Hazel, 189
　Linda Jean, 301
　Mildred Lorraine (Hillman), 301
　Walter, 301
Colson, Bonnie Sue, 393
　Cleo (Longard), 393
　Vernon, 393
Comacho, Angela Louise, 346
　Colleen Joyce (Haynes), 345
　Dawn Marie, 346
　Paul, 345
Comer, Cathy Elizabeth, 231
Comstock, Donald, 225
　Muriel, 225
Conant, Betsey, 78
　Lewis, 78
Conford, — (Austin), 443
　Ormul, 443
Congdon, Edna Elizabeth, 299
Conklin, Rebecca, 48, 77
Conkling, Shirley, 394
Conner, Inez (Roseth), 358
Connor, Barbara, 432
　Charles Richard, 358
　Michelle Inez, 358
　Nichole Elizabeth, 358
Contreras, Rita Ann, 382
Conway, Ina Belle (Cates) (Tognoni), 166
　Leslie R., 166
Conwell, Laurie Ann, 369
Cook, Abby E., 98
　Eunice (Dayton), 78
　George W., 78

Lorenzo, 78
Mary Marie (Reed) (Wingate), 78
Cooper, Alvie (Roseberry), 431
　Cornelia, 441
　Cornelia (Smith), 26
　Dorothy Ellen, 431
　Howard Marvin, 431
Cope, Zula, 211
Copp, Nat, 58
　Nathaniel, 57
Coppinger, —, 61, 64
Copus, Cheryl Rae, 396
　Hank, 396
　Harriet Christina (Boch), 396
Corbett, Ida, 176
Corn, August, 273
　Cheryl Lynn, 274, 400
　Donna Rae (Schroeder), 273
　Elizabeth (Bucklew), 273
　Josephine, 272
　Laurie June, 274, 399
　Norman, 273
Coryell, Charles, 173
　Martha Jane (Ingle), 173
　Ruby Blanche, 173
Cothern, —, 314
　Becky Ann (Trimble), 314
Cottrell, Carrie F., 118
　Mark, 119
Courch, Troy Lee, 321
Courchaine, Sandra Jean, 275
Courtice, John S., 78
Courtney, Bob, 248
　Cleora (McNamie), 248
　Deborah Ann, 249, 380, 445
　J. W., 248
　Mark Alan, 248
　Mary Gertrude (Robertson), 248
　Mary Robertson, 380
　Pamela Sue, 249
　Sandra Lynn, 248
Covert, Herbert A., 252
　June (Cates) (Zunino) (Wolford), 252
　Lucy Margaret (Cates) (Perchetti), 250
　Pete, 250
Cowley, Eliza Jane, 146
Cox, Alan Wayne, 257, 388
　Bonnie Jane (Kennedy), 193
　Brian Howard, 388

Carol Jean, 257, 389
Clarence, 257
Dorothy Elizabeth (Morris), 193
Eileen (Rooney), 193
Gertrude E. (Reed), 257
Gloria Mae, 257, 389
Jason Alan, 388
Jesse, 257
Karen, 420
Katherine (Hearley), 388
Kenneth Allen, 257, 388
Marilyn (Palmer), 388
Mayme (Frank), 257
Paul Edward, 193
Sheila Marie, 193
Tirrell Jason, 388
Cozart, Helen Mertie, 317
Crafton, Debra Jane, 312
  Dennice Jean, 312
  Jerry Leon, 312
  Larry, 312
  Larry Lynn, 312
  LaVon Elaine (Crouch), 312
Crane, —, 42
  Amy (Pike), 105
  Charles James, 105
  John, 105
  Mary Ann (Ames), 105
  Percy, 105
  Stella, 105
Crates, Nelson, 113
Crawford, Gerald, 165
  Gerard N., 165
  Hannah, 99
  Jessie, 165
  Jessie Anna (Cates), 165
  Mary Louise, 285
Croch, Angeline (Austin), 35
Crocker, Elizabeth, 15, 16
Cross, Aurillo, 16
Crossen, Lawrence A., 305
  Nora Marie, 305
  Ruth Marie (Sterling), 305
Crotty, Irene (Oros), 413
  Madeline, 413
  Michael, 413
Crouch, Agnes Abbie (Briggs), 98
  Alberda Lazetta (Keune), 140
  Allen George, 139, 205
  Angeline (Austin), 43
  Anola, 138
  Bernice (Holtan), 204
  Bertie Lorn, 98
  Bette Germaine (Draper), 205
  Betty Jane, 140, 208
  Beulah (Hollingsworth), 139
  Brenda Eileen, 205, 320
  Byron Ross, 205, 320
  Carol Diane, 205
  Cecilia (Cassutt), 98
  Charles, 98
  Charles Henry, 98, 139
  Charles Wesley, 35
  Chelsea Kaley, 321
  Cheryl Mavis, 139, 207
  Clarence, 136, 200
  Clarene Elmina, 201, 312
  Collin Kermit, 320
  Connie (Butterfield), 318
  Connie (Van Der Borgh), 205
  Debra Sue, 205
  Donald William, 139
  Elaine Marlys (Peterson), 139
  Eliza Jane (Castle), 97
  Elizabeth, 204, 318
  Elizabeth Louise (Ross), 205
  Elna Nadene, 139, 206
  Elsie Belle (Cartwright), 138
  Emma (Burch), 97
  Emma A., 35, 99
  Erin, 318
  Evelyn, 136, 201
  Evelyn Faith (Garlow), 201
  Floyd Allen, 98, 139
  Frank Nelson, 98
  Garth, 204, 318
  Genevieve (Irwin), 138
  George Henry, 35, 97
  Grace Mae, 136
  Grace May, 98, 136
  Harlie Laverne, 138, 204
  Harrison, 136
  Harrison Morton, 98, 138
  Harvey, 138
  Hattie M. (Leach), 98
  Hazel Nordstrom, 138
  Henry, 35, 43, 99
  Irvin H., 98, 136
  James Harrison, 35
  Janet Carlaw (Abernathy), 98

Jennie Adell (Garrison), 136
Jennifer, 318
Jerald Allen, 205
John Wilbur, 98, 140
Kathryn, 204, 318
Kathy Lorraine (Hall), 321
Kermit, 138, 205
Kim (Weikle), 321
Kurt Jeffrey, 205, 321
LaVon Elaine, 201, 312
Leora Belle, 138, 204
Lettie Adell, 98, 137
Lila Belle, 98, 138
Linda Kay, 201, 314
Lindsey Jo, 321
Lois (Quick), 320
Lois Marie (Peterson), 205
Marcia Jean, 205, 320
Marie Lois, 139, 206
Mary Louise, 139
Maud Pearl (Griffin), 200
Mertie Ann, 98, 136
Mildred, 136
Mildred (Moreland), 139
Mildred Abby, 98, 140
Mildred Adell, 201
Mildred Mary (McGoon), 140
Nelson Reasoner, 35, 98
Norman Carroll, 136
Quentin, 138, 204
Quentin Vincent, 321
Richard Jay, 201
Roni Jo (Neppl), 321
Ruth Mildred, 139, 205
Sharon Lu, 201, 313
Steven Douglas, 205
Thelma, 136
Todd Gregory, 205
Vernon, 136, 201, 313
Vernon George, 98, 138
Vincent Joshua, 321
Vincent Kevin, 205, 321
Virginia Lee, 205, 320
Walter Irvin, 35
Wilberda Lazetta (Keune), 140
Croughers, William, 288
Crouthers, Betty, 288
  Janet Loraine (Reed), 288
  Karen, 288
  Lula (Blake), 288
  Richard Dean, 288
Crowe, Heather Lyn, 374
  Jennifer Lyn, 374
  Mary Jane (Abel), 373
  Thomas Earl, 373, 445
  Todd Brian, 374
Crump, Gertrude Estelle, 131
Cue, Deloris J. (Cates) (Weeteling), 252
  Gordon B., 252
Cuff, Clara (Day), 222
  Lester, 222
  Mary Lois, 222
Culbert, Aaron Lee, 429
  Adrienne Leanna, 429
  Bessie (French), 365
  Bessie Ann (French), 238
  Bonnie Lou (McKnight), 365
  Brian, 366, 430
  Carolyn Lisa (Rogers), 429
  Celeste Joy (Ropelt), 429
  Charles Edward, 238
  Charles Lee, 238, 365
  Dale Leslie, 366
  Daniel William, 429
  Daryl Lynn, 366, 429
  David Lyle, 366, 429
  Douglas Lee, 365, 429
  Francis Lee, 238
  Gary Allen, 430
  Jeffrey, 366
  Jennifer Lacy, 430
  Jerald Lance, 238, 366
  Judith Mabel (Halbom), 366
  June (Froelich), 430
  Katherine (Hayes), 238
  Katherine O. (Hayes), 156
  Kim, 366
  Kristin Tara, 429
  Lydia Ann (Cagle), 429
  Mary Layne, 238, 366
  Shari Lynette, 366, 429
  Sheila Ann (Holbrook), 429
Cumming, Nancy Susan, 328
Cummings, Virginia, 91
Cunningham, Elizabeth, 431
  Julie (Sparrow), 351
Currie, Hannah (Ames), 44
  Hannah Marie, 44
  John, 44
  Robert, 44

Index

Curtis, —, 312
    Allen, 336
    Esther Lois, 210
    Gladys (—), 336
    Lois Iciphene (Puleston), 210
    Lyman, 210
    Paul Allen, 336
    Paul Rocky, 336
    Sandra Leigh (Rogers), 312
    William, 336
Curtiss, Bessie, 159
Custer, George A., 90
Cyr, Ruby Minnie, 201

D

D'Agostino, Pasqualina, 213
Dajani, Heather Ann, 365
    Margaret Elaine (Kroeplin), 365
    Talal, 365
Dale, Douglas John, 356
    Esther (Schekel), 356
    Harriet, 144
    Jennifer Lynn, 356
    Jo Ann (Sigmont), 356
    Michael Scott, 356
    Richard Ryan, 356
    Ronald Everet, 356
Dalke, Andrew, 213
    Dorothy Margaret, 213
    Magdalene (Sina), 213
Dalton, Danny D., 343
    Darcy D., 343
    Darin D., 343
    Dolores Janette, 221, 342
    Etta (Smith), 221
    Jeffery S., 343
    Laura Ann (Ferguson), 343
    Mark, 221
    Mildred (Bunk), 343
    Monna Elaine, 221, 343
    Nola (Moore), 343
    Orin D., 221
    Richard O., 343
    Richard Orin, 221, 343
    Russell Charles, 221, 343
    Ruth Janette (Roberts), 221
D'Amico, Lucretia, 190
Daniel, Charles Wesley, 154
    Emil, 109
    Evelyn Lenoi (Olson) (Peckham), 154
Daniele, Bob, 420
    Lisa Marie, 420
    Mary (—), 420
Daniels, Adele (Wyman), 137
    Ashlie Noelle, 419
    Barbara Jean (Goar), 317
    Benjamin Edward, 317
    Bert Jacob, 137
    Bethel June, 138, 203
    Constance Diane, 203, 317
    David Blake, 317, 419
    David Wynott, 203, 317
    Edna Anita (Gunnufson), 203
    Edwin Alec, 317
    Eric Christopher, 317
    Juanita Mae, 138, 203
    Julie Kay, 317, 419
    Kay Rose (Block), 317
    Lettie Adell (Crouch), 137
    Robert Blake, 203, 317
    Stephen, 137
    Tryphena, 28
    Whittnie Nicolle, 419
    Wynot Berdell, 138, 203
Danne, Karon Rae, 282
    Lawrence William, 282
    Nona Marion (Ruthroth), 282
Danz, Arlene P. (Weisensel), 342
    Brent, 342
Daugherty, Dorothy (Austin), 443
    Ronald, 443
Daus, Barbara Jean (Vancaster), 260
    Robert, 261
Dausman, Diane Elyse (Clarke), 296
    John Arthur, 296
    Kirk William, 297
    Robert W., 296
    Ruth Claire (MacGowan), 296
Davenport, Mildred, 294
David, Irma Belle (Lowry), 289
    Jacklin Kim, 289
    Jay Drexel, 289
    John Bruce, 289
    Sue Bernadine (Reed), 289
Davis, —, 122
    Charles, 122
    Charles Henry, 121
    Jennie, 122
    Jennie L. (Wadley) (Surback), 121

John, 11
Mary, 11
Sarah (Carter), 11
Dawkins, Alice, 93
  Beatrice M., 93
  Edward, 93
Dawley, Dora, 121
Dawson, Blake Alyn, 234
  Brooke Allyn, 234
Dawn Paige, 234
  Donna Jean (Peckham), 234
  Kimberly Layne, 234, 359
  Wayne Paul, 234
Day, Barbara, 228
  Barbara June, 352
  Charles Herbert, 227
  Clara, 222
  Ellis Milton, 227
  Hazel Viola (Peckham), 227
  Helen (—), 407
  Leo, 407
  Martha, 228
  Martha Joan, 352
  Mary Alice, 205
  Mary Sue, 228, 352
  Pamela Ann, 407
  Sylvia B. (Fogelberg), 227
Dayton,
  Eunice, 78
Dean, Delores Maxine, 303
  Elvira (—), 312
  Frank, 312
  John Harold, 303
  Lois Maxine (Ross), 303
  Norma Ethel, 312
De Baere, Kathy Harriet, 310
  Margaret (—), 310
  Raymond, 310
DeBauch, Aaron Clyde Joseph, 400
  Gary, 400
  Joyce (Operman), 400
  Shiloh David Lee, 400
  Tammy (Grignon), 400
  Vincent, 400
Debrucque, Joyce, 415
Defazio, Gail (Beavert), 414
  Scott, 414
DeGuire, Anna Maria Irene (Gillis), 402
  Barbara Ann, 402
  Jeffrey J., 402

Marvin, 402
Melinda Sue (Prothero), 402
Michael John, 402
Dellon, Robyn, 328
DeLowe, Elizabeth, 167
DeMain, Albine, 267
DeMars, Anita, 200
  Charlotte Lauren, 200
  Mitchell, 200
Demuling, Dorothy, 335
Denison, America Elizabeth (Haggard), 142
  E. Glenn, 191
  George Taylor, 191
  Grace (Taylor), 191
  James, 142
  Jean Martha (Canfield), 191
  Mary Ethel, 142
Denny, Rhonda Lynn, 378
Dentino, Louise, 153
DeSeyn, Jacob, 195
  Leroy Jerome, 195
  Lillian (Beach), 195
  Marla Ann, 196, 305
  Martha Louise (Kennedy), 195
  Melanie Mae, 196
  Roy Jerome, 196
  Scott William, 196
  Sharon Leigh, 196
Desroches, Philomine, 206
Dettling, Nick, 283
  Patricia Ann, 283
  Veronica Mary (Perrault), 283
Devlin, Mary, 399
DeWolf, Polly, 34
Dewsnap, Amy Leigh, 360
  Calvin Roger, 235, 360
  Carol Ann (Clark), 234
  Carolyn Henrietta E. (Eager), 235
  Christopher Adam, 360
  Cory Allan, 360
  Daniel Ryan, 360
  David Charles, 235
  Dawn (Anacker), 360
  Dennis Dean, 235, 360
  Douglas Wayne, 235, 360
  Freeman, 235
  Linda (Friedly), 360
  Linda Diane, 235
  Lucy Jean (Duell), 360

Michael Stewart, 361
Nicholas Jon, 360
Sheldon, 234
Steven Clark, 360
Stewart Harold, 235, 360
Susan Nelson, 360
Tammy Sue, 360
Deyarmond, Gregory, 288
   Jack, 288
   Jeffery Lee, 288
   John William, 288
   Lynn Marie (Grosshams), 288
   Marilyn Carol (Reed), 288
   Roger, 288
   William, 288
Deyoung, Michael, 367
   Patricia G. (Hanson), 367
Diaz, Guadalupe (Unzueta), 283
   Manuel Enreques, 283
   Mary Lou, 283
Dick, Fern (Rose), 297
   Louis, 297
   Martha Josephine, 187
Dickerson, Louise, 347
Dies, Anna (Mertens), 179
   Charles, 179
   Frederick, 179
   Isabelle Jane (Reed), 179
Dillenbeck, Blanche Pearl, 120
   Jennie, 120
   Joshua, 120
Dillon, Hattie, 115
Dilts, Lorena (Reed), 130
   Oa, 130
DiLullo, Barbara, 338
DiSalvo, Giacomo, 299
   Jack, 299
   Janice Lynn, 300
   Joyce Marie (Lane), 299
Dispanza, Brent Stanton, 296
   Penelope Lee (Nickle) (Philhower), 296
   Ronald, 296
Dix, —, 55
Dixon, Pamela Renea, 391
   Raymond, 403
   Rhonda, 403
   Ronald, 403
   Ruth Ann (Andekain), 403
   Shane, 403

   Sharon (Beyer), 403
Doberstine, Candace, 412
   Cheryl (Jorgensen), 412
   Clifford, 412
   Marcie Ann, 412
   Rose (LaGuire), 412
Dobson, Sarah Jeanette, 144
Dohlmon, Natalie, 398
Dominquez, Teresa Ann, 359
Donahue, Charles H., 437
   Dennis J., 437
Donaldson, Bea (—), 353
   Bobbie Ray, 259
   Curt, 353
   Gavin Douglas, 353
   Glen, 353
   June Adeline (Carey) (James), 259
   Keri Ann (Ronning), 353
   Myrtle Adelia (Mosley), 259
   Nicholas, 353
   T. J., 259
Donilay, Marietta (Smith) (Reed), 46
Donnelly, Emma Augusta, 112
   Marian, 419
   Marietta, 112
   Marietta (Smith) (Reed), 46
Donohue, Charles, 435, 436
   Dora, 437
   Dora (Wadley), 436
   John, 436
   Margaret (Williams), 436
Doppenberg, Barbara, 328
   Garrett, 328
Dore, Aldea Marie, 207
Dorseh, Patricia, 329
Dougherty, Rachel Minerva, 27
Douglas, Alice, 248
   Diana Gail, 248
   John, 248
Douglass, Ruth Elaine, 329
Dow, Mabel, 211
Downey, Geoffrey Thomas, 407
   Mary Ann (Minor), 407
Draeger, Ervin, 363
   Ethel Ann, 363
   Irene (Matthews), 363
Drake, Carol Susan, 244
Draper, Bette Germaine, 205
Driggs, Bob la Dian, 301
   Syotha Jean, 301

Drolet, Elsie, 310
Dubois, David Arthur, 206
   Eugene William, 206
   Frederick, 206
   Marie Lois (Crouch) (Marquette), 206
   Philomine (Desroches), 206
DuBuque, Joan, 377
Dudley, —, 53
   Lottie Irene, 157
Duell, Alice (—), 360
   Lucy Jean, 360
   Sidney, 360
Duess, Clara, 223
Duke, Leola, 388
Dunk, Bonnie, 388
Dunn, Betty May (Beavert), 295
   Eddie L., 431
   Frances (—), 431
   Gladys, 295
   Jeannie, 295
   John E., 295
   John F., 295
   John Frank, 295
   Judy, 295, 414
   Shannon Gale, 431
Dunton, Florence S., 166
Duran, Jane, 25
   Joyce, 203
Duranso, Esther (Thompson), 405
   Jacqueline Ann, 405, 434
   Jeffrey Allen, 405
   John, 405
   Lori (Baierl), 405
   Mary (Mentz), 405
   Orville, 405
Durkee, Florence W., 145
   Franklin E., 145
   Huldah (Carpenter), 34
   James H., 34
   Mary (Wakeman), 145
   Valnett Miriam, 34
Dye, Wm. McE., 86
Dyer, Cathy Jo, 314
   Kenneth Elbert, 314
   Keron Lene, 314
   Mark Jeffrey, 314
   Sharon Lu (Crouch), 313
   William H., 314

E

Eades, Donna Jean (Brandenhoff), 391
Eads, Eli, 391
   Frances (Hartley), 391
   Kerry Rae, 391
   Lawrence, 391
   Torey, 391
Eager, Carolyn Henrietta Elizabeth, 235
Early, Evelyn, 268
East, Jean Marie, 244
Eastman, Mary, 106
Ebbesmier, Lyman, 318
   Margaret (Welch), 318
   Sally Jo, 318
Eck, Casper Leroy, 128
   Claire Evan, 128
   Eva Belle (Reed), 124, 125, 126
   Lee, 124
   Mary A. (Clark), 124
   William N., 124
Eckhard, Shirley, 299
Ectes, Nelson, 81
Edmonds, Annie Gertrude, 294
Efferdahl, Diane, 276
Egan, James L., 139
Eggebrecht, Elsa Josephine, 264
Eggleston, Mary, 445
Ehler, David, 330
   Debra May (Badtke), 330
Eisen, Shirley (Phelps) (McKeig), 323
   Thomas, 323
Eisenhauer, Bessie (Curtiss), 159
   Donald, 158, 378
   Donald Keith, 246, 378
   Donald Leslie, 159, 246
   Ethel Edna (Phillips), 158
   Frank, 159
   Garry, 378
   Mary Sue (Peckham), 246
   Patricia Jean, 159, 246
   Peggy (Light), 378
   Terri Ann, 246
   Terry Ann, 378
Ekwinski, Margaret Theresa, 388
Elder, Lenora, 219
Elie, Aldea Marie (Dore), 207
   Edmond Joseph, 207
   Rolande Marie, 207
Elkins, Asbury, 285

Jo Lynn, 285, 406
Joyce Ann (Reed), 285
Linton, 285
Mary Louise (Crawford), 285
Ellingboe, Lurene, 311
Ellinson, Ann, 151
Elliott, Mabel B., 107
Ellis, Christopher Shawn, 301
Susan Maria (Kent), 301
Elquest, C. A., 111
Charlie, 111
Willis, 111, 112
Engebose, Edmund Louis, 275
Nancy, 275
Ruth
(LeGrave), 275
Engelman, Elizabeth Jane (Roseth)
(Casey), 232
Gladys Otha (Holt), 232
John, 232
Morton Valentine, 232
Engen, —, 244
Nina (Pepin), 244
Englemann, Johanna Amelia, 177
English, Angela, 410
Marcia Joan (Pryor), 409
Michael Ray, 409
Michelle, 410
Enselman, Beverly Anne (Beavert) (Vallentyne), 294
Iris (Ball), 294
Joseph, 294
Ray, 294
Ericcson, Amanda Carolyn, 264
Erickson, Charles A., 174
Cheryl (Wolf), 279
Christel Lynn, 372
Craig, 279
Cynthia Lee, 279, 404
Gary Allen, 279
Georgia (Plautz), 279
Hilma (Anderson), 174
Janet Marie, 174, 279
Jean Mildred, 174, 279
Melinda Ann, 372
Michael, 279
Mildred Agnes (Reed), 174
Norman, 372
Norman Aaron, 372
Raymond Charles, 174

Ruth Elizabeth, 220
Sharon Nadine (Abel), 372
Vern Charles, 335
William Charles, 174, 279
Wilma Maxine (Jelmeland), 335
Ernst, —, 165
Jessie (Crawford), 165
John, 245
Linda (Wester) (Theien), 245
Esker, Linda Eileen, 300
Robert Raymond, 300
Shirley Eileen (Hulbert), 300
Esselstein, Jane, 283
Lynn Ellen, 284
Marlene Ellen (Grassens), 283
Walter, 283
William, 283
Evans, Carol (Schmiege), 315
David Wayne, 203, 316
Deborah Lynn, 316
Glenn William, 203
Ira, 203
Jennifer Lynn, 376
Joyce (Duran), 203
Juanita Mae (Daniels), 203
Judy (O'Konek), 316
Matthew, 419
Michael Allen, 316, 419
Michel Cae, 316
Nancy (Seehusen), 419
P. W., 74
Patricia Kay, 316
Peggy Susan, 316
Richard Allen, 203, 315
Robert Thomas, 316
Sarah (Paul), 203
Sarah Adell, 203, 316
Sharon Elizabeth, 203, 316
Shirley (Weldon), 316
Steven Wayne, 316
Thomas Glenn, 203, 316
Timothy Glen, 316
Todd David, 316
Tom, 376
Victoria Lynn (Wester), 376
Everitt, Audrey, 176, 281
Betty Jo (—), 176
Floyd, 176
Ford, 176
Ida (Corbett), 176

Ida (Landis), 176
Irma Jean, 176
Lee, 176
Malanthken, 176
Martha Pauline (Rieumes), 176
Mildred Desilva (Wadley), 176
Olley (—), 176
Ewing, Donald Glen, 338
  Glenda, 338
  Helen Marie (Vining), 338
  Janet Marie, 338, 424
  Karen Sue, 338
  Kurtis Glen, 338

F

Fagundes, Florence, 357
Fairchild, Brenda Eileen (Crouch), 320
  David, 320
  Kyle Nathan, 320
  Lucille (—), 320
  Mark, 320
Farnsworth, Amanda (Newman), 120
  Florence Evelyn, 253
  Nathan, 120
  Rosemary, 304
  Ruby Grace, 120, 445
Farrara, Rena Annette, 233
Farrell, Greg, 313
  Janice Adell (Crouch), 313
  Joe, 313
  Timothy, 313
Fascia,
  Cherubina, 286
Fate, Beatrice (Baker), 243, 363
  Chan, 243, 375
  Dayton Andrew, 376
  Denise Jean, 375
  Erin Nicole, 376
  Irene Anne, 243, 363
  Jean (Wilke), 375
  Martin James, 243, 375
  Mattie (Langdon), 243
  Melody Ann, 376
  Michael Todd, 376
  Nathan, 376
  Randy (Urkmann), 376
  Ray, 243, 363
  Starr, 243
  Thomas Daniel, 375

  Troy, 376
  Troy Allen, 243
Faust, Elsie (Wolcholz), 331
  Shirley Ann, 331
  William, 331
Fazenden, —, 172
  Ilene Ruth (Reed), 172
Felt, —, 314
  Mary Colleen (Meeker), 315
Fendley, Opaline, 280
Fenety, Beatrice (—), 406
  Jo Lynn (Elkins) (Hamilton), 406
  John, 406
  Linden Harris, 406
Fenske, Edna, 149
  Lillie (Winne), 149
  William, 149
Ferg, Adrienne Ann, 402
  Elmer, 402
  Marie (LaFave), 402
  Robert James, 402
  Ruby Lynn (Prothero), 402
  Tracy Marie, 402
Ferguson, E. Joyce, 367
  Laura Ann, 343
  Mary Margaret (Vining) (White), 338
  Myril, 338
Fernandez, Angela Rose, 272
  Dawn, 272
  Elisa Joy, 272
  Francis, 272
  Josephine (Corn), 272
  Maureen Martha (Reed), 272
  Quintin Roger, 272
  Robert Francis, 272
  Roger Louis, 272
  Travis Lee, 272
  Valerie Joyce (Reed), 272
  Virgil Francis, 272
  Wade Robert, 272
  Wendy Mae, 272
Ferrill, Grace, 284
Fessler, Beatrice (Beekman), 167
  Flora Etta, 167
  Frank, 167
  Wilbur Nicholas, 167
Fetcha, Euloda, 8, 435
Fetterely, Grace Irene, 301
Fidler, Carol Lynn (Brandenhoff), 390
  Howard, 390

Index 471

Marit (Carter), 390
Michael, 390
Shannon Leanne, 390
Shawn Gregory, 390
Filek, Beverly P. (Roseth) (Waite), 231
  Edwin J., 231
Fillmore, Betty, 291
  John Allen, 291
  Liza May (Gleason), 291
Fingulin, Carolyn Sue (Campbell), 305
  Joseph Paul, 305
  Michelle Grace, 305
Fink, Beau, 402
  Brian Alan, 402
  Sheryl Lynn (Hawkins), 402
Finster, George, 387
  Loretta (—), 387
  Mary, 387
Finstune, Cheryl, 367
Fischer, Aaron, 270
  Barbara Sue (Reed), 270
  Chad Lee, 270
  Debora, 410
  Heather Sue, 270
  Karen, 423
  Katie Marie, 270
  Martha (Krueger), 270
  Ralph, 270
  Robert, 270
  Stephen, 270
Fisher, Carol Jean, 356
  Debra Sue (Crouch), 205
  Gary, 205
  Henry, 356
  Lydia (Wagner), 356
Fitzgerald, Colleen, 366
  Ken, 366
  Mary Layne (Culbert) (Hyslop), 366
  Terri, 366
Fitzsimons, G. T., 82, 84, 86
Fiveash, Phoebe, 174
Flaig, Delores L. (Utke), 269
  Deloris L. (Utke), 171
  Edward H., 171, 269
  Joan, 269
  Judy, 171
Flaven, Laurel, 369
Fletcher, Frank E., 92
Florey, Irma Jean (Everitt) (Johnson), 176

Paul, 176
Florio, Laurie (Waite), 356
  Marc, 356
  Serena Marie, 357
Fobes, Charles, 99
  Elmira M. (Canfield), 99
  Ida B. (Lange), 99
Fogarty, Mary Ann, 208
Fogelberg, Sylvia B., 227
Fogner, Daniel, 337
  David, 337
  Davida Marie, 337, 423
  Douglas, 337
  Gwendolyn, 337
  Shirley Ann (Vining), 337
Foote, Myrtle, 141
Foral, Antoinette Marie, 265
  Barbara (Graff), 265
  Harlan, 265
Forbes, Angela Vonn, 336
  Danny, 219, 336
  Darcy, 336
  Elenor (Mattner), 218
  Henry, 147
  Lulu (Hewitt) (Vining), 147
  Ralph Jess, 218
  Terre (Arndt), 336
  Vivian (Beck), 218
  Wayne, 219, 336
Ford, Henry, 111, 188
  Judy (Bond), 283
  Lisa Marie (Johnson), 283
  Robert H., 283
  Robert Shields, 283
Forney, Jesse, 210
Fortier, Bessie May (Kroeplin), 364
  Michael H., 364
Foss, Bonnie, 336
  Esther (—), 336
  Oscar, 336
Foster, Dana Kay, 281
  Edith Evelyn, 382
  George Earl, 335
  Greg Robert, 281
  Hilbert Joyce, 176
  Karen (Stamstad), 335
  Lera Edwina (Wadley), 176
  Lera Jean, 177, 281
  Lois Ann (Griffeth), 281
  Marie (Thomson), 176

Patricia Kay (Hawkins), 281
Paul Hilbert, 176
Robert Paul, 177, 281
Vera June, 335
Fox, —, 18
  Arthur, 217
  Dorothy Jeanette (Ryburn), 217
  John Richard, 217
Franch, Danal Charles, 367
Frank, Alan, 341
  Carole Ann, 200
  Elizabeth, 423
  Mayme, 257
  Sharon A. (Pogue), 341
Franklin, Albert Lloyd, 210
  Alice Sylvia (Miller), 211
  Bida Bell (Osborn), 141
  Clark Mason, 142
  Donald Lincoln, 142, 210
  Esther Lois (Curtis), 210
  Gordon W., 142
  Gordon William, 210
  Horace, 141
  Kent Gordon, 210
  Marcia Jane, 210
  Marjorie Helen (Kaldahl), 210
  Marjorie May, 142
  Norman Dale, 142, 211
  Paul Dwight, 210
  Rie, 211
  Rilla Bell, 142, 211
  Robert Lois, 210
  Sarah (Schramm), 141
  William, 141
Frazer, Shirley, 254
  Fredenthal,
  Wanda, 351
Freeman, Amy Elizabeth (Ames), 42
Freer, Bernice M., 304
French, Allen Flavel, 156, 238
  Anna (Roff), 156
  Anthony Raymond, 367
  Bessie Ann, 156, 238
  Beverly Ann, 238, 366
  Charles Robie, 156
  Cheryl (Finstune), 367
  Clara Alverette, 156, 239
  Craig Charles, 240
  Danal Charles, 238
  Dawn Renee, 240, 370

  Denise Margaret, 366, 430
  Dennia Allen, 366
  Dennis Allen, 238
  Dorothy Belle, 156, 239
  Emma Viola (Lampland), 239
  Erika, 277
  Estina May (Abel), 156
  Evan Lynette, 240
  Evelyn Mae, 156, 240
  Evon Lynette, 370
  Helene (—), 238
  Jane (—), 367
  Jason, 367
  Jayne Marie (Reed), 277
  John Flavel, 156
  Joshua Curtis, 370
  Julie (Weitzenkemp), 370
  June Carol, 156, 241
  Kelly Lynn, 366
  La Verna (Tienter) (Westphal), 240
  Lara, 367
  LeRoy Edward, 238
  Margaret (Rasmussen), 366
  Mary, 277
  Michelle Jean, 371
  Muriel (Loguia), 367
  Nathan, 367
  Nyal June (Martin), 238
  Richard, 277
  Richard Andrew, 156, 239
  Rodney Lee, 240
  Ronald Richard, 239, 367
  Ruth Lilyan, 240, 370
  Scott Benjamin, 240, 370
  Sharyn Lynn, 240
  Toni Grant (Wilkinson), 240
Frey, Leona, 278
Friedhoff, Barbara Lee (Peckham), 217
  Bart, 217
Friedly, Linda, 360
Fritz, Marie Ann, 325
Froelich, June, 430
Frost, Annise, 46
Fuller, Ann Eliza, 103
  Barron Bradley, 393
  Bonnie Louise (Johnson), 393
  Darwin Follett, 284
  Dennis, 393
  Doris (Hamilton), 393
  Earl, 393

Kelly Lynn, 393
Michael Ann, 393
Mina Ann, 149
Nola Mae, 284
Oreada Emgard (Peterson), 284
Fultz, Carl Buck, 381
Cloma (Ratliff), 381
Louise Fay, 381

G

Gaerger, Donna, 420
Gahagan, Margaret, 263
Galer, Mary, 343
Galewski, Edward, 423
Grace (—), 423
Mary Louise, 423
Galgoczy, David John, 334
John, 333
Kalman, 333
Mary Elia (Peckham), 333
Stephan Kalman, 334
Terez (—), 333
Gallagher, —, 426
Jenni Kay, 426
Lisa Kay (Peckham), 426
Gallaglier, Bernard, 438
Margaret (Muldowney), 438
Marguerite Cecilia, 438
Gallenberger, Andrew Bernard, 391
Bernard, 391
Lois Ann (Missall) (Kumhala), 391
Mary Ann (Shwanke), 391
Nicholas Andrew, 392
Gamble, Rosalie Luella, 405
Ganzer, Gail (Beavert) (Defazio), 414
Jeffery Raymond, 414
Morgan Elizabeth, 414
Garcia, Debra Kay (Kruse), 355
Michael, 355
Gardner, Alta (Bright), 107
Garison, Gerald Kenneth, 163
Marcelle R. (Olson), 163
Ronnie Lee, 163
Wilma Jean (Hart), 163
Garloch, Catherine (Hassler), 135
David, 135
Ina E. (Cheeseman), 135
John, 135
Lorena A., 135

Garlow, Evelyn Faith, 201
Joshua Franklin, 201
Ruby Minnie (Cyr), 201
Garrison, Anona Bell, 137
Barbara, 202
Chrysandra Dell (Hudson), 315
Clare Faye, 137
Darion Wayne, 315
David, 202, 315
Dee Ann Robin, 314
Donald, 137, 202, 315
Donald Lloyd, 202, 314
Donna (More), 314
Dora (Hodge), 202
Dorothy Carol (Smith), 202
Edmond E., 136
Elizabeth (Goss), 315
Frederick L., 137
George Edmund, 137
Grace May (Crouch), 137
Jennie Adell, 136
John Michael, 203
Josiah, 315
Judy, 202
Kathy La Vonne, 203, 315
Lillian (Leseuer), 202
Lillian M. (Stovee), 137
Lloyd Henry, 137, 202
Lois (Newcomb), 137
Lucinda (Taft), 136
Lynda Kay (Grip), 315
Mary G. (Yearly), 137
Myrtle Adell, 137, 202
Nona Lou, 202, 314
Patricia Ann (Petrick), 202
Steven Ritchard, 314
Vernon, 137, 202
Vicky, 202
Wayne, 137
Garten, Lorie, 375
Gates, Beverly Ann (Peterson), 336
Duane Leon, 336
Harriet (—), 336
Leon, 336
Michael, 336
Wilma, 302
Gault, Daniel, 384
Lisa Karen, 384
Mary Ellen (Carling), 384
Gaw, Betty (Weaver), 411

Colene Ann (McMannis), 411
Lewis William, 411
Rodney, 411
William, 411
Gay, Carolyn Elaine, 207, 322
Cheryl Mavis (Crouch), 207
Emma, 157
Kevin Wyatt, 207
Lila Joni (Hammaker), 322
Mary (Coker), 207
Thomas Charles, 207
Warren Kenneth, 322
Wayne, 207
William Kenneth, 207, 321
Wilton Kenneth, 207
Geer, Betty Carolyn, 317
Gehm, Lydia (Sorenson), 269
Susan, 269
Victor, 269
Geise, Charles, 206
Elna Nadene (Crouch), 206
Genesy, Elizabeth (Bahari), 183
Irene Hanak, 183
John, 183
Geoffrion, Joseph Paul, 345
Lucas Michael, 345
Michael, 345
Vivian Carol (Jenkins), 345
George, Drinkwater, 125
Frank, 125
Lucy (Plaster), 125
Mary, 125
May, 125
Gergen, Bill, 253
Neva Faye, 253
Gerky, Darlene Ruth, 363
Gerrish, William, 9
Giannoni, Isolina, 241
Gibson, Annie Gertrude (Edmonds), 294
Dava E., 391
David, 391
Dianne Lee (Stroud), 294
Donna Jean (Archibald), 294
Douglas Loy, 294, 413
Earl William, 294
Joseph Harold, 294
Kaylin Ashley, 413
Sharilyn Autumn, 294, 413
Steven Earl, 294
Susan (Stultz), 413

Gilberson, Annie, 117
Gilbert, Caroline Almira, 139
Gillis, Anna Maria Irene, 402
Gilmer, Maybelle Gertrude, 208
Gittings, —, 58
Glass, Beda, 47, 435
Gleason, Liza May, 291
Glenn, Matel Emma, 220
Glover, —, 12
Goar, Barbara Jean, 317
Gordon Mims, 317
Helen Mertie (Cozart), 317
Goebel, Adam, 332
Cecilia (Stahl), 332
Clarabell Margaret, 332
Dennis, 362
Geraldine Edna (Zaszczurynski), 362
Sharon, 362
Goerl, Eugene, 78
Goff, Alice Virginia, 304
Gonzales, Elizabeth Ann (Kutzner), 410
Eugene, 410
Gabriel Adam, 410
Jacob Eugene, 410
Gooderham, Janet, 216
Kathryn Leigh (Peckham) (Aune), 216
Kenneth John, 216
William, 216
Goodrich, A., 112
Anne, 159, 246
Grace (Austin), 159
Jane, 159, 247
Leon, 159
Gordon, Ruth, 298
Gorsuch, Eunice (Ross), 149
Floy Beatrice, 149, 224
Freeman Wesley, 149
Harold, 149
John Wesley, 149
Maysel Elizabeth, 149, 224
Mina Ann (Fuller), 149
Stuart, 149
Wilfred, 149
Winnie Blanche (McElroy), 149
Goss, Elizabeth, 315
Goutermont, Heather, 372
Helen May (Abel), 241
Jerold LeRoy, 241
John, 241

Loretta Alice, 241, 372
Lynne (White), 372
Nettie (Barber), 241
Roy Luverne, 241, 372
Shawn Aaron, 372
Grabanski, Albina, 262
Alexander, 262
Wilhelmina, 262
Graber, Ann, 247
Leland, 248
Graff, Barbara, 265
Graham, —, 73
Harry, 110
Grahn, Brian, 329
Emma (Sanders), 214
Ervin, 213
Evelyn (Quick), 213
Gary, 214, 329
Henry, 214
Jayne (Sanderson), 329
Michael, 329
Patricia (Dorseh), 329
Robert, 329
Grams, Elizabeth, 171
Grandhom, John, 313
Grant, Brenda Gail, 290
Francis LeBaron, 290
Grace Katherine (Stackley), 290
Nancy, 275
Granthom, Beverly Ann (Lee), 313
James Roy, 313
John Allen, 313
John Lee, 313
Thomas Allen, 313
Verna, 313
Grassens, Johanna Amelia (Englemann), 177
Joseph John, 177
Marlene Ellen, 177, 283
Pauline Lois (Wadley), 177
Roland, 177
Graves, Bette Lorraine, 350
Harold, 350
Ruth (Smith), 350
Green, Barrie Jo, 327
Jeanne Ann (Quick), 327
Michael, 327
Patricia, 428
Shayna Lynn, 327
Greene, Jacq. M. (Simmons) (Reinhart), 181
Warren, 181
Greenfield, Carolyn Rae (Vining), 337
Robert, 337
Roberta Rae, 337
Griffeth, Jacob W., 281
Lois Ann, 281
Pearl E. (Wiggs), 281
Griffin, Catherine, 200
John, 200
Mattie, 240
Maud Pearl, 200
Griffith, Austin Thomas, 379
Dorothy (—), 379
Ivan, 379
Kenneth Alan, 379
Lucinda Jean (McDaniel), 379
Zachery Eugene, 379
Grignon, Darla, 274, 400
Darwin, 274
Donna Rae (Schroeder) (Corn), 274
Inez (Adams), 274
Michael, 274
Patrick, 274
Selena, 274, 400
Tammy, 274, 400
Grimes, Mary Sue, 367
Grinley, Anna S., 226
Audrene (Skarperrid), 226
Ben, 226
Grip, Ben, 315
Lynda Kay, 315
Maxine, 315
Grizzard, Beverly (—), 314
Dana, 314
Linda Kay (Crouch) (Beck), 314
Thomas Norman, 314
Groslimond, Andrew Mitchell, 359
Gery Will, 359
Jeffrey Paul, 359
Pamela Ann (Mitchell), 359
Grosshams, Lynne Marie, 288
Grout, Austin, 143
Irma L. (Quick), 143
Grubb, Barbara Jean (Verriden), 398
Fred, 398
John Hiram, 398
Joshua, 398
Mary Ann (Mazanec), 398
Gudahl, Berthanna, 217

Gudmondson, Elaine, 265
Guenchner, Beverly Jeanette (Shipton), 331
   Kenneth, 331
   Otto, 331
   Sue Ellen, 331, 422
Guererro, Angela, 432
Guilford, John, 34
Guiliano, Louise (Dentino), 153
   Victor, 153
Guillory, Denver Imo, 373
   Karen Marie (Pardini), 373
   Tyler Wayne, 373
   Wayne, 373
Guiney, Bonnie J. (Pogue), 424
   Christy Lynn, 424
   Shawn, 424
   Stephen, 424
Guiterrez, Anita, 319
Gulbrand, Burdette, 287
   Emma (Benhke), 287
   Hans, 287
   June Rose (Reed), 287
   Sara Esther Patricia, 288
Gunderson, Caroline (Siegel) (—), 401
   John, 401
Gunnufson, Aletta Sophia (Anderson), 203
   Edna Anita, 203
   Edward Andrew, 203
Gustafson, Lezlie Marie, 371
   Lizbeth, 371
   Mark, 371
   Theodore Charles, 371
   Vicki Lea (Urch), 371
Gustag, Mary, 179
Gustavison, Majel, 292
Gustavson, Jo-Lynn, 410
   Mildred (Hedstron), 410
   Robert, 410
Gustrowsky, Floyd H., 341
   Ione Pearl (Pogue), 341
   Linda G., 341, 425
   Lloyd H., 341
   Ramona M., 341, 424
   Verna G., 342
   Wanda P., 341, 424
Guthrie, Alice, 162
   Edith Harriet (Smith), 162
   James B., 162

Gutzmann, Sandra Lee, 332
Gwiazda, Beatta (Huth), 427
   Cheryle Ann, 362, 427
   Duane Walter, 362, 427
   Eric Daniel, 427
   Gloria (Welner), 427
   Gregory Gene, 362, 427
   Irene Mary, 362, 427
   Jeanine Lynn, 427
   Mary, 362
   Nicholas, 362
   Nicholas Walter, 427
   Regina Camille, 427
   Walter, 362
   Waneta Beth (Meeker), 362

H

Haag, Beverly Jean (Jenkins), 346
   Gerald David, 346
   Paul Michael, 346
   Randall Alan, 346
   Ronald, 346
   Victoria Lynn, 346
   William Richard, 346
Hack, Gladys Leona (Powell), 105
   Glenmore W., 105
   Mary E. (Onley), 105
   Thorton Onley, 105
Hackbarth, Amelia, 224
Hadala, Dorothy Elizabeth, 237
   Jacob, 237
   Mary (Telatko), 237
Haggard, America Elizabeth, 142
Hagopian, Bonnie Ann (Reed) (Rudelich), 402
   Danim, 402
   Mary (Chardukian), 403
   Milton, 403
Hagreen, Barbara, 389
Halbom, Johanna (—), 366
   John, 366
   Judith Mabel, 366
Hall,
   Beatrice (Rose), 184
   Charles S., 183
   Cynthia (Rowland), 183
   E. Leona, 184
   Elsie, 257
   Karl Stanley, 183

Index

Kathy Lorraine, 321
Marion Jessie (Rider), 183
Mary Ann, 353
Shirley Gay (Simmons) (Webb), 290
Wayne C., 184
William, 290
Halverson, Charles, 121
   Christina (Swensen), 121
   Mabel Rose, 121
Hamilton, Annette Dora, 406
   Dora Alice (Hudson), 406
   Doris, 393
   Eleanor Merle, 199
   Halsey Hobert, 406
   James, 406
   Jo Lynn (Elkins), 406
   Sara Celeste, 406
Hammaker, Lila Joni, 322
Hammerstad, Lois (Archibald)
      (Thompson) (Raleigh), 293
   Lynn, 293
Hammond, Daphne Marie, 415
   Lucille Katherine (Smith), 415
   Mary Ann (Mason), 421
   Stephanie Ann, 421
   Steven, 421
   Walter Joseph, 415
Handlin, Lillian May, 168
Handricki, —, 244
   Janice (Pepin), 244
Haney, Alan, 278
   Dorothy, 316
   Elizabeth, 278
   John, 278
   John Louis, 278
   Judith (Reed), 278
   Marjorie Janet (Woodward), 278
Hansen, Bessie, 361
   Carl Holger, 116
   Dorothy E. (Buschenfield), 312
   Hans, 287
   Mary, 261
   Orpha (Carrie), 116
   Sharon, 312
   Virgil John, 312
Hanslin, Nettie, 154
Hanson, Aaron J., 369
   Andrew L., 367
   Anna, 235
   Anna Louise, 239, 368
   Anola Gayle, 239, 369
   Arvena, 303
   Barbara A. (Vangness), 368
   Brenda K. (Johnson), 369
   Brittany Lynn, 369
   Carla S., 368
   Clara, 43
   Clara Alverette (French), 239
   Curt D., 368
   Darla R., 368
   David Bruce, 239, 369
   Debbie (Speaks), 430
   Denise K., 368
   Douglas A., 368
   E. Joyce (Ferguson), 367
   Edward Jefferson, 239
   Glenn Eldon, 239, 367
   James Mark, 239
   Jill G., 367
   Joanne, 390
   Larry Kay, 239, 367
   Laura (Pierce), 239
   Laura Lynn, 368
   Laurie Ann (Conwell), 369
   LeRoy, 239
   Leslie E., 367
   Levi D., 369
   Linda L., 295
   Loren Richard, 239, 367
   Lyle, 390
   Mark J., 369
   Mary Lou (Urch), 367
   Mary Sue (Grimes), 367
   Matilda, 284
   Matthew, 430
   Michael, 430
   Michael C., 367, 430
   Pamela R., 367
   Patricia G., 367
   Penny L., 367
   Philip, 368
   Phillip, 239
   Rebekah J., 369
   Rilla Margaret, 228
   Rodney E., 239
   Roger Arlen, 239, 368
   Sharon (Reynolds), 368
   Steven Joel, 239
   Teri L., 368
   Timothy Clayton, 239, 369

Tina Marie, 368
Todd P., 368
Harden, Beryl Jo (Sigmont), 356
   Jeffrey Todd, 356
   Richard, 356
Hardin, Marie, 218, 335
Hardt, Andrew E., 382
   Barbara April Rachael, 431
   Bradley W., 382
   Daniel Oliver, 431
   Darrell Oliver, 381, 431
   David Oliver, 251, 381
   Dorothy Ellen (Cooper), 431
   Elayne Jeanne, 251
   Emma Mary Magdaline (Weber), 251
   Gary James, 251
   Gay Jeanette, 381, 431
   Gustave Andrus, 251
   Ivan Thomas, 381, 431
   Jenifer Ann, 383
   Joeline Nicole, 383
   Laura Ann (Bohmfalk), 382
   Linda Susan, 251, 382
   Louise Fay (Fultz), 381
   Meredith Angelee, 383
   Michelle Elizabeth, 383
   Nina Louise, 381, 431
   Phillip Joel, 251, 382
   Phillip Thomas, 383
   Ronald "Mickey" Michael, 382
   Ronald Michael, 251
   Shannon Gale (Dunn), 431
   Timothy V., 382
   Tyler Thomas, 431
   Vernaline Marie, 251, 381
   Winnie Mae (Alexander), 382
Hardwick, John Milton, 80
   Sarah Higgins (Chandler), 80
   Susan Belle, 80, 91, 123
   Susan Josephine, 92
Harkness, Audrey, 411
   Ellen (—), 411
   Emerson, 411
Harkum, Emily, 138
Harnish, Dora Thea, 219
Harper, Helen Agnes, 249
Harrington, Barbara, 390
   Doris (Larivee), 390
   Francis, 390
Harris, —, 312

Jeanette, 336
Karen (Rogers), 312
Louisa L., 87
Louisa O., 91
Louise, 79
Harrison, Nellie Sarmia, 188
Hart, Arlina or Aroline Bell (Cates), 251
   Bobby Jo, 319
   Burdette, 204
   Cherelyn Lea, 204, 319
   David Burdette, 204, 318
   David Dean, 319, 420
   Deborah Jo, 319
   Grover Franklin, 204
   Harmony Lee, 420
   Jason David, 420
   Johanna Magdalena (Pfeiffer), 204
   Kevin Bradley, 319
   Larry Duane, 204, 319
   Leora Belle (Crouch), 204
   Lisa Marie (Daniele), 420
   Mary Kay (Wampler), 319
   Michael, 319
   Nancy Kay, 204, 319
   Richard Kennedy, 319
   Sally Jo (Ebbesmier), 318
   Steven Craig, 319
   Sue Ranal, 204, 320
   Tami Lea, 319
   Todd, 319
   Vernon Oliver, 251
   Wilma Jean, 163
Hartley, Frances, 391
Hartwell, Alice Edna (Preston), 236
   Betty Jean, 236, 361
   Eugene Joseph, 236
   Mary Ann (Spratt), 236
   Stephen Walter, 236
Hassell, Julie A., 404
   Russell, 404
Hassler, Catherine, 135
Hatch, Jean Helene, 432
Hatfield, Hazel, 236
Hathorn, Betty (Hock), 215
   Betty Jean, 215, 332
   Clarence Millard, 215
   Frank E., 215
   Harriet (Peckham), 215
   John Clarence, 215
   Lida (Smith), 215

Hauge, Ella, 137
Haugen, Danny, 246
  Dena, 246, 378
  Donald Christian, 246
  Linda, 246
  Margarette (Howell), 246
  Oscar Christian, 246
  Patricia Jean (Eisenhauer), 246
Have, Clara, 222
Haver, Amanda, 123
Hawkins, Artie (Name), 172
  Barbara (Wright), 276
  Diane (Efferdahl), 276
  Gale Michael, 172, 275
  George, 172
  Ilene Ruth (Reed), 172
  Jackie, 275
  Jackie (Rodefer), 275
  Jennifer Irene, 276
  Linda June, 172, 276
  Nancy (Engebose), 275
  Nancy (Grant), 275
  Patricia Kay, 281
  Ralph Clayton, 172
  Ralph George, 172, 275
  Randal Clarence, 275
  Robert Carl, 172, 276
  Rochelle Marie, 275
  Rodney Ralph, 275
  Ruth Ann, 276
  Sara Lee, 276
  Scott Allen, 275
  Shannon Ralph, 275
  Sharon Lou (Brauer), 275
  Shawn Michael, 275
  Sheryl Lynn, 275, 401
  Tonya Jean, 276
  William Michael, 276
Hayden, Florence Helen (Montgomery), 295
  Lester Raymond, 295
  Sharon Louise, 295
Hayes, Alice Caroline, 156
  Henry, 156
  Katherine, 238
  Katherine O. (Culbert), 156
Haynes, Caroline May, 222, 345
  Colleen Joyce, 222, 345
  Debra Lucille, 222
  Emma (Hughes), 222
  Howard, 222
  Katherine, 102
  Lucille Elizabeth (Jenkins), 222
  Stanley, 222
Haynie, Angela (Guerrero), 432
  Barbara (Connor), 432
  Bonnie Ann (Clark) (Carter), 432
  Byron Jerome, 382
  Cara Ann Marie, 432
  Clinton DeWayne, 382, 432
  Dee Ann, 382, 432
  Dorene Marie, 382, 432
  Jessica Dalene, 432
  Jessie Dewayne, 432
  Joseph Lyn, 432
  Katherine Marie (Jackson), 432
  Kelly Jeanette, 382
  Mary Eileen (Udell), 381
  Robert, 381
  Roberta Joleen, 432
  Roger Koy, 381, 382, 431, 432
  Talen Eric, 432
  Thomas Glenn Stan, 432
  Vernaline Marie (Hardt), 381
  Walter Lyn, 382, 432
Hays, Corrie Ann, 419
  James, 419
  Kelly Thomas, 419
  Rosean Marie (Widendorf) (Parks), 419
  Scott Alan, 419
Heard, Kathrine Jean, 358
Hearley, Bonnie (Dunk), 388
  Harold, 388
  Katherine, 388
Hearn, Daniel, 181
  Edwin, 181
  Louise (Van Keuren), 181
  Olive Marinda (Reed) (Simmons), 181
Heath, Allen, 271
  Andrea, 422
  Christine (Warrington), 271
  Janice Marie, 271
Hebb, Donna (Gaerger), 420
  Ivan Glenn, 420
Hecht, Brian Kelly, 326
  Elizabeth Jo (Walenga), 326
  Jessica Lynn, 326
Heckes, Fred, 214

Gordon, 214
Ida (Splitgerber), 214
Jennifer, 330
Melody, 330
Naomi Mary (Quick), 214
Ronald Gordon, 214, 330
Sharon Mae, 214, 329
Shirley (Cluppert), 330
Hedgecock, Fred, 440
    James, 440
    Jamie, 440
    Judith Gloria (Wadley), 440
    Virginia (Martin), 440
Hedstron, Mildred, 410
Hefke, Hulda, 287
Heidamann, Wilma, 405
Heimberger, Alice Virginia (Goff), 304
    James Earl, 304
    James Robert, 304
    Sharon Joy (Kennedy) (Kendall), 304
Heiser, Anna, 414
    Helgeland,
    Dennis, 399
    Dennis Troy, 399
    Kym Marie (Reed), 399
Helson, Harriet, 118
Hendricks, Marion, 398
Hendron, Ella, 227
Henkel, Bonita Jean (Stafford), 323
    Heidi Jo, 324
    Jason Andrew, 324
    Joseph Eugene, 209, 323
Henlrey, David, 18
Henry, June Barbara, 235
Hensey, Kathryn, 327
Henton, James, 54
Herbert, Amy Elizabeth, 431
    Brandi Lynn, 431
    Christin Louise, 431
    Elizabeth (Cunningham), 431
    Milton, 431
    Nina Louise (Hardt), 431
    Thomas Joseph, 431
Herich, Arnold Alfred, 266
    Christian Peter, 266
    Gay Laurel, 266
    Holly Anissa, 266
    Laurel Gay (Johnson), 266
    Maria Vilma (Piovarchy), 266
    Mark John, 266

Herick, Emil Peter, 266
    Laurel (Johnson), 169
Hermans, Bernard, 426
    Candase Marie, 426
    Cheryl Lynn (Peckham), 426
Hernandez, Raymunda, 326
Herrin, Mark Allen, 315
Herrington, Rosetta, 292
Hertzler, Betty Jo (McDaniel), 248
    Dean Brent, 248, 379
    Diana Gail (Douglas), 248
    Eileen (Higgins), 248
    Gary Lee, 248
    Glen Jay, 248
    Gregory Lloyd, 248
    Hazel (Schwab), 248
    Joshua Brent Zacharia, 379
    Myrlan L., 248
    Pamela (Michael), 379
Hess, Delina, 230
    Marcella, 230
    Nick, 230
Hetts, Eva, 171
Hewen, Madeline, 336
Hewitt, DeEtta, 97
    Elbert, 147
    Elizabeth (—), 387
    Eva (Lane), 147
    John, 387
    Lulu, 147
    Sandra Ann (Tognoni), 387
    William Nelson, 387
    Winston Jonathan, 388
Heyerdah, Annie (Gilberson), 117
Heyerdahl, Clemet, 117
    Helga Lydia, 117
Hickman, Clifford O., 324
    Cyrus, 324
    Nancy (Palmer), 324
    Pamela, 324
Hicks, Anne Sheridan, 430
Higgins, Eileen, 248
Higginson, Sarah, 10
Hill, Arlene May (Reed) (Snively), 289
    James Russell, 289
    Joe Paul, 289
    Ruby Louise (Atkins), 289
Hilligoss, Billy, 217
    Donny, 217
    Jerry, 217

Index 481

Leota Vernette (Ryburn), 217
Omar, 217
Hillman, Mildred Lorraine, 301
Myron, 269
Hilmoe, Gudrun Borghild, 352
Hilty, Al, 92
Hinajosa, Consuelo Guadalupe, 277
Joyce Lynn (Reed), 276
Nestor, 276
Nestor Ernesto, 276
Veda (Vela), 276
Hindenburg, Sophia, 155
Hines, Beth (Breneman), 347
Brian Zachary, 348
Clarence, 347
Keith Marshall, 347
Marilyn (—), 347
Rebecca Jo, 348
Hinton, R. J., 91
Hinz, Amanda Mathilda (Schmidt), 242
Elsie, 242
Michael, 242
Hjelmeland, Britha (Instefjord), 217
Sjur Knutsen, 217
Hochreiter, Carol Ann (Urch), 371
Dustin Richard, 371
Richard, 371
Wendi Ann, 371
Hock, Betty, 215
Margaret, 215
Paul, 215
Hockenberry,
Doris A. (Buchanan), 357
John E., 357
Judy Lilith, 357
Hockman, Julia, 408
Hodge, Daniel Robert, 263
Dora, 202
Fred, 202
John Henry, 263
Margaret (Gahagan), 263
Millie (Allen), 202
Neva Angeline (Johnson), 263
Robert Neal, 263
Hofstad, Betty Jane (Schuffenhauer), 311
Bruce Dennis, 311
Cheri Lyn, 311
David, 311
Randy, 311
Hogen, Martin, 86

Holbrook,
Sheila Ann, 429
Holcomb, —, 55
Holden, Beverly Jean (Simmons), 289
Clarence, 223
Eunice (Ramaker), 223
Grant, 289
Mark Wallace, 290
Ronald Wallace, 289
Ronda Jean, 290
Winifred, 223
Holdren, Bob Ray, 335
Wilma Maxine (Jelmeland) (Erickson) (McDonnell), 335
Holland, Amanda, 425
Amy, 426
Brandon, 426
David Leslie, 350, 425
Delores Helen (Peckham), 349
Diane Laurel, 350
Diane Lee (Musgrave), 390
Janet Kay, 349
Johnny (Townsend), 390
Kenneth Paul, 390
Kurt, 425
Lester, 349
Martin, 349
Michael Douglas, 390
Myrtle (Birget), 349
Patsy Lynne, 349, 425
Ramona M. (Gustrowsky), 425
Ronald, 390
Wilford, 390
Holley, Francis, 439
Julia, 439
Margaret (Rado), 439
Hollingsworth, Beulah, 139
Marvin David, 139
Myrtle Dell (Johnson), 139
Hollister, Frances, 48
Lydia, 48
Holloway, Claude S., 327
Joan Barbara, 327
Kathryn (Hensey), 327
Holmberg, Bradley Allan, 340
David Vining, 341
Kristi Vining, 341
Kyle Vining, 341
Nancy Dale (Vining), 340
Holme, Andrea Marie, 349

John, 349
Sonja (Bates), 349
Holmes, Eleanor Louise, 386
Holt, Gladys Otha, 232
Holtan, Alfred, 204
    Bernice, 204
    Minnie, 204
Holtorf, David, 320
    Lenora (Schmidt), 320
    Marcia Jean (Crouch), 320
    Norman, 320
    Renee Marie, 320
Homer, Alan Matthew, 432
    Dee Ann (Haynie), 432
    Matthew Alan, 432
    Patricia Ann (Page), 432
    Richard Leslie, 432
Hommen, Annie (Austin) (Kefer)
    (Vivian), 442
    Henry, 442
Honzu, Alyce Mae, 394
Hooker, Elsie (Rogers), 250
    John, 250
    Julia, 164
    Robert N., 250
Hooper, David, 26
    Lucinda (Peterson), 26
    Nancy, 26
Hopkins, —, 13
Hoppe, Boyd Mark, 224
    Lloyd J., 224
    Maxine Elizabeth (McElroy), 224
Hopper, James, 344
    James D., 344
    Kim Renee, 344
    Marilyn (Stollfus), 344
Horn, Caroline, 267
    Charles L., 267
Horneday, W. T., 40
Hosche, Frederick Elmer, 411
    Patricia, 411
    Rosemary (Spencer), 411
Hoskins, Phoebe (Bailey) (Clarke), 298
    Robert, 298
Hotchkiss, Alta (Rhodes), 96
    Benjamin Vaughn, 96
    Debra Diane, 402
    Gut, 402
    Marguerite, 96
    Marguerite (Purkey), 402

Sarah Ann, 28
Stephen, 28
Tryphena, 28
Houghton, Ann Louise, 212, 327
    Doris Iva (Quick), 212
    James V., 212
    James Vernon, 212
    Jessie Fremont (Sharp), 212
    Lois Jean, 212, 327
    Marian Delores, 212
House, Dulsie Mae (Taylor), 157
    Lysander George, 157
    Mary Ann, 93
    Pearl Eliza (Rhodes), 157
Houska, Darryl Daniel, 396
    Frank, 396
    Isaiah Franklin John, 396
    Lora Jean (Slang), 396
    Megan Jean, 396
    Rose A. (Nemacheck), 396
    Scott Daniel, 396
    Sean James, 396
Houston, Wendy, 361
Howard, Bernice (Roark), 303
    Donna Sue, 303
    Jarvie, 303
Howe, Sarah, 25
Howell, Margarette, 246
Howser, Peggy (Bullock) (Ash), 280
    Stacey, 280
    Steve, 280
Howzdy, Mickey, 387
Hudson, Chrysandra Dell, 315
    Dora Alice, 406
    Frances (Watson), 315
    John, 315
Hughes, Amber Michelle, 382
    Barbara Ann (Layton), 382
    Christopher Shawn, 382
    Edith Evelyn (Foster), 382
    Edna Marie (Vaughn), 382
    Emma, 222
    John, 382
    Linda Susan (Hardt), 382
    Ronald Lee, 382
Huguelet, Mildred, 290
Hulbert, Shirley Eileen, 300
Hull, Nancy Ann, 151
Humrickhouse, Eunice M., 205
Huninston, —, 150

Index

Hunn, Brian, 375
    Joel, 375
    Laura Lucille, 375
    Robert, 375
    Robert Leroy, 375
    Rose Alveretta (Baker), 375
Hunt, Amy, 318
    Bethel June (Daniels), 204
    Blanche (Seefelt), 204
    Christopher, 318
    Diane (Wilson), 317
    Drusilla, 318
    Gary Dean, 204, 318
    Irene (Klebacha), 318
    Jack Reed, 204
    Kathleen Marie, 265
    Orvil, 265
    Ricky Reed, 204, 317
    Sarah, 318
    Smith, 204
    Thadius, 318
    Winifred (Igoe), 265
Huntington, Judith Lynne, 266
    Mildred (Kupke), 266
    Parke Frederick, 266
Hunziker, Sylvia, 413
Hurdle, Robert, 277
Hurlbut, Agnes Martha, 191
    John Clinton, 191
    Mildred Marie (Rice), 191
Huschka, Gertrude, 343
Huston, Alice Melinda (Austin), 38
    Charles Frank, 38
Huth, Beatta, 427
Hutson, John, 38
    Mary, 38
Hyde, Alvin, 21
Hyska, Alphonse, 267
    Clifford Robert, 267
    Diana Lynn, 267, 399
    Lois Elaine (Paulsen), 267
    Maria Ann, 267
    Rosalie (Boulange), 267
Hyslop, Barbara, 366
    Brandie, 430
    Brenda, 366, 430
    Lee, 366
    Mary Layne (Culbert), 366
    Pamela, 366

I

Iglinski, Cecilia, 410
Igoe, Winifred, 265
Ilgen, Carrie (Snook), 213
    Christine (Littleton), 329
    Colin Thomas, 329
    Irene (Quick), 213
    James, 213
    Jane Ellen, 213, 329
    Joe S., 213
    Jonathon Seth, 329
    Thomas Lee, 213, 328
Ingersoll, Alice Ivena (White), 246
    Cindy Lou, 246, 377
    Ilene Ruth, 246
    Joyce Ann, 246, 377
    Kenneth Marland, 246
    Marland Grover, 246
    Nancy Kaye, 246, 377
    Steven Ray, 246
Ingham, Elsie Viola, 299
Ingle, Martha Jane, 173
Instefjord, Britha, 217
Ironima, Cherubina (Fascia), 286
    Nicholas, 286
    Sylvia, 286
Irwin, Genevieve, 138
    Mary (Porter), 138
    William H., 138

J

Jackling, Gertrude, 274
Jackson, Heather Lee, 337
    Henry, 12, 18
    Katherine Marie, 432
    Lorina Emeline, 33
    Ronald, 337
    Royal G., 33
    Shirley Ann (Vining) (Fogner), 337
    Sophie, 33
Jacobi, Barbara, 403
    Muriel, 403
    Robert, 403
Jacobs, Augustus, 82, 84, 85
Jacobson, Cheryl, 321
    Hazel, 194
    Lorraine Elsie (—), 321
    Oral, 321

Jacques, Jesse Myrtle, 165
Jahns, Dennis, 421
    Kiel, 422
    Lorene (—), 421
    Raymond, 421
    Ryan, 422
    Susan (Retzlaff), 421
Jameison, Eva, 292
James, Dava E. (Gibson), 391
    Elizabeth Jo (Peters), 391
    Jesse, 259
    Jesse Curtis Ray, 391
    Jesse Franklin, 259, 391
    Jesse Lee, 259
    June Adeline (Carey), 259
    Maggie (—), 259
    Olympia Laura, 259, 391
    Shilo Christopher, 391
    Woodson Lee, 259, 391
    Zachara Nathan, 391
Jammen, Eddie, 192
    Ralph, 192
    Sadie, 192
    Sandra Joyce (Canfield), 192
Jansen, Frank, 261
    Lois Marie, 261
    Nora (Scheuttpeltz), 261
Jarstad, Ardell, 403
    Caroline (Cibourski), 403
    Donna Rae, 403
Jeffalone, Angelo, 260
    Ann, 260
    James, 260
    Lylis Margaret (Wright), 260
Jefferson, Daniel, 354
    Jesse, 354
    Rebecca Lynn (Peckham), 354
Jelmeland, Amy, 423
    Berger Sjursen, 217
    Bernetta May, 218
    Carie, 423
    Coy, 423
    David, 335, 423
    Donald Kenneth, 218, 335
    Ethel (Jennings), 218, 335
    Harvey Vincent, 218, 335
    Jenny, 423
    La Rae (Rainville), 423
    Lennis Ann (Neinast), 423
    Nettie May (Palmer), 217

    Richard Kenneth, 335, 423
    Vera June (Foster), 335
    Wilma Maxine, 218, 335
Jenkins, Alan Ray, 223, 346
    Alyson (Tasch), 344
    Amber Louise, 347
    Amie Elizabeth, 347
    Barbara, 358
    Barbara Walker), 344
    Benjamin Neal, 344
    Bess, 221
    Beverly Jean, 223, 346
    Brian James, 346
    Carrie Marie, 347
    Cheri Ann, 223
    Cynthia Sue, 222
    Daniel Lee, 346
    Debra (Kaas), 223
    Dennis Lee, 223, 346
    Donald, 148
    Donald Earl, 148, 223
    Donalee Ann, 223
    Douglas Lee, 222, 345
    Edward David, 148
    Elaine Mary, 222
    Gary Lee, 223, 347
    George Ronald, 222
    Gladys Fern, 149
    Gordon Lyle, 222, 344
    Gregory, 344
    Harold Kenneth, 222
    Howard, 222
    James Orris, 222, 344
    Jason Lee, 345
    Jeffery, 344
    Jerry Vern, 223
    Jessica Lynn, 347
    Joseph Alan, 346
    Joshua Donald, 347
    Joshua Lee, 344
    Judith (Morrison), 346
    Justin Lyle, 347
    Karen Jean, 346
    Kathleen (Meyer), 345
    Kathryn Ann, 223
    Kathy (Meyer), 346
    Kenneth Duane, 223, 346
    Kenneth James, 344
    Larry Lynn, 223, 347
    Laura Lorraine, 344

Index 485

Linda Rae, 222, 345
Louise (Dickerson), 347
Lucille Elizabeth, 148, 222
Lucy Jean, 223
Lucy May (McElroy), 148
Mary (McTier), 223
Mary Lois (Cuff), 222
Mary M. (Redeker), 344
Michael Wayne, 223
Monica Marie, 346
Natalie Ruth (Wagner), 222
Nathanial Michael, 347
Neal Edward, 222, 344
Noreen (Sweet), 223
Orris Durwood, 148, 222
Pamela, 344
Patricia (Wehrmann), 346
Paula (Stier), 346
Richard Carl, 346
Ronald Ralph, 148, 222
Russell Earl, 223, 346
Rustin James, 344
Sarah Ann, 345
Sarah Elizabeth (Reynolds), 148
Scott Stephen, 345
Shane Roy, 345
Shannon Carol, 345
Sharon (Terbeest), 345
Sharon Louise, 223
Shawn Ray, 345
Sheila Sue, 345
Stanley William, 148, 222
Stephen Roy, 222, 345
Theresa Rene, 346
Valorie Louise, 345
Vernon Jess, 149, 223
Vivian Carol, 222, 345
William Donald, 222
Winifred (Holden), 223
Jennings, Ethel, 218, 335
    Marie (Hardin), 218, 335
    William, 218, 335
Jensen, Arnold, 389
    Bruce, 389
    Carol Jean (Cox), 389
    Daman, 420
    Edna (Bahrke), 389
    Jens Paeter, 389
    Johanna, 178
    Kara Krista, 389

    Kristina Matia, 389
    Lee Harlene, 420
    Lida Leigh (Lokoen), 420
    Phadrah Rae, 420
    Robert, 420
Jessel, Tekla Frances, 315
Jesusito, Susie, 254
Jezak, Gregory Bernard, 405
    Kevin Gregory, 405
    Sherry Lynn (Reed), 405
    Stephanie Lynn, 405
Jodarski, Margaret Mary, 212
    Martha (Tramph), 212
    Martin, 212
John, David Virgil, 396
Johns, Annette, 182
Johnson, —, 45
    Alfred Willard, 236
    Alice (Szymanski), 262
    Alice May (Bond), 158
    Andrew Edward, 416
    Angeline Irene (Reed), 169
    April, 343
    Audrey Dorothea, 169, 264
    Bertha, 122
    Beverly June, 169, 265
    Bonnie Louise, 262, 393
    Bonnie Sue (Colson), 393
    Brenda K., 369
    Carol Ann (Micelli), 199
    Cecilia Jean, 262, 394
    Charles, 300
    Charles Garth, 282
    Charles J., 122
    Cheryl Rae (Copus), 396
    Clara (Wilson), 416
    Clyde Lyle, 169, 263
    Connie McCoy (Anderson), 393
    Crystal Ann, 199
    Cynthia Marie, 265, 396
    Cynthia S., 136
    Dale Raymond, 169, 266
    Daniel Arling, 265
    Darrell, 372
    David Erik, 396
    David S., 136, 199
    David Virgil, 265
    Dean Patrick, 245
    DeEtta (Hewitt), 97
    Dora Jeanette, 169, 264

Doris, 190
Doris Lilian (Noel), 263
Edith Marie (Reece) (Spratt), 236
Eliza, 168
Ellen, 8, 26, 34
Ellen Louis, 97
Ester, 300
Fay Ann, 263, 394
Florence, 226
Floyd Perry, 97
Frank M., 97
Gary, 263, 394
Geoffrey Garth, 283
Gerald Garth, 282
Gladys, 437
Heidi Elizabeth, 266
Inez, 143
Irma Jean (Everitt), 176
Iver Otto, 158
Jackie Carol, 401
Jeffery Allen, 263
Jenny, 116
Jessica Ann, 416
John C., 169
John Robert, 265
Joshua Wade, 372
Joy Lynn, 382
Judith Lynne (Huntington), 266
Julie Mae, 393
Kara Ann, 393
Karen Kathryn, 262, 394
Karin Marlis (Wackenagel), 394
Karsten Dale, 266
Katherine Christina, 414
Kathy Lynn (Pardini), 372
Kenneth LeRoy, 169, 262
Larry Lars, 262, 393
Lars, 143
Lars Christian, 169, 262
Laurel (Herick), 169
Laurel Gay, 169, 265
Le Anne Michelle, 282
Lenna, 33
Lenna Sherman (Cheeseman), 97
Leota (Wester), 245
Linda, 263, 395
Lisa Marie, 283
Louis F., 136
Louis Frank, 97, 136
Louise, 26, 34
Lyman, 176
Lynn Renea, 245
Mae Carolyn, 169, 263
Marie Alice (Krause), 264
Marilyn, 300
Mark Andrew, 265
Marlene Josephine, 262, 393
Mary (Sorenson), 143
Matthew Ronald, 377
Merlyn John, 393
Merlynn John, 262
Michael Shawn, 416
Morris, 185
Myrtle Dell, 139
Nancy Ann (Ticknor), 282
Neva Angeline, 169, 263
Patricia, 263, 394
Patsy (Beyers), 185
Rebecca, 263
Richard, 316, 401
Richard Lawrence, 307
Ronald, 377
Ronald Eugene, 169, 262
Ruth, 8
Ruth Ann, 158, 245
Ruth Elizabeth, 97
Ruth Elizabeth (Stewart), 136
Sara Ann, 393
Sarah Adell (Evans), 316
Sharon Beth (Kent), 416
Shawn Wesley, 416
Stacey Christa, 316
Tammara Kay (Wester), 377
Timothy James, 393
Valerie, 263
Verna (Bartz), 262
Viola (Charles), 401
Violette Marie (Brewer), 282
Virgil Arling, 169, 264
Wendy Marie, 372
Wesley, 416
Wilhelmina (Grabowski), 262
William Hayes, 416
Wilma Fern, 169, 261
Johnston, Kerry, 349
  Micah, 349
  Robert, 349
  Scott, 349
  Susan (Bates), 349
Johonnot, Ralph, 378

Ralph Helm, 378
Samantha, 378
Terri Ann (Eisenhauer), 378
Jonas, Bertha (Bowery), 301
Bette Eileen (Canfield), 301
David Walter, 302
Homer, 301
Jonathan Robert, 302
Samuel Walter, 301, 302
Jones, Bessie, 201
Margaret, 104
Jonson, Betty Louise (Turner), 307
Jorgensen, Audrey (Harkness), 411
Betty Rae, 184, 292
Bryan Wayne, 292, 411
Cheryl, 292, 412
Chris, 184
Christopher, 292
Curtis, 292, 411
Danielle, 411
Donna (—), 292
Ellen Marinda (Rider), 184
Eric, 411
Irene Lucille (Richardson), 292
John Reed, 292, 411
Joshua Reed, 412
Karen (Nichols), 411
Louise Arlene (Rockafellow), 292
Majel (Gustavison), 292
Mary, 411
Mindy, 411
Patricia (Hosche), 411
Pearl Irene, 184, 291
Reed Carlyle, 184, 292
Robert Stanley, 184, 292
Scott, 411
Sherry Rae, 292, 411
William Bryan, 184
Jozwiak, Frances, 406
Frank, 406
Margaret (Poe), 406
Julian, Carl, 153
Wilda Floy (Roseth), 153
Junk, Margrite, 155

K

Kaas, Debra, 223
Kaczmarowski, Antoinette, 273
Kaiser, Ellen, 322

Zella (Austin) (Kegler), 442
Kaldahl, Clarence, 210
Jesse (Forney), 210
Marjorie Helen, 210
Kalloth, Lorrene, 264
Karasti, Agnes Irene, 267
Karlstad, Anne, 153
Karow, Beverly May (Clark), 235
Ellen (Schultz), 361
Gregory Lee, 235
Joshua Lorence, 361
Lorence Orville, 235, 361
Myrtle, 235
Orville, 235
Richard Clark, 235
Walter, 235
Kasper, Betty, 397
Katzenmeyer, Carole Jane (Peckham), 334
Donald, 334
Jason Curtis, 334
Katherine (Caspers), 334
Kelly Elaine, 335
Kim Elizabeth, 335
Robert Peckman, 335
Kawanabe, Hisayo, 296
Phyllis, 296
Thomas, 296
Keating, Anjelina Michelle, 388
Bruce, 388
Leonard, 388
Lynne Marie (Tognoni), 388
Margaret Theresa (Ekwinski), 388
Xandon Xaviree, 388
Keck, Friederike, 175
Keegan, Sarah, 335
Keenan-O'Keefe,
Beatrice, 440
Kefer, Annie (Austin), 442
Fred, 442
Kegler, Zella (Austin), 442
Keighly, Lilly, 129
Keipper, Margaret Emma, 173
Keithley, Ann Louise (Houghton)
(White), 327
Tom, 327
Kelley, Luana Cecilia America, 122
Melinda Jo (Abel), 374
Thomas Charles, 374
Kellogg, John A., 125

Kelly, Karen Ann, 325
  Leo James, 325
  Marie Ann (Fritz), 325
  Matthew Gregory, 374
  Nicholas Leonard, 374
Kendall, —, 63
  Ashley Rosemary, 305
  Charles Harry, 304
  David Charles, 305
  David Wayne, 304
  Jamie Earl, 305
  Rosemary (Farnsworth), 304
  Sharon Joy (Kennedy), 304
Kennedy, Alta, 28, 94
  Alta Canfield, 7, 31
  Alta May (Canfield), 132
  Amoret Ida, 133
  Benjamin Kevin, 305
  Bonnie Jane, 193
  Brant Dow, 193, 302
  Christine Lee Ann, 302
  Clara (Sherman), 132
  Cynthia Kay, 197, 306
  David Martin, 195, 305
  Delores Maxine (Dean), 303
  Donna Sue (Howard) (Scheeler), 303
  Effie Lou (Wade), 196
  Elaine Joann (Myers), 302
  Eric Paul, 193
  Florence Eliz. Minnie (Baker), 192
  Florence Theresa (Moen), 197
  Francia (—), 305
  Gloria Carolyn (Schanzle), 195
  Gloria Dawn, 195, 304
  Gwen Ann, 197, 306
  Helen Sarah (Peterson), 194
  Hugh Irving, 134, 196
  Hugh Scott, 197
  Jason Neil, 303
  Jessica Marie, 305
  Joyce Elaine, 303
  Julie Lynn, 197, 307
  Justin Peter, 303
  Karen Jean, 194, 303
  Kayla Renee, 305
  Kenneth Scott, 302
  Laurel, 8
  Laurel Nadeen, 133
  Marilyn Naomi (Brown), 303
  Mark William, 193
  Martha Louise, 134, 195
  Mary Jane, 387
  Michael, 132
  Michelle Grace (Fingulin), 305
  Neil Craig, 194, 302
  Neil Dow, 133, 194
  Nora Marie (Crossen), 305
  Roger Belden, 134, 194
  Roger Bruce, 195, 303, 304
  Sharon Joy, 195, 304
  Sherman L., 195
  Sherman Lloyd, 132
  Sherman Walter, 193
  Sherman Wilbur, 133, 192
  Stephen Scott, 195, 305
  Tami Louise, 197, 306
  Tamra Lynn, 304
  Valerie Nicole, 304
  Wilma (Gates), 302
Kent, Carol Ann (Canfield), 301
  Edward, 190
  Edward Arthur, 301
  Gladys, 190
  Sharon Beth, 301, 416
  Susan Maria, 301
  Tiny (Wood), 190
Kepley, Kate, 37
Kerens, Patrick, 59
Kerns, —, 67, 68
Keune, Alberda Lazetta, 140
  Wilberda Lazetta, 140
Kiefer, Fred, 443
  George, 150
  Georgetta, 150
  Nellie (Merrill), 150
Kiesner, Agnes, 392
Kiesschnick, Esther L., 163
Kilbourn, Rita Irene, 416
Killips, Edna, 277
Kilmer, E. J., 61
Kilroy, Gerald, 439
  James, 439, 440
  Joyce, 440
  Lillian (Wadley), 439
  Lynn, 440
  Maureen, 439
Kimball, Ernest, 394
  Kenneth, 394
  Patricia (Johnson), 394
  Ruth (Schemmel), 394

Todd, 394
Ward, 394
Kimble, Josephine (Lichtenberg), 214
   Lois Lorraine, 214
   Merwin, 214
Kindschy, Armin, 375
   Chester Armin, 375
   Christopher Aris, 375
   Curtis Allen, 375
   Donna Marie, 375
   Lorie (Garten), 375
   Ona Marie, 375
   Roger Lee, 375
   Ruth Lucille (Baker), 375
Kinser, Alice, 422
Kirk, Dorcus Marie, 415
Kitzmiller, Andi Bruce, 430
   Jesse Allyn, 430
   Martin Willus, 429
   Shari Lynette (Culbert), 429
Klawitter, Bonita, 330
Klebacha, Blanche (Zavatsky), 318
   Henry, 318
   Irene, 318
Klein, Elsbeth Dorothy, 114
   Emma Mary Annie (Kroeplin), 155
   Harry Frederick, 155
   Henry, 155
   Herman, 114
   Louise (Bahn), 114
   Margrite (Junk), 155
Kleven, Anna, 200
   Matthew, 200
   Myrtle, 200
Klugen, Agatha, 212
Klumb, Jackie, 275
Knapp, Anna Marie, 186
   H. R., 32
Knutson, Cathleen Sarah, 316
   Charles Gary, 316
   Gary, 316
   Sarah Adell (Evans) (Johnson), 316
   Stacey Christa, 316
Koch, Ella Louise, 317
   Jody Lynn, 220
   Joseph August, 220
   Joyce Carol, 220, 340
   Lilas Jane (Vining), 220
   Margaret Ann (Schuth), 220
   Raymond Joseph, 220
   Sheryl Ann, 220, 340
Kocherer, Angela Michelle, 364
   Clarence, 364
   Crystal Lynn, 364
   Dale Arthur, 364
   Myrtle (White), 364
   Sharon Alice (Meeker), 364
Koehler, Patricia Louise (Quick), 213
   Wallace, 213
Koenig, Barbara, 348
   Charles, 348
   Daniel, 349
   David, 348
   Jim, 349
   Judy (Bates), 349
   Julie, 349
   Krissy, 348
   Nancy (Bates), 348
Kohn, Cindy (Antognini), 229
   Terry, 229
Kolberg, Bruce Howard, 335
   Michaela Wynne (McDonnell), 335
Kolisch, Emma, 412
Konen, Betty, 310
   Margaret (Kraft), 310
   Werner, 310
Konop, Anna, 269
Kootaka, Jeanette Carol (Slang), 395
   Sam, 395
   Sanjen Lo'iki Mei Ling Jo Slan, 395
Kopalecki, Stella, 438
Kopp, Edward Dewey, 362
   Kathryn May (Simonson), 362
Koslowski, Carol, 351
Kosmoski, Ben, 392
   Ellen Marie (Vancaster), 392
   Jack, 392
   Steven, 392
Kozar, Susan, 392
Kozou, Mary, 262
Kraft, Margaret, 310
Kralovetz, Gregory Virgil, 264
   Kralovetz, Henry, 264
   Lorrene (Kalloth), 264
Kramer, Mattie, 351
   Rosabell, 156
   Rosilian, 138
Krause, Arthur Gustave, 264
   Elsa Josephine (Eggebrecht), 264
   Marie Alice, 264

Mary Alice, 264
Kreft, Beverly Ann (French), 366
   David, 366
   Ronyle, 366
   Sarah, 367
Kreischer, Florence Margaret, 266
Kretschmer, Jessie Irene (Baker), 381
   Joan Gayle (Perchetti), 381
   Kenneth Lee, 381
   Larci April (Yates), 381
   Roy Allen, 381
   Tamra Gaye, 381, 430
   William Dean, 381
   William George, 381
   William Harvey, 381
Krielcamp, Kathleen, 409
   Robert, 409
   Ruth (Wolf), 409
Kroeplin, Benjamin Jacob, 365
   Bessie May, 237, 364
   Betty (—), 237, 243
   Cindy (Schneider), 365
   Cora Malinda Matilda, 155
   Delano James, 237, 243
   Delia Ann (Abel), 155, 243
   Dorothy Elizabeth (Hadala), 237
   Edna Sophie Ann, 155, 236
   Elmer Thomas John, 155, 237
   Emma Mary Annie, 155
   Esther May (Warner), 237
   Henry, 155, 243
   Henry Albert Neil, 155, 237
   Ilene Joyce (Richardson), 238
   Jason Ernest, 237, 243
   John Louis, 155
   Karen Joyce, 365
   Kevin Elmer, 237
   Leona Marie, 237, 243
   Lorraine (Baker), 237, 243
   Luvern Adelbert, 237, 243
   Margaret Elaine, 238, 365
   Mark William, 237, 243
   Martin Louis, 237, 243
   Mary Elizabeth, 238, 364
   Nathan, 365
   Noel Elizabeth, 365
   Palmer James Louis, 155, 238
   Randy Edward, 237, 244
   Robert Neil, 237, 243
   Roxanne, 365

   Sophia (Hindenburg), 155
   Thomas William, 238, 365
   Timothy Warren, 238, 365
   Violet Louise, 237, 243
   Wendy (Shadis), 365
   William, 243
   William Henry Frederick, 155, 237
Kronschnable, Linda Marie, 324
Krueger, Caroline (Vegue), 274
   Florence, 235
   Geraldine, 274
   Larry, 235
   Linda Diane (Dewsnap), 235
   Martha, 270
   Martin, 274
   Marvin, 235
Krupinski, Darcy (Forbes), 336
   Keith, 336
Kruse, Alicia Orel, 355
   Amanda Christine (Meyer), 230
   Beverly (Beardsley), 355
   Cathy Elizabeth (Comer), 231
   Cynthia (Chico), 427
   David Alan, 231
   Debra Kay, 355
   Henry Herman, 230
   James Wesley, 231, 355
   Janice Marie (Marx), 355
   Kevin Lee, 355, 426
   Kristel Ann, 355, 427
   Kurt William, 355
   Leslie William, 231, 355
   Lisa, 355
   Mark James, 355
   Marvel, 355
   Marvel Gustav, 230
   Marvel Keith, 231, 426
   Michele Dawn, 355
   Nancy Orel, 231
   Orel Luvia (Roseth), 230
   Roxanne (Barnes), 355
   Samantha Lee, 427
   Scott Alan, 355
   Shane Franklin, 355
Kubly, Susan R. (Pogue), 341
   Todd, 341
Kuhl, Brett Lee, 360
   Flynn James, 360
   Lee William, 359
   Peri Anne (Peckham), 359

Kuhn, Aldo, 172
    Norma Mae (Reed) (Siegel), 172
Kuhnast, Vena, 160
Kumhala, James Clifford, 392
    John David, 391
    Lois Ann (Missall), 391
    Richard Jon, 392
Kunz, Bettina, 400
    Crystal (—), 400
    Richard, 400
Kupke, Mildred, 266
Kurnizki, Andrew Paul Dawson, 359
    Anna Sophia, 359
    Kimberly Layne (Dawson), 359
    Vasile, 359
Kutzner, Adolf Anton, 287
    Barbara Kay, 288
    Clifford Henry, 287, 410
    Elizabeth Ann, 288, 410
    Hulda (Hefke), 287
    Jennifer Jean, 288
    Jo-Lynn (Gustavson), 410
    June Rose (Reed), 287
    Katherine Sue, 287, 410
    Paul Herman, 287

L

Lachapelle, Cheryl Lynn (Corn), 400
    Curt, 400
    Teir Rae, 400
Lack, Aaron Isaac, 422
    Harry Lawrence, 422
    Mildred (Sur), 422
    Sue Ellen (Guenchner), 422
LaClair, Loren, 433
    Marilyn (Bliner), 433
    Ralph, 433
    Rhonda Lee (Spaun), 433
    Robert Michele, 433
    William Loren, 433
LaFave, Marie, 402
LaFayette, —, 13
Lagness, David, 284
    Gail Ann (Pack), 284
LaGuire, Rose, 412
Lake, John, 168
    Margaret Eva, 168
    Theresa (Reidenger), 168
Lakemacher, Anola Gayle (Hanson), 369
    Jeffrey J., 369
    Jeremy W., 369
    Justin S., 369
    William G., 369
LaMarche, Delore, 179
    Dora Marie, 179
    Pauline, 179
Lamb, April McCall, 414
    Donald, 414
    Elizabeth Jane (Clarke), 414
    Evelyn (—), 414
    Joseph, 414
Lambert, Opal, 122
Lambright, Casey John, 249
    Nina Noel (Austin), 249
Lampereur, Clifford, 399
    Doris (Amenson), 399
    Susan, 398
Lampland, Emma, 239
    Emma Viola, 239
    Henry, 239
Lampson, Sam'l, 85
Landenberger, Cynthia Marie (Johnson), 396
    Doris Elaine (Merkel), 396
    Lane Gene, 396
    Leonard Walter, 396
    Lisa Marie, 396
Landis, Catherine, 302
    Ida, 176
Landwehr, Jacqueline Ann (Duranso), 434
    Stephanie Ann, 434
    Steven Benjamin, 434
Lane, Clarence, 189
    Eugene Dills, 189
    Eva, 147
    Hazel (Collins), 189
    Janice Lynn, 190
    Joyce Marie, 190, 299
    Marcia Jean, 189, 299
    Thelma Ann (Canfield) (Oatman), 189
    Thelma Canfield Oatman, 299
Langdon, Jeanette, 148
    Mattie, 243
Lange, Ida B. Fobes, 99
Langeland, Bertha Augusta, 350
Langland, Barbara Louise, 339
Largent, Edith Marie, 236

Larivee, Doris, 390
Larsen, Joyce (Lehman), 277
Larson, Lynda, 334
    Sandra Lee, 243
Lasher, Janice Diane, 371
Lawyer, Sonya Ann, 340
Lawton, Ruth, 36
Layer, Dolores, 380
Layton, Barbara Ann, 382
    Delbert Scott, 382
    Joy Lynn (Johnson), 382
Leach, Frances, 37
    Frances Jane, 37
    Hattie M., 98
Leair, Arlene, 285
    Elsie Tunie (Visser), 285
    William Albert, 285
LeBaron, Charles, 174
    V. (Bullock) (Adel) (Snyder), 174
Lee, Bessie (Hansen), 361
    Beverly Ann, 201, 313
    Florence Hazel, 209
    Howard Monroe, 201
    Janet May, 320
    John, 361
    John Donald Hansen, 361
    John William, 362
    Kristin Marie, 362
    Lynn Monroe, 201, 312
    Mildred Adell (Crouch), 201
    Norma Ethel (Dean), 312
    Olga Gamena, 230
    Pamela, 105
    Pamela Louise (Spratt), 361
    Randall Howard, 312
    Ronald Dean, 312
    Rosa Bell (Turley), 201
    W. F., 201
Leese, Pilot, 40
Lefferdink, Gertrude Johanna, 293
Legge, Mary Mundy, 146
LeGrave, Ruth Ann, 275
Lehman, George, 277
    Joyce, 277
    Margaret (Victoor), 277
Leitch, Agnes Newell, 190
Leitha, Doris Evelyn, 245
Lemon, Kimberley Anne, 378
LeNoble, Frances Catherine, 397
Leonard, Hannah, 42

Leseuer, Lillian, 202
Lester, Barbara (Harrington), 390
    Clarence, 258
    Geneva Viola (Beekman), 258
    Grace (Putman), 258
    Joanne (Hanson), 390
    Lawrence Arthur, 258, 390
    Loraine, 258, 389
    Robin, 390
    Russell Milo, 258
    Terry, 390
Lethco, Anona Bell (Garrison), 137
    Paul Bernie, 137
Leverson, Eric Day, 352
    Gudrun Borghild (Hilmoe), 352
    Hartwick Nicholai, 352
    Mary Sue (Day), 352
    Sarah Christine, 352
    Verne Hartwick, 352
Lewis, Harley, 209
    Lois (Mason), 209
    Mary (Barthelow), 209
    Rowena Harlene, 209, 324
    William James, 209
Lichtenberg, Josephine, 214
Light, Clifford, 191
    Mabel Alberta (O'Dell), 191
    Mabel Sarah, 191
    Peggy, 378
Lincicum, Beulah, 343
Lindburg, Beranard Lee, 249
    Donald Maxwell, 249
    Joyce (Austin), 249
    Karen Lynn, 249, 380
    Mabel (Stegeman), 249
    Ronald Lee, 249
    Valan Nicole, 380
Lindell, Lois Ann (McElroy), 224
    Terence, 224
Lindhart, Frances, 139
Lindley, Naida, 413
Link, Charles J., 327
    Doris J., 327
    Lois Jean (Houghton), 327
    Mitzi (Sweet), 327
    Phillip, 327
    Phillip J., 327
    Terry, 327
    Zachary J., 327
Lipton, Arlene (Weise), 330

Index

Ralph, 330
Sandra, 330
Liswoe, Elizabeth, 268
Litrenta, Mary, 277
    Sophie (Romano), 277
    Tony, 277
Littleton, Christine, 329
Lochnew, Wm., 85
Locke, —, 61
Loeper, Ernice, 389
Loewen, Anna Ruth, 207
Loguia, Muriel, 367
Lokoen, Floyd, 324
    Laura Ann, 325
    Lida Leigh, 325, 420
    Lisa Diane, 325
    Rowena Harlene (Lewis), 324
    Rowena Lewis, 420
Long, Annie, 150
    Pansy, 282
Longard, Cleo, 393
Longstreet, —, 58
Looking Elk, Lora (Noble), 379
    Paula Victoria, 379
    Talbert Lloyd, 379
Lopez, Ambrosio Saldana, 432
    Julio James, 432
Lord, Audrey (Everitt), 281
    Mary, 46
    Ray, 281
Lord-Simmons, Linda, 404
Loreno, Josephine, 270
Loring, Patricia, 306
Louis, Bonnie Jane (Barone), 439
    Laura, 439
    Luelle (Avery), 439
    Robert, 439
    Stewart Melvin, 439
    William, 439
Lowell, —, 30, 74
    Abbott Lawrence, 10
    Abigail (Proctor), 10
    Amanda, 17
    Amy, 10, 11
    Asa, 12, 16, 17, 31
    Aurilla, 31
    Aurillo (Cross), 16
    Benjamin, 10, 11
    Benjamin Davis, 17
    Charles, 11
    Ebenezer, 10
    Elizabeth, 10, 16, 17, 19, 20, 21
    Ella Fear, 17
    Francis Cabot, 10
    Hannah, 12
    Hannah (Proctor), 10
    James, 10
    James Russell, 11, 23, 31
    Joan, 9
    John, 9, 10, 11, 15, 16, 17, 20, 21, 22, 31, 126, 127
    John Messer, 7, 9, 12
    John Reed, 18
    Joseph, 10, 11
    Lydia, 12
    Lydia (Messer), 11, 12
    Mary, 10
    Mary (Davis), 11
    Mollie, 12
    Pauline Reed, 17
    Percival, 9, 10, 11, 15
    Peter, 10
    Rebecca, 9
    Rebecca (Tyng), 10
    Reuben, 16
    Richard, 9
    Robert, 126
    Robert Traill Spence, 11
    Ruth, 12, 16
    Ruth (Woodman), 11
    Sarah (Higginson), 10
    Stephen, 11, 12
    Susan, 12
    Susanna (Cabot), 10
    Thomas, 10
Lowle, Richard, 9
    William, 9
Lowry, Irma Belle, 289
Lucas, Hazel, 195
Lueckfeld, Erick Paul, 400
    Kenneth, 400
    Paul, 400
    Raven Star, 400
    Renata (Priez), 400
    Selena (Grignon), 400
Lundy, Douglas, 354
    Karen Joy (Arntz), 354
    Matthew Douglas, 354
Lusardi, — (Scholz), 268
    Matthew, 268

Susie, 268
Lyannas, Eva Lonea, 179
  George, 179
  Mary (Gustag), 179
Lyman, Orrin, 26
Lyon, Lulu, 121
Lyons, Margaret, 409

M

Maack, Hedwig (Sievert), 116
  Henry, 116
  Ida, 116
Maass, Brian Michael, 393
  Johannes, 393
  Marlene Josephine (Johnson), 393
  Sean Bradley, 393
McAtee, Anne (Goodrich), 246
  Christopher Mark, 378
  Daniel Alexander, 246
  Jane (Petty), 247
  John Christopher, 247
  Kimberley Anne (Lemon), 378
  Leon Paul, 247
  Margaret, 247
  Mark Daniel, 247, 378
  Thomas Austin, 247
McBain, Jennie, 192
McBride, Amy Elizabeth (Aldrich), 343
  Patrick, 343
McCarran, Pat, 255
McCarthy, Gerry Ann, 325
  Jerimah, 325
  Mary Ann (McCormick), 325
McCartny, Alice Lois, 363
  Dorothy (Westaky), 363
  Merl, 363
McCellan, Mary Alice, 284
McClenaghan, Donald, 406
  Gertrude Joy (Seabrook), 406
  Jo Lynn (Elkins) (Hamilton)
    (Fenety), 406
  Robert S., 406
McCloskey, Georgia Mae (Quick), 211
  James Wood, 211
  Minnie (Sanderson), 211
  William Herbert, 211
McCloy, Audra Lynn, 364
  Earl Darl, 364
  James William, 364

Lena Ruth Anne, 364
  Mary Elizabeth (Kroeplin), 364
McCormick, Ann Elizabeth, 412
  David, 293, 412
  Donald Albert, 185, 293
  Elizabeth, 185
  Ina Fae (Schneider), 293
  James A., 185
  Laura May, 185
  Mary Ann, 325
  May (Beavert), 185
  Nancy, 293
  Paul William, 412
  Sarah (Bruns), 412
  William, 185
McCowen, Charlotte Ann, 252
  Donna Kay, 252
  Katherine, 252
  Lawrence, 252
  Willetta (Cates), 252
McCullick, Betty Lillian (Martin), 395
  Glenn Wisdom Eldon, 395
  Jason Glenn, 395
  Linda (Johnson), 395
  Max Eldon, 395
  Melanie Mae, 395
McDaniel, —, 160
  Ann (Graber), 247
  Betty Jo, 162, 248
  Danald Robert, 110
  Deborah Jean (Moore), 379
  Essie May, 108
  Frances Roberta, 162, 247
  Frank, 108
  Gertrude, 44, 110
  Gertrude Pauline (Austin), 108
  Harry, 161
  Harry Austin, 107, 110, 159
  Harry Lee, 108
  Henry, 162
  Jamie Lee, 379
  Jay Scott, 247
  Jeffery Lane, 379
  Jennifer Lynn, 379
  Katherine (Thomas), 247
  Leah (Powell), 110
  Lucinda Jean, 247, 379
  Lynsey Jean, 379
  Mabel Margaret, 110, 162
  Margaret Amanda (Barnes), 108

Mattie Enochs (Rawles), 108
Maud (Bright), 107
Maud Bright, 161
Robert Austin, 162
Robert Thomas, 379
Thomas Lane, 247, 379
Vena Margaret, 162
Ward Emery, 162, 247
William Edwin, 108
William Franklin, 108
McDaniels, Gordon, 252
   Willetta (Cates) (McCowen), 252
   William, 109
McDearmon, Dorothy (Haney), 316
   Jeremy Joseph, 317
   Julie Marie, 317
   Kelly Lynn, 317
   Sharon Elizabeth (Evans), 316
   Taft, 316
   William Joseph, 316
McDermott, Mary, 175
McDonald, Angus M., 187
   Elizabeth, 187
   Emily (Yecny), 187
   Pamela, 331
MacDonald, Esther, 306
   Marjorie Jean, 348
McDonnell, James M., 335
   Maynard William, 335
   Michaela Wynne, 335
   Sarah (Keegan), 335
   Wilma Maxine (Jelmeland) (Erickson), 335
McDowell, —, 64
McElroy, —, 103
   Alice Grace, 103, 148
   Ann Eliza (Fuller), 103
   Berwin Ralph, 150, 225
   Boyd Wayne, 149, 223
   Carol Ann, 150, 225
   Donna Kay, 224
   Edith (Rye), 223
   Edna (Fenske), 149
   Edna Joyce, 103
   Elizabeth Ann (Peckham), 103
   Evalyn Elizabeth, 150, 224
   Georgetta (Keifer), 150
   Lois Ann, 224
   Lucy May, 103, 148
   Maxine Elizabeth, 149, 224

Muriel (Comstock), 225
Myrtle Elizabeth, 103
Ralph Donald, 225
Ralph Fay, 103, 150
Steven Edward, 225
Susan Marie, 225
Wanda Elaine, 150, 225
William, 103
William Boyd, 103, 149
William George, 150
William Gerald, 149
William Henry, 103
Winnie Blanche, 103, 149
McFarland, Dean, 321
   Lorraine (—), 321
   Maureen, 321
McGettigan, Amy Elizabeth (Aldrich) (McBride), 343
   Michael, 343
McGoon, Iola (Thibode), 140
   John, 140
   Mildred Mary, 140
MacGowan, Ruth Claire, 296
McIntosh, —, 76
   C. E., 75
McKay, Debra Beth, 192
   Ruth L. (Clemenson), 192
MacKay, Phyllis, 390
   Stanley A., 192
McKee, Justice, 70
McKeig, James, 323
   John D., 323
   Shirley (Phelps), 323
McKittrick, Donna M., 229
   Glen, 229
   Mildred, 229
McKnight, Bonnie Lou, 365
McMannis, Austin Claire, 292
   Colene Ann, 292, 411
   Pearl Irene, 292
   Rosetta (Herrington), 292
   Walter Edgar, 292
McMullen, Gertrude (McNeely), 185
   Laura May (McCormick), 185
   William Henry, 185
McNally, Frances, 413
McNamie, Cleora, 248
McNatt, James, 377
   Jamie Marvin, 377
   Jason Lee, 377

Jodie Ilene, 377
Joshua Andrew, 377
Joyce Ann (Ingersoll), 377
McNeely, Gertrude, 185
McQueen, Bonnie Ester, 385
   Joseph Sidney, 385
   Patricia Linda (Tognoni), 385
   Rebecca Renee, 385
   Ronald Sidney, 385
   Ruth Esther (Ranch), 385
   Sidney Clifford, 385
McTavish, Sara, 226
McTier, Mary, 223
Madden, Donald, 407
   June (Schooltz), 407
   Katherine Marie, 407
Maddox, Kathryn, 389
Madonna, Carmella, 206
Maier, Mary Jane, 180
Main, B. J. (Crouch) (Schoenfelder), 208
   Cleon, 208
   Maybelle Gertrude (Gilmer), 208
   William A., 208
Maldari, Mary, 213
   Pasqualina (D'Agustino), 213
   Philip, 213
Malecki, Cheryl Ann (Gwiazda), 427
   Corey James, 427
   James, 427
   Russell Louis, 427
Malnor, Agnes (Karasti), 267
   Kevin Paul, 267
   Lawrence, 267
   Lisa Ann (Verriden), 267
Manley, Kathy, 311
Manteufel, Meta, 442
Manwarren, Charles, 130, 131
   Lorena (Reed), 130
Marble, Alice Juliet (Cheeseman), 96
   Chauncey, 96
   Clara (Cobb), 96
   Homer, 34
   Homer Wilder, 96
   Junior, 97
   Marguerite (Hotchkiss), 96
   Olive, 96
   Paul, 96
   Warren W., 96
March, Ella Oella (Murphy), 132
   Hulda Oella, 132

James Hiram, 132
Marcy, Bessie Louise, 276
   Cora, 292
Marquette,
   Edwin, 206
   Marie Lois (Crouch), 206
Marring, Donna May, 291
Marsh, Hattie (Dillon), 115
   John H., 115
   Mary Louise, 115
Marshall, —, 293
   Brenda Lee, 301, 416
   Carissa LeRay, 417
   Grace Irene (Fetterely), 301
   Harry William, 301
   Jean Canfield, 416
   Jean Kitty (Canfield), 301
   Joseph, 307
   Julie Lynn (Kennedy), 307
   Lois (Archiald) (Thompson)
      (Raleigh) (Hammerstad) (Tate),
      293
   Milton Eugene, 307
   Nellie (Taylor), 307
   Patti Sue, 301, 416
   Robert Fred, 301, 417
   Sharleen Rae (Rodgers), 417
Martell, Marla, 398
Martin, Adelbert, 36
   Amanda Elizabeth, 36, 100
   Amanda Melissa (Austin), 36
   Bert, 175
   Betty Lillian, 395
   Carroll Lee, 174
   Deborah Denise, 280
   Della, 113
   Della Elsie Berdine (Bullock), 174
   Derick Edward, 440
   Edward, 238
   Ellen M., 36, 99
   Esther M., 36
   Forrest Lee, 175, 280
   Kathleen (O'Neal), 440
   Lansing, 36
   Laurie Michelle, 280
   Lennie Dale, 440
   Loren, 36
   Louise, 175, 280
   Mae, 175
   Marriett, 36

Mary (McDermott), 175
Nyla June, 238
Opaline (Fendley), 280
Phoebe (Fiveash), 174
Virginia, 440
Wesley, 36
William E., 174
Worthy, 36
Marx, Edward, 355
  Elizabeth (—), 355
  Helena, 229
  Janice Marie, 355
Mason, Alicia Marie, 325
  Berkley Alvin, 141
  Cephas James, 326
  Charles R., 107
  Darlene Faye, 210, 325
  Deborah Thais, 326, 421
  Florence Hazel (Lee), 209
  Gerry Ann (McCarthy), 325
  Jeremiah James, 325
  John, 141
  John Gerald, 210, 325, 421
  Karen Ann (Kelly), 325
  Laura Gertrude, 107
  Lida Elizabeth (Osborn), 141
  Lillie (Brouillette), 107
  Lois, 141, 209
  Mary Ann, 325, 421
  Merle, 141
  Myron, 141, 209
  Myrtle (Foote), 141
  Patricia Lee, 325
  Phyllis Marie (Nieto), 325
  Robert Myron, 210, 325
  Rose Ann, 325
  Veronica, 325
Massey, Cheryl Jeannine, 324
Mastenbrook, Gail, 322
Mathers, Doris (Johnson), 190
  Lynette Joan, 190
  William, 190
Mathis, Elizabeth, 164
Matthews, Irene, 363
Mattner, Elenor, 218
Mattoon, Dorothy (Cheeseman), 309
  Dorothy May (Peck), 309
  Dorothy Merle, 309
  Gordon Dayton, 309
  Harry Dayton, 309

  Karen Lynn, 309
  Patricia Ann, 309
  Robert Vaughn, 309
  Roland Harry, 309
Maxwell, Belva, 282
  Omer, 282
  Pansy (Long), 282
Maytum, Crystal, 215
  Lillian Mae (Syferd), 215
  Thelma, 215
  Wellington James, 215
Mazanec, Mary Ann, 398
Meacher, —, 104
Mead, Dorothy Ellen, 191
  Esther Clara (Northrup), 191
  Lloyd James, 191
Meadows, Bernadine, 827
Meeker, Alice Lois (McCartny), 363
  Betty June, 202, 314
  Candy (Biddle), 363
  Cecil Emmett, 236
  Charles, 202
  Chester Eugene, 237, 363
  Chester Kenneth, 202
  Darlene Ruth (Gerky), 363
  Deanne Marie, 363
  Debbie Ann, 363, 428
  Dora (Pearson), 202
  Edna Sophie Ann (Kroeplin), 236
  Elsie May (Parker), 236
  Ethel Ann (Draeger), 363
  George Allen, 363
  George Anthony, 236
  George Henry, 236, 363
  Irene Ann (Fate), 363
  Jeffrey John, 363
  Joseph Michael, 363
  Josephine Penny, 363
  Judith Ann, 237, 364
  LaDonna Bea, 363, 428
  Lester David, 237, 363, 364
  Marvin Cecil, 236, 363
  Mary Colleen, 315
  Myrtle Adell (Garrison), 202
  Nancy Elizabeth, 364
  Rose Blanche, 236, 362
  Sabrina Louise, 363
  Samuel Marvin, 363
  Sandra Louise (Turner), 363
  Sharon Alice, 237, 364

Sharon Lee (Myers), 363
Susan Kay, 363, 429
Trinity Eric, 363
Waneta Beth, 236, 362
Meeks, Arthur, 242
Esther, 242
Ruth, 242
Mefford, Dawn, 399
Donald, 399
John Devlin, 399
Karen Marie (Verriden), 399
Mary (Devlin), 399
Mehaffey, —, 160, 162
Meiller, April (Johnson), 343
Arthur, 342
Brian, 343
Dolores Janette (Dalton), 342
Lillian (Bruce), 342
Mary (Galer), 343
Ricky L., 343
Wayne, 342
Melby, Jennifer Maytum (Peckham), 332
Ruth (—), 332
Todd Leslie, 332
Tom, 332
Meligan, Mildred Marie, 384
Mendez, Amanda Lynn, 385
Anthony Tobias, 385
Antonio Joseph, 254, 385
Cindy Jill, 254, 386
Damon Miguel, 386
Derek Jonathan, 386
Edith Holmes (Prentice), 386
Ian Archer, 385
Joey Ann, 254, 385
John Frank, 254, 385
John George, 254
Joseph Navarro, 254
Karen (Smith), 385
Neva June (Tognoni), 254
Mentch, Blanche, 177
Mentink, Eric, 429
Susan Kay (Meeker), 429
Travis Eric, 429
Mentz, Gilbert Michael, 284
Mary, 284, 405
Matilda (Hanson), 284
Michael, 284
Ruth, 7
Ruth Elizabeth (Reed), 284

Mercer, Olga Marie, 362
Richard, 12
Sharon, 362
Merkel, Doris Elaine, 396
Merker, Audrey Lenore (Becker), 420
Bernard, 420
Melody Ann (Breit) (Brunswick), 420
Steve Lee, 420
Merrill, Nellie, 150
Mershom, Lorilla, 37
Mershon, Clarissa, 37
Theron, 37
Mertens, Anna, 179
Merwyn, David, 374
Faye Etta (Baker), 374
Gary Robert, 374
Robert, 374
Messer, John, 11
Lydia, 11, 12
Sarah (Barker), 11
Metcalf, Grace, 196
Meyer, Amanda Christine, 230
Andrea, 361
Derek, 361
Herbert, 361
Kathleen, 345
Kathy, 346
Marsha, 353
Nancy Marie (Audiss), 361
Richard, 361
Viva (—), 361
Meyers, —, 96
Alice Juliet, 96
Carrie (Cheeseman), 95
Will, 95
William, 95
Williams, 96
Micelli, Carol Ann, 199
Michael, Chris, 379
Pamela, 379
Sharon (Beede), 379
Michaelsen, Caroline (Nielsen), 147
Gertrude, 147
Hans J., 147
Michelson, Curtis Allen, 430
Dale, 430
Denise Margaret (French), 430
Michelstetter,
Wm., 56
Miles, Bernice Vernetta (Roberts), 148

Index

Jaxon, 148
Miller, Alice Sylvia, 211
  Allen, 269
  Anna (Konop), 269
  Bernard, 224
  Brenda (Riehl), 399
  Bruce Allan, 269, 399
  Cameron Scott, 399
  Charles E., 342
  Cheryl (Jacobson), 321
  Christopher Douglas, 321
  Doris Geneil, 252, 383
  Ethel, 218
  Evalyn Elizabeth (McElroy), 224
  Flora Bell, 144
  Gary Ralph, 224
  Gloria Jean, 252, 383
  Gordon Ralph, 206
  Heidi, 342
  Janice (Roberts), 342
  Jasmine Elizabeth, 321
  Jeffery, 342
  John Edward, 211
  Judy Kay, 252, 383
  Kathleen Evalyn, 225
  Kenneth Gordon, 206
  Lillian Maria (Watson), 211
  Lisa, 269
  Lloyd, 224
  Louie, 252
  Maureen (McFarland), 321
  Nathan James, 399
  Nellie Elizabeth (Proper), 206
  Nina Sue, 225
  Norma Jean (Reed), 269
  Pamela Ruth, 206, 321
  Ralph Vernon, 206
  Ruth Mildred (Crouch), 206
  Steven Douglas, 206, 321
  Sylvia Joy (Cates), 252
  Viola Marie, 204
  Walter H., 269
Mills, Florence M., 118
  Harriet (Helson), 118
  R. Frank, 118
Minor, Anthony Lee, 407
  Carla Marie (Willoughby), 409
  Christopher, 407
  Cindy (Castle), 408
  Corrie Ann, 409
  Darlene Margaret, 286, 408
  Donald Gerard, 286, 408
  Donna Marie, 286, 408
  Douglas Allen, 286, 408
  Dyanne Patricia, 286, 408
  Frances (Jozwiak), 406
  Gerald, 407
  Gerald Anthony, 286, 406
  Jennifer, 407
  Jessica Marie, 407
  John Thomas, 286, 409
  Joseph Michael, 407
  Julie Kristin, 409
  Justin Thomas, 407
  Katherine Marie (Madden), 407
  Linda (—), 408
  Margaret (Murphy), 285
  Marilyn (White), 407
  Mary Ann, 286, 407
  Michael, 407
  Michael Herbert, 286, 407
  Pamela (Weber), 286
  Pamela Ann (Day), 407
  Richard Charles, 286
  Robert, 408
  Roxanne Louise (Blackstone), 407
  Spring Marie, 408
  Tammy Ann, 406
  Thomas, 285
  Thomas John, 286, 406
  Timothy James, 406
  Virginia Charlotte (Minor), 285
  Virginia Reed, 406, 408
  William David, 286, 407
Misner, Fern (Rose) (Dick), 297
  Jill, 297
  William, 297
Missall, Alvina (Robenhorst), 260
  Clarence Eva (Wright), 260
  Clifford William, 260
  Dennis John, 260
  Dion John, 392
  Jean Marie, 260
  Kristi Lynn, 392
  Lois Ann, 260, 391
  Otto, 260
Missell, Peggy Jean (Weber), 260
Mitchell, Caitlin Patricia, 359
  Cameron Paddock, 359
  Elizabeth Jane (Peckham), 234

Lashelli Sue, 340
Mark Steven, 234, 359
Matthew Brant, 234
Pamela Ann, 234, 359
Robert Laverne, 234
Sonya Ann (Lawyer), 340
Susan Sanborn (Paddock), 359
Tamara Allyson, 234
William L'Dell, 340
Modgner, Barbara Ann (Visser), 275
Modrell, Ida Edna, 177
    Moen, Borghild Nicholina (Nelson), 197
    Florence Theresa, 197
    Olaf, 197
Mohr, Helen (—), 347
    Merlyn, 347
    Sandra Jean, 347
Molgner, Bob, 275
    Craig, 275
    Sandra Jane (Siegel), 275
    Steven, 275
    Troy, 275
Monroe, Lizzie, 38
Montgomery,
    Florence Helen, 295
    Mary Katherine, 401
Montoya, Davida Marie (Fogner), 424
    Gloria Jean (Miller) (Beckwith) (Roberts), 383
    John, 424
    Rudy, 383
Monty, Ruth, 408
Moore, Ava, 293
    Beulah (Lincicum), 343
    Dale, 343
    Deborah Jean, 379
    Earl, 281
    Earlyne, 281
    Harold, 379
    Martha (Penley), 281
    Nola, 343
    Shirley (—), 379
More, Angela Joy, 340
    Charles Robert, 340
    Donna, 314
    Joyce Carol (Koch), 340
    Kelly Rae, 340
    Lucille (Vaughn), 314
    Thomas Charles, 340

    Verne, 314
Morehead, Alene Eleanor (Taylor), 181
    Brenda Gail (Grant), 290
    Bruce Bennington, 181
    Bruce Reed, 182
    Charles Francis, 181
    Clayton Bennington, 290
    Ernest Lee, 182, 290
    Vivian Medora (Reed), 181
    Wesley Lebaron, 290
Morehouse, Anna Augusta, 132
Moreland, Caroline Almira (Gilbert), 139
    John William, 139
Morey, Harry, 412
    June, 412
    Wilma (Bilsby), 412
Morris, —, 76
    Dorothy Elizabeth, 193
    Joyce Ann (Reed) (Elkins), 285
    Mary Evaline (Witcher), 285
    Orville, 285
    Sylvia, 298
    William Newton, 285
    William Reed, 285
Morrison, Judith, 346
    Morrone, Bridget Mary (Schoenfelder), 323
    Rossi, 323
    Seamus Rosario, 323
    Sean Rossi, 323
Mortensen, Doris Virginia, 232
    Jack, 232
    Muriel (Noonan), 232
Morton, Betsy, 45
    Gad W., 45
    Martha J., 45
Mortuary, Martin, 250
Mosley, Myrtle Adelia, 259
Mote, Nathan Scott, 307
    Sarah Elizabeth, 307
    Scott Leslie, 307
    Tami Louise (Kennedy), 307
Moxness, Mary Jo, 426
Moyer, Daniel Norman, 417
    Mary (—), 416
    Melissa Sue, 416
    Norman, 416
    Patti Sue (Marshall), 416
    Peggy, 313
    Scott Douglas, 416

Susan Elizabeth, 416
Tamera Myra, 417
Mudge, Mabel, 292
Mueller, Amy Lynn, 400
  Blake Irwin, 400
  Cory Robert, 270
  Doris (Buhrandt), 270, 399
  Irvin, 399
  Lacey Nicole, 270
  Laurie June (Corn), 399
  Lorna Foy (Reed), 270
  Nick, 101
  Russell, 270
  Ryan Russell, 270
  Walter, 270, 399
Muldowney, Margaret, 438
Mulone, Anthony, 310
  Anthony F., 309
  Carol Edna (Cheeseman), 309
  Frank, 309
  Linda, 310
  Teresa, 309
Munson, Bill, 151
  Goldie (Bates), 151
  Greta (Bates), 151
  Justin Scott, 151
Murphy, Anna May, 298
  Cathy, 388
  Ellen Oella, 132
Margaret, 285
Musgrave, Brady Alexander, 390
  Charles Anthony, 258, 390
  Charles Brady, 258
  Christopher, 390
  Clarence Arthur, 258
  Diane Lee, 258, 390
  Mary Caroline (Wennell), 258
  Robbin (Scharmag), 390
  Versa (Barker), 258
Musolf, Clara (Tweton), 310
  Hans, 310
  Harry, 310
  Karlene, 419
  Kimberly, 419
  Norma Ruth (Wiedendorf), 310
  Ronald Richard, 310, 419
  Sandra (Yentsch), 419
Myers, Catherine (Landis), 302
  Elaine Joann, 302
  Sharon Lee, 363

Wilford Leon, 302
Myszkewicz, Arthur, 408
  Donna Marie (Minor), 408
  Joseph, 408
  Julia (Hockman), 408
  Kenneth Joseph, 408
  Mark Philip, 408

N

Nagel, Jacob F., 281
  Lera Jean (Foster), 281
  Lori Jean, 281
  Paul, 281
  Sara W. (VanWinkle), 281
  Steven, 281
Name, Artie, 172
  Nappo, Gwendolyn (Fogner), 337
  Paul, 337
Nardiello, Cynthia Lee, 271
  Fiona (Skinner), 270
  Frank, 270
  Frank Nicholas, 270
  Josephine (Loreno), 270
  Nicholas, 270
  Renee Jean, 271
  Vivian Ann (Reed), 270
Nasby, Serena, 216
Nave, James David, 293
  Nancy (McCormick), 293
Naylor, Brett, 370
  Evan Lynette (French), 370
  Justina, 370
Nehring, Bertha, 221
Neiliert, Amber Nicole, 326
  Kevin, 326
  Lora Marie (Walenga), 326
Neinast, Harold, 423
  Lennis Ann, 423
  Marie (Woombill), 423
Nelessen, Jane, 397
  Marion (Hendricks), 398
  Robert, 398
Nelson, Beth (Abel), 157
  Betty (—), 360
  Borghild Nicholina, 197
  Cindy, 322
  Cory, 339
  Glen, 339
  Jamie, 339

Layton, 360
Linda (Vining), 339
Matthew, 339
Robert, 157
Susan, 360
Tena, 244
Nemacheck, Rose A., 396
Neppl, RoniJo, 321
Nesbitt, Betty Jean (Hathorn) (Baal), 332
   W. H., 332
Ness, Barbara (Schroeder), 404
   Jodenne Kay, 404
   John, 404
Nestle, Ben Heath, 412
   Benjamin, 292
   Betty Rae (Jorgensen), 292
   Carl, 293, 412
   Constance Ellen, 292, 412
   Heather Rae, 412
   June(Morey), 412
   Mabel (Mudge), 292
Neudeck, Eva (Carey), 254
   George-Ann, 254, 255
   Louis Merrill, 254
Neuens, Amy Lynn, 276
   Linda June (Hawkins), 276
   Maxine (Bouressa), 276
   Nicole Ruth, 276
   Peter, 276
   Randall Gordon, 276
   Robb Randall, 276
Neumann, Carol (—), 332
   Paula Eileen, 332
   William, 332
Neva, Ruth (Reed) (Prothero), 277
Neve, Fred, 277
Newby, Hearn, 313
   Janice Adell (Crouch) (Ferrell, 313
   Kevin, 313
Newcomb, Betty Jo, 137
   Dolores, 137
Hazel Delight, 202
   Lois, 137
Newman, Amanda, 120
Newsome, Elia Leigh, 216
Nichols, Charles Oscar, 226
   John Henry, 226
   Karen, 411
   Luvia I. (Chowen) (Williamson), 225
   Sara (McTavish), 226

Nicholson, —, 187
   Gladys P. (Baurer) (Weston), 187
Nickle, George, 188
   Leota, 80
   Leota Lorraine (Plasteur), 188
   Martha Jane (Stanton), 188
   Nellie Sarmia (Harrison), 188
   Penelope Lee, 188, 296
   Stanton Alexander, 188
   Stanton Harrison, 188
Niebaum, Ellen Eliz. (Quick) (Brown), 212
   Herman, 212
Nielsen, Caroline, 147
   Kirsten, 158
Nieto, Phyllis Marie, 325
   Raymunda (Hernandez), 326
   Simon Cantu, 325
Niman, Doris Geneil (Miller), 383
   Duane Lee, 383
   Nicci Lin, 383
   Ronald, 383
Nissen, Christene, 258
Nitzband, Matilda, 170
Noble, Bess (Jenkins), 221
   Carlton, 221
   Christopher Scott, 378
   Frances Roberta (McDaniel), 247
   Grant Lee, 247, 378
   Harold, 247
   Lila Jean, 247, 378
   Lora, 247, 379
   Patricia Ann (Risor), 247
   Rhonda Lynn (Denny), 378
   Russell Eugene, 247
   Verna, 221
Noel, Doris Lilian, 263
   Mae (VerBunker), 263
   Wilfred, 263
Nold, Cindy Lou (Ingersoll), 377
   Edward, 377
   John Edward, 377
Nolen, James, 85
Noonan, Muriel, 232
Norburg, Dennis, 220
   Laurie (Vining), 220
Nordstrom, Hazel, 138
Norling, Ada, 163
Norman, Lucille, 248
Norris, Alice (Kinser), 422

Charity Grace, 422
Henry Brantley, 422
Jacob, 422
Leah Beth, 422
Ruth Ellen, 422
Sue Ellen (Guenchner) (Lack), 422
Tony, 422
North, —, 18
Northrup, Esther Clara, 191
Nuthals, Bernard, 267
Karen, 267
Millie (Bissick), 267
Nygard, Delores, 174, 278
Ruby Blanche (Reed), 173
Victor, 173
Wayne John, 173

O

Oatman, Emma, 219
Kenneth Newell, 189
Mabel, 189
Newell, 189
Roger Kevin, 299
Roger Newell, 189, 299
Shirley (Eckard), 299
Thelma Ann (Canfield), 189
O'Connell, J. D., 59
John D., 62
O'Connor, Arlene (—), 318
Betty Jane, 294
Daniel K., 294
David, 318
Joshua, 318
Kathryn (Crouch), 318
Margaret A., 294
Steven, 318
O'Dell, Mabel Alberta, 191
O'Donnell, Anthony James, 358
Carolyn Jeanne (Wiley), 358
Dianne, 233, 358
Vashti Rose, 359
O'Downally, Helen Beatrice, 439
Oftedall, Amanda E., 243
O'Konek, Judy, 316
Olick, Emil, 263
Mae Carolyn (Johnson), 263
Pamela, 264, 395
Randall, 264
Virgil, 263

Olinyk, Davida Marie (Fogner) (Montoya), 424
Greg, 424
Oliver Z., 424
Oliver, Joan (Lowell), 9
John, 9
Olm, Bill, 422
Dianna Marie (Retzlaff), 422
Kay (—), 422
Steve, 422
William, 422
Olmsted, Elsie Viola (Ingham), 299
George LeRoy, 299
Joyce Marie (Lane) (DiSalvo), 299
Robert C., 299
Olsen, Barbara Joanne, 217, 334
Bette, 228
Chris, 216
Christopher Reed, 334
David Peckham, 217, 334
Dean Stanton, 216, 334
Elaine (Gudmondson), 265
Emma Pernilla, 152
Francis R., 216
Jeffrey David, 334
Jennifer Lyn, 334
Judy (Thompson), 334
Kjersti, 152
LaVerne, 265
Lynda (Larson), 334
Michael James, 265
Norma Florence (Peckham), 216
Otto Gottlieb, 228
Peter, 152
Rebecca Ann, 334
Rika Sophia (Tvite or Twite), 228
Serena (Nasby), 216
Wendy Elizabeth, 334
Olson, Ada (Norling), 163
Dianne (Rathgeber), 163
Eleanor, 327
Eva (Ash), 153
Evelyn Lenoi, 153
James Bertil, 163
Jeanette, 311
John B., 163
Joseph, 311
Lurene (Ellingboe), 311
Marcell R., 163
Marjorie Ruth (Austin), 163

Ole, 153
Verner, 163
O'Neal, Edward Kyle, 439
   Edward Paul, 439
   Helen Beatrice (O'Downally), 439
   Helen Margaret (Barone), 439
   Karleen, 439
   Kathleen, 439, 440
O'Neil, Kathy, 404
   Sam'l, 86
Onesti, Carl John, 266
   Florence Margaret (Kreischer), 266
   Gregory John, 266
   Lisa Nageline (Arneson), 265
Onley, Mary E., 105
Operman, Joyce, 400
Orlando, Paul, 171
   Virginia (Reed), 171
Oros, Irene, 413
Orr, Claude, 146
   Helen (Ryburn), 146
Osborn, — (Caukins), 99
   Abraham, 99
   Bida Bell, 99, 141
   Daisie (Prall), 140
   Earl, 141
   Emma A. (Crouch), 99
   Emma Angeline, 99, 141
   Henry A., 99
   Lida Elizabeth, 99, 141
   Wilie L., 99
   William, 141
   William Edgar, 99
   William L., 140
Owes, Erin Elizabeth, 378
   Lila Jean (Noble), 378
   Ronald J., 378

P

Pack, Barbara Kathelene (Sweeney), 284
   Charles M., 178
   Gail Ann, 284
   Grace (Ferrill), 284
   Harold L., 178
   Harold Laurence, 284
   Harold Lloyd, 178, 284
   Karen, 405
   Kathy (O'Neil), 404
   Mary Alice, 284

   Mary Alice(McCellan), 284
   Pearl Eunice (Reed) (Sones), 178
   Rhonda Marie, 284
   Terry Lynn, 284
   Thomas, 178
   Thomas Alexander, 284, 404
Paddock, Susan Sanborn, 359
Padgett, Andrea Lynn, 352
   Carol Diane (Crouch), 205
   Clarence, 352
   Jean (Shelp), 352
   Neta (Westendorf), 352
   Robert Kenneth, 205
   Terry, 352
   Timothy, 352
Page, Juanita May, 294
   Patricia Ann, 432
Painter, Bennett, 322
   Carolyn Elaine (Gay), 322
   Matthew Seth, 322
Paioni, Betty Mae (Quick), 326
   Brandon, 421
   Charles H., 326
   Darrell Edwin, 326, 421
   Denise (Salo), 421
   Dwayne Charles, 326
   Jessica Ann, 421
   Roe, 326
   Rose (Sqhezia), 326
Palluck, Bernie, 354
   Marie (Peckham), 354
   Samantha, 354
   Tony, 354
Palmer, Allie (Rieken), 209
   Benjamin, 146
   Benjamin Wade, 146
   Chester, 147, 218
   Cleo Patra Eloise (Plasteur), 129
   Clinton (Red) Orwin, 141
   Clinton Owen, 209
   Dale, 209, 324
   Eliza Jane (Cowley), 146
   Emma Angeline (Osborn), 141
   Ethel (Miller), 218
   Eva Reed, 141, 208
   Herbert, 129
   Howard, 388
   Jason Owen, 324
   Jeremy Alan, 324
   Laura May, 146

Index 505

Laura May (Vining), 146
Leola (Duke), 388
Linda Marie (Kronschnable), 324
Marian Nadean, 141, 208
Marilyn, 218, 388
Nancy, 209, 324
Nettie May, 146, 217
Owen Leon, 141
William, 146
Palochuk, Mary, 348
Pardini, Alice (Abel), 241
    Amanda Rose, 372
    Debbie Haggerman (Turner), 372
    Guisippie (Joe), 241
    Imo, 241
    Isolina (Giannoni), 241
    Karen Marie, 242, 372
    Kathy Lynn, 242, 372
    Keith Thomas, 242, 372
    Phillip Haggerman, 372
Parker, Elsie May, 236
Parks, Glenn, 419
    Jennie, 435
    Rosean Marie (Wiedendorf), 419
    Rowena (Rugh), 435
    Warren, 435
Patchett, Alice, 100
    Amanda, 100
    Amanda Maude (Clark), 143
    Clarence H., 143
    Clarence Maude, 100
    Donald, 143
    Earl, 143
    Eleanor, 143
    Frank, 143
    George Leroy, 100, 143
    John, 100, 143
    Julia (Sear), 100, 143
    Ruth Mae (Clark), 143
Patterson, Henry H., 86
Patton, Gail Marie (Theien), 376
    Mike, 376
Paul, Sarah, 203
Paulsen, Beverly (Petrie), 398
    Caroline (Horn), 267
    Carrie Lynn, 398
    Christopher, 170
    Christopher Harold, 267
    Eugene, 398
    Harold R., 170, 267

Janet Marie (VerVooren), 398
Jed Roy, 398
June Ione, 170, 267
Lena (Christiansen), 170
Lois Elaine, 170, 267
Marla (Martell), 398
Randall Roy, 267, 398
Roy, 170
Scott, 267, 398
Verna (Verwey), 170
Peacha, Irene, 186
Pearson, Dora, 202
    Lois (Archibald) (Thompson)
        (Raleigh) (Hammerstad), 293
    Palmer, 293
Peck, Dorothy May, 309
    Sol, 49, 50
Peckham, Aaron Kenneth, 23
    Abigail (Waite), 104
    Adam Paul, 333
    Almira Bray (Staves), 100
    Anne Christine, 333, 423
    Anne Rosella, 151, 227
    Anthony James, 233
    Areta Virginia (Caldwell), 228
    Audrey Susan, 228
    Barbara Lee, 217
    Beatrice Marguerite, 144, 214
    Benjamin James, 233
    Bert, 101
    Beth Ann, 333
    Bette (Olsen), 228
    Bette Lorraine (Graves), 350
    Beulah M. (Arneson), 217
    Beverly May, 154
    Bradley Rex, 350
    Brett Michael, 350
    Carol M., 154
    Carole Jane, 217, 334
    Charles Herbert, 101, 144
    Charles W., 152
    Charles Wesley, 37, 103, 104, 154, 234
    Cheryl Lynn, 350, 426
    Christopher Reed, 353
    Cindy, 230, 354
    Clarabelle Margaret (Goebel), 332
    Clayton Maurice, 152, 229
    Crystal (Maytum), 215
    Dale, 230

Daniel Jonathan, 233
Daniel Phillip, 332
Darla Dean, 354
Darwin Dennis, 229, 353
Daryl Dean, 229
David, 230
David Andrew, 423
David Ellsworth, 332
David Elwyn, 233
Dean, 333
Dean Aaron, 332
Deanna, 333
Delores Helen, 226, 349
Dennis James, 354
Diana, 230, 354
Dianne (O'Donnell), 233
Dolores (Pederson), 333
Donald Dean, 216, 333
Donald Orville, 226, 350
Donald Seth, 145, 215, 333
Donna Jean, 154, 233
Donna M. (McKittrick), 229
Douglas, 230
Douglas Jesse, 230
Edith May, 101, 145
Edna Pearl, 104, 150
Elizabeth, 37, 104
Elizabeth Ann, 103
Elizabeth Jane, 154, 234
Elizabeth Jane (Smith), 103
Ellsworth L., 145, 215
Elwyn Kay, 154, 233
Emma Pernilla (Olsen), 152
Erin Christine, 359
Evelyn Lenoi (Olson), 153
Fern Isabelle, 152, 229
Flora Bell (Miller), 144
Florence W. (Durkee), 145
Floy Valanda, 104, 153
Francis Herbert, 145, 217
Frank Durward, 101, 145
Gene Ralph, 151, 228
Geraldine (Sanders), 227
Gertrude Anne (Aker), 333
Gertrude Primrose, 104, 152
Gladys (Watson), 152
Gladys Evelyn (Randall), 246
Grace Elizabeth, 151, 226
Harold, 152
Harold S., 104

Harriet, 145, 215
Harriet (Rednik), 144
Hazel Viola, 151, 227
Hilda (Schumacher), 333
Howard John, 145, 216, 333
Ida Maude, 101
Irwina (Wahl), 226
J. E., 100
Jacqueline (Urdahl), 230
James, 152, 230
James John, 332
James Maytum, 216, 333
Janelle Marie, 351
Janet May, 216, 333
Jean Carolyn, 226, 350
Jean Elizabeth (Ross), 332
Jennifer Maytum, 332
Jesse Lawton, 104
Jesse Vernon, 152, 229
Joan Elaine, 217
John Eber, 36, 100
John Richard, 215, 332
John Wallace, 101, 144
June Barbara (Henry), 235
Kathryn Leigh, 216
Kay Lynn, 227
Keith, 227
Kenneth, 227, 233
Kenneth Eric, 234
Kenneth Nathan, 151, 227
Kirk Andrew, 234
Kristi Kae, 350
Lane Ray, 350
Leigh Anna, 351
Leith James, 144
Lela Eldora, 104, 154
Linda, 230, 355
Lisa Kay, 350, 426
Lucretia M., 37, 102
Marcella (Hess), 230
Marcus John, 332
Margaret, 228
Marie, 230, 354
Marie Caroline (Bakken), 151
Marjorie May, 152
Marlene Carole (Blow), 351
Marsha (Meyer), 353
Mary Ann (Hall), 353
Mary Elia, 216, 333
Mary Ina, 104

Mary Kathryn, 333
Mary Kathryn (Price), 216
Mary Louise (Galewski), 423
Mary Margaret, 228
Mary Sue, 246
Matthew, 228, 353
Maude Susan, 104, 151
Melinda Ann, 353
Merlyn Clyde, 236
Merlyn Emery, 154, 235
Michelle Cecile, 332
Minerva (Austin), 36
Morris William, 154
Myrtle Ann, 102
Nancy Ann, 216
Nettie (Hanslin), 154
Norma Elaine, 154
Norma Florence, 145, 216
Orrie, 104
Orville Charles, 151, 226
Orville Kenneth, 104, 153
Patty, 227
Paula Eileen (Neumann), 332
Peleg Lawton, 36
Percy Donald, 151, 228
Peri Anne, 234, 359
Phillip Durward, 215, 332
Ralph William, 246
Raymond Charles, 104
Rebecca Lynn, 229, 354
Rex Maynard, 226, 350
Richard, 230
Rilla Margaret (Hanson), 228
Robert, 152, 230
Robert Frank, 217
Ronnie Kirk, 228
Ruth (Lawton), 36
Ruth Marie, 151, 228
Sally Ann, 228
Samuel Charles, 233, 359
Sandra (Thompson), 350
Sandra Lee (Gutzmann), 332
Sara, 228
Sarah Jeanette (Dobson), 144
Scott Allen, 333
Scott David, 423
Shirley (—), 333
Sibil, 101
Stephen, 36
Steve, 333

Steven Louise, 332
Steven Wayne, 351
Sybil (Vickers), 144
Teresa Ann (Dominquez), 359
Thelma (Maytum), 215
Thomas, 228
Thomas Arthur, 228
Thomas John, 333
Thomas Ralph, 104, 151
Timothy Joseph, 332, 423
Vance Lester, 350
Vera Etta (Roth), 229
Vicki Lee, 350, 426
Vicki Renee, 229, 354
Vieva May, 104
Virginia Cleone, 152, 230
Walter Eugene, 102
Wayne Russell, 226, 351
Wendy Jeanne, 350
William Emery, 104, 154
William Eugene, 101
William Harrison, 37, 104
Yvonne (Speer), 234
Pedersen, Anne Elizabeth (Vining), 220
  Dolores, 333
  Nathaniel, 220
Pederson, Gloria, 351
  Henry, 351
  Mabel (Anderson), 351
Penke, Linda Rae (Jenkins), 345
  Michael Ray, 345
  Norman, 345
  Sandra Rae, 345
Penley, Martha, 281
Pepe, David, 446
Pepin, Aaron, 244
  Claudia L. (Baker), 244
  Edward, 244
  Janice, 244
  Karen, 244
  Nina, 244
Percha, Claudine Lee, 385
  Frank, 385
  Irene (—), 385
  Joey Ann (Mendez), 385
  Julie Irene, 385
  Laurie Neva, 385
  Marvin Arnold, 385
  Michelle Marie, 385
  Perfidia Loretta, 385

Perchett, Donald A., 250
Perchetti, Joan Gayle, 250, 381
   Joseph Anthony, 250
   Lucy Margaret (Cates), 250
   Mary Louise (Boot), 250
Perkins, Dorothy, 289
Perrault, Veronica Mary, 283
Perry, Kenneth, 212
   Ronnie, 212
   Vera Evelyn (Quick), 212
Person, Karen Lynn (Lindburg), 380
   Matthew Shane, 380
   Matthew Thomas, 380
   Valan Nichole, 380
Peters, Elizabeth Jo, 391
   Joe, 391
Peterson, Albert, 139
   Beverly Ann, 218, 336
   Bonnie (Foss), 336
   Carol, 252
   Charles, 194
   Clarence D., 205
   David, 252
   Dona Jane, 218, 336
   Donald Gordon, 218, 335
   Elaine Marlys, 139
   Eunice M. (Humrickhouse), 205
   France S. (Lindhart), 139
   George Alfred, 218
   Hazel (Jacobson), 194
   Helen Sarah, 194
   John Franklin, 366
   Judith Ann, 274
   June (Cates) (Zunino), 252
   Kim (Culbert), 366
   Laura (Vining), 336
   Laura May (Vining), 218
   Lois Marie, 205
   Lucinda (Hooper), 26
   Maren Oline (Anderson), 147
   Mark, 336
   Oreada Emgard, 284
   Paul, 147
   Selma Christine, 147
   Steven, 336
   Tim, 336
   Victor Woodrow, 274
   Walt, 252
Petrick, Ida Florence (Woodworth), 202
   John Frank, 202

   Patricia Ann, 202
Petrie, Beverly, 398
Petty, Adeline (Woody), 111
   Jane, 247
   John, 111
   Sarah, 111
Peyton, Bruce Almy, 421
   Bryan Judd, 421
   Deborah Thais (Mason), 421
   Mary Elaine (Abdoo), 421
   Stacy, 421
Pfeiffer, Johanna Magdalena, 204
Phelps, Barbara Jean, 370
   Carol (Schacht), 323
   Constance Faye, 239, 370
   Corey Lynn, 369
   Dale Loren, 239, 369
   Darrel Frederick, 239
   Darrell Frederick, 369
   Dorothy Belle (French), 239
   Eva Reed (Palmer), 208
   Frederick, 239
   Guy, 208
   Hattie A. (Burk), 208
   Karen (Renner), 369
   Katherine Elizabeth (Thomas), 239
   Keith Dale, 370
   Kelly Jean Phelps, 323
   Kent David, 369
   Laurel (Flaven), 369
   Lawrence, 208, 323
   Maria, 95
   Reuben, 208
   Shirley, 208, 323
   Shirley Ann, 370
   Steven Darrell, 369
   William Henry, 239
Philhower, Amber Lee, 296
   Claire, 296
   Herman, 296
   Herman Norwood, 296
   Penelope Lee (Nickle), 296
Phillips, —, 90
   Brandon Wayne, 424
   Clara, 331
   Estrina Louesta, 43
   Ethel Edna, 107, 158
   Janet Marie (Ewing), 424
   Jonathan, 43
   Lorena Delina, 43

Lorilla Ann, 43, 106
Lyman Addison, 43
Mabel B. (Elliott), 107
Malinda Alvaretta, 43, 106
Martha Emma, 43
Matilda, 43
Matilda (Austin), 42
Nelson Ray, 43, 106
Thomas, 43
Thomas Boston, 42
Wayne, 424
Phillipson, Karen (Peterson), 169
Lars Christian, 169
Pieper, Augusta (Riemes), 441
Bertha, 441
Fred, 441
Pierce, Laura, 239
Pietsch, Bonnie (Bullock), 280
Pete, 280
Robert, 280
William, 280
Pike, Amy, 105
Pilon, Elizabeth Mary, 232
Piovarchy, Marie Vilma, 266
Piper, Pearl Amelia, 189
Pirlot, Edward, 268
Evelyn (Early), 268
Jodie, 269
Marcella Mae (Reed), 268
Wade, 269
Wayne, 268
Pitsch, Frances, 278
Plaster, John, 125
John H., 125
Lucy, 125
Plasteur, Cleo Patra Eloise, 128
Eva B., 19, 127
Eva Belle, 31
Eva Belle (Reed), 125
Leota Lorraine, 129, 188
Rudoloph Culmore Thomas Peter, 125
Rudolph, 128
Rudolph Culmore, 125
Rudy, 125
Plautz, Elisie (Schultz), 279
Georgia, 279
Rhinehard, 279
Plewnarz, Paul, 350
Wenty Jeanne (Peckham), 350

Poe, Margaret, 406
Pogue, Arlene, 221
Barbara J., 341, 424
Beulah Elizabeth (Roberts), 221
Bonnie J., 341, 424
Dale E., 341
Daniel J., 341
Darcy (Surprise), 341, 424
Delores A. (Scheel), 341
Everett J., 221
Fay F., 341
Ione Pearl, 221, 341
Irene, 342
Irene C., 221
John, 221
John O., 341
Juanita P., 341
Kathleen R., 341
Michael Steven, 424
Paul D., 341
Pearl (Stocks), 221
Roy Roger, 221, 341
Ruth (Shaben), 341
Sharon A., 341
Steven V., 341, 424
Susan R., 341
Vernon Everett, 221, 341
Popal, Susan, 100
Porter, Iola Gladys (Abaney), 255
Joseph Aubrey, 255
Mary, 138
Nancy Orel (Kruse), 231
Pearl Marie, 255
Robert, 231
Portner, Ruth, 190
Post, Anna, 169
Powell, Ann Janette (Austin), 104
Edna Margaret, 105, 154
Edward Harrison, 437
Gladys Leona, 105
Helen (Wadley) (Blake) (Barone), 437
Leah, 110
Margaret (Jones), 104
Thomas, 105
Thomas James, 104
William, 104
Prahl, Jerry, 404
Warren, 404
Prall, Clinton, 140
Daisie, 140

Mary, 140
Prausa, Carolyn, 262
Prentice, Edith Holmes, 386
    Eleanor Louise (Holmes), 386
    William Hardy, 386
Preske, Mary Lou (Slack), 196
    Raymond, 196
    Robert, 196
    Sharon Leigh (DeSeyn), 196
Preston, Alice Edna, 236
Pretz, Deborah Ann (Courtney), 380
    John, 380
    Lisa Marie, 380
    Robert J., 380
    Rosemarie, 380
    Stacey Lynn, 380
Price, Elia Leigh (Newsome), 216
    Mary Kathryn, 216
    Walthal Wooldridge, 216
Priez, Renata, 400
Procknow, Augusta, 166
Proctor, Abigail, 10
    Hannah, 10
Proper, Nellie Elizabeth, 206
Prothero, Debra Diane (Hotchkiss), 402
    Edna (Killips), 277
    Leah Ruth, 402
    Melinda Sue, 277, 402
    Miles, 277
    Ruby Lynn, 277, 402
    Russell, 277
    Russell David, 402
    Russell LeRoy, 402
    Ruth (Reed), 277
    Tabitha Renee, 402
Proutsos, Crintina Maria, 383
    Georgene, 383
    Johanna Lin, 383
    John, 383
    Judy Kay (Miller), 383
Pruitt, —, 160
    Doris June, 356
Pryor, Bernadine (Meadows), 827
    Cheryl Lynn, 287, 409
    Christopher James, 409
    James Robert, 287, 409
    Janet Louise, 287
    Judith Lorraine, 287, 410
    Kathleen (Krielcamp), 409
    Marcia Joan, 287, 409

Mary Jean, 287
Patricia, 8
Patricia Jean (Reed), 287
Patricia Reed, 53
Paula, 409
Virgil Robert, 827
Przybykski, Dustin Bernard, 427
    Jessica Mary, 427
Przybylski, Bernard, 427
    Irene Mary (Gwiazda), 427
Pschorr, Adeline Mary, 332
Pudell, Barbel Ingried, 277
    Berta (Walter), 277
    Daniel James, 277
    Edward, 277
    Erich, 277
    Ilsa, 277
    Peter Eric, 277
    Ruth (Reed) (Prothero) (Killips), 277
Puleston, Lois Iciphene, 210
Pulsinelli, Lillian, 295
Purkey, Marguerite, 402
Putman, Grace, 258
Putnam, George W., 48

Q

Quandt, Ann (Ziereis), 260
Quast, Nancy Ellen, 209
    Chris, 260
    Melvin Chris, 260
Quick, Amy Beth, 328
    Ann Marie, 328
    Barbara (Doppenberg), 328
    Benjamin, 328
    Bernice (Trowbridge), 212
    Betty Mae, 212, 326
    Bruce, 213, 328
    Calvin, 142, 212
    Darlene Lois, 214
    David, 213, 328
    Deborah Lee, 327
    Dennis Lee, 212, 327
    Doris Iva, 142, 212
    Dorothy, 143
    Dorothy Margaret (Dalke), 213
    Dorothy Mary Ellen, 214
    Ellen Elizabeth, 142, 212
    Ellen M. (Martin), 99
    Ellen Martin, 142

Elmer, 143, 212
Esther, 100
Eugene, 100, 143
Eugene James, 142, 211, 326
Evelyn, 143, 213
George Martin, 100, 142
Georgene (Bednarek), 328
Georgia Mae, 142, 211
Gina, 326
Ginette Kathleen, 328
Gladys Vivian (Bush), 142
Hannah (Crawford), 99
Harry Denison, 142
Howard, 36, 100
Ida B. (Fobes) (Lange), 99
Ida B. Fobes (Lange), 99
Inez (Johnson), 143
Irene, 143, 213
Irma L., 143
Jacob, 99
James R., 99
James Russell, 213, 328
Jamie Ann, 328
Jeanne Ann, 213, 327
Jennifer, 328
Jesse James, 100, 142, 212
Jesse Russell, 328
Joan Barbara (Holloway), 327
Kelly Jean, 327
Kylan Michael, 328
Leland, 143, 213
Linda, 326
Lois, 320
Lois Lorraine (Kimble), 214
Lyle James, 143, 214
Mabel (Dow), 211
Margaret Mary (Jodarski), 212
Mary (Maldari), 213
Mary Ethel (Denison), 142
Mary L., 213, 328
Mary Moletna, 142
Nancy Susan (Cumming), 328
Naomi, 143
Naomi Mary, 214
Patricia Louise, 212
Phyllis, 214, 329
Robert Alan, 213, 328
Robyn (Dellon), 328
Russell, 143
Russell E., 213

Shane, 326
Susan Marie, 327
Vera Evelyn, 142, 212
Virginia Jean, 211, 326
Zula (Cope), 211

R

Raddant, Alicia Mae, 395
  Jason David, 395
  Pamela (Olick), 395
  Ronald, 395
Rado, Margaret, 439
Radomski, Allison, 340
  James, 340
  Lauren, 340
  Mary Curtis (Vining), 340
Rael, Sarah, 319
Rainville, Elizabeth (Frank), 423
  La Rae, 423
  Lloyd, 423
Raleigh, Ava (Moore), 293
  Hubert Adair, 293
  James Ebert, 293
  Lois (Archibald) (Thompson), 293
  Richard Orin, 293
  Roxanne Lee, 293, 412
Ramaker, Eunice, 223
Ramsey, Diana Lynn (Hyska), 399
  Elenore (Bauder), 399
  James Eugene, 399
Ranch, Ruth Esther, 385
Randall, —, 26
  Gladys Evelyn, 246
Rapp, Hattie, 227
  Melinda Ann, 342
Rasmussen, Anker Conrad, 384
  Caroline Joyce, 384
  Margaret, 366
  Mildred Marie (Meligan), 384
Rathgeber, Dianne, 163
  Edward Richard, 163
  Esther L. (Kiesschnick), 163
Ratliff, Cloma, 381
Rawles, Mattie Enochs, 108
Ray, —, 84, 85
  Euretta, 114
Rayl, Keith Allen, 207
  Laura Abby (Raymond), 207
Raymond, Anna Ruth (Loewen), 207

Jettie Susan, 140
John Walker, 140, 207
Jonathan Moses, 207
Joseph Walker, 140
Laura Abby, 207
Linda Gail, 207
Mildred Abby (Crouch), 140
Mildred Crouch, 207
Peter Thomas, 207
Rolande Marie (Elie), 207
Thomas Hamilton, 140, 207
Wilbur Hamilton, 140
Read, Amanda, 16
  Anne, 15, 19
  Fear, 15, 16
  John, 16, 28
  Lee, 16
  Manda, 15
  Michael, 46
  Pauline, 15, 16
  Ruth, 15
Reardon, David James, 441
  Francis, 441
  Fred, 441
  Geraldine Dolores (Wadley), 441
  Josephine (Amerelli), 441
  Ryan, 441
Reb, Johnny, 62
Redeker, Mary M., 344
Rednik, Harriet, 144
Reece, Edith Marie (Largent), 236
  Homer Adam, 236
Reed, —, 89, 90
  Aaron Lee, 273
  Adelbert, 48
  Adelbert George Lowell, 183, 291
  Adelbert Lowell, 77, 122
  Alan, 269
  Alfred, 268
  Alfred Allen, 170, 269
  Alfred Floyd, 93
  Alfred Michael, 117, 170
  Amanda, 17
  Amy Rosina (Andrus), 180
  Angeline Irene, 115, 168
  Anne, 16
  Anthony Alan, 403
  Arlene (Leair), 285
  Arlene May, 180, 289
  Arnold James, 118, 172

Arthur, 46, 114, 118
Arthur James, 46, 113
Audrey Ethel (Becker), 173
B. L., 89
Bailey Yourell, 405
Barbara (Jacobi), 403
Barbara Sue, 171, 270
Beatrice M. (Dawkins),93
Bert, 7, 28, 47, 123
Betty (Fillmore), 291
Beverly Ann, 171, 269
Bonnie (Starks), 273
Bonnie (Warschkow), 268
Bonnie Ann, 277, 402
Bradley, 268
Bradley Michael, 269
Brandon Jay, 269
Brenda Jean, 285
Brian M., 285, 405
Brigham Ryan Lowell, 405
C., 80
Candace Pearl, 258
Charles, 173
Charles Anthony, 278, 403
Cleo (Seipel), 405
Clifford, 184
Clifford Lowell, 123, 179
Clinton, 269
Clyde, 125
Clyde Laverne, 93, 129
Colleen Kay, 171, 273
Cynthia Amy, 286
Cyrus, 7, 18, 19, 22, 29, 30, 32, 71, 78, 79, 80, 82, 84, 85, 86, 87, 88, 89, 90, 112, 125, 126, 129
Dale Adelbert, 291
Daniel, 285
Darla, 173, 278
David Dewitt, 171
David Roland, 285, 405
Delbert Lowell, 180
DeWitt, 45, 46
DeWitt Cornelius, 46, 117
Donald Adelbert, 123, 182
Donald Allen, 291
Donna May (Marring), 291
Donna Rae (Jarstad), 403
Dora Marie (LaMarche), 179
Dwight Dale, 171, 272
Effie Maud, 46, 118

Index

Elizabeth, 15, 19, 20, 21, 22
Elizabeth (—), 18
Elizabeth (Crocker), 15, 16
Ella Fear, 25
Elsbeth Dorothy (Klein), 114
Emerald DeWitt, 117, 170
Emily Hulda (Shuettpelz), 170
Emma Augusta Donnelly, 46
Ethan Dewitt, 271
Eva, 141
Eva (Hetts), 171
Eva Belle, 15, 92, 124
Eva Lonea (Lyannas), 179
Fear, 19
Florence M. (Mills), 118
Florence S. (Dunton), 166
Floyd, 30
Fred, 46, 115, 118
Freda Rose (Vorpahl), 171
Geneva, 123
Gerald Scott, 287
Geraldine Ann (Weslowski), 273
Gertrude E., 166, 257
Gladys Lastrella (Allman), 182
Glynn, 166
Gordon Elmer, 166, 257
Gordon F., 93
Gordon Harold, 258
Grant, 269
Gregory, 268
Harold Arthur, 114, 166
Heath Allan, 273
Heather, 273
Heather Lynne, 271
Helga Lydia (Heyerdahl), 117
Herald Lincoln, 123
Holly Ann, 273
Ida, 31
Ida Adella, 32, 93
Ida May, 46, 116
Ilene Ruth, 118, 172
Irene Hanak (Genesy), 183
Irma Jean (Burdeau), 171
Isabelle Jane, 179
Isaiah Ashlin, 272
Jacqueline Jane, 278
Janet (Zandt), 268
Janet Loraine, 180, 288
Janice Margaret, 173
Janice Marie (Heath), 271

Janine Ann, 173
Janis, 285
Jaqueline Jane, 173
Jayne Marie, 173, 277
Jeffrey Allen, 278, 403
Jenifer Nicole, 403
Jennie Adell, 46, 114
Jewell, 115
Joan (Flaig), 269
Joanne May, 173
Joel Gene, 273
John, 7, 15, 19, 20, 21, 22, 27, 30, 31, 32, 126, 127
John Lowell, 7, 15
Jolene Leigh, 271
Joyce (Lehman) (Larsen), 277
Joyce Ann, 180, 285
Joyce Lynn, 173, 276
Judith, 173, 278
Julia, 46, 115
Julia Agnes, 46
July (Flaig), 171
June Anne Marietta, 118, 172
June Rose, 180, 287
Karen Marie (Schultz), 271
Katie Lynn, 291
Kelly Marie, 291
Kim Teresa, 291
Kym Marie, 271, 399
Lance, 268
Leona (Bashina), 170
Linette Fay, 272
Lorena, 129
Lorna Joy, 171, 270
Louise (Harris), 79
Lowell Vaughn, 271
Luanne Marie (Carey), 405
Lynelle, 171
M., 18, 22, 23, 57, 61, 66, 70, 72, 73, 75
Marcella Mae, 170, 268
Marietta, 112, 113, 117, 167
Marietta (Smith), 45
Marilyn Carol, 180, 288
Marinda, 122, 178, 182
Marinda (Wingate), 48
Martha, 29, 32, 47, 435, 445
Martha J. (Morton), 45
Marvin Lee, 170
Mary, 29

Mary (Litrenta), 277
Mary Louise (Marsh), 115
Mary Marie, 32, 77
Mary Marie (Wingate), 78
Maud, 80
Maud Edna, 92, 123
Maureen, 257
Maureen Martha, 171, 272
Maydora Cecilia (Robinson), 122
McKenzie Kathryn, 405
Melissa Jean, 276
Michael, 29, 31, 32, 44, 45, 46, 126
Michele Faye, 271
Michelle Lynette, 406
Mike, 126
Mildred Agnes, 118, 174
Mitzi Kay, 258
Morma Mae, 118
Morris, 7, 8, 15, 17, 18, 28, 29, 30, 31, 32, 45, 48, 53, 56, 74, 126
Morris Herbert, 180, 286
Myrna (Blair) (Schlais), 117
Myrtle Minnie, 77, 123
Nelda Jean (Varnell), 276
Neva, 125
Neva (Sisson), 129
Nola Mae (Fuller), 284
Norma Jean, 170, 269
Norma Mae, 172
Norman, 48
Norman Wilder, 123, 180
Olive Marinda, 123, 180
Patricia Ann (Riley), 257
Patricia Jean, 180, 287
Pauline, 26, 441
Pearl, 80
Pearl (Young), 166
Pearl Eunice, 123, 177
Pearl Reed, 92
Philip Edmund, 171
Phillip, 273
Phillip Edmund, 271
Rachelle Lynn, 273
Ragna Antine (Anderson), 129
Raymond Edgar, 117, 171
Richard Morris, 179, 284
Robert Adelbert, 179
Roger Allan, 173
Roland Lowell, 179, 285
Roland Morris, 123, 178

Ronald James, 173, 276
Ronda, 268
Rosalie, 170, 268
Roy, 118
Roy Albert, 46, 118
Ruby Blanche, 118, 173
Ruby Blanche (Coryell), 173
Russell, 173
Russell Sadell, 118, 173, 277
Ruth, 17, 19, 20, 22, 27, 28, 173, 277
Ruth Ann (Chapin), 271
Ruth Elizabeth, 179, 284
Sarah Ann (Hotchkiss), 28
Scott, 268
Sharlene Lyn, 271
Sharon Lynn, 258, 389
Shawn James, 271
Sherry Lynn, 285, 405
Sidney, 170
Stanley DeWitt, 171, 271
Sue Bernadine, 180, 289
Susan (Gehm), 269
Susan Belle (Hardwick), 80, 91, 123
Susie (Lusardi), 268
Susie Belle, 125, 129
Sylvan, 171, 273
Sylvia (Ironima), 286
Tami Jo, 269
Thomas B., 23
Timothy Wayne, 269
Todd Johnson, 173
Tom, 171
Treana Lea, 271
Valerie Joyce, 171, 272
Vincent, 170, 268
Virginia, 171
Virginia Charlotte, 180, 285
Vivian Ann, 171, 270
Vivian Medora, 123, 181
Wallace, 273
Wallace Clemet, 117, 171
Wallace James, 171, 271
Warren James, 170, 268
Wayne Carl, 171, 269
Whitey, 172
Yvette Marie, 271
Zoe Olive, 91
Reeder, Lorraine (Wadleigh), 438
  Robert, 438

Reese, Absalom Hobcomb, 259
   Clara Mae (Rutherford), 259
   Edith Marie, 236
   Frances Dolores, 259
Reeves, Rhoda, 103
Regall, Dyanne Patricia (Minor), 408
   Ella (Westphal), 408
   Gregory Scott, 408
   Helmet, 408
   Karl, 408
   Kevin Karl, 408
   Renee Dyanne, 408
Reichard, Dale, 176
   Gail (Bullock), 176
Reidenger, Theresa, 168
Reiley, Elizabeth (—), 435
   John, 435
Reindl, Laura Lynn, 368
   Leo, 368
   Mary Sue (Grimes) (Hanson), 368
   Tim L., 368
   Tina Marie, 368
Reinhart, Jacqueline Mae (Simmons), 181
   Ralph, 181
Rendahl, Carl, 419
   Earl, 419
   Marian (Donnelly), 419
   Rosean Marie (Wiedendorf) (Parks) (Hays), 419
Renner, Karen, 369
Replogle, Mable Marie, 188
Retzlaff, Caroline Dorothy (Badtke), 330
   Christopher Donald, 330
   Dianna Marie, 330
   Donald, 330
   Dora (Slotffus), 330
   Otto, 330
   Susan, 330, 421
Reynolds, Hannah (Warner), 199
   John F., 54
   John Francis, 199
   Marion Edna, 199
   Sarah Elizabeth, 148
   Sharon, 368
Rhodes, Alta, 96
   George, 280
   Jennifer Ellen, 280
   Lawrence M., 280
   Minnie, 280
   Pearl Eliza, 157
   Sandra Lorraine (Springman), 280
Rice, Mildred Marie, 191
Richardson, Blache (Brown), 238
   Eva (Jameison), 292
   Ilene Joyce, 238
   Irene Lucille, 292
   Isaac Bruck, 238
   James Alvin, 340
   Jason James, 340
   Karen Joyce, 238, 365
   Oscar, 292
   Sheryl Ann (Koch), 340
   Wanda Faith (Brown), 197
Richey, Archie Pruett, 254
   John Frank, 254
   Maureen Patricia, 254, 386
   Nancy (Ballinger), 254
   Nancy Lynn, 254, 386
   Neva June (Tognoni) (Mendez), 254
Ricky, Emy D., 33
Riddle, Linda Louise, 339
Rider, Ellen Marinda, 184
   Marion Jessie, 183
   S. D., 72
Riehl, Brenda, 399
Rieken, Allie, 209
   Kate, 209
   Michael, 209
Riemes, Augusta, 441
Rieumes, Martha Pauline, 176
Riley, Elsie (Hall), 257
   Gladys Leona (Powell) (Hack), 105
   Jack, 105
   John Harold, 257
   Patricia Ann, 257
   Rosa Reiley, 435
Risor, Patricia Ann, 247
Roark, Bernice, 303
   Robenhorst,
   Alvina, 260
Roberts, Alice Grace (McElroy), 148
   Amber Irene, 148, 221
   Arthur Lee, 250
   Arthur Thomas, 250
   Asa Christopher, 148
   Bernice Vernetta, 148
   Beulah Elizabeth, 148, 221
   Carol Ann, 250
   Clarence Henry, 288
   Diana Lee, 250

Dustin William, 342
Eathel Maude (Williams), 288
Felicia Mae, 433
Gloria Jean (Miller) (Beckwith), 383
Jack Paul, 383
Janette Danean, 250
Janice, 221, 342
Jeanette (Langdon), 148
Jeffery Lee, 288
Jennie Roberts, 433
Jessica, 342
John Henry, 288
Kevin Gene, 383, 433
Margery W. (Rogers), 250
Marilyn Carol (Reed) (Deyarmond), 288
Marilyn Eathel, 288
Mark, 436
Markus, 148
Melinda Ann (Rapp), 342
Mellissa Carroll, 288
Richard L., 383, 433
Rickie Roberts, 433
Roger Wayman, 148, 221
Roger William, 221, 342
Ruth Janette, 148, 221
Stanley Paul, 383
Thomas Henry, 288
Verna (Noble), 221
Robertson, Asahal (Ace) B., 162
Cynthia Lucille, 248, 379
Floy Valanda (Peckham), 153
Hugh Linley, 153
Janice Ranee, 248
Lucille (Norman), 248
Mabel Margaret (McDaniel), 162
Mary (Sandercook), 162
Mary (Whitney), 153
Mary Gertrude, 162, 248
Maxine, 153, 233
Smoke, 153
Thomas, 153, 162
Thomas Earl, 162, 248
Robinson, Annie, 107
Betty, 439
Florence Anne, 107
Franics Morris, 122
Luana Cecilia America (Kelley), 122
Maydora Cecilia, 122
Phillip, 107

Virgie, 176
Rock, Colin, 278
Cortney Crystal, 403
Erin, 278, 403
Frances (Pitsch), 278
Harold, 278
Jacqueline Jane (Reed), 278
Jennifer Anne, 403
Kathleen Mary, 278
Kevin, 278
Patrick, 278, 403
Sue (Baele), 403
Rockafellow, Cora (Marcy), 292
Earl, 292
Louise Arlene, 292
Rodefer, Jackie, 275
Rodger, Agnes, 154
Rodgers, Sharleen Rae, 417
Rodriguez, Patsy Lynn (Holland), 425
Victor, 425
Roff, Anna, 156
Rogers, Carolyn Lisa, 429
Charles Wesley, 312
Clarene Elmina (Crouch), 312
Elizabeth (Mathis), 164
Elizabeth Jane, 164, 250
Elsie, 164, 249
George, 164
Gladys, 164, 249
Helen, 164
Julia (Hooker), 164
Julia Cates, 250
Julia Mae (Cates), 164
Karen, 312
Margery W., 164, 250
Michel, 312
Robert Bruce, 164
Sandra Leigh, 312
Thomas, 250
Thomas Jefferson, 164
Rognrud, Artha Jane (Shipton), 331
Bradley Thomas, 331
Christopher Brian, 423
Evelyn (—), 331
Glenn Dennis, 331
Jason, 423
Karen (Fischer), 423
Mark Shipton, 331
Mary Ann (—), 331
Pamela (McDonald), 331

Index 517

Steven Dennis, 331, 423
Susan Kay, 332
Walter, 331
Rohde, Anna (Post), 169
   Laura C., 169
   Paul, 169
Rolfson, Mary, 311
Rollins, John Dee, 383
   Kami Jo, 384
   Pauline Yvette (Bass), 383
   Todd James, 384
   William Dee, 383
Rolls, Arthur Wayne, 412
   Frances (McNally), 413
   Opal, 412
   Roxanne Lee (Raleigh) (Thomas), 412
Romano, Carmella (Madonna), 206
   Elna Nadene (Crouch) (Geise), 206
   John, 206
   John Anthony, 206
   Neil Vincent, 206
   Nicholas Allen, 207
   Rachelle (Schwalm), 206
   Sophie, 277
   Susan Carmella, 206
Ronning, Amy (Bazeley), 228
   Kari Ann, 228, 353
   Kristin Amy, 229, 353
   Laura (Ulrich), 353
   Oscar, 228
   Rachel Ulricka, 353
   Richard Royce, 228, 353
   Royce Russell, 228
   Ruth Marie (Peckham), 228
Rooney, Eileen, 193
Roots, Amber Adora, 380
   Beauford Alba, 249, 380
   Chadrick Arthur, 249, 380
   Chadrick Arthur Joseph, 380, 430
   Crystal Maria, 380
   Dolores (Layer), 380
   Erin Lee (Appleton), 430
   Gladys (Rogers), 249
   James, 249
   Jeffery, 380
   Jesse Joseph, 430
   Joe, 381
   Loretta Mary (Yank), 380
   Mike, 380
   Nicholas Anthony, 380
   Patricia (—), 381
   Paula, 381
   Wilford Accord, 249, 380
   William, 381
Ropelt, Celeste Joy, 429
Rose, Beatarice, 184
   Fern, 297
Roseall, Al, 92
Roseberry, Alvie, 431
Rosenstengle, Frances, 386
Roseth, Andrew, 152
   Anne (Karlstad), 152
   Annette, 232, 358
   Beryl Smith, 153, 231
   Beverly Peckham, 153, 231
   Billie Gae, 153
   Debra Lynn, 232, 357
   Dolores Anna (Bellenbaum), 232
   Doris Virginia (Mortensen), 232
   Elizabeth Jane, 153, 232
   Gertrude Primrose (Peckham), 152
   Harold Merwyn, 153, 232
   Holly Breeze, 358
   Inez, 232, 358
   James Harold, 232, 357
   Jessica Aileen, 357
   Jon Harold, 357
   Jon Henry, 232
   Judy Lilith (Hockenberry), 357
   Kathleen Dawn, 232, 357
   Kim (Russo), 357
   Minard Wesley, 153
   Nancy Dawn, 153, 233
   Orel Luvia, 153, 230
   Ronald Darwyn, 153
   Summer Gabriel, 358
   Thomas William, 232, 357
   Wilda Floy, 153
   William A., 152
Ross, Adeline Mary (Pschorr), 332
   Carole Mavis (Williamson), 348
   Donald Alexander, 205
   Elizabeth Louise, 205
   Eunice, 149
   James Alexander, 348
   James Carlyle, 348
   Jean Elizabeth, 332
   Joseph Ambrose, 332
   Lois Maxine, 303

Marjorie Jean (MacDonald), 348
Mary Alice (Day), 205
Nancy, 309
Norman Alexander, 348
Rosthe, Jon Henry, 153
Roth, George, 229
   Helena (Marx), 229
   Vera Etta, 229
Rowe, Kody Alan, 427
   Kristel Ann (Kruse), 427
   Ronald, 427
Rowell, Anna Augusta (Morehouse), 132
   Grace Naomi, 131
   Herbert, 132
Rowland, Cynthia, 183
Rucker, Thos. A., 112
Rudelich, Bonnie Ann (Reed), 402
   Joseph, 402
   Joseph John, 402
   Lisa Marie, 403
   Lucille (Catapano), 402
Rugh, Rowena, 436
Runyan, Margie Obedience (Scott), 162
   Thomas Wayne, 162, 445
   Vena Margaret (McDaniel), 162
   Vera, 8
Rupnow, Doris (—), 330
   Dorreen, 330
   Robert, 330
Russell, John, 31
   Leann Marie, 446
Russo, Jean (Vaughn), 357
   Jim, 357
   Kim, 357
Rutgowski, Gertrude, 407
Rutherford, Clara Mae, 259
Ruthroth, Nona Marion, 282
Ryan, Beatrice (Keenan-O'Keefe), 440
   Beatrice Ann, 440
   Elizabeth, 185
   Martin Francis, 440
Ryburn, Dorothy Jeanette, 146, 217
   Edith May (Peckham), 146
   George, 145
   Helen, 146
   Leota Vernette, 146, 217
   Mary Mundy (Legge), 146
   Neva, 146
   William, 146
   William Legge, 146

Ryder, Amanda (Haver), 123
   David, 123
   Ellen Marinda, 123
   Marion Jessie, 123
   Myrtle Minnie (Reed), 123
   Sidney David, 123
Rye, Clara (Duess), 223
   Edith, 223
   Ralph, 223

S

St. Pierre, Alfred, 298
   Louise, 298
   Ruth (Gordon), 298
Salazar, Lorena (Reed), 130
   Manual, 130
Salbro, Arie, 310
   Cheryl, 310
   Lea Etta (Stevens), 310
   Sheldon, 311
Salisbury, Lisa Ann, 323
   Maxine Paula (Stafford), 323
   Stanley Craig, 323
   Steven Michael, 323
Salo, Denise, 421
Saltvedt, Larry, 320
   Laura Lynn, 320
   Shane Eric, 320
   Shara Lee, 320
   Virginia Lee (Crouch), 320
Salvaggio, Angeline, 190
   Anna Marie, 190
   Frank, 190
Samplawski, Clarence, 236
   Edna S. A. (Kroeplin) (Meeker), 236
   Edward, 236
   Hazel (Hatfield), 236
Sandberg, Dorothy Olga, 242
Sandercook, Mary, 162
Sanders, Emma, 214
   Geraldine, 227
   Hattie (Rapp), 227
   Michael G., 227
Sanderson, James, 329
   Jayne, 329
   Joanne (—), 329
   John, 248
   Minnie, 211
   Sandra Lynn (Courtney), 248

Index 519

Valda, 248
Vernon, 248
Sandon, Lynelle (Reed), 172
    Richard A., 172
Sanford, Louisa, 136
Sargent, Adelaide Marion, 95
    Alfred, 95
    Maria (Phelps), 95
Saunders, Clara (Westaky), 364
    Floyd, 364
    Judith Ann (Meeker), 364
    Lisa Lynn, 364, 429
    Raymond Eugene, 364
    Sheila Ann, 364
Saykally, Rebecca, 260
Schacht, Carol, 323
Schanzle, Arthur, 195
    Gloria Carolyn, 195
    Hazel (Lucas), 195
Scharhag, Herman, 390
    Phyllis (MacKay), 390
    Robbin, 390
Schauman, Alfred, 279
    Cathy, 279
    Delores (Nygard), 278
    Edward, 279
    Eric, 404
    Julie A. (Hassell), 404
    Randy, 279
    Sandra, 279
    Terry, 279, 404
Scheel, Delores A., 341
Scheeler, Aaron Ronald, 304
    Adam Michael, 304
    Donna Sue (Howard), 303
    Jennifer Marie, 304
    Jeremy Todd, 304
Schekel, Esther, 356
Schemmel, Ruth, 394
Schermerhorn, Peter, 17
Scheuttpeltz, Nora, 261
Schiding, Bertha, 170
Schlais, Myrna (Blair), 117
Schliep, Bernice, 273
Schlueter, Dale L., 279
    Janet Marie (Erickson), 279
    Joel R., 280
    John, 279
    June, 279
    Ronald Todd, 279

Schmidt, Amanda Mathilda, 242
    Carl Albert, 245
    Daniel Ryan, 377
    Dennis James, 245, 377
    Duane Herbert, 245
    Herbert Carl, 245
    Joan (DuBuque), 377
    Lenora, 320
    Lillian (Pulsinelli), 295
    Patricia Lee, 295
    Robert, 295
    Ruth Ann (Johnson), 245
    Vivian May (Severson), 245
Schmiege, Carol, 315
Schneider, Benjamin, 293
    Cindy, 365
    Gertrude Johanna (Lefferdink), 293
    Ina Fae, 293
Schoenfelder, Betty Jane (Crouch), 208
    Bridget Mary, 208, 323
    Cindy (Nelson), 322
    Daniel John, 208, 322
    Ellen (Kaiser), 322
    Emily (Tikton), 322
    Erin Nicole, 323
    Gail (Mastenbrook), 322
    Gerald Phillip, 208
    Jason Daniel, 322
    Jeremy John, 322
    John Wilbur, 322
    Kathleen Carmel, 208
    Kevin Peter, 208, 322
    Lindsey Ann, 322
    Marla Joy (Bockelman), 322
    Mary Ann (Fogarty), 208
    Mary Elizabeth, 208
    Michael Kaiser, 322
    Nora Anne, 208
    Patrick Gerald, 208, 322
    Sheila Marie, 208
    Timothy William, 208, 322
    William Alfred, 208
Schoening, Cecil Martin, 329
    Chad Austin, 329
    Dean Martin, 329
    Gary Martin, 329
    Phyllis (Quick), 329
    Ruth Elaine (Douglass), 329
Schoewe, Agnes (Kiesner), 392
    Margaret, 392

Walter, 392
Scholz, —, 268
School, Lylis Margaret (Wright), 260
  Margaret Ann, 260
  Norman, 260
Schooltz, June, 407
Schramm, Sarah, 141
Schroeder, Bannon James, 274, 400
  Barbara, 404
  Bernard W., 261
  Bessie (Wilson), 172
  Beth (—), 401
  Bettina (Kunz), 400
  Bjorn Torben, 401
  Bobbi Lee, 401
  Carol Bernadette, 261
  Charity Ann, 375
  Clint Duran, 401
  Clyde Gust, 172
  Cynthia Lee (Erickson), 404
  Donna Rae, 172, 273
  Duane, 339
  Duran Vernon, 274, 401
  Faron Reece, 274
  Gladys Irene (Baker), 375
  Gust, 172
  Herman, 114
  Jackie Carol (Johnson), 401
  Jason, 375
  Jeffery, 339
  Jennie Adell (Reed) (Wright), 114
  John Wesley, 375
  Judy (Vining), 339
  June Anna Marietta (Reed), 172
  Laurel (Chapin), 274
  Melissa Joy, 375
  Ralph, 404
  Rodney, 404
  Shane, 404
  Shane Sheldon, 274, 401
  Shannon, 404
  Steven, 339
  Vernon Clyde, 172, 274
  Violet (Wren), 261
  Zackery Shane, 401
Schubert, Agnes Newell (Leitch), 190
  Margaret Isabell, 190
  Paul F., 190
Schuettpelz, Martha, 396
Schuffenhauer, Ann Elizabeth, 312

Betty Jane, 311
Dawn Marie, 311
Debra Lyn, 311
Jeanette (Olson), 311
Jo Ann, 311
Kenneth Roy, 311
Margaret Illene (Tuttle), 311
Mary Kay, 311
Michael Frank, 311
Robert Donald, 311
Ronald Dean, 311
Sharon (Hansen), 312
Steven John, 312
Schultz, Albert, 412
  Constance Ellen (Nestle), 412
  Donna Rae (Schroeder) (Corn)
    (Grignon), 274
  Edward William, 271
  Ellen, 361
  Emma (Kolisch), 412
  Harry, 412
  Karen Marie, 271
  Kimberly Sue, 412
  Mary Elizabeth (Bricco), 271
  Richard, 274
Schumacher, Hilda, 333
Schuth, Margaret Ann, 220
Schuffenhauer, Betty Jane, 200
  Carole Ann (Frank), 200
  Charlotte Lauren (DeMars), 200
  Gayle James, 200
  Jo Ann, 200
  Kenneth Roy, 200
  Louise (Stopp), 200
  Norman Charles, 200
  Otto, 200
  Robert Donald, 200
  Ronald Dean, 200
  Thelma Belle (Stevens), 200
  William Paul, 200
Schwab, Hazel, 248
Schwalm, Rachelle, 206
Schwartz, Anna May, 298
Schwartzotte, Anna May (Murphy), 298
  George L., 298
Schwarzkopf, Erwin, 353
  Kristin Amy (Ronning), 353
  Lisel Marie, 353
  Marie (—), 353
  Seth David, 353

Index

Stan, 353
Schwittay, Martha, 263
   Rudnia, 263
Scott, Margie Obedience, 162
   Russell LeRoy, 277
Seabrook, Gertrude Joy, 406
Seaman, Ronald, 306
Sear, Julia, 100, 143
Seefelt, Blanche, 204
Seehusen, Nancy, 419
Seipel, Cleo, 405
   Richard James, 405
Serier, Cornelius, 166
   Florence S., 166
   Florence S. (Dunton), 166
   Mary Ann (Allcox), 166
Seth, Daniel Lee, 414
   Jordan Michael, 414
   Judy (Dunn), 414
   Katherine Christina (Johnson), 414
   Richard Lee, 414
   Tyler Lee, 414
Severn, Patricia, 387
Severson, Vivian May, 245
Severud, Anna Louise (Hanson), 368
   Joshua A., 368
   Kristin E., 368
   Shawn M., 368
   Todd M., 368
Shaben, Ruth, 341
Shadis, Wendy, 365
Shaffer, Cora M. M. (Kroeplin), 155
   Ferris, 155
Shahinian, Nevart, 192
Sharp, Jessie Fremont, 212
Shaw, Andrew, 282
   Barbara, 282
   Herbert, 282
   Le Anne Michelle (Johnson), 282
Shelp, Ann, 351
   Anne Rosella (Peckham), 227
   Carol (Koslowski), 351
   Cheri, 351
   Darron, 351
   David Scott, 227, 351
   Florence, 227
   George, 227
   Glenn, 227
   Jack, 351
   Jean, 227, 352

   John, 227, 351
   Kristi, 351
   Lynn, 227
   Pat (Wiswell), 352
   Ralph, 227, 351
   Richard, 227
   Roger, 351
   Tricia, 352
   Wanda (Fredenthal), 351
Shepardson, Donald, 413
   Naida (Lindley), 413
   Richard Carl, 413
   Sharilyn Autumn (Gibson), 413
   Tawnya Ann, 413
Sherman, Clara, 132
   Cynthia Jean, 358
   Deborah Elizabeth, 34
   Elizabeth E., 34
   Jean (Toole), 358
   John Sackett, 34
   Polly (DeWolf), 34
   Richard, 358
Shilts, Edward L., 365
   Karen Joyce (Kroeplin), 365
   Karen Joyce (Richardson), 365
   Rodney, 365
   Samuel, 365
   Tracy, 365
Shipton, Artha Jane, 215, 331
   Arthur Randolph, 214
   Beatrice Marguerite (Peckham), 214
   Beverly Jeanette, 215, 331
   Edith, 214
   George, 214
   Virginia Lola, 215, 331
Shoemaker, Sarah, 97
Short, —, 233
   Cynthia Diane (Bell), 233
   Quanita, 261
Shove, —, 105
   Stella (Crane), 105
Shreve, —, 144
   James Bird, 144
   Sarah Jeanette (Dobson) (Peckham), 144
Shuettpelz, Carl, 170
   Emily Hulda, 170
   Matilda (Nitzband), 170
Shultz, Elisie, 279
Shurtleff, —, 243

Sophronia, 35
Shwanke, Mary Ann, 391
Sidney, —, 75
   Ellen, 75
   Marion, 75
Siegel, Caroline, 274, 401
   Cecil, 172
   Donaven Louis, 275
   Donna, 274
   Ella, 172
   Geraldine (Krueger), 274
   Gerett, 401
   Heidi, 274
   James Brian, 275
   Jeffery, 275, 401
   John, 172
   Jolene Lee, 275
   Jon, 275, 401
   Jordan Lee, 172, 274
   Judith Ann (Peterson), 274
   Mary Katherine (Montgomery), 401
   Norma Mae (Reed), 172
   Patti Renee (Clark), 401
   Raymond Cecil, 172, 274
   Rhonda, 274
   Sandra Jane, 172, 275
   Sandra Jean, 275
   Sandra Jean (Courchaine), 275
Siegfried, Billie Jean (Spaun), 433
   Donald, 433
   Doris (—), 433
   Dusty Jean, 433
   Paul, 433
Siepel, Beulah Helen (Yourell), 405
Sievert, Hedwig, 116
Sigmont, Bertha (Stemelski), 231
   Beryl Jo, 231, 356
   Beryl Smith (Roseth), 231
   Carol Jean (Fisher), 356
   Dawn Marie, 356
   Jo Ann, 231, 356
   Jodi Ann, 356
   Lori Jean, 356
   Nikki Lynn, 356
   Ruth Ann (Beckert), 356
   Walter, 231
   Walter Theodore, 231, 356
   Wendy Rhena, 356
   William Charles, 231, 356
Siminoe, Fred, 250

   Glen, 250
   Josephine (Vincent), 250
Simmons, Audrey (Everitt) (Lord), 281
   Beverly Jean, 181, 289
   Bill, 281
   Eleanor (Patchett), 143
   Emma Rose (Staeben), 180
   Jacqueline Mae, 181
   Judith Lee, 181, 290
   Olive Marinda (Reed), 180
   Robert, 143
   Sanford, 181
   Sanford Staeben, 180
   Shirley Gay, 181, 290
   William Alfred, 180
Simonson, Kathryn May, 362
Simpkovitz, Mary Sheridan, 374
Simpson, Ira, 25
   Mary A., 25
   Mary Etta (Cheeseman), 25
   Milward L., 163
Sina, Magdalene, 213
Sisson, Henry Charles, 129
   Lilly (Keighly), 129
   Neva, 129
Sitter, Lisa Lynn (Saunders), 429
   Michael, 429
   Renee Marie, 429
Skaare, Angela Marie, 426
   Bertha Augusta (Langeland), 350
   Carol Doreen (Webb), 426
   Eric David, 426
   Jean Carolyn (Peckham), 350
   Jeffrey Lee, 350, 426
   Jerald Wayne, 350, 426
   Joan Elaine, 350
   John Leo Irving, 350
   John Richard, 350
   Joshua Jerald, 426
   Joy Kathleen, 350
   Julie Ann, 350
   Mary Jo (Moxness), 426
   Tiffany Jeanne, 426
Skarperrid, Audrene, 226
Skinner, Fiona, 270
Slack, Harvey, 111
   Mary Lou, 196
Slang, Amanda Carolyn (Ericcson), 264
   Carol Lea, 264, 395
   James Oscar, 264

Jeanette Carol, 264, 395
Lora Jean, 264, 396
Orvil John, 264
Slangon, Dora Jeanette (Johnson), 264
Slotffus, Dora, 330
Smith, Amy-Lynn Marie, 440
   Angela, 421
   Annise (Frost), 46
   Arthur, 45
   Bessie, 237
   Cornelia (Cooper), 26, 441
   Dorothy Carol, 202
   Edith Harriet, 162
   Elias, 112
   Elizabeth Jane, 103
   Emma, 45
   Etta, 221
   Helen Marie, 382
   Isaac, 46
   Juliana, 45, 112
   Karen, 385
   Lida, 215
   Lucille Katherine, 415
   Lyman, 112
   Marietta, 45, 46
   Marthena, 247
   Mary Jane, 104
   Michael, 440
   Rhoda (Reeves), 103
   Ruth, 350
   Samuel, 45, 112
   Shawn, 421
   Stephanie Marie (Wadley), 440
   Susan Emerson, 376
   Teresa Hebb, 420
   Thomas, 103
Snively, Arlene May (Reed), 289
   Bradley Allen, 289
   Dennis, 289
   Dorothy (Perkins), 289
   Heidi Marie (Binion), 289
   Julie, 289
   Leo, 289
   Richard, 289
Snook, Carrie, 213
Snow, —, 26
Snyder, Betty Jane (O'Connor) (Beavert), 294
   Joe, 174
   John A., 174

   Ken, 294
   Marietta (Springman), 174
   Verna (Bullock) (Adel), 174
Sokol, Paula, 392
Sommers, Carol, 344
Sones, P. E. (Reed) (Christopherson), 178
   Peter, 178
Sorenson, Lydia, 269
   Mary, 143
Spanenberg, Ryan Scott, 304
Spangenberg, Barry, 304
   Bernice M. (Freer), 304
   Gloria Dawn (Kennedy), 304
   John D., 304
   Julie Ann, 304
   Marc Aaron, 304
Sparrow, Craig, 351
   Ella (Hendron), 227
   Gloria (Pederson), 351
   Grace Elizabeth (Peckham), 227
   Joseph L., 227
   Julie, 351
   Len, 351
   Monica, 351
   Sara, 351
   William Donald, 227, 351
   William Walter, 227
Spaun, Ammie Dawn, 434
   Billie Jean, 390, 433
   Deborah Kay, 389, 433
   Kathryn (Maddox), 389
   Lois Marie, 389
   Loraine (Lester), 389
   Rhonda Lee, 389, 433
   William, 389
   William Alvin, 389
Speaks, Debbie, 430
Speer, Yvonne, 234
Spelce, Cynthia (Vance), 282
   Gary, 282
   Jason, 282
   Tiffany Rae (Ticknor), 282
Spencer, Jenny, 137
   Rosemary, 411
Splitgerber, Ida, 214
Sporleder, Alyce Mae (Honzu), 394
   Andrea, 394
   Fay Ann (Johnson), 394
   Lea, 394

Raymond John, 394
Raymond Lee, 394
Spradling, Frances, 411
Spratt, Edith Marie (Reece), 236
   Edna Margaret (Powell), 155
   George Walter, 155
   Kay Kopp, 362
   Laura (Clowen), 155
   Mary Ann, 155, 236
   Oscar, 155
   Pamela (Lee), 105
   Pamela Louise, 236, 361
   Philip, 105
   Philip Reece, 362
   Phillip Reece, 236
   Sharon (Mercer), 362
   Sharon Kay (Kopp), 362
   William, 155, 236
Springman, Carolee (Christian), 175
   Friederike (Keck), 175
   Johann Georg, 175
   Marietta, 174
   Marietta Eleanore (Bullock), 175
   Martha, 175
   Otto, 175
   Paul, 175
   Sandra Lorraine, 175, 280
Sqhezia, Rose, 326
Squadrito, James L., 296
   Jennie (Campolo), 296
   Natalie, 296
Stackley, Grace Katherine, 290
Staeben, Emma Rose, 180
Stafford, Betty Kay, 209, 324
   Bonita Jean, 209, 323
   Cheryl Jeannine (Massey), 324
   Isabelle (Bartholomew), 209
   Kyle Markie, 209
   Marian Nadean (Palmer), 209
   Mark Owen, 209
   Markie, 209
   Marvin Kyle, 209, 324
   Maxine Paula, 209, 323
   Michael Ryan, 324
   Nancy Ellen (Quast), 209
   Sarah Jeannine, 324
Stahl, Cecilia, 332
Stallings, LaVon Elaine (Crouch), 312
   Phillip, 312
Stamstad, Karen, 335

Stanley, Clarence E., 302
   Sharon Kay, 302
Stanton, Edward M., 188
   Martha Jane, 188
Starks, Bonnie, 273
Starrow, —, 54
Staves, — (Bray), 100
   Almira Bray, 100
   John, 100
Stayback, Jeffery Paul, 261
   Joseph Wayne, 261
   Julie Ann Margaret, 261
   Lewis, 261
   Patricia Ann (Wright), 261
   Quanita (Short), 261
   Wayne Lewis, 261
Stearn, Hazel Jennie (Wennell) (Brandenhoff), 258
   John Atlee, 258
Stearns, James, 258
   Lucy (Stevens), 258
Steele, Fannie Mayrice, 431
Steesy, Walt, 8
Stegeman, Mabel, 249
Stemelski, Bertha, 231
Stennett, Michelle Ivena, 377
   Nancy Kaye (Ingersoll), 377
   Ray, 377
   Shane Ray, 377
Stephans, Genevieve, 135
   Joshua, 135
Stephson, Bernice Vernetta (Miles), 148
   Bernice Vernetta (Roberts), 148
   Gerry, 148
Sterling, Ruth Marie, 305
Stevens, Frank, 136
   Grace Mae, 199
   Lea Etta, 200, 310
   Louisa (Sanford), 136
   Lucy, 258
   Mertie Ann (Crouch), 136
   Myrtle (Kleven), 200
   Norman C., 136
   Norman Carroll, 200
   Thelma Belle, 200
Stevenson, Alonzo, 78
   Harriet, 78
Stewart, Ruth Elizabeth, 136
Stier, Paula, 346
Stigsell, Gary Allen, 311

Jo Ann (Schuffenhauer), 311
John, 311
Mary (Rolfson), 311
Terri Lyn, 311
Wallace John, 311
Stilwell, Donna, 413
Stocks, Pearl, 221
Stollfus, Amber Irene (Roberts), 221
  Amber Roberts, 343
  Bertha (Nehring), 221
  Brennen, 344
  Carol (Sommers), 344
  Fred, 221
  George, 221
  Marilyn, 221, 343
  Nathan, 344
  Wayne George, 221, 344
Stone, Brenda Suzanne, 260
Stopp, Louise, 200
Stout, Barbara Louise (Langland), 339
  James Martin, 339
  Joan, 339
Stovee, Ella (Hauge), 137
  Lillian M., 137
  Nordahl, 137
Stowel, Harvey, 86
Strachan, Adam Winston, 233
  Albert George, 233
  Dawn Alison, 233
  Drew Marshall, 233
  Nancy Dawn (Roseth), 233
  Rena Annette (Farrara), 233
Strack, Chester, 155
  Cora M. M. (Kroeplin), 155
Strang, Anthony Joseph, 425
  Brian, 425
  Cory Alan, 425
  Rebecca G. (Weisensel), 425
Street, Cynthia Lucille (Robertson), 379
  Don, 379
  Lorene (—), 379
  Marcia Lu, 380
  Rodney C., 379
Strong, B. T., 56
Stroud, Dianne Lee, 294
  Juanita May (Page), 294
  Norman Frederick, 294
Strutz, Donald, 398
  Natalie (Dohlmon), 398
  Sally, 398

Stucky, Donovan Daniel, 242
  Dorothy Olga (Sandberg), 242
  Marilyn Dorothy, 242
Stultz, Charles, 413
  Donna (Stilwell), 413
  Susan, 413
Sturges, William, 42
Sullivan, —, 13
Sundsmo, Hilda (—), 347
  John, 347
  Rosalind Gail, 347
Suprise, Darcy, 341
Sur, Mildred, 422
Surback, Jacob, 121
  Jennie L. (Wadley), 121
  Joseph, 121
Suring, Aaron James, 396
  Carol Lea (Slang), 395
  Erik John, 396
  Louis, 396
  Lowell Howard, 395
  Martha (Schuettpelz), 396
Surprenant, Angeline (Vigen), 339
  Barbara Joyce (Wilson), 339
  Ernest James, 339
  Ernest Leon, 339
  Glenn James, 339
  Lee Ray, 339
Surprise, Darcy, 424
Sutherland, David, 220
  Ruth Elizabeth (Erickson), 220
  Virginia, 220
Sivage, Wynnie, 233
Swanson, Laura Mae (Vining) (Peterson), 218
  Melvin John, 218
Sweeney, Barbara Kathelene, 284
  James, 284
  Kathelene, 284
Sweet, Mitzi, 327
  Noreen, 223
Swensen, Christina, 121
Swindle, Mary Lou, 178
Syferd, Lillian Mae, 215
Szymanski, Alice, 262
  Frank, 262
  Mary (Kozou), 262

T

Taft, Louise, 188
　Lucinda, 136
Tallent, Barbara J. (Pogue), 424
　Richard, 424
Tangen, Susan Margaret, 373
Tarter, Amy, 422
　Lloyd, 422
　Michael, 422
　Shari Bea (Bauer), 422
Tasch, Alyson, 344
Tate, Delmar (Worthington), 293
　Jesse, 293
　Lois, 124
　Lois (Archibald) (Thompson)
　　(Raleigh) (Hammerstad), 293
　Robert, 293
Taylor, Alene Eleanor, 181
　Dulsie Mae (House), 157
　Floyd, 157
　Fred, 157
　Grace, 191
　Herbert, 157
　John, 157
　M. E., 121
　Nadine, 157
　Nellie, 307
Tead, Leota L. (Plasteur) (Nickle), 188
　Richard D., 188
Teetz, Jane, 374
Telatko, Mary, 238
Telen, Daniel A., 295
　Donald A., 295
　Erik J., 295
　Sharon Lee (Weston), 295
Terbeest, Sharon, 345
Terry, Brian Lee, 361
　Gary, 361
　Sally Jane (Audiss), 361
Teschke, Gail Marie (Zaszczurynski), 428
　Lena Marie, 428
　Michelle Ann, 428
　Richard, 428
Theien, Brenda Lee, 245
　Erin Marie, 377
　Gail Marie, 245, 376
　John Gustoff, 245
　John Kevin, 245
　Linda (Wester), 245
　Theresa Kay, 245
Thelan, Arthur, 129
　Cleo Patra Eloise (Plasteur), 129
Thibode, Iola, 140
Thiel, Fred, 145
Thill, Regina, 147
Thomas, Billy Jo, 412
　Deanna Charlene, 413
　Doris Elaine (Woodruff), 412
　G. W., 109
　Gerald Wayne, 412
　Jeffrey Paul, 413
　Kainen Braun, 413
　Katherine, 247
　Katherine Elizabeth, 239
　Marthena (Smith), 247
　Roxanne Lee (Raleigh), 412
　Steven Earl, 412
　William Eugene, 247
Thompson, Brenda Suzanne (Stone), 260
　Carol Ann (McElroy), 225
　Cassie Elizabeth, 391
　Charles, 293
　Chester, 350
　Dennis, 260
　Donald Andrew, 259
　Eliza (Johnson), 168
　Elston, 168
　Esther, 405
　Florence (Wagner), 350
　Frances Dolores (Reese), 259
　Irene Orpha (Wright) (Carey), 168
　James, 225
　Jane Ellen, 225
　John, 168
　John Calvin, 260, 391
　John Norman, 168, 259
　Judy, 334
　Julie Ann, 225
　Lois (Archibald), 293
　Marion Robert, 168
　Mark Vail, 225
　Mary Louise, 168
　Pamela Renea (Dixon), 391
　Sandra, 350
　Timothy James, 225
　Vail, 225
Thomsen, Barbara June (Day), 352
　Eli (Zapek), 352

Hans Day, 352
Richard N., 352
Tom Wayne, 352
Thomson, Marie, 176
Thorpe, Page, 8
Thrasher, Edna Marie (Williams), 253
Martha Jane, 253
Norman Glen, 253
Ticknor, Ashley Rae, 404
Belva (Maxwell), 282
Blanche (Mentch), 177
Christopher Weyburn, 282
Cole Thomas, 404
Cynthia Diane, 282
Edythe Martha (Wadley), 177
Harry W., 177
Jodenne Kay (Ness), 404
John Weyburn, 177, 281
Karon Rae (Danne), 282
Nancy Ann, 177, 282
Scott Alan, 282
Steven William, 282, 404
Tamara Jeanne, 282
Tiffany Rae, 282
William Alan, 177, 282
Tienter, Ben, 240
Gertrude (Urieze), 240
La Verna (Westphal), 240
Tikton, Emily, 322
Titus, Arthur, 186
David, 186
Dianne Short, 186
Elizabeth (Winklesky), 186
Nancy Schoner, 186
Tognoni, Becky Lou, 255, 387
Brian Hale, 255, 387
Caroline Joyce (Rasmussen), 384
Cassandra, 388
Cathy (Murphy), 388
Christine Joyce, 384
David Quentin, 255, 387
Dayle Christine, 387
Gary, 387
George-Ann (Neudeck), 254
Hale, 164, 166, 254
Hale Christopher, 166, 254
Ina Belle (Cates), 165
Ina Cates, 253
Jeffery R., 255, 388
Jesse Myrtle (Jacques), 165
Joseph, 254
Joseph Christopher, 165
Joseph R., 256
Joseph Russell, 165
Keith Irvin, 257
Louis Christopher, 254, 384
Lynne Marie, 257, 388
Marie Faye, 384
Mary (Finster), 387
Michael Angelo, 254
Mickey (Howzdy), 387
Nathan, 387
Neva Faye (Gergen), 253
Neva June, 166, 254
Nicholas Ford, 388
Nye Woodrow, 166, 253, 254, 384
Patricia (Severn), 387
Patricia Linda, 254, 384
Pearl Marie (Porter), 255
Robert, 256
Robert Joseph, 254
Robert Louis, 166, 255
Sandra Ann, 255, 387
Sean Bradley, 387
Shirley (Frazer), 254
Susie (Jesusito), 254
Wesley, 387
Tomlinson, Delbert, 443
Sylvia (Austin), 443
Toole, Jean, 358
Torgerson, Lenice Margaret, 265
Towner, —, 95
Jay W., 95
Jennie (Cheeseman), 95
Townsend, Johnny, 390
Tracey, Elizabeth Ann, 349
Kathy (Bates), 349
Tim, 349
Tramph, Martha, 212
Trecartin, George Henry, 46
John, 46
Marietta (Smith) (Reed), 46
Mary (Lord), 46
Trescott, —, 18
Lemuel, 12
Tress, Cynthia Amy (Reed), 287
Timothy Mark, 287
Trimble, Becky Ann, 314
Betty June (Meeker), 314
Jack B., 314

Martha, 314
Steven C., 314
Trinidad, Efran, 428
　Gabrielle M. (Zaszczurynski), 428
　Roselenna Michelle, 428
Trochanowski, Alexander, 348
　Annie, 348
　Mary (Palochuk), 348
Troff, Bryan Jeffery, 241
　Frances (Alberts), 241
　Gary Allen, 241
　Harold, 241
　Hemme, 241
　June Carol (French), 241
　Wayne Harold, 241
Tronsdall, Betty Jean (Hartwell), 361
　John, 361
　Mary Louise, 361
　Peggy Ann, 361
Trowbridge, Agatha (Klugen), 212
　Bernice, 212
　Frank, 212
Trudell, Lula-Mae, 300
Trueax, Edith Velma, 241
Tubbs, Peter, 74
Tucker, Charles, 130
　Lorena (Reed), 130
Tunnell, Madge, 436, 437
Turchiarulo, Esther, 190
　Lawrence, 190
　Lucretia (D'Amico), 190
Turk, Dorcus Marie (Kirk), 415
　Stanley, 415
　Tammy Marie, 415
Turley, Rosa Bell, 201
Turner, Amelia (—), 363
　Betty Louise, 307
　Cleo Patra Eloise (Plasteur), 129
　Debbie Haggerman, 372
　George, 129
　Gerald, 237
　Herbert, 129
　John, 363
　Leona Marie (Kroeplin), 237
　Sandra Louise, 363
Tuttle, Kathy (Manley), 311
　Margaret Illene, 311
　William, 311
Tvite or Twite, Rika Sophia, 228
Tweton, Clara, 310

Twohig, Abigail (Young), 438
　Ellen, 438
　John, 438
Tyng, Rebecca, 10

U

Udell, Mary Eileen, 381
Ulrich, Laura, 353
　Martha (—), 353
　Walter, 353
Unzueta, Guadalupe, 283
Upton, Laurie Dawn Warren, 431
Urch, Barbara Jean, 240
　Carol Ann, 240, 371
　Evelyn Mae (French), 240
　Fred G., 240
　Frederick Charles, 241
　Harvey, 240
　Jared Michael, 371
　Laurelie Mae, 371
　Lowell Earl, 240, 371
　Mary Lou, 367
　Mattie (Griffin), 240
　Mavis (Bender), 371
　Rachel Lynn, 371
　Rebecca Marie, 240
　Suzan Marie, 371
　Vicki Lea, 240, 371
Urdahl, Jacqueline, 230
　Myrtle, 230
　Oscar, 230
Urieze, Gertrude, 240
Urkmann, Randy, 376
Utke, Delores L., 269
　Deloris L., 171

V

Valenta, Adam, 392
　John, 261
　Joseph Clyde, 262, 392
　Joseph Peter, 261
　Laurel Fern, 262, 392
　Margaret (Shoewe), 392
　Melvine (Brazean), 261
　Paige, 392
　Sherry Jean, 262
　Wilma Fern (Johnson), 261
Valentine, Theodora, 321

Valette, Bethel June (Daniels) (Hunt), 204
  Henry Clement, 204
  Henry Louis, 204
  Viola Marie (Miller), 204
Vallentyne, Beverly Anne (Beavert), 294
  Debra, 294
  Diane, 294
  Howard Judson, 294
  John, 294
  Mildred (Davenport), 294
  Shannon, 294
Van Ark, Adam John, 270
  Beverly Ann (Reed), 269
  Bobbie Jo, 270
  Joseph James, 270
  Kenneth, 269
  Kiva Marie, 270
  Lee Michael, 270
VanAsdale, Janice, 303
Vanburkleo, David, 318
  Elizabeth (Crouch), 318
  Francis, 318
  Gladys (—), 318
  Natalie, 318
Vancaster, Aaron, 392
  Alice (Boehm), 260
  Barbara Jean, 260
  Delores Dorothy (Wright), 260
  Donald Raymond, 260, 392
  Ellen Marie, 260, 392
  Jolene, 392
  Junior Louis, 260
  Louis Joseph, 260
  Mark Andrew, 260
  Mike James, 261
  Rebecca (Saykally), 260
  Susan (Kozar), 392
Vance, Cynthia, 282
Vanden Boogart, Amy Lynn, 398
  Arnold, 266
  David John, 266
  Gloria Verwey, 397
  Jane (Nelessen), 397
  Jay Martin, 266, 398
  Kim Marie, 267
  Margaret, 266
  Matthew Robert, 398
  Rick Charles, 266, 397
  Robert, 266
  Sally (Strutz), 398
  Scott Robert, 266
  Sharon Lynn, 266, 397
  Todd Joseph, 266
Van Der Borgh, Connie, 205
Vanderhyde, Emily (Harkum), 138
  Frank S., 138
  Hila, 138
  Lila Belle (Crouch), 138
  Melva, 138
Vangness, Barbara A., 368
Van Keuren, Louise, 181
Van Ooyan, Wilhelmina, 115
Van Schoch, Elisea J., 442
  Elizabeth (—), 442
  Frederick, 442
VanWinkle, Sara W., 281
Varnell, Bessie Louise (Marcy), 276
  Edward Leon, 276
  Nelda Jean, 276
Vaughn, Edna Marie, 382
  Jean, 357
  Jessie Lawrence, 382
  Lucille, 314
  Minnie, 250
  Myrtle (—), 382
Vegera, Mary L. (Quick), 328
  Ricky, 328
  Tony, 328
Veglianti, Corrine J., 309
Vegue, Caroline, 274
Vela, Veda, 276
Vendetti, Adele, 325
VerBunker, Mae, 263
Vernon, —, 55
Verriden, Albine (DeMain), 267
  Allan Roy, 267, 398
  Alvin, 267
  Barbara Jean, 267, 398
  Donald John, 267
  June Ione (Paulsen), 267
  Karen (Nuthals), 267
  Karen Marie, 267, 399
  Larry John, 267
  Leah, 399
  Lisa Ann, 267
  Susan (Lampereur), 398
  Trisha, 399
Ver Vooren, Constance (Buchanan), 398
  Janet Marie, 398
  Richard, 398

Verwey, Dudley Gilbert, 116
　Emma Florence (Benson), 116
　George, 115
　George Leroy, 116
　Gloria Ann, 169, 266
　Ida (Maack), 116
　Julia, 113, 118
　Julia (Reed), 46, 115
　Laura C. (Rohde), 169
　Peter, 115
　Richard, 115
　Verna, 116, 170
　Victor Richard, 116, 169
　Wilhelmina (Van Ooyan), 115
Vickers, Harriet (Dale), 144
　John, 144
　Sybil, 144
Victoor, Margaret, 277
Vigen, Angeline, 339
Villwock, Cheryl Lynn (Pryor), 409
　Diana, 409
　Edward, 409
　Henry, 409
　Scott, 409
　Tammy, 409
　Thomas, 409
Vincent, Josephine, 250
Vining, Anne Elizabeth, 220
　Barbara (DiLullo), 338
　Benjamin W., 102
　Carolyn Rae, 219, 337
　Charles, 102
　Charles Lester, 147, 219
　Cory, 339
　Curtis Harry, 148, 220
　Eddue, 339
　Edward, 102
　Edward Harrison, 147, 219
　Edward Warren, 219, 338
　Gertrude (Michaelsen), 147
　Harry Edward, 102, 147
　Helen Marie, 219, 338
　Holly Jo, 338
　Janet Lee (Washburn), 338
　Jason Edward, 338
　Jesse L., 102, 147
　Joanne, 220, 339
　Joyce Marvel, 148, 220
　Judy, 220, 338
　Katherine (Haynes), 102
　Laura May, 102, 146, 147, 218
　Laurie, 220
　Lena (—), 338
　Lenora (Elder), 219
　Lester Eugene, 102
　Lilas Jane, 148, 220
　Linda, 220, 339
　Lucretia M. (Peckham), 102
　Lulu (Hewitt), 147
　Mabel Caroline, 147, 219
　Martha M. (Wudel), 219
　Mary Curtis, 220, 340
　Mary Margaret, 219, 338
　Nancy Dale, 220, 340
　Paula Marie, 338
　Ralph Jesse, 147
　Raymond Hans, 147, 219
　Rene Lynn, 338
　Regina (Thill), 147
　Selma Christine (Peterson), 147
　Shirley Ann, 219, 337
　Thomas, 102
　Thomas Ray, 102, 147
　Thomas William, 219, 338, 445
　Velma Ruth (Ashley), 219
　Vickie Lee, 338
　Virginia (Sutherland), 220
　Wendy, 339
Visser, Adam Ryan, 397
　Barbara Ann, 275
　Elsie Tunie, 285
Vissers, Frances Catherine (LeNoble), 397
　Gregory George, 397
　James, 397
　Sharon Lynn (Vanden Boogart), 397
Vivian, Annie (Austin) (Kefer), 442
　William, 442
Volante, Adam Joseph, 386
　Cindy Jill (Mendez), 386
　Michael, 386
　Monica Michelle, 386
Vorpahl, Edmund John, 171
　Elizabeth (Grams), 171
　Freda Rose, 171

W

Wabbel, Geneil Naomi, 384
　Harold Wayne, 384

Index

Karen Geneil (Carling), 384
Wackenagel, Erick, 395
  Fritz, 394
  Heika, 395
  Inge (—), 394
  Karin Marlis, 394
  Keith, 395
Wade, Effie Lou, 196
  Grace (Metcalf), 196
  Robert, 196
Wadleigh, Lester P., 438
  Lester Parks, 438
  Lorraine, 438
  Margaret (Walker), 438
  Marguerite, 438
  Marguerite C.(Gallaglier), 438
Wadley, Beatrice Ann (Ryan), 440
  Beda (Glass), 47, 435, 445
  Bill, 74, 89
  Blanche Pearl (Dillenbeck), 120, 445
  Brent William, 283
  Deborah Chere, 283
  Dora, 436
  Douglas Lee, 283
  Douglass Lee, 177
  Edythe Martha, 121, 177
  Elizabeth, 47, 48
  Elizabeth (—), 435
  Ellen, 438
  Ellen (Twohig), 438
  Geraldine Dolores, 440
  Helen, 437
  Jennie (Parks), 435
  Jennie L., 47, 121
  Jerry Arthur, 438, 440
  Joshua, 28, 47, 435, 445
  Joshua L., 47, 435
  Judith Gloria, 440
  Laurie Anne, 283
  Lera, 47, 445
  Lera Edwina, 121, 176
  Lester Wadleigh, 437
  Lillian, 438, 439
  Lizzie, 47
  Mabel Rose (Halverson), 121
  Marianne Kay, 283
  Martha (Reed), 47, 435, 445
  Mary Lou (Diaz), 283
  Mildred DeSilva, 121, 176
  Moses, 47, 435, 445
  P. L., 90
  Pamela Jane, 440
  Patricia Ann (Dettling), 283
  Paul, 120
  Paul Lowell, 121
  Pauline Lois, 121, 177
  Pearl, 7, 17, 29, 121
  Pearl Lera, 47, 120, 445
  Rex, 437, 438
  Richard Norlin, 177, 283
  Rosa Reiley (Riley), 435
  Ruby Grace (Farnsworth), 120
  Seymour, 437
  Stella (Kopalecki), 438
  Virgie Norine (Wolfe), 177
  William, 47
  William Irwin, 121, 177
Wagner, Christine, 404
  Clara (Have), 222
  Darrell, 404
  Edwin, 222
  Florence, 350
  Gary, 404
  Linda (Lord-Simmons), 404
  Lydia, 356
  Marylu, 404
  Natalie Ruth, 222
Wahl, Edwin, 226
  Florence (Johnson), 226
  Irwina, 226
Waite, Abigail, 104
  Andrew, 104
  Beverly Peckham (Roseth), 231
  Laurie, 231, 356
  Lorin, 231
  Mary Jane (Smith), 104
  Randy, 231
Wakeling, James, 252
  June (Cates) (Zunio) (Wolford), 252
Wakeman, Mary, 145
Walden, Hillman Alexander, 280
  Hilman Alexander, 280
  Louise (Martin), 280
  Teresa Luan, 280
Waldo, Charles, 309
  Dorothy Merle (Mattoon), 309
Waldoch, Betty (—), 332
  David, 332
  Michelle Cecile (Peckham), 332
  Robert, 332

Walenga, Edward Leo, 211
    Elizabeth Jo, 211, 326
    Jaqueline Kay, 211
    John, 211
    Lora Marie, 211, 326
    Mark Gregory, 211
    Minnie Mary (Albert), 211
    Rilla Bell (Franklin), 211
    Yvonne Carol, 211
Walker, Barbara, 344
    Cecilia Jean (Johnson), 394
    Dawn, 394
    James, 394
    Margaret, 438
    Patrick, 394
    Patrick William, 394
    Roger, 394
Waller, —, 314
    Martha (Trimble), 314
Walls, Esther Marie, 188
    James H., 188
    Mable Marie (Replogle), 188
Walske, Clarence, 269
    Margaret, 269
Walter, Berta, 277
Wampler, Mary Kay, 319
Wandrey, Alfred, 321
    Gary, 321
    Gary Scott, 321
    James Gordon, 321
    Kellie Lynn, 321
    Pamela Ruth (Miller), 321
    Regina Ann, 321
    Theodora (Valentine), 321
    Tricia Lee Miller, 321
Ward, Tilla, 152
Wargo, Justin James, 305
Warner, Bessie (Smith), 237
    Claude, 237
    Esther May, 237
    Hannah, 199
    V., 18
Warren, G. K., 58
Warrington, Christine, 271
Warschkow, Bonnie, 268
    Elizabeth (Liswoe), 268
    Gordon, 268
Washburn, Janet Lee, 338
Wathen, C., 301
    Toni Lynn, 301

Watson, Frances, 315
    George, 152
    Gladys, 152
    Lillian Maria, 211
    Tilla (Ward), 152
Weaver, Betty, 411
Webb, Carol Doreen, 426
    Daniel Scott, 290
    Debora (Fischer), 410
    J. B., 290
    Jason, 410
    Jerod, 410
    Michael David, 290, 410
    Shirley Gay (Simmons), 290
    Steven Clark, 290
Weber, —, 438
    Emma Mary Magdaline, 251
    Julanne, 286
    Marguerite (Wadleigh), 438
    Michael, 286
    Pamela, 286
    Peggy Jean, 260
Webster, —, 419
    Bryan David, 420
    Carrie M., 135
    Daniel, 135
    Floyd Stanley, 413
    Julie Kay (Daniels), 419
    Kenneth, 413
    Marinda, 135
    Micah Daniel, 420
    Sharilyn Autumn (Gibson) (Shepardson), 413
    Sylvia (Hunziker), 413
    Travis, 413
    Troy Douglas, 413
Weeks, Sherrill, 189
    Wendy Lou (Clarke), 189
Weeteling, Deloris Jane (Cates), 252
    John J., 252
    Richard, 252
    Terrance, 252
Wehrmann, Patricia, 346
Weikle, Kim, 321
Weise, Arlene, 330
Weisensel, Arlene P., 342
    Bruce L., 342
    David C., 342
    George B., 342
    Irene (Pogue), 342

Irene Pogue, 425
Jill E., 342
Joseph M., 342
Lisa M., 342
Margaret R., 342, 425
Natalie C., 342
Peggy R., 425
Phyllis E., 342
Rebecca G., 342, 425
Tina E., 342
Weiss, Janice Adell (Crouch) (Ferrell) (Newby), 313
    Walter, 313
Weitzenkemp, Julie, 370
Welch, Margaret, 318
Weldon, Shirley, 316
Welner, Gloria, 427
Wennell, Caroline, 167
    Hazel Jennie, 167, 258
    Mary Caroline, 167, 258
    Nellie Beatrice (Wright), 167
    Oscar, 167
    Peter, 167
Wenzel, Esther (—), 352
    Katie Day, 353
    Mark David, 352
    Martha Joan (Day), 352
    Stirling Albert, 352
Wesolowski, Antoinette (Kaczmarowski), 273
    Geraldine Ann, 273
    Norbert, 273
West, Edna Elizabeth (Congdon), 299
    Joseph Charles, 299
    Joseph Leroy, 299
    Lisa Marie, 299
    Marcia Jean (Lane), 299
Westaky, Clara, 364
    Dorothy, 363
Westcott, Al, 88
    Allen, 93
    Asa, 28, 31, 93
    Mary, 28, 31, 93
    Mary (Wing), 93
Westendorf, Neta, 352
Wester, Anna (Callahan), 376
    Anna Marie, 245
    Barry Victor, 245
    Brian Phillip, 244
    Carol Susan (Drake), 244
    Curt Allen, 244
    Deborah Kay, 244, 376
    Donald, 158, 244, 376
    Doris Evelyn (Leitha), 245
    Ethel Lorilla (Abel), 158
    Glen Andrew, 244
    Harry, 158, 244
    Ingvard, 158
    Jean Marie (East), 244
    Jensen Christian, 158
    Julie Ann, 245
    Keith Douglas, 244
    Kirsten (Nielsen), 158
    Lee Anne, 244
    Leota, 158, 245
    Linda, 158, 245
    Marcus Allen, 376
    Mary Edith (Botton), 244
    Melissa, 376
    Michael Lee, 244, 376
    Mitchell Allen, 244, 376
    Phillip, 158, 244
    Scott Allen, 245
    Susan Emerson (Smith), 376
    Tammara Kay, 245, 377
    Tena (Nelson), 244
    Victor, 158, 245
    Victoria Lynn, 244, 376
Weston, Andrew, 91, 187
    Andrew Medford, 124
    Cecil, 187
    Esther Marie (Walls), 188
    Gladys Pauline (Baurer), 187
    James Merle, 188, 295
    Jan Michael, 296, 446
    Jay Bradley, 295
    Jeni Marie, 296
    Joshua Michiel, 446
    Leann Marie (Russell), 446
    Linda L. (Hanson), 295
    Marvin L., 187
    Marvin Laverne, 124
    Marvys Jane, 187, 295
    Maud Edna (Reed), 124
    Merle Vincent, 124, 187
    Mindi A., 295
    Patricia Lee (Schmidt), 295
    Sarah (Beavert), 124
    Sharon Lee, 187, 295
    Sharon Louise (Hayden), 295

    Steven Craig, 187, 295
    William J., 124
    Zoe Olive (Reed) (Zane), 91
Westphal, Darrell, 240
    Ella, 408
    Phyllis, 240
    Walter, 240
Whatley, Brayton, 391
    Blair Ann, 391
    Clifton Alan, 391
    Charles C., 391
    Olympia Laura (James), 391
    Roxie (—), 391
Wheat, Genevieve, 332
Whirry, Mary Jane, 224
Whitacre, Adam Thomas, 329
    Jane Ellen (Ilgen), 329
    Russell William, 329
Whitcomb, Ann, 38
White, Alice Bond, 246
    Alice Ivena, 158
    Ann, 106
    Ann Louise (Houghton), 327
    Anna Laura (Bond), 158
    Cindy (Peckham), 354
    Dan R., 327
    Derek, 327
    Diana (Peckham), 354
    Eleanor (Olson), 327
    Jeff, 354
    Jon, 355
    Krista Anne, 338
    Leonard, 338
    Leslie Michelle, 338
    Lindsey, 354
    Linette Marie, 338
    Lynne, 372
    Marilyn, 407
    Mary (—), 407
    Mary Margaret (Vining), 338
    Mike, 355
    Monte, 354
    Myrtle, 364
    Nathaniel, 327
    Nicholas, 354
    Norman, 407
    Ralph, 327
    Richard, 158
    White Eagle, 89
Whiteside, Alice, 232

Whitlock, Ellen Eliz. (Quick) (Brown), 212
    Jack, 212
Whitney, Mary, 153
Wiedendorf, Andrew, 199
    Betty (Konen), 310
    David, 200
    Earl, 199
    Geryl Earl, 200, 310
    Grace Mae (Stevens), 199
    Julia, 199
    Kathy Harriet (De Baere), 310
    Lorraine Frances (Brow), 310
    Norma Ruth, 200, 310
    Rosean Marie, 310, 419
    Tammie Ann, 310
    Timothy Alan, 310
    Wayne Andrew, 200, 310
Wiggs, Pearl E., 281
Wilbur, Carl Blane, 315
    Jillian Jacqueline, 315
    Kathy LaVonne (Garrison), 315
    Mason Kenyon, 315
    Patricia Ann, 315
    Tekla Frances (Jessel), 315
Wilcox, Perry, 132, 133
Wiley, Carolyn Jeanne, 358
Wilke, Jean, 375
    Leona E., 275
Wilken, Alec Victor, 282
    Tamara Jeanne (Ticknor), 282
Wilkinson, Toni Grant, 240
Williams, Barbara Joanne (Olsen), 334
    Eathel Maude, 288
    Edna Marie, 253
    Elizabeth Lynn, 334
    Erwin L., 334
    H. B., 125
    Laurie Lee, 334
    Margaret, 436
    Mark Talbot, 334
Williamson, Annie (Trochanowski), 348
    Carole Mavis, 226, 348
    Clifford Carlyle, 225, 226, 348
    Craig Alexander Clifford, 348
    Deborah Lynn, 348, 425
    Edward Thomas, 225
    Kyle Thomas, 425
    Lizzie (Buchanan), 225
    Luvia Imogene (Chowen), 225

Index 535

Teri-Ann Theresa, 348
Willoghby, Eugene, 409
    Margaret (Lyons), 409
Willoughby, Carla Marie, 409
    Eugene, 409
    Margaret (Lyons), 409
Wilson, Barbara Joyce, 220, 339
    Bessie, 172
    Brandy Lynn, 386
    Cecelia Sunshine, 339
    Celeste Rose, 340
    Clara, 416
    David Christopher, 339
    Diane, 317
    Doreen A. (—), 317
    Drue, 267
    James Richard, 220, 340
    Joan (Stout), 339
    Jodie Jacqueline, 387
    Joe E., 317
    John David, 220, 339
    John Glenn, 220
    John Vining, 340
    John Walter, 220
    Joyce Marvel (Vining), 220
    Justin Teria, 340
    Krishna Robert, 339
    Lashelli Sue (Mitchell), 340
    Linda Louise (Riddle), 339
    Lois Elaine (Paulsen) (Hyska), 267
    Matel Erma (Glenn), 220
    Nancy Lynn (Richey), 386
    Nicolette Sunshine, 340
    Shawn Eric, 387
    Steven Eric, 386
Wilton, Ruth, 326
Windedall, LaVonne, 433
Wines, Brenda Lee (Marshall), 416
    Elizabeth Jean, 416
    Elizabeth Nette (Brockway), 416
    Raymond John, 416
    Raymond Robert, 416
    Robert David, 416
    Robyn Lee, 416
Wing, Mary, 93
Wingate, Anna, 78
    Charles, 77
    Charles Cyrus, 78
    Cyrus, 77, 78
    Cyrus Charles, 78

    George, 78
    John, 48, 77, 78
    John S., 77
    Marinda, 48
    Mary, 78
    Mary Marie, 78
    Mary Marie (Reed), 77
    Rebecca (Conklin), 48, 77
Winklesky, Elizabeth (Titus), 186
    Irene (Peacha), 186
    Paul, 186
Winne, Lillie, 149
Winnery, Floyd, 251
    Miriam (Coleman), 251
Wiswell, Pat, 352
Witcher, Mary Evaline, 285
Witter, Corey Lee, 389
    Ernice (Loeper), 389
    Gloria Mae (Cox), 389
    Harry, 389
    Lee Allen, 389
    Paul Robert, 389
Wolcholz, Elsie, 331
Wolf, Cheryl, 279
    Ruth, 409
Wolfe, Ida Edna (Modrell), 177
    Maxwell Leo, 177
    Virgie Norine, 177
Wolford, Colleen, 253
    J. (Cates) (Zunino) (Peterson), 252
    Keith, 253
    Merrill, 252
Wolske, Darla (Grignon), 400
    Logan Lane, 400
    Regan, 400
    Seth Taylor, 400
Wood, Rosanne, 373
    Tiny, 190
Woodcock, Eugene, 415
    James Harold, 415
    Jamie Marie, 415
    Joyce (Debrucque), 415
    Leona Norene (Chase), 415
    Norene Cora, 415
Woodman, Edward, 11
    Joanna, 11
    Ruth, 11
Woodruff, Doris Elaine, 412
    Kerry Brent, 405
    Mary (Mentz) (Duranso), 405

William, 405
Wilma (Heidamann), 405
Woodward, Marjorie Janet, 278
Woodworth, Ida Florence, 202
Woody, Adeline, 111
Woombill, Marie, 423
Worthington, Delmar, 293
Wray, Euretta, 114
Wren, Violet, 261
Wright, Alice, 168
   Anne Christine (Peckham), 423
   Austin Scheffel, 423
   Barbara, 276
   Berl (—), 423
   Carol Bernadette (Schroeder), 261
   Clarence Alfred, 276
   Clarice Eva, 168, 260
   Clark, 114, 167
   Dalores Dorothy, 168
   Delores Dorothy, 260
   Eugene Thomas, 168, 261
   Euretta (Ray), 114
   Euretta (Wray), 114
   George, 114
   George McGill, 114
   Gertrude Mary Etta, 114, 166
   Irene Minnie (Calkins), 276
   Irene Orpha, 115, 168
   Jack, 423
   Janet, 168
   Jennie Adell (Reed), 114
   Jennie Reed, 168
   Judith Ann (Carroll), 168
   Kim Marie, 261
   Lois Marie (Jansen), 261
   Lylis Margaret, 168, 260
   Margaret Eva (Lake), 168
   Mary Hansen, 261
   Nellie Beatrice, 115, 167
   Patricia Ann, 168, 261
   Randall Eugene, 261
   Rhonda Jean, 261
   Richard Frank, 261
   Robert Herman, 168
   Robert Scheffel, 423
   Ronald Thomas, 261
   Thomas Martin, 115, 168, 261
Wudel, Dora Thea (Harnish), 219
   Martha M., 219
   Nathaniel, 219

Wyman, Adele, 137
Wynn, Hiram, 189
   Loretta Marie, 189
   Pearl Amelia (Piper), 189

Y

Yank, Loretta Mary, 380
Yates, Larci April, 381
Yearly, Mary G., 137
Yecny, Emily, 187
Yentsch, Benita (—), 419
   Sandra, 419
   Wayne, 419
Young, Abigain, 438
   Augusta (Procknow), 166
   E. R., 443
   Elias Roy, 442
   Evelyn (Bamberg), 297
   Graham, 166
   Marcia Louise, 297
   Michael, 297
   Myrtle (Austin), 442
   Pearl, 166
Youngs, Bruce Brian, 190
   Jeffery Scott, 190
   Kenneth, 190
Yourell, Beulah Helen, 405

Z

Zandt, Janet, 268
Zane, Jesse Thomas, 91
   Thomas W., 91
   Virginia (Cummings), 91
   Zoe Olive (Reed), 91
Zapek, Eli, 352
Zaszczurynski, Cecil Joseph, 428
   Cora M. M. (Kroeplin), 155
   Gabrielle Michelle, 362, 428
   Gail Marie, 362, 428
   Geraldine Edna, 362
   Glenda Emma, 362
   Gwen Rose, 362, 428
   Leon John, 155
   Patricia (Green), 428
   Rose Blanche (Meeker), 362
   Rose Meeker, 428

Index

Sharon (Goebel), 362
Terrance Emmet, 362, 428
Theodore Eugene, 362
Theodus, 362
Yaritza Iris, 428
Zavatsky, Blanche, 318
Ziellow, Leona, 100
Ziereis, Ann, 260
Zimmerman, Brent, 354
   Frank, 118
   Jacob, 354
   Kara, 354
   Tiffany, 354
   Vicki Renee (Peckham), 354
Zunino, Avald, 252
   Gordon, 252
   June (Cates), 252
   William, 252